THE FIFTY YEARS WAR

THE FIFTY YEARS WAR

The United States and the Soviet Union in
world politics, 1941–1991

Richard Crockatt

London and New York

First published 1995
by Routledge
11 New Fetter Lane, London EC4P 4EE

Simultaneously published in the USA and Canada
by Routledge
29 West 35th Street, New York, NY 10001

© 1995 Richard Crockatt

Typeset in Garamond by
J&L Composition Ltd, Filey, North Yorkshire
Printed and bound in Great Britain by
TJ Press (Padstow) Ltd, Padstow, Cornwall
Printed on acid free paper

British Library Cataloguing in Publication Data
A catalogue record for this book is available from the British Library

Library of Congress Cataloging in Publication Data has been applied for.

ISBN 0–415–10471–8

This book is for
Clara,
Sam, Martha, and John

CONTENTS

CONTENTS

CONTENTS

FIGURES

PREFACE AND ACKNOWLEDGEMENTS

What follows is a history of US–Soviet relations between 1941 and 1991, viewed in a global perspective. It is thus neither simply a study of bilateral superpower relations nor a comprehensive world history. The theme is rather the ways in which the United States and the Soviet Union have adapted, or failed to adapt, to global change.

The writing was begun in the autumn of 1989 and completed in January 1994. Inevitably, the revolutionary changes of these years informed every phase of the writing. In response to questions from friends about how it was possible to keep pace with events, my reply was always the same: rather than making my task more difficult, the collapse of communism and the end of the cold war served to give shape to the subject. It was possible finally to view the post-war years with some detachment. The cold war really was now history.

Keeping pace with the volume of scholarship and journalistic commentary on the cold war and its end was another matter. The amount of relevant literature in a project of this scope is vast and quickly growing. No one could hope to master it all. I have arrived at what I hope is a judicious sampling of the available material. At points I have interrupted the narrative to discuss the scholarly literature where interpretation of events is particularly disputed or where new knowledge has radically altered perceptions of major events. An example of the former is the debate about the origins of the cold war; an example of the latter is the Cuban missile crisis.

Though heavily reliant on secondary sources, I have also made use of government publications, edited collections of documents, journals, newspapers, and memoirs. I owe a debt to a great number of scholars and journalists who have written on the subjects covered by this book, though two in particular deserve mention – John Lewis Gaddis and Raymond Garthoff. Their writings meet researchers of the cold war at practically every turn. An exceptionally valuable resource for cold war historians is the Cold War International History Project at the Woodrow Wilson International Center for Scholars in Washington D.C. The project publishes working papers and a Bulletin which contains reports of findings in newly opened archives in the Soviet Union and Eastern Europe.

At all times I have been guided by the necessity of giving shape to a mass of events of often bewildering complexity. Two priorities have been uppermost in my mind. The first is a commitment to viewing Soviet–American relations as an interactive process rather than as a matter of one power acting on the other. There are many histories of American policy in the cold war, rather fewer of Soviet policy, and even fewer which attempt to give balanced treatment to both. Of course, the relative absence of sources for Soviet policy and the abundance of sources for American policy in part account for this imbalance. Even now, as new sources from the Soviet Union become available on an almost daily basis, the imbalance remains. Though some startling revelations have already been made, it will take years to unearth Soviet sources of the kind and on a scale which are available for the United States, assuming they exist, and many more to organize and digest them. Many conclusions about Soviet policy must necessarily remain provisional.

However, this lack should not be used as a reason for failing to address Soviet policy both on its own terms and in relation to the United States. The record of Soviet actions is there for all to see, even if interpretation of them must remain matters of dispute. But interpetation of American policy too is subject to fierce differences of opinion, despite the richness of source material, or perhaps in part because of it. This is not to celebrate our relative ignorance of Soviet policy-making or to say that primary sources do not matter. It is simply to say that more goes into the interpretation of events than the issue of sources; at least as important is a prior decision about how the subject in question is to be conceived or conceptualized. 'Where you stand is where you sit', the sociologists of knowledge tell us, and with some notable exceptions historians have sat intellectually if not physically in Washington or Moscow. In this book I have located myself somewhere between these two poles, a project made easier by the accident of birth and the accident of history which has allowed for a measure of detachment not available to historians writing before 1989.

My second priority has been to integrate history with the insights of international relations theorists. To a considerable extent these two approaches have developed along separate tracks, asking different sorts of questions and speaking different languages. Historians are traditionally suspicious of systematizers, whose schemes, it is held, impose an artificial simplicity on the complexity, the sheer messiness, of events. Theorists for their part sometimes question the value of the painstaking empirical research of the historian. At the very least theorists will challenge historians to say what all those researches add up to, what they might reveal about relations between states, the origins of wars, or the conditions of peace.

It will be said that in practice each draws on elements of the other's approach. There is no history, no good history, which is devoid of organizing ideas or whose conclusions do not bear some relation to philosophical or social issues of perennial concern. By the same token, the abstractions of the theorist are nothing without the detailed information and analysis of the empirical researcher. All this is true. To a surprising degree, however, historians and political scientists have remained at arm's length from each other. This may be because historians are convinced that theorists are incapable of explaining change, while theorists are convinced that historians ignore the structural contexts within which foreign policy is made. The end of the cold war has surely served to undercut this artificial divide. The sudden collapse of apparently stable structures has focused our minds precisely on the relationship between change and the structures of international politics.

This book, while certainly not making a contribution to international relations theory as such, employs certain theoretical approaches in the conviction that they provide routes to an understanding of historical problems. In particular, the concept of a system of states helps to make sense of the global context in which US–Soviet rivalry took place. Crucial questions such as the origins of the cold war take on new shapes when they are lifted out of the usual analytical framework of the individual nation-state or purely bilateral US–Soviet relations. Chapter 1, the first section of Chapter 4, and Chapter 14 address these issues explicitly and provide the main organizing ideas of the book. At various points I have drawn on other theoretical perspectives – including decision-making theory and the theory of 'complex interdependence' – to illuminate particular historical issues.

Inevitably, in crossing boundaries in the way suggested, I risk disappointing both historians and theorists. It should be clear, however, that at every point my criterion for employing one or another theoretical perspective has been whether it helps in an understanding of historical change.

Chapters 1–5 are a heavily revised and expanded version of my *The United States and the Cold War, 1941–1953* (1989), published by the British Association for American Studies. Chapter 14 contains some material from my 'Theories of Stability and the End of the Cold War' in Mike Bowker and Rob Brown (eds) *From Cold War to Collapse: Theory and World Politics in the 1980s* (1993), published by Cambridge University Press.

My thanks to both publishers. Several institutions, friends and colleagues have helped during the writing of this book. The University of East Anglia granted me a term of study leave midway through the writing, and over the years has given me scope to develop my interests in history and political science. I owe a good deal to successive years of undergraduates who have taken my special subject on the cold war, and to graduate students on the MA course in International Relations. I am grateful to Dickinson College, Carlisle, Pennsylvania for providing me with a very congenial place to teach and write during the academic year 1992–93, and to the Fulbright Commission for granting funds which allowed that stay in Carlisle to go ahead.

My largest intellectual debt is to Steve Smith, formerly of the University of East Anglia and now of the University of Wales, Aberystwyth. I have learned an enormous amount from working with him on an earlier book project and on the MA in International Relations at the University of East Anglia. In his willingness to read large sections of the book and to answer endless questions he has been the best of friends and colleagues. It was largely owing to him that I ventured into the field of international relations, though he is in no way responsible for the uses to which I have put it.

Others too gave freely of their time and advice. Edward Acton read Chapter 2, Russell Bova Chapter 13, and Mike Bowker read most of the text. All are Soviet/Russian specialists and, since I am an Americanist by training, I found their detailed comments especially valuable. Rosemary Foot and Andrew Patmore, both specialists on superpower politics in Asia, read Chapter 5 and Chapter 10 respectively. Douglas Stuart's expertise on the arms race and security policy was applied to a careful reading of Chapters 7 and 11. He and Russell Bova, both of the Political Science Department at Dickinson College, were always willing to listen to my half-formed ideas and helped to make the writing of the later chapters a pleasure rather than a chore. I am grateful to the readers of the original proposal and in particular to Richard Aldrich for his wide-ranging and thoughtful comments. Needless to say, none of the above can be held responsible for the final result, which is mine alone.

Gordon Smith of Routledge has been an unfailingly encouraging and patient editor. I am happy that chance and the mysteries of take-overs and mergers, which took us in different directions from Unwin Hyman some years ago, should have brought us together again at Routledge.

Thanks are due to Stephanie Harry for word-processing assistance and to Gladys Cashman who helped in the preparation of the manuscript and was an ever-cheerful presence in the History Department at Dickinson College.

Certain friends who have read little or nothing of this book nevertheless deserve warmest thanks for their interest in it and for their morale-boosting conversation – John Ashworth, Legs and Oli Knowland, Litty Paxton, Roger Thompson, and Bob Winston. Graeme Winn generously allowed me to use his flat for a period of uninterrupted writing. Conversation with Leonid Gozman was invaluable at a late stage in the writing. I owe a good deal to a course taught by Michael Dunne over twenty years ago at the University of Sussex. Some of the seeds planted there bear fruit in Chapter 2.

Clara and our three children, Sam, Martha, and John, have given me the kind of support without which this book could not have been written. The book is dedicated to them, with love.

The author and publishers have made every effort to trace copyright holders of the sources from which the maps in this volume are derived. Individual sources are given beneath each map. In addition we wish to acknowledge Hamish Hamilton and W.W. Norton for Figure 0.1; W.W. Norton for Figures 2.2, 8.2 and 10.1; Basil Blackwell for Figure 0.2; D.C. Heath for Figures 2.1 and 3.1; A. & C. Black for Figure 4.1 (originally published by Ernest Benn); HarperCollins for Figure 5.1 (originally published by Harper & Row); McGraw-Hill for Figures 8.1, 11.1 and 11.2. Any copyright holders not acknowledged here are asked to contact the publishers.

ABBREVIATIONS

ABM	anti-ballistic missile
AIOC	Anglo-Iranian Oil Company
ALCM	air-launched Cruise missile
BMD	ballistic missile defense
BPA	Basic Principles Agreement
CDU	Christian Democrats
CIA	Central Intelligence Agency
COMECON	Council for Mutual Economic Assistance
CPD	Committee on the Present Danger
CSCE	Conference on Security and Cooperation in Europe
DRV	Democratic Republic of Vietnam
EDC	European Defence Community
EEC	European Economic Community
END	European Nuclear Disarmament
ERP	European Recovery Program
ERW	enhanced radiation weapon
FBS	Forward Base System
FMLN	Farabundo Marti National Liberation Front
FRG	Federal Republic of Germany
GATT	General Agreement on Trade and Tariffs
GDR	German Democratic Republic
HUAC	House Un-American Activities Committee
IAEA	International Atomic Energy Agency
IBRD	International Bank for Reconstruction and Development
ICBM	intercontinental ballistic missile
IMF	International Monetary Fund
INF	Intermediate Nuclear Forces
IRBM	intermediate-range ballistic missile
JCS	Joint Chiefs of Staff
KOR	Workers' Defence Committee (Polish)

LDCs	less-developed countries
MAD	mutual assured destruction
MAS	mutual assured survival
MFN	Most Favoured Nation
MIRV	multiple independently targetable re-entry vehicle
MRBM	medium-range ballistic missile
NCA	National Command Centre
NICs	newly industrializing countries
NIEO	New International Economic Order
NLF	National Liberation Front
NORAD	North American Aerospace Defense Command
NSC	National Security Council
OAS	Organization of American States
OECD	Organization for Economic Cooperation and Development
OPEC	Organization of Petroleum Exporting Countries
OSS	Office of Strategic Services
PCF	French Communist Party
PCI	Italian Communist Party
PNW	Prevention of Nuclear War
PPS	Policy Planning Staff
PRC	People's Republic of China
RDF	Rapid Deployment Force
SAC	Strategic Air Command
SALT	Strategic Arms Limitation Treaty
SAM	surface to air missile
SDI	Strategic Defense Initiative
SEATO	Southeast Asia Treaty Organization
SLBM	submarine-launched ballistic missile
SPD	Social Democrats
START	Strategic Arms Reduction Treaty
UFCO	United Fruit Company
WEU	Western European Union

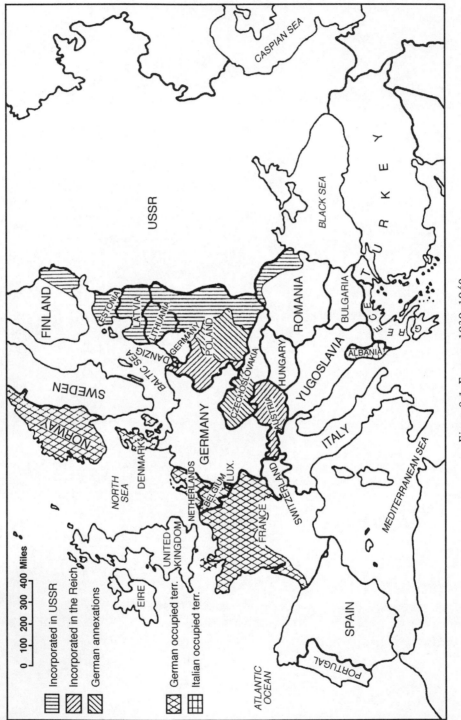

Figure 0.1 Europe, 1939–1940
Source: Derived from R. Edmonds, *The Big Three*, New York: Norton, 1993.

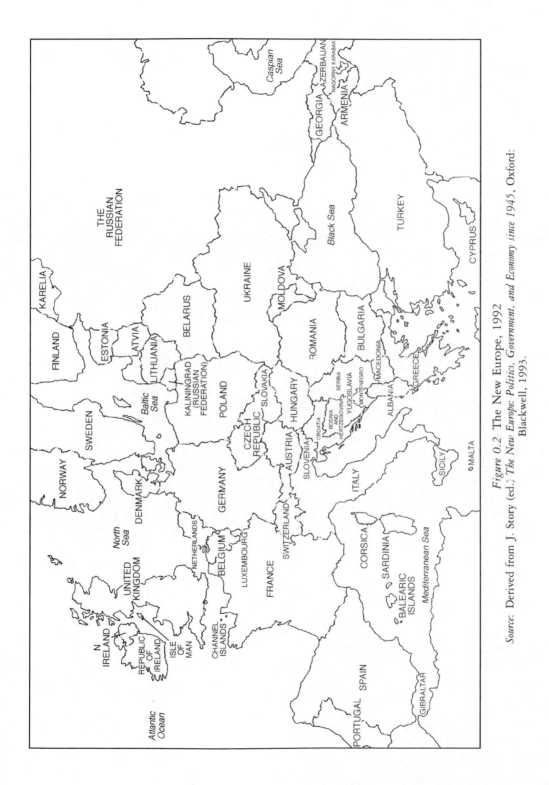

Figure 0.2 The New Europe, 1992

Source: Derived from J. Story (ed.) *The New Europe: Politics, Government, and Economy since 1945*, Oxford: Blackwell, 1993.

Part I

PERSPECTIVES

1

INTRODUCTION
The Fifty Years War

For fifty years relations between the United States and the Soviet Union were the deciding factor in international affairs. War against Germany brought them together in 1941 in an alliance which was decisive in securing Germany's defeat, but victory ultimately drove them apart, giving rise to the state of continuous, if fluctuating, antagonism which we know as cold war. No open hostilities took place between the United States and the Soviet Union, yet for the bulk of the period each armed against the other as if for war. Even their brief alliance against Germany was plagued by mistrust and misgivings. Since these loomed ever larger as the hot war against Germany gave way to cold war, and since the US–Soviet relationship was the determining factor in both the anti-Axis alliance and the shaping of the post-war world, it seems appropriate to view both within the same frame. In short, the upheaval of the Second World War set the geopolitical scene for the cold war.

In December 1991, following the re-drawing of the political map of central Europe, the Soviet Union itself finally disintegrated and with it the cold war. In the space of little more than a generation the international system of states had undergone two earthquakes, the epicentres of which both lay in Europe, the seat of the modern system of states dating from the seventeenth century.

Such transformations demand explanations of the kind which could not be fully offered while the cold war was still in progress. Research into the various episodes of US–Soviet relations over the past fifty years has grown to unmanageable proportions. It is now accompanied by equally urgent questioning of the reasons for the Soviet collapse, spurred on by bafflement at its sheer suddenness and the consequent shock it supplied to assumptions about the durability – the apparent givenness – of the cold war system. Notoriously, few commentators predicted the collapse of the Soviet Union. Faced with the enormity of such events we grasp for metaphors where the facts are so legion and diverse in their implications.

The great temptation is to read history backwards. Knowing the outcome of events, we are inclined to construct accounts of history which lead inevitably to the known conclusion. Nor is hindsight necessarily always blind or partial. It is in fact one important advantage which the historian possesses over participants in historical events. Nevertheless, an adequate account of the origins, growth, and collapse of the cold war will be one which balances hindsight against awareness of the contingencies of events as they were experienced by contemporaries. That demands of the historian both detachment and engagement. It may be that the present moment is peculiarly apt for such a balancing act, since the events in question are close enough for their pulse still to be felt but distant enough – by reason of the radical discontinuity supplied by the Soviet collapse – to be grasped as history. As suggested above, the major premise of this book is that the half century from 1941 to 1991 is best understood as a whole. In destroying the pre-war balance of power the Second World War created the conditions under which US–Soviet rivalry would come to form the basis of a new world balance of power. For all the manifest global shifts and upheavals between 1945 and 1991 US–Soviet rivalry was a constant and for much of the period dominated international politics. Such schematic statements clearly demand justification. It is the purpose of this chapter to outline the aims and methods adopted in the book as a whole, providing a general mapping of US–Soviet relations within the framework of global political change.

A QUESTION OF SCALE

Understanding the recent past is like trying to read a map which lacks a scale. Events which loom large as they occur often prove to be of minor importance when viewed in retrospect. On the other hand, apparently minor shifts of policy assume major proportions when, with the passage of time, their full ramifications become visible. Unfortunately, providing an appropriate scale is much more difficult for the historian than for the cartographer. The cartographer simply settles on a framework whose dimensions remain fixed and uniformly applicable. A ruler is all that is needed to establish the true proportions between the features on the map.

By contrast, the historian's scale is constantly in motion. The calendar, the historian's only fixed point of reference, indicates when events occurred but not precisely how important they are, since that involves judgements which vary according to the position and experience of the observer. Even the most obviously global events – such as the Second World War – affected nations in fundamentally different ways, and in some cases scarcely at all. The location of the historian both in space and time critically affects the scale adopted and the character of the map which results.

A sequence of events from the recent past will illustrate the dimensions of the problem. In the early 1980s, as the superpower *détente* of the late 1960s and 1970s wound down, it became common to speak of the emergence of a 'new' or 'second' cold war (Chomsky *et al.* 1982; Halliday 1983). Whoever was to blame for the downturn in US–Soviet relations, it seemed clear that *détente* was dead. The succession of crises from the Angolan revolution in 1975, to the Soviet invasion of Afghanistan in 1979, the Sandinista victory in Nicaragua in the same year, in addition to Soviet intervention in the Horn of Africa and insurgency in El Salvador, seemed to indicate that *détente* had done little to moderate superpower rivalry in the Third World. These events, coupled with the deployment of new intermediate-range nuclear weapons by both sides in Europe and the halt in the SALT (Strategic Arms Limitation Treaty) process, ushered in a period of hostility in US–Soviet relations comparable in scope and intensity with the early post-war years. *Détente*, already moribund in the later years of the Carter administration, was apparently buried by the time of the election of President Reagan in 1980. The new president embarked on rhetoric and policies which were more nakedly confrontational than anything since the days of John Foster Dulles in the mid-1950s. There is room for much debate about the interpretation of these events, an issue which will be addressed later in this book, but there can be little doubt that US–Soviet relations had entered a new and dangerous phase. The resurgence of the long quiescent anti-nuclear movement in the West was one indication of the depth of popular concern over the revival of cold war politics.

Within a few years, however, these events appeared in a very different light. In 1987 President Reagan, who in 1983 had labelled the Soviet Union an 'evil empire', put his signature to the first arms reduction (as opposed to arms control) treaty ever negotiated between the superpowers, he had established a cordial, even warm relationship with the new Soviet leadership, and relations between the United States and the Soviet Union in general were perhaps closer than during the period of *détente* in the early 1970s. The second cold war looks to have been a minor blip on the changing graph of US–Soviet relations, a matter of rhetoric rather than substance, and an event whose significance has been exaggerated by political observers.

How are these different perspectives to be explained, let alone reconciled? Evidently much depends on the length of the time-scale adopted. Viewed in the short term, the second cold war did represent a novel departure in US–Soviet relations. The Soviet invasion of Afghanistan, for example, was in line with a general expansion of Soviet intervention in the Third World during the latter half of the 1970s. These developments, like the build-up of Soviet naval power and other categories of armaments, were matters of fact not rhetoric. On the American side one need only look at the substantial increases in the American defence budgets adopted by the Reagan administration to be aware that here too we are speaking of matters of substance. Furthermore, the US arms build-up was associated with a distinct swing to the right in domestic politics, expressing a repudiation of permissive social values at home and a distaste for compromise abroad. The Reagan presidency brought revised assumptions about the nature of the Soviet threat and the appropriate means of dealing with it. Reagan's Manichaean vision of the world order as a moral battleground between the principles of good and evil, and not merely an arena for competition between nation-states, was at several removes from the complex *Realpolitik* of the Nixon–Kissinger approach to world politics during the years of *détente*. In short, it is arguable that there was a qualitative change in the US–Soviet relationship during this period. It was not, of course, entirely novel, in that it disinterred old cold war attitudes dating

5

from the 1940s and 1950s, but it was to be sharply distinguished from the period of *détente*.

The alternative way of viewing the second cold war is to place it firmly within the overall framework of US–Soviet relations since the Second World War. From this standpoint the oscillations between periods of confrontation and *détente* are less significant than the fact that both issued from a fundamental pattern or structure which was continuous from the mid-1940s to the late 1980s. That structure was defined by the geopolitical conditions and ideological rivalry established after the Second World War. The division of Europe, the growth of parallel alliance systems, the arms race, and the extension of superpower competition to the Third World constituted a cold war 'system', so it can be argued, which underlay periods of *détente* no less than the periods of more overt conflict between the superpowers (Cox 1990: 30–1). From this viewpoint *détente* itself was conditioned by cold war relations; it was an episode in the cold war rather than a departure from it. This interpretation does not deny that significant changes in the behaviour of the superpowers took place in the early 1980s, but it does question whether they signalled a basic alteration in the underlying conditions of superpower relations.

If, to adopt another change of scale, we take as our benchmark, not the signing of the Intermediate Nuclear Forces (INF) Treaty in 1987 but the collapse of communism in Eastern Europe and the Soviet Union since 1989, then the second cold war looks even less like the fundamental upheaval it appeared to be at the time. The comprehensive demise of communism now allows us to see more clearly than ever that cold war was the defining characteristic of the US–Soviet relationship. Like the shooting star which shines most brightly just before it burns out, the second cold war might from this perspective be seen as the dying phase of the cold war.

Furthermore, the upheavals since 1989 have exposed an instructive ambiguity in the term 'cold war' itself which helps the historian to gain a perspective on the whole post-war period. 'Cold war' has been used in two distinct ways. In its more restricted sense it refers to (roughly) the two decades following the Second World War during which the main outlines of the US–Soviet relationship were established and in which open antagonism predominated. By the late 1960s some commentators began to ask what was left of the cold war and concluded that not much remained (Thomas 1969; Buchan 1972: 34–5). The second cold war of the 1980s was so called precisely because it recalled that earlier period and seemed out of line with the *détente* of the 1970s.

In the first meaning of the term, then, cold war refers to particular periods and a particular type of behaviour. It is to be contrasted sharply with *détente*. The second meaning of the term refers to the underlying conditions of the US–Soviet relationship which persisted until what has been called 'the second Russian Revolution' (Roxburgh 1991). When in the late 1980s commentators and political leaders began to talk of 'the end of the cold war' it was this structural condition they meant. They meant also, to be sure, declining antagonism and a growing climate of cooperation, but what distinguished this climate from the *détente* of the 1970s was the fact that it went along

6

with fundamental structural change: nothing less than the entire geopolitical order which had been established in the early post-war years. *Détente*, by contrast, involved a ratification of the post-war European *status quo*, including mutual *de facto* recognition by East and West Germany. The price of *détente* in the early 1970s was formal acknowledgement by both sides of the division of Europe. As was suggested above, this places *détente* firmly within the cold war framework.

THE COLD WAR AND INTERNATIONAL POLITICS

The above example illustrates some of the choices open to the historian in attempting to understand the recent past. The argument for employing a long perspective on the period can be reinforced by reference to the writings of certain international relations theorists who have engaged rather more explicitly than historians with the underlying principles of international politics. Since in the course of this book some of these principles will be invoked, it may be as well to refer briefly to them here.

The dominant theoretical perspective in the study of international relations, established in the early post-war period, was 'Realism'. It posited that the key units of analysis in international politics were nation-states, that nation-states presented themselves to the outside world as coherent, integrated units pursuing rationally conceived objectives, and, furthermore, that conflicts of power (particularly military power) based on clashing national interests provided the driving force of international politics. Historians largely shared this state-centric approach and characteristically also the Realists' preoccupation with the 'balance of power' as the feature of international politics which made for stability, or the lack of it, within the international system.

However, while historians, who were generally area or single nation specialists, tended to retain the emphasis on the nation-state, some theorists developed alternative ways of conceiving the international context within which nation-states operated. Two lines of development deserve particular mention. The first, termed 'Neorealism', was, as its name suggests, an outgrowth of Realism. While retaining the view that nation-states were the basic units of international politics, Neorealists denied that the character of the units determined the structure and behaviour of the international system. The functioning of the system was determined not by the capabilities of the units but by the particular position they assumed relative to each other within the overall system. Nation states, that is to say, could be considered as being essentially alike for the purposes of analysing the characteristics of the system. In the words of the most prominent Neorealist theorist, Kenneth Waltz:

> To define a structure requires ignoring how units relate with one another (how they interact) and concentrating on how they stand in relation to one another (how they are arranged or positioned). Interactions . . . take place at the level of the units. How units stand in relation to one another, the way they are

arranged or positioned, is not a property of the units. The arrangement of units is a property of the system.

(Waltz 1979: 80)

The characteristics of any particular international system are set by two main features: anarchy and polarity (multipolarity or bipolarity). Anarchy exists in international politics because there is no overarching sovereign body which exerts governmental or organizing power over the states which compose it. There exists, that is to say, no body in the international system which exerts power comparable to that which national governments wield over their own territory. International law and such bodies as the United Nations are limited in their effects by the willingness of sovereign nations to accede to their rulings. There is as yet no compulsion to do so.[1] For this reason the international system reflects any particular given distribution of power. This generally takes the form either of a multipolar system, in which several Great Powers form the peak of a hierarchy of powers (such as existed between the world wars), or a bipolar system, whose shape is set by the presence of two dominant powers (such as existed for much of the cold war) (Hollis and Smith 1991: 101–4).

On the face of it, adoption of the most rigorous form of systems theory would seem to place the bulk of diplomatic history on the rubbish heap, since the latter is premised on the assumption that what goes on inside nation-states – not least policy-making, personalities, ideology, national traditions and so on – are causal factors in producing change in the international system. Indeed, one of the criticisms levelled at systems theory (at least in its most rigorous form) is that it has not been able satisfactorily to explain how change in the international system is possible without some reference to the inner workings of nation-states (Ruggie 1986: 141–52).

There is much, however, which systems theory can offer the historian. The chief gain lies in the concept of system itself, in that it allows us to understand the foreign policies of states as being determined, at least in part (a qualification we shall return to) by constraints and opportunities supplied by the given distribution of power. For example, many historians write as if the origin of the cold war is to be explained wholly by reference to the intentions of the nations in question. This has frequently meant that interpretations have rested on ascribing blame to one or another of the major powers. Depending on one's political or national viewpoint, either the Soviet Union or the United States was regarded as the initiator of the cold war and the other as the reactive power. In particular, histories written during the first two decades of the cold war tended to adopt this approach. This was a consequence not simply of national or ideological bias but of the framework of analysis itself which served to abstract the nation-state from its international setting.

A systems approach, furthermore, offers insights into how different structures tend to produce different types and levels of international conflict and different forms of alliances among nations. Much debate has taken place about whether multipolar or bipolar systems are more conducive to stability (Deutsch and Singer 1964; Waltz

8

1964). For present purposes, however, the important point is that bipolarity in the post-war international system, in conjunction with nuclear weapons, tended to lock the superpowers into tense relations at the centre and extend international conflict to the 'periphery' of the system. That may or may not be described as stability; doubtless it depends on one's location within the system. At any rate, according to the Neorealist approach, as compared with multipolar systems, bipolar systems are less likely to produce war between the major powers.

However, such a conclusion is warranted only if one assumes that structures determine the behaviour of states. Two modifications to this position are necessary for the historian to be able to make use of the systems approach. One indeed comes from Kenneth Waltz himself who, in a revised version of his theory, has conceded that 'thinking in terms of systems dynamics does not replace unit-level analysis nor end the search for sequences of cause and effect' (Waltz 1986: 344). In short, Waltz acknowledges that it is necessary to analyse what goes on inside nation-states in order to understand the full workings of the system.

A second modification of the systems approach is to insist, against the advice of some theorists, that it is necessary specifically to relate the system and nation-state levels of analysis. 'We may utilize one level here and another there,' argues J. David Singer, 'but we cannot afford to shift our orientation in the midst of a study' (Singer 1969: 28). The historian, however, will often find that this is precisely what is required. The most important questions for the historian of international relations arise in the interaction between the international system and the nations of which it is composed, not least because the internal character of nation-states, their ambitions, policies, and capacities to exert power are manifestly causal factors in producing system change. It would be a strange history of twentieth-century international relations which did not examine the internal sources of Germany's bid for world power in the decades prior to 1914 as a major cause of the First World War; or Germany's renewed bid in the 1930s as a cause of the Second World War. We need to study structures in order to understand how things endure and we need to study nation-states in order to understand how things change.

The second main strand of international relations theory from which the historian can profit is 'pluralism' or 'neoliberal institutionalism'. This approach does not entirely dispense with the notion of structures or with nation-states as a focus of analysis, but it does question Realist and Neorealist assumptions in two fundamental ways. Firstly, Pluralists reject the notion that structure – bipolarity or multipolarity – determines the behaviour of nation-states, and in doing so they undermine the Realist belief that it is possible to separate the international environment from the domestic environments of nation-states. Secondly, Pluralists question the Realist assumption that nation-states are the only significant actors in world politics.

Positively, Pluralism takes the analysis of international politics in two new directions. In the first place, it is argued that 'non-state actors' such as international organizations and multinational companies are important independent actors in their own right. *Trans*-national processes are as important as *inter*-national processes in world politics. Indeed nation-states are increasingly losing control over their destinies. Non-state actors often set the agenda for the policies of nation-states. One example might be the conditions which the International Monetary Fund (IMF) sets for loans to nations. Another is the influence which powerful multinational companies can exert on the taxation and trade policies of nation-states by exacting concessions from governments as a condition for establishing manufacturing plants in those countries. Furthermore, Pluralism challenges the Realist view that there is a hierarchy of interests in the policies of nation-states, with national security and military power at the top. For the Pluralist, economics, trade, energy, and environmental issues are often equally significant items on the international agenda. In place of the Realist idea of a balance of power among competing sovereign nations, the Pluralist offers the notion of 'complex interdependence'. In the words of the most prominent Pluralist theorists, adopting the concept of complex interdependence 'we can imagine a world in which actors other than states participate directly in world politics, in which a clear hierarchy of issues does not exist, and in which force is an ineffective instrument of policy' (Keohane and Nye 1977: 24).

The second way in which Pluralist theory has altered the agenda of international relations theory and research has been to re-direct attention to the internal processes within nation-states. Contrary to Realist claims, Pluralists argue that nation-states are neither unitary nor rational actors. Policy outcomes are more likely to be the product of bureaucratic bargaining and political conflict than of ordered, rational processes. There is thus a danger in using shorthand such as 'Washington' or 'Moscow' or even 'the United States' or 'the Soviet Union'. From this perspective has developed the 'bureaucratic processes' model of international relations theory, to which we shall refer in more detail in Chapter 7 in discussing the Cuban missile crisis. For the moment, we must pause to assess the bearing which the theoretical perspectives described above have on the task of understanding the history of the cold war.

Readers might reasonably ask how such an assemblage of often contradictory perspectives can hope to issue in coherent explanation. We can begin to answer this question by noting that none of the theorists mentioned above claim that their particular theories explain every aspect of international politics. Neorealism and Pluralism represent models, or 'ideal types', which seek to explain reality according to factors which are taken to be salient. Indeed, that is the point. These theories attend to different aspects of international politics, and both are justified within the terms of the realities they set out to explain. Specifically, it is proposed here that Neorealism best fits the dynamics of the cold war system, with its characteristics of US–Soviet bipolarity and the primacy of national security concerns in policy-making. Pluralism, however, best explains the expansion of world capitalism which grew alongside the cold war system but was not coterminous with it. It is no accident that Pluralist theory should have emerged in the 1970s as US–Soviet relations became, so to speak, infected by complex transnational pressures. *Détente*, it will be argued later, represented an attempt on the part of the superpowers, which was only partially successful, to reshape their relations in the light of the emergence of 'complex interdependence'. In short, the development of international relations theory since the Second World War mirrors the shift in international politics from a bipolar, security-centred system dominated by US–Soviet conflict to a multipolar system which was characterized by increasingly complex and multi-level interactions. Crucially, the United States and the Soviet Union experienced these changes in quite different ways. We shall conclude this chapter with a sketch of the overall picture.

The decisive effect of the Second World War was to destroy the multipolar balance of power which in varying forms had characterized the international system since the seventeenth century. The end of the Second World War found the old pillars of the pre-war system of states incapable of sustaining that structure, and in its place grew a new bipolar structure founded on the predominance of the United States and the Soviet Union. For fifteen years or more the disproportionately large economic, military, and political power wielded by the United States and the Soviet Union heavily influenced, even where it did not wholly determine, the political alignments of other nations. This period of high cold war was followed by a transitional period during which both superpowers experienced relative economic decline, as Europe and Japan recovered from wartime devastation and the process of decolonization brought numerous new independent states into the world system. The result by the late 1960s was the decay of bipolarity and the emergence of a more complex, multipolar world system in which transnational economic forces and institutions played an increasing role. To be sure, this was not a uniform process. Effective military bipolarity, based on nuclear weapons, continued long after the growth of new centres of economic power, a point to which we shall return.

As mentioned above, the United States and the Soviet Union experienced these changes in different ways, corresponding to their different strengths and weaknesses. In fact, fundamental asymmetries had existed between the United States and the Soviet Union from the earliest post-war years. The cold war was never an equal contest. Even the period of 'high' cold war in the late 1940s and 1950s was in actuality characterized by basic imbalances between the superpowers. The most significant of these was economic. It has two aspects, the first being simply the Soviet Union's economic weakness relative to the United States, a weakness for which the Soviet Union could compensate only by maintaining military strength and hence the capacity to impose political and ideological conformity within the sphere of influence which it established in Eastern Europe after the war. In the absence of a socio-economic system which exerted attractive power by virtue of its capacity to generate growth, repressive means were necessary to ensure political and ideological compliance. Secondly, economic growth was pursued in the Eastern bloc in virtual isolation from the global, capitalist-dominated economy. Economic autarky was in any case firmly within the Soviet tradition, in part forced upon it by the capitalist powers and in part chosen by the Soviet leadership in order to defend the Revolution against penetration from outside, the hoped-for global communist revolution having failed to materialize out of the Bolshevik success.

In so far, then, as the early cold war balance of power developed elements of stability, it did so within the framework of imbalances: complementary imbalances, to be sure, but imbalances nevertheless.[2] So long as the Soviet Union was able to sustain growth on the basis of autarky and the command economy, it could both maintain the integrity of the Eastern Bloc and present an effective military and political challenge to the West. And indeed it did so for a time. In the late 1950s, at a time when Soviet growth rates actually exceeded those of the United States, both enemies and friends of the Soviet Union foresaw a time when Soviet economic achievement might outstrip that of the West. 'Stalin's isolationism, protectionism, and Iron Curtain', wrote Isaac Deutscher in 1960, had been designed 'to keep the Soviet people immune from the impact of higher Western efficiency and higher Western standards of living'. This era, however, was drawing to a close. Within a decade it was likely that the Soviet bloc would be producing 'half the world's industrial output', and would be competing on equal terms with the capitalist nations (Deutscher 1960: 90).

Needless to say, this estimate was wildly astray. The Soviet Union both failed to maintain its 1950s rates of growth – which in any case are to be understood in light of the low base from which it started and the chronic weakness of its agricultural and consumer goods sectors – and subsequently fell sharply behind Western Europe and the United States in relative economic terms (Kennedy 1988: 329–32). Soviet successes in heavy industrial production and in missile and space technology in the late 1950s and 1960s gave a false impression of the health of the overall economy, which by the late 1960s was experiencing the costs of its inefficiency and isolation from the world economy. Soviet recognition of these costs was acknowledged in the late 1960s when as part of the goal of *détente* the Soviet Union sought increased trade with the West and in particular the transfer of new technology.

The full implications of the fragility of Soviet power were only realized in the 1980s, when it became clear that military power could no longer compensate for economic weakness or for the declining hold of communist ideology over Soviet and Eastern bloc peoples. The cold war system began to unravel as the Soviet command economy proved quite unable to respond to the high-tech industrial revolution of the 1970s and 1980s. The United States too experienced serious economic problems from the early 1970s, but because it had always been integrated into the world economy, indeed had dominated it for two decades after the war, it caused no corresponding upheaval at home. Economic crisis, that is to say, did not lead to a disabling crisis of political legitimacy within the United States. Another way of putting this is to say that the United States possessed a marked advantage by virtue of its full integration into the world system as distinct from the cold war system. The Soviet Union's position, by contrast, was defined and limited by the cold war system. It had the status of a Great Power primarily by virtue of its military strength. It was, in Paul Dibb's words, an 'incomplete superpower' (Dibb 1988).

The above account clearly leaves much out, most obviously the extent to which the Soviet Union was successful in promoting communism, or at least anti-Westernism, as a model for Third World development. Nor is it claimed that the end of the cold war is to be explained wholly in economic terms. The intention is to highlight certain broad distinctions which need to be made when one tries to relate the US–Soviet relationship to the changing world order. The key distinction is between the cold war system and the world system, the claim being that even during the period of high cold war, when the bipolar superpower relationship was at its most dominant, the two systems were not entirely coterminous. From the outset the United States possessed a superior capacity to project itself on the world arena. It had the largest stake and the dominant influence in the major international economic institutions set up at the end of the war, pre-eminently the International Monetary Fund and the World Bank, in neither of which the Soviet Union participated. It is even arguable that the world system in the initial phase of the cold war is best described as uni-polar, were it not for the fact that America's manifest economic superiority did not of itself guarantee achievement of its goal of containing Soviet power in Europe. The Marshall Plan of economic aid to Western Europe (1948–52) was quickly supplemented by a military alliance in the form of NATO (1949), in part because of a basic asymmetry in the US–Soviet relationship which in this case worked to Soviet advantage: namely, Soviet proximity to the potential theatre of military conflict, coupled with Soviet superiority in conventional troop strength.

There was, in short, no automatic translation on either side of their peculiar strengths into clear political advantage. Each nation experienced constraints on the exercise of the particular level of power which appeared most advantageous to it. This had the effect of locking the superpowers into tense relations with each other. In that sense they were bound to each other by their differences even as they were pushed apart by them.

Clearly the cold war system, which is the form that the bilateral US–Soviet relationship took, initially exerted a significant influence on the international system and continued (until at least the beginning of the 1990s) to absorb much of the attention of foreign policy-makers in the United States and the Soviet Union. Cold war bipolarity did not entirely disappear as more complex patterns emerged. It was sustained in the nuclear relationship between the superpowers, in the geopolitical fact of a divided Europe (until 1989), and in rivalry at various points in the Third World.

However, the superpowers paid a considerable price for their mutual absorption in the cold war system. Cold war politics served to ossify the US–Soviet relationship, hindering both from responding creatively to the growing diversity within the world system, though evidently at greater cost to the Soviet Union than to the United States. In the end, the Soviet Union's attempt to sustain its separate development in the face of an increasingly interdependent world proved impossible.

As the above sketch makes clear, the bilateral relationship between the superpowers is only part of the story told in this book. The guiding theme is of the interaction between the superpower relationship and the larger movements in world politics. In the chapters which follow, detailed narratives are embedded within interpretive frameworks appropriate to each phase of US–Soviet relations since 1941. The periodization adopted rests on the conviction that certain clusters of events constitute important turning points in both the global system and in US–Soviet bilateral relations. We begin, however, with a discussion of the foreign policy traditions of both powers, since these provide essential clues not only to superpower behaviour but to the form which the post-war international system assumed.

2

THE AMERICAN AND SOVIET FOREIGN POLICY TRADITIONS

Individual nations, as we have seen, occupy positions within systems of states, and the nature of the system has a direct bearing on the making of foreign policy. The limitations on the behaviour of states and the opportunities open to them, however, are also influenced by historical experiences of long standing. The origins of the cold war cannot be wholly explained by reference to events which immediately precipitated it. Both the United States and the Soviet Union brought to those events sets of assumptions and practices which had their roots in the experience of nation-building. It is worth reminding ourselves, as Michael Howard has done recently, that the study of world affairs is about international relations, not merely interstate relations. International relations is about how nations deal with foreign cultures, about nations which speak different languages, think different thoughts and respond to common challenges in quite different ways (Howard 1989a).

The aim of this chapter is to examine the historical sources of the leading principles which have informed the foreign policies of the United States and the Soviet Union since the Second World War.

THE UNITED STATES

Inured as we are to the presence of the United States as a dominant power in world politics, it was nevertheless the case that for much of its history America proclaimed 'isolationism' as its chief principle in foreign relations. The story of American foreign policy in the twentieth century has often been described as the ultimate triumph of involvement over isolationism. Dragged unwillingly into the First World War in a belated recognition that it was destined to play an international role which matched its already huge economic power, it then 'retreated into isolationism' in the 1920s and 1930s, only to be forced once again in 1941 to enter a world war in order to restore the global balance of power. From 1945 onwards there could be no question of a second retreat into isolationism. Such is the story-book account of American foreign relations.

There are two problems with this picture. In the first place, despite its professed isolationism during the nineteenth century, the United States was manifestly an

15

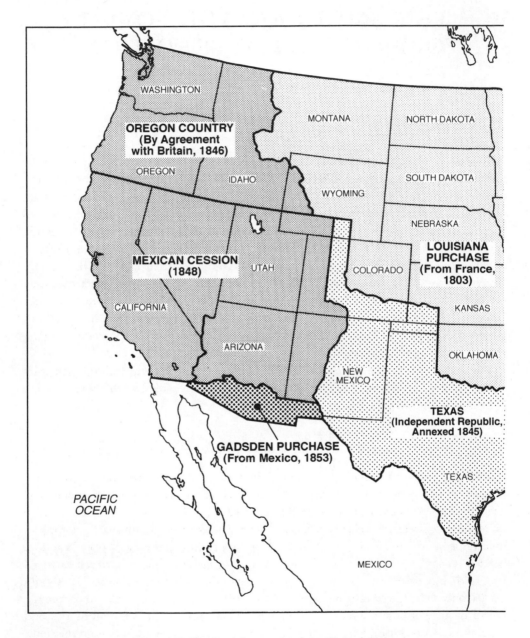

Figure 2.1 Territorial growth of the United States
Source: Derived from P. Boyer *et al.*, *The Enduring Vision: A History of the American People*, 2nd edition, Lexington, Mass.: D.C. Heath, 1993, front endpaper.

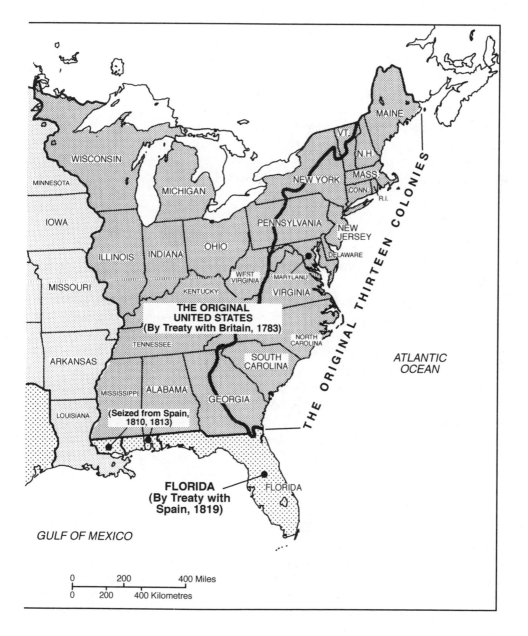

expansionist power, extending its territory from the banks of the Mississipi river to the Rocky Mountains in 1803 with the purchase of the Louisiana territory from France, to the gulf of Mexico in 1819 with the acquisition of Florida from Spain, and to the Pacific in the 1840s with the acquisition of the Oregon territory from Britain and the seizure of California and the Southwest from Mexico in the war of 1846–48. There were also powerful voices at various times urging the extension of American territory further into Mexico, Cuba, and even Canada. Equally striking were America's first territorial gains outside the North American continent with the annexation of Hawaii in 1896, followed by the Philippines, Puerto Rico, Guam and other Pacific islands after the war with Spain in 1898. Even if one accepts that most of the newly acquired territory involved extension of America's frontiers to its natural continental limits – the justification generally offered by apologists of this process – it must be admitted that the dynamism of America's outward thrust sits oddly with the profession of isolationism. The first problem, then, is to explain the connections between these two apparently contradictory motions.

A second problem with the conventional picture outlined above is that, while the United States has manifestly become involved in world politics during the twentieth century, isolationist sentiment has nevertheless remained a powerful force. A leading historian of isolationism, writing in 1956, concluded his study on an ambivalent note. By 1945, he wrote, 'authentic isolationism was all but gone,' but he also noted that 'any number of possible foreign calamities could once more render isolationism a feasible and even an attractive policy'. American economic and military commitments abroad were fervently opposed by a significant minority in Congress, such that 'if isolationists could recapture control of the GOP [Republican Party], they could rejuvenate the insular tradition with the help of provincial Dixiecrats [conservative Southern Democrats] and other Democrats willing to make capital of the foreign aid issue' (Adler 1961: 428, 432). Since then, at various times of strain during the cold war, notably in the aftermath of Vietnam, commentators have voiced fears of the rise of 'neo-isolationism'. Nor has isolationism been the exclusive preserve of the right. It has a long and continuing history among those on the left who deplore what they see as the unprincipled extension of American power around the world (Paterson 1988: Ch. 11).

It seems clear that isolationism is not a simple notion, once we try to apply it to the development of the United States. The policy, if not the term, originates with George Washington's famous 'Farewell Address' of 1797, in which he counselled future American administrations thus: 'the great rule of conduct for us in regard to foreign nations is, in extending our commercial relations to have with them as little political connection as possible' (Fitzpatrick 1940, Vol. 35: 233). This was followed up four years later by Thomas Jefferson, who urged 'equal and exact justice to all men, of whatever state or persuasion, religious or political; peace, commerce, and honest friendship with all nations, entangling alliances with none' (Padover 1943: 386). These statements represent not merely expressions of sentiment but pragmatically conceived policies designed to consolidate American independence at a time when Napoleon's France was unleashing war in Europe. At the outset isolationism was a policy of survival in a world whose conflicts threatened to involve the United States, as indeed they did eleven years later when British violations of American neutrality provoked President Madison into war against Britain. The experience of the War of 1812 only entrenched the doctrine of non-entanglement further and, moreover, confirmed the American disposition to elevate the pragmatic desire for non-involvement into a matter of principle. America, it was held, was different; it was founded on novel principles of individual liberty and republican government. The European way of diplomacy, based on corrupt bargains between leaders who were unaccountable to their peoples, was productive of war. American republican diplomacy embodied a peaceful principle, founded on the belief, expressed by Adam Smith in his *Wealth of Nations*, that commerce, in contrast to political intercourse, was conducive to friendly relations with other nations. If this meant that America must withhold support from other fledgling nations seeking independence from imperial powers, then so be it. America 'goes not in search of monsters to destroy', declared Secretary of State John Quincy Adams in justifying his decision to turn down a request for aid from Greek insurgents fighting for independence from Turkey in the 1820s (Seward 1849: 132).

Isolationism, then, began life as a policy tailored to meet particular circumstances and became an article of faith. It could hardly have been sustained, however, had it not been for America's uniquely favourable geographical position. Three thousand miles of ocean did for the United States what the best intentions of its leaders could hardly have achieved unaided: provided a cushion of distance and time between themselves and the chief sources of danger to their own peace. Three further conditions helped to promote the policy of isolationism into a doctrine. The first was the possession of vast areas of land and natural resources which allowed the United States to be virtually self-sufficient in many vital goods. The second was the fortunate circumstance that the hundred years from 1815 to 1914 saw no major European wars. The 'long peace' of the nineteenth century happened to coincide with the period in which America was engaged in nation-building. That it was able to come close to destroying itself in civil war (1861–65) without damaging intervention from foreign powers was due in part to the state of relative peace in Europe. Finally, the waves of immigrants which America absorbed during the nineteenth century created a society which was peculiarly vulnerable to splits along ethnic lines, rendering its leaders correspondingly wary of foreign policies which might provoke such divisions. While in the twentieth century domestic ethnic interests have on occasion exerted a powerful influence on foreign policy, during the nineteenth the other favourable conditions mentioned above held the ethnic factor below the threshold where it might have dictated the direction of foreign policy.

The end result of these favourable circumstances was a frame of mind which contained two remarkable features: the belief that America could remain economically

19

in the world but politically out of it, and the belief that the extension of American influence was a benign and natural process to which no right-thinking person could take exception. That this involved the destruction or removal of native Americans from their ancestral lands and the absorption of Mexicans and others into the expanding republic, was conceived to be a natural and inevitable consequence of America's civilizing mission. Democracy and economic growth created their own justification. It was, as a newspaper editor put it in the 1840s, America's 'manifest destiny' to extend the area of freedom where she might (Merk 1966: Ch. II). In Michael Hunt's persuasive account of American foreign policy ideology, a commitment to 'racial hierarchy' was welded to 'an active quest for national greatness closely coupled to the promotion of liberty' to form a powerful engine of expansion. A third element – a suspicion of revolutionary movements which did not conform to America's own – 'defined the limits of acceptable change overseas' and became particularly important during the twentieth century (Hunt 1987: 17–18 and *passim*). This will be considered below. For the moment, it is enough to emphasize the conjunction between the cultural assumptions which grew during the period of nation-building and the international setting in which this took place.

Isolationism and expansionism, in short, were mutually reinforcing rather than contradictory principles. Isolationism in fact expressed not so much a rejection of the world as a conviction that America could pursue its legitimate interests without compromising its own values or provoking the unwelcome attentions of other nations, above all the Great Powers of Europe.

The American way of diplomacy had very different results in the hugely altered circumstances of the twentieth century. In the first place, America's own interests expanded in line with its economic growth. To take only one indicator, by 1910 United States steel production surpassed that of Britain and Germany combined. Still less dependent than other industrialized countries on imports, America nevertheless sought outlets for its exports, which inevitably led to competition with other powers, most notably in China, where in 1899 the United States proposed adherence to the principle of an 'open door' for the goods of all interested powers. The second, and closely related, factor affecting American diplomacy at the close of the nineteenth and the beginning of the twentieth century was what could be called the contraction of the world consequent upon the improvement of communications and transport. The Atlantic no longer insulated the United States so effectively from the troubles of Europe. Like it or not, the United States was becoming a factor in the European balance of power no less than in the Pacific and the Far East. The task of American diplomacy in the twentieth century was to respond to these developments in ways which were, as far as possible, consistent with its inherited traditions.

Latin America was the region in which American interests were most tangibly at stake, and the Monroe Doctrine proved an eminently flexible instrument in meeting the challenge. Originally devised in 1823 as a warning to European powers not to attempt further colonization of Latin America, or to attempt re-colonization of newly independent nations, the Monroe Doctrine was enforceable only because it was in Britain's interest too to prevent France and Spain from recapturing their former colonies. British sea power underwrote the Monroe Doctrine for much of the century. By the turn of the century, however, following the war with Spain over Cuba and with the prospect of a strategically important canal being constructed across the isthmus of Panama, the negative 'hands off' doctrine was transformed into a positive claim of an American interest in the 'stability' of Latin America.

Speaking the unmistakable language of imperialism, in 1904 President Theodore Roosevelt announced, in what came to be known as the Roosevelt Corollary to the Monroe Doctrine, that 'chronic wrongdoing, or an impotence which results in a general loosening of the ties of civilized society, may in America, as elsewhere, ultimately require intervention by some civilized nation, and in the Western Hemisphere may force the United States, however reluctantly, in flagrant cases of such wrongdoing or impotence, to the exercise of an international police power' (Smith 1964, Vol. 2: 350). Despite the emergence of a domestic anti-imperialist movement, neither then nor since has the assumption of America's special responsibility in this region been questioned by American policy-makers. Isolationism has never applied to Latin America.

Less easy to justify was the annexation of Hawaii, the seizure of the Puerto Rico and the Philippines (former Spanish possessions) and the tight supervision the United States exercised over the newly independent Cuba following the war with Spain in 1898. Was this not imperialism in everything but name? Not so, claimed successive American administrations, for whom the promise of eventual American statehood (for Hawaii) and of independence (for Cuba and the Philippines) relieved American policy of the odium of imperialism. Whatever the validity of these justifications, the key point is the degree to which these expansionist moves were of a piece with the growth of the United States during the nineteenth century. The American disclaimer of imperialism was nevertheless significant for the development of its future interests around the world in that it betrayed an unwillingness to acknowledge either the intrusive nature of its own power or the legitimacy of independence movements which did not conform to the American model.

More difficult problems were posed by the abandonment of the hallowed principle of non-entanglement in 1917, when the United States entered the First World War. Woodrow Wilson, furthermore, declared his determination to take part in, indeed take the lead in, the peace conference which would resolve the issues of war and peace once victory had been achieved. Non-entanglement and isolationism, it seemed, had been comprehensively buried.

Appearances, however, were deceptive. The terms on which the United States participated in the war were carefully tailored to maintain a certain detachment from the Allies. America entered the war as an 'associated', not an 'allied' power. Nor was there any question of integrated military commands, which proved to be a potent source of conflict and frustration among the co-belligerents (Kennedy 1980: 170ff.).

More substantively, however, Wilson defined American war aims in language which was designed to dissociate them from those of the Allies and maintain American freedom of movement. 'The World must be made safe for democracy,' Wilson announced in his message to Congress requesting a declaration of war on Germany. 'We have no selfish ends to serve. We desire no conquest, no dominion. We seek no indemnities for ourselves, no material compensation for the sacrifices we shall freely make. We are but one of the champions of the rights of mankind' (Wilson 1983, Vol. 41: 525).

The question of precisely why the United States entered the war is much disputed and cannot be addressed here. Suffice it to say that nominally she went to war in order to safeguard the rights of neutrals to trade freely. The important point for our purposes is the recurrence of the assumption, which goes back to the War of 1812 and ultimately to the pronouncements of Washington and Jefferson, that the United States should be able to pursue its economic and trading interests without incurring political costs. The evident collapse of that assumption in 1917, however, scarcely removed the need to justify participation in terms which retained some vestige of the original principle. The solution was to take the moral high ground by casting American war aims in terms which not only distanced them from the aims of Britain and France but in terms which explicitly repudiated them: in effect to Americanize the war. Non-entanglement and isolationism were not so much abandoned as translated into unilateralism.

The same impulse is apparent in Wilson's vision of the future peace, as outlined in the Fourteen Points of January 1918. These included provisions for open diplomacy, freedom of the seas, free trade, national self-determination, 'impartial adjustment of all colonial claims', and, crucially, a League of Nations as a framework for a new world order. None of these principles, not even the League of Nations, was original to Woodrow Wilson. Many were drawn from the British nineteenth-century liberal agenda so much admired by the Anglophile Wilson. Taken as a whole, however, and in the context of 1918, they represent a bid for an American definition of a new world order.

A significant feature of the context of 1918 was the Bolshevik Revolution of the previous year. The announcement of the Fourteen Points was in fact prompted by the Bolsheviks' publication of the 'Secret Treaties', which revealed the existence of bargains among the European powers providing for the parcelling out of former German colonies among the Allies. Provoked into dissociating the United States from the corrupt diplomacy of the old world, Wilson found himself ironically in alignment with Lenin in this one respect. Both leaders, as Geoffrey Barraclough has pointed out, adopted a new democratic diplomacy, appealing to the people of other nations over the heads of politicians. Both were competing 'for the suffrage of mankind' (Barraclough 1967: 120, 118). They were competing, of course, on behalf of different ideologies, but it is important to note that this early intimation of the cold war found America and Russia curiously at one in their determination to seize the political and moral high ground from the old Great Powers of Europe. Neither at this stage was able to make good its claim to win the hearts and minds of the peoples of the world: Russia, as we shall see later, because she was unable to do so, the United States because she was unwilling to do so. With the US Senate's rejection of the Treaty of Versailles, largely because of Wilson's refusal to compromise on inclusion of the League of Nations within the Treaty, the Wilsonian vision of the new world order proceeded without the participation of the United States.

America's 'retreat into isolationism' in the 1920s and 1930s was only in part a retreat and in important respects was hardly isolationist. Broadly, the picture is of a continuing American effort to pursue maximum overseas economic activity at minimum political cost. Such internationalist commitments as the United States entered into – the Washington naval disarmament conference of 1921–22 and the Kellog–Briand Renunciation of the War Pact of 1928 – entailed few burdensome obligations. Both expressed a revulsion against the horrors of the last war rather than a realistic calculation that the next one could be prevented by legal fiat. More significant was the surge of American overseas investment during the 1920s, above all in Europe and Latin America. The decade has justifiably been viewed as the seedtime of the multinational corporation. Furthermore, the tenacity of America's devotion to its primary articles of faith was well illustrated during the 1930s. As the Versailles settlement crumbled in the face of German rearmament and Japanese expansionism, and as the steady drift towards renewed world war began in the mid-1930s, the United States passed a series of neutrality acts designed to insulate itself from these developments. These acts, one of which contained the key provision that trade with nations at war was permissible if belligerents collected the goods in their own ships and paid 'cash on the barrel head', reflected, as one historian has put it, 'the contradictory desire of the American people to remain economically in the world and politically out of it' (Divine 1965: 37).

In short, though a Great Power in economic terms, the United States as yet saw no good reason to abandon the political independence which had brought it such advantages in the previous century and a half. On the threshold of World War in the mid-twentieth century the United States thus looked out on the world with assumptions born in the eighteenth. International conditions, however, had changed radically. The global reach of the United States had long outstripped the capacity of eighteenth century rhetoric to comprehend reality. Nevertheless, such vestiges of the rhetoric as were left remained important in domestic political debate. Franklin Roosevelt was forced to affirm in the presidential election of 1940 that he would never send American boys to fight overseas, and this at a time when his policies of aid to Britain and his increasingly stiff stance towards Japanese expansionism were already eating at the foundations of neutrality.

This review of America's foreign policy assumptions will have served its purpose if it has illustrated the gap between the United States' growing capacity to influence world politics and its perception of its role in the world system. Its capacity was based on raw economic power, which, however, the United States viewed as fundamentally benign and untainted by the imperial ambitions associated with the old Great Powers of Europe. What has been called America's 'diplomacy of principle' was not merely a matter of couching policy in idealistic terms (Spanier 1977: Ch. 1; Kuniholm 1987: 51–4). It was the product of a culture which had experienced revolution and national growth as a natural process. America had achieved revolution, as Louis Hartz has observed, without a major class upheaval (Hartz 1955: Ch. 1). It had expanded across a continent without damaging conflict with major powers. It had achieved economic growth, so it was believed, through the natural operations of the market. What more logical than to assume that liberal democracy, *laissez-faire* economics, and a diplomacy based on the application of self-evident principles should suffice for all nations? Given its traditions, it is not hard to see why the United States should have experienced difficulty in accepting the consequences of twentieth-century revolutions. It was not merely that they often drew on ideas which were inimical to American traditions, but that they did not possess the option, which had been open to the United States, of nation-building in a gradual and unforced fashion. In former colonial territories the requirements of national independence and consolidation of governmental power frequently produced a combination of political instability and endemic war, both national and civil.

A curious consequence of American growth has been the conviction that she has no ideology. The United States, suggests the prominent liberal intellectual Arthur Schlesinger, 'has had the good fortune not to be an ideological society'. In its 'finest hours' America has pursued 'ideals' rather than ideology. To this extent, the argument goes, America's world role has been radically distinct from that of such ideologically motivated powers as the Soviet Union and Germany during the upheavals of the mid-twentieth century (Schlesinger 1963: 533–6). Free from the destructive ambitions of the more dogmatic powers, according to this view, America has characteristically been drawn into world conflict in order to 'contain' the ambitions of aggressive nations. From John Quincy Adams's statement that 'America goes not in search of monsters to destroy', to Woodrow Wilson's 'we have no selfish ends to serve', and Harry Truman's 1947 announcement that 'great responsibilities have been placed upon us by the swift movement of events' (Truman 1963: 180), there is a strong thread of continuity, despite the vast changes in the conditions of world affairs. It lies in the conviction that the initiative for events which might involve the United States has lain elsewhere. Hence the frequent protestations that other nations have nothing to fear from the exertion of American power; hence also the intensity of the American reaction to the establishment in Russia of an ideologically motivated society, whose principles were explicitly opposed to those of the United States. American ideals, it could be said, became explicitly ideological in the encounter with the Soviet Union.

RUSSIA AND THE SOVIET UNION

Certain parallels have often been noted between the growth of the United States and Russia. Both expanded over large continental land masses, each eventually reaching the Pacific Ocean. The experience of pushing back the frontiers of settlement, which involved absorbing or destroying native populations, was common to both, as was the problem of reconciling control from the centre with the ever expanding extent of new territories. Russia's system of serfdom was matched by America's slavery; both persisted until the mid-nineteenth century and were abolished within two years of each other (1861 and 1863). Each nation had deep roots in European civilization but also developed strong Pacific and Far Eastern interests. Geography, combined with a powerful nationalist dynamic, thus dictated that each would become a global power and, moreover, that they would eventually encounter each other as the one pushed eastward and the other westward. When they did so during the early nineteenth century in the Pacific Northwest of America and in Alaska, such conflicts of interest as existed were resolved without acrimony. A 'habit of cooperation', as one historian has put it, had been established between America and Russia during the Napoleonic wars which lasted until the late 1860s when the United States purchased Alaska from Russia (Gaddis 1990a: 8).

The harmonious relations between Russia and America in the first half of the nineteenth century, however, scarcely hid the fundamental divergence in the character of their political and social systems. Beyond the obvious difference in their historical starting points, which meant that Russian culture and institutions were set in firm moulds well before the United States came into existence, an important difference in their processes of growth lay in the relative poverty of Russian society, the low yield of its land, and the high proportion of resources which had to be directed towards defence from ambitious neighbours. Russia possessed few natural advantages. Hence the slowness and difficulty of Russian expansion when compared with that of the United States. 'It took the Russians six centuries to reach the Ural mountains,' writes A. Lobanov-Rostovsky, 'and then a century more to reach the Pacific. The reason for this was the onrush of counterinvasions from Asia, which like breakers submerged the Russians or blocked their advance, while in the westward drive in America the greatest resistance came from local Indian tribes' (Lobanov-Rostovsky 1965: 82).

An enduring legacy of these twin processes of eastward expansion and the need to counter successive invasions from Asia was the establishment of powerful autocratic rule from the centre. With the overthrow of the Mongols, who had dominated Russia from the thirteenth to the fifteenth centuries, a Russian state based on Moscow was consolidated under Tsar Ivan III in the 1480s and subsequently extended to the Volga river under Ivan the Terrible by the mid-sixteenth century. While modern historians tend to minimize the effect of the Mongol invasion and occupation in moulding Russian autocracy, it is nevertheless acknowledged that 'the urge to overthrow the

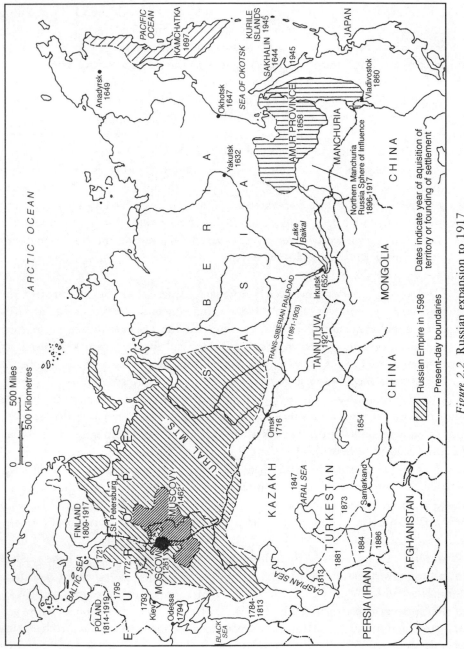

Figure 2.2 Russian expansion to 1917

Source: Derived from W. LaFeber, *The American Age*, New York: Norton, 1989.

[Mongol] yoke served to strengthen the desire for unity among the princes' (Acton 1986: 10). The growing ascendancy of Moscow among the Russian principalities during the resistance to the Mongols laid the foundations for its subsequent dominance in the post-Mongol period. Maintaining that ascendancy and expanding the scope of Moscow's rule led in turn to the establishment of the characteristic features of Russian autocracy: a highly centralized monarchy, the increasing dependence of the church on the state, a relatively dependent nobility, and the institution of serfdom (Acton 1986: Ch. 2).

By contrast with the early struggles to expand Moscow's rule, the conquest of Siberia was relatively easy, if slow because of the enormous distances involved and the difficulties of communications and transport. By 1640 Cossack adventurers had reached the Pacific and the Amur River, the boundary with China. The use of Siberia as a penal colony was well established by the mid-eighteenth century, though settlement on a substantial scale had to await the completion of the Trans-Siberian railway in the 1890s. The development of Russia's Far Eastern zone, however, brought new conflicts with neighbouring Asiatic powers. The weakness of the declining Manchu dynasty in China enabled Russia to achieve the virtual absorption of Manchuria in the 1890s, while, by contrast, the encounter with Japan brought a disastrous defeat in the war of 1905. Severe as the Russian defeat of 1905 was in exposing the fragility of Tsarist rule – the revolution of that year providing a foretaste of the war-born Revolution of 1917 – territorially Russia emerged relatively unscathed. Further expansion was checked, but Russian spheres of interest in the Far East, including northern Manchuria, Mongolia, and part of the strategically important Sakhalin Island, were secured in the treaty following the war with Japan. Each of these territories would feature large in the calculations of Soviet leaders during the upheavals of the twentieth century.

Russian imperial ambitions looked West as well as East, and the formation of the Russian state owed as much to successive wars with Western powers as to the struggles involved in the drive towards the Far East. On the northern flank of Russia's western border lay Sweden and Poland. Both were effectively neutralized as serious threats by the middle of the eighteenth century as a result of campaigns initiated by Peter the Great. The subsequent dismantling of the Polish state served both Russian imperial purposes and the interests of Prussia and Austria, who likewise desired a weak Poland. On the southern flank lay the Ottoman Empire, which constituted an obstacle not only to Russian territorial expansion but to the extension of Orthodox Christianity. 'Predating Peter's reign and going back to the earliest days of Muscovy,' observes Adam Ulam, 'there is the notion of the historical mission of the Russian nation as the representative and defender of eastern Christianity as against Catholicism and also (and especially) as against Islam. The concrete expression of this mission was the goal of expelling Turkey from Europe and regaining Constantinople and the Straits for Christendom' (Ulam 1968: 4, 5). During the nineteenth century Russia profited from the upsurge of nationalism among the Balkan Slavs (many of whom lived under Austro-Hungarian or Turkish rule), enabling the Tsars to satisfy the growing Pan-slavist sentiment within Russia and to promote Russian territorial interests. In this instance, however, Russian ambitions came into sharp conflict with those of Austria-Hungary.

By the end of the nineteenth century a fundamental realignment of the European powers had taken place. Russia's historic common interest with Austria and Prussia in containing Polish nationalism had been overridden by the ramifications of the 'eastern question'. The growth of German power following unification in 1871, the decline of Ottoman power, and the growing ambitions of Austria-Hungary and Russia in the Balkans forced Russia to seek new allies in the West in the form of France and Britain, both historic enemies of Russia.

Three things stand out in the record of Russian national growth. The first is the degree to which the process was associated with the maintenance of autocratic rule. The historic mission of the Tsars was indissolubly linked with the mission of the nation to the extent that an opponent of Tsarist rule must necessarily be an opponent of Russian imperial expansion, if only for tactical reasons. The 'revolutionary defeatism' advocated by Lenin in 1905 and in 1917 was a logical consequence of the need to break the spell of Tsarist autocracy.

A second feature of Russian growth was its ambivalent stance towards the West. The policy of Westernization initiated by Peter the Great never obliterated the deep Eastern imprint on Russian society and culture. The Enlightenment established only tenuous roots in Russian society and then only among the intelligentsia, which was both small in number and relatively isolated from the vast army of the peasantry which made up the bulk of the Russian population. Perhaps more important was the awareness of the gap between Western and Russian economic advancement. It was Peter the Great's ultimate ambition to close it, but he never succeeded in doing more than adding a small manufacturing sector to the largely peasant economy. The control of manufacturing and trade by the government itself, furthermore, decisively limited the scope for individual entrepreneurs. By the time Russia had begun to industrialize in the late nineteenth century, it did so within the framework of antiquated social and political institutions, producing a portentous clash between the old and the new.

The ambivalent stance towards the West and modernization manifested itself notably within the revolutionary movement which eventually overthrew Tsarist rule. The conflicts between the various factions in successive phases of the revolutionary movement were, Bertram Wolfe has written, 'changing forms of the protean battle between Westernizer and Slavophile. One path led closer to the parties and trade unions of the West, which were democratically organized . . . The other led to concentration on conspiracy and insurrection under the leadership of a self-selected, rigidly centralized, secret and conspirative band of revolutionary intellectuals under a self-appointed leader' (Wolfe 1964: 160–1). Arguably the Bolshevik Party contained both tendencies through the period of the Revolution itself, and developed to the full its conspiratorial 'Slav' character only during the subsequent consolidation of the

Soviet state. In any event, the later history of the Soviet Union suggests that the 'protean battle' between Westernizer and Slavophile did not stop there; indeed it could be said to have been at the root of the upheaval produced by Mikhail Gorbachev's efforts to reform the Soviet Union (Roxburgh 1991: 81).

The third noteworthy feature of Russian development lies in the tension between the urge to expand and the fear of being attacked. Two centuries of domination by the Mongol Khans inclined the Russian leaders and the Russian people to deep suspicion of predatory powers on its borders, or rather to the suspicion that any power on its borders must be predatory. Extending the frontiers of the nation was, from this point of view, a defensive necessity rather than an act of aggression. The wider the circle of Russian power, the wider the circle of powers which posed potential threats. The fear of encirclement, so prominent a feature of Soviet foreign policy during the twentieth century, thus had a long history. The result was that, while the Russian 'mission' to extend its rule far and wide often produced bold foreign policies, fear of encirclement just as often induced caution. A similar duality appears in Soviet foreign policy.

It is tempting, in turning from Russian to Soviet foreign policy, to say that the one is simply a continuation of the other. According to some historians, the only thing which really changed in 1917 was the personnel of the Kremlin. The combination of cultural insularity and aggressiveness, of rigid control from the centre coupled with highly personalized rule, the denial of individual rights and resistance to Western democratic ideas, the machinery of political repression and cultural censorship, and, not least, the fear of encirclement combined with the outward expansionist thrust – all these are replicated, it is said, in the development of the Soviet state, above all in the period of Stalin's rule (1928–1953). Indeed, because there was so much continuity between Russian and Soviet history, it is important to identify its limits precisely in order that the novel Soviet elements can be recognized.

The argument for continuity could well rest its case by referring to a speech given by Stalin in 1931:

> One feature of the history of old Russia was the continual beatings she suffered because of her backwardness. She was beaten by the Mongol Khans. She was beaten by the Turkish beys. She was beaten by the Swedish feudal lords. She was beaten by the Polish and Lithuanian gentry. She was beaten by the British and French capitalists. She was beaten by the Japanese barons. All beat her – because of her backwardness, military backwardness, cultural backwardness, political backwardness, industrial backwardness, agricultural backwardness . . . That is why we must no longer lag behind.
> (Daniels 1985, Vol. 1: 230)

Three years later Stalin took this logic one step further in his assertion that 'the defence of the fatherland is the supreme law of life' (Daniels 1985, Vol. 1: 243). Russian nationalism, it would seem, had triumphed over Marxist internationalism.

Furthermore, there are significant instances in the inter-war period when the Soviet Union manifestly pursued pragmatic policies which appeared to be dictated by motives of self-interest and survival rather than ideology. The most striking of these was the short-lived non-aggression pact with Nazi Germany, formed in August 1939 and ended in June 1941, when Germany invaded the Soviet Union. The fact that the Soviet Union took the opportunity provided by this two-year breathing spell to absorb eastern Poland and the Baltic states, and to attack Finland, seems to suggest that the Soviet Union was nothing more nor less than a traditional Great Power acting in its own national interest.

There are, however, important features of the Soviet approach to foreign policy which bear the imprint both of Marxist ideas and of the specific conditions under which the Soviet Union was established. The key to Soviet foreign policy lies in the process whereby the original doctrines of Marx and Engels were adapted to the internal and external circumstances surrounding the birth and early growth of the Soviet Union. Marxism in its original form was internationalist, in that it was believed that the international proletariat had a common interest in the overthrow of capitalism. But Marx posited no mechanism for achieving this. It was assumed that revolution would take place in the most advanced capitalist countries first and spread to others as they reached the requisite stage of growth, which is to say, the stage at which the contradictions of capitalism reached crisis point. Marx had little to say about international relations. Conflict between classes rather than between nations was conceived to be the chief motor of the historical process. He also assumed that capitalist powers had little interest in warring with each other, since the ruling classes within each nation shared an interest in promoting economic well-being and in suppressing their respective proletariats (Ulam 1968: 13–14).

The internationalism implicit in Marxism achieved much sharper definition with the growth of the international socialist movement from the 1870s onwards and more especially in the revolutionary movement in Russia. Indeed Lenin and Trotsky believed in 1917–18 that revolution was imminent in Western Europe and that the success of the Bolshevik Revolution was vitally dependent upon socialist victories in those other centres. Lenin, however, was not prepared to leave things to chance. If Marxist internationalism remained the primary intellectual force behind Bolshevism, organizationally it owed much to Lenin's own distinctive contribution.

Lenin's innovations were twofold. In the first place he proposed and put into practice a mechanism for the formation of a revolutionary regime under conditions which did not conform to those specified by Marx. Without abandoning Marx's assumption of the inevitability of revolution and the ultimate victory over capitalism, Lenin reconceived the means necessary to achieve it. He advocated the formation of a vanguard party, composed of dedicated professional revolutionaries, whose function was to create a revolutionary consciousness among the proletariat and direct it towards a recognition of its own interests. If the vanguard party was the instrument of revolution, Marxism, with its conviction of the necessity for revolution and of ultimate triumph in the coming war between capitalism and socialism, nevertheless remained the doctrinal and emotional core of the faith which the vanguard preached to its followers. In this sense, Marxism, as employed by Lenin, served the purpose of revolution rather than the reverse.

Lenin's second innovation was to explain the links between imperialist wars and the advance of revolution within individual nations. The outbreak of war between capitalist powers in 1914 was the catalyst for this revision of Marx's thought. For Lenin, the world war proved that at an advanced stage of capitalism, characterized by the growth of monopolies in finance and industry, monopoly capitalists would seek to expand their markets by exploiting opportunities in less developed parts of the world. There, inevitably, the interests of capitalists would come into conflict. Class conflict within capitalist nations was thus exported to the developing world, which would hence become a central battleground between capitalists and the international working class.

Both these Leninist principles reflect the immediate exigencies of mounting and, where possible, extending the revolution. The first illustrates the importance of the connection between survival of the Bolshevik regime and survival of the nation. Weakened by civil war, the new government was also faced in March 1918 with the humiliating Treaty of Brest-Litovsk with Germany, under which Russia surrendered the Ukraine, Finland, the Baltic states, the Caucasus, White Russia, and Poland – more than a third of her European territory. (All but the Baltic states, Finland, and Poland reverted to Russia when the Treaty of Versailles invalidated Brest-Litovsk.) Moreover, intervention in Russia by the Allied powers between 1918 and 1920 could only be viewed by the Bolsheviks as an attempt to strangle the Revolution in its cradle. Under these circumstances there could be no question of the 'inevitability' of the revolutionary process without an employment of iron will, particularly following the failure of the temporarily successful revolutionary movements in Germany and Hungary. What came to be known under Stalin as the doctrine of 'socialism in one country' was a policy dictated to the new regime by the pressure of circumstances. These circumstances also provided the Bolsheviks with a powerful justification for their own hold on power. Born in war, Bolshevik rule entrenched itself with the instruments of war – mass mobilization guided by a tightly organized central body. The Leninist period of rule (1917–24) thus established a continuum between defence of the nation, of the Revolution, and of the Communist Party. If Stalin later produced his own innovation, it was to extend this continuum to defence of his own personal rule. Lenin's second principle, concerning the links between international capitalism and international revolution, governed the long-term goal of the Soviet Union in advancing the cause of global communism. In this case the instrument was the Third Communist International (Comintern), established in 1919. The maximum communist programme is well illustrated in Lenin's uncompromising statement that: 'as long as capitalism and Socialism remain, we cannot live in peace. In the end one or another will triumph' (Lenin 1925: 398). No timetable, however, was set for the achievement

31

of this goal. Western statesmen (and historians) who interpreted Soviet policy wholly in the light of assertions such as Lenin's were doubly deceived. On the one hand, during the 1920s and 1930s the Soviet Union lacked the capacity to expand the realm of communism significantly (Mongolia was the one success story of the inter-war years); on the other hand, it was prepared to bend ideology in order to promote anti-Western movements in the developing world.

We come full circle here to the coalescence in Soviet foreign policy of expansive long-term ideological goals and a preoccupation with the Soviet national interest. Inter-war circumstances – isolation as a communist nation and a limited capacity to extend its power and influence – dictated a practical policy of prudence, but without abandonment of ideological militancy. The latter was necessary as much to maintain conformity at home as to promote revolution abroad. In ascribing all manifestations of internal opposition to a foreign conspiracy to destroy the Soviet Union, Stalin was only carrying to brutal extremes in the purges of the 1930s the old principle of statecraft that troubles at home could be cured by the manufacture of a threat from abroad. The result from the Western point of view, at any rate, was a confusing duality in Soviet policy. In truth, it had been there from the beginning. Lenin, the author of militant expressions of war to the death with capitalism, was also the coiner of the term 'peaceful coexistence'.

One's conclusion must be that the attempt to make a clear separation between the Soviet national interest and Soviet ideology is doomed to fail. Without doubt Soviet foreign policy displayed strong elements of continuity with Tsarism, and that is what one would expect, given that the Bolshevik leadership did not possess the power to transform by fiat the international system. The Soviet state took its place as a state among others in a system which offered both constraints and opportunities. It did so, however, in a manner which betrayed its revolutionary origins. 'All revolutionary states', writes Fred Halliday, 'have tried to promote revolution abroad, to "export" it' (Halliday 1990b: 215). They may not always have succeeded, as the Soviet Union did not between the world wars, but they have posed a challenge to the existing international order by virtue of their promotion of an alternative principle of political organization. Internal and external forces feed on each other.

Paradoxically, the effect of the Bolshevik Revolution on the international system in the inter-war years is most apparent in Soviet relations with Germany, a state with which on the face of it the Soviet Union had little in common. For much of the inter-war period both were pariah states among the European powers: Germany as a defeated nation, stigmatized with the responsibility for the First World War; the Soviet Union as the national embodiment of militant and subversive principles. First at Rapallo in 1922 and then, in very different circumstances, in 1939, the Soviet Union and Germany concluded treaties in defiance of the other European powers. It is hard to imagine that, had the Russian Revolution not taken place, these alignments would have been conceived or desired by either power. Soviet foreign policies may not have followed a Marxist blueprint, if such a thing is conceivable in the real world, but its political options were decisively influenced, as was the international system, by the events and ideas of the Revolution.

Comparison of the processes of nation-building in the United States and the Soviet Union throws up important points of difference which were to play a decisive role in their relations after the Second World War. The United States possessed a large and increasing capacity during the twentieth century to influence events around the globe, but also a conviction that such political power as it wielded was a natural and benign extension of its economic and cultural dynamism. To adopt Marxist terms, America's perception of itself was a classic instance of 'false consciousness': the promotion of a partial and self-interested view of the world as if it were of universal validity. American ideals were from the start strictly speaking ideological, in that they were the product of self-deception. Doubtless all powers (and individuals) engage in comparable efforts of self-justification. The distinctive feature of the American case, as far as its international role is concerned, lies in the potent combination of the capacity to effect change and possession of a 'revolutionary' tradition proclaiming universal principles. The fact that these principles had their roots in the eighteenth century made the United States a politically 'conservative' power in the twentieth, even as its economic and cultural dynamism helped to revolutionize social and economic conditions around the world. None of these factors ensured that American influence would be automatically converted into political gains. Indeed the illusion of power could just as easily provoke failure, as in Vietnam – an instance, if ever there was one, of the illusory assumption that what was good for Kansas City must necessarily be good for Saigon or Hanoi.

The Soviet Union, by contrast, combined politically revolutionary principles, more explicitly formulated than those of the United States, with a continually embattled posture towards the outside world. Relative economic and military weakness in the period immediately following the Revolution inclined the Soviet leadership to exploit propaganda as a major instrument of political power. 'Soviet Russia', wrote E.H. Carr some fifty years ago, 'was the first national unit to preach an international doctrine and to maintain an effective world-propaganda organisation' [the Comintern] (Carr 1942: 175). Unlike the United States, which had been able to consolidate its revolution in relative detachment from external pressures, the Soviet Union was bound to reject the existing international order and seek to change it. Two opportunities were presented to the Soviet Union in the twentieth century to promote such change: the depression of the 1930s and the spate of colonial independence movements after the Second World War. In the first case, the chief beneficiaries of capitalist crisis were fascism, on the one hand, and social democracy, on the other. In the second case, despite notable gains, the Soviet model was no more successful than the 'Westminster model' in directing the course of change in the Third World. True, the Soviet Union was able to capitalize on a variety of anti-Western (as opposed to communist) movements in the Third World, but these rarely resulted in stable allegiances. In this sense, the limits of

Soviet power were set as much by the character of its own internal development as by the conditions of international politics.

Two revolutions, two states with great principles at stake, two large nations with expansive tendencies: these do not of themselves make for cold war. While its beginnings can be discerned in the years 1917–20, it took another world war and an alliance between the United States and the Soviet Union to ignite the cold war proper. In the inter-war years the decisive factors in international relations were the efforts of Germany and Japan to reorder the balance of power in their favour within their respective spheres. Until the late 1930s the United States played a peripheral role in these dramas, while the Soviet Union, more directly threatened by German resurgence, attempted a holding action: first by the promotion of collective security via the League of Nations, and second, when that failed, by entering into the Non-Agression Pact with Germany in August 1939. Throughout the 1930s relations between the United States and the Soviet Union themselves were cool, despite American diplomatic recognition of the Soviet Union on Franklin Roosevelt's assumption of the presidency. Relations were also distant. There were neither major areas of agreement nor pressing conflicts of interest.

The war changed that picture out of all recognition. Agreement within the 'Grand Alliance' on the goal of defeating Germany (the Soviet Union did not declare war on Japan until August 1945) and the achievement of that goal in May 1945 left Europe at the disposal of the victorious powers. But it also placed a high premium on the continuance of unity if a post-war settlement were to succeed. As we know, Great Power unity broke down. The cold war was thus in important respects an outgrowth of the Second World War. The ideological antagonism stemming from 1917 was, so to speak, energized by the demands placed upon the United States and the Soviet Union for cooperation during the war and its aftermath. To this we now turn.

Part II

THE EMERGENCE OF A BIPOLAR WORLD, 1941–1953

INTRODUCTION

The most ambitious schemes for peace and international harmony have often arisen from the depths of war. The Second World War was no exception. Though the divided world which was well established by 1953 was undoubtedly a consequence of decisions taken during and immediately after the war, the declared intention of the Allied leaders was the continuation of Allied unity into the post-war period.

One indication of American thinking was the publication in 1943 of a compendium of four books by prominent American politicians under the collective title *Prefaces to Peace*. While it had no official status, it represented an important strand within official thinking about the post-war world. Wendell Wilkie, Republican presidential nominee in the 1940 election, ex-President Herbert Hoover, incumbent Vice-President Henry Wallace, and Under-Secretary of State Sumner Welles collectively affirmed the necessity of planning for peace in the midst of war. Despite differences of emphasis, two imperatives were shared by all: the determination not to repeat the error of 1919–20, when the United States had repudiated membership of the League of Nations, and a conviction that economic considerations (effectively ignored in the Versailles settlement) were as important as politics in framing the new world order. Broadly, this meant, firstly, that the United States must participate in a new international political organization and, secondly, in the words of Henry Wallace, that the United States must collaborate 'with the rest of the world to put productive resources fully to work' (Wallace 1943: 415). Political and economic internationalism were subsequently embodied in the United Nations organization and the Bretton Woods machinery, which included the International Monetary Fund (IMF) and the International Bank for Reconstruction and Development (commonly known as the World Bank).

Of course it was possible even at this stage to discern self-interested motives in these proposals, and it has not been difficult for historians to mount an argument that the seeds of the cold war are to be found in an American determination to put its stamp on the new world order. This is, however, to read history backwards to an excessive degree. For one thing, the record of discussions at Bretton Woods shows that British suspicions of American intentions were as deep as those of the Soviet Union

(Hathaway 1981: Chs 2 and 10). For another, the positive desire for 'one world' was reinforced by an equally powerful negative: the fear that a world split between two opposing camps would be inherently unstable and likely to lead to further war. The internationalist idea was not merely the projection of American idealism or of an urge for American hegemony, but an expression of the view that future peace and prosperity depended on the maintenance of wartime unity among the Allies. The United Nations Organization was conceived as the continuation in spirit and in name of the wartime alliance, 'United Nations' having been the term used to describe the alliance (Edmonds 1991: 208, 550 n.2).

Soviet statements expressed comparable aspirations. The only way to prevent fresh aggression by Germany, noted Stalin in 1944, was 'to set up a special organization consisting of representatives of the peaceful nations, for the protection of peace and for ensuring security'. It must not be 'a replica of the League of Nations of sad memory . . . [but] . . . a new, special, fully-empowered organization which will have at its disposal all that is necessary for protecting peace and preventing further aggression'. It would be effective, he concluded, 'only if the Great Powers who have borne the brunt of the war against Hitler continue to act in a spirit of unanimity and harmony' (Daniels 1985, Vol. 2: 128).

To be sure, the Soviet Union too approached this question from its own angle. It was both more urgently concerned about the possibility of German resurgence and less convinced of the value of international organizations than was the United States. Stalin, like Churchill, was more inclined to place faith in Great Power leadership than in untried organizations. It was also the case that American leaders were excessively credulous about the extent to which the Soviet Union had abandoned the goal of spreading communism. However, there is little reason to doubt that during the last year of the war the Soviet Union sincerely hoped to participate in and benefit from membership in the new international bodies.

The broad question to be answered in the following three chapters is how the internationalist aspirations of the wartime years were transmuted within two years of the war's end into belligerent pronouncements of 'two ways of life' (Truman) and 'two camps' (Zhdanov). But the issue of the origins of the cold war is arguably composed of two distinct, if closely related questions: why did the wartime Alliance break down, and why did allied disunity become institutionalized on a global scale? The first looks backwards to the nature of the Alliance itself (discussed in Chapter 3) and the second looks forward to the conditions confronting the major powers in the aftermath of military victory (the subject of Chapters 4 and 5).

3

THE SECOND WORLD WAR AND THE STRUGGLE FOR PEACE, 1941–1946

GLOBALISM AND THE CHANGING BALANCE OF POWER

The Second World War was more truly global than the First in the geographical scope of military conflict and in its effects on nations which were not primary belligerents. While in both wars Europe was the major theatre, in the Second, the Far East came close to Europe in significance (and in the eyes of some Americans exceeded it), largely because of Japan's role. In 1914 Japan had entered the First World War on the Allied side chiefly in order to pursue its interests at China's and Germany's expense, and at Versailles Japan succeeded in gaining former German territories in the Far East and important concessions from China. From the point of view of the major powers, however, these issues were of regional rather than global significance. The same could not be said of the Second World War. Japan's vigorous expansionist drive from 1940–42 displaced Western rule (at least temporarily) from a host of colonies, including French Indo-China, Hong Kong, Malaya, Singapore, British Borneo, most of Burma, Thailand, the Dutch East Indies, the Philippines, and a scattering of islands in the Western Pacific, many of them American. Japan's eventual defeat did not check, but rather stimulated, the urge for independence among many of these territories. The overall effect of Japan's participation was to provoke a redrawing of the political map of Asia.

A second important difference between the two world wars lay in the character of American and Soviet participation. In the First, important as American productive power was in ensuring the defeat of Germany and the Central Powers, the United States played a relatively minor military role, effectively only in the last six months of the war. Russia, by contrast, having been in at the beginning and having sustained enormous losses against Germany, succumbed to revolution in 1917 and was taken out of the war by the new Bolshevik leadership early in 1918. Though the United States aspired to moral leadership among the victorious nations in peace-making, this was not translated into political power, for reasons which have already been discussed. The political centre of gravity within the world system of states remained in Europe, despite the destructive effects of the war on the European economies.

The beginning of the Second World War found both future superpowers on the sidelines and for a period of close to two years they remained there, until Hitler's invasion of Russia in June 1941 and the Japanese attack on Pearl Harbor in December of the same year drew both irrevocably into war. Within a short time the scale of the Soviet and American contribution to the defeat of Germany dwarfed that of Britain and the British Empire, which, following the fall of France in 1940, had been Germany's sole adversary. The Second World War completed the process begun in the First of shifting the centre of the world system of states away from Europe.

The United States and the Soviet Union, however, were not fighting identical wars. The United States from the outset was forced to take a global view, since it was at war with both Germany and Japan. The Soviet Union remained neutral towards Japan and declared war only after the dropping of the first atomic bomb on Hiroshima on 6 August 1945. The war aims and strategies of both powers showed a marked divergence, despite the common goal of defeating Germany. The chief difference lay between what might be called the United States' 'extensive' and the Soviet Union's 'intensive' goals. The near catastrophic effects of the German invasion of the Soviet Union concentrated Soviet efforts on the task of national survival, inclining the Soviet leadership to think of victory in territorial terms. United States territory had also been attacked – at the Pearl Harbor naval base – but there was no question of enemy occupation of Hawaii, far less of the continental United States itself. Beyond the immediate goal of achieving the unconditional surrender of Germany and Japan, America sought the establishment of certain principles of international behaviour, most famously expressed in the Atlantic Charter (August 1941).

Much debate surrounds the Atlantic Charter. It was formulated by Churchill and Roosevelt some months before the United States entered the war and announced their joint adherence to a set of apparently clear-cut principles: the affirmation that neither sought territorial aggrandizement, that any territorial changes should reflect the interests of the peoples concerned, that all peoples should have the right to choose the form of government under which they would live, and that free trade and freedom of the seas should be enjoyed by all states. Both parties, furthermore, desired collaboration between all nations to produce economic growth and social welfare, and they affirmed their commitment to the abandonment of the use of force in international disputes and to the establishment of a 'wider and permanent system of general security' with sufficient power to enforce the disarmament of nations which threatened the peace. Comparisons with Woodrow Wilson's Fourteen Points of 1918 are inevitable, with the singular difference that the Atlantic Charter was a joint rather than a unilateral endeavour.

Questions arise, however, about precisely what Roosevelt and Churchill believed they were committing themselves to. Stalin's subsequent endorsement of the Charter compounded rather than clarified these questions. Each party harboured important reservations, reflecting their conceptions of where their interests lay. At the draft stage Churchill had managed to include alterations of wording which safeguarded the interests of the British Empire and British international trade. Stalin was similarly keen to protect Soviet interests, though he couched his reservations in more general terms. Practical application of the Charter's principles, he declared, must adapt itself to 'the circumstances, needs and historic peculiarities of particular countries' (Taubman 1982: 47). Though Roosevelt for his part had watered down Churchill's original draft of the clause regarding a new international security framework, reflecting his anxiety about isolationist sentiment in the United States, he subsequently swallowed these doubts as Congress and public opinion proved amenable to internationalism. It seems safe to say that of the three leaders Roosevelt was most committed to the universalism of the Atlantic Charter.

It is tempting to regard the Charter's statement of grand principles as no more than empty rhetoric, and certainly British officials expressed irritation, as they frequently have before and since, at the American propensity to indulge in high-flown phrases. (Actually, in this case they were mostly the work of Churchill, himself no mean phrase-maker.) But this is to underestimate the extent to which the Charter, once signed, created a momentum of its own. To be sure, neither Roosevelt nor Churchill appears to have begun their talks at Argentia Bay in August 1941 with the intention of publishing a general statement of war and peace aims. Churchill's primary goal in meeting Roosevelt, in the words of Robert Sherwood, was 'the establishment of a common policy of resistance to further Japanese aggression' (Sherwood 1948: 350). This he did not achieve, but he did establish a close personal relationship with Roosevelt, of which the Charter itself was ample testimony, and which in the long run may have been more important than agreement on specific policies.

From Churchill's point of view, the Charter spelled out a broad agenda in advance of what he took to be an inevitable and much desired event: the entry of the United States into the war. Roosevelt, who had originally proposed the idea of a joint statement, was no less concerned to solidify the relationship with Britain. The United States was already acting as the 'arsenal of democracy', having through lend-lease and other measures committed considerable resources to the British war effort. One further consideration, not mentioned in the Charter but nevertheless of great significance, had a bearing on the Atlantic Conference. Roosevelt and Churchill agreed that both nations should send aid to the Soviet Union, which was reeling in the face of Germany's invasion deep into Soviet territory. In short, the building blocks of the wartime coalition of anti-Axis powers were put in place at the Atlantic Conference.

It is useful to think of the Atlantic Charter as a point of intersection of Allied goals, but also as a focus of their differences. It remained a key reference point throughout the war. Many of its phrases appeared word for word in the United Nations Charter. It was also referred to in the frequent disputes which arose in the later stages of the war over the treatment of the liberated areas of Europe and the Far East, a point to which we shall return. Above all, however, the Charter represented an attempt to register the vast shift in the world balance of power which the war had effected and, furthermore, a determination to dictate the shape it would assume. We can think of the Charter, and the Alliance which followed, as a bid to create a concert of powers as a framework, not only for wartime strategy but for a new world order.

The overriding context was the destruction of the pre-war balance of power by Germany and Japan in conjunction with Italy. Ironically, it was the Axis powers who initiated a bipolar division in the world system, a point noted by Stalin in a speech given in 1942 on the twenty-fifth anniversary of the Bolshevik Revolution. The world, he declared (in terms which uncannily anticipate the rhetoric of the 'Truman Doctrine' speech of 1947), was now divided into 'two camps':

> The programme of the Italo-German coalition may be characterized by the following points: race hatred; domination of the 'chosen' nations; subjugation of other nations and seizure of their territories; economic enslavement of the subjugated nations and spoliation of their national wealth; destruction of democratic liberties; universal institution of the Hitler regime.
>
> The programme of action of the Anglo–Soviet–American coalition is: abolition of racial exclusiveness; equality of nations and inviolability of their territories; liberation of the enslaved nations and restoration of their sovereign rights; the right of every nation to manage its affairs in its own way; economic aid to war-ravaged nations and assistance in establishing their material welfare; restoration of democratic liberties; destruction of the Hitler regime.
>
> (Daniels 1985, Vol. 2: 122–3)

Doubtless it comes as no surprise to find that during wartime leaders should present the conflict in a polarized fashion. The double need to vilify the enemy and to justify one's own cause prescribed the use of such devices. However, taken in conjunction with the key strategic goal agreed by the Allies – that of 'unconditional surrender' of the Axis powers – the Allied commitment to a new concert of powers placed a heavy burden on unity of resolve. The goal of total dictation to the defeated powers would leave total discretion to the Allies about how the resulting power vacuum should be filled. No less important was the explicit ideological component in the Allied conception of conflict with the Axis powers. The Second World War was, in a fuller sense than the First, a war 'to make the world safe for democracy', however divergent the meanings of 'democracy' might later prove to be among the Allies. This factor again intensified the problem of shaping a new world order, precisely because success relied on the maintenance of ideological consensus among nations with differing interests and values. In sum, both the structure and the mind-set of what turned into the cold war were initiated by the challenge posed by Axis belligerence and the Allied response to it. In this sense, Germany and Japan were at least co-authors of the cold war.

THE GRAND ALLIANCE AND THE WAR IN EUROPE

How cooperative was the Grand Alliance? The Roosevelt administration certainly made efforts to present the Soviet Union in a favourable light to American public opinion. Though publically he resisted endorsing some of the more extreme portrayals of 'our gallant ally' in films and newspapers, Roosevelt shared the prevalent impression among America's liberal elite that the trend in the Soviet Union was towards a convergence with Western democracy (Gaddis 1972: 41). Lend-lease, as we have seen, was made available to the Soviet Union before the United States herself had entered the war. Roosevelt, furthermore, made long trips to meet Stalin at Tehran in 1943 and Yalta in 1945 at considerable risk to his health and security, Stalin insisting that he himself must stay on or close to Russian soil. Beyond that, Roosevelt indicated repeatedly his desire for cooperation in both the political and military spheres. The decision to pursue a Europe-first strategy, rather than concentrate the American effort on defeating her attacker, Japan, was in part prompted by Roosevelt's awareness that the Soviet Union was bearing the main military and civilian burden of the war against Germany. Finally, Roosevelt set much store by his capacity to develop a personal relationship with Stalin, whether through his personal emissary, Harry Hopkins, who made frequent trips to Moscow on Roosevelt's behalf, or directly in his meetings with Stalin himself.

Stalin gave some indication that he too valued the personal link with Roosevelt. Roosevelt, said Stalin in 1944, was someone he could communicate with. Following Roosevelt's death in April 1945, the Soviet leadership's first encounters with President Truman's blunt style of diplomacy led Soviet Foreign Minister, Molotov, to declare that the disputes over Eastern Europe would not have occurred had Roosevelt still been alive. The same view was echoed by Khrushchev in his memoirs and by later Soviet commentators; it clearly represented Soviet orthodoxy (Gaddis 1972: 205; Khrushchev 1990: 82; Arbatov 1983: 66). Nor perhaps is it surprising to find 'revisionist' historians of American foreign policy presenting similar views (Horowitz 1967: chs 1–3).

It is doubtful, however, whether Stalin placed as much emphasis as Roosevelt on the personal factor. Nor is it clear that the cold war could have been avoided had Roosevelt lived beyond April 1945. Though historians frequently quote Roosevelt's last message to Churchill to the effect that 'I would minimize the Soviet problem as much as possible', this must be weighed against Roosevelt's last communication to Stalin which was a stiff complaint that the Soviet Union was failing to fulfil promises made at Yalta on progress towards democracy in Poland (Kimball 1984, Vol. 3: 630; FRUS 1945: 194–6). Furthermore, one must take into account the fact that Truman was forced to deal with issues such as Poland at a later and more difficult stage of their evolution. Personal contacts between international statesmen then and since have certainly helped to cement relationships when the needs were pressing, but they have rarely served to prevent fissures when interests seriously diverged. As an aide of Churchill's remarked following the Prime Minister's meeting with Stalin in August 1942, 'I should say that to make friends with Stalin would be equivalent to making friends with a python . . . the Prime Minister's relationship with Stalin would only be close and personal as long as Stalin thinks that his interests will be served thereby' (Edmonds 1991: 303).

As it happened, during the war Stalin had indeed a pressing interest in conciliatory moves towards his wartime allies. While making clear at an early stage his desire for 'friendly' governments on Russia's western border following the war, Stalin gave at least nominal consent to the Atlantic Charter and later to the Declaration on Liberated Europe (1945), one of whose provisions was self-determination for all peoples. The dismantling of the Comintern in 1943, moreover, was presented by the Soviet Union and perceived in the West as a gesture of goodwill, implying a suspension of the ideological goal of spreading communism.[1] Finally, Stalin indicated at the Tehran Conference that he would declare war on Japan as soon as the war in Europe was over. At Yalta this was converted into a firm pledge.

The divergent interests among the Allies, however, were apparent even in the commitments they made to each other. Two issues loomed large. The first was Stalin's request for acknowledgement of Soviet vital interests in Eastern Europe (essentially a ratification of the gains Stalin had acquired in the Nazi–Soviet Pact of 1939, above all the Baltic States and Eastern Poland). The Western Allies resisted making firm commitments on this point at the outset of the Alliance, and Stalin agreed to postpone agreement on this issue upon receipt of an assurance that the Western Allies would mount a 'second front' in Western Europe with all speed. This in turn became a second point of friction since the major assault in North-west Europe which Stalin desired was repeatedly postponed, pre-eminently at Churchill's insistence. During a stormy meeting between Churchill and Stalin in Moscow in July 1942, at which Churchill announced that a second front was impossible that year, Stalin voiced the accusation that 'the British Prime Minister will once again prove to us that his country is not in a position to sacrifice men' (Deutscher 1960: 478). The same charge was levelled, with some justification, at Roosevelt, who, despite his anxiety to commit American forces against Germany, yielded to Churchill's insistence that too early an assault on 'Fortress Europe' would be unlikely to succeed and would involve enormous casualties. The Western Allies settled instead on a North African campaign in 1942, followed in 1943 by landing in Sicily and the Italian mainland.

Despite Stalin's praise for the Allied landings in Normandy when they came in June 1944, the damage to the Alliance caused by the repeated postponements was enormous. As the Soviets saw it, Churchill's strategy was politically motivated. After Churchill's departure from Moscow in July 1942 (which took place at the onset of the decisive but costly battle of Stalingrad) Stalin is reported as saying that 'all is clear. A campaign in Africa, Italy. They simply want to be the first in reaching the Balkans. They want us to bleed white in order to dictate to us their terms later on . . . Nothing will come out of this! The Slavs will be with us . . . They hope that we shall lose Stalingrad and lose the springboard for an offensive' (Deutscher 1960: 479). Even if this was to read too much into Churchill's motives, Stalin's suspicion that Churchill and Roosevelt had their own agenda, which excluded him, proved to be a potent source of mistrust within the Alliance. (In the case of atomic bomb development, to be discussed later on pp. 54–8, Stalin had grounds for doubt about the good faith of his Allies.)

In actuality, however, Roosevelt was acutely conscious of the disproportionate burden borne by the Soviet Union and this led him in the later stages of the war to go to great lengths to be conciliatory to Stalin. It also inclined him to be wary of associating himself too closely with Churchill's clear preference for a Mediterranean strategy. By the time of the Tehran Conference at the end of 1943, as Keith Sainsbury observes, a turning point had been reached within the Alliance, coincident upon the shift of military power in the Anglo-American alliance in favour of the United States: 'the United States turned its main attention within the alliance from Britain to the Soviet Union: Western strategic policy changed from a Mediterranean focus, largely inspired by British ideas, to a Western European focus reflecting largely American concepts' (Sainsbury 1985: 307).

Much as Stalin may have resented the delay in the second front, it worked decisively to his political advantage in the long run. It ensured that the bulk of Eastern Europe would be liberated by the Red Army. This, in combination with Roosevelt's inclination to defer consideration of political issues until military victory had been achieved, helped to set a pattern in which military decisions would come to have major political repercussions. Roosevelt has frequently been accused of political naivety in this regard. Firmer efforts earlier in the war, it is implied, to tie Stalin down to agreements on the composition of future governments in the liberated nations, might have prevented, or at least moderated, the subsequent sovietization of Eastern Europe. Such views receive apparent confirmation in a frank remark made by Soviet diplomat, Maxim Litvinov, to the American journalist Edgar Snow in June 1945: 'Why did you Americans wait till now to begin opposing us in the Balkans and Eastern Europe? . . . You should have done this three years ago. Now it's too late and your complaints only arouse suspicion' (Mastny 1979: 218).

It is hard to believe, however, that such pressure could have been applied on Stalin without splitting the alliance. Roosevelt was worried enough that in the absence of firm support from the United States Stalin might seek a separate peace with Germany. (Indeed Stalin had considered making a separate peace with Germany following the decisive Soviet victory over Germany at Stalingrad in 1943; see Mastny 1979: 73ff.) Demanding that Stalin make agreements in advance on the governments and borders of the Eastern European nations as a price of the Alliance might have produced just that outcome. In fact, while it is true that Roosevelt preferred to leave detailed discussion of territorial questions until the German surrender was within sight, he had clear political motives for doing so. Chief among these was his conviction that the best foundation for post-war reconstruction lay in the continuance of big power unity, and that depended, in his view, on the swift prosecution of the war to a successful military conclusion. To press forward on territorial issues too early, above all on Eastern Europe, would be to risk exposing serious differences between the Western

Allies and Stalin. In any case Roosevelt had little quarrel with the general proposition that the Soviet Union was justified in seeking friendly governments on its western border. He would doubtless, though, have been less sanguine about the chances of avoiding a wholesale Soviet domination of Eastern Europe if he had been able to overhear Stalin's oft-quoted remark to Milovan Djilas in early 1945: 'this war is not as in the past: whoever occupies a territory also imposes his own system as far as his army can reach' (Djilas 1962: 114).

In essentials Stalin proved to be right. By the time Roosevelt, Churchill, and Stalin gathered at Yalta in Soviet Crimea in February 1945 to discuss the major questions arising from the imminent prospect of victory over Germany, the broad framework of the territorial arrangements had been decided by the disposition of forces. The American decision not to engage in a race with the Russians for Berlin and Prague, decisions made partly on military and partly on political grounds, reinforced the emerging pattern of divided responsibility between the zones of occupation. The Western Allies had already set a precedent in Italy, where the Allied Control Council, on which a Soviet representative sat, was accorded only advisory status, the real power lying with the Western Allied commander of the occupying forces. The more comprehensive European Advisory Commission, charged with overseeing joint military and political control of all liberated areas, was similarly limited in its capacity to enforce a unified approach to the treatment of liberated areas.

THE DISINTEGRATION OF THE WARTIME ALLIANCE

In one sense there is no mystery about the disintegration of the wartime Alliance. Brought together in adversity, the Allies naturally reverted to the pursuit of their own interests once the emergency was over. The United States and the Soviet Union had had little in common prior to the war – indeed much had divided them – and from a long perspective the Alliance was an abberration in their relations. 'Political alliances', writes Martin Wight, 'are always contracted with third parties in view' (Wight 1979: 122). The destruction of the third party – in this case the Axis powers – inevitably exposed the largely utilitarian purpose which had led to the formation of the Alliance. Furthermore, to anticipate discussion of the onset of the cold war, the historical record illustrates what common sense would suggest: that in a system of states where there are two dominant powers, they tend to move towards opposite poles, around which the smaller powers range themselves. If, as theorists have argued, large powers seek hegemony on their own terms, which includes the urge for homogeneity within the system as a whole, the limits to such ambitions will be set by the presence of other large powers pursuing comparable ambitions.

Looked at in this way, both the disintegration of the Alliance and the onset of the cold war are explicable in terms of (a) the dynamics of alliance politics, and (b) the dynamics of power within systems of states containing two would-be hegemonic powers.

Figure 3.1 The new Poland, 1945
Source: Derived from D.M. Smith (ed.), *Major Problems in American Diplomatic History: Documents and Readings*, Lexington, Mass.: D.C. Heath 1964, Vol. 2, p. 537.

Useful as these perspectives are, they do not encompass all the complexities of the actual processes which concern us. In the first place, the western pillar of the Alliance was not a single, unified pole. An important sub-theme in the story of the war was the shift in economic, military, and political power from Britain to the United States. Adopting Martin Wight's terms once again, the Anglo-American relationship was an instance of an association 'between powers that seem to be deeper than formal alliances, to be based on affinity and tradition as much as interest, to be not so much utilitarian as natural' (Wight 1979: 123). This clearly did not ensure a conflict-free relationship. On the contrary, if anything it made the assumption by the United States of a global leadership role more complex, since this inevitably involved clashes with Britain's interest in retaining some vestige of such a role. Furthermore, if we read history forwards from the war rather than backwards from the cold war, it is evident that the United States leadership did not envisage the forward political and military role it later assumed in containing Soviet power in Europe or indeed elsewhere (Leffler 1992: 16). Roosevelt had intimated at Yalta that the United States planned to withdraw its occupation forces from Europe within two years. During the latter stages of the war and until the middle of 1946, moreover, Britain rather than the United States was regarded by the Soviet Union as its chief antagonist (McCagg 1978: 255). For its part, the United States conceived of itself, though evidently with waning conviction as 1946 wore on, as a mediator between the other two, much as Roosevelt had done at Yalta. In short, within the western arm of the Alliance a delicate transition was taking place. To adapt a statement later used by Dean Acheson to describe Britain's post-war dilemma, in 1945–46 the United States had found new power but not yet a role.

The second qualification to the scheme offered by international relations theory outlined above is that the wartime Alliance contained the seeds of two possible systems of states. One was globalist, based on chiefly American ideas, but subscribed to nominally by the Soviet Union and Britain. It is best expressed by Roosevelt's wartime Secretary of State, Cordell Hull, in his comments upon the Four Power Declaration agreed at Moscow in 1943. With the signing of the Declaration, he said, 'there will no longer be need for spheres of influence, for alliances, for balances of power, or any other of the special arrangements through which, in the unhappy past, nations strove to safeguard their security or to promote their interests' (Sainsbury 1985: 117). The other possible system emerging from the war was precisely of the type which Hull hoped had been ruled out by wartime agreements: one based on traditional balance of power and spheres of influence arrangements. In the event the outcome was neither of these in a pure form, but a unique amalgam of the two. The United States, globalist by persuasion and by virtue of its economic power, was drawn into a spheres of influence arrangement by the late 1940s; the Soviet Union, inclined for security and political reasons to the establishment of a sphere of influence in Europe, nevertheless emerged from the war as a global power in a double sense, both by virtue of its ideology and its commitment, however nominal, to a joint reshaping of the world order with its wartime allies.

There existed, then, in the crucial last year of the war and the first of 'peace' a delicate balance between forces tending to undermine the alliance and attempts to sustain it as the basis for a new world order. We can observe the interplay of these forces in five major problems which dominated the agenda in 1945–46: (1) the establishment of the United Nations Organization, (2) the reconstruction of the world economy, (3) the settlement of borders and the establishment of new governments in Poland and Eastern Europe, (4) the treatment of Germany, and (5) the issue of atomic weapons and atomic energy. By the middle of 1946 the mould was set in which the best that could be achieved was fragile agreement: the worst was rank failure to find common ground.

The United Nations

On the face of it the United Nations represents the least unsuccessful joint venture of the post-war years. Having repudiated Woodrow Wilson's cherished League of

Nations in 1919, the United States was now determined to play a leading role in the new international organization. Bipartisan support in Congress for participation and widespread public sentiment in favour of internationalism were decisive in making up Roosevelt's mind. By the summer of 1942 three out of four Americans favoured United States membership in some form of collective security organization (Gaddis 1972: 26). Not that this meant a reversion to the Wilsonian idealism of 1919. Convinced that the League of Nations had been based on the unrealistic assumption that all nations deserved equal status in decision-making, Roosevelt favoured Big Power predominance. This priority was reflected in the Dumbarton Oaks Plan of 1944, in which pre-eminent power was given to the Security Council with its five permanent members – the United States, the Soviet Union, Great Britain, France, and China – while the universalist principle of the old League of Nations was retained in the form of the Assembly. Stalin, though less inclined to trust Soviet interests to an international body, was prepared to countenance a scheme which acknowledged the reality that some powers were more equal than others.

Early disputes arose over procedural issues and the Soviet Union's claim to sixteen votes in the Assembly, based on its sixteen 'autonomous republics' and designed to match the separate votes accorded to the nations within the British Empire and Dominions. Agreement on these points, however, scarcely removed crippling weaknesses from the organization. The founding conference at San Francisco in April 1945 provided a shop window for some of these. Serious disagreements arose over the American move to seat Argentina, which had been pro-Nazi during the war, and over the Soviet demand that Poland, still ruled by the Soviet-installed 'Lublin' government, also be included. The veto power available to the five permanent members of the Security Council, desired as much by the United States as by the Soviet Union, meant that each could forestall decisions perceived to be against its interests (Sherwood 1948: 854).[2]

In so far as the effectiveness of the organization depended upon Big Power unity, disagreement on major issues would undermine its capacity to act. Such proved to be the case. The UN became a mirror of the growing disunity among the major powers, but above all between the Soviet Union and the other members of the Security Council plus their respective clients and supporters. Furthermore, there was scepticism about the UN among American leaders. Dean Acheson, Assistant Secretary of State in 1945 and later Secretary of State, was responsible for preparing the government's case for ratification of the UN Charter by the US Senate, and records in his memoirs that 'I did my duty faithfully and successfully but always believed that the Charter was impracticable' (Acheson 1969: 111). Though subsequently the administration was careful to ensure that its major initiatives, such as the Truman Doctrine and NATO, were compatible with the UN Charter, there was never a chance that matters of vital interest would be submitted to UN decision. The organization's singular success in the early post-war years, at least as a collective security organization – namely, the Council's endorsement of the American decision to resist the North Korean invasion of

South Korea in June 1950 – was possible only because at that time the Soviet Union was boycotting the organization in protest at the refusal of the UN to admit Mao Zedong's government as the legitimate government of China. (The nationalist government of Chiang Kai-shek had been overthrown by the communists in 1949 and driven out to the island of Formosa.)

Reconstruction of the world economy

Cooperation to produce a new economic order proved even more elusive, despite initial signs of progress. The Roosevelt administration was convinced that the political instability of the inter-war years had been rooted in economic nationalism and had been a major cause of the Second World War. Roosevelt's closest advisers believed, therefore, in the words of Treasury official Harry Dexter White, that 'the absence of a high degree of economic collaboration among the leading nations, will, during the coming decade, inevitably result in economic warfare that will be but the prelude and instigator of military warfare on an even vaster scale' (Pollard 1985: 8). The outcome was the formulation at Bretton Woods in 1944 of a plan to provide for international currency stabilization and the distribution of loans to needy countries with a view to promoting international trade. The key principle, as far as the United States was concerned, was openness, its global applicability to capitalist, communist and developing nations alike. Indeed the United States anticipated more resistance from Britain, with its jealously guarded system of imperial preference, than from the Soviet Union. Britain signed the Bretton Woods accords only after receiving the promise of a post-war loan from the United States (Pollard 1985: 67–8). The Soviet Union for its part 'sought larger political objectives, such as the recognition of its great power status, maximum influence in the IMF and IBRD at the smallest possible price, and assurance that the Bretton Woods system would not interfere with its internal policies' (Pollard 1985: 15). The resulting provisions, which gave the Soviet Union voting power and influence in the new institutions out of proportion to the volume of its world trade, reflected a willingness on both sides to compromise. The promise of a US post-war loan to the Soviet Union, as in the British case, helped to smooth the passage of the agreements. The Bretton Woods conference ended, as far as the US–Soviet relationship was concerned, in an atmosphere of considerable amity.

Economic self-interest undoubtedly played a role in the United States' promotion of the system. As by far the largest subscriber of funds to the proposed IMF and IBRD, the United States was in a position to determine the shape and operation of the new institutions. It stood to gain from an increased demand for American exports in the period of post-war reconstruction, given the decisive shift of financial and commercial power to the United States as a result of the war. It was also thought that the new system would obviate the need for large-scale loans to other countries for post-war reconstruction. In practice, while the United States did become the world's economic and financial powerhouse, this was less because of the establishment of the Bretton

Woods machinery than because of the simple fact that the United States emerged from the war as the dominant and expanding economic power. Nor could the wretched economic condition of the bulk of the rest of the world be resolved overnight by the fledgling Bretton Woods institutions. Despite the short-term, one-off loans to Britain and other nations immediately following the war, a much larger scheme was needed subsequently in the form of the Marshall Plan for Europe and the 'Point IV' programme for developing countries (see Chapter 4).

The Soviet Union meanwhile, having endorsed the Bretton Woods agreements in 1944, failed to ratify the accords by the deadline of 31 December 1945. This decision seems to have arisen less from objections to the plan itself than from growing rifts with the United States on other issues. The American refusal to grant a post-war loan without stringent conditions, coupled with the peremptory cut-off of lend-lease aid in May 1945, exacerbated relations which were already marked by serious disputes over Eastern Europe. In this sense, as John Gaddis has remarked, the Soviets' withdrawal from participation in the Bretton Woods system 'was an effect rather than a cause of the cold war' (Gaddis 1972: 23). Nevertheless, the result was to encourage the development of separate economic blocs to match the political divisions which were fast appearing.

The Polish question

Confrontation over the establishment of borders and new governments in Poland and other Eastern European countries lay at the root of the Alliance's problems. Agreements of a sort, however, were reached on Eastern Europe and to that extent tension arose as much from problems of interpretation and implementation of agreed policies as over the character of the policies themselves. An important background influence in the discussions at Yalta on Eastern Europe was the so-called 'percentages deal' reached by Stalin and Churchill in October 1944. According to this arrangement, hurriedly drafted by Churchill on a half sheet of paper, Soviet and Western spheres of responsibility in the Balkan nations and Hungary were divided along the following lines: Romania: Russia 90 per cent, others 10 per cent; Greece: Great Britain in accord with the US 90 per cent, Russia 10 per cent; Yugoslavia: 50–50 per cent; Hungary: 50–50 per cent; Bulgaria: Russia 75 per cent, others 25 per cent (Churchill 1953: 227).

Two questions suggest themselves. Why, given his long-standing anti-Bolshevism, was Churchill apparently prepared to concede so much to Stalin in Eastern Europe? Churchill's own answer was that this was conceived of purely as a temporary wartime measure to clarify transition arrangements, permanent settlements being left for a later peace conference (Churchill 1953: 227). It is just as likely, however, that Churchill believed that this was realistically the best that could be achieved, given the military dispositions at the time, and furthermore that it was necessary to safeguard Western interests in Greece. Churchill had already settled on a policy of sending British parachute troops to Greece in the wake of the German withdrawal with the purpose of ensuring an orderly transition of power in a nation which was deeply divided. In the event, civil war broke out between the communist-backed forces which had led the resistance to German occupation and rightist forces which wanted the return of the monarchy. Surprisingly, Roosevelt endorsed the British policy of supporting the rightists, a policy which was highly unpopular with liberal public opinion in the United States (Gardner 1993: 194–6). This raises the second important question regarding the percentages deal: namely, Roosevelt's attitude towards it.

Spheres of influence was not what he had led the American public to expect. 'The Americans', noted a British official, 'have an astonishing phobia about "spheres of influence"' (Gardner 1993: 188). The Americans were deeply suspicious of the Churchill–Stalin talks in October 1944, believing with some justification as it turned out, that Churchill would make commitments which might tie the Western Allies' hands. The Americans therefore insisted on having an observer in Moscow. Though the observer did not attend the Churchill–Stalin conversations themselves, he was briefed fairly fully about their content. In short, Roosevelt was certainly aware of the essentials of the percentage deal. In the event, as with other issues relating to future political settlements in Europe, Roosevelt's philosophical opposition to spheres of influence did not prevent him from accepting realities for the moment in the hope that they could be changed later. Into that gap between total repudiation and total endorsement of the percentages deal Stalin and military realities drove a large wedge. In the words of a recent study of wartime diplomacy, the percentages deal 'cast a shadow over resistance to Russian claims to dominate Poland, however much the prime minister or the president sought to maintain the illusion that Europe was not being divided among the Big Three' (Gardner 1993: 206).

The long and tortuous dispute over Polish boundaries was 'solved' by Stalin's presentation to the Western Allies of a military *fait accompli*, by which Poland was moved bodily westwards some 150 miles – the Soviet Union gaining Poland's former eastern territories and Poland gaining comparable territory from Germany. Several million Germans were displaced from former German lands which now became part of Poland. The result was to make the new Poland firmly dependent on the Soviet Union for protection against possible future German claims for return of former Polish territory.

Implicit Western agreement to these arrangements, however, did not extend to approving Stalin's proposals for the composition of the Polish government. Churchill and Roosevelt each had powerful reasons for insisting on a democratic Poland, consistent with the Atlantic Charter and the Yalta Declaration on Liberated Europe. Defence of Poland had been the immediate cause of Britain's declaration of war on Germany in 1939, while Roosevelt was ever conscious of the five million voters of Polish origin in the United States. At the Yalta conference provision was made for the establishment of a new provisional government based on the existing Soviet-backed 'Lublin' government but with the addition of 'democratic leaders from Poland

and from Poles abroad'. Free elections and the formation of a government with full powers were to follow as soon as the military situation would permit. Even before Roosevelt's death on 8 April 1945 wrangles had developed over observance of the agreement, as the Soviet Union made it clear that it was unprepared either to accord the non-communists any real role or to conduct the kind of elections which would satisfy the West. Roosevelt's successor, Harry Truman, introduced a more abrasive style in relations with the Soviet Union, but in substance he sought to continue Roosevelt's preference for dealing independently with Stalin rather than tying America to British policy and arousing Stalin's suspicions of a Western Allied bloc against him. Truman dispatched Harry Hopkins to Moscow in May 1945 in an effort to persuade Stalin to make good the Yalta pledges on Poland. The meeting produced minor Soviet concessions, enough to lead the United States to recognize the new Polish government by the middle of the summer, but in essence little had changed. The truth was that Truman was left with the alternative of accepting an unsatisfactory agreement or provoking an open breach with Stalin.

A similar pattern followed in Romania and Bulgaria. In a series of Foreign Ministers' conferences held in late 1945, during which Stalin managed to exploit disagreements between the United States and Britain, a framework was established for settlements on Bulgaria and Romania. These provided nominal self-government but little in the way of genuine democracy. Indeed the communist hold had been established on these two countries within a few months of the arrival of Soviet troops in summer 1944 (Taubman 1982: 75). Only in Czechoslovakia and Hungary did non-communists still retain real power but, as events were to prove, the Western powers possessed as little leverage in those countries as they did in Bulgaria and Romania. (This is discussed in Chapter 4.)

An important result of the tangled and often acrimonious negotiations over Eastern Europe was to draw the United States and Britain closer together. British objections that American Secretary of State James Byrnes was willing to pay too high a price for agreement with Stalin (ironic in the light of Churchill's Moscow deal with Stalin), coupled with criticism within the United States of the agreements on Bulgaria and Romania, provoked a reassessment of policy towards the Soviet Union. By early 1946 a new and tougher American line was developing, characterized by a growing partnership between the United States and Britain. More precisely, the United States was beginning to assume leadership in the Anglo-American partnership as both moved further away from Moscow.

Germany

On the German issue American policy shifted from an initial desire to reduce that nation to virtual political and economic impotence to a recognition that an impoverished and resentful Germany could prove a potent source of instability in Europe. The Soviet Union's paramount interest – shared by France – in preventing German resurgence and gaining recompense for the destruction Germany had wreaked ran counter to the United States' growing preference for 'rehabilitation' over 'repression' (Gaddis 1972: Ch. 4). Once again the issue of joint control was the focus of dispute. By 1944 zonal boundaries of occupation had been agreed, though within a framework of joint supervision of Germany as a single unit. The story of the following two years is of the hardening of these temporary zones of occupation into rigid boundaries.

Of the many disputed questions reparations presented the largest difficulty. Given its enormous human and material sacrifices in the war against Germany – it is now estimated that the Soviet Union suffered 27 million military and civilian casualties (Volkogonov 1991: 505) – the Soviet Union had most at stake, and at Yalta proposed the substantial sum of $20 billion as a basis for the joint Allied claim on Germany, half to go to the Soviet Union. Fearful of German economic collapse (and the drain on the American taxpayer once the bill for German recovery was presented), the United States proposed instead at the Potsdam meeting in July 1945 that the occupying powers should each exact reparations from its own zone. The consequence of this decision was a *de facto* division of responsibility for the transition period. As with the settlements in other areas, temporary and transitional expedients became the basis for permanent arrangements. The Allied Control Council for Germany, riven by disputes over denazification policies, access by the occupying powers to each other's zones, and the interzonal transfer of reparations, was hardly in a position to enforce joint administration of Germany. Though the United States and the Soviet Union continued to advocate a united Germany – a policy which the Soviet Union persisted in longer than the United States – neither was willing to risk its potential cost: the absorption of Germany into the other's camp.

The atom bomb

Debate about the use of atomic bombs on Hiroshima and Nagasaki on 6 and 9 August 1945 began almost as soon as they were dropped and has continued unabated. The official justification was that the immediate dictates of the military situation supplied the primary motivation. Defeating Japan by conventional means, it was believed, would involve a costly and bloody invasion of the Japanese homeland. There seemed no immediate prospect of a Japanese surrender, despite the imminent entry of the Soviet Union into the war against Japan (agreed at Yalta). 'Let there be no mistake about it,' Truman recalled in his memoirs, 'I regarded the bomb as a military weapon and never had any doubt that it should be used. The top military advisers to the President recommended its use, and when I talked to Churchill he unhesitatingly told me that he favored the use of the atomic bomb if it might aid to end the war' (Truman 1955: 419). In support of this contention one could add that from the start the Manhattan Project (the code name given to the programme to produce the bomb) had been designed to produce a usable weapon and that there was an inexorable technological and military logic driving the process forward. As one historian put it, the bomb was used 'because it was there' (Ambrose 1988: 51). Crucially, despite his position as Roosevelt's Vice-President, Truman had been kept ignorant of the Manhattan Project and therefore had had little time to reflect on the wider implications of atomic weapons before he was confronted with the decision to use them. Perhaps it would have made no difference to his decision if he had been informed earlier. Nevertheless, his isolation from earlier decision-making on the atomic bomb surely reinforced his inclination to view it narrowly as a military matter.

However, few commentators at the time or historians since then have been satisfied with such an uncomplicated interpretation. Questions were raised about whether the bombs were in fact necessary to force a Japanese surrender. Was there not the option of a demonstration atom test to convince the Japanese of its overwhelming power? Were there not indications that Japan was interested in peace talks in early August and in particular after the first bomb was dropped? Perhaps, it has been argued, the surrender owed more to Russian entry into the war on 8 August than the effect of the bombs. It was, after all, five days after the second bomb before the Japanese surrendered, by which time Russian forces were already deep into Manchuria. There is some evidence, furthermore, that estimates of likely American casualties in a conventional invasion of Japan were wildly inflated by Truman in restrospect. Rather than Truman's figure of 500,000 casualties, military planners during the war projected no more than 46,000, casting doubt on the claim that the bomb was used to save American lives. There is even some, admittedly contradictory, evidence from Truman's private diaries that he was aware that the bomb might not be necessary to end the war (Walker 1990: 103–5). Nevertheless, though with hindsight some historians may be convinced that alternatives to the use of the bombs were available, there is little reason to argue with the conclusion that at the time 'there were no moral, military, diplomatic, or bureaucratic considerations that carried enough weight to deter dropping the bomb and gaining its projected military and diplomatic benefits' (Walker 1990: 111).

If military necessity was not the only issue involved, what were the projected 'diplomatic benefits' of the bomb? Though historians vary in the significance which they ascribe to the diplomatic implications of the bomb's use, most accept that this was an important element in the decision. In fact political considerations had been there from the beginning, when the decision was taken to exclude the Soviet Union from knowledge of the Manhattan Project. Furthermore, as Martin Sherwin has pointed out, as the war progressed, 'the diplomatic implications of the weapon's development came steadily to the fore'. Roosevelt and Secretary of War Stimson 'became increasingly anxious to convert it to diplomatic advantage', and in December 1944 'they spoke of using the "secret" of the atomic bomb as a means of obtaining a quid pro quo from the Soviet Union' (Sherwin 1977: 5). Furthermore, it seems clear that the Americans hoped the demonstration of the bomb's power in bringing about the defeat of Japan might incline the Soviet Union to be more compliant in negotiations over political and territorial issues. News of the first successful test of the A-bomb, which reached Truman while he was at Potsdam in late July 1945, reportedly had the effect of stiffening Truman's resolve not to yield to the Soviets on the composition of new governments in Bulgaria and Romania.

Evidence that certain political considerations were present as a penumbra around the decision to use the bomb on Japan has not, however, proved the contention of one revisionist historian that from the time he assumed office in April 1945 Truman employed a concerted strategy of 'atomic diplomacy'. According to this view, Truman pursued a strategy of 'delayed showdown', designed to postpone negotiations with the Soviet Union and ensure that a bomb could be developed and used before the Soviets entered the war with Japan (Alperovitz 1985: 103–9). Few scholars have been convinced by such categorical conclusions in a field in which the evidence remains complex and often contradictory. As things stand, in the words of a recent commentator, despite disagreements about specific points, there is a rough consensus that 'the bomb was used primarily for military reasons and secondarily for diplomatic ones' (Walker 1990: 111).

If anything, Truman might be accused of having given insufficient thought to the political implications of the atomic bomb. Others, including a group of scientists at the Chicago Laboratory of the Manhattan Project, had given thought to this question – in particular to the dangers of an unrestricted arms race – should the bomb be used unannounced on Japan. The so-called 'Franck Report' of June 1945, which was effectively ignored by the administration, spelled out in advance what actually eventuated – the collapse of attempts to produce international control of atomic energy and the advent of an atomic arms race (Sherwin 1977: 210–19).

In any event, to whatever degree it was believed that possession of the bomb would incline the Soviets to be more compliant, such hopes appear to have been stillborn. The Soviet position on Eastern Europe showed no sign of moderation in response to the American atomic monopoly (Taubman 1982: 110).

There are several possible reasons for the inability of American possession of the bomb to dictate relations with the Soviet Union. In the first place, because of successful Soviet penetration of the Manhattan Project, the Soviet leadership was aware of the progress the Americans had made in this field. According to one authority, Soviet scientists had been aware of the possibility of exploiting nuclear physics to make bombs well before the Second World War and before the war had ended they had resumed work on the project (Zuckerman 1987: 27–8). At any rate, Stalin showed little surprise or dismay on being told by Truman at Potsdam that the Americans had a powerful new weapon, simply replying that he hoped they would use it on Japan. Doubtless there was an element of pure bluff in this. Stalin was not one to betray weakness, even when he was at a disadvantage. The chief effect of the American test was probably to encourage the Soviet Union to step up its own nuclear programme.

A second problem faced by American policy-makers was that wielding the bomb as a threat over the Soviet Union would have been hard to justify morally and politically. Open use of atomic coercion or blackmail was hardly an option at a time when strenuous attempts were being made to reach agreements with the Soviet Union in other areas, to say nothing of the widespread sense of the awesome destructive power of the new weapon. Pressure for international control was strong within the government and public opinion. Conscious that the exclusion of the Soviets from the Manhattan Project must have aroused Soviet suspicions of an Anglo-American combination against them, Under-Secretary of State Dean Acheson counselled cooperation with the Soviet Union to produce international control of atomic energy if an arms race were to be avoided. Since, he reasoned, atomic science could not be kept secret, agreements must be reached (Gaddis 1972: 251–2).

A third consideration affecting American policy on atomic energy looked in the opposite direction from the second: towards maintenance of American superiority, as far as that was possible. Even those favouring some form of international control did not envisage simply opening the books to the Soviet Union, if only because the United States was clearly ahead in atomic development. Estimates about how long this would last varied. Many scientists thought the United States had at most a four-year advantage. Those, such as Secretary of State Byrnes and General Groves, head of the Manhattan Project, who were reluctant to cooperate with the Soviet Union, by contrast held highly optimistic forecasts about the likely duration of the American atomic monopoly: anything from ten to twenty years (Herken 1980: 98–100). While these estimates proved to be wildly out (the first Soviet test was achieved in 1949), the thinking which prompted them had a profound effect on discussions of atomic energy, as the climate of cooperation between the United States and the Soviet Union worsened in the year following the war. Of particular significance was the discovery early in the year of a Soviet-run Canadian spy ring which trafficked in atomic secrets.

The resulting debate on international control within the UN Atomic Energy Commission during the summer of 1946 displayed both the growing dominance of a hardline within the United States government and continuing Soviet resistance to any hint of atomic diplomacy. The so-called 'Baruch plan' (named after America's representative on the UN Commission) proposed the establishment of an international authority to oversee all phases of the development and use of atomic energy. Provision for inspection and control was integral to the plan, as was the American insistence that the United States could contemplate ending manufacture of its own weapons and disposing of its own stockpile only when the machinery was in place. In response the Soviet Union not only objected to on-site inspection, but called for the destruction of existing stockpiles prior to the establishment of the machinery of control. Deadlock ensued, ensuring that separate and competitive development of nuclear weapons would be the outcome. On the face of it, the period of the American atomic monopoly (1945–49) was precisely the time in which atomic diplomacy might have been expected to succeed. In the event the atomic bomb proved to be a very blunt diplomatic instrument, and the will to contemplate its use as a weapon of war was probably decreased by its employment against Japan.

One final point deserves mention. The waning of cooperation with the Soviet Union was evident also in relations with Britain on the issue of atomic energy. Having participated fully with the United States in the Manhattan Project, Britain now found itself barred by the McMahon Act of 1946 from any exchange of information with the United States in the field of atomic energy. The US military and its supporters in Congress gained this provision as the price for agreeing to civilian control of atomic power. That it contravened the spirit and the letter of wartime agreements between Roosevelt and Churchill providing for future joint development meant little to legislators, who had been kept almost wholly in the dark about these commitments (Hathaway 1981: 262–3). Though subsequently the ban on cooperation was partially lifted, in the climate of 1946 it conveyed a clear signal that the 'special relationship' forged in the war would not override America's own interests where it was felt these might be in conflict with each other. Just as important was the evidence this issue supplied of the desire of Congress to reassert power after several years of dominance of the policy-making process by the executive branch. In both the United States and the Soviet Union domestic politics appeared resurgent in the aftermath of war and exerted a powerful influence on diplomacy.

1946: DOMESTIC POLITICS AND INTERNATIONAL CONFLICT

The decisive change during 1946 was a growing public acknowledgement by both sides that the Grand Alliance was moribund. The change was not immediate. Within the United States conflicting opinions were apparent in the early months of 1946. One strand of opinion took the form of mounting criticism of the Truman administration's 'soft line' on Eastern Europe, focusing on Secretary of State James Byrnes who had negotiated the agreements on Bulgaria and Romania. Byrnes himself, shifting with the times, signalled a new hard line in early February 1946 when he acknowledged deep differences between the United States and the Soviet Union. On the other hand, the unsettled nature of American public opinion was manifest in the public reaction to Churchill's 'Iron Curtain' speech at Fulton, Missouri in early March. His vision of a divided world, and his full-blooded anti-communism, aroused intense anger within American public opinion for its belligerent tone. Truman and his closest advisers, however, did little to disown the speech, not least because Churchill's sentiments were close to those which the Truman administration was fast coming to hold. Less often remembered is Churchill's plea in the same speech for a 'fraternal association of the English-speaking peoples'. Because it seemed to imply a wilful disregard of the United Nations, it attracted as much ire among internationalists in the United States as did his strident denunciation of the Soviet Union.

Just as telling, as far as views within the administration were concerned, was the receipt in February of the so-called 'Long Telegram' from George Kennan, senior American diplomat in Moscow. This document painted a dark picture of a Soviet Union 'fanatically committed to the belief that with the US there can be no permanent *modus vivendi*, that it is desirable and necessary that the internal harmony of our society be disrupted, our traditional way of life destroyed, the international authority of our state be broken if Soviet Power is to be secure' (Jensen 1991: 28). With these words Kennan uttered the as yet unspoken thoughts of the Truman administration, and it brought him swiftly, though briefly as it turned out, to the centre of the policy-making process. Kennan's assessment had been prompted by a request from the State Department for an interpretation of Soviet policy in the light of a speech by Stalin at the beginning of February. Though given as an electoral address for a domestic audience, its strident denunciation of capitalism, its picture of the war as having been the product of capitalist imperial designs, and its claim that the war proved that 'our Soviet social system has triumphed', were hardly calculated to improve cooperation and understanding with the West (Daniels 1985, Vol. 1: 295). It was perceived in the United States as a declaration of cold war.

International events intervened to confirm the worst fears of the Truman administration. During March a crisis developed in Iran. Soviet delay in withdrawing troops from Iran (deployed there during the war along with British forces in order to prevent the Iranian oilfields falling into Axis hands), coupled with its seeming design to annex the northern Iranian province of Azerbaijan, provoked an angry American response. Not content that the problem should be resolved by bilateral negotiations between Iran and the Soviet Union, which appeared close to success by the end of March, the United States insisted on placing the issue before the UN Security Council. In the event the Soviet Union backed down amid a flurry of resentment at the American decision to throw a public spotlight on the issue.

The degree to which the range of permissible views within the Truman administration was narrowing during 1946 can be gauged by the reaction to an address by Secretary of Commerce Henry Wallace given in September. 'The real peace treaty we now need is between the US and Russia', he declared, going on to suggest that, while Americans may not have liked what was going on in Eastern Europe, 'we should recognize that we have no more business in the political affairs of Eastern Europe than Russia has in the political affairs of Latin America, Western Europe, and the US' (Siracusa 1978: 210). Such even-handedness was unacceptable and Wallace was forced to resign. His error was to endorse a Soviet 'sphere of influence' in Eastern Europe. In practice, the United States was left with little alternative, short of war, to accepting Soviet predominance in Eastern Europe. The situation was unpalatable, however, for a number of reasons: it left countries recently liberated from Nazi rule subject to a new form of domination, and it risked alienating the large section of the American population whose ethnic roots lay in Eastern Europe. Nor were Truman and his advisers convinced that Soviet ambitions would rest with Eastern Europe. Communist parties were ominously strong in France and Italy and seemed likely to benefit from the economic and social disruption caused by the war. But Wallace committed the further error of equating the Soviet position in Eastern Europe with the United States' position in Latin America. While, as Eduard Mark has pointed out, the Truman administration might have been willing to countenance an 'open' Soviet sphere in

Eastern Europe, comparable to America's 'benign' influence in Latin America, events had dashed such hopes. The reality in Eastern Europe was Soviet domination, and Wallace's remarks seemed to Truman wilfuly oblivious of that fact (Mark 1981–82: 316–36).

Wallace's enforced resignation in September 1946 registered a marked shift of mood in America. Within a month the mid-term Congressional elections had produced Republican majorities in both Houses, overthrowing a Democratic dominance of sixteen years. Into the legislature came a new cohort of Congressmen, many of them war veterans (among them Richard M. Nixon and John F. Kennedy) who had learned the lesson of 'appeasement' from the war and readily transferred their hatred of Hitler's totalitarianism to Stalin's version of it. The death in January 1946 of Harry Hopkins, the embodiment of Rooseveltian aspirations for maintenance of the Grand Alliance, symbolized the passing of the wartime ethos. The exposure of the Soviet spy ring in Canada earlier in the year had sensitized Americans to the threat of communist subversion, and within a few months of the elections Truman came under great public pressure to introduce a 'loyalty program' for all Federal employees. These developments laid fertile ground for the subsequent activities of the House Un-American Activities Committee and of Senator Joseph McCarthy, ensuring that the cold war at home would preoccupy American public opinion as much, if not more, than the conflict abroad.

Less often noticed by historians of American policy is the fact that a parallel process was taking place in the Soviet Union. The downplaying of communist ideology during the war and the elevation of Russia's national (especially military) traditions was speedily reversed after the defeat of Germany. As a British diplomat in Moscow observed at the time, the Soviet election campaign of March 1946 'also included a tremendous revival of orthodox Marxist ideology, which left the impression that the Soviet peoples were a chosen people, and that they were surrounded by a hostile world composed largely of reactionary capitalists and their willing tools in the social democratic movement' (Jensen 1991: 40; and see Volkogonov 1991: 503). Fearing the effects of the Soviet troops' exposure to non-communist Europe as they drove westward, the Soviet security services saw to it that those who had lived for periods abroad or had been imprisoned were rigorously screened, sent to labour camps, or simply shot. 'The contact with foreign countries', one historian has written, 'generated moral ferment . . . a new vague yearning for freedom and a novel curiosity about the outside world.' As the only organization capable of 'translating the new ferment into political ideas', the army aroused Stalin's particular suspicions. National heroes such as Marshal Zhukov, the architect of Soviet military victory, were demoted to minor posts within a few months of the end of the war. By 1948 Pravda was celebrating the third anniversary of the taking of Berlin without mentioning Zhukov (Deutscher 1960: 560–2). (Zhukov was later rehabilitated under Khrushchev, becoming Defence Minister.) More broadly, under the leadership of Andrei Zhdanov the Party began what amounted to a 'Kulturkampf', designed to eliminate all vestiges of 'unprogressive' ideas from literature, art, films, and scholarship, all of which had enjoyed a certain freedom during the war (Hosking 1985: 305ff.). Though the post-war purges were more selective than those of the 1930s, they were no less draconian and betrayed Stalin's determination to impose ideological conformity upon Soviet life and to insulate the country from all possible external influences.

Equally significant was a communication from an official in the Soviet Embassy in Washington to the Foreign Ministry in Moscow which in many respects matches Kennan's long telegram. Nikolai Novikov, writing in September 1946, pictured an America bent on 'world domination'. Reactionaries had displaced those within the Democratic Party who advocated cooperation with the Soviet Union, the development of a far-flung military base system indicated the 'offensive nature' of American strategy, and the United States and Britain were establishing what amounted to a condominium to divide up the world 'on the basis of mutual concessions'. Novikov's conviction that 'internal contradictions' in the Anglo-American relationship meant that it could not last, was no comfort, since American power was dominant. Talk in the American press of a 'third war', meaning a war against the Soviet Union, and the promotion of a 'war psychosis' within public opinion, were making it easier for the government to carry out its militarist goals. The only bright spot in an otherwise grim picture was that 'the USSR's international position is currently stronger than it was in the prewar period'. It was all the more important in this climate that the Soviet Union consolidate its position in Eastern Europe (Jensen 1991: 3–16).

These developments raise important questions about the relationship between domestic politics and the formulation of foreign policy. By the end of 1946, if the cold war 'mind-set' had not fully matured, its outlines were emerging in both countries. It included the imputation of conspiratorial designs to the other side, a declining toleration of dissent within official circles, and a growing tendency to think in terms of simple dichotomies. In the United States the picture was complicated by two factors which posed fewer difficulties for Stalin: the re-emergence of partisan politics and the conflict between a desire to 'return to normalcy' and pressure on the United States to assume a major and permanent international role.

The first of these was manifested in the Congressional elections of 1946. The Republican victories represented an attack, not only on Truman's leadership but on the entire reform legacy of Franklin Roosevelt's 'New Deal'. This left Truman (an unelected President and not himself due to face an election until 1948) with the task of proving his fitness to deal with the Soviet Union without abandoning his party's reform tradition, to which he was firmly committed. The Republican Party's tactic of implying that New Dealism was dangerously socialistic thrust Democrats, the labour unions, and liberal intellectuals on to the defensive. By 1950, despite the Democrats' recapture of Congress and Truman's victory in the election of 1948, Republicans and conservative Democrats had successfully oriented the agenda of domestic politics around the issue of anti-communism and resistance to any new reforms along the lines of the New Deal.

The second complication for the Truman administration lay in creating a consensus for a major international role for the United States. Paradoxically, many of those conservatives, both Republican and Democrat, who favoured a stiff stand against the Soviet Union were also isolationist in general orientation and were reluctant to vote large sums for defence or aid to needy countries. The concern, which rapidly mounted to an obsession, with communist subversion within the United States arose from a conviction that communist victories abroad must be put down to the presence of a fifth column at home. Truman, then, was forced to pursue a narrow path between, on the one hand, alienating liberals by adopting a firm stance against the Soviet Union and, on the other, alienating conservatives by failing to crack down on communism at home.

Much debate has revolved around the question of the extent to which Truman himself created the climate in which virulent anti-communism could flourish. Historians have had little trouble in showing that Truman strove hard to create a consensus for a hard line towards the Soviet Union, that he engaged in a vigorous campaign to discredit critics such as Henry Wallace, and that his preference for unambiguous solutions to complex problems often served to raise the temperature of public debate (Paterson 1988: Chs 1–3, 5 and 6). As Lyndon Johnson found later in the Vietnam War, though with very different results, Truman had a war on two fronts – one with the Soviet Union and one with American public opinion which, as he saw it, needed to be persuaded of the Soviet threat. To that extent Truman engaged in the manufacture of consent, thereby helping to promote a cold war mentality. However, this is not to say that the Soviet threat was a figment of his imagination or that he wilfuly exaggerated its extent. The truth is that Truman was subject to multiple pressures: Soviet actions in Eastern Europe which he perceived to be aggressive, requests from Britain to make a commitment to the stability of Western Europe in the face of Soviet intransigence, Communist Party strength in France and Italy, and the need to justify to the American Congress and the American public an unprecedentedly active role for the United States in international affairs. Nor is it clear that he can be charged with the major responsibility for fuelling domestic anti-communism. Congress initiated the demand for a domestic loyalty programme and Truman's own proposals were made in the face of a more sweeping plan devised by conservatives within Congress.

The Soviet Union too, as we have seen, underwent major domestic changes in the transition from war to peace. As in the United States these arose from internal as much as external pressures. Stalin too had a 'war' on his home front and he may have underestimated the extent to which his method of fighting it would be interpreted abroad in the light of disagreements with his former allies in the field of diplomacy. Indeed, the most thorough investigation of Stalin's foreign policy in the years 1943–48 concludes that Stalin's anxieties about his domestic position lay at the root of his stance towards the outside world (McCagg 1978: 14). Soviet anxiety was doubtless also triggered by American actions in the Iran crisis, by the perception that the United

States was employing economic and atomic pressure, and by Churchill's Iron Curtain speech, rekindling the fear of 'encirclement' aroused during the inter-war period. As in the United States, domestic and foreign issues reacted upon each other, with the consequence, noted in 1949 by the American Ambassador in Moscow, Walter Bedell Smith, that 'the time has passed when foreign affairs and domestic affairs could be regarded as separate and distinct' (Smith 1950: 327).

Smith meant by this that the United States must gear all its domestic resources to a long struggle with the Soviet Union, but the statement has wider applications than Smith had in mind. The erosion of the boundary between foreign and domestic affairs substantially raised the stakes of diplomacy, making the cold war a conflict of cultures no less than of nation-states. '[The cold war] has really become a matter of the defence of western civilization', wrote a British Foreign Office official in 1948 (Gaddis 1987: 46). In the United States the publication of an abridgement of Arnold Toynbee's *A Study of History* (1947), a sweeping survey of the decline of civilizations throughout world history, jangled raw American nerves. Toynbee's message that only a spiritual regeneration in the West could prevent it going the way of the Roman Empire was eagerly absorbed by an American intelligentsia seeking a counterweight to Marxism. A similar sense of urgency was found in the Soviet Union. The task of Soviet writers, said Andrei Zhdanov in 1946, was not only 'to reply, blow for blow . . . to the assaults on our Soviet culture and socialism, but also to lash out boldly and attack bourgeois culture which is in a state of emaciation and depravity' (Daniels 1985, Vol. 1: 300). In the end the striking feature of US–Soviet relations in the immediate post-war years is the acute sense of vulnerability on both sides and the inability of each to comprehend the fears no less than the interests of the other.

In the year following the war the wartime alliance disintegrated but the cold war had not yet fully broken out. It might be called a time of cold peace, in the sense that the war was over but in the absence of a comprehensive peace settlement. Already, however, both sides had framed answers to the question of who was responsible for the growing division between West and East. In the half century since these events took place historians have debated this issue intensively and it is with this that the following chapter begins.

4

'TWO WAYS OF LIFE'
The cold war in Europe, 1947–1953

PERSPECTIVES ON THE ORIGINS OF THE COLD WAR

Was the cold war inevitable? Was it given in the circumstances surrounding the end of the war? If not, which side was to blame? Which particular decisions determined the direction of events? Did the character of the leaders make any difference? Who, more specifically, was to blame for the divisions of Europe? Did the West give away Eastern Europe at Yalta? What precisely were the goals of the United States and the Soviet Union at the end of the war? Certain answers to these and related questions have been implied in the previous chapter, but it may be well to address them directly at this point in order to illustrate the range of issues involved.

The record of historical writing on the origins of the cold war proves the difficulty of arriving at a total explanation of the events. The ascription of blame to one side or the other, for example, tends to underestimate the influence of forces over which individual decision-makers may have had little control. While ascribing blame accords with our predisposition to believe that individuals (and by extension, nations) are free moral agents and that things therefore could have been otherwise, few historians can be unaware of the extent to which the options available to decision-makers at a particular point in time have been set by circumstances, which include the effects of earlier decisions. Events, that is to say, are at least to some extent determined. But how far? At the opposite extreme from the pure voluntarist model – the one which seeks to lay blame – lies pure determinism. 'If', writes one historian, 'you put a scorpion and a tarantula together in a bottle the objective of their own self-preservation will impel them to fight each other to the death.' From this point of view, as the same writer puts it, 'the Cold War represents an historical necessity' (Halle 1967: xiii, 12).

Broadly speaking, the first generation of historians (often termed 'orthodox'), writing in the period of high cold war, blamed the Soviet Union for the cold war and regarded American policy as a justifiable reaction to Soviet aggression. The second generation (generally termed 'revisionist'), stimulated in part by opposition to the Vietnam War, reversed this picture: Soviet policies were essentially defensive and limited in scope, while those of the United States were expansionist and uncompromising. This revisionist position bore close comparison with the writings of Soviet historians of the cold war.

There were many variations of emphasis within these schools. Nor is it the case that these approaches were simply reflexes of the historical circumstances in which they were written; the historiography of the cold war has been a continuing conversation in which the participants have increased in number and diversity of views without silencing all the previous voices.[1] However, an important feature unites the apparently opposed orthodox and revisionist viewpoints. Both tend towards the voluntarist end of the interpretive spectrum, in that they imply that the cold war resulted from essentially unilateral actions by one or another power and that therefore the cold war was an avoidable tragedy. To be sure, from the early 1970s, as the Vietnam War wound down and the period of *détente* opened, some of the ideological heat was removed from the historical debate. This, in conjunction with the publication of new American documents and a new attention given to European nations as independent actors in the early post-war years, tended to enlarge the focus of historical inquiry and to blur the outlines of US–Soviet relations supplied by previous interpreters. This so-called 'post-revisionist' phase of historical writing has introduced a new complexity and diffuseness into the historical debate.

A further important input into debate about the cold war generally has come from psychologists and political scientists interested in the role of perceptions, misperceptions, and belief systems (Larson 1985; Jervis 1976). These writings have produced clear evidence of perceptual gaps in the encounters between cultures, the extent to which these gaps became institutionalized in decision-making processes, and the degree to which decisions were often made on the basis of fundamental misreadings of the antagonist's intentions and motives. Studies of group psychology have demonstrated the role of 'groupthink' – the tendency for decision-making groups to strive for consensus and to limit consideration of alternative courses of action (Janis 1972). The psychological approach has proved most fertile in case studies of particular decisions and in analysis of the cultural assumptions and mind-sets of particular decision-makers. It is easier, however, to state that psychological factors are important than to establish precisely how much they can explain about the behaviour of states as opposed to individuals. Psychological analyses have tended to focus on single nations and policy-makers within them – and generally the United States. To that extent, this approach has reinforced the single-nation bias of much cold war history. The problem remains of finding an approach which allows us to understand American and Soviet national interests in relation to the international system.

To illustrate the point we can take the division of Europe and, more particularly, the place of Eastern Europe in the policies of the United States and the Soviet Union. It is arguable that if the United States had been prepared to concede Eastern Europe to the Soviet Union – to consider it as a Soviet counterpart to the American Monroe Doctrine – the tensions and antagonisms of the cold war need not have eventuated. What, then, was the American stake in Eastern Europe? Revisionist historians have claimed that, although the United States had little investment in Eastern Europe at the time, it was not prepared to see the opportunity for future investment foreclosed. America's post-war plans, which according to one account were dictated by the goal of expanding capitalism (in part prompted by fears of a post-war recession), simply could not tolerate American exclusion from a major potential market. Furthermore, it is suggested, the Soviet Union did not emerge from the Second World War 'with a determination to take over Eastern Europe and then embark upon a cold war with the United States' (Williams 1972: 228). The Soviet hold on Eastern Europe was tightened after 1947 only in response to concerted attempts by the United States to gain a foothold there, above all by holding out the offer of Marshall aid to Eastern European countries in the hope of detaching them from the Soviet Union (Williams 1972: 272–3). In the crucial transitional period of 1945–47, it is held, the Soviet Union was chiefly concerned with rebuilding its shattered economy and reaching a *modus vivendi* with the United States. The United States, by contrast, 'proceeded rapidly and with a minimum of debate' to translate its traditional outlook of open-door expansion 'into a series of actions and policies which closed the door to any result but the cold war' (Williams 1972: 229).

This approach has the merit of logic and consistency, assuming that its major premises regarding the motives and policies of the United States and the Soviet Union can be accepted. Suspicions about its validity may be raised in the light of the fact that it effectively inverts the picture offered by orthodox historians. The latter present Soviet policy as swift in execution and uncompromising, while American policy-makers are seen as slow to awake to the Soviet threat, albeit firm once the scale of the threat was recognized. Nevertheless, an interpretation need not be wrong simply because it is one-sided. Events may themselves have been one-sided. Any attempt to prove that they were not must shift the grounds of judgement. Three issues must be addressed: (1) conditions in Eastern Europe, (2) the motives of Soviet policy, and (3) the motives of American policy.

Eastern Europe

Concentration among historians on superpower politics has tended to obscure the extent to which the division of Europe arose from internal conditions in Eastern Europe. From the late Middle Ages the region which came to form the Soviet bloc had been an arena of conflict between Russia in the east, the German states in the west, and the Ottoman Empire in the south-east. Of the future Soviet bloc states, only Romania and Bulgaria were independent nations by the end of the nineteenth century (1877 and 1878 respectively). Poland, partitioned in the late eighteenth century, and Hungary, incorporated into the Habsburg Empire in the sixteenth century and granted partial autonomy under the 'Dual Monarchy' of Austria-Hungary in 1867, gained full independence only after the First World War. Yugoslavia and Czechoslovakia, carved out of former Austro-Hungarian territory, were new creations of the First World War settlement. With the exception of Czechoslovakia, during the bulk of the inter-war period all these states were led either by authoritarian monarchies or virtual dictators, having first engaged in brief flirtations with democracy. During the Second World War Hungary, Romania, and Bulgaria sided with the Axis Powers, with the result that all were invaded by the Soviet Union and treated as conquered powers.

Clearly, the military presence of the Soviet Union throughout Eastern Europe was a powerful enabling factor for communist dominance. But, as Jacques Rupnik has observed, Soviet presence alone 'does not satisfactorily explain the relative weakness of resistance to the Communist takeovers':

> The answer varies with the political culture of each country: the legacy of pre-war authoritarian patterns, the relative weakness of civil society, the appeal of Marxist ideology among the intellectuals (or the discrediting of conservative or liberal alternatives), and, of course, the indigenous base of the Communist Parties. But the crucial factor was the impact on these societies of the war itself. The Nazi occupation and the agonies of liberation represented a radical breach in the social and political structures and helped to create the conditions for post-war Communist takeovers.
>
> (Rupnik 1989: 76)

In short, while few Eastern Europeans outside the communist parties themselves might have wished for the regimes which were firmly established by 1948, few wished to return to the pre-war regimes. East Europeans, a recent account concludes, were not entirely passive agents in the events which led to sovietization. In addition to Soviet force and structural weaknesses within those nations, East Europeans made critical mistakes. Finland, by contrast, which experienced some of the same conditions as other nations of Eastern Europe, managed to resist Soviet power (Schöpflin 1993: Ch. 3). Furthermore, as an American journalist noted at the time, the communist parties of Eastern Europe made efforts to address immediate needs. 'The strength of the iron curtain regimes', wrote Joseph Harsch in 1950, 'lies not in their communism but in that when they took power they had ready at hand scores of housekeeping tasks and overdue reforms. They did not neglect their opportunities' (Harsch 1950: 47). The combination of these internal conditions and Soviet ambitions sealed the fate of Eastern Europe. But what were Soviet ambitions?

Soviet motives

Revisionist historians have rightly pointed out that full sovietization was not immediately imposed. It was embarked on in a wholesale way only in 1948 with the communist coup in Czechoslovakia, though it had been signalled clearly the previous year by the establishment of the Communist Information Bureau (Cominform), which sought to coordinate policies among the Soviet bloc. Events preceding full sovietization, however, some going back to the war, suggest that the distinction between full sovietization and the state of relative fluidity which existed in some Eastern European nations between 1945 and 1948 is not clear-cut. In Poland at least, Soviet intentions were evident even before Germany invaded the Soviet Union. At Katyn in Poland the advancing German army discovered mass graves containing some 15,000 Polish officers, massacred in 1940, the Soviet government has now admitted, by Soviet troops, with the apparent intention of eliminating the Polish officer class (Remnick 1993: Ch. 1).

Later, in 1944, a Soviet army paused before Warsaw while an uprising by the people of Warsaw against the Germans took place. Western requests that they be allowed to use airfields in Soviet-occupied territory to send relief supplies to Warsaw were denied by the Soviet Union until the uprising had been virtually quelled. Again, despite Soviet claims that logistical and supply problems prevented them from going to the aid of the Warsaw insurgents – an explanation which Churchill accepted at the time – it is possible that an equally important motive was to allow the Germans to destroy the most active elements in the Polish resistance. Though militarily, it has been pointed out, the rising was directed at the Germans, 'politically, [it] was directed against the Soviet Union' (Edmonds 1991: 385). The formation of the so-called 'Lublin Committee' by the advancing Soviet army in July 1944 and official Soviet recognition of the Lublin Government as the provisional government of Poland in January 1945 (a month before the Yalta conference), also indicate a determination to make the running in Poland. In the light of this there was little for the West to 'give away' at Yalta, since it had already been taken.

It is arguable that these events can be put down to the exigencies of war and, furthermore, that it was of particular importance to the Soviet Union to establish control in Poland because its northern plain had historically been the invasion route into the Soviet Union from the West (by Napoleon in 1812, the Germans in 1914, and the Germans again in 1941). The pattern of Soviet actions in other Eastern European countries, however, was similar in emphasis, if not in detail. In each nation the Allied Control Commissions were controlled by the Soviets (as those in Western Europe were controlled by the Western Allies), giving them effective control over day to day administration and, crucially, the economies. By the beginning of 1946 communist-dominated governments had been established in Bulgaria and Romania, following brief periods of rule by restored monarchs. In Hungary the appearance of pluralism lasted a good deal longer. In elections held in 1946 the communists gained only 17 per cent of the votes. However, communists held a number of ministries (most importantly the Ministries of the Interior and Commerce) and controlled the police and trade unions.

Even in Czechoslovakia, where non-communists remained in the majority in the government until 1948, the Ministry of the Interior, the police and the trade unions were headed by communists. The three-year breathing space for Czechoslovakia can be explained in part by the legacy of the Munich agreement of 1938. At Munich Britain and France had endorsed Germany's annexation of the Czech Sudetenland (a

German-peopled region) and subsequently stood by while Hitler invaded Czechoslovakia itself the following year. In consequence Czechoslovakia mistrusted the West and trusted its future rather to reaching an accommodation with the Soviet Union. Czechoslovakia, the 'freest' of East European nations between 1945 and 1948, was also by inclination the most pro-Soviet. Finally, in Yugoslavia the Soviet Union had no need to tread cautiously, since Tito's administration out-Stalined Stalin in its determination to eliminate non-communists, first from the wartime resistance movement and then from the post-war political scene. Even Stalin wondered in 1942: 'Are there really no Yugoslav patriots apart from Communists and Communist sympathizers?' (Rupnik 1989: 79). Not that Tito's unimpeachable communist credentials saved him from Stalin's ire. Rather the reverse. Alone among the East European countries Yugoslavia's liberation had not been dependent upon the Red Army, giving Yugoslavia a measure of freedom (at least with respect to relations with the Soviet Union) not open to the other nations of Eastern Europe. Stalin's desire to bring Yugoslavia to heel and Tito's equally strong desire to resist provoked the breach between the Soviet Union and Yugoslavia in 1948, to be discussed later (see p. 85).

There was, then, a time lapse between a measure of pluralism in Eastern Europe and the full imposition of Soviet-style rule. It was not, however, a matter of a simple choice on Stalin's part between allowing freedom and imposing domination. It was rather a process, sometimes described as 'salami tactics', whereby control was established by stages, according to the circumstances in each country. Nor is it necessary to see this simply as the outcome of the desire to spread the ideology of communism as such. For Stalin, as has been said of Lenin, communism was organization rather than ideology *per se*. This priority helps to account for Stalin's qualified toleration of power-sharing in much of Eastern Europe and his deep suspicion of independent sources of communist power, such as Yugoslavia and later China. Power-sharing with non-communists within Eastern Europe was tolerable as long as control was firm. Once that was in doubt, the organizational imperative took over.

It is not necessary to believe that Stalin was intent on provoking cold war in order to accept that his motives in Eastern Europe were always to ensure tight control. He was both afraid of the United States and determined to maintain 'friendly' governments in Eastern Europe. In his memoirs Khrushchev recorded the strength with which Stalin expressed both these motives. How Stalin 'trembled', Khrushchev wrote, at the prospect of war with the United States, which the Soviet leadership believed was bound to come; on the question of relations with the 'fraternal countries', Khrushchev recalled, 'Stalin's understanding of friendship with other countries was that the Soviet Union would lead and they would follow' (Khrushchev 1990: 100, 102). That Stalin moved cautiously to extend control bespeaks his fear of the United States and its putative design to undermine the Soviet position in Eastern Europe; that he continued to extend control bespeaks his determination to do what was necessary to safeguard Soviet territory and interests.

American motives

The details of America's 'containment' policies – the Truman Doctrine, the Marshall Plan, and NATO – will be discussed later in this chapter. The purpose here is to address the broad question of the motives behind American actions with respect to the division of Europe. Why did the United States contest, at least verbally, Soviet control in Eastern Europe? Part of the answer has been given in the previous chapter: a divided Europe went against all the assurances given to American public opinion about the prospects of a new world order based on self-determination for all nations and collective security founded on the continuance of cooperation between the wartime Allies. The American reaction to Soviet policies arose also from the perhaps inevitable fading of the illusion, which the Roosevelt administration had done much to promote, that agreements such as the one reached at Yalta were solidly based and heralded post-war friendship with the Soviet Union. A Congress and a public which was told by Roosevelt on his return from Yalta that 'on every point, unanimous agreement was reached' could only react with bafflement and frustration to the unfolding antagonisms of the coming years.

Not that everyone in the United States was surprised by events. George Kennan, a leading authority on the Soviet Union within the diplomatic service and based in Moscow during the war, had been sending warning signals to the State Department about the character of the Soviet Union since the middle of the war. They made little impression, since this was not the message Roosevelt and his closest advisers wanted or were primed to hear. In any case, it was Roosevelt's habit to bypass the government departments, notably the Department of State, and retain a tight personal hold on decision-making. Even Truman, his Vice-President, was not told of the existence of the Manhattan Project. The result, when Roosevelt died, was a policy vacuum which Truman filled with, on the one hand, his own blunt style and, on the other, advice from figures who in many instances had come to doubt the possibility of cooperation with the Soviet Union. This did not mean, as some have claimed, that Truman set about reversing Roosevelt's broad goals. But it did mean that he was not inclined to engage in the subtleties of what one historian has called Roosevelt's dual foreign policy: a 'foreign' foreign policy, characterized by realism and designed for negotiating situations, and a 'domestic' foreign policy, designed for home consumption and characterized by idealism (Yergin 1980: 68).

These issues tell us something about the mood of the times and about the significance of institutional and personnel changes in the transitional period from war to peace. They do not, however, of themselves account for the specific direction of policies. Indeed, beyond its obvious displeasure with Soviet policy in Eastern Europe, it is not clear that the United States had a coherent East European policy. One historian has called it a 'non-policy' (Lundestad 1978).

What were American goals in Europe generally? It would appear, in the first place, that the United States did not envisage a long-term political and military presence in

Europe beyond the time taken for reconstruction. Roosevelt's observation to Stalin at Yalta that the United States expected to withdraw its troops from Europe within two years is one item of evidence for this. Another, as we shall see later, was the initial reluctance of Congress to vote money for mechanisms of containment when these came up for discussion.

Secondly, as a counterpart to these expectations, was the hope that, once rebuilt, Europe (Western Europe at least and the rest if possible) would constitute a 'third force' between the United States and the Soviet Union. Thirdly, US policy-makers undoubtedly envisaged the vigorous expansion of American economic interests, not only in Europe but throughout the world. But as far as possible this goal was to be pursued at minimum political and military cost – very much in line with America's traditional approach to foreign policy. Those revisionist historians who place emphasis on the American desire for an economic open door are correct, but so also are those post-revisionists, such as John Gaddis (1972), who stress the indecisiveness of American policy in the transition period. Each separates out two basic elements of American policy: its combination of economic dynamism and political caution. Once, however, it appeared that diplomacy could not achieve the conditions required for America's vision of an open world order, political caution – which is to say the vestiges of isolationism – was abandoned. This point was approached in 1947 with the Truman Doctrine, and confirmed in the establishment of the Marshall Plan and NATO (1948 and 1949).

More specifically, American anxieties about the sovietization of Eastern Europe cannot be separated from their anxieties about the stability of Western Europe and its capacity to resist the inroads of communism. The chief fear in the late 1940s was not of a Soviet invasion of Western Europe – even American military leaders discounted this – but of the strength of the communist parties in France and Italy and the degree to which post-war economic and social disruption in Western Europe generally rendered it vulnerable to communist ideas. Doubts about the ability of Western Europe to reconstruct itself unaided presented a political as well as an economic challenge. Furthermore, the pressures inclining the United States to fill the power vacuum in Western Europe arose not only from within the American policy-making establishment but from within Europe itself. As a historian of French foreign policy has written, 'it was the pull of the French, rather than the push outward from Washington, that characterized the different aspects of American involvement, diplomatic, economic, political, and military between 1945 and 1954', even if it was the case that, once having invited the Americans in 'the French quickly became dissatisfied with what their guests brought with them' (Wall 1991: 300). To that extent there is an analogy with the situation in Eastern Europe *vis-à-vis* the Soviet Union: the consolidation of American influence in Western Europe is to be explained in terms of internal European conditions as well as in American ambitions.

The key element in the structure of the post-war world order influencing the policies of the United States and the Soviet Union was not merely their emergence as superpowers and the establishment of bipolarity, but the asymmetry in the types of power they possessed and in their first order goals. Misperception of each other's aims was not the main problem, though it undoubtedly played a part. The overriding problem was the tendency of each power to push its policy goals farthest and fastest in those areas in which it possessed greatest leverage and which the other could not effectively meet. In the case of the Soviet Union this meant its military and political hold over Eastern Europe; in the case of the United States this meant its economic power and capacity to project it on a global scale. In striving to compensate for their weaknesses and to match the other's strength, each power pursued policies which made for the global institutionalization of their differences. The outcome was cold war.

CONTAINMENT AND THE TRUMAN DOCTRINE

Roosevelt had returned from Yalta in February 1945 declaring in his message to Congress (in words borrowed from Cordell Hull) that the agreements 'ought to spell the end of unilateral action, the exclusive alliances, the spheres of influence, the balances of power, and all the other expedients that have been tried for centuries – and have always failed' (Siracusa 1978: 34). Roosevelt's hopes for a clean slate were, as we have seen, quickly undermined in the events of 1945–46, but some fluidity still remained in US–Soviet relations. In 1946 and into 1947 they were still talking to each other, trying to give tangible form to their aspirations for cooperation. In the event, the outcome of these efforts was precisely those despised talismans of the bad old politics – spheres of influence, exclusive alliances, and the rest. By 1950 they had become firmly institutionalized, and management of cooperation had given way to management of conflict.

'Containment' supplied the philosophical rationale for the Truman administration's new orientation and was classically expounded by George Kennan in his anonymously published article 'The Sources of Soviet Conduct' ('X', *Foreign Affairs*, July 1947). In effect it was a public version of his 1946 'Long Telegram'. Both in turn presented views of the Soviet Union which, in broad outline, he had held for a number of years (Kennan 1967: 246–51). The key to the influence of the 'Long Telegram' and subsequently the 'X' article, as Kennan pointed out in his memoirs, was timing (Kennan 1967: 295). The first reached government circles at a critical moment, as policy-makers sought an explanation for the breakdown in communication with the Soviet Union over Eastern Europe. The second offered a public rationale for the containment policies already embarked upon in the form of the Truman Doctrine.

Kennan did not view the Soviet Union as bent upon immediate fulfilment of its ideological goals. While Soviet ideology assumed the inevitable downfall of capitalism, no timetable was laid down by the Kremlin. The Soviets were prepared for the long haul. Given the doctrine of the infallibility of the Kremlin and the iron discipline of the Party, the Soviet leadership was 'at liberty to put forward for tactical purposes any particular thesis which it finds useful to the cause at any particular moment and require the faithful and unquestioning acceptance of that thesis by the members of the movement as a whole'. Caution and persistence characterized Soviet policy, and America must respond with 'policies no less steady in their purpose, and no less variegated and resourceful in their application, than those of the Soviet Union itself'. In these circumstances the United States must seek to contain Soviet power by the 'adroit and vigilant application of counterforce at a series of constantly shifting geographical and political points' (Kennan 1947: 573, 575, 576).

Kennan's prescriptions for American policy appear to be unmistakably global in scope and to carry strong military implications. In fact Kennan, the supposed architect of containment, dissociated himself from many aspects of its implementation, emerging as a critic of both the Truman Doctrine and NATO. Since Kennan played such an important and ambiguous role in policy-making during these years, we can usefully employ his writings as a vantage point from which to view the institutionalization of the cold war.

Containment had already been enacted in the form of the Truman Doctrine before Kennan supplied the policy with a label. In March 1947 Britain announced that it could no longer afford to sustain its support for the Greek government in the civil war which had raged intermittently after the liberation of Greece from the Germans in 1944. Greece had been conceded by Stalin as a Western sphere of influence in the percentages agreement with Churchill in October 1944. It is now clear that Stalin held to this agreement and not only withheld support from the Greek communists but was disturbed by the prospect of a communist revolution with indigenous roots. Such distinctions, however, meant little to American leaders who could only see in the flow of arms from Yugoslavia and Albania to the Greek rebels the hand of the Soviet Union. In Turkey too, although not at risk domestically to the same degree as Greece, Soviet pressure for control of the Black Sea straits was perceived as a bid not merely for influence in Turkey but as a stepping-stone to gains in the Middle East.

The striking feature of the American response to the announcement of British withdrawal is not so much the actual decision to send military and economic aid to Greece and Turkey as the manner in which Truman strove to create a consensus for a fundamental reorientation of American policy. Presenting a stark contrast between two alternative ways of life, 'one based upon the will of the majority and one based upon the will of a minority forcibly imposed upon the majority', he declared in his speech to Congress on 12 March 1947 that 'it must be the policy of the United States to support free peoples who are resisting subjugation by armed minorities or by outside pressures' (Truman 1963: 178–9).

There seems little doubt, as historians have shown, that one of Truman's motives for pitching the rhetoric of his message so high was the need to convince a cost-conscious Congress and an American public opinion not yet fully cognizant of the extended role the United States was about to assume that the stakes in Greece and Turkey were indeed as high as he claimed. But it is equally clear that Truman and his advisers sincerely believed that the crisis was much wider than the situation in Greece and Turkey. To that extent, as Daniel Yergin has pointed out, while the message to Congress was conceived as a 'sales job', it was not a cynical manoeuvre (Yergin 1980: 283). A second consideration lay behind the presentation of the Truman Doctrine – the need to 'avoid the appearance of standing in for London in the Middle East, of simply taking over traditional British responsibilities'. Aid to Greece and Turkey must be promoted as an American policy, based upon consideration of its own interests, and not as a matter of 'pulling British chestnuts out of the fire once again' (Hathaway 1981: 303). The occasion thus demanded a comprehensive statement of a distinctively American purpose.

In the congressional hearings on the Greece and Turkey Aid Bill the administration was pressed on the extent of the commitment the United States was undertaking. Under-Secretary Dean Acheson sought to calm fears that the Truman Doctrine was a blank cheque to be drawn on at will in other comparable situations, but he barely succeeded. Each case, he said, would be considered according to the specific circumstances, but he could not disguise the fact that the Truman Doctrine speech had established the framework within which such cases would be judged. This is clear in an exchange with Senator Vandenberg, a leading Republican Senator whose influence in this and other crucial policy initiatives laid the basis for bipartisan support for Truman:

> Vandenberg: . . . In other words, I think what you are saying is that wherever we find free peoples having difficulty in the maintenance of free institutions, and difficulty in defending against aggressive movements that seek to impose upon them totalitarian regimes, we do not necessarily react in the same way each time, but we propose to react. Acheson: That, I think, is correct.
>
> (Jones 1955: 193)

George Kennan objected strongly to the universalist character of the message but also to the specifics of the aid to Greece and Turkey. He opposed any aid to Turkey and felt that the emphasis in the proposals for Greece was excessively military (Kennan 1967: 314–17). These distinctions appear puzzling in the light of his 'X' article with its apparent globalism and military terminology ('adroit and vigilant application of counterforce . . .'). In his memoirs Kennan admits to serious deficiencies in his exposition of containment: the failure to make clear that he considered containment as primarily political and economic, and 'the failure to distinguish between various geographic areas and to make it clear that the "containment" of which I was speaking was not something I thought we could, necessarily, do everywhere successfully' (Kennan 1967: 359). Much debate has revolved around whether Kennan's after-the-fact 'correction' of his 'X' article statement can be accepted at face value, an issue which need not be resolved here. Suffice it to say that his overriding intention was evidently to underline the seriousness of the Soviet threat which he felt was insufficiently appreciated. Certainly his other writings at the time, in his new capacity from 1947 as head of the State Department's Policy Planning Staff (PPS), show a much more nuanced and pragmatic grasp of the Soviet challenge and of options open to the United States (Gaddis 1982: Ch. 2). In the July article, perhaps anxious to promote his salient point, he overplayed his hand. Attention was thus deflected from arguably his most important suggestion, that 'the issue of Soviet–American relations is in essence a test of the overall worth of the United States as a nation among nations' (Kennan 1947: 582). By extension the West's strongest card in its conflict with communism was the health and vigour of its own democratic traditions and values. This view became central to the Marshall Plan. Kennan himself has noted the irony that his name should be associated with the Truman Doctrine, about which he had serious reservations and in which he was scarcely involved, rather than the Marshall Plan, in which he was a prime, if largely unseen mover (Kennan 1967: 361).

The Truman Doctrine was of profound significance for a number of reasons. Firstly, it set a precedent for the tendency of superpower policy-makers to view all global conflict within the framework of the cold war. Bipolarity was not merely a matter of the structure of international relations but a state of mind. Thinking and acting in terms of simple dichotomies became second nature, even when actual conflicts, such as those in the Middle East, fitted awkwardly within this mould. In part this was a question of rhetoric, a necessary simplification of complex realities for the purpose of explaining unfamiliar commitments to domestic audiences. Rhetoric was not the whole story, however, since in the aftermath of the war the United States and the Soviet Union did in fact possess a disproportionately large power to affect the destinies of other nations. Less-favoured nations indeed looked to the superpowers, but above all to the United States, to authenticate their own aspirations, whether it be Ho Chi Minh seeking endorsement in 1945 of his goal of an independent Vietnam or the Western European nations seeking aid for economic recovery. There was an element of illusion in this, only fully exposed when the unusual conditions of the immediate post-war years had passed: the illusion that the United States could or would supply precisely what other nations wanted. So long as basic interests coincided, as was broadly the case between the United States and Western Europe, reality sustained the illusion, though even here as time went on interests diverged. In the case of Vietnam and many other former colonial territories of European powers, however, the gap between illusion and reality quickly appeared. Despite the possession of enormous power, the United States was not always able to dictate the direction of events in the Third World and elsewhere, but because it possessed enormous power the United States continued to believe that this was possible.

The second significant feature of the Truman Doctrine lies in its connection with the United Nations. Why, asked many Congressmen and commentators, had the United States government not sought to resolve the crisis in Greece and Turkey through the United Nations? Truman had stated in his message to Congress that 'in helping free and independent nations to maintain their freedom, the United States

75

will be giving effect to the principles of the United Nations'. Truman did not, however, risk actually relying on the United Nations to achieve these goals. The pragmatic reason for acting unilaterally is clear: the certainty that the Soviet Union would use its veto. The end result, though, was the devaluation of the original aspiration for collective security as the basis for the new international order.

Finally, it is noteworthy that the occasion for this major departure in American policy concerned not the heartland of Europe but its south-eastern rim. Taken in conjunction with the Iranian crisis of 1946, it shows the susceptibility of what has been called the 'Northern Tier' of the Middle East to superpower conflict (Kuniholm 1980: xv–xxi). The reason is not far to seek: Turkey and Iran bordered the Soviet Union directly while Greece bordered Soviet bloc territory (i.e.: Bulgaria, Yugoslavia, and Albania). The possibility of the extension of Soviet power to the Middle East proper was an added reason for American concern, though, as it turned out, there was a delay of several years before this materialized. American fears that the Soviet Union would take the Arab side in the conflict over the establishment of the state of Israel in 1948 were unfounded. The Soviet Union promptly recognized the new state and gave it substantial military aid at a critical time during the first Arab–Israeli war of 1948–49. It was the early 1950s before the increasingly close relations between the United States and Israel led to the Soviet Union's shift towards firm support of the cause of Arab nationalism (Saivetz and Woodby 1985: 25–6.) Meanwhile, in 1947 both the United States and the Soviet Union were more preoccupied with events in Europe. The Truman Doctrine was only the opening gambit in the development of containment.

THE MARSHALL PLAN, GERMANY, AND THE DIVISION OF EUROPE, 1947–1949

The Marshall Plan was not to all appearances designed to divide Europe but such, in conjunction with Soviet actions, was its effect. The growth of the much despised 'spheres of influence' was hastened by the Marshall Plan and consolidated in the division of Germany and the establishment of NATO. Once again Kennan's role is instructive. John Gaddis has drawn attention to an exchange of letters in early 1945 between Kennan and Charles Bohlen, the State Department's other leading Soviet expert. Kennan expressed the view that, given the Soviet Union's determination to dominate Eastern Europe, 'why could we not make a decent and definite compromise with it – divide Europe frankly into spheres of influence – keep ourselves out of the Russian sphere and keep the Russians out of ours?' Bohlen shared Kennan's assessment of Russian intransigence but replied that 'foreign policy of that kind cannot be made in a democracy . . . Only totalitarian states can make and carry out such policies' (Gaddis 1987: 48, 49). In the event American policy combined both these perspectives, producing a fundamental duality described by Jacques Rupnik as a 'verbal refusal to accept the Sovietization of East-Central Europe, without having the means or the determination actually to oppose it (Rupnik 1989: 67).

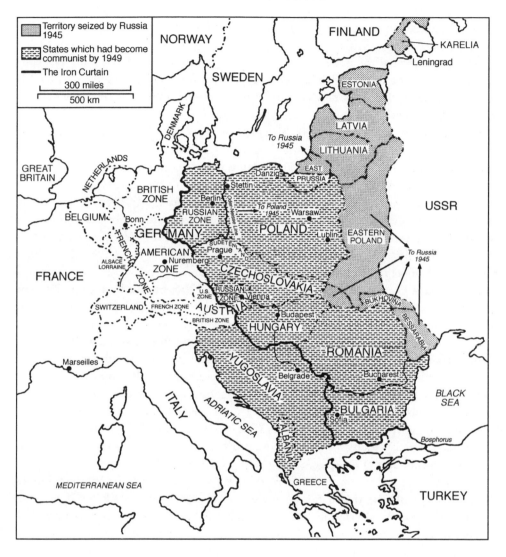

Figure 4.1 Divided Europe in 1949
Source: Derived from P. Hastings, *The Cold War: 1945–69*, London: Ernest Benn, 1969.

European recovery plans were already under discussion while the Truman Doctrine was being formulated. Indeed the two policies were related in the minds of the Truman administration from the start – 'two halves of the same walnut', as Truman put it. Three things provoked a reconsideration of policy towards Europe: deepening dismay at the consolidation of communist power within Eastern European governments, failure to agree on a German settlement, and economic disarray in Western

Europe, apparently threatening the political stability of, in particular, France and Italy.

The last presented the most urgent problem. Returning from Europe in May 1947 from a fact-finding mission, Under-Secretary of State for Economic Affairs William L. Clayton declared that 'it is now obvious that we grossly underestimated the destruction to the European economy by the war . . . Europe is steadily deteriorating.' The plight of Europe, however, was not his only preoccupation. In addition to the awful implications a European collapse would have for the future peace and security of the world, he wrote, 'the immediate effects on our domestic economy would be disastrous: markets for our surplus production gone, unemployment, depression, a heavily unbalanced budget on the background of a mountainous war debt. These things must not happen.' Concluding that the United States must therefore initiate a substantial programme of aid, he remarked (with emphasis): 'The United States must run this show' (FRUS 1947: 230, 231, 232).

Clayton represented the hard-nosed side of the Marshall Plan, its economic bottom line. The State Department's Policy Planning Staff (PPS), headed by George Kennan, was less bald in its perception of the consequences for the US economy of Europe's decline, and emphasized, rather, the goal of restoring Europe's faith in its future. In a document which was heavily drawn on by Marshall in his public announcement of the European Recovery Program (ERP) in June, Kennan was at pains to stress that 'the American effort in aid to Europe should be directed not to the combatting [sic] of communism but to the restoration of the economic health and vigor of European society'. He also insisted that the initiative must come from Europe and be jointly conceived by all participating countries (FRUS 1947: 225, 226-7). The conception was thus of a plan which would promote European unity as well as economic revival, with the overall aim of creating a stable and independent European bloc.

But how much of Europe? The PPS addressed itself primarily to Western Europe but, in line with the desire not to invite the charge that the ERP was an anti-communist measure, also felt it necessary to consider the possibility of Soviet and East European participation. The way in which Soviet bloc participation was discussed, however, shows that it was neither genuinely desired nor really anticipated. It was essential, Kennan believed, that the proposal for general European cooperation 'be done in such a form that the Russian satellite countries would either exclude themselves by unwillingness to accept the proposed conditions or agree to abandon the exclusive orientation of their economies' (FRUS 1947: 228). Not surprisingly, the Soviet Union was unwilling to accede to conditions which would involve opening its economy to Western penetration. Having accepted the invitation to attend the opening ERP meeting in Paris, the Soviet representative withdrew, once the conditions had been made explicit, and placed pressure on the Poles and Czechs to follow suit.

One can only speculate what the conseqences would have been had the Soviet Union called the United States' bluff and agreed to participate in the ERP. The Soviet decision has been called 'a blunder of major proportions' (Nogee and Donaldson 1988:

86). It is clear, however, that the shape of Europe would have been radically different if the ERP had been operated in a way which would have satisfied the Soviets. Their preference was for a series of bilateral treaties, rather than the coordinated plan favoured by the Americans. Central to the American conception was the idea of a single European market. While this was only partially achieved – Britain's Labour Government proving adamantly opposed (Pelling 1988: 98–102) – the ERP gave a powerful impetus towards the creation of the European Coal and Steel Community (1951), the forerunner of the EEC itself. It is doubtful in any case whether the American Congress would have approved a plan along Soviet lines which left Western Europe prey to political particularism. The Marshall Plan, though nominally an economic programme, was inseparable from the political dynamic which was producing a divided Europe, as can be seen in Soviet actions following their withdrawal from the ERP conference in Paris.

Four days after his return from Paris, Foreign Secretary Molotov announced the establishment of the Cominform, designed to strengthen Soviet control in Eastern Europe. In Hungary non-communists within the government were purged, and Cominform leader, Andrei Zhdanov, embarked on a campaign of ideological vilification of the West which included a call to French and Italian communists to foment disruption and seek the elimination of all non-communist leftists in their countries. Whether one interprets these actions as a defensive response to a perceived threat of Western encroachment on Eastern Europe or as an aggressive design for the destabilization of Western Europe makes little difference to the essential point: that the Marshall Plan forced Stalin to reassess his stance towards Europe East and West (Taubman 1982: 172–3).

The communist coup in Czechoslovakia in February 1948 was the most dramatic outcome of this process, removing the only remaining non-communist leader in Eastern Europe. Since 1945 President Beneš had trodden a careful path between remaining on good terms with the Soviets and resisting communist control. The fall of his government under the pressure of Soviet troops stationed on the Czech border, coupled with the suicide of his Foreign Minister Jan Masaryck under suspicious circumstances, profoundly shocked the West. Its immediate effect within the United States was to hasten the vote on appropriations for the Marshall Plan which had languished in Congress for some months. Amidst a war scare Truman went before Congress to impress upon legislators that the survival of freedom was at stake.

The German issue too was inseparable from the Marshall Plan. In January 1947 the British and American zones had been formally merged, an acknowledgement that four-power control of Germany was not working and was unlikely to work. American policy was now aimed frankly at rebuilding the West German economy. An important goal of the Marshall Plan was to calm French fears about a revived Germany by integrating West Germany into a Europe-wide system. German recovery, the Americans argued, was vital to the economic health of Europe. Two important steps were then taken at a conference of the United States and five West European nations

79

held in London in February 1948: the decision to introduce a new currency into the western zones of Germany to provide financial stability for economic revival, and an as yet tentative move towards West German statehood. Again France's anxieties were aroused about German revanchism and were soothed in this instance by an American commitment to retain some troops indefinitely in Europe. Though aimed at containing Germany rather than the Soviet Union, this decision coincided with discussion on the establishment of NATO. The militarization of containment followed inexorably from the logic supplied by the economic and political decisions of 1947–48.

The Soviet reaction to the introduction of the new currency in western Germany (including West Berlin) ensured that this logic would be played out. The day after the new Deutschmark was introduced, the Soviets cut the land routes between the western zone and West Berlin. The Berlin Blockade began on 24 June 1948, and lasted for nearly a year until the airlift mounted by the United States and Britain convinced the Soviet Union that the only alternative to accepting the 'illogic' of a Western enclave deep within the Soviet zone was war. Indeed at no time since the end of hostilities in 1945 had war seemed so likely. While the blockade stretched out, as one historian has remarked, 'sixty long-range bombers of the US airforce were quietly moved across the Atlantic to the British Isles', to remain there and be subsequently reinforced (Halle 1967: 164). The German, though not the Berlin, problem was 'solved' by the adoption in May 1949 of a constitution which established the Federal Republic of Germany (FRG). The Soviet Union responded by the end of the year with the formation of the German Democratic Republic (GDR).

These events show a cycle of action and reaction which makes the identification of ultimate causes difficult and probably impossible. It is striking that the United States moved more swiftly than the Soviet Union to establish formal institutions. The Marshall Plan, the FRG, and subsequently NATO all preceded their Soviet counterparts – the Council for Mutual Economic Assistance (COMECON), the GDR, and the Warsaw Pact – and it is possible to make the case that the United States initiated the cycle. This, however, may in part be attributed to the difference in political styles between the United States and the Soviet Union: a consequence of the Western democratic emphasis on consent and its ratification through formal documents and institutions. The Soviet Union, by contrast, it can be argued, already possessed the substance of control within its bloc by means of the communist parties and political–military occupation. From this point of view formalization of control was aimed as much at legitimizing its rule in Eastern Europe *vis-à-vis* the West as within the Soviet bloc itself. Nevertheless, in the coming years the United States would prove vulnerable to the charge that it had rushed to consolidate a Western bloc in Europe.

NATO, NSC 68 AND THE MILITARIZATION OF CONTAINMENT

Daniel Yergin has identified the growth of a 'national security state' within the United States in the post-war decade – the organization of the United States 'for perpetual confrontation and for war' (Yergin 1980: 5). At a time in mid-1946 when the United States was demobilizing fast, Truman's Special Counsel, Clark Clifford, wrote a paper for the President which looked to a very different future from the one implied in the urge to 'bring the boys home' from Europe and the Far East. 'In restraining the Soviet Union,' Clifford wrote, 'the United States must be prepared to wage atomic and biological warfare. A highly mechanized army, which can be moved either by sea or air, capable of seizing and holding strategic areas, must be supported by powerful naval and air forces' (Etzold and Gaddis 1978: 66). A year later a new Defense Act created a more integrated defence organization, including a single Department of Defense to replace the separately run branches of the armed services, and a National Security Council to coordinate overall security planning. The Act also created a Central Intelligence Agency (CIA), successor to the wartime Office of Strategic Services (OSS), designed to centralize intelligence gathering and create a counter-intelligence capability. Following the Czech coup of March 1948, Truman requested Congress to pass a bill providing for universal military training and the restoration of selective service. War plans in the event of conflict with the Soviet Union were being formulated as Europe fractured down the line of the Iron Curtain (Leffler 1992: 221–6).

As yet, however, there was no consensus in Congress, to say nothing of the country at large, on the desirability or need for an extensive commitment to the defence of Western Europe. Isolationism remained a factor which American policy-makers had to take account of in presenting requests to Congress, particularly when it involved entering binding political and military commitments in time of peace. Furthermore, there was an American insistence that Europe be seen to be willing to expend resources on its own defence rather than relying wholly on the United States. In fact the beginnings of a Western European defence organization did exist – the Western European Union (WEU), established under the Brussels Pact of 1948, signed by Britain, France and the Benelux countries. Conceivably this organization, supplemented by United States membership and military assistance, could have become the major instrument of Western European defence. The fact that it did not, and that future efforts to create an intra-European system of defence also failed, says much about the US–European relationship at this time, no less than internal divisions within Western Europe.

In the first place, American military planners were convinced that the composition of the WEU was too limited to provide adequate defence against Soviet aggression. 'Without the Azores [Portuguese territory], Iceland, and Greenland,' declared an American official, 'help could not be got to Europe in sufficient quantities at all', and this meant inclusion at the very least of Iceland, Denmark, and Portugal. Furthermore, the American Congress would be unlikely to favour becoming simply a member of a European organization, and one which they would be expected in large part to finance. In short, the WEU was both 'too "European" for American isolationists to accept and too small to be an appropriate deterrent to Soviet aggression'

(Kaplan 1985: 115). The paradoxical outcome, notes Michael Howard, was 'that the American insistence, accepted reluctantly by the leading European actors, that this should be an Atlantic rather than a European entity, in fact committed the Americans to a far closer involvement with European defence than would have been the case if they had been dealing simply with a limited grouping of powers on the American mainland' (Howard 1985: 18).

The debate in Congress on NATO itself reflected American ambivalence towards the commitment to Europe. While there was a good measure of agreement on the need for American participation in some sort of security pact with West European nations, there was little appetite for a large US force permanently stationed in Europe. When asked whether the administration planned to send 'substantial' numbers of troops to shore up European defences, Dean Acheson assured the Senate that 'the answer to that question . . . is a clear and absolute no' (LaFeber 1993a: 83). The Senate was similarly assured that there was no plan for the rearmament of Germany. The NATO pact was conceived by the administration, or at least presented publicly, as a confidence booster to Europe to prevent it succumbing politically to appeasement or neutrality under Soviet pressure.

A marked change in the conception of NATO was produced by the detection in September 1949 of a Soviet atom bomb test. News of the test threw to the winds the more optimistic calculations of the likely duration of the American atomic monopoly, which had ranged from about five years among Truman's scientific advisers to as much as twenty years among some administration officials (Bundy 1988: 199; Herken 1980: 98–9, 301). The news also set off a frantic search for the traitors whose help, it was presumed, must have accounted for the speed with which the Soviets acquired their own bomb. In Klaus Fuchs (a naturalized Briton who had worked on the Manhattan Project and who was captured by the British and found guilty of espionage in March 1950) and the Rosenbergs (also convicted of espionage in early 1950 and subsequently executed) such traitors were found. Historians have always assumed, without conclusive evidence to back it up, that information from Fuchs and the Rosenbergs probably accelerated the Soviet atom programme but that the Soviets would have reached their atomic goal before long (Gaddis 1992: 98). These conclusions have been partially confirmed and partially superseded by evidence published in 1993 which indicated that the first Soviet atomic bomb was in fact a copy of the first American bomb, based on plans supplied by Klaus Fuchs (*New York Times*, 14 January 1993).

The military and strategic implications of the ending of the American monopoly profoundly affected the calculations of American policy-makers. In conjunction with the 'loss' of China in 1949 and the beginnings of Joseph McCarthy's attacks on the Truman administration's supposed weak response to the communist threat, news of the Soviet test produced pressure for a fundamental reassessment of America's strategic objectives. The immediate result was Truman's decision to order a crash programme to develop the hydrogen or thermo-nuclear bomb. Equally important for the future was an extensive security policy review prepared in 1950, known as National Security

Council Resolution 68 (NSC 68) and generally considered by historians as equal in significance to the Truman Doctrine speech.

NSC 68 illustrated the inseparability of military and ideological concerns in this critical year of the cold war. The challenge presented by the Soviet Union was conceived to be moral as much as material. With the eclipse of freedom in Czechoslovakia two years before, 'it was in the intangible scale of values that we registered a loss more damaging than the material loss we had already suffered'. However, in order to convince the Soviet Union of the American determination to uphold the idea of freedom ('the most contagious idea in history'), the United States must match its capabilities to its intentions. 'Without superior aggregate military strength, in being and readily mobilizable, a policy of "containment" – which is in effect a policy of calculated and gradual coercion – is no more than a policy of bluff' (*FRUS* 1950: 240, 239, 253). It has been argued that little of the theory behind NSC 68 was new; that it reproduced in essentials an NSC document of 1948 (Leffler 1992: 355–6). However, the changed global situation, and in particular the Soviet acquisition of the atomic bomb, lent urgency to NSC 68's major recommendation: the need to embark upon a rapid build-up of political, economic, and military strength in what by now was routinely being referred to as the 'Free World'.

NSC 68 was commissioned by Truman in January 1950, forwarded to the President in April, and approved in September. Of central importance in converting the document from a blueprint for a substantial arms build-up into practical policy was the outbreak of the Korean War in June of the same year. (This is discussed in Chapter 5.) The North Korean attack not only confirmed the logic of NSC 68 regarding the communist threat but eased its implementation by providing a justification for the new expenditures entailed by NSC 68. 'We were sweating over NSC 68,' recalled one of Acheson's aides, 'and then, thank God, Korea came along' (Whelan 1990: 74). If the communists were prepared to breach the 38th parallel dividing North and South Korea, might they not also attempt the same in Europe? Once engaged in Korea, American policy-makers moved to build up the defences of Western Europe, which included quadrupling military aid and prolonging economic assistance beyond the end of Marshall Plan aid, coupled with an increase in American troop strength and a substantial supplement to the US defence budget. Moreover, the United States began the delicate process of promoting the rearmament of West Germany in the teeth of French opposition (Leffler 1992: 383–90).

Above all, NSC 68 was explicitly global in scope and military in application. Negotiation with the Soviet Union was not abandoned as a goal but remained carefully circumscribed by military priorities. As the authors of NSC 68 put it, 'negotiation is not a separate course of action but rather a means of gaining support for a program of building strength, of recording, where necessary and desirable, progress in the cold war' (*FRUS* 1950: 276). In short, Kennan's beliefs in the need for selectivity in American commitments, for the primacy of the political over the military, and for a policy based on Soviet intentions rather than capabilities were firmly sidelined with the adoption of NSC 68.

NSC 68 epitomized the militarization of containment. It was not, however, wholly lacking in flexibility. Indeed it failed to provide clear criteria for engaging in military action. 'Recording progress in the cold war' was a vague formula which allowed for strategic retreats from exposed positions. Equally, where American policy-makers felt that the United States' interests could be advanced at acceptable cost, then NSC 68 proved capacious enough to accommodate them. A comparable combination of militancy and opportunism was evident in Soviet policy in the critical years from 1949–53.

STALINISM AND THE COLD WAR AT HOME AND ABROAD, 1947–1953

The establishment of the Cominform in 1947 led to the Stalinization of Eastern Europe. Politically each of these nations were forced to introduce new constitutions on the Soviet model which outlawed all political groupings but the communist parties. The leaders were selected on the basis of their acceptability to the Kremlin and all dissident or otherwise questionable figures were rigorously purged. Internal security forces followed the Soviet pattern and were subject to continuous Soviet supervision. Economically, centralization and nationalization were imposed on the Eastern bloc states and they became tied to the Soviet Union by means of highly unequal arrangements which allowed the Soviet Union to extract goods and raw materials to its own considerable advantage. Direct control of key East European industries was established via joint-stock companies in which the Soviet Union held controlling shares, and (with the exception of Poland) the Soviet collectivist model of agriculture was likewise imposed (Gati 1990: 9–23).

Stalin had considered absorbing the Eastern bloc into the Soviet Union itself but concluded that he could reap the same advantages without the costs such an upheaval would inevitably entail. Nevertheless, it is worth noting that relations with the Eastern bloc were administered not by the Ministry of Foreign Affairs but by a special department devoted to relations with the People's Democracies. Soviet relations with the so-called fraternal nations thus fell somewhere between formal empire and an association of like-minded states.

The scale of the terror imposed on East European nations was enormous, comparable in scope and intensity with the purges within the Soviet Union during the 1930s. To give only one example, it is estimated that 387,000 opponents – or alleged opponents – of the Hungarian regime were imprisoned between 1950 and 1953, approximately 5 per cent of the total population (Brzezinski 1989: 110). The process in Hungary and elsewhere, however, was aided by the complicity of significant numbers of communists within these nations whose 'seemingly unshakable confidence and faith were inspired by Stalin's charisma' (Gati 1990: 26). It was also the case that sovietization served the interests of radicalized agricultural and industrial workers who had gained little from the pre-war regimes (Brzezinski 1989: 108). Nevertheless, the short-term stability produced by the enforcement of sovietization had its costs, not least in the absence of legitimacy of the communist regimes which were so clearly beholden to Moscow. By the time of Stalin's death in 1953, disaffection was already apparent in several East European nations. The uprisings in East Germany in 1953 and in Poland and Hungary in 1956, to be discussed in Chapter 6, were only the most obvious manifestations of general discontent.

The exception to this pattern, of course, was Yugoslavia. Indeed Yugoslavia's expulsion from the Cominform in 1948 arose precisely from the Soviet attempt to determine the leadership in that country. Stalin's manoeuvring to unseat Tito, however, fell foul of the Yugoslav leader's firm hold on power. Not only had the liberation of Yugoslavia from German wartime occupation been achieved largely without the aid of the Soviet Union, but in the aftermath of the war Tito had imposed his own communist regimen in Yugoslavia which was as tight as Stalin's own within the Soviet Union. At the time of the break with Stalin, Tito had not yet declared his own path to socialism, but he soon announced measures which would take the Yugoslav system towards decentralization and economic self-management while still maintaining the principles of state ownership of major enterprises and the leading role of the Party (Nogee and Donaldson 1988: 221–2).

Tito's crime in Soviet terminology was 'nationalism', or deviation from 'internationalism' which was code for the leading role of the Soviet Union within the international communist movement (Lowenthal 1964: 6). More was at stake, however, than disloyalty to the Soviet Union. As Yugoslavia consolidated its position as an independent socialist state, it developed an ideology of its own founded on the perception that the Soviet urge to dominate neighbouring states grew from bureaucratization and oppression within the Soviet system. Tito thus presented a doctrinal challenge to the Soviet Union which threatened the ideological cohesion of the international communist movement. It was hardly surprising that in imposing conformity on the Eastern bloc the Soviet leadership should have used 'Titoism' as a whipping boy to keep the other nations in line. Of particular concern was Tito's desire to open trading links with capitalist countries, in direct defiance of the Stalinist two-camps theory of international relations. The demonstration effect of Titoism, should it be followed elsewhere, posed a clear threat to security as well as ideological cohesion within the bloc.

The authors of NSC 68 had estimated that by 1954 the Soviet Union would probably possess the capacity to deliver atomic bombs and possibly also a thermonuclear (H-bomb) capability. In the light of this potentially 'disastrous situation' the United States must 'launch a build-up of strength which will support a firm policy directed to the frustration of the Kremlin design' (*FRUS* 1950: 287). Ironically, according to the testimony of the Czech Defence Minister, during a meeting of Soviet bloc leaders in January 1951, Stalin presented an analogous prognosis:

No European army is capable of seriously opposing the Soviet Army, and one can even assume that there will be no resistance. The current military strength of the United States is not very great. The Soviet camp thus enjoys a temporary superiority in this field. But it is only temporary, for three or four years. After that the United States will have at their disposal rapid means of transport to bring troops to Europe and could exploit fully their nuclear superiority. It will be necessary therefore to make good use of this short period to complete the systematic preparation of our armies by devoting to them all the economic, political and human means at our disposal. During the three or four years to come the whole of our domestic and international policy will be subordinated to this goal. Only a total mobilization of our resources will allow us to seize this unique occasion to spread socialism to the whole of Europe.

(Rupnik 1989: 127)

It would be foolish to place too much emphasis on this document alone as a guide to Stalin's policies in the early 1950s. Only six months before, Stalin had decided against a military invasion of Yugoslavia to oust Tito, on the grounds that the swift American response to the North Korean invasion of South Korea might be repeated in Europe (Charlton 1984: 77). Stalin's very different estimate of the relative military strengths of the Soviet Union and the United States in January 1951 was similarly related to the course of events in Korea. At this point, following the Chinese entry into the war, things were going badly for the Americans and Stalin felt correspondingly confident about his chances of exerting pressure in Europe. As it happened, at precisely this time, in line with NSC 68 the Americans were making the decision to increase their troop and air-force strength in Europe, which would take it from one infantry division, three armoured cavalry regiments, and two fighter–bomber groups in June 1950 to five divisions and seven air wings at the end of 1952 (Wells 1985: 189).

The significant point about Stalin's January 1951 statement is not only that it would have confirmed the Americans' worst fears had they known of it, but that, taken in conjunction with signs of his caution at other moments, it shows a Soviet pattern of tactical shifts in relation to the perceived strength or weakness of the West. A major instrument of Stalin's foreign policy between 1948 and 1953 was his promotion of a world-wide 'peace movement'. Launched in 1948 as discussion on the formation of NATO was taking place in the West, it was channelled through the French and Italian communist parties. Its initial effect, however, was to isolate communists in the West even further, particularly after the provocative statement by the General Secretary of the French Communist Party that if the Soviets marched into Western Europe he would support them. Having failed to thwart the etsablishment of NATO by a policy of militancy, Stalin shifted ground by using the peace movement to appeal to liberal 'bourgeois' elements in the West – a revival in effect of the pre-war 'popular front'. Hoping to exploit splits within public opinion in the West on the issue of the atomic bomb, the Soviet Union sponsored a World Peace Congress and a 'ban the bomb' petition which reportedly gained over 500 million signatures (most of them in the Soviet bloc). Despite gaining some adherents among prominent liberals in the West, the peace movement failed to check the West's military mobilization (Shulman 1963: 54–61, 91–100).

On the diplomatic front there was a similar oscillation in tactics between phases of uncompromising militancy and more conciliatory moves. As Marshal Shulman observed, Soviet policy towards Korea shifted with the course of battle, Stalin being inclined to harden his stance on a Korean settlement when the communist forces were in the ascendant and more accommodating when the United States regained the initiative (Shulman 1963: 158–75).

More puzzling is the proposal Stalin made in 1952 for a German settlement, his last major policy initiative before his death in March 1953. In a series of notes to the West he proposed a reunited Germany, permitted to possess its own army on condition that it remain permanently neutral. Was this, as Western (including West German) leaders believed, a device to destabilize West Germany and undermine Western defence plans by exploiting divisions within the West on the proposed rearmament of West Germany? Or was it a genuine attempt to resolve the German problem by means of concessions by both sides: i.e.: Soviet willingness 'to sacrifice communist East Germany for the larger objective of preventing Germany's rearmament'? (Nogee and Donaldson 1988: 99). No definitive answer can be given, but both motives may have been at work. It is significant that during this last year of Stalin's life the growing prominence given to 'peaceful coexistence' in Soviet policy coincided with the emergence of Georgi Malenkov as a force within the Soviet leadership. On the death of Stalin, Malenkov was to figure, if only briefly, as the dominant force within the Soviet hierarchy and the chief spokesman for the policy of peaceful coexistance. On these grounds it is possible to interpret the Soviet proposals on Germany as a genuine effort to reach an accommodation with the United States, though of course this is not inconsistent with the aim of destabilizing Western defence plans.

CONCLUSION

Historians have often been reluctant to apply the term 'balance of power' to the cold war relationship between the United States and the Soviet Union. It smacks too much of European cabinet diplomacy, of the cynical manipulation of other nations' destinies by diplomats operating behind closed doors. Above all, it is felt, to describe the cold war as a balance of power conflict scarcely does justice to the great clash of political principles and ethical values involved in the encounter between East and West. Interestingly, revisionist historians have repudiated a balance of power or 'realist' interpretation of the cold war as strongly as the most strident apologists of American policy. What was the source of this tendency to make a rigid distinction between traditional balance of power politics and cold war politics, and is it justified?

The distinction came in part from the ideological intensity of the cold war itself. It came also from the long-standing American predisposition to regard the United States as representing unique and anti-European principles. But, given that the Bolshevik Revolution was thirty years old in 1947 and that most Americans had been firmly opposed to it from the start, why do we not habitually date the cold war from 1917? If ideology were the main ingredient of the cold war, 1917 would be the logical starting date. That 1947 rather than 1917 is generally chosen lies in the structure of the international system – in the changing balance of power.[2] Until 1945 the configuration of major powers was not such as to make US–Soviet antagonism a determining factor in international relations. The decisive result produced by the war was the destruction of Germany as a Great Power, and that necessitated a new solution to the old problem of creating and preserving stability in Central and Eastern Europe. Historically that region had been a battleground between German (including Austro-Hungarian) and Russian ambitions. With the removal of Germany and the weakness of France and Britain no power other than that of the United States existed on the Continent to contain Soviet power. Ideological antagonism was to that extent a result rather than a cause of the bipolar cold war structure. The particular form which the balance of power took after 1945 – a bipolar system after all is simply a balance of power system in which there are only two main players – served to exacerbate the ideological divide which had existed, but only in a latent form, since 1917.

The structure of the post-war international system does not tell us everything about the nature of the cold war, but it did set the basic conditions within which governments had to operate. The precise form the cold war assumed was not inevitable, but some form of American participation in the European balance undoubtedly was, as was an enhanced Soviet role in Eastern Europe. The ideological conflict certainly gave the cold war its characteristic quasi-religious intensity, but it is difficult to believe that the US–Soviet relationship would have been conflict free, even had they possessed similar political systems and social values. In short, to adopt Kenneth Waltz's terms, in broad outline the roles of the superpowers were set by the positions they occupied in the international system as a whole in 1945, in particular by their disproportionately large power and influence (Waltz 1979: 80).

By 1953 the cold war in Europe had achieved a measure of definition, even stalemate, despite continuing tension during the 1950s. The same was not true of Asia, where the lines of conflict were more complex and less amenable to superpower control, as will become clear in the next chapter.

5

COLD WAR
The Far Eastern dimension, 1945–1953

ASIA AND EUROPE COMPARED

It was relatively easy for policy-makers in the United States and the Soviet Union to arrive at definitions of their interests in Europe. Having by 1948 abandoned the attempt to produce a joint and comprehensive settlement, they sought to stabilize their influence within their respective spheres of interest. Their methods of control differed greatly, but geography, history, and the needs of the moment combined to make division the least unacceptable alternative to open conflict. The Iron Curtain was as much a psychological as a political barrier. It defined the limits of the possible with painful clarity, particularly after the Soviet acquisition of the atom bomb. The bomb raised the potential costs of a breach in the line by either side, with the result that mutual antagonism was displaced into the nuclear arms race, the propaganda war, and the espionage war.

Each of these closely related spheres of conflict thrived on stalemate in the central political theatre, creating an adversarial frame of mind which entered deep into the cultures of the West. Fears of atomic war issued in a burgeoning disarmament literature and a body of apocalyptic novels and films which had precedents in the writings of Jules Verne and H.G. Wells but which now had a new sense of reality and urgency. Fear of communism fed the vogue in the 1950s for revelatory docudramas about the fight against subversion and for Hollywood's science fictional representations of nameless threats from outer space which were defeated only by a combination of an affirmation of Western values and massive technological know-how. Spy novels and films joined the techniques of detective fiction to the *frisson* supplied by reality itself: reports of defection and betrayal, and revelations about the techniques of espionage. While it is true that these genres thrived on the deceptiveness of appearances, hidden dangers, and possibility of annihilation, the ultimate sources of fear could be identified; they lay in the machinations of international communism. More particularly, the stalemate in Europe provided the international backdrop for these projections of national fears. It became a given of the international scene, a focus for

89

the reinforcement of the West's cultural identity in contradistinction to that of the 'East'.

However, the real East – lumped together in the Western mind for centuries as 'the Orient' – was less amenable to the methods used to make sense of the situation in Europe. The lines between hostile and friendly territory were rarely as clear as in Europe both in the geographical and political sense. There was no single 'Bamboo Curtain' in Asia comparable with the Iron Curtain in Europe. While the 38th parallel dividing North and South Korea and the Taiwan Strait dividing Communist from Nationalist China came to mark boundaries in Asia between communism and capitalism, in many other parts of Asia the lines were far less clear. Attempts to establish similar lines, for example on the 17th parallel between North and South Vietnam, proved ultimately impossible to sustain. In Indo-China and the rest of Asia, in so far as the situations within individual countries were reducible at all to the terms of the cold war, the lines of conflict were as varied in their nature as were the nations themselves. Western, and particularly American, attempts to press Asian conflicts into the mould of the cold war fell foul of this diversity.

After Stalin's death the Soviet Union pursued a more flexible line, often backing anti-Western and non-aligned rather than communist states and groups within states – a consequence, in part, of relative weakness in projecting itself globally and, in part, of its historical pragmatism. Both superpowers in any case experienced difficulty in applying policies devised for Europe to situations in Asia and the Third World. The geopolitics of European conflict allowed for, indeed invited, a concentration of interests; the geopolitical diversity of Asia produced multiple spheres of interest and posed the problem for both superpowers of achieving coordination amongst them.

Underlying these problems was the pressure within Asia for radical political change. The growing movement for independence among former European colonial territories eventually produced a situation not unlike that in East-Central Europe between the world wars: an increasing number of more or less unstable states, subject to a greater or lesser extent to the desires of the Great Powers to create order in the service of their own interests. The difference in Asia in the post-war period lay not only in the sheer number of new and would-be new states but in the nature of their historical ties with the Great Powers and in the nature of the international situation in which they sought to achieve independence. Colonial dependence had created little scope for indigenous political activity, however successfully cultural institutions and values had survived the onslaught of the West. This ensured that decolonization would involve nation-building from the ground up, meaning a necessary concentration on internal con-solidation at a time when international economic and political forces were exerting powerful external pressures on new states. It was a potent mixture of forces. In these circumstances, internal political conflict frequently turned Asian and other Third World nations into arenas for superpower rivalry, not least because many of the revolutionary movements adopted communism, or versions of it, as their guiding philosophy.

The overriding economic imperative was modernization. This must be achieved, wrote a liberal Western economist in 1955, 'because Western influence has wiped out the old economic system and has vastly increased the birth rate. The choice now is: modernize or perish' (Ward [1955] 1962: 57). But which route to modernization: the capitalist or the Soviet communist model? The Soviet model was preferable to many Asian leaders both because the Soviet Union was not associated with the legacy of Western imperialism and because it offered an example of how 'a nation can drag itself up by its own bootstraps . . . without any intervention or help from the West' (Ward [1955] 1962: 73). But there were limits to the applicability of the Soviet model. Whatever the success of the Soviet Union in forcing the pace of industrial growth through its five-year plans, agriculture remained a problem sector in the Soviet economy and hardly offered a promising example to Asian nations whose economies were based pre-eminently on agriculture. Furthermore, even those nations, such as China, which did adopt communism as a national ideology developed the system in their own ways, subsequently establishing a rival communist model for Third World growth. Finally, former colonial nations, such as India, many of whose leaders had been educated in the English-speaking world, rejected communism for political and social as well as economic reasons.

Perhaps the overriding difficulty faced by Third World nations was that of establishing the necessary political stability on which to build economic growth. Regional, ethnic and religious differences within newly independent states undermined the consensus on which national growth would depend. Civil war was an ever-present possibility. 'Most of the political violence that has inflamed human society since 1945', observes Richard Barnet, 'has been of a special character:

> Its source has not been conflict between states, but conflict within societies. The wars of our time have not been primarily fights for territory, raw materials, colonies or the preservation of the King's honour, although all of these have at some time been involved. Essentially, contemporary wars have been fights for the rights of various political groups within the former colonial appendages of Europe to take political power and to exercise it on their own terms.
>
> (Barnet 1972: 15–16)

It is only necessary to add that 'exercising power on their own terms' was limited not only by internal conflict but by the ambitions of former European colonial powers and the superpowers. Newly independent states possessed neither the cushion of time nor distance enjoyed by the United States in its period of nation-building. Globalism was the inescapable condition of Asian and Third World growth.

DEFINING SUPERPOWER INTERESTS IN ASIA

The language of NSC 68, as we have seen, was global, but limitations of resources and the primary concern at this stage with Europe combined in practice to create a hierarchy of interests in the minds of American policy-makers. Prior to the Korean War Asia came low on the list of American priorities. In a Joint Chiefs of Staff (JCS) Paper of April 1947 on 'United States Assistance to Other Countries from the Standpoint of National Security' countries were listed according to two criteria: 'importance to our national security' and 'urgency of need'. When considered separately, the first criterion produced the following outcome:

1. Great Britain	7. Italy	13. Japan
2. France	8. Canada	14. China
3. Germany	9. Turkey	15. Korea
4. Belgium	10. Greece	16. The Philippines
5. Netherlands	11. Latin America	
6. Austria	12. Spain	

(Etzold and Gaddis 1978: 79)

When the two criteria were combined, however, Japan moved up to eighth place, the other countries remaining broadly in the same positions.

Two important points emerge from this document: the primacy in the eyes of the JCS of Japan among the Asian nations and the low significance in terms of US national security accorded to Korea and China. Of Korea it was felt that 'if the present diplomatic ideological warfare should become armed warfare, Korea could offer little or no assistance in the maintenance of our national security. Therefore, from this point of view, current assistance should be given Korea only if the means exist after sufficient assistance has been given the countries of primary importance to ensure their continued independence and friendship for the United States and the resurgence of their economies.' Of China it was said that, while a communist China would pose serious problems, even in the event of war with the Soviet Union, it might be possible to isolate communism in the Far East by means of an economic quarantine of China (Etzold and Gaddis 1978: 78–9).

Of course, the leading assumption behind this document was that war against communism meant war with the Soviet Union, which indicates that at this stage American thinking about Asia was dictated by the European situation. The decisive change over the next three years, brought about by the revolution in China and the beginning of the Korean War, was towards the perception that war against communism would not necessarily begin in the central European theatre and spread out to the periphery, but could well begin on the periphery. This did not obviate the need for the strongest possible defences in Europe, but it did expand the sphere of American interests and commitments. As we shall see shortly, the Europe-first policy of the period 1945–50, essentially a continuation of America's priorities during the Second World War, came under severe attack within the United States as the cold war was extended to Asia.

In so far as it is possible to ascertain Soviet interests in Asia in the aftermath of the Second World War, it would appear that until Zhdanov's 'two camps' speech of 1947 the Soviet Union was cautious in offering support to communist movements, but thereafter shifted towards open and unequivocal denial that former colonial territories could adopt a position of neutrality in the struggle against imperialism. Asian communist parties were urged to take an oppositionist line rather than join with non-communist nationalists to form united fronts in independence movements or governments in newly independent states. In part this was determined by growing expectations of a communist victory in China and in part by the outbreak of cold war in Europe. But this policy also reflected Stalin's memory of what has been described as his 'disastrous experience' of supporting the non-communist Nationalist movement in China in the 1920s (Nogee and Donaldson 1988: 149). Under Comintern guidance in 1925 the Chinese Communist Party had entered into alliance with the Nationalists under the leadership of Chiang Kai-Shek, who was waging a struggle to unite China under his rule. In 1927, however, once victory was in sight, Chiang turned on the Communist Party, slaughtering thousands of its members.

The legacy of this experience dictated that Stalin would press communist parties in Asia to uncompromising opposition to 'bourgeois' rule. This led to communist insurrectionist movements in the Philippines, Burma, Indonesia, and Malaya in the late 1940s and early 1950s, as these countries achieved or moved towards independence. (They gained independence respectively in 1946, 1948, 1949, and 1957.) There seems little reason to quarrel with the judgement that this policy involved Stalin in a 'sterile conflict with the first new states', and this included India which demonstrated its independence from the West in Nehru's attempt to mediate in the Korean War (Lowenthal 1964: 326).

In the long run this policy proved self-defeating and following Stalin's death was abandoned. Its pursuit, however, at a crucial divide in relations with the United States raised the stakes of the cold war. It inclined the United States to see in all Asian insurgent movements the hand of the Soviet Union. Above all, it encouraged the process by which the United States would come to interpret conflict in Asia less in terms of threats to its security as such than in terms of global cold war between East and West. Clearly the two are intimately related, but one of the striking features of American policy in Asia over the whole post-war period is the difficulty experienced by policy-makers in justifying military intervention in countries which did not obviously pose a threat to American security. Vietnam was the most significant case, but that lay in the future. Meanwhile, attention was focused in 1950 on North-east Asia – China, Japan, and Korea.

McCARTHYISM AND THE FAR EASTERN TURN IN AMERICAN POLICY

Truman was politically vulnerable in the early months of 1950. The twin blows of the Soviet atom test and the Chinese revolution had shaken public confidence in the administrations's policies, exposing it to charges of negligence and worse. The conviction of Alger Hiss for perjury in January 1950 seemed to confirm suspicions that the Truman and Roosevelt administrations had harboured traitors in key policy-making positions. Hiss had worked at the State Department during the 1930s, had been a member of the American delegation at Yalta, and after the war had been appointed president of the Carnegie Endowment for International Peace. The specific charge against him was that he had perjured himself before the House Un-American Activities Committee in denying that he had passed information to the Russians while employed at the State Department in 1937–38. (Thanks to the Statute of Limitations he could not be charged with espionage as such.) In actuality Hiss's role had been a minor one, but the case became a convenient peg on which critics of the Truman administration could hang a series of accusations, amounting to a comprehensive denunciation of the whole Roosevelt–Truman record in foreign policy.

For figures such as Senator Joseph McCarthy, who rose to prominence in the wake of the Hiss conviction, the case provided an explanation for the succession of American defeats in the cold war, beginning with the 'sell-out' of Eastern Europe to the Soviets at Yalta and culminating in the 'loss' of China. No note is more consistently sounded in McCarthy's speeches than his belief in America's 'impotency' in the face of communism, 'the feeling of America's weakness in the very air we breathe in Washington'. The present situation could only be accounted for as the product of 'a great conspiracy, a conspiracy on a scale so immense as to dwarf any previous such venture in the history of man'. Alger Hiss's cultured, urbane demeanour, his association with the east coast liberal elite, and his deep roots in Roosevelt's New Deal offered easy targets for Republican attacks on the betrayers of true Americanism and heralded the end of bipartisanship on foreign policy within Congress. Dean Acheson, George Marshall's successor as Secretary of State, blackened the Democrats' record still further when he announced, following the conviction of his old friend, that 'I will not turn my back on Alger Hiss.' With this statement, said McCarthy, 'this pompous diplomat in striped pants, with a phony British accent . . . awakened the dormant indignation of the American people' (Matusow 1970: 22, 59, 26). For four years McCarthy pressed home his message, throwing the administration on to the defensive and ensuring that the communist issue would dictate the agenda of domestic affairs.

McCarthy did not invent anti-communism. His genius was to dramatize the issue, to put his personal imprint upon it by a combination of adroit self-publicity and unscrupulous exploitation of the media's appetite for sensational copy. His targets were many – the State Department, the Democratic Party, and subsequently the army and the presidency. By 1954 he had become an embarrassment to his own party. Republicans who had been content to go along with McCarthy's attacks on the Democrats, especially for their handling of the Korean War, balked at his increasingly indiscriminate charges against such hallowed institutions as the army and the (now Republican) presidency. In 1954 he was censured by the Senate and effectively silenced. Within three years he was dead, a broken man mired in alcoholism.

There are many contexts in which McCarthy and McCarthyism can be viewed. A rich literature on the political and sociological roots of the American anxiety about communism began to appear within months of McCarthy's censure by the Senate. From the standpoint of foreign relations, however, the significance of McCarthy's career lies in the coincidence of his brief period of notoriety with the shift of attention from Europe to the Far East, a shift which he helped to promote. Two figures appear repeatedly in his catalogue of traitors – George Marshall, who had attempted in 1946–47 to negotiate a truce between the Nationalists and Communists in China, and Owen Lattimore, an oriental scholar who had also been an adviser to Chiang Kai-shek during the Second World War. Both, it was claimed, had been instrumental in the disastrous policy of denying adequate support to the Chinese Nationalists under Chiang, hence paving the way for the Communist victory of 1949. The Korean War would never have happened, it was argued, if the Truman administration had given due attention to the danger of communism in the Far East rather than devoting its resources to Europe in the crucial years after 1945.

Once again, McCarthy was not the initiator of the 'Asia first' view. Its roots lay in the controversy over the United States' wartime Europe-first strategy and gained powerful advocates within Congress and among prominent publishers and business-men in the immediate post-war years. Henry Luce, publisher of *Time* and *Life* magazines, was an ardent supporter of the Chinese Nationalists and a critic of the Truman policy of seeking to resolve the civil war in China by bringing the Nation-alists and Communists together. Madame Chiang, a Christian with close ties to American businessmen and legislators, lobbied energetically on behalf of the Nation-alist cause both before and after the Revolution. Within Congress Senator Knowland's role in this cause was such that, following the Nationalists's flight to Formosa (Taiwan), he was dubbed 'the Senator from Formosa'. The links which the Asia firsters and the China lobby managed to forge between the communist threat in Asia and inside America had profound effects upon the future of America's involve-ment in the Far East. It ensured that diplomatic recognition of Communist China would remain off the agenda for a long time to come, in fact until 1978. It removed from office the cream of America's China specialists in the purge of the State Department which followed the Chinese Revolution. It also encouraged a heightened sensitivity to the dangers of further losses to communism in Asia. Thereafter com-promise or accommodation to Asian communism was tantamount to abject surrender.

CHINA AND THE FERMENT IN ASIA, 1945–1950

The Asia firsters' contention that the Truman administration had lost China is justified only if one accepts their premise that China was America's to lose. This view was based on the romantic notion that the United States had a record of benign concern for China, stemming from the 'Open Door' notes of 1899. In opposing the European nations' plans to parcel up China in line with their own economic interests, the United States, it was felt, had demonstrated an enlightened concern for China's territorial integrity. While extensive cultural and educational ties did exist between the United States and China, in actuality the United States had done little to enforce the principle of the open door, which in any case could be seen as a self-interested claim for an economic stake by a latecomer on the Chinese scene. In other spheres too China had little reason to feel beholden to the United States. Discriminatory American immigration laws and maltreatment of the Chinese population within the United States had been a constant source of friction from the 1880s onwards. Nor did successive American administrations do much to aid China in the face of Japan's growing aspirations to dominance in the Far East. With the (admittedly reluctant) support of the United States, Japan gained concessions in the Shantung Peninsula at China's expense at the Treaty of Versailles (1919); the Japanese invasion of Manchuria (the northern province of China) in 1931 produced only verbal protests from the United States; and when full-scale war broke out between China and Japan in 1937 Roosevelt shrank from imposing sanctions on Japan.

American policy towards China changed substantially with the deterioration of American–Japanese relations in 1940–41. Indeed the cause of this deterioration was increasing encroachment by Japan on China as well as on Southeast Asia. In this sense the United States' 'special relationship' with China was a late development; too late, it might be said, given that China was burdened with internal conflict in addition to the war with Japan. Having once made the decision to build up China as a major power by including her in the councils of the anti-Axis nations, the United States was confronted by the problem of supporting a leader – Chiang Kai-shek – whose hold on power was distinctly fragile. The central issue for American policy-makers in the wartime and immediate post-war years was their attitude towards the relations between the Chinese Nationalists and the Communists.

Contradictory advice was reaching Washington from China as the war drew to a close. Ambassador Hurley (appointed in January 1945) advocated unreserved support for Chiang. In so far as Hurley conceded a role at all to the Communists it was to be wholly on Chiang's terms. Meanwhile counsellors within his embassy, such as John Stewart Service and John Paton Davies, doubted Chiang's ability to produce stable government and were critical of his dictatorial style. Ironically, McCarthy's *bête noire*, Owen Lattimore, held a more favourable view of Chiang than many other old 'China hands', perhaps because he had worked as Chiang's political adviser during the war. (However, contrary to McCarthy's claim, Lattimore was never a State Department employee and exerted influence after his post with Chiang during the war primarily through his writings.) In a widely read book published in 1945 Lattimore wrote that Chiang was not at present 'losing control'. Nevertheless he felt that there was a case for political compromise with the Communists. The Communists, he wrote, 'have done well enough in the territory they control to stand comparison with the Kuomintang [Nationalists]' (Lattimore 1945: 122). Hurley was incensed at signs of what he took to be pro-Communist learnings among the Embassy staff, and on 26 November 1945 he resigned in protest. 'It is no secret', he wrote in a letter of resignation to Truman, 'that

the professional foreign service men sided with the Chinese Communist armed party
. . . Our professional diplomats continuously advised the Communists that my efforts
in preventing a collapse of the National Government did not represent the policy of
the United States' (Kahn 1975: 174–5).

In truth the policy of the United States government was more ambiguous than
Hurley believed or desired. It was essentially one of 'wait-and-see', though with a
definite tilt towards the Nationalists (Stueck 1981: 36). In 1946 Truman dispatched
General Marshall to China supposedly to mediate between the Nationalists and the
Communists and to encourage the formation of a coalition government. After a largely
fruitless year Marshall returned empty-handed. (He, in common with John Paton
Davies, John Stewart Service and other State Department China specialists, subsequently paid dearly for his efforts at the hands of McCarthy, who in 1951 launched a
60,000-word diatribe against him in Congress, later published as a book – see
McCarthy 1951.) By 1947 the United States had resolved on a course of recognition
of the Nationalist government, coupled with moderate military and economic aid. As
the civil war raged and the Communists advanced, aid to China was gradually scaled
down and in January 1949 the American Military Advisory Group was withdrawn.
The climax of the civil war coincided with the Berlin Blockade, and the prospect of a
Communist victory in China did not seem to weigh heavily enough to warrant a large
allocation of military resources (Dulles 1972: 31–2).

By the early months of 1949, as a Communist victory seemed imminent, angry
Republicans produced a 'round robin' letter in Congress accusing Acheson of
'irresponsibility' in his China policy, and followed it up by introducing a series of
China aid bills in Congress with the aim of pressuring the administration into action.
These efforts achieved partial success, since the administration needed Congressional
support for continuance of aid to Europe under the Marshall Plan. A moderate package
of assistance to Chiang was passed as an amendment to a European aid bill. It would
appear, however, that by the middle of the year the administration was more or less
reconciled to a Communist victory in China and was bracing itself for the inevitable
reaction within the United States. In August the State Department published the
China White Paper, a lengthy history and justification of American policy accompanied by extensive documentary evidence. In the appended Letter of Transmittal
from Acheson to Truman it was argued, to the consternation of the administration's
critics, that 'the ominous result of the civil war in China was beyond the control of the
government of the United States' (Department of State [1949] 1967, Vol. 1: xvi).
That this was no more nor less than the truth did not mollify Truman's opponents,
who believed that the policy of heavily qualified support for Chiang had been a self-
fulfilling prophecy. A new set of battle lines was thus drawn around the related
question of recognition of Mao's China and the United States' attitude towards the
Nationalist regime which at the end of the year fled to the island of Formosa.

Non-recognition of Mao and unequivocal support for Chiang was by no means a
foregone conclusion. For one thing, this policy would incur the risk of war in support

of Chiang, and neither Truman nor the Joint Chiefs of Staff favoured such a course. A strong lobby within the State Department argued for a 'realistic' policy of recognizing whoever was in control. (Britain recognized Mao's government in 1950, albeit sending only a chargé d'affaires rather than an ambassador.) The scales were tipped away from Truman's preference for disengagement from the China conflict by the influence of McCarthy and the Asia firsters, as we have seen, but more decisively by a sequence of international events during 1950: the signing of a treaty between China and the Soviet Union in January, the North Korean attack on South Korea in June, and the entry of China into the Korean war in October.

From the United States' point of view the first of these confirmed their worst fears about the scale of the threat posed to the West by communism. In fact, however, Sino–Soviet relations before and after the Revolution were more complicated than Americans were able to perceive. For one thing, the Soviet Union had been noticeably lukewarm in its support for Mao's Communists since 1945, continuing to recognize the Nationalists as the legitimate government of China until as late as mid-1949. This policy was apparently based on doubts about whether Mao possessed the power to unify China under Communist rule and possibly also an overestimation of the Nationalists' strength and the level of American support for them. Moreover, the Soviet Union had been able to achieve important territorial ambitions in China without the aid of the Communists. At the Yalta conference, and subsequently in a treaty with Nationalist China, the Soviet Union regained rights in China which it had possessed prior to the Russo–Japanese War of 1904. These included use of the commercial port of Dairen and the naval base at Port Arthur in the northern Yellow Sea between the Korean peninsula and the Chinese mainland, and control of the Chinese Eastern and South Manchurian railroads, which formed the Soviet Union's links to its Pacific coast. A Nationalist-run China thus held out certain advantages for the Soviet Union.

Finally, even after the decision was taken in mid-1949 to throw firm support to Mao, the Soviet Union, as one account has it, 'took pains to deny Mao Zedong's authorship of the Chinese strategy' (Nogee and Donaldson 1988: 94). Given the Soviet experience with Tito, it can be assumed that Stalin harboured suspicions of a large and independent centre of communist power. Certainly it would appear that the hand of friendship was extended only so far to the Chinese Communists. On his arrival in Moscow to negotiate the Treaty of Alliance, Mao was met at the airport, not by Stalin but by Molotov. Mao's visit was also short by comparison with those of other communist leaders. China certainly emerged from the Revolution and from the alliance negotiations as a power to be reckoned with, but, so far as the Soviet Union was concerned, as a decidedly junior partner. Mao appeared to acknowledge this in his declaration in July 1949 that 'the Communist Party of the USSR is our best teacher from whom we must learn,' but there was no question of the Soviet Union establishing the same position of dominance over China which it wielded over the nations of Eastern Europe (Daniels 1985, Vol. 2: 183).

The terms of the Treaty itself, which was signed in February 1950, were finely balanced. On the one hand, Stalin undertook to return to Chinese control those rights to Port Arthur, Dairen, and the Manchurian railroads which he had gained at Yalta. On the other hand, the handover was not to be immediate and was to be dependent upon conclusion of a Chinese treaty with Japan. Furthermore, Mao's hope for substantial economic aid was not realized, though he did gain some. Perhaps the most important clauses of the Treaty, however, concerned the mutual security guarantees in the event of aggression from Japan 'or any other state that may collaborate in any way with Japan in acts of aggression' (Text of Treaty in Grenville and Wasserstein 1987: 165). The Treaty has been described as 'in essence a propaganda instrument condemning the danger of a Japanese military revival' (Lowe 1986: 121). Doubtless the Soviet Union's main gain in the Treaty, and the feature which compensated for the territorial concessions, was the addition to communist political and military power in the Far East in the face of the consolidation of American power in Japan. Before looking at the way in which the Korean War affected the calculations of the major powers we must consider the role of Japan in American policy after 1945.

THE AMERICAN OCCUPATION OF JAPAN

In many respects Japan's place in American Asian policy paralleled that of Germany in Europe. Early designs for a punitive settlement were quickly shelved as it became clear that communism was on the march in Asia. Initially the reconstruction of Japan was based on the need to remove the entrenched elites and institutions which had given rise to militarism in the 1930s. Democratization of the political system, dismemberment of the family-based industrial monopolies (or *zaibatsu*), and the elimination of Japan's capacity to produce heavy industrial goods (including, of course, war material) were all aimed at uprooting authoritarianism and encouraging a wider distribution of wealth and power. To a degree each of these policies was embarked upon but, as Michael Schaller has observed, they gradually 'lost momentum or changed direction in 1948' (Schaller 1986: 51). The *zaibatsu* essentially survived efforts to break them up and the new constitution, while establishing formal democracy and liberal principles, allowed ruling conservatives to retain their position. The plan to de-industrialize Japan was never realized since it soon became clear, as was the case in Germany, that a weak and unstable Japan would invite communist inroads and would undermine America's broader goal of setting up a counterweight to communism in Asia. The change of policy towards Japan coincided with the mounting of the Marshall Plan and the Truman Doctrine. Japan became the keystone of containment in Asia.

The development of the occupation policy in Japan bears directly on the administration's reluctance to get involved too deeply in the internal affairs of China. The United States was able to exert control over the Japanese situation to an extent which it was not able to do in China. Indeed the United States insisted from the outset that the Soviet Union should have only a nominal role in the occupation of Japan, a point which the Soviets exploited to the full in their claim for a similar role in the Balkans and Eastern Europe (Schaller 1986: 58–61). Though it would be going too far to say that the administration viewed China as expendable, it is the case that Japan was increasingly regarded as the strategic key to the American position in Asia. From the evidence of PPS and NSC documents in 1948–49, policy was formulated in anticipation of the fall of the nationalist regime, and the recurring theme is the danger of an extensive commitment to preventing its defeat (see documents 25–34 in Eztold and Gaddis 1978).

When in January 1950 Dean Acheson announced the 'defensive perimeter' which the United States must be prepared to defend in Asia, it excluded not only Formosa but also Korea. America's policy in Asia was an offshore policy, reflecting the prevailing conventional wisdom that the United States should resist being drawn into a land war in Asia. In the event, the North Korean attack not only undermined this policy but also removed any obstacles to the conclusion of a peace treaty with Japan, formally ending hostilities and establishing Japanese independence. Ironically, as Schaller points out, the North Korean attack 'set the stage for the termination of the Occupation' (Schaller 1986: 290). Any qualms about reaching a separate peace with Japan were now brushed aside. Though the Treaty was signed amid the trappings of an international conference in San Francisco in September 1951 (attended also by the Soviet Union), its provisions – which included a security pact and the granting of base rights to American forces – reflected largely bilateral interests between the United States and Japan. The Soviet Union refused to sign.

THE KOREAN WAR

Much obscurity surrounds the opening of the Korean War, in particular the question of Soviet motives. Western observers assumed that the Soviets had engineered the North Korean attack, encouraging the North Korean leader, Kim Il-sung, to achieve by force what negotiation had failed to achieve since the temporary partition of Korea in 1945 – namely, the reunification of Korea (Foot 1985: 58–9). Khrushchev, on the other hand, asserted in his memoirs that 'the war wasn't Stalin's idea, but Kim Il-sung's', though Stalin 'didn't try to dissuade him' (Khrushchev 1971: 368). Recent scholarship, based on new evidence from Soviet archives, supports the view that the idea for the invasion was Kim's but that the North Korean leader actively sought and received the endorsement of the Soviet Union. While there is as yet no conclusive evidence explaining the Soviet decision, it would appear that a strong motive was concern not to be seen to be doing less than the Chinese in promoting the cause of revolution in the Far East. In the event of a Soviet refusal to give help to the North Koreans, Stalin's 'position as leader of the communist camp', it has been pointed out, 'would be weakened while the authority of Mao, to whom Kim would obviously turn . . . would rise'. In any event, it seems clear that Kim's policy of reunifying the peninsula by force represented a more militant position than Stalin had wished for. Of

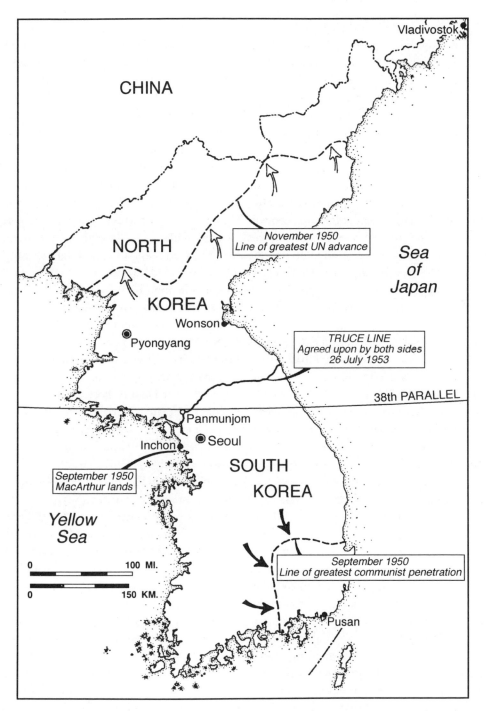

Figure 5.1 Military phases of the Korean War
Source: Derived from R.H. Ferrell (ed.), *America in a Divided World, 1945–1972*, New York: Harper and Row, 1975.

particular significance here was Stalin's concern about potential American reaction. Stalin reportedly approved Kim's plan 'only after having been persuaded that the US would not intervene in the conflict' (Weathersby 1993: 30, 31–2). That the United States did intervene meant that the Soviet Union was drawn into a larger commitment than it had contemplated.

A further puzzle is the Soviet boycott of the UN Security Council at the critical moment in late June when the Council made the decision to label North Korea as the aggressor and to support military moves by the United States to repel the invasion. Several more or less subtle explanations have been offered. Stalin may have wanted to embroil the United States in conflict with China, thereby ruling out the possibility of Communist China being admitted to the UN. On this view, Soviet policy was driven by fear of a large rival communist power. The problem with this explanation is that the Soviet Union had been boycotting the UN since January 1950, nominally at least, precisely because of the United States' opposition to Communist Chinese membership of the UN. Besides, a policy of seeking to isolate China would seem to sit oddly with the treaty which Stalin had signed with Mao only six months earlier.

Another suggestion is that 'Stalin may have hoped that cloaking American intervention in the UN flag would destroy this body or at least would reveal it to be an American tool' (Halliday and Cumings 1988: 78). The problem here is that by August 1950 the Soviet representative had returned to the UN and was using its position on the Security Council to obstruct American initiatives. The simplest and most plausible explanation has been offered by Andrei Gromyko, Soviet Deputy Foreign Minister at the time. Reportedly indignant at what he took to be an insulting letter from the United States government to the UN Security Council on the subject of Korea, Stalin simply acted on angry impulse. 'On this occasion', wrote Gromyko, 'Stalin, guided for once by emotion, had not made the best decision' (Gromyko 1989: 102).

It seems safe to say that the Soviet Union had no master plan and that it was making policy 'on the hoof'. The swiftness of the American response threw Soviet policymakers into some confusion. After all, only six months earlier Secretary of State Dean Acheson had given the impression that the United States did not consider Korea an area of vital interest. Furthermore, it appears that the Soviet Union soon 'regretted the North Korean invasion, were eager to distance themselves from it, and to prevent any widening of the war'. It was doubtless this which led the Americans, assuming as they did that China would act in concert with the Soviet Union, to discount the possibility of China acting on her own in support of the North Koreans (Hastings 1987: 142).

As it happened, the Truman administration showed little hesitation in revising its assumptions about involvement in a land war in Asia. Within a few days of the North Korean attack the United States had committed ground troops to the defence of South Korea, pushed a resolution through the UN Security Council labelling North Korea as the aggressor, and interposed the 7th fleet between Formosa and the mainland in order to prevent an attack by the People's Republic of China. Militarily the course of the war fluctuated wildly in the first few months. The initial push by the North Koreans took them deep into the South by the middle of September and left only a corner of the peninsula beyond their reach. General MacArthur, seconded from his post as occupation commander in Japan, responded with an outflanking amphibious landing at Inchon, a port half way up the west coast, and within a month had retaken Seoul and driven the North Koreans back to the line dividing North and South Korea at the 38th parallel. MacArthur's military success raised the question of America's political aims – whether to re-establish the *status quo* or to revise it by reunifying Korea?

The division of Korea had followed the pattern of Germany since 1945 – provisional partition following the removal of the Japanese wartime occupation forces, failure of the United States and the Soviet Union to agree on means of unification, and the establishment of separate governments in North and South. The initial UN resolution on the Korean War envisaged only the restoration of the 38th parallel, but the success of MacArthur's northward drive held out the inviting prospect of reunification by force of arms. Containment, it appeared, was giving way to 'roll-back' as Truman endorsed military operations north of the 38th parallel and gained UN approval for it. At this point the character of the war changed. Ignoring Chinese warnings that they would intervene if the Americans continued north towards the Korean border with China, MacArthur pushed further north, reaching the Yalu river by the end of October. As promised, and clearly against all the expectations of the Americans, the Chinese entered the war and by the end of the year had forced the UN forces into a headlong retreat down the peninsula to a point south of the 38th parallel.

Three considerations appear to have weighed with the Chinese in their decision to join the North Koreans. The first was simply the threat to Chinese security posed by the possibility of a reunified Korea under Western auspices on their border. Secondly, several thousand North Korean volunteers had fought with Mao's army in the civil war with the Chinese Nationalists, and support for Kim Il-sung in 1950 can be interpreted as recompense for this assistance. Finally, it has been suggested that Mao saw an opportunity to enhance Chinese influence in North Korea at the expense of the Soviet Union and to establish Chinese claims to Great Power status in the region (Halliday and Cumings 1988: 113). Doubtless the most important of these reasons was the first. From the beginning of the war China had been warning the United States, in public speeches and via the Indian Ambassador in Peking, that they could not accept the presence of hostile troops so close to their border. American indifference to these warnings and subsequent talk among some Americans of carrying the war beyond the Yalu river into China itself can only have increased Chinese anxieties. China does not seem to have been eager to enter the war, not least because it could not fight it without substantial military aid from the Soviet Union, thus increasing its dependence on its ally. This might tend to cast doubt on the view that Chinese entry was predicated on the aim of replacing Soviet influence in North Korea.

Truman's response to the Chinese entry was a combination of strident verbal aggression against China – including a hint that the United States reserved the option of using the atomic bomb – and a strategic retreat to the initial goal of restoring the 38th parallel. Truman's aggressive rhetoric aroused deep anxiety among America's UN allies. The British Prime Minister, Attlee, rushed to Washington in early December to express his dismay at the direction of American policy. In a series of conversations with Truman, Attlee urged him to open negotiations with Peking in order to avoid an all-out war with China. Though the Truman administration ceased making public atomic threats, Attlee failed to convince Truman and Acheson that a less belligerent policy towards China might cool the situation in Korea and also encourage a split between Peking and Moscow. The United States was now too committed to Chiang and to the view that accommodation to communism in one sphere meant capitulation everywhere to find Attlee's arguments acceptable.

In practice, however, Truman was as concerned as Attlee to avoid all-out war with China. Without conceding Attlee's point about the possible advantages for policy in Asia in general of negotiating with China, he acknowledged the narrower point about the danger of an all-out war. A serious obstacle in the way of this policy was General MacArthur, whose bellicose pronouncements and evident desire to extend the war into China became a serious embarrassment to Truman. Though it could be said that MacArthur was simply following through the logic of the decision to press forward north of the 38th parallel, after the Chinese entry the costs of that policy looked to Truman to be excessive. By April 1951, with MacArthur now back at the 38th parallel, eager to cross it once again onto the North, Truman ordered his recall. Containment was re-established as the reigning orthodoxy.

Having escaped one set of costs, however, by ruling out war with China, Truman then incurred another – the storm of protests within the United States which greeted his dismissal of MacArthur. At a time when Senator McCarthy's attacks on Truman were at their most strident, MacArthur returned to the United States as a conquering hero denied his booty, to be fêted by Congress and public opinion. Whether these protesters would really have welcomed a war with China is open to question. It was enough that MacArthur offered a sounding board for public frustration with the conduct of the war. As the front stabilized around the 38th parallel, military stalemate ensued, though at enormous cost in casualties. It was two years before negotiations, continually stalled over the issue of the return of prisoners of war, brought a conclusion to the conflict.

The political costs of the Korean War to Truman and his party were substantial. The military stalemate ensured that the presidential election of 1952 would be fought in part on the issue of the war. The Democrats suffered a severe defeat, both in the presidency and Congress, while the Republican candidate, Dwight Eisenhower, was able to exploit his great prestige as a military leader to advantage. Declaring during the election campaign that, if elected, 'I will go to Korea', he was able to convey the impression that his presence alone would ensure the ending of the conflict.

In fact, between Eisenhower's inauguration in January 1953 and the conclusion of the armistice in late July some of the bitterest fighting of the war took place. Manoeuvring by both sides, including desperate efforts by the South Korean leader,

Syngman Rhee, to obstruct the negotiations, stretched out the war. The conclusion of the armistice has often been attributed to the American threat, conveyed to the Chinese by the new Secretary of State, John Foster Dulles, via the Indian Prime Minister, that they would employ the atomic bomb unless the North Korean side was prepared to come to a peace agreement. Doubtless this threat played a role, though equally important was the death of Stalin in March 1953, which brought the more accommodating Malenkov to power. Discussions at Stalin's funeral among Chinese, Soviet, and North Korean leaders may have resulted in proposals which broke the deadlock on exchanges of prisoners of war. Increasing American pressure on Syngman Rhee also played its part, though in the event Rhee continued to do all he could to sabotage the negotiations and ultimately refused to sign the armistice agreement when it was concluded. This proved to be only one of a succession of instances in which 'pro-Western' leaders would exploit American anti-communism for their own ends, forcing the Americans to choose between becoming tied to political leaders of questionable value or bypassing them and assuming the direct commitment of containment themselves. In this case the United States assumed a massive direct commitment. The outcome in the long term was a kind of stability which bore a curious resemblance to the situation in Europe: a divided country, whose stability was guaranteed less by the character of the South Korean government than by the fact that the United States, the Soviet Union and China all had their own reasons for wanting the continuance of the *status quo*. The overriding reason was the perception that the attempt to change it would involve the possibility of a major war. We shall see in Chapter 10 why the same conditions did not obtain in Indo-China.

Understanding the policies and interests of the participants in this complex of events is not easy. Korea has been described as a 'limited war', an exemplary case of containment in action. But, as we have seen, it also illustrates the fine line in American policy between containment and rollback. The words used by Walter Lippmann to characterize Soviet intentions in the cold war seem to apply equally well to the United States in the case of Korea: 'They will expand the revolution, if the balance of power is such that they can; if it is such that they cannot, they will make the best settlement they can obtain for Russia and the regime in Russia' (Blum 1985: 505). The best the Americans could obtain in Korea was a return to the lines which existed in 1950. It was not in all respects, however, a return to the *status quo ante*, since it was associated with deepened commitment to holding the line in Asia generally. The geo-strategic and ideological assumptions which had led to the original formulation of containment in Europe were now firmly adopted in Asia. These included the 'domino theory' – that a loss of one country to communism would set up a chain reaction in its neighbours – and the belief that, by whatever devious route, all manifestations of communism were to be traced to the activities of the Kremlin.

There is, to be sure, evidence to suggest that some within the American administration were aware that the differences between Peking and Moscow might be exploited to America's advantage. Perhaps Mao could be considered a potential 'Asian Tito'. It has been argued that, contrary to the common view that American policy-makers considered the Soviet Union and China as a monolithic bloc, the Americans pursued a 'wedge through pressure' strategy with the aim of provoking a split between the two communist powers. Pressure on China, it is suggested, was exerted in order to push them into making demands on the Soviet Union for aid which the Soviets would be unwilling to satisfy (Gaddis 1987: 152–94; Foot 1985: 237–8). While this may have been the long-term aim, in the short term it is arguable that the strategy had the opposite effect. Moreover, within American public opinion, as opposed to government circles, it seems clear that the combination of the Sino–Soviet Treaty and Chinese entry into the war intensified the assumption of monolithic communism. In short, from the American point of view the Korean War had the effect of reinforcing the bipolar conception of the world already established in the antagonism with the Soviet Union in Europe.

The war also deepened American anxieties about the insidious and subversive character of communism. The evidence that considerable numbers of American prisoners of war had been 'brainwashed' by their communist captors provoked two sorts of reactions. One led to heightened fears of the devilish and inhumane nature of, in particular, Asian communists. The other led to much soul-searching about the shallowness of young Americans' adherence to their own value system. Americans seemed to lack the solidity of belief which would enable them to resist the pressures of interrogation. Either way, the effect was to screw American ideological fervour a notch higher. It was under Eisenhower's administration that the words 'under God' were added to the pledge of allegiance to the American flag, a ritual which children performed every morning at school assemblies. Finally, the still undecided issue of whether the United States used germ warfare in the Korean War and the evidence that maltreatment of prisoners took place on the American as well as the Sino–North Korean side muddied the moral waters surrounding this war which already, because of its equivocal military outcome, failed to conform to classic notions of military victory (Halliday and Cumings 1988: 174–86). The moral simplicities of the fight against Germany and Japan were not to be reproduced in this first major military conflict of the cold war, despite efforts to present it in this light. The Korean War produced few films and novels in the heroic mould. The film and subsequent television series *M.A.S.H.*, the major celluloid memorial to the Korean War, was made in the Vietnam era and made little reference to the realities of the war in Korea itself. Nor did returning veterans from Korea find that their compatriots showed much interest in their experience of the war. 'The war', Max Hastings has written, 'seemed an unsatisfactory, inglorious, and thus unwelcome memory' (Hastings 1988: 409). Furthermore, as we have already seen, the war proved disastrous for Truman and the Democratic Party. If the Korean War represented a victory for the West – and it could be presented as such, given the original intention of containing communism – it was nevertheless of a highly equivocal sort.

For the Soviet Union also the war had important negative effects. Not only did the North Korean attack invite a powerful Western response in Korea itself, but it cemented the American commitment to the security of Japan and of Taiwan. The three years of the war also provoked a decisive build-up of American forces in Europe and prepared the way for the rearmament of West Germany. The prospect of reopening bargaining with the United States on the as yet uncompleted Second World War settlements on Japan and Germany was thus further reduced. Nor could the Soviet Union be entirely happy with the enhanced prestige of the People's Republic of China (PRC). Despite enormous losses of people and resources, the outcome of the war strengthened the PRC's hand *vis à vis* the Soviet Union, enabling it to ask for fulfilment of the terms of the Sino–Soviet Treaty of 1950 – above all the withdrawal of Soviet forces from the naval base at Port Arthur (Low 1976: 66). The PRC's renewed self-confidence was manifested in a growing predisposition to act independently, both in exerting pressure on Taiwan and in seeking influence among underdeveloped countries. The Korean war, it has been said, was 'pivotal in undermining the relationship between Peking and Moscow', though it was several years before their differences developed into an open split (Foot 1985: 27).

If there were 'winners' in the Korean War they were the leaders of North Korea, South Korea, and Taiwan. The first two, albeit at enormous cost, and the last at virtually no cost, gained guarantees of their continued rule as a result of the interests of the Great Powers in maintaining the *status quo* (Halliday and Cumings 1988: 202–3). The Korean settlement proved surprisingly long-lasting. It outlived the end of the cold war in Europe, despite important changes along the way, including an as yet unfulfilled agreement, reached between North and South Korea in 1972, to seek reunification by peaceful means.

CONCLUSION

The extension of the cold war to Asia was, as in the case of Europe, a consequence of the shift in balance of power caused by the Second World War. It was a multi-layered process, involving fundamental changes both at the system level and the level of the nation-state. The vast expansion of Japanese power after 1940 cut a swathe through European colonialism, while the sudden demise of Japanese power in 1945 left three often contending forces in play: the superpowers, independence movements, and, not least, former colonial powers – pre-eminently Britain, France, and Holland – which sought either to re-establish colonial rule or to manage the road to independence in ways which safeguarded their interests.

Within this context the lines drawn in the Korean War were relatively clear when compared with, for example, Indo-China. Korea had been occupied by Japan from 1911 until 1945, with the consequence that its liberation did not involve the European powers directly. The conflict in Korea shaped up as an East–West confrontation and its resolution took the form which the cold war had taken in Europe, essentially of a spheres of influence arrangement. Geography played a large part in the superpowers' perceptions of their interests in Korea. 'When the Americans took over from the Japanese the burden of Japanese defense,' Louis Halle has written, 'they took over, as well, the conflicts which that defense involved.' That included Korea, which, because of its proximity to Japan on the one hand and to China on the other, 'had been for centuries . . . a strategic point of the utmost sensitivity' in the historic conflict between the two major Asian powers (Halle 1967: 192, 193).

The Soviet interest was less tangible, but, given its ideological alignment with China and its resentment at exclusion from Japan, the Soviet Union too had an interest in 'containing' Western power in Korea. In this sense Korea formed the front line of the cold war in Asia.

In those Asian nations which had previously been subject to European colonial rule, however, the pressures were different. Cutting across the East–West divide were, firstly, the efforts of the former colonial powers to reassert their influence, producing conflict within the Western camp, and, secondly, the presence of powerful independence movements which aspired to a measure of detachment from Great Power influence. In Asia, and more generally in what came to be known as the Third World, conflict was not wholly contained within the framework of the cold war, despite the ambitions of the superpowers. In many instances the 'enemy', as far as newly independent or would-be independent nations were concerned, was not one or another of the superpowers but the cold war system itself.

Part III

GLOBALISM AND THE LIMITS OF BIPOLARITY, 1953–1964

INTRODUCTION

Of all the phases of post-war US–Soviet relations the period from the mid-1950s to the mid-1960s is the least susceptible of easy categorization. One suggestion, that the period is characterized by 'oscillatory antagonism', has the merit that it captures the contrary motions of events and processes but it leaves us with the problem of understanding the dynamics which underlay them (Halliday 1983: 6). Unlike the formative period of cold war which preceded it and the shift towards *détente* which followed it, the Eisenhower/Kennedy–Khrushchev years do not obviously lend themselves to generalization.

Taken individually, for example, both Eisenhower and Khrushchev presented apparently contradictory faces to the world at different times and in different facets of their policies. Eisenhower the 'man of peace' and prophet of the dangers of the military–industrial complex also advocated a defence policy which gave a high profile to nuclear weapons. By the same token, while Eisenhower was cautious about intervening in situations which might lead to extensive US troop commitments overseas, he also presided over the development of the CIA into a routine instrument of foreign intervention by covert means.

Khrushchev's duality is quite as obvious. An advocate of 'peaceful coexistence', he also made dramatic and bellicose pronouncements about the irreconcilable nature of the conflict between East and West and took pride in parading Soviet achievements – such as its impressive economic growth rates in the mid-1950s and the launch of Sputnik – which seemed to suggest that the Soviet Union was capable of beating the West at its own game. Moreover, while Khrushchev announced to an astonished Party Congress in 1956 that Stalin had committed grave errors and that much of his legacy must be repudiated, later the same year he ordered Soviet troops into Hungary to suppress an uprising which was fuelled by his own de-Stalinization speech. In short, both leaders could be openly provocative and accommodating.

The character of US–Soviet relations as a whole during this period was decidedly mixed. Signs of *détente*, such as the conclusion of the long-delayed Austrian State Treaty in 1955, the Geneva summit of the same year (the first meeting of American and Soviet leaders since Potsdam in 1945), and the signing of the partial Test Ban

Treaty in 1963 vie with sharp crises over Berlin and Cuba and with the inexorable progress of the nuclear arms race. Nor did summitry imply the suspension of competition in the Third World, and indeed a salient feature of these years was the emergence of the Third World as a major theatre of superpower conflict.

Clearly something more is needed than a listing of discrete events and tendencies. To what extent in fact can one speak of these years as a defined period? While there is an element of arbitrariness in all attempts at periodization, certain marker points suggest themselves. Changes in the leadership of both powers lend a degree of continuity to the period. It opens with the inauguration of Eisenhower (January 1953) and the death of Stalin (March 1953) and closes with the removal of Khrushchev (October 1964) and the election of Johnson (November 1964). (Though of course Johnson had assumed the presidency in November 1963 on the assassination of Kennedy, his own personal mandate is most appropriately dated from the election of 1964.) Coinciding with these boundaries are the conclusion of the Korean War in 1953 and the beginning of the large-scale commitment of American ground troops to Vietnam as a result of decisions taken in 1964.

The justification for dividing the material up this way, however, also lies in the particular character of the superpower relationship during this period. The oscillatory motion of events already referred to marks a specific phase in the relationship in which areas of relative stability, such as broad acceptance of the division of Europe, coexisted with areas of profound instability, pre-eminently competition in nuclear arms and in the Third World. Cold war competition became more intensive as a technological and political dynamic drove both superpowers to seek ever-greater security through the development of nuclear weapons, but it also became more extensive as the arena of competition expanded to the 'periphery' of the international system. A feedback loop operated to redirect the tensions generated at the periphery back to the centre. The resulting increase in the potential for crisis also, however, produced pressure for crisis management and control. Hence the efforts to reach solutions across the board of the superpower agenda via negotiation.

More concretely, we can identify three areas of superpower competition, each of which is treated in turn in the following three chapters. The first is the central ideological conflict, focusing on Europe and on the process of summitry initiated by the Geneva conference of 1955. On both sides of the divide the continued leadership of the United States and the Soviet Union was combined with a growing diversity within them. 'Polycentrism' within the communist bloc and, with less dramatic consequences, the economic revival of Europe and the formation of the EEC produced pressures which cut across the bipolar cold war system without, however, effectively dislodging it.

In the second area – nuclear weaponry and strategic doctrine – bipolarity continued to dominate, despite the acquisition by Britain and France of limited nuclear capabilities. The decade from 1953 to 1963 (when the partial Test Ban Treaty was signed) was one of extraordinary anxiety about nuclear war, matched only in the post-war period by the early 1980s. If by the end of the period both superpowers had concluded that avoidance of nuclear war was their paramount priority, there was no let up in the arms race. The Soviet Union's awareness of its nuclear inferiority, clearly exposed in the missile crisis, was the spur to a massive arms build-up in the following years which by 1969 had created the necessary conditions for comprehensive arms negotiations – rough Soviet parity with the United States. This process, in combination with other developments, laid the groundwork for *détente* and is best considered in conjunction with *détente* itself in Part IV.

The third area of contention – the Third World – was less amenable to direct superpower control, the chief stimulus arising from de-colonization and the attempt of new nations to establish forms of neutrality with respect to the superpower blocs. Though this effort was only partially successful, weakness could on occasions become strength, given the capacity of Third World nations to play on the superpowers' anxieties about each other's ambitions. Here, as in the other issues under consideration in Part III, there proved to be limits to superpower dominance of the international system. If we cannot speak of a multipolar world, the lineaments of multipolarity were becoming visible. Nowhere were the changes in the international system more apparent than in economics, and for this reason Chapter 6 opens with a discussion of this issue.

6

PEACEFUL COEXISTENCE AND IRRECONCILABLE CONFLICT, 1953–1964

THE ECONOMICS OF SUPERPOWER STATUS

During the 1950s the global economy not only recovered from the crises of the 1930s and the Second World War but embarked on a period of sustained growth. World industrial production came close to doubling between 1953 and 1963, a performance which was repeated in the following decade. Equally important, until the early 1970s annual growth rates actually increased as the global economy grew – an indication of impressive levels of production, productivity, and consumption. Of course, growth was unevenly distributed, but even the so-called LDCs (less developed countries) shared to some extent in the economic boom (Kennedy 1988: 413–16).

What of the performance of the United States and the Soviet Union, relative to each other and to other nations? The answer to this question is important because both powers, despite the heavy emphasis on moral values in the public statements of both leaderships, also subscribed in their different ways to materialist views of history. Waging the cold war demanded high levels of production and productivity if a balance was to be struck between 'guns and butter'. In one sense the problem was greater for the United States than for the Soviet Union, since in a time of peace, as compared with the Soviet Union, there were political limits to America's capacity to divert production from civilian consumption to military uses, a point noted in a Rockefeller Fund report published in 1958: 'although the rate of growth of these countries [the communist bloc] may slow down, the economic superiority of the West will become less and less significant militarily at our present levels of effort. By sacrificing the civilian sector of its economy, the Soviet Union has caught up with the United States in major fields of technology' (Rockefeller 1958: 16).

This statement indicates why the United States could not be content with raw statistics which told a story of impressive Western growth. In any case, while the figures were indeed striking, they also showed that other parts of the West were growing faster than the United States. In absolute terms United States GNP grew (in constant 1958 dollars) from $355.3 billion in 1950 to $487.7 billion in 1960, representing an average annual growth rate of 3.2 per cent. During the same

114

period, however, Japan's annual growth rate was 9.5 per cent and West Germany's 7.8 per cent (Roskamp 1977: 58; Van der Wee 1987: 50). Just as telling was the decline in America's share of world GNP, from a high of around 50 per cent in 1945 to 25.9 per cent in 1960 (Kennedy 1988: 432). Clearly America's relative decline was to be expected as the shattered economies of Europe and Japan recovered from the war, and it was not yet apparent how substantial Japanese and West European competition would prove to be. The United States economy remained by a considerable margin the world's largest, and despite periodic minor recessions in the 1950s and early 1960s, the pattern of growth was sustained at even higher levels in the 1960s until 1968.

An important structural change was taking place, however. While American exports of capital and goods rose markedly, so also did imports, producing for the first time in its history a balance of payments problem. The United States, wrote a prominent contemporary economist, was becoming 'daily more dependent upon the outside world – in particular upon the raw-material producing countries'. Economic self-interest, no less than political prudence, demanded that the United States increase exports, and this could only be achieved by promoting 'the rapid economic growth – and especially the rapid industrial growth – of the raw-material producing countries' (Drucker [1956] 1971: 557, 561). Economic isolation was at an end or, as later analysts would have it, interdependence was becoming a fact of life.

Whatever qualms American policy-makers may have had about these developments, they were dwarfed by concern about the Soviet Union. Thriving capitalist economies after all meant markets for American goods and expanded possibilities for trade. Thriving communist economies, and the sovietization of new regions, offered no benefits to the United States and a potential contraction of the area of world free trade. The fact that the Soviet economy had serious problems which were not exposed in a reading of the gross statistics was less important than the perception that the Soviet Union was an expanding economic power and hence an expanding political and military threat. While there are doubts among Western observers about the validity of Soviet economic statistics (Nove 1970: Appendix), nominally Soviet GNP grew at an annual rate of 6.7 per cent between 1953 and 1958, exceeding the rates of all but Germany and Japan, slowing to 5.2 per cent between 1958 to 1965 (Munting 1982: 132, 137). Hidden behind these figures were slow rates of technological innovation and development of new products, combined with inefficiency in production, and above all a disproportionate growth of heavy industry as compared to consumer goods (Munting 1982: 133). On the other hand, the Soviet Union was devoting an estimated 20–23 per cent of national income to investment, compared to the United States' 12–13 per cent (Mosely 1960: 416) and in the military and aerospace fields at least showed itself capable of striking advances, as manifested in the launch of Sputnik in 1957. The American perception was of an increasing momentum in Soviet economic growth, as indeed was to some extent the case.

A worried Eisenhower wrote to his Secretary of State, John Foster Dulles, in December 1955 that the Soviets had apparently abandoned the Stalinist tactic of

115

using force to achieve their objectives and had turned instead to economics, so that 'it would appear that we are being challenged in the area of our greatest strength' (Ambrose 1984: 283). Six years later, in his famous speech to the 22nd Party Congress of the Soviet Union, Khrushchev invoked Lenin's formula, 'communism is Soviet power plus electrification', and went on to predict that 'in the current decade (1961–70) the Soviet Union, in creating the material and technical basis of communism, will surpass the strongest and richest capitalist country, the USA, in production per head of population' (Daniels 1985, Vol. 1: 339).

Given our knowledge of the stagnation of Soviet growth in the 1970s and 1980s, and its catastrophic decline in the 1990s, it takes an effort of imagination to reconstruct the circumstances of the 1950s, during which communism appeared as a genuine competitor to Western capitalism. The communist bloc did not at that time seem to suffer unduly from its virtual detachment from the global capitalist system. On the contrary, the Soviet bloc's capacity to generate its own economic dynamic rendered it immune from Western economic pressure.

American policy under Truman and Eisenhower in fact tended to reinforce the separation of the two systems. A sequence of presidential initiatives, culminating in the passage in 1951 of the Mutual Defence Assistance Control Act (popularly known as the Battle Act), not only denied the Soviet bloc strategic materials but required the President to 'terminate aid to countries that exported goods to communist states of a kind embargoed by the United States'. Moderate liberalization of this policy during the Eisenhower administration under pressure from Britain, which was less inclined to employ economic warfare for ideological purposes, left the essentials of the embargo system in place. Even Kennedy, who favoured a more liberal policy, initially found Congress firmly opposed to any easing of the highly restrictive terms of the legislation, not surprising in the light of the sharp downturn in US–Soviet relations in 1961 following the unsuccessful American-backed attempt to unseat Fidel Castro in the Bay of Pigs invasion. Only after the successful conclusion of the Cuban missile crisis and the signing of the Test Ban Treaty was Kennedy sufficiently secure to challenge Congressional conservatives and mount a relaxation of the strategic embargo policy. The immediate outcome was an agreement to sell wheat to the Soviet Union, heralding a significant shift in the overall framework of US–Soviet economic relations. While exports to the Soviet Union did not increase dramatically, there was, as Alan Dobson has put it, a 'widespread realization . . . that the US embargo policy was harming the United States more than the Soviet Union'. From then until the late 1970s, Dobson concludes, 'emphasis within the executive shifted away from having to justify taking items off the embargo list to justifying keeping items on it' (Dobson 1988: 601, 603–5, 613–14, 615).

That growing element of interdependence lay in the future. Meanwhile, in the mid-1950s the superpowers were like two boxers sizing each other up and engaging in those pre-fight verbal slanging matches which are designed to convince the public as well as each other of their strength and will to compete. Of the two powers the Soviet

Union had the greatest difficulties to surmount. Prior to the death of Stalin in March 1953 the Soviet Union had experienced only one change of leadership – Stalin's assumption of power after Lenin's death – and that had proved messy and drawn-out. It had taken four years (1924–28) for Stalin to acquire undisputed power, but in the succeeding years he had stamped his imprint on every aspect of Soviet life. 'Stalinism' was more than a name for Stalin's personal rule. It represented the form which communist ideology had assumed as a result of his personal leadership. His death therefore raised the question of the continuity of communist ideology within the Soviet Union and the cohesion of the international communist movement itself. De-Stalinization was to prove as momentous as the process of Stalinization had done.

DE-STALINIZATION AND INTERNATIONAL COMMUNISM, 1953–1964

Between 1947, when the Cominform was established, and 1953, Eastern Europe, with the exception of Yugoslavia, had undergone a thorough process of Stalinization. Stalin's death threw the issue of his management of the Soviet external and internal empire into the melting pot. Though it was three years before Khrushchev's momentous attack on Stalinism and the cult of personality at the Twentieth Party Congress of 1956, cracks within the Stalinist edifice were apparent from the moment the new leadership took power. They emerged in the jockeying for position within the new leadership, a process which over a period of two years eventually found Khrushchev as the dominant figure, owing in large part to his tight control over the Communist Party. Even then it was not until 1957 with his defeat of the 'anti-Party' group that his domestic position was relatively secure. Casualties along the way included Lavrenti Beria, head of the Interior Ministry and hence responsible for the NKVD (predecessor of the KGB or security police). His peremptory removal and execution in July 1953 signalled a turning away from Stalinist repression and it provoked 'a flood of demands for the rehabilitation of prisoners and victims of Stalin's campaigns of terror' (Medvedev 1982: 67).

The sidelining of Georgi Malenkov, who as Chairman of the Council of Ministers (or Prime Minister) initially appeared to be Stalin's chief successor, was a more complex affair. Malenkov was tainted by his close friendship with Beria, but more importantly, as far as Khrushchev was concerned, Malenkov was the leading advocate of the so-called 'New Course' of economic reform which proposed a shift of emphasis from heavy industry towards production of consumer goods. Khrushchev's problem was not with the policy itself but with Malenkov's leadership of it. Khrushchev's tactic, cutting a long and devious story to its bare essentials, was initially to oppose the New Course, use his leverage over the Party to exalt its power and purify its ranks, engineer the removal of Malenkov, and subsequently adopt many of his policies (Crankshaw 1966: 192–7).

By the early months of 1955 the outlines of Khrushchev's new agenda were becoming plain. His policies involved controlled political and economic liberalization, coupled with the extension of these benefits to the People's Democracies. Not that they were always perceived as benefits by the Eastern bloc leaderships. After all, most of them owed their positions and their allegiance to Stalinism and found that the new policies undercut their own power by promoting internal dissent (Fejtö 1974: 33). In any event, a pattern was emerging in the People's Democracies featuring the nominal institution of the separation of government power from Party power (the chief plank of the call for collective leadership and the ending of the cult of personality), an economic shift from heavy industry to consumer goods, and the rehabilitation of former opponents of Stalinism. Moscow's economic controls were also eased with the winding up of the hated Soviet-controlled joint-stock companies, devised to integrate the Soviet and East European economies.

The Soviet Union was treading a fine line. Going too far and too fast in this direction risked destabilizing East European regimes and severing Moscow's bonds with the People's Democracies. Not to follow through on the course already set in Moscow risked inviting explosions of frustration which would have the same destabilizing effect. The problem was compounded by the fact that conditions in the Eastern bloc nations varied considerably. The liberalizing trend was much more firmly rooted in Poland and Hungary than, for example, in Bulgaria or Albania. No single formula could be applied to all. Crises in the Eastern bloc thus appeared in succession and, despite the generally consistent aim of balancing change against the need for continuity of the Soviet system, the crises were resolved in a piecemeal fashion.

The potentially contradictory nature of Moscow's priorities surfaced first in its policies towards East Germany and Yugoslavia. East Germany's critical location on the geopolitical front line of the cold war left little scope for toleration of dissent from the centre. A workers' uprising in Berlin in 1953 against the repressive Ulbricht regime was crushed by Soviet tanks, albeit with Moscow's insistence that henceforth Ulbricht should 'follow the new course and acknowledge his mistakes through self-criticism' (Fejtö 1974: 37). Yugoslavia presented the opposite case of an independent centre of communist power whose allegiance could be won only by efforts at conciliation. Khrushchev personally undertook the rehabilitation of Tito on a visit to Belgrade in 1955. It took place during a thaw in the cold war between the Soviet Union and the United States, and was sandwiched between the signing of the Austrian State Treaty and the opening of the Great Power summit conference in Geneva. In a speech on his arrival in Belgrade Khrushchev ascribed the regrettable split of 1948 to the machinations of Beria and 'other exposed enemies of the people' (Daniels 1985, Vol. 2: 223).

However, while each side had an interest in repairing the split, each also wanted things which the other party could not give. The Soviet Union, with one eye on the People's Republic of China, was concerned to reassert the leading role of the Soviet Union and the essential indivisibility of the communist ideological bloc, albeit with the recognition that rigid Stalinist control was no longer viable over states which had already achieved a measure of independence.

For his part, Tito firmly insisted that he could not subscribe to the Soviet concept of a communist ideological bloc. 'The partition of the world into ideological blocs', the Yugoslav Party newspaper editorialized during Khrushchev's visit, was 'not the path that leads to peace.' Behind this statement, Richard Lowenthal notes, lay a dispute between Yugoslavia and the Soviet Union on the meaning of 'co-existence' with non-communist powers: between the Soviet concept of 'co-existence in the sense of some temporary truce between hostile blocs, created by an ideological division' and the Yugoslav concept of 'active co-existence' or 'the active co-operation of all countries regardless of differences in their internal systems' (Lowenthal 1964: 15). With differences such as these there could be no real meeting of minds, and indeed the truce lasted a bare two years. In the interim, however, Khrushchev's 'secret' speech to the Twentieth Party Congress in February 1956 sent a shock wave through Eastern Europe. It served to foster diversity within the bloc – or 'polycentrism' as it came to be called – without, however, defining clearly where its limits might lie.

Khrushchev's speech was chiefly designed to consolidate his own reformist position within the Soviet leadership and to discredit the residual Stalinist elements, represented above all by Molotov, Minister for Foreign Affairs. The speech involved considerable risks. Khrushchev after all was deeply implicated in Stalinism, having risen up through the Party ranks through the period of the purges in the 1930s. There was also the danger that excessive zeal in uncorking the bottle of Stalinism might expose the emptiness of the Soviet system itself.

His strategy was twofold. He would firstly personalize his attack on Stalinism, ascribing the violence, illegality, and repressiveness of the Stalinist regime to Stalin's 'cult of personality'. This in itself was shocking enough to his immediate audience and to the wider communist world once the content of the speech was made known. Stalin, he said, had originated the concept of the 'enemy of the people' and used it as a device to engage in 'the most cruel repression, violating all norms of revolutionary legality', and consigning thousands of loyal Party members to imprisonment or execution. He had criminally decimated the officer corps of the Red Army through the purges, leaving the Soviet Union fatally weakened in the face of the German invasion of June 1941. The poor state of Soviet agriculture, the split with Tito, and numerous other errors in Soviet domestic and foreign policy were all laid at Stalin's door. The recitation of detail was so relentless, the tone so impassioned, that it was perhaps not immediately apparent how carefully circumscribed the charges were. Nothing was said about the collectivization of agriculture between 1928 and 1933 and the elimination of the Kulaks (rich peasants) which this involved. Nor, despite throwing a floodlight on the purge of Party members and old Bolsheviks during the 1930s, did Khrushchev address the wider issue of the terrorization of ordinary Soviet people.

Given the risks to his own position and the danger of discrediting the Soviet system itself, it is not surprising that Khrushchev should have set limits to his exposure of

Stalinism (Medvedev 1982: 88–9). He had done enough in any case to send a shiver through communist nations and communist parties around the world. His task was to balance his attack on Stalinism with a restoration of the legitimacy of Marxism–Leninism in a purified, non-Stalinist form. Hence the second element of his strategy, one followed several decades later by Mikhail Gorbachev during the first years of his rule: the recourse to Leninism as the true fount of Soviet communism. 'It is necessary', Khrushchev announced, 'to restore completely the Leninist principles of Soviet socialist democracy, expressed in the Constitution of the Soviet Union, to fight willfulness of individuals abusing their power' (Daniels 1985, Vol. 1: 323, 327).

The repercussions of Khrushchev's speech were felt within a short time throughout the Eastern bloc, but particularly in Poland and Hungary. The constellation of competing forces in both countries was similar, though the outcomes were very different. Three elements were in contention: a Stalinist leadership, liberal opposition leaders who had been rehabilitated since Khrushchev's February speech, and popular workers and student movements supported by prominent intellectuals. Initially also, the pattern of events in both countries showed significant parallels. Public demonstrations, bloodily put down by troops, were followed by pressure on the Stalinist leaderships to stand down. In the Polish case, however, the new 'liberal' leader, Wladislav Gomulka, was able to maintain control of the popular movement and avoid military intervention by the Soviet Union, if only by the skin of his teeth. In part this was because Gomulka had a firmer base of support in the Party and the factories than was the case with his Hungarian counterpart, Imre Nagy (Fejtö 1974: 95). It was in part also because Gomulka showed no signs of wanting to go as far as the new Hungarian leadership in disassociating his country from the Soviet Union. Nor was it realistic for Poland to seek separation, given the extent to which the post-war border changes had left it beholden to the Soviet Union for its security. Finally, as the crisis in Poland resolved itself in late October 1956, Soviet troops were crushing the rebellion in Budapest and demonstrating what Poland's own fate would be, should the Polish leadership fail to control the popular movement.

Nagy's fate was to be installed in power in Hungary at a time when the momentum of the uprising was reaching its peak and when the Communist Party itself was the chief target of the rebels. Within days of Nagy's appointment as Prime Minister on 23 October, after attempting to hold out against the more extreme demands of the rebels, he yielded to the revolutionary momentum, announcing the establishment of a multi-party system, withdrawal from the Warsaw Pact (created only the year before), and complete Hungarian independence and neutrality. The sequel was inevitable. On 4 November the Soviet tanks moved in. 'Separate paths to socialism' was never meant to sanction rank defection. Even the Chinese, who had supported Nagy prior to the announcement of his full de-sovietization plans, balked at the idea of a parliamentary-style 'neutral' Hungary. Austrian neutrality, established only the previous year, showed that this could only mean an orientation towards the West. More surprising perhaps was Tito's initial endorsement of Soviet intervention, which Khrushchev had been particularly anxious to gain. The reopening of the Soviet–Yugoslav split arose not out of the Soviet action itself, but from the subsequent Soviet treatment of Nagy. Having sought refuge in the Yugoslav Embassy in Budapest, Nagy was then snatched by Soviet agents as he was being driven to the airport for a flight to Belgrade. Over Yugoslav protests Nagy was brought to trial and shot. 'The whole deplorable episode', writes Roy Medvedev, 'led to a worsening of relations between the Soviet Union and Yugoslavia' (Medvedev 1982: 109).

The fruits of these events in Poland and Hungary were somewhat paradoxical. Having established the outer limits of polycentrism for these nations, and by implication for others inclined to enter on the same course, Poland and Hungary were permitted, indeed encouraged, to develop the most liberal economic and political systems of all those in Eastern Europe. As François Fejtö points out, in Hungary 'it became evident that Stalinist methods of repression had been used, not to restore Stalinism, but to institute a Khrushchevist regime similar to Gomulka's' (Fejtö 1974: 122–3). The most oppressive Eastern European regimes remained those, such as Albania, Romania, Bulgaria, and Czechoslovakia, which were in least need of the hand of Soviet oppression. This did not prove to be an unmixed blessing for the Soviet Union. While Bulgaria remained for historical reasons the staunchest of Moscow's allies, in Czechoslovakia de-Stalinization proved only to have been delayed rather than comprehensively checked, as the events of 1968 would prove. Albania and Romania, on the other hand, were able to exploit the split between the Soviet Union and the PRC which developed after 1957 to manoeuvre themselves into more independent positions with respect to Moscow. From the time of Khrushchev's 1956 speech until his removal from the Kremlin in 1964 relations with Communist China were never far from the top of his political agenda.

In retrospect it seems incredible that it was believed two nations with such different histories, cultures, and geopolitical interests as China and the Soviet Union could be anything but rivals. Hindsight, however, must yield at least provisionally to an understanding of contemporary perceptions and aspirations if the story of the split is to be comprehended. From the Western, and particularly the American point of view, any suggestion that it might be possible to drive a wedge between the two communist powers confronted the reality that they aspired to unity within the international communist movement and that they had signed a mutual security treaty at a critical moment when the West was still struggling to absorb the implications of the Chinese Revolution. As the split developed in the late 1950s and even as it went public in the early 1960s, it was regarded by most except academic specialists as 'noises off', a sideshow to the centre-stage drama of East–West conflict.

It is a mistake to view the split as purely ideological but it is equally erroneous to regard it simply as the result of clashing national and geopolitical interests. These elements were inseparable. The ideological intensity of their struggle from the late 1950s onwards certainly bore the marks of a theological dispute, each side regarding the other's version of Marxist-Leninism as heretical. On the other hand, differences of perspective on pragmatic policy issues were evident, as we saw in Chapter 5, as early as the Korean War. These increased as the People's Republic of China consolidated its revolution and aspired to its own role within world communism. Indeed, ideology and national interest were both present in the ambition of each 'to be the leader, to wield the greatest influence, if not actually to dominate world Communism' (Low 1976: 25).

If there was one issue which brought into focus the differences between the two nations, it was the campaign which Mao Zedong began to mount in 1958 against Soviet 'revisionism' – in essence everything associated with de-Stalinization within the Soviet Union and peaceful coexistence abroad. Mao's campaign represented a sudden turn from his earlier 'let a hundred flowers blossom' movement which had been broadly in line with Soviet liberalization. The shift occurred initially for domestic reasons, chiefly because of the growth of discontent within the Party and the country at agricultural collectivization, discontent which his 'hundred flowers' policy had allowed to flourish (Deutscher 1970: 144–9). The 'Great Leap Forward' of 1958 was designed both to restore Mao's control of the Party and to institute a new form of agricultural organization based on the commune, a system of regimentation which went beyond anything contemplated even by Stalinist collectivization. More importantly, Mao's new course involved a doctrinal departure from the orthodox Soviet interpretation of Marxist-Leninism. Mao claimed that China could bypass the intermediate stage of socialism on the road to communism and move directly to communism itself. Moreover, as Klaus Mehnert observed in one of the first extended analyses of the Sino–Soviet split, 'with the "Great Leap Forward" Peking was at last to make up for the bitter experiences of the recent past, during which it had to be content to play second fiddle in the Communist bloc and to be a grateful pupil of the complacent Russians' (Mehnert 1964: 384).

During the next four years this explosion at the core of communist doctrine spread out in waves until by the end of 1962 the crust of the international communist movement itself was effectively broken. The process took place largely in Communist Party Congresses and bilateral Soviet–Chinese meetings, only fragments of which were visible to the outside world. Furthermore for much of this time it was carried on in code, neither side wanting to provoke an irrevocable separation. While Khrushchev fulminated against 'dogmatism' (code for Mao's failure to recognize changing realities), Mao attacked 'revisionism' (code for Khrushchev's betrayal of revolutionary Marxist-Leninism). Both sides chose to deflect their attacks by directing them onto third parties: Mao onto Tito and Titoism and Khrushchev onto Albania, which by 1960 was detaching itself from the Eastern bloc and moving towards China (Crankshaw 1963: 66–7).

On international policy there was a steady drift away from the ringing statements of unity in the 'Moscow Declaration' of 1957 which had asserted that the struggle for peace was the 'foremost task' of the communist parties (Daniels 1985, Vol. 2: 249). Within a short time Mao regarded Khrushchev's peaceful coexistence and summitry with the United States as the appeasement of imperialism. Indeed, according to one historian, at the root of the Sino-Soviet split was Mao's fear 'of a Soviet–American accommodation at [China's] expense' (Zagoriu 1967: 21–2). The Soviet Union's refusal to help China develop its own nuclear weapons was a particular bone of contention, as was, from Khrushchev's point of view, Mao's increasing tendency to adopt positions on key international issues which were at variance with those of the Soviet Union. Among these was Mao's rejection of Khrushchev's sudden shift in 1959 towards support for De Gaulle's solution for ending the Algerian War; another was Mao's attack on Moscow's backing for Nehru in India's dispute with Tibet, a conflict in which China had a direct interest of its own. More generally, China was consistently promoting communist militancy in the Third World at a time when the Soviet Union was content to back 'bourgeois' leaders so long as they espoused neutrality in the cold war (Crankshaw 1963: 91, 126–7; Deutscher 1970: 263). In short, both on the central issue of relations with the West and in Third World conflicts China presented an open challenge to Soviet leadership of the international communist movement. Despite periodic efforts at accommodation, by early 1963 both sides were openly acknowledging the split, each claiming to be the true heir of Marx and Lenin (Crankshaw 1963: 136–7). If the implications of this earthquake in international communism were largely unappreciated in the West, the reason must lie in the tenacity of its conviction that communism was one thing wherever and whenever it appeared.

THE EISENHOWER ADMINISTRATION AND THE NEW SOVIET LEADERSHIP

It is only one of the many ironies in the story of US–Soviet relations that the post-Stalin liberalization in the Eastern bloc should occur at a time when the new leadership in the United States was embarking on a more aggressive cold war stance. Eisenhower's vocal and determined Secretary of State, John Foster Dulles, indicated at the outset of the new administration that he had serious reservations about the containment policy he had inherited from Truman. In his Senate confirmation hearing as Secretary of State he spoke of the need for the 'liberation of these captive peoples' of Eastern Europe. A year later he introduced the concept of 'massive retaliation' as a means of deterring potential aggressors. 'The way to deter aggression', he said, 'is for the free community to be willing and able to respond vigorously at places and with means of its own choosing.' Both these priorities, which constituted the main planks of the so-called 'New Look' policy of the Eisenhower administration, were premised upon a dissatisfaction with the supposed negativity and passivism of Truman's containment. Containment held out no hope for rolling back communism or creating peace: 'we shall never have a secure peace or a happy world so long as Soviet communism dominates one-third of all the peoples that there are'. Nor did containment enable the West to seize the initiative in the cold war so long it meant 'in the main emergency action, imposed on us by our enemies' (Smith 1964: 648, 650, 651).

Taken at face value, the New Look represented a radical break with the Truman years. As we shall see in Chapter 7, there are some grounds for accepting this view in relation to nuclear policy, though even here there are strong elements of continuity. In the area of US relations with the communist world, despite Dulles's rhetorical flourishes, liberation proved impossible to implement. As the tanks rolled into Budapest, the United States voiced loud protests but did nothing beyond accepting thousands of Hungarian refugees. Whatever modifications it underwent, containment remained the cornerstone of US policy.

If, as has recently been suggested, 1953 represented a 'lost opportunity' to end the cold war, why was it not seized (Bialer and Mandelbaum 1988: 41ff.)? Firstly, as was the case some three decades later on Gorbachev's assumption of power, there was much American scepticism about the capacity and the willingness of the Soviet leopard to change its spots. Furthermore, the new leadership was largely an unknown quantity, and what was known was hardly encouraging. Molotov, Stalin's closest associate during the period of the sovietization of Eastern Europe, remained in his post as Foreign Minister. Early events, such as the suppression of the uprising in East Berlin within a few months of Stalin's death, also invited doubts about the liberal character of the new regime.

A second set of factors arose from domestic issues within the United States. Electoral politics in 1952 dictated that the Republican Party distance itself from the Democrats' foreign policy agenda. Besides, the Congressional elections returned Republican majorities in both houses in 1952, offering the chance, so it appeared to some Republican leaders, to reverse the West's 'losses' in the cold war. An indication of the thinking of the Republican Old Guard is provided by its efforts during Eisenhower's first month in office to push a resolution through Congress repudiating the Yalta agreement and following it up with action to free the peoples of Eastern Europe. Eisenhower resisted this move, since he felt it would tie his hands in negotiations with the Soviets and incline them to block settlements on outstanding problems such as Austrian neutrality and the German question. In the event the resolution died with Stalin, but it was a foretaste of the struggles which Eisenhower would have with Congressional conservatives, Democrat as well as Republican, throughout his period of office (Ambrose 1984: 65–7). Like Khrushchev, Eisenhower had to keep looking over his shoulder as he planned his foreign policy moves.

The third constraint on American policy-makers was built in to the mind-set which they brought to relations with the Soviet Union. Perceptions of the global ideological conflict born in the first phase of the cold war could not be discarded at the drop of a hat. Psychologists have established the powerful resistance which an *idée fixe* can offer to empirical changes in the real world. The result is what might be called 'ideological lag': a delay in response time to changes which might tend to disprove the postulates of the established mind-set. The point, of course, is equally applicable to Soviet policy-makers. In their case they were presented in Dulles's rhetoric with what they could only view as confirmation of their perception of American aggression.

The final point to be considered is the overarching structural or systemic condition of cold war rivalry. If anything, given its economic growth and nuclear weapons development, the Soviet Union was a more potent rival of the United States in the mid-1950s than it had been in 1945. The addition of China to the communist bloc in 1949 weighed heavily in the scales of the cold war, particularly since, in the light of ideological lag, the United States was slow to see the developing Sino–Soviet split and to recognize its implications. During the 1950s and early 1960s, it could be said, the cold war became institutionalized in the form of the geopolitical division of Europe, the alliance systems, the arms race, and habits of mind which extended out from these central points to the whole globe.

None of these factors meant that there was no scope for change in US–Soviet relations. Any tendency to stasis or equilibrium was always liable to be upset by the movement of events, and within the limits set by continuities in the system individual policies and policy-makers could make a difference. Khrushchev's volatile personality, in combination with his obvious commitment to breaking the Stalinist mould in domestic and foreign policy, was undoubtedly a factor in achieving such accommodations with the United States as were arrived at during this period. But Khrushchev's brashness also gave rise to moments of serious crisis. On the American side Dulles's Wilsonian moralism and tendency to extreme statement was tempered by Eisenhower's generally more pragmatic style, though he, like Khrushchev, was also capable of the politics of grand gesture. Moreover, as recent scholarship on Eisenhower has shown, despite appearances Eisenhower maintained a firm hand over foreign policy and was in his way as confirmed a cold warrior as his publicly more forceful Secretary of State (Greenstein 1982: 89; Ambrose 1984: 442; Rabe 1988: 174).

TOWARDS THE GENEVA SUMMIT

The convening of the Geneva summit of July 1955 was testimony less to the sudden emergence of a spirit of conciliation than to a certain logic of events. The events contained both positive and negative elements, but all seemed to indicate the need for a high-level acknowledgement that in important respects the climate of the cold war had changed.

Three developments are important in understanding the background to the summit. The first was the growth since Stalin's death of a new and more flexible Soviet approach to diplomacy, which had repercussions in Asia and Africa as well as in Europe. In line with de-Stalinization at home Khrushchev launched a three-pronged foreign policy offensive based on 'peaceful coexistence', the abandonment of the idea of the inevitability of war with capitalism, and the promotion of revolution in the Third World through peaceful means, all of which indicated, as Robert Tucker suggests, 'the tremendous emphasis upon the function of persuasion' rather than force in the new diplomacy (Tucker 1972: 238).

In Asia, Soviet pressure on North Korea had been an influence on the conclusion of the armistice in July 1953, and at the Geneva Conference on Indo-China in 1954 once again Soviet (and Chinese) pressure had been instrumental in producing agreements which, if only temporarily, brought an end to the fighting in Vietnam. In Europe the fruits of the new diplomacy were manifested in Soviet agreement in May 1955 to the ending of the Four-Power occupation of Austria and its establishment as a neutral, independent state. The breaking of the diplomatic log-jam over Austria which, as Townsend Hoopes has written, 'had been an explicit American test of Russian good intentions for several years', cleared a large obstacle in the way of a summit meeting (Hoopes 1974: 293).

The second major development bearing on the Geneva summit was the growing cohesion of the communist bloc, short-lived as it proved to be. In a striking departure from Stalin's reluctance to leave Soviet soil, Khrushchev made a visit to China in September 1954 during which he returned Port Arthur and the Chinese Eastern Railway to the People's Republic, and negotiated an agreement to supply China with large quantities of capital goods. In May 1955 he made his fence-mending visit to Belgrade. In short, by mid-1955 the communist bloc appeared united and buoyant. Khrushchev, furthermore, having seen off Malenkov earlier in the year and consolidated his position within the leadership, felt secure enough to embark on a major diplomatic move. The Americans for their part had an interest in establishing precisely who was in control in the Soviet Union and in testing the extent of the Soviet commitment to a resolution of US–Soviet differences. At the summit itself Eisenhower made it his business to probe into these issues, and he satisfied himself that indeed Khrushchev was pulling the policy strings and that he was seriously interested in moving closer to the United States (Ambrose 1984: 262–6).

The third and perhaps overriding set of considerations affecting the summit were the related issues of the nuclear arms race and security in Europe. The race to produce the hydrogen or thermo-nuclear bomb had followed swiftly on the Soviet atom test of August 1949. According to recent statements by Soviet scientists, they won the thermo-nuclear race, achieving a hydrogen bomb test in August 1953 ahead of the Americans. The American thermo-nuclear explosion conducted in 1952, it is pointed out, was only a 'device', not a true bomb (Khariton and Smirnov 1993: 29). In any event the prospect was of a spiralling arms race and strategic deadlock.

In such circumstances peace was hardly a luxury but an urgent necessity. Besides their genuine and almost visceral distaste for the destructive power of nuclear weapons, both Eisenhower and Khrushchev had economic reasons for wanting to check the arms race. Eisenhower, a convinced budget balancer, fought a continuous battle with the Defense Department and the Joint Chiefs of Staff to limit defence spending. In this he largely succeeded, though ironically at the price of heavy reliance on nuclear weapons. Nuclear weapons, as one of his aides put it, provided 'a bigger bang for the buck'. Khrushchev, who required substantial conventional forces to police the Eastern bloc and defend its borders, needed to cut costs in order to promote his internal economic reforms. A nuclear arms race would put that priority seriously at risk.

The situation in Europe, above all in Germany, provided a further incentive to come to terms. In 1954, despite strenuous promotion by the Eisenhower administration of a free-standing European defence pillar to complement the Atlanticist emphasis of NATO, the proposal for a European Defence Community (EDC) collapsed in the face of French objections. The EDC had been designed originally as a means both of promoting European integration (including a rearmed West Germany) and encouraging Europe to take greater responsibility for its own defence. Following the French repudiation of the plan, Dulles threatened an 'agonizing reappraisal' of the American commitment to Europe, but the chief effect of the French action was to make the United States even more insistent upon the rearmament of West Germany and its admission to NATO (Cromwell 1992: 7–12). In May 1955 the Federal Republic of Germany was admitted into NATO and rearmament begun, following lengthy and disputatious negotiations during which the United States managed to convince France that its defence against possible German resurgence would be guaranteed by a large and permanent commitment of American troops to Western Europe. This was precisely the outcome which Soviet diplomacy had sought to forestall, and failure to do so left the Soviet Union with little alternative but to accept the fact and respond in kind by formalizing its defence of Eastern Europe in the shape of the Warsaw Pact, established also in May 1955. If this meant that there was little chance of serious progress on the reunification of Germany – still nominally the policy of both sides – at least the lines were clearly drawn.

Given the contradictory nature of the evidence regarding Soviet intentions, it is not surprising to find a certain reluctance among Eisenhower's advisers to engage in negotiations with the Soviet Union. Dulles was sceptical about the value of the summit before it happened and remained so afterwards. Eisenhower had his doubts too, but the nuclear issue was probably decisive in his decision to agree to the meeting. Strong pressure also came from Britain, where an election was due in May. Anthony Eden, Churchill's successor as leader of the Conservative Party, hoped to campaign on the basis that he had helped bring about peace. 'Eisenhower's readiness to help Eden', observes Hoopes, 'was a key factor in Washington's ultimate willingness to go to the summit' (Hoopes 1974: 287).

THE GENEVA SUMMIT

The summit itself perhaps inevitably served to illustrate the chasm between East and West on the key issue of Germany and, more generally, on the ideological divide between communism and capitalism. In his opening statement Eisenhower proposed a reunified Germany, free elections, and Germany's right to choose its own means of security – implying that it could join NATO. He also wanted to discuss the Soviet Union's failure to implement the Yalta agreement, doubtless knowing that there was slim hope of the Soviets' willingness to yield any ground. His broad attack on the Soviet Union's efforts to spread communism around the world was likewise somewhat speculative – a matter of setting out the West's maximum demands rather than a realistic negotiating position. Khrushchev responded similarly, advocating a demilitarized and neutral Germany, and rejecting any suggestion that the conference could discuss Soviet 'internal affairs', meaning the status of Eastern Europe (Eisenhower 1963: 515–16; Ambrose 1984: 264). In the event, the final communiqué of the conference papered over these differences and in the case of Germany produced a formula which appeared to represent agreement on the principle of free elections. No procedures were laid out for progress towards this goal, however, and given the pre-conference moves towards a hardening of the lines between the two parts of Germany – the East's inclusion within the Warsaw Pact and a rearmed West brought into NATO – the communiqué's vague phrases bore little relation to the reality.

The Geneva summit, however, is generally remembered not for its effective ratification of a divided Europe and a divided Germany but for Eisenhower's startling 'open skies' proposal. It was launched in the context of deadlock over the issue of mutual inspection of each other's armaments as a step towards disarmament and the lowering of military tension. Soviet proposals were limited to fixed ground inspection points, which, as Eisenhower noted, could easily be bypassed both by air and ground forces. Could not both sides agree, Eisenhower said, to aerial inspection coupled with an exchange of blueprints covering the character and location of all military installations both within their territorial boundaries and in overseas bases? Detailed regulations would govern the operating heights, routes, and frequency of flights, and, perhaps most daringly of all, 'each plane would be authorized to include in its crew one or more representatives of the nation under inspection' (Eisenhower 1963: 520).

Eisenhower had hoped for maximum surprise, and he certainly achieved it. The room broke out into spontaneous applause and his proposal was quickly endorsed by Britain and France. The Soviet response was initially encouraging. Bulganin, the Soviet Prime Minister, felt that the plan had 'real merit' and assured the conference that his delegation would give it close and sympathetic consideration. During an adjournment, however, Khrushchev told Eisenhower, 'I don't agree with the Chairman [Bulganin]', a retort which convinced Eisenhower of 'the identity of the real boss of the Soviet delegation'. The open skies proposal made no further progress and in the final communiqué all parties merely agreed 'to work together to develop an acceptable system of disarmament through the Subcommittee of the United Nations Disarmament Committee' (Eisenhower 1963: 521, 527).

If the value of the conference is measured by practical consequences in the form of hard agreements then it can hardly be called a success. If, however, one views it as the beginning of a dialogue, the significance of which lay in the talking itself, then it can be said to have served a purpose in reducing tension. The open skies proposal illustrated the temptation and the dangers of trying to go too far too fast. While there seems no reason to doubt Eisenhower's sincerity in making the offer, it could not have escaped his attention, or Khrushchev's, that the United States was ahead in the field of aerial inspection. The U-2 'spy plane' was in an advanced stage of development and with its capacity to fly at over 70,000 feet would be immune to attack, given the current state of anti-aircraft technology. In this respect the open skies idea fell foul of the uneven rates of development in military technology achieved at turns by each side in the cold war. Within only two years the Soviet launch of Sputnik would provoke a similar disinclination on the part of the United States to enter into negotiations to slow the arms race. As the record of the test-ban negotiations would prove, such agreements could only be reached after long and painstaking preparation and in carefully limited areas. (These are discussed in Chapter 7.)

CRISIS AND ITS MEANING, 1956–1961

When viewed from the perspective of the second half of the 1950s and the early 1960s, 1955 appears a year of exceptional calm and perhaps unrealistic hopes. Within a short time the dynamics of superpower competition had re-established themselves and the word 'crisis' became charged with new meaning as events unfolded: from the crises over the Chinese offshore islands, Quemoy and Matsu, in 1954 and again in 1958, to the suppression of the Hungarian revolt and the Suez crisis in 1956, to the launch of Sputnik in 1957, the Berlin crisis of 1958–9 (only to re-emerge in Kennedy's first year of office), the Cuban revolution of 1959 and its sequels in the Bay of Pigs invasion (1961) and the missile crisis (1962). In the light of the Geneva summit agenda – Germany and European security, the nuclear arms race, and promotion of East–West dialogue – the above events represent a seemingly comprehensive failure of the exercise to reduce tension. Why did the impetus towards accommodation represented by the Geneva summit prove so fragile?

Excessive hopes about the effectiveness of high level personal diplomacy must count for something. It could hardly have been expected that this first excursion into summitry since the Potsdam conference could do much more than clarify the areas of difference between the powers. The post-summit litany of crises illustrates the complex dialectic which existed in this period between the urge to resolve tension and the desire to reap maximum national advantage in the highly competitive superpower relationship. Furthermore, the days were gone when the superpowers could hope to dispose of a range of problems over which increasingly they had only indirect control, above all in the Third World. They had difficulties enough with the issues which lay directly within their own domain, such as the arms race and Germany. The bilateral relationship was increasingly subject to multiple cross-cutting pressures which raised the stakes of the cold war without necessarily supplying the superpowers with the means of matching them.

The 'spirit of Geneva' may have contained a large element of illusion, but both sides nevertheless aspired to sustain it. Geneva did at least establish the principle that high level contact was of some value in confirming the desire of each side to avoid the worst possible outcome of tension between them – nuclear war. Eisenhower and Khrushchev met next at Camp David near Washington in 1959, during which they engaged in lengthy and seemingly good-natured reminiscences about their wartime experiences, besides laying the groundwork for a future summit to be held in Paris the following year.

The Paris summit itself, however, proved the frailty of reliance on personal diplomacy, however well-intentioned. The shooting down of an American U-2 over the Soviet Union a few days before the meeting was due to open destroyed the summit. Questions can be raised about the good faith of both sides in this incident. Why did Eisenhower allow an inevitably provocative U-2 flight to take place at this critical moment and, once it had been shot down, refuse to take the option Khrushchev offered him of denying knowledge of the flight? Why for his part did Khrushchev choose to shoot it down (there had been many other such flights) and subsequently release the information to the world in a way which caused the Americans maximum embarrassment?

Khrushchev's motives in this incident are obscure. One plausible suggestion is that his action was related to the growing Soviet dispute with China, which in the early months of 1960 was markedly stepped up with the publication in Peking of a strident manifesto entitled 'Long Live Leninism'. It took the form of a barely disguised attack on Soviet 'revisionism'. Khrushchev may have calculated, in the light of the damage a split with China would cause in the communist bloc as a whole, that he had more to gain at this juncture by a tough policy towards the United States. This seems likely, particularly if one accepts Edward Crankshaw's judgement that 'from 1960 until the end the course of Khrushchev's career was dominated by the Chinese quarrel' (Crankshaw 1966: 272–3).

An equally strong influence on Khrushchev's actions may have been anxiety about domestic pressure, particularly from his generals, who were concerned that Khrushchev's attempts to reach accommodation with the United States and his proposed reductions in Soviet conventional forces were undermining the Soviet Union's defence. Taking a tough stand in this instance was therefore designed to placate his critics and to secure his own political base (Beschloss 1986: 376–7, 381). For his part, Eisenhower evidently made the decision to go ahead with the flight at this critical time on the advice of officials such as the Secretary of Defense and the CIA Director whose interests were narrowly military and who were not inclined to question the possible effects of this form of intelligence-gathering on the political relationship with the Soviet Union. Eisenhower later conceded that this had been a lapse of judgement on his part (Beschloss 1986: 370).

In his thorough investigation of the U-2 incident Michael Beschloss concludes that both governments were responsible for 'the shattering of *détente*'. A basic gap in their perception of the significance of the flights lay at the root of the problem. Eisenhower, believing that the Soviets had come to accept that they could do nothing about the flights, saw no reason not to authorize another. Moreover, he could not take advantage of Khrushchev's offer of a way out – i.e. acknowledging that the U-2 was a spy-plane but that he had not authorized the flight – since that would imply that he was not in control of his defence policy. For Khrushchev, however, the flights had always been an intrusion which exposed the Soviet Union's vulnerability; anything which could be done to reduce that vulnerability could and should be done. Though there is no conclusive evidence that either Eisenhower or Khrushchev deliberately provoked the incident in order to scuttle the Paris summit, both sides acted in ways which seemed designed to provoke the other (Beschloss 1986: 371–2, 376-7). The U-2 incident in that sense was the focus of antagonism which already existed over other issues such as Germany and arms control. In any event, the Eisenhower administration closed with US–Soviet relations in a state of disarray, the goal of accommodation seemingly as distant as at any time during his tenure of office.

KENNEDY AND KHRUSHCHEV

Kennedy injected a new dynamism into the cold war, beginning with the election campaign in which the notorious issue of the 'missile gap' played a central part. The launch of Sputnik in 1957 had engendered deep anxiety in the United States since it demonstrated that the Soviet Union was ahead in missile technology. The shooting down of the U-2 was further evidence of Soviet advances in rocketry. In actuality these dramatic instances belied the reality that the gap was very much in the United States' favour by the time of the election of 1960, as Eisenhower well knew from CIA photo-espionage. He refused, however, to provide hard evidence since that would involve revealing the extent of the U-2 programme and showing the photographs to the public (Ambrose 1984: 562). The result was that Kennedy was able to stoke the fire of public anxiety about Russia's lead in the arms race which had been building during Eisenhower's second administration.

In truth the issue was about more than numbers of missiles. In a striking reprise of the 1952 election, during the 1960 election campaign the incumbent administration was accused of losing the initiative in the cold war, while the challenging party, in this case the Democrats, presented itself as the party of dynamism and change. In March 1960 Senator Fulbright, who within a few years was to emerge as a leading opponent of the Vietnam war, gave a speech which is virtually a replay of John Foster Dulles's most strident 'New Look' speeches of the early 1950s. 'We endure in an era of total crisis', he said, adding that 'we have never faced an antagonist quite like this one. The Soviet Union swiftly leaped from the oxcart to the moon. It rose from a second-rate underdeveloped country to loom menacingly over the world.' For all its riches, the United States had failed to use them to maintain its defences at a level appropriate to its economic power and to the level of the Soviet threat. The fault lay with President Eisenhower – with his complacency and refusal to heed the advice of his military advisers. Furthermore, communism was on the offensive in Asia and the Soviet Union was mounting a 'worldwide trade offensive aimed primarily at us' (Smith 1964: 653, 655, 656).

The scene was set for Kennedy's inaugural address, which in its rhetorical flourishes set the tone for that curious mixture of tough-minded pragmatism and idealism which characterized the Kennedy presidency. Aiming his words at a world rather than simply an American audience, Kennedy announced that 'we shall pay any price, bear any burden, meet any hardship, support any friend, oppose any foe to assure the survival and the success of liberty' (Kennedy 1962: 1). More specific about what this meant in policy terms, however, was his State of the Union Address given a few days later. After surveying the world scene in terms very much like those of Fulbright, he proposed that in order to meet the challenges the United States must 'first . . . strengthen our military tools'. He promised enhanced and more flexible conventional forces, coupled with an acceleration of missile and Polaris submarine programmes. Second came an improvement in 'our economic tools', involving expanded foreign aid to developing countries, an Alliance for Progress for Latin America, and the opening of trade links with Eastern Europe 'in order . . . to help reestablish historic ties of friendship'. The scale of the challenge was such, he observed, that 'the response must be towering and unprecedented, much as lend-lease and the Marshall Plan were in earlier years'. Finally, 'we must sharpen our political and diplomatic tools', by expanding the disarmament effort, supporting the United Nations, and cooperating with the Soviet Union and other nations 'to invoke the wonders of science instead of its terrors' (Kennedy 1962: 23, 24, 26).

If this sounded like a pure cold war agenda, Kennedy was nevertheless at pains to stress that 'our greatest challenge is still the world that lies beyond the cold war' – by which it appears he meant the developing nations – and that the United States must increase its support of the United Nations 'as an instrument to end the cold war instead of an arena in which to fight it'. The bottom line, however, was indicated by his statement that 'the first great obstacle is still our relations with the Soviet Union and Communist China' (Kennedy 1962: 23). While the crises over the arms race, Cuba, and other areas of the Third World are covered in the following two chapters, at this point we can attempt an assessment of Kennedy's overall stance towards the problems which dominated his in-tray.

Kennedy, as he himself admitted, came late to 'liberalism': 'some people have their liberalism "made" by the time they reach their late 20s. I didn't. I was caught in cross currents and eddies. It was only later that I got into the stream of things' (Heath 1976: 24). As a young Congressman, and subsequently Senator, he had been in the van of those calling for a tough anti-communist stance both domestically and overseas. He had been prominent among those decrying the 'loss' of China and had temporized over McCarthyism, suggesting, along with his lukewarm support of black civil rights during the 1950s, a less than solid commitment to the agenda of the Democratic Party's liberal wing. By the 1960 election, however, he had identified himself with the liberal agenda, if only cautiously.

Of course, given the fluidity of party lines, liberalism in its American guise admits of multiple applications. In its broad meaning it can refer to the whole tradition of

American political culture stemming from its Lockean and eighteenth-century roots (Hartz 1955: 3–32). In its narrower twentieth-century meaning it refers to the reform tradition identified with the 'progressivism' of Theodore Roosevelt and Woodrow Wilson, through Franklin Roosevelt's 'New Deal' to the 'New Frontier' and 'Great Society' programmes of Kennedy and Johnson. A yet narrower application of the term is to the leftward end of this reform tradition, but characteristically those who termed themselves liberals (and there was a time when it was not considered a dirty word) exploited the multiple levels of the term. In calling himself a liberal Kennedy was thus aiming at inclusiveness, not exclusiveness in defining his political position. He was in effect redefining the centre of the political spectrum. At any rate, by the time he came to office, domestically liberalism meant active government to manage the economy and to promote civil rights, combined with a rhetoric of social idealism. Abroad it similarly implied activism in pursuit of American interests but in conjunction with the goal of cooperation with the Soviet Union and the principle of self-determination for all nations. In essence it differed little from the characteristic American amalgam of nationalism and internationalism enunciated so clearly by Woodrow Wilson some forty years earlier. Kennedy's personality, however, and the context of international affairs gave it a new stripe.

Doubtless it is possible to overplay Kennedy's 'youthful idealism' in accounting for his foreign policy. Without reference to the fresh injection of pace and drive which Kennedy brought to the presidency, however, it is impossible to understand the peculiar mixture of combativeness and conciliation which characterized his policy-making. In some respects he was no less cautious in practice than Eisenhower had been – indeed he was more so if we reflect that he never attempted anything as grandiose as Eisenhower's open skies proposal – but many of his statements and policy positions served to heighten the profile of cold war antagonism within the arena of world politics. The inaugural address itself, which was aimed at a world as well as a domestic audience, was a political and moral call to arms designed to wrest the high ground from the Soviet Union. Conciliatory gestures were wrapped up in crusading rhetoric.

The world Kennedy faced in 1961 was more diverse and in many respects more volatile than the one faced by Eisenhower in 1953, posing particular difficulties in assessing the various threats to American interests and in formulating policies to deal with them. What exactly did self-determination mean in a world in which newly independent nations were subject to the Soviet goal, as Kennedy put it in an interview with the editor of *Izvestia*, of 'communizing the world' (Kennedy 1962: 742)? What could 'peace' mean in a world in which the superpowers had the capacity to destroy each other and perhaps the globe itself? What was to be made of the split between the Soviet Union and China? Could it be exploited to America's advantage or was it simply a family quarrel which made no difference to the essential reality that communists were communists the world over?

If in each of these areas the threat issued from a single source – world communism – then there could be no let up in the cold war. If, however, as Kennedy and his advisers were aware, there was a process of fragmentation in the communist bloc, if developing nations had their own national agendas and were not eager to rush into the arms of the Soviet Union or China, and if the real danger in the arms race was nuclear war itself, meaning that nuclear weapons could hardly be considered to be usable, then the cold war policy agenda needed substantial revision. Policy must be more flexible, more 'particularist' in its focus, more accommodating to the diversity of the threats. 'Flexible response' indeed became the label applied to the declared policies of the Kennedy administration. Actual policy, however, as we have seen in Kennedy's State of the Union message, represented a strengthening of America's means of fighting the cold war across the board of political, economic and defence policy. Why the gap between the apparent acknowledgement of diversity and the promotion of policies which seemed premised upon the vision of an essentially unitary threat?

John Gaddis has offered a plausible explanation. 'What happened during the Kennedy administration', he writes, 'was a contraction of the threats mixed with a proliferation of means over and above what the previous incumbent had been willing to supply.' This was so, he continues, because 'what the Kennedy and Johnson administrations came to fear most, was not communism, which was too fragmented, or the Soviet Union, which was too committed to *détente*, or even China, which was too impotent, but rather the threat of embarrassment, of humiliation, of appearing to be weak' (Gaddis 1982: 213, 212).

Considerations of prestige, of being seen to be standing firm in the eyes of allies as well as potential enemies, undoubtedly played an important role. There is, however, another way of reading the Kennedy dilemma, and this is to start from the proposition that the formulation of positive foreign policy goals is ultimately determined by negative priorities. The chief negative in question here was the need to deny to communism opportunities to expand its spheres of influence. Positive goals – disarmament, the reduction of East–West tension, and the promotion of self-determination in developing countries – were forced to run the gauntlet of the fundamental need to deny communism opportunities to advance. When it came to a choice between promotion of the positive and adherence to the negative, the latter frequently won out simply because the uncertainties inherent in the competitive relationship with communism dictated strategies of denial where the risks of failure were so great. However real the reduction in the communist threat appeared to be, it could rarely override the possibility that its moves were merely tactical, its moderation a mask for expansion.

Viewed in this light, the remarkable feature of Kennedy's policy-making as compared with his predecessor was the size of the gap between his positive aspiration to reduce tension and the enhanced means adopted to wage the cold war. The gap was filled, it could be said, by 'liberalism', which gave a positive, activist, and idealist gloss to the strategies of denial. In actuality, while Gaddis's assessment of the narrowing of the communist threat may hold for the last year of Kennedy's administration – by which time the Sino–Soviet split was in the public realm and the conclusion of the missile crisis had broken the log-jam in the test-ban negotiations – Kennedy's first two years in office were profoundly crisis-ridden. The consolidation of Castro's revolution in Cuba represented a large breach in the wall of the Monroe Doctrine. The missile crisis arose seemingly from an attempt by the Soviet Union to reorder the nuclear balance in its favour. Soviet pressure in Berlin tested the West's commitment to that anomalous feature of an otherwise tidy division of Europe. The eruption of conflict in Laos in 1961 posed a threat not only to efforts to create a neutral Laos but to the stability of South Vietnam, since the North Vietnamese supported the radical Pathet Lao as part of the larger struggle to liberate Indo-China. Across the entire policy agenda communist initiatives seemed to undermine any hope that accommodation might be possible.

Khrushchev himself gave out contradictory signals. At his meeting with Kennedy in Vienna in June 1961 little progress was achieved on matters of substance, though the two leaders established a respectful, if not warm, relationship which was followed up in a remarkably frank and sustained exchange of letters over the next two years (Beschloss 1991: 318-20, 326). Hanging like a cloud over the Vienna meeting was the crisis over Berlin, a repeat of the events of 1958–9. Leaving discussion of the arms race and Third World confrontations to the following chapter, we must consider here that piece of unfinished business left over from 1945.

Khrushchev's threat in 1961, as it had been in 1958, was to dictate a solution to the as yet unresolved issue of the status of the two Germanys and within that of West Berlin. Though in a *de facto* sense the two Germanys were sovereign states, in the absence of a treaty formalizing their existence, they were still subject to Four-Power control under the Potsdam agreement of July 1945. This included the question of Western access to West Berlin which lay some one hundred miles inside East German territory. West Berlin had become an escape route for East Germans. particularly among the professional classes. It was also a base from which the West could conduct propaganda and espionage. Khrushchev's threat was that he would sign a separate treaty with East Germany, recognizing its sovereignty over its own territory and turning over control of access to Berlin to the new East German government. Four-Power rights would thus be terminated, though Berlin itself would become a 'free city'.

In 1961, as in 1958, Khrushchev set a deadline of six months for Western agreement to these terms. In the earlier case the tension was resolved following Eisenhower's agreement to set a date for a summit meeting (the abortive Paris summit of 1960). In 1961, however, after the stalemate at Vienna, there was no room for movement, and as anxiety rose during the summer Kennedy braced himself and the American public for crisis, much as Truman had done in 1948. 'The immediate threat to free men is in West Berlin', Kennedy declared in a television broadcast, 'but that isolated outpost is not an isolated problem. The threat is world-wide.' He called on Congress to pass an emergency defence appropriation, to increase army manpower, step up draft calls, and reactivate ships and planes destined to be retired. A civil defence programme, already planned, was speeded up (Kennedy 1962: 533, 535–6).

The Soviet response, which was to erect a barbed wire barrier between East and West Berlin on the night of 13 August and subsequently a wall, was both provocative and ultimately decisive in resolving the immediate crisis, if not the issue of West Berlin's formal status. Neither side gained its positive goals but each gained a negative: Khrushchev in sealing off West from East Berlin and Kennedy in denying to the Soviets a revision of the agreement on the status of the city. The result, as it had been in Korea, was in one sense a return to the *status quo ante*, but also a hardening of the lines, which meant that the divided city would become a potent symbol of the global differences between the superpowers. Kennedy's famous assertion, made during a visit to the city in June 1963, that 'all free men, wherever they may live, are citizens of Berlin' and that therefore 'as a free man I take pride in the words "Ich bin ein Berliner"' confirmed that Berlin would remain a test of the West's global resolve (Kennedy 1964: 525).

It is an indication, however, of the deep contradictions inherent in superpower relations that this statement should have come only ten days after an equally significant public pronouncement in which Kennedy had presented a very different face to the world. His American University address of 10 June had counselled a rededication to peace and a re-examination of Americans' attitudes towards the Soviet Union and the cold war. Lacking the rhetorical expansiveness of his inaugural address, the tone was measured and conciliatory; it accentuated the positive. It was redolent, not of the uneasy stalemate over Berlin but of the post-missile crisis thaw in relations with the Soviet Union, signalled by the establishment of a 'hot-line' between Washington and Moscow enabling swift communication in times of crisis and by the encouraging progress towards the conclusion of a test ban treaty (signed in July). Significantly, in an adaptation of Woodrow Wilson's call in 1917 to 'make the world safe for democracy', Kennedy hoped to enlist the Soviet Union's help to 'make the world safe for diversity' (Kennedy 1964: 462).

As a statement of Kennedy's aspirations the American University speech was both forthright and consistent. As a guide for action, however, it was bedevilled by two entrenched features of cold war rivalry. In the first place, the limits to diversity had already been set by both sides in ways which precluded any agreed definition. As regards those nations of the world which were already included within one or another of the blocs, toleration of diversity was conditional upon broad acceptance that the cold war divide was still the determining factor in world politics. Even departures from within the blocs – China's from the communist bloc and France's withdrawal from NATO – did not mean defection to the other side. In those nations, predominantly in the Third World, which sought detachment from one or another bloc or where the struggle was unresolved there was always the danger, as superpower policy-makers saw it, that toleration of diversity might mean a concession to the other side.

Secondly, since the key points of conflict between the United States and the Soviet Union developed at different speeds and raised quite different issues, a solution in one area, even if it were achievable, did not necessarily carry over into the others. The (albeit temporary and partial) *détente* in the arms race in 1963 had no influence, for example, on the conflict in Vietnam where during the summer and autumn of that year political crisis in the South and stepped-up pressure from the North combined to set the United States on its course of large-scale intervention. In short, each of the three major areas of contention – Europe, the arms race, and the Third World – had a dynamic of its own. It would be some years before Richard Nixon and Henry Kissinger would attempt to resolve that dilemma via the concept of 'linkage'.

7

THE NUCLEAR ARMS RACE, 1945–1963

INTRODUCTION

Arms races are nothing new in human history. There are countless previous examples of technological breakthroughs granting a massive temporary advantage to one side, provoking others eventually to reply in kind and restore some sort of balance. One common feature of such innovations in recent times was the conviction that one or another new weapons system was so appalling in its destructive power that it would never be used and would provoke all parties into a recognition that war must be outlawed. Prior to the First World War it was believed that the submarine, especially when used against civilian shipping, would be so indiscriminate in its effects that no power would seriously contemplate its use. The same was believed of mass aerial bombardment. The German submarine campaigns in the First World War, the German bombing of Guernica in the Spanish Civil War, and mass bombing of civilian targets by all sides in the Second World War put paid to these optimistic hopes. It seemed that the capacity of human beings to make mental adjustment to their physical capacity to destroy each other was infinitely elastic.

Until, that is, the advent of nuclear weapons. The inhabitants of Hiroshima and Nagasaki have reason to doubt whether any limits exist to the willingness of political leaders to use nuclear weapons, but the experience has not been repeated. Significantly, the only occasion on which they have been used was at a time when one nation held a nuclear monopoly. It is also significant that it came at the end of a long war during which both sides had become inured to ever-higher levels of destruction. Finally, despite the knowledge that one atomic bomb vastly multiplied the power of one conventional bomb, the framework of assumptions which guided its use was still 'conventional'. Little was known about the dangers of fall-out, delivery was by conventional means (the manned bomber), and the bombs used on Japan were small by the standards which soon developed with the advent of the hydrogen, or thermo-nuclear, bomb.

Even so, there could be little doubt that something radically new had entered the human scene. Within a short time some were sufficiently persuaded of this fact to begin agitating for the old liberal panacea of world government (*New Republic* 1945: 366–7). John Hersey's *Hiroshima*, a powerful first-hand report on the effect of the bomb on seven individuals, commanded a huge readership both in its original serial form in the *New Yorker* magazine and in book sales when it was published in 1946 (Hersey [1946] 1986). Equally significant, though less visible to the public at large, was a pamphlet published in November 1945 by Bernard Brodie, who was to become perhaps America's leading nuclear strategist. In *The Atomic Bomb and American Security* Brodie observed that atomic weapons heralded a change 'not merely in the destructiveness of modern war but in its basic character'. In the first place, the atomic bomb was not just 'another and more destructive weapon adding to an already long list. It is something which threatens to make the rest of the list relatively unimportant.' Secondly, there was no conceivable defence against these weapons. They appeared to erase the distinction between offence and defence. Above all, 'the essential change introduced by the atomic bomb is . . . that it will concentrate the violence in terms of time. A world accustomed to thinking it horrible that wars should last four or five years is now appalled at the prospect that future wars may last only a few days' (Brodie [1945] 1989: 65, 67). There are few features of the coming nuclear arms race which are not adumbrated in Brodie's pamphlet – the theory of deterrence (including in an embryonic form Mutual Assured Destruction or MAD), missile development, nuclear proliferation, problems of arms control and verification.

Brodie's central insight was into the concentration of 'violence in terms of time'. In effect he anticipated that nuclear strategy, unlike traditional military strategy, would come to be premised on the necessity to prevent the use of the chief weapons in a nuclear power's arsenal. The key to the nuclear arms race lies in this paradoxical feature: that 'success' would come to be measured, not by defeat of another power in war but by the avoidance of war.

Despite the ever-present possibility of miscalculation or accident, nuclear war has not taken place, which has inclined some recent commentators to call the last forty years 'the long peace' rather than the cold war (Gaddis 1986; Kegley 1991). This may or may not serve us well as a way of understanding the last forty years from our own particular vantage point (an issue taken up in the last chapter of this book), but it hardly does justice to the prospects as they appeared to policy-makers and ordinary citizens during the early years of the nuclear age. One thing alone unites present expressions of relief that nuclear war has not taken place with the anxious forebodings of the immediate post-Hiroshima years: the large element of speculation involved in making judgements about the significance of nuclear weapons. We cannot be sure that it has been nuclear weapons themselves, as opposed to some other factor, which has kept the nuclear 'peace'; they could not be sure that knowledge of the destructive power of nuclear weapons would restrain nations from war.

Since the end of the cold war, understanding of the incalculable element in the superpower nuclear relationship has been enhanced by studies of the possibility of nuclear accidents. Studies by Bruce Blair and Scott Sagan have uncovered deep flaws in the command and control systems of nuclear weapons. By and large, theorizing about deterrence by politicians and academics during the cold war was premised on the notion that the key determinant in any crisis was the political intentions and capacities of the leaderships. The evidence presented by Blair and Sagan suggests that even the most strenuous efforts by both sides to ensure against inadvertent launches of missiles left much to chance. Not only were safety procedures inherently subject to error but the necessity to maintain active readiness and the capacity to respond to a nuclear attack inevitably pushed safety to the limits. Both the United States and the Soviet systems, for example, 'contrary to widespread belief, were geared for launch on warning', meaning in effect that the authority to launch nuclear weapons was delegated to military commanders. In sum, writes Blair, 'their nuclear postures were accidents waiting to happen' (Blair 1993: 8, 9; Sagan 1993: 3–4).

While it is too early to give a definitive assessment of such conclusions, it is worth noting that Blair and Sagan in a sense offer academic respectability to views which anti-nuclear activists, and some film directors and novelists have held since early in the nuclear age – namely, that the nightmare scenario was most likely to be the product of an accident rather than malign intention. Clearly, given that such accidents as did occur during the cold war (and there were many) did not issue in catastrophe, it is arguable how far such conclusions need alter one's interpretation of the historical record. At the very least, however, from this perspective the cold war was more fraught with danger than has generally been assumed.

Given the absence of actual experience of nuclear war between the superpowers, the history of the arms race has a dual character. The history of the nuts and bolts can be recounted in terms of the number and type of weapons on each side; the history of nuclear strategy, however, is largely the history of hypotheses about how nuclear weapons *might* be employed. In the absence of any experience of the consequences for individual nations and the human community itself of a nuclear exchange, strategy has taken the form of projections, scenarios, and, in its most arcane form, game-theoretical exercises. The emergence of the 'defence intellectual' in the United States was a measure of the highly political character of military strategy in the nuclear age. If nuclear hardware remained the preserve of the military and of defence contractors, the software betrayed the influence of the civilian defence analyst to a degree unusual in the history of warfare. All of which is to suggest that the issues raised by the nuclear arms race go to the heart of the societies engaged in it. The ultimate weapon raises questions of an ultimate character. In this chapter we shall outline the development in the United States and the Soviet Union of nuclear doctrines and subsequently measure these against the record of confrontation and negotiation between 1953 and 1963. The guiding theme is the dynamic and unstable nature of the arms race during this period and the corresponding fluidity in the development of strategic doctrines and proposals for arms control.

AMERICAN NUCLEAR STRATEGY

Truman and negative deterrence

Despite the writings of figures such as Bernard Brodie, recognition of the radical implications of nuclear weaponry for military planning was not immediate. For one thing, the use of the atomic bombs over Japan appeared to confirm the Air Force view that strategic bombing was the key to success in warfare (Freedman 1981: 22–4). For another there was an absence of hard evidence over the next four years that the United States' atomic monopoly had exerted any discernible influence on Soviet behaviour beyond inclining them to move as quickly as they could to develop their own atomic weapons. However 'special' atomic weapons might be – and the Truman administration certainly regarded them as such – they did not appear to reap the political benefits their specialness would seem to promise. Nuclear weapons could not thus be considered as an alternative to conventional forces. While by 1948 atomic weapons were included in military planning, Truman, in David Rosenberg's words, was unwilling or unable 'to conceive of the atomic bomb as anything other than an apocalyptic terror weapon, a weapon of last resort' (Rosenberg 1983: 11).

The legacy which Truman handed on to Eisenhower was mixed. Following detection of the first Soviet atom test in September 1949, Truman had taken decisions to step up research and development on the thermo-nuclear or 'super bomb' and to produce 'tactical' nuclear weapons, but operational plans for use of these weapons in war were couched in general terms. In so far as one can speak of a theory of deterrence at this point in time it was premised on the general threat of reprisal in the face of a possible Soviet attack. There was no expectation that with the Soviet Union's newly developed atomic capacity mutual deterrence would eventuate. On the contrary, wrote the authors of the 1950 strategic reassessment NSC 68, 'when it [the Soviet Union] calculates that it has a sufficient atomic capability to make a surprise attack on us, nullifying our atomic superiority and creating a military situation decisively in its favor, the Kremlin might be tempted to strike quickly and with stealth. The existence of two large atomic capabilities in such a relationship might well act, therefore, not as a deterrent, but as an incitement to war' (*FRUS* 1950: 266).

As this statement suggests, despite the recognition that atomic weapons represented a new order of destructive power, it was envisaged that they might be used. NSC 68 explicitly ruled out a declaration of 'no first use' by the United States. Just as important was the perception that the Soviets would not hesitate to use them, if they believed it was to their advantage. This made preparation for a surprise attack an urgent necessity, raising the question of the circumstances in which the United States would mount a nuclear response. To wait until the Soviets had actually delivered their own weapons would be to risk destruction of America's own capacity to reply, given that there was no known defence against nuclear weapons. Even if one enemy bomber got through it could wreak enormous havoc. To engage in a preventive war, taking advantage of the Soviet Union's as yet limited ability to deliver its nuclear weapons, would violate American cultural norms and would hardly be acceptable to world opinion. A possible intermediate position was a 'pre-emptive', as opposed to a preventive, strike, meaning that in a situation in which war already seemed imminent the United States must be prepared to strike the first blow. This, however, would require accurate intelligence about the enemy's movements, and this was not yet available.

By the time Truman left office the dynamics of the nuclear stand-off were already appearing in outline form, even if they had not yet produced settled strategic doctrines: vulnerability to surprise attack, the need to retain the ability to retaliate after an enemy first strike, the crucial significance of accurate intelligence, and the difficulty of conceiving of any defence against nuclear weapons. Each of these elements would in the course of the 1950s become integrated into nuclear planning.

From negative to positive deterrence

We can term the American nuclear posture during the Truman administration 'negative deterrence', in that it was premised upon a generalized threat of an American nuclear response to a Soviet attack, whether conventional or nuclear. In the Eisenhower/Dulles years, in line with the Republican critique of Truman's containment, the United States moved towards 'positive deterrence'. This more strident posture of massive retaliation and brinkmanship is generally associated with John Foster Dulles, but in actuality Dulles had little to do with nuclear planning policy.

A more precise guide to nuclear policy during the Eisenhower administration is the National Security Council document NSC 162/2 (1953). As in NSC 68, political, ideological, economic, and military considerations are closely linked. In the later document, however, the nuclear anxiety is sharper and economic constraints more prominently foregrounded, betraying both the advent of the H-bomb era and the Eisenhower administration's insistence on moderation in defence costs. The task of policy-makers was to meet the Soviet threat without 'seriously weakening the US economy or undermining our fundamental values and institutions'. Given that the authority of the Soviet regime did not appear to have been weakened by the change in leadership and that the capacity of the Soviet Union to attack the United States with nuclear weapons was growing, the United States must develop 'a strong military posture, with emphasis on the capability of inflicting massive retaliatory damage by offensive striking power', enhance its conventional forces, improve its intelligence gathering, maintain a sound and growing economy, and enlist the support of its allies for these policies (*FRUS*, 1952–54: 578, 582–3).

Explicit mention of the term 'massive retaliatory power' is not the only significant departure from NSC 68. In several other respects already existing and projected developments in nuclear technology had altered perceptions of the threat and the means of dealing with it. In the first place, in contrast to the view taken in NSC 68, it was now believed that the prospect of 'atomic plenty and ample means of delivery . . . could create a stalemate, with both sides reluctant to initiate general warfare'. Secondly, 'although Soviet fear of atomic reaction should still inhibit local aggression, increasing Soviet atomic capability may tend to diminish the deterrent effect of US atomic power against peripheral Soviet aggression'. One significant danger was the possibility of local conflicts escalating into general war, to avoid which 'it will in general be desirable for the United States to make clear to the USSR the kind of actions which will be almost certain to lead to this result, recognizing, however, that as general war becomes more devastating for both sides the threat to resort to it becomes less available as a sanction against local aggression' (*FRUS*, 1952–54: 581). Massive retaliation, that is to say, was governed by the law of diminishing returns, the limits being set by the credibility (or lack of it) of a threat which was out of proportion to the provocation. A third important feature of this document, however, was the implication – and it is no more than that – that tactical nuclear weapons might offer an alternative in local conflicts where the threat of massive retaliation would be excessive (Freedman 1981: 82–4).

Subsequent developments during the 1950s served to complicate rather than clarify the problems raised in NSC 162/2 regarding the threat of surprise attack, the relationship between strategic and tactical nuclear weapons, and the possible dynamics of a nuclear stalemate. The chief engine of uncertainty was advancing technology or, more precisely, anxiety about the consequences of technological change. The period between 1955 and 1962 was one of feverish theorizing both within and outside government. The one certainty appeared to be that, whatever the actual numbers of deliverable nuclear weapons on each side, something like a 'balance of terror' was emerging, which left the United States in the unfamiliar position of feeling vulnerable to direct attack from the Soviet Union (Brands 1989: 964).

The technological stimulus to new thought was the combined prospect of deployment by both sides of thermo-nuclear bombs and missile development. Consideration of the likely impact of missiles came in advance of the launch of the Soviet Sputnik in 1957. Here, as in all phases of the arms race, policy was anticipatory, based on projections of likely Soviet capabilities within various time periods. An important NSC study undertaken in 1957 – the Gaither report – shows this anticipatory dynamic clearly at work.

To the Gaither panel the prospects were alarming. The Soviet economy was apparently growing faster than that of the United States, investment being concentrated on heavy industry and arms production, holding out the prospect that within a decade Soviet military expenditure would be double that of the United States. Building on this foundation, the Soviets had made 'spectacular progress' in military strength. They had produced enough fissionable material for 'at least 1500 nuclear weapons', created from scratch a long-range air force, while also developing a large short-range air force, developed a range of short and medium range ballistic missiles, submarine-based cruise missiles, a sophisticated air defence and early warning system, and, to cap it all, 'probably surpassed us in ICBM development' (*FRUS*, 1955–57: 640–1).

In order to meet these threats the committee proposed sweeping measures to speed up ICBM production and provide them with hardened attack-proof bases, accelerate production of all categories of missiles, improve the Strategic Air Command's (SAC) alert status, explore the possibilities of limited nuclear war, develop an anti-ballistic missile (ABM) system, and, not least (since the committee's original brief was to investigate civil defence against nuclear attack), embark upon a massive programme of building fallout shelters (*FRUS*, 1955–57: 642–4). The committee had begun work in April 1957; by early November, when it was submitted to the NSC, the launch of Sputnik was already public knowledge, as if to confirm the committee's most pessimistic predictions.

Much has been made of Eisenhower's less than enthusiastic response to these alarmist predictions. Eisenhower himself concluded in his memoirs that the committee's estimates of Soviet power had been excessive and that the report could not be accepted as a 'master blueprint for action'. 'In the final result', he wrote, 'the Gaither report was useful; it acted as a gadfly on any in the administration given to complacency; and it listed a number of facts, conclusions, and opinions that provided a checklist for searching examination' (Eisenhower 1966: 221, 223). Eisenhower's biographer, Stephen Ambrose, is more categorical. Eisenhower, writes Ambrose, 'rejected the Gaither report. He refused to bend to pressure, refused to initiate a fallout shelter program, refused to expand conventional and nuclear forces, refused to panic. It was one of his finest hours' (Ambrose: 1984: 435). The facts do not bear out this judgement in its entirety. The more extreme recommendations of the committee – such as the crash fallout shelter proposal – were shelved, but most of the others were implemented, if in a modified form. Paul Nitze, one of the chief authors of the Gaither report, notes in his memoirs that 'the high priority recommendations of the report were carried out . . . In the course of the next few years we perfected our early warning capabilities and put a substantial part of our SAC bomber force on fifteen-minute alert status, deployed our first Atlas ICBM squadron, successfully flight-tested the Titan ICBM, accelerated the Minuteman development program, and placed two Polaris submarines at sea' (Nitze 1989: 169).

Perhaps the chief consequence of the Gaither report and the events surrounding it was to establish firmly in the minds of policy-makers and the public the significance of technological and scientific innovation as the driving force behind the arms race and the corresponding necessity to seek and maintain superiority. The Gaither committee believed that up to 1960 the United States might still be ahead. But projecting its estimates forward to 1970 and beyond, the committee saw, not a stalemate but 'a continuing race between the offense and the defense. Neither side can afford to lag or to fail to match the other's efforts. There will be no end to the technical moves and counter-moves.' What the Gaither report did not address in any detail, however, were

144

the conditions under which fruitful negotiations on arms control might take place. True, it was suggested that the period up to 1960 offered an opportunity for the United States to negotiate from strength, but no assessment was offered of whether the Soviets might find it in their interest to negotiate under such conditions. Also, it was felt that the prospects for a spiralling technological arms race suggested 'the great importance of a continuing attempt to arrive at a dependable agreement on the limitation of armaments', but in the face of the overwhelming military and technological imperatives emphasized in the report this statement seems almost incidental, a ritual nod in the direction of a perhaps desirable but presumably unrealistic goal (*FRUS* 1955–57: 651, 652, 653).

In actuality, some, even within the committee, came to doubt whether technology alone could guarantee security and advocated instead political solutions in the form of arms control. One such was Jerome Wiesner, later scientific adviser to President Kennedy (Nitze 1989: 168–9). Wiesner's reaction represented one possible response to the prospect of a balance of terror, and while Lawrence Freedman may be right that arms control only became an entrenched feature of the superpower relationship in the 1970s, it began to make its mark on policy in the late 1950s, most notably in the test-ban negotiations, treated later in this chapter (Freedman 1981: 200). The other possible response to the balance of terror was 'formal strategy', a term which covers a spectrum of considerations from targeting policy to theoretical models of nuclear conflict.

Towards balance deterrence

The distinguishing feature of strategic thinking between roughly 1957 and 1967 was the transition from positive deterrence, associated with massive retaliation, to balanced deterrence, associated with 'flexible response'. This new approach, which was not finalized by NATO until 1967, also envisaged a more prominent role for conventional forces.

At the time Kennedy entered the presidency official doctrine was still premised upon massive nuclear retaliation against both Soviet military targets and Soviet and Chinese cities. The key factor making for change in doctrine was the enhancement, or rather projected enhancement, of Soviet capabilities. In 1961 the United States possessed a six to one lead over the Soviet Union in nuclear warheads (3,267 to 500) and the missile gap was very much in the United States' favour (Sagan 1989: 27). The issue of balance thus arose not from equality of forces but from the recognition that each side had the potential to survive a first strike and deliver a retaliatory blow.

Once this possibility was accepted, it became a question of what kind of conditions might produce war, what kind of war might be fought, and what kind of 'rules' might govern the behaviour of each side. 'Thinking about the unthinkable', in Herman Kahn's words, thus became as important as deterrence. Indeed deterrence could only work if each side were convinced that the other was prepared to act on the threat

145

implied in the deterrent stand. Since the threat of massive retaliation implied an all-out attack on cities, it might lack credibility in situations short of extreme provocation such as the Japanese attack on Pearl Harbor (Kaufmann [1956] 1989: 174). Strategists thus turned their attention in the late 1950s to the idea of limited nuclear war, involving (in the early stages at least) tactical (or battlefield) rather than strategic nuclear weapons and focusing on attacking the enemy's nuclear and other forces rather than cities. Once this possibility was entertained, it was logical (and a presumed rational logic was an essential component of formal strategy) to think of war-fighting as involving a politico-military process in which successive stages of escalation would 'signal' the United States' determination to match the enemy's moves at each point in the escalation ladder. Deterrence, that is to say, could continue to operate within war itself. As Henry Kissinger put it in an influential book published in 1957, 'the prerequisite for a policy of limited war is to reintroduce the political element into our concept of warfare and to discard the notion that policy ends when war begins or that war can have goals distinct from those of national policy' (Freedman 1981: 102).

Much depended in these scenarios on assumptions about how the other side would perceive the moves in the superpower stand-off. Game theory was offered by some civilian analysts as a model for superpower conflict. The prisoner's dilemma was felt to be particularly appropriate to the US–Soviet relationship. In this game a prosecutor, having placed two prisoners suspected of a serious crime in separate cells, presents them with the alternatives of confession or remaining silent. In Freedman's succinct summary the sequel is as follows:

> If both remain silent he will prosecute them on a minor charge and they will receive light sentences (1 year). If both confess they will be prosecuted but with a recommendation for a sentence below the maximum (5 years). If one confesses and the other does not then the confessor will get a lenient sentence (3 months) while the other will be prosecuted for the maximum sentence (10 years). The two players are left alone in separate cells to think things over . . . The answer is that they both confess. A unable to conspire with B knows that if he remains silent he risks 10 years' imprisonment; if he confesses he risks only 5 years. Furthermore, if B decides to go for the solution that would be of greatest mutual benefit and so remains silent, by confessing A can improve his own position, though in a sense double-crossing B. Game theory predicts that B will follow the same reasoning. This is known as the minimax strategy, in that it guarantees the best of the worst possible outcomes.
>
> (Freedman 1981: 185–6)

The rules of the game, of course, are loaded against the possibility of cooperation. Extrapolating from this to the real world of US–Soviet relations, we could say that the game mirrored the actual divergence in superpower interests and also the veil of ideology and mistrust which was cast over their intentions. For practical purposes they were in separate cells and it was this which prevented them from adopting the most obvious mutually beneficial solution of cooperating to achieve a reduction in armaments and tension.

In another sense, however, the game was quite unlike the nuclear arms race. In the real world there was no third party capable of imposing or withholding punishment, no set of rules imposed from outside. Indeed the 'lesson' of the game might be that it was within each side's power to arrive at the best possible solution – an agreed strategy to limit arms. Why didn't they at this point in the arms race? The answer surely is that they were prisoners, not of some rule-setting third party but of their own doubts about each other's motives. Each side imputed to the other motives which it did not apply to itself. More specifically, each believed that it was capable of self-restraint, or self-deterrence, and that the other was not. In this sense, the assumption adopted by game theorists regarding the rational character of both party's approaches to the dilemma of the arms race was not easily convertible into political reality. In the real world, given the absence of hard evidence about Soviet intentions and real doubts about whether they could be trusted, it was safer to judge Soviet actions by their capabilities, potential as well as actual.

Robert McNamara, Kennedy's Secretary of Defense, accepted some of the conclusions of the civilian strategists, in particular the critique of the inflexible doctrine of massive retaliation and the idea of intrawar deterrence. He also accepted, at least initially, the 'no cities' approach on the grounds that it might serve to 'preserve the fabric as well as the integrity of allies' society' while destroying the enemy's military forces (McNamara [1962] 1989: 206). However, as Gregory Treverton has pointed out, 'MacNamara himself began to back away from the approach almost as soon as he had adopted it' (Treverton 1989: 193). There were two main reasons for this. In the first place, the provocative no cities (or 'counterforce') idea put the nuclear relationship with the Soviet Union on a hair-trigger basis, since it seemed to imply the adoption of a first strike strategy. (In a crisis each side would be tempted to strike first in order to ensure the survivability of its nuclear forces.) Secondly, 'there was little evidence that the Soviet Union was prepared to play the 'no cities' game (Treverton 1989: 195). In these circumstances, and given the absence of reliable forms of defence against ballistic missiles, McNamara moved towards the doctrine of 'assured destruction' and eventually 'mutual assured destruction' (or MAD), under which deterrence would work 'through the punitive threat of irresistible hurt to the enemy's social and economic structure, rather than through the prospect of victory in combat' (Freedman 1981: 192–3).

It is easy to exaggerate the significance of changes in strategic terminology. Assured destruction did not mean the abandonment of counterforce targeting but rather a change of emphasis (Sagan 1989: 11–13). The key point to be grasped here is the acknowledgement by the Kennedy and later the Johnson administrations of the necessity to cater for a range of possible threats. At one extreme lay limited war which admitted the possibility of graduated deterrence even within war itself; at the other extreme lay all-out nuclear war which would involve massive destruction on both sides – the threat of ultimate mutual destruction presumably serving as a deterrent against use of the ultimate weapon. By a curious logic, vulnerability, the nightmare prospect envisaged by the Eisenhower administration, had come to be seen as the guarantor of national security, however fragile it might be. Not that this checked the demand for ever more sophisticated and powerful means of offence and defence. If anything, acknowledgement of vulnerability only intensified the search for means of overcoming it, not least because it could not safely be assumed that deterrence did not work. Building a nuclear arsenal was not unlike taking out health insurance to cover all contingencies from a mild case of measles to a disabling car accident. Even if it were not the case that larger and larger arsenals increased security – just as taking out health insurance does not create health – the sense of security could be enhanced by this means.

In theory, an enhanced conventional defence could increase NATO's options in the event of a Soviet conventional attack. In fact, such an approach had been advocated at a NATO conference in Lisbon in 1952, but the 'Lisbon force goals' had been abandoned. None of the NATO countries was prepared to incur the costs which the projected quadrupling of NATO's conventional force strength would have involved. Subsequent reliance on tactical nuclear weapons in Europe and the United States' strategic nuclear weapons, however, meant that in the event of a sub-nuclear Soviet attack NATO would have no option but a nuclear response. So long as the Soviet Union was incapable of reaching the United States with missiles, arguably the threat of an American nuclear response remained credible. The argument for flexible response grew during the early 1960s in part out of growing doubts whether, given the Soviet Union's capacity to strike the United States directly, the United States would be prepared to go nuclear first and hence risk its own destruction in order to save Europe from a conventional attack (Cromwell 1992: 18–19).

The problem was one of 'extended deterrence', and its roots lay in geography – the Soviet Union's proximity to the likely theatre of war and the United States' distance from it. If anything, however, flexible response deepened the Western security dilemma. Unless NATO were willing to spend far more on conventional armaments than they currently were spending, the West could never afford to abandon the option of first use of nuclear weapons in the event of a conventional attack, and indeed NATO never did abandon this option. We shall encounter further instances of this dilemma in later chapters. For the moment we must note that France's solution to this problem was to signal its independence from the American design for Europe by withdrawing from NATO's integrated military structure. Though the process was not completed until 1966, as early as 1959 De Gaulle had decided to withdraw the French Mediterranean fleet from NATO command, to ban American nuclear warheads from French soil, and to deny to the Americans French rocket-testing sites (Werth 1965: 311).

SOVIET NUCLEAR STRATEGY

Like many aspects of Soviet policy in the immediate post-war years, military strategy was hamstrung by Stalinism. Soviet strategy reflected Stalin's own interpretation of the catastrophic German invasion of the Soviet Union in 1941 and the subsequent triumphant struggle to repel the German armies. On the face of it the threat of surprise attack should have featured large in post-war Soviet strategy, but this would have involved an admission by Stalin that he had erred in 1941 in not heeding the many warnings he had received about German mobilization. Rather than admit this, Stalin held that the Soviet retreat in the face of the German attack had been a premeditated strategy designed to draw the Germans into a trap. The Soviet Union's checking of the German advance and subsequent defeat of the German armies proved that surprise was a 'fortuitous' and 'transitory' factor in deciding the outcome. Of far more importance were certain 'permanently operating factors' such as 'stability of the home front, morale of the army, quantity and quality of divisions, equipment of the army, the organizing ability of the commanding personnel of the army' (Holloway 1984: 36). Ideology was as important as military strength and skill in producing the Soviet victory. 'Our victory means', Stalin declared in a speech given in 1946, 'that our Soviet social order has triumphed, that the Soviet social order has successfully passed the ordeal in the fire of war and has proved its unquestioned vitality' (Daniels 1985, Vol. 1: 295).

Well before Stalin's death these ideas were already dated. By 1953 the Soviet Union had already developed its own atomic weapons, was on the verge of achieving the thermo-nuclear breakthrough, and was engaged on research on long-range rockets. As yet the Soviet Union was probably incapable of delivering an atomic strike, but the significance of surprise must already have been evident to Soviet military planners. The result, at any rate, during the latter years of Stalin's rule, was a growing gap between a military doctrine which was 'conventional' in character and heavily overlaid with ideological doctrine regarding the superiority of the Soviet system, and the facts of the nuclear arms race. As David Holloway has put it, 'weapons development and military doctrine existed in separate worlds; the former was pushed at a rapid pace, the latter was stifled' (Holloway 1984: 28).

Stalin's death unfroze the orthodoxies associated with his name in the military as in other fields. Two factors helped to speed a change in military doctrine: firstly Khrushchev's damning criticism of Stalin's leadership during the German invasion of 1941 allowed for a general reassessment of inherited military doctrine, and secondly, the advent of missiles confirmed that surprise could be decisive in nuclear war. The two other chief elements in Stalinist military thought – the permanently operating factors and the inevitability of war between capitalism and communism – similarly underwent review and were rejected (Freedman 1981: 145–54). Regarding the first, military planners pressed for a strategy which challenged the doubtful assumption that socialist countries would triumph in war simply because they were

149

socialist. As regards the inevitability of war, Khrushchev explicitly repudiated the idea at the Twentieth Party Congress, albeit still acknowledging the possibility that the imperialists might provoke war (Daniels 1985, Vol.2: 226).

Ideology continued to play a central role in Soviet doctrine but it was now embedded in a notion of deterrence which contained two cardinal principles: the necessity to prevent war and to be prepared to fight a nuclear war (and prevail), should it occur. Arguably, in the development of the Soviet nuclear strategy, one factor was paramount – the fact that until the late 1960s the Soviet Union lagged behind the United States in all fields of nuclear weapons. Despite the apparent lead represented by the launch of Sputnik, this was not converted into military advantage, since the rocket used for the launch – the SS-6 – was 'too primitive, hence unreliable for military purposes'. During the period of American anxiety about the missile gap (1957–61) American estimates of projected Soviet ICBM deployment were 500 at the end of 1960 and 1,000 by the end of 1961, while the Americans had only 30 in 1960 and 70 in 1961 (Newhouse 1989: 122).

In actuality, as photographic intelligence showed, the Soviet Union possessed fewer than 50 ICBMs in 1961, only four of which, according to a later report, were actually deployed (Holloway 1984: 85). Khrushchev's boasts about Soviet ICBM capability during the late 1950s, in short, were pure bluff. 'The Soviet Union', writes Holloway, 'could not take the deterrent power of its own forces as much for granted as the United States – hence the attempt to hide Soviet vulnerability' (Holloway 1984: 56). Among the Kennedy administration's most provocative acts, as far as the Soviet leadership was concerned, was its revelation that the missile gap had been a myth, exposing the Soviet Union to public embarrassment and Khrushchev to the fury of his generals. One of Eisenhower's reasons for not exposing the truth had been to forestall the outcome which did actually eventuate: a marked stepping-up of Soviet ICBM development (Beschloss 1991: 66, 328–9, 350–1).

The implications of Soviet nuclear inferiority for its overall military strategy were doubtless complex, though one priority was abundantly clear: the need to catch up with the Americans. Another was the capacity to 'wage and win' a nuclear war, a policy announced by Khrushchev in 1960 (Holloway 1984: 39–40). Since that time American policy-makers have pointed to the war-fighting aspect of Soviet military doctrine as a threatening and offensive principle, to be met only with an enhancement of America's own deterrent power. The Soviet Union's civil defence plans, which envisaged large-scale evacuation of cities, seemed further proof of Soviet willingness to contemplate waging and winning a nuclear war.

As many commentators have pointed out, however, prevention of war, a political rather than a military principle, was as important in Soviet doctrine as preparing to wage it and grew logically from the view that war between capitalism and communism was no longer considered to be 'fatalistically inevitable'. It also arose, one can assume, from memories of the human and economic costs borne by the Soviet Union in the Second World War, costs which the United States did not bear in the same measure. At any rate, while prudence dictated that the Soviet Union be prepared for war, it also dictated that positive promotion of the forces of peace, combined with the requisite capacity to deter imperialist aggression, would serve to prevent the outbreak of war. In short, the Soviets regarded their essential posture as defensive. The result, however, was a bifurcation in Soviet thinking about nuclear strategy productive of much confusion and misunderstanding in the West. As Raymond Garthoff has described it:

> Soviet military doctrine at the political level has always been held to be defensive, but until recently (1987) at the 'military-technical level' governing strategy, operations, and tactics it has been unabashedly offensive (as incidentally the comparable doctrine of most great powers has been). There is no necessary contradiction between a defensive policy (or in Soviet terms, the political level of military doctrine) and an offensive strategy for waging war should it come.
>
> (Garthoff 1990: 40; and see Holloway 1984: 32–3)

'No necessary contradiction', one might add, as far as the Soviets were concerned, but from the point of view of American planners potentially a deep contradiction. We are confronted with the problem of mutual perception of each other's deterrent postures, a problem complicated by the fact that the Russian language possesses two words used to translate the English 'deterrence'. The word *sderzhivaniye*, which is generally used to describe Soviet policy, means 'constraint', 'holding in check', 'containment', 'deterrence', and carries an essentially defensive overtone. *Utrasheniye*, the term generally employed to describe the American concept of deterrence, on the other hand, implies intimidation, coercion, compellence. The distinction is, of course, as Garthoff points out, self-serving, but, he suggests, 'it also does reflect and embody a different real Soviet perception' (Garthoff 1990: 24–5).

One can legitimately ask, however, whether misperception, real as it undoubtedly was, is a sufficient explanation for the gap between American and Soviet deterrence doctrines. Both sides surely regarded their own basic doctrines as defensive, but given the fine line in nuclear deterrence between defence and offence, both also engaged in planning for the possibility that deterrence would break down. This is not to say that Soviet and American strategies were mirror images of each other. On the contrary, the gap in perception reflected real differences in defence requirements and capabilities. Garthoff notes that 'paradoxically, the only period in which the Soviets claimed superiority and brandished their nuclear weaponry for political pressure was at the time of greatest relative weakness, in the late 1950s and early 1960s' (Garthoff 1990: 19). Is this a paradox, or is it not rather the posture one could expect from a power finding itself at a vital disadvantage in a life or death contest? Moreover, was not this period between the launch of Sputnik and the Cuban missile crisis precisely the time during which the fundamental dynamics of the nuclear arms race, particularly in missiles, were established?

151

The case is not of an either/or interpretation of Soviet nuclear strategy – either offensive or defensive deterrence; nor is it useful to say that despite appearances Soviet strategy was 'in reality' defensive. One is confronted rather with an unstable mixture of offensive and defensive deterrence and more broadly of adventurism and caution. Adventurism, as in Khrushchev's ICBM bluffing and missile deployment in Cuba, represented maximum goals arising from the perceived necessity to take risks to counterbalance the American advantage. Soviet caution, however, was manifested in the tendency to back away from the brink of a crisis – as in Berlin and Cuba – and to insist, as Khrushchev did on many occasions, that prevention of war was the governing principle of Soviet defence policy.

Geopolitics played a role in Soviet strategy, as it did in American. The Soviet Union reaped some advantage from the West's dilemma of extended deterrence, in that the Soviet combination of superior conventional forces and capacity to strike at American bases in Europe enabled it to hold Western Europe 'hostage' to American good behaviour (Freedman 1981: 266). However, if this gave the Soviet Union some leverage, its own vulnerability to attack inclined it to dismiss over-subtle distinctions between general and limited war and conventional and nuclear war. For political purposes the Soviet Union might be able to exploit the ambiguities in Western defence policies, but militarily it could only rely on aggregate military strength, conventional and nuclear, to deter a Western attack. The Soviets were never so inclined as the Americans to envisage a neatly staged process of escalation (with its attendant concepts of intrawar deterrence and bargaining) as a likely scenario for war between NATO and the Warsaw Pact, not least because the primary and direct threat was always to its own territory. For the same reason the Soviets have refused to believe that limited war was possible between the major powers. As Khrushchev put it in his memoirs, 'to those people who claim that the development of nuclear weapons precludes war, I say that the development of nuclear weapons precludes limited war – that is, it precludes war fought with conventional weapons' (Khrushchev 1974: 528).

The implication of the above discussion is that the chief differences between the American and Soviet strategic doctrines arose not primarily from the gap in perception, real as it was, but from the practical and structural conditions which these doctrines were designed to meet. No amount of clarification of each other's positions could remove the fundamental divergence of interests arising from their different security requirements. It was this, surely, which made negotiation on arms control and crisis management so difficult.

DISARMAMENT OR ARMS CONTROL?

International control of atomic energy had been tried in 1946 and had failed, as we saw in Chapter 3. Soviet acquisition of the atomic bomb in 1949 caused the United States to go ahead with a crash programme to produce the 'super' or thermo-nuclear bomb, to which the Soviets responded in kind. The result was a round of efforts by both sides to resurrect proposals to check the arms race and even to end it altogether. It was characteristic of the fluid state of the nuclear stand-off in the 1950s that the rush to achieve maximum security through the production of arms and refinement of strategic doctrines should have been accompanied by what look in retrospect to have been excessively optimistic proposals for disarmament and grand gestures of conciliation. This combination of impulses is testimony less to the belligerence or naivety of the superpower leaders than to the virtual absence of a negotiating culture. The rules of the game had not yet been established.

By the end of the period certain rules had taken root, even if their most obvious fruit – the Limited Test Ban Treaty of 1963 – exerted only a marginal effect on the arms race itself. As it happened, the most important 'rules' may well have been tacit rather than explicit understandings that each side would refrain from actions likely to take them to the brink of war. This was probably the main fruit of the Cuban missile crisis. Equally important was each side's growing awareness that satellite reconaissance might play a stabilizing rather than a destabilizing role by providing an unofficial means of establishing each other's military capabilities and later on of verifying compliance with arms control treaties. This too can be attributed to the change in atmosphere after the missile crisis (Gaddis 1987: 203–6). These understandings, however, were hard won. In the ten years preceding the Test Ban Treaty peace offensives alternated with naked threats.

Eisenhower came into office determined to seek some means of moderating the arms race. Drawing on ideas of J. Robert Oppenheimer, former head of the Manhattan Project and Chairman of the Atomic Energy Committee's General Advisory Council, Eisenhower planned a major speech at the UN. It drew on Oppenheimer's anxiety at the 'terrible immediate peril' of the arms race and his conviction that 'candor' with the American public was vital if the full dimensions of the arms race were to be understood and public support for measures to end it be forthcoming (Oppenheimer 1953: 529, 530–2). Eisenhower set his advisers to work on 'Operation Candor', the outcome of which was the 'Atoms for Peace' address to the UN on 8 December 1953.

In the first part of the speech Eisenhower cited the facts of life of the nuclear arms race, at least to the extent of noting that the destructive power of America's nuclear arsenal exceeded by many times the total of all the bombs dropped during the Second World War. He resisted the suggestion of Oppenheimer and other advisers that he reveal the actual figures for America's stockpile. Noting then that the Soviet Union sought a comparable nuclear capability, he proceeded to outline a means of diverting the military uses of nuclear power to civilian uses. Both powers would contribute fissionable materials to an International Atomic Energy Agency (IAEA) – small amounts in the initial phase. A staff of scientists from many nations would devise ways of employing the material in production of electricity, in medicine, agriculture, and a host of other fields. It was an ingenious scheme for beating nuclear swords into ploughshares and, as Eisenhower observed, it avoided the 'irritations and mutual suspicions incident to any attempt to set up a completely acceptable system of worldwide inspection and control'. Lest the Soviet Union be worried that, given America's lead, the Soviet Union would be at a disadvantage, Eisenhower proposed that the United States contribute five units of fissionable material for every one contributed by the Soviet Union (Ambrose 1984: 147–9).

Like the 'Open Skies' proposal discussed in the last chapter, this one met with an overwhelmingly enthusiastic response from his audience but was rebuffed by the Soviet Union. The IAEA was established but not until 1957 by which time the arms race had moved on. Stephen Ambrose may be justified in saying that 'the Communists allowed their suspicions to overcome their judgement' (Ambrose 1984: 149), but the times were hardly propitious for the kind of mutual under-standing which would have been necessary for such a far-reaching proposal to succeed. Though the Soviet leadership had been advised that Eisenhower was about to make an important announcement about disarmament at the UN, the plan itself was as much a surprise to them as it was to the American public. Even if one acknowledges that Eisenhower conceived of the plan as a modest beginning on a long road towards cooperation, less important for its details than as a statement of intent, as the President himself later observed, 'in the circumstances of the time the proposals were revolu-tionary' (Eisenhower 1963: 254). Furthermore, there was scant follow-up from Eisenhower himself, who seemed satisfied that with the address delivered he could rely on his officials to take it further. Finally, and perhaps most importantly from the Soviet point of view, the proposal contained no provisions for checking the production of nuclear arms or limiting their use (Bundy 1988: 293–5).

Some perspective can be gained on this and other disarmament proposals by reference to the record of overt or implied nuclear threats issued by both sides between 1953 and 1963. These were often veiled in such phrases as 'we shall use all necessary means' or 'we can deliver a smashing rebuff' but the implication was clear – the other side should recognize that *in extremis* no weapon could be considered unusable. On at least four occasions the Eisenhower administration employed nuclear 'compellence', each, significantly, with reference to local conflicts which did not involve the Soviet Union directly. In none of them is it absolutely clear that the nuclear threat rather than some other influence was the deciding factor in producing the desired outcome, but the administration appeared to believe that it was. All four instances related to the Far East: the ending of the Korean War in 1953, the Geneva Accords on Vietnam in 1954, and the two crises over the Chinese offshore islands of Quemoy and Matsu in 1954–5 and 1958, in which Communist China sought to retake the Nationalist-held islands. In all these cases Communist China (a non-nuclear power at this stage) was the chief target, though in at least one instance – during the second crisis over Quemoy and Matsu in 1958 – Khrushchev replied to the United States with a threat of his own.

A far more serious Soviet effort at nuclear pressure came in the summer of 1961 over Berlin. At the height of the tension Khrushchev announced that 'we shall sign the peace treaty [with East Germany] and order our armed forces to administer a worthy rebuff to any aggressor if he dares to raise a hand against the Soviet Union or against our friends'. Such an encounter, he noted, could easily lead to nuclear war (Bundy 1988: 365). The Americans, too, brandished their nuclear power. In response to a question about whether the United States was considering use of nuclear weapons in connection with the Berlin crisis MacNamara replied: 'yes . . . we will use nuclear weapons whenever we feel it necessary to protect our vital interests. Our stockpile is several times that of the Soviet Union' (Newhouse 1989: 157).

On balance it would seem that nuclear threats were used as a reinforcement of other means of exerting pressure. For the United States an important constraint was the knowledge that her allies would oppose actual use of nuclear weapons short of a catastrophic breakdown in East–West relations. More generally, each side accompanied nuclear threats with assurances that it would not be the one to trigger nuclear war. The art of nuclear diplomacy, in so far as one can interpret it as a deliberate strategy, meant allowing room for the other side to retreat from an exposed position without losing all credibility in the eyes of the world.

It is against this background of threat and counter-threat that the test-ban negotiations must be viewed. They took five years of complex and often acrimonious meetings (1957–63), but the event which precipitated concern about the effects of fall-out goes back to 1954. Some days after the United States' BRAVO test of a hydrogen bomb on Bikini atoll it was reported that the crew of a Japanese fishing boat were suffering from the classic symptoms of radiation sickness. Six months later one of them died. Worldwide publicity about the incident touched off heated debate about disarmament in general and nuclear testing in particular. Efforts by the American administration to calm public fears only increased them when the Chairman of the US Atomic Energy Commission, Lewis Strauss, revealed in reply to a question at a press conference that one H-bomb could wipe out the metropolitan area of New York (Divine 1978: 6–9, 13). This was not quite what J. Robert Oppenheimer had meant by the need for 'candor' about nuclear weapons, since the admission was sprung on a largely unprepared public. In any event, it ensured that the issue of nuclear weapons and fall-out would never be far from the headlines over the next few years. Ban the bomb movements had their start in these events and gathered momentum during the 1950s and early 1960s, paralleling the test-ban negotiations themselves. Significantly, they lost impetus once the Test Ban Treaty was signed.

The full story of the negotiations is too detailed to be told here. Three considerations will help to place them in perspective. The first is that initial discussions of a test ban were linked to general nuclear disarmament. Indeed the American position until April 1958 was that a commitment to nuclear disarmament must precede agreement on a test ban, a policy which reflected the military's reluctance to stop testing and in which they were supported by Lewis Strauss. The Soviet Union, by contrast, tended to see a test ban as an end in itself. Several influences conspired to reverse the American position in 1958 – increased public anxiety about fall-out, following a series of

H-bomb tests by both the United States and the Soviet Union during 1957, the suspension by the Soviet Union of its atmospheric tests in March 1958, exposing the United States to the charge that it was less cognizant of the nuclear danger than the Soviet Union, and a change in personnel of Eisenhower's scientific advisers. The creation of a new body, the President's Scientific Advisory Committee, headed by James Killian and staffed by scientists who were persuaded of the value of arms control, released Eisenhower from dependence on Lewis Strauss and devotees of the H-bomb such as Edward Teller (Divine 1978: 211–12). The result was a shift towards separating test-ban negotiations from general nuclear disarmament. This would make agreement on a test ban more likely but, of course, at the cost of leaving weapons production effectively unchecked.

The second important consideration regarding the test-ban negotiations grows directly out of this last point. At a time when the arms race was in a highly dynamic phase no country – and this includes the British and French who were engaged on their own H-bomb tests – would readily contemplate the end of testing if that would leave them at a disadvantage. A competition among the parties to the negotiations ensued, involving the tactical suspension of tests designed to take the political and moral high ground but at a minimal cost to their own weapons development. 'As one side completed a series,' writes John Newhouse, 'its willingness to stop would rise, while its adversary would turn away from the idea until it too had conducted its next scheduled round of tests' (Newhouse 1989: 139–40).

The technology of detection also played a role in this political dynamic. Once it became evident that underground tests up to a certain level could remain undetected in the absence of intrusive means of inspection, efforts to produce a comprehensive ban on tests fell foul of Soviet resistance to American inspection proposals. By the spring of 1960, when it appeared that both sides were willing to move towards an agreement which would ban all atmospheric tests and all but the smallest underground tests, the U-2 spy plane incident intervened to destroy such trust as had been built up (Divine 1978: 31–41). It took the Cuban missile crisis to concentrate the minds of Soviet and American leaders sufficiently to produce the final Treaty in 1963. It was limited, however, to atmospheric tests, indicating the continuing force both of technological competition and the limits of mutual trust.

The missile crisis points to the third important consideration in the test-ban issue. The link between the two reveals the extent to which the test-ban negotiations were a barometer of the wider relations between the superpowers and between them and their allies. In one sense the Test Ban Treaty represents a modest triumph of the spirit of compromise, providing, as one commentator has put it, 'an important learning experience and the confidence to make progress in other areas'. The Treaty 'generated the necessary impetus for the series of arms-control agreements that followed in the late 1960s and early 1970s' (White 1987: 104). When the final result is compared with the earlier aspirations for nuclear disarmament, however, the Treaty looks far less impressive. Agreement was possible only because of a progressive narrowing of the focus, and then in large part because the missile crisis had provoked recognition in Washington and Moscow that the nuclear danger demanded something more than the ritual parading of their differences. Yes, the Treaty institutionalized *détente* within specified bounds but it also served to legitimate the wider framework within which it was set – the arms race itself.

Indeed for this reason arms control was acceptable to many who opposed disarmament. It was and is one of the signal features of arms control agreements that they tend to undermine the rationale for disarmament, relegating it to the level of fantasy. It is even arguable that arms control agreements promote the arms race, in that in specifying what is impermissible all else is deemed to be permissible. Doubtless this is to go too far, since it takes no account of the informal behavioural constraints generated by the commitments entailed in any arms agreement. Certainly while the weapons were piled up ever higher on both sides after 1963 there were few if any instances in the coming years of the kind of nuclear *machismo* so characteristic of the 1950s and early 1960s.

Finally, in connection with the test-ban talks as a barometer of superpower relations, the Test Ban Treaty pointed up the growing dominance of the US–Soviet bilateral relationship in arms talks. The test-ban talks had begun under the aegis of the UN and took place primarily in Geneva. In these Britain played a significant mediating role once the Macmillan government had swallowed its doubts about the likely effect of a test ban on Britain's independent nuclear deterrent. Ironically, Macmillan's most important contribution to breaking the deadlock in negotiations – his suggestion in March 1963 that the United States and the Soviet Union negotiate directly in Moscow rather than Geneva – may have served to heighten the bilateral superpower profile of the talks. Thereafter, with the exception of the Nuclear Proliferation Treaty of 1968, which by its nature was a multinational treaty, nuclear arms talks have taken place on a bilateral basis (Sanders 1990: 192–3).

Moreover, the period of the test-ban negotiations marked important shifts within the blocs. The conclusion of the Treaty confirmed and deepened the Sino–Soviet split, Soviet unwillingness to give China nuclear weapons having been a major bone of contention since the late 1950s (Crankshaw 1966: 116). Firmly embarked now on its own nuclear programme, the Chinese could only view the Treaty as a superpower conspiracy to prevent other powers from acquiring their own nuclear deterrents. The Chinese had affirmed in 1960 that they would not be bound by 'an international agreement concerning disarmament' (Newhouse 1989: 195). By 1966 China had made its first test.

France viewed the Treaty in a similar light. Signing the Treaty would have seriously impaired France's nuclear programme. Besides, the legacy of the Suez crisis of 1956 still rankled. It was this which had led France to develop its own nuclear deterrent in the first place and to begin its process of detachment from the United States. Furthermore, De Gaulle was furious at the so-called 'Nassau agreement' of 1962 under which the United States had agreed to sell the Polaris submarine missile system to Britain. France too had been offered Polaris but on less favourable terms, confirming De Gaulle's view that Britain had become an American 'satellite'. De Gaulle's 'cult of independence' saw fruit in a sequence of decisions – from its refusal to sign the Test Ban Treaty, its blocking of British entry into the Common Market, its recognition of Red China, and withdrawal from NATO's military structure (Werth 1965: 327, Ch. 10).

Britain meanwhile had recemented its relations with the United States after Suez with surprising speed, the work largely of Macmillan. Though not as subservient to United States interests as De Gaulle claimed, Britain continued to place great reliance on the Atlantic connection even after the election of a Labour government in 1964 and Britain's studied detachment from America's Vietnam policy had led to a cooling of the 'special relationship'. The Test Ban Treaty, however, marked an important divide. It is hard to think of any instance after 1963 in which a British statesman played the role in US–Soviet relations which Eden did at Geneva in 1954 or Macmillan did in the test-ban talks. Curiously, as the world became more multipolar and the blocs less rigid, the bilateral superpower relationship became more salient and exclusive, at least as regards the nuclear issue.

THE CUBAN MISSILE CRISIS

The Cuban missile crisis embodied all the dynamics which had characterized the development of the arms race in the previous decade: its competitive nature, the uncertainties inherent in the nuclear stand-off, the fear that conflict 'on the periphery' might trigger war at the centre, and not least the significance of individual leadership and of domestic factors influencing decision-making. But the missile crisis also crystallized these tensions in a peculiarly stark fashion, making it an event to which analysts have returned again and again in seeking clues to the nuclear danger in the superpower relationship, and above all to the behaviour of the superpower leaderships in moments of crisis. Here the debates can only be touched on. A brief outline of the events of October 1962 will serve to introduce the main issues involved.

The Cuban revolution was close to four years old in October 1962. Fidel Castro had consolidated his power internally, having within a year of his victory over the Batista dictatorship resolved any ambiguity about his relation to communism. Mutual hostility between Castro and the Americans, signalled by expropriation of American assets in Cuba and an American trade embargo on Cuba, soon removed any basis for accommodation. A Cuban economy almost entirely dependent on American trade prior to 1959, within three years of the revolution was effectively integrated into the Soviet bloc. By the beginning of 1962 the Soviet Union and Eastern Europe accounted for 80 per cent of Cuba's trade. Soviet arms defended Cuban soil which, as the Americans hardly needed reminding, lay a mere 90 miles off the Florida coast.

It was, of course, Soviet arms which triggered the missile crisis. During the summer of 1962 enough Soviet hardware and personnel arrived in Cuba to produce calls from

Senator Goldwater and others for an immediate invasion. Kennedy moved cautiously – there was as yet no evidence of 'offensive' missiles – gaining an assurance from Khrushchev as late as 17 October that he had no intention of installing offensive missiles in Cuba. The date is significant. The previous day American photographic intelligence had confirmed the existence of intermediate and medium-range ballistic (IRBM and MRBM) missile sites in Cuba. Kennedy moved quickly to set up a crisis team, formally designated as the 'Ex-Comm' (or Executive Committee of the National Security Council), which met almost continuously until the crisis was resolved.

The bare facts of the crisis can be quickly summarized. Relatively little debate took place about the goal of seeking the removal of the missiles. Their deployment was considered to be a provocative and aggressive threat to American security, an unacceptable unilateral change in the military and political *status quo*. The Ex-Comm swiftly narrowed down the range of possible options to two: an air strike or a blockade (more precisely a 'quarantine', since technically a blockade could be considered an act of war). By Saturday 20 October Kennedy had firmly decided upon a quarantine, which was publicly announced on the evening of Monday the 22nd and over the next five days produced the desired effect of checking the flow of missiles to Cuba. Several Soviet ships bound for Cuba, including one which was known to be carrying nuclear warheads, turned back to Soviet ports. The quarantine, however, was only one of the potential flash-points. In Cuba itself work on the missile sites was continuing, with the likelihood that they might soon be operational. It could not be assumed that no warheads had got through. Plans for an American invasion of Cuba were prepared and US bases around the world put on a high state of alert in the expectation that an American move in Cuba might produce a Soviet response, most probably in Berlin.

The resolution of the crisis was as tense as the operation of the blockade had been. On the evening of Friday the 26th a letter was received from Khrushchev, containing the seeds of a solution acceptable to the United States – removal of Soviet offensive weapons from Cuba in return for lifting the quarantine and an American pledge not to invade Cuba. As the Ex-Comm considered its reply, however, a second letter was received from the Kremlin which was markedly less conciliatory than the first. It also raised the stakes, demanding as a quid pro quo for the removal of Soviet missiles from Cuba the removal of recently installed American Jupiter and Thor missiles in Turkey. Tension reached a peak on the evening of Saturday 27 October as the Ex-Comm deliberated, heightened by news of the shooting down of an American U-2 spy plane over Cuba with the death of the pilot. After much agonizing the solution adopted was to reply positively to the first letter as if the second had not been received, coupled with a strong warning of the consequences should the Soviet Union continue on its present course. The ploy paid off. On Sunday morning Khrushchev communicated his agreement on the basis of the terms set out in his first letter. The Americans for their part let the Soviets know that the missiles in Turkey would be removed, though this was not included as part of the formal agreement between the governments. Though implementation of the agreement took some months, the immediate crisis was over by the morning of 28 October.

The crisis has proved a magnet for theorists of international relations and for historians. Among the theorists, Graham Allison employed the missile crisis as a means of studying decision-making processes. Of course he was also concerned to elucidate the facts of the crisis, and, despite the mass of recent research, his study remains an important starting point for knowledge of the events. The theoretical purpose, however, remains primary. Factual knowledge of the events has received a great boost in recent years from the revelations which have emerged from joint US–Soviet study groups on the crisis, made possible by the climate of *glasnost* in the Soviet Union. It may be that we can use this new knowledge to reflect back on the questions raised by Allison.

In essence, Allison's question is: what can the missile crisis tell us about the relationship between particular policies – the Soviet emplacement of missiles in Cuba, for example – and their outcomes? In seeking explanations of the origins and consequences of foreign policy initiatives, what intepretative frameworks are most likely to yield the most adequate results? Allison elaborates three conceptual schemes, the first being the 'common sense' approach employed by most analysts and laymen alike. He terms this the 'rational actor model' (or Model I). Those employing this model 'attempt to understand happenings in foreign affairs as the more or less purposive acts of unified national governments' (Allison 1971: 4–5).

Models II and III dispense with the notion of a unitary decision-making body in different ways, arguing instead that analysts must confront the 'intra-national mechanisms from which governmental actions emerge'. Model II, termed the 'organizational process model', replaces Model I's assumption of purposive acts and choices with a focus on the 'outputs of large organizations functioning according to regular patterns of behaviour', the question being: 'from what organizational context and pressures did this decision emerge?' (Allison 1971: 6). Model III, termed the 'bureaucratic decision-making model', bears a close relation to Model II, in that it emphasizes intra-governmental processes, but explains events, not in terms of choices or outputs, but as the 'resultant of various bargaining games among players in the national government'. Politics rather than organizational processes are thus conceived by the Model III analyst to be the central explanatory concept (Allison 1971: 6–7).

As Allison is aware, the test of an explanatory scheme lies in how much of reality it is capable of explaining. Here we can examine only one of the many questions posed by Allison, the question of why the Soviet Union installed the missiles in Cuba. Even limiting ourselves to this one area, only a sketch of Allison's richly detailed account can be given. With reference to Model I, in examining the various reasons for the Soviet decision to place missiles in Cuba, Allison settles on the view that it was primarily designed to rectify the imbalance in missile capacity between the superpowers and more specifically to enhance the Soviet capacity to reach American soil with its missiles (and thus compensate for the Soviet Union's relative weakness in

ICBMs). Such a hypothesis, he writes, 'permits an understanding of the Cuban venture as another application of the strategy that the Soviets had been pursuing for the previous five years: the strategy of bluff and deception designed to rectify the adverse strategic balance' (Allison 1971: 55). There are several puzzles, however, which are not resolved by the Model I approach. The method and the timing of the installation of the missiles does not square with the assumption of a planned and purposive strategy. Among the puzzles Allison cites are that surface-to-air anti-aircraft batteries (SAMs) were installed after rather than before work on the MRBM sites was finished, the reverse of what one would expect; there was no attempt made to camouflage the missile sites, nor did the Soviets apparently take account of American U-2 flights; furthermore, the Soviets ignored Kennedy's repeated warnings about the consequences of placing offensive missiles in Cuba (Allison 1971: 55–6).

What can Model II do to clarify some of the problems not solved by Model I? 'Many pieces of this maze of seeming contradictions', writes Allison, 'become considerably less puzzling if one assumes the perspective of an observer of the outputs of Soviet organizations.' Standard Soviet operating procedures, most notably the premium on secrecy in Soviet decision-making in general and nuclear policy in particular, can account for some of the anomalies: 'each organization's tendency to "do what it knows how to do" was reinforced by a lack of information about the activity of other organizations and the impossibility of an overview of the whole operation'. Shipping, unloading, and transport to the missile sites was under the eye of military intelligence and the KGB, but once on site the personnel of the Strategic Rocket Services took over. Never having installed missiles outside the Soviet Union, they chose the deployment format they were familiar with (and which was familiar to American intelligence), and felt no need to camouflage the missiles because it had never been done in the Soviet Union. Besides, that would take time and risk failure to meet the schedule for completion. The SAM batteries in turn were under another command – the Air Defence Command – which proceeded according to its familiar pattern, independently of the IRBM and MRBM installations (Allison 1971: 109–11). In short, however clear cut the decision may have been in the mind of Khrushchev himself, implementation of policy was subject to pressures which substantially affected outcomes.

What of Model III? Allison concedes that assessment of the internal political background to the decision to install missiles must be largely speculative, since so little is known about Soviet decision-making processes. In the light of the Model III approach Allison begins by noting that American public response to the Soviet build-up of arms in Cuba during the summer of 1962 was sufficiently ambiguous to leave some doubt as to how seriously its warnings to the Soviet Union should be taken. Into this grey area it was possible for various Soviet leaders possessing very different motives to come to agreement on a policy which served not a single purpose but several. From the Model III perspective, writes Allison, 'it seems likely that the decision emerged not from global grand planning – the Soviet government (or

Khrushchev) standing back and considering, for example, where to probe the United States – but rather from a process in which a number of different individuals' quite distinct perceptions of separable problems snow-balled into a solution' (Allison 1971: 237). These could range from Party leaders who had been urging specific Soviet security guarantees to Cuba for two years, to military leaders anxious to close the missile gap, and to economic planners attracted to the missile emplacement as a cheaper way of meeting Soviet strategic needs (Allison 1971: 238–44).

The differences between these three approaches lie not in the fact that they give different answers to the same question but that they yield differently formulated questions. While Model I, for example, asks the question 'why were the missiles placed in Cuba?' and answers that 'Khrushchev' or 'Moscow' or 'the Kremlin', acting with calculated rationality, believed that it was a useful means of rectifying the strategic imbalance, Models II and III shift the ground by asking respectively 'what kinds of processes led to the missile decision?' and 'whose interests did the decision serve?' Doubtless, as Allison points out, 'the best analysts of foreign policy manage to weave strands of each of the three conceptual models into their explanations', but while they may be complementary in some respects, in other respects their implications may be incompatible (Allison 1971: 258–9). Allison's broad aim indeed is to question the common assumption that Model I is an adequate all-purpose approach. What Model I does best is analysis of long-term policy trends, for which the assumption of rationality is a useful shorthand (Allison 1971: 257–8). In analysing the details of events, however, Models II and III represent a marked gain because they give more attention to the institutional contexts of events and processes. Perhaps the differences between the models are most obviously revealed in assessments of the lessons of the missile crisis drawn by the three models. The Model I lesson is that nuclear crises are 'manageable'; leaders will have little difficulty in thinking through alternative courses of action and arriving at satisfactory limited policies. The lessons of Models II and III, however, are that 'nuclear crises between machines as large as the United States and Soviet governments are inherently chancy', making the process of crisis management 'obscure and terribly risky' (Allison 1971: 259–60).

Much of the new information which has been published about the missile crisis tends to confirm Allison's assessment of the significance of Models II and III for an understanding of the events, though it has by no means displaced Model I. As one would expect, the most important new revelations refer to Soviet decision-making, though there are some important new findings about American policy too. Much of the evidence is complex and contradictory and, since it is still appearing, will take years to digest. It is sufficient, however, to suggest that both sides made decisions which were based on scanty information, guesswork, or misinterpretation of each other's actions and motives.

In the first place, it seems clear from the record of the sequence of conferences held since 1987 – attended by participants in the crisis from both sides – that Soviet motives for installing the missiles were mixed, and that even now Soviet individuals disagree on whether the prime reason was to protect Cuba (as Khrushchev stated in his memoirs, 1971: 494) or to right the strategic imbalance (Blight and Welch 1990: 238–43; Lebow 1988: 15–16). On the other hand, much greater emphasis is now given to the Soviet aim of protecting Cuba, as research on American attempts to destabilize Cuba has proceeded. Even Robert McNamara, while protesting that the Kennedy administration had no intention of invading Cuba, conceded that 'if I was a Cuban and read the evidence of covert American action against their government, I would be quite ready to believe that the U.S. intended to mount an invasion' (Blight and Welch 1990: 329–30). One historian has taken this same point further and argued, on the basis of the United States' efforts 'to harrass, isolate, and destroy the radical government in Havana', that without these 'there would not have been a Cuban missile crisis'. 'The origins of the crisis, then,' it is concluded 'derived largely from the concerted campaign to quash the Cuban revolution' (Paterson 1990: 256). An argument which began as an attempt to understand the source of the crisis in Soviet policy thus ends by locating it in American policy. A later analysis concluded that 'the new evidence suggests that Moscow and Havana were justified in suspecting that Washington was considering an invasion of Cuba, although it does not confirm that a decision to order an invasion was, in fact, ever made' (Hershberg 1992: 238). At the very least, however, this line of argument has redirected attention to the Cuban factor in the crisis, a point to which we shall return.

Secondly, an interview conducted with Sergo Mikoyan (son of deputy Prime Minister Anastas Mikoyan at the time of the crisis) confirms Allison's hypothesis about the method and timing of emplacement of the missiles and the absence of camouflage. The technicians, Mikoyan states, 'were military men and they only knew the order to build it, and they were used to building these sites at home. They acted in Cuba as if they were in the USSR' (Greiner: 1990: 214). Model II, with its emphasis on standard operating procedures in defiance of changed conditions, yields positive results here.

Thirdly, there were far more Soviet troops deployed in Cuba during 1962 than American intelligence had known at the time. Its highest estimate during the crisis was 12,000–16,000, upped to 22,000 in a restrospective estimate made in 1963. In fact the number was 42,000 in October 1962 (Garthoff 1988: 67). If, as Garthoff notes, the American government had known the true number, the troop issue 'would have stretched tension still tighter' (Garthoff 1989: 121).

Fourthly, much new information has been revealed about the shooting down of the American U-2 plane. On the basis of somewhat inconclusive evidence, one claim is that the finger on the trigger of the SAM missile battery in question was Cuban rather than Soviet. The SAM site, it is said, had been forcibly seized by Cuban troops, with the implication that Castro's determination to press the Soviets into the strongest possible response to the Americans was an important and dangerous factor in the crisis. This view has been firmly rejected by other scholars on the basis of statements by Soviet officials, who confirm that the order to shoot down the U-2 was given by the local Soviet commander (Trachtenberg 1990: 244–5). Differences of opinion exist also on the significance of this apparent loss of control between the decision-making centre in Moscow and the Soviet commander on the ground. Some scholars suggest that, since the Americans assumed the order came from Moscow and that it therefore represented a 'conscious provocation and escalation by Khrushchev', this incident was among the most inflammatory of the crisis. A different reading of the evidence, however, indicates that the Ex-Comm made no categorical assumption about where the order to shoot down the U-2 came from. In any case, not only did the Ex-Comm choose to respond in a moderate fashion but the Americans were assured by the Soviets at the time that 'it had been an accident and that it would not be repeated' (Trachtenberg 1990: 245, 246).

This incident, of course, took place at a critical juncture in the crisis: at the moment when the Ex-Comm was puzzling over how to respond to the two letters which had been received from Khrushchev. Until recently it had been thought that the first more moderate letter was the work of Khrushchev himself, while the second bore the stamp of hardliners in the Kremlin, a view which would seem to illustrate the dynamics of Model III. In fact, it now appears, the difference in tone and substance of the letters reflected a change in Soviet intelligence estimates of the likelihood of an American attack on Cuba. The first was written when it was believed that an American attack was imminent, leaving no time for diplomatic bargaining, the second when it appeared that the danger of an immediate attack was past, in which case the Soviet leadership could now afford to up the ante and spin out the bargaining process (Blight and Welch 1990: 342). In this they were forestalled by the American decision to ignore the second letter. One could perhaps, then, interpret this particular incident in the light of Model I with its assumption that policy is based on a rational calculation of advantage.

Among the most contentious issues raised by new evidence concerns the role of short-range Soviet nuclear missiles designed for use in a possible American invasion of Cuba. The debate is not about whether they were present in Cuba – it seems clear that they were – but whether, as some scholars claim, the local Soviet commander had authority to use them without reference to Moscow. The debate is highly technical and cannot be rehearsed here, but the question bears on assessments of the level of risk in the crisis. Indeed, this particular debate is the clearest case of a divide which has always existed in studies of the missile crisis but which has widened considerably since 1987 between those who tend to point up the risk of nuclear war in the crisis and those who are more inclined to downplay such dangers. On balance, on the particular issue of authority to order the use of tactical nuclear missiles in Cuba the weight of evidence and argument would seem to lie with Mark Kramer's view that the local commander was specifically prohibited from firing the missiles on his own authority (Kramer 1993: 40, 42–6; cf. Blight *et al.* 1993: 41, 47–50). This conclusion seems warranted, however, not merely on technical–historical grounds but because it is more consistent with the overall patterns of interaction during the crisis.

As it happens, the most important piece of new evidence regarding American policy tends to confirm the view that there were important forces at work making for restraint. It had always been assumed that Kennedy was unwilling to trade the American missiles in Turkey for the Soviet missiles in Cuba, since this would have been visibly to back down under Soviet pressure, indeed to legitimize the Soviet action by equating their Cuban missiles with the American missiles in Turkey. The chosen tactic, as mentioned above, was to convey to the Soviets that the Turkish missiles would be removed but that this was not to be considered part of the Cuban deal. It has now emerged that Kennedy held in reserve a message to be passed to the UN Secretary-General, U Thant, which proposed the removal of the missiles in Turkey and in Cuba. As Dean Rusk (Kennedy's Secretary of State) remarked in retrospect, 'I think this . . . ploy would have been used before we landed troops in Cuba, because landing those troops in Cuba with thirty thousand or more Russian troops in there and Russian missiles there would have been a major escalation from the Soviet point of view' (Blight and Welch 1990: 173–4). In the event, of course, the Soviets accepted Kennedy's offer of the 27th October which left the removal of the Turkish missiles as an informal verbal assurance. The UN ploy therefore was never activated. It does show, however, that Kennedy was prepared to go to greater lengths than was previously believed to check a possible escalation of the crisis beyond control. To this evidence of positive moves for restraint one could add negative instances – such as Khrushchev's decision not to respond aggressively to an American U-2 flight which strayed into Siberian airspace on the 27th or to the action of American naval vessels forcing a Soviet submarine to the surface near the quarantine line around Cuba. These cases are comparable with the Ex-Comm's decision not to allow the downing of the U-2 over Cuba to arrest the moves towards a resolution of the crisis.

Numerous other details have emerged from recent studies, but the above points will serve to show the kinds of issues which they raise. The 'what-ifs' multiply as more evidence appears, suggesting that in many respects Allison's call for a reorientation of international relations scholarship towards study of foreign policy processes was salutary. So much of the evidence points towards the significance of procedures and bureaucratic processes, of personalities, perceptions and misperceptions. The simple assumption that policy was unitary, rational, and purposive in character cannot stand as a catch-all explanation. Nevertheless, as we have seen, the evidence points in several directions, and much of it tends to support the view that, despite the many incalcul-able elements in the decision-making processes, in crucial instances the leaders on both sides chose courses of action which were both non-provocative and allowed room for retreat from exposed positions.

We might think of the decision-making process as composed of a core around which much peripheral and often random activity took place which might tend to distract attention from the core and even threaten to disintegrate it. If we picture the core as control, the integrity of the decision-making process itself, then little conclusive evidence has so far been produced to indicate that either side was prepared deliberately to pursue actions which would provoke a loss of control. On the contrary, in the main the reverse was true. Intentions, of course, were not everything. Indeed, even at the time and without access to the knowledge we now have, the decision-makers could hardly have been unaware that they were walking on a knife edge between maintenance of control and catastrophe. This awareness was enough to stimulate efforts in the aftermath of the crisis to find ways of reducing the force of the incalculable, of misperceptions, and the role of potentially dangerous contingencies. The institution of a 'hot-line' connection between the White House and the Kremlin, the move towards conclusion of the Limited Test Ban Treaty, the joint US–Soviet agreement to support a UN resolution banning the placing of nuclear weapons in space, and even the resolve to seek a Nuclear Non-Proliferation Treaty (not signed until 1969) all owed much to the shock of the missile crisis (Garthoff 1989: 134–5). *Détente* itself showed the impress of the missile crisis.

In sum, if it is no longer adequate to picture the crisis as a masterpiece of crisis management, it is equally wrong to exaggerate the risks of a breakdown of control – of nuclear war itself.

There is an important twist in the tale. Neither Castro nor his revolution was unseated by the crisis. Indeed for this reason Khrushchev had some justification for his claim that the Soviet Union had 'achieved . . . a spectacular success without having to fire a single shot!'(Khrushchev 1971: 504). The Cuban revolution remained a substantial breach in the wall of the Monroe Doctrine which the United States was never able to plug. In 1970 and again in 1979 mini-Cuban crises erupted, both arising from apparent attempts by the Soviet Union to increase its military presence in Cuba, and in both cases the United States invoked what might be called the 'spirit of '62' to check these moves. The military stalemate over Cuba, however, did not prevent Castro from dispatching troops to Angola in 1975 to support the revolutionary regime there following Portugal's withdrawal from Africa. The implication of these points is that missile crisis must be viewed within the context of revolutionary change in the Third World and not merely of the arms race. This is the subject of the next chapter.

8

THE UNITED STATES, THE SOVIET UNION, AND THE THIRD WORLD, 1953–1963

PATTERNS OF DEPENDENCE AND INDEPENDENCE

By comparison with the United States' own period of nation-building the new nations of the post-war years possessed few advantages. Distance from the major powers counted for far less in an age of global communications and transport. Economically many of the new nations continued to be restricted by the arrangements under which colonies had been managed to the benefit of the mother countries. As in the main producers of raw materials, former colonies remained dependent upon the prices the developed nations were prepared to pay for raw materials and by the necessity to buy many of their manufactured goods on the world market. Politically the new nations, with some exceptions such as India, were thrown on their own devices without much administrative or political experience among the indigenous populations. Furthermore, many (including in this instance India) contained diverse ethnic, tribal and religious groupings which undercut efforts to create cohesive national institutions and sentiments – testimony to the arbitrary fashion in which colonial boundaries had been drawn by the colonial powers.

These and other associated difficulties led so-called 'dependency theorists' in the 1960s and 1970s to argue that former colonies had merely exchanged direct imperialism for 'informal' imperialism or neo-colonialism. While there is much justice in this view, the full story is more complex. If we consider the reasons for the decline of colonialism, it is apparent both that the processes of decolonization varied considerably in different parts of the world and that the emergence of what came to be called the 'Third World' became an important independent factor in the world balance of power.

The combined effect of the 'psychological and spiritual awakening' among Asian and African, Carribean and Pacific peoples and the declining will and capacity of colonial powers to maintain their ascendancy must count as the chief forces at work. The upheavals of the two world wars hastened both processes, the Second World War in many cases completing what the First had begun. The example of the Bolshevik Revolution and the rise of the Soviet Union to world power offered an alternative model of political and socio-economic development which, moreover, in the context of the cold war was explicitly anti-Western. Even where the Soviet model was considered inappropriate, aspiring or newly independent nations could under certain circumstances play one superpower off against another, thereby increasing their own political options. Finally, the increased legitimacy of the principle of self-determination and its embodiment along with universal principles of human rights in the charter of the United Nations was a powerful challenge to the old order, even where such values were not observed in practice (Bull 1984: 224–8).

Clearly these general factors must be refined down in order to take account of the variety of specific cases, but they do offer a framework for understanding the conditions affecting Third World nations in the two decades following the Second World War. The most important refinements to be made lie in recognizing regional differences and the intersection between decolonization processes and the development of the cold war.

Decolonization took markedly different forms in Asia and Africa. In India the issue was not so much whether independence should be granted as how it should be managed. As R.F. Holland has observed, 'the breakdown of the Raj's administrative control, the demands on the UK's military resources in other parts of the world and the Labour party's victory in the 1945 British general election all pointed towards an early decolonization' (Holland 1985: 74). The Philippines, acquired by the United States in 1898, gained independence in 1946 in conformity with a pledge made in 1934. Elsewhere Japan's wartime occupation of large areas of East, Southeast, and South Asia dealt a blow to Western colonization from which the Western colonizers never fully recovered. The stimulus to independence provided by Japan's displacement of Western rule was if anything heightened by the evidence that Japanese dominance was no more congenial than that of Western powers. Having been initially welcomed, for example, in the Dutch East Indies (later Indonesia) as liberators from Western rule, the Japanese soon squandered their credit 'as the Japanese military began to harness the Indonesian economy to meet Japan's wartime needs' (McMahon 1981: 35). In Southeast Asia the issue was immediately raised in 1945 of whether the European powers would be able to re-establish colonial rule. The French (in Indo-China), the British (in Malaya), and the Dutch (in the East Indies) moved quickly to regain their hold over these territories but soon found themselves engaged in bitter guerrilla wars with nationalist movements.

The cold war dimension was manifest in these cases in two important respects. Firstly, within each of these territories communist insurgency was a powerful destabilizing influence even where (as in the Dutch East Indies) the dominant nationalist movement was non-communist. Furthermore, the Stalinist policy, which held sway until his death in 1953, of dismissing all non-communist nationalists as bourgeois and of giving strong support to communists, exacerbated the tensions within the nations seeking independence. Secondly, the patterns of decolonization were affected by American perceptions, not only of the role of communists in these Southeast Asian nations but of the European balance of power. The United States was prepared to put much more pressure on the Dutch to grant independence to the East Indies than on the French to concede self-rule to Vietnam, both because in Sukarno Indonesia possessed a strong non-communist nationalist leader and because the Dutch were less capable than the French of resisting American demands to conform to its policies in Europe. By contrast, not only was the strongest force for independence in Vietnam communist led, but the United States needed France's agreement to its policy of rebuilding West Germany economically and politically in the late 1940s. Part of the price of this agreement was a soft-pedalling of America's declaratory policy of anti-colonialism and effective endorsement of France's desire to resume control of Vietnam. In short, from the outset the fate of independence struggles was influenced by external Great Power machinations as well as by internal factors. Later in this chapter we shall examine precisely how these forces interacted.

Africa presents a wholly different case. Except for the military campaigns in North Africa between 1941 and 1943 Africa was not a major theatre of battle during the Second World War, and there was no radical disruption to the pattern of colonial rule such as was produced in Asia by the Japanese occupations. Certainly the main European colonial powers in Africa – Britain, France, Belgium, and Portugal – envisaged no change in the direction of a speedy granting of independence to the colonies. In fact, writes Holland, 'the late 1940s and early 1950s were the heyday of African empire, when it seemed to have a coherence and a dynamic of its own' (Holland 1985: 128). Since neither the United States nor the Soviet Union had a history of involvement in Africa, they scarcely possessed African policies and largely left the European colonial powers to their own devices. As late as 1957 the American foreign service had only 248 officers in its 33 African posts, compared to its 256 officers in West Germany alone (Ferrell 1975: 193). In the 1940s and 1950s Africa was not an important factor in the cold war. The event which changed the face of Africa was the Suez crisis of 1956, which for Britain and France at least proved to be a turning point in the history of empire no less than in their relations with the United States. The details will be discussed later. For the moment it is enough to point out that in the years immediately following Suez, the combination of the loss of European colonial nerve and the rising tide of nationalism in Africa led to a rash of grants of independence between 1957 and 1964. (Among the major new nations were Ghana, 1957; the Congo, later Zaïre, 1960; Uganda, 1962; Algeria, 1962; Kenya, 1963; Nigeria, 1963; Zambia, 1964.)

As compared with Asia, Africa continued to provoke little direct superpower interest or intervention, though the Congo crisis between 1960 and 1965 was an important exception. In combination with other insurgencies and independence struggles in the Third World – the Cuban Revolution of 1959, conflict in Laos and Vietnam, and the tide of nationalism in Africa being among the most significant – the Congo crisis supplied the stimulus to President Kennedy's pledge in his inaugural address to help 'those peoples in the huts and villages of half the globe struggling to break the bonds of mass misery'. Africa was to remain, however, a distinctly marginal sphere of interest for both superpowers until in the mid-1970s the ending of Portuguese rule over Angola and Mozambique and conflict between Ethiopia and Somalia produced a new and more critical round of superpower confrontation in Africa. (This is discussed in Chapter 11.)

For the Middle East, as for Asia, the Second World War proved decisive in breaking the mould of empire, though the process had begun after the establishment of the mandate system under the League of Nations, and in some cases (Egypt, Iraq, and Saudi Arabia) independence preceded the Second World War. The strength of Arab nationalism ensured that the vestiges of Western colonialism would all but disappear, though Britain in particular continued to believe that its extensive and long-standing economic and political interests in the region would allow it to retain substantial influence (Holland 1985: 113). Until the Suez crisis of 1956 Britain retained a large military base in Egypt to protect its control of the canal, and until 1967 a British presence was maintained in Aden. It was not until 1971, with the grant of independence to the Gulf Emirates (collectively known on independence as the United Arab Emirates), that Britain departed from the Middle East.

Britain's slow and conflict-ridden retreat from the Middle East coincided, however, with two developments which had the effect of transforming the region from a sphere of old-style imperialism into one in which cold war competition would become significant. The first was the creation of the state of Israel in 1948 which inflamed the Arab world by raising to new levels of intensity the traditional enmity of Arab and Jew and by reintroducing what Arab nations regarded as a Western-oriented wedge of influence into the Middle East. The second was the exploitation of oil resources on a new and massive scale. Both developments, as far as the superpowers were concerned, sharply raised the political and economic stakes in the region. A volatile mixture of increasing superpower interest, Arab nationalism, Israeli assertiveness on behalf of its own defence, and British (and French) determination to maintain control over the Suez Canal resulted in 1956 in a crisis which resolved the issue of vestigial European influence by effectively removing it but left the other elements very much in play. In the aftermath of 1956 the Soviet Union cemented its relations with Egypt (not entirely, as we shall see later, to the satisfaction of either party) and extended its connections with other Arab states, while the United States announced the 'Eisenhower Doctrine' which was essentially an extension of Truman's containment into the Middle East. The cold war had come to the Middle East.

In Latin America the issue, with certain small exceptions, was not formal independence as such. The major countries of Latin America had achieved independence during the nineteenth century. (Exceptions are Guyana, formerly British Guiana, and Surinam, formerly Dutch Guiana. They became independent in 1966 and 1975 respectively.) The issue was rather what kind of internal political structures and external policies could ensure stable political and economic development. Generalization about such a large and diverse continent as South America is hazardous, but certain broad features shared by most countries can be identified. The general pattern was of a highly unequal tripartite division of social, economic and political power between the mass of rural and urban poor, a small but growing middle class, and a smaller but dominant landowning class which in most countries possessed the bulk of the productive land and resources. The officer class might be considered a fourth category but for the fact that it tended to support the *status quo* and in moments of crisis moved to restore it.

Industrial development, which might have served to limit the economic and political power of the landowning oligarchy, was initially constrained by the fact that the landowners controlled the bulk of the export-earning primary resources, the returns from which were devoted to reinvestment in their own enterprises and in importing manufactured goods from overseas. Nevertheless, the impact of the depression of the 1930s was to produce demands for political and economic change. With the support of the armed forces, nationalist revolutions were carried out in several countries during the 1930s which forced the old political elites to share power more equally with the urban middle classes. The Second World War served as a further stimulus to domestic industrial development, not only because of increased demand for Latin American raw materials but because manufactured imports were less available. Industrialization did not, however, resolve the rural crisis of low prices and unequal land tenure. The rapid growth of population and large-scale migration of the rural poor to the cities produced a potentially explosive situation in many Latin American countries. Nor did the nationalist revolutions and industrialization produce political stability but rather a fragmentation of power among competing groups (Williamson 1992: 330–42).

The most important external factor governing Latin American development was the interest of the United States in maintaining political stability and economic influence within the hemisphere as a whole. To the long-standing justification of this interest supplied by the Monroe Doctrine and its Roosevelt corollary must be added the history of direct intervention in Latin American nations from the 1890s onwards: from Cuba in 1898, to the Dominican Republic, Panama, Mexico, and Nicaragua in the first thirty years of this century. Franklin Roosevelt's 'Good Neighbour' policy had shifted the emphasis from military intervention towards economic and political pressure, but the essentials of the hemispheric system, based on a resistance to changes which would threaten American influence, remained firmly in place.

The advent of the cold war if anything deepened these commitments, despite the American declaratory policy of an open world economic system as envisaged in the Bretton Woods discussions of 1944 on international economic institutions. Three new inter-American institutions, established in 1947 and 1948, testified both to the Truman administration's recognition of the strength of nationalist feeling in Latin America and to his determination to maintain the high level of American influence in the region. The first was the Rio security pact of 1947, which subsequently provided a model for the NATO treaty. The second was the Organization of American States (OAS) and the third the Economic Agreement, negotiated like the OAS at a

171

conference in Bogota in 1948. Each of these agreements, in particular the last two, were the subject of fierce contention with the Latin American states. The Latin American negotiators pressed for inclusion of articles in the OAS charter which 'prohibited political, military, or economic intervention in the affairs of any state by any other state or group of states', but this was counterbalanced by American insistence upon a resolution condemning 'international communism or any other totalitarian doctrine' as 'incompatible with the concept of American freedom' (Green 1974: 177). This latter resolution was the ground on which the United States intervened in the Dominican Republic in 1965. Similarly the parties clashed over the status of private property, particularly foreign-owned property, the level of Latin American state control over their own economic resources, and terms of inter-American trade. Despite United States concessions to Latin American demands in the wording of the Economic Agreement, as Walter LaFeber has put it, 'the unchallengeable US economic power could largely set the actual conditions of trade and investment' (LaFeber 1993b: 99).

On the threshold of the 1950s the United States had effectively cemented its hemispheric influence while making marginal concessions to Latin American demands. Truman's 'Point Four' foreign aid and technical assistance programme, announced in 1949, made only a small impact on Latin America's economic problems. The level of aid bore little relation to the amounts being devoted to Europe via the Marshall Plan. Besides, as the cold war progressed, military aid tended to take precedence over economic aid, a trend which increased over the next decade in Latin America, as in other parts of the Third World. Private American investment, meanwhile, was attracted to obviously profitable enterprises such as the development of Venezuelan oil and far exceeded investment in Latin American manufacturing (Green 1974: 180–1). In short, the combination of traditional American interest in the region and the pressures supplied by the cold war tended to reinforce American assumptions of its special rights and responsibilities in Latin America. It also made the United States correspondingly sensitive to any threat of radical change within this sphere, whether its sources lay in Latin American nationalism or in Soviet communism. Increasingly, the United States would acknowledge no real distinction between the two.

The dilemma for Third World nations, in so far as it can be generalized, arose from the conflict between their aspirations for national development, which were hugely varied in character, and the rigidities imposed by superpower cold war competition. It must not be thought, however, that this made Third World nations simply putty in the hands of the superpowers. From an early stage in the cold war the notion of non-alignment developed out of Yugoslavia's detachment from the Eastern bloc and from the efforts of India and Egypt to pursue a neutral course with respect to the superpowers. Though formally the Non-Aligned Movement was established only in the early 1970s, in an *ad hoc* way non-alignment dates from the Bandung Conference of 1955. The conference was attended by a number of nations which were clearly aligned to one side or another in the cold war – for example, Japan and China – but the agenda reflected the belief of Asian and African nations that their interests were not being met by current international organizations. Not only had the pace of decolonization slowed since 1950, notes one historian, but the UN was slow to open membership to new states, it was 'dominated by Cold war rivalries, and was not in practice giving effect to the principle of universality of membership' (Lyon 1984: 229).

Subsequent non-aligned conferences in Belgrade in 1961 and Cairo in 1964 saw increased participation, largely as a result of the addition of new African states. Inevitably, splits among such a heterogeneous group were evident on many issues, and such agreements as were possible grew from broad opposition to 'imperialism, colonialism, and neo-colonialism' and from the negative priority of opposing the dominance of the two cold war blocs (Lyon 1984: 230–2). Non-alignment, however, represented a challenge to both superpowers, and set certain limits to the superpowers' capacity to control events in the Third World.

THE SUPERPOWERS AND THE THIRD WORLD: BASIC ASSUMPTIONS

Anti-colonialism was as central to American declared foreign policy during the nineteenth century as was non-entanglement with other powers, hardly surprising in the light of its own origins. Even the event which precipitated America's acquisition of overseas territories – the war with Spain over Cuba in 1898 – was justified in anti-colonial terms. Nominally America went to war in order to free Cuba from Spanish imperialism. That the United States thereby acquired a number of former Spanish territories – most importantly the Philippines and Puerto Rico – did not wholly displace the inherited assumption that America's form of rule was different in kind from that of European powers. It was held to be both enlightened and benign, where it was not conveniently forgotten that the United States was now effectively an imperial power. And forgotten it generally was, despite the efforts of a small but vociferous anti-imperialist movement in the early twentieth century. As compared with the extent of Britain's overseas empire, America's was both small in itself and, unlike Britain's, marginal to its international economic and political status.

It was thus also marginal to the American public's perceptions of its role in the world. American conceptions of the outside world, it has been observed, 'arose from and remained tied to the domestic political culture'. In the absence of any urgent need to take account of the internal character and needs of its overseas dependencies, no less than of other nations such as China where it sought influence, American perceptions were based overwhelmingly on the moral values developed in its own growth: belief in American exceptionalism, in its special mission as an exemplar of democracy (Darby 1987: 170). To the extent that the United States was a world unto itself, ethnocentrism tended to flourish.

Doubtless these observations apply in some measure to all nations and cultures. The special significance of the American experience was twofold: firstly its sheer intensity, the degree to which the expression of moral idealism was intertwined with conceptions of the national interest, and secondly, the extent to which during the twentieth century this intensity became a factor in world politics. Inevitably, the realities of power politics and economic interest intervened, and the story of America's relations with the Third World after the Second World War is of the accommodation, or trimming, of its anti-imperialist self-image to the demands of specific situations and interests.

Even Roosevelt, who was loud in his condemnation of imperialism, did not envisage immediate independence for colonial territories. He was a gradualist who believed that a period of preparation for full independence was necessary (McMahon 1981: 61). At the Yalta conference in February 1945, he had agreed that trusteeships under the UN for former colonies need be established only with the consent of the mother country. This effectively allowed France, for example, to repossess the territory of Vietnam, and it paved the way for the Truman administration's recognition of the French claim to Vietnam. The United States was similarly cautious in pressing Britain to de-colonize. Finally, and most important of all, with the onset of cold war, anti-imperialism was downgraded as anti-communism progressively assumed primacy in American foreign policy.

These developments did not entirely remove the rhetoric of anti-imperialism from American policy-making, and there is no doubt that, other things being equal, the United States favoured de-colonization. In certain instances, such as the Suez crisis, furthermore, it explicitly dissociated itself from manifestations of European imperialism. It was also the case that the United States had much to gain economically from the end of European colonialism and the termination of preferential trading conditions which the colonial relationship granted to the mother countries. All this said, however, the United States' fear of communism on the march set clear limits to its acceptance of the principle of self-determination. Or perhaps more accurately, the United States felt that it could not be indifferent to the internal forms which Third World governments assumed. Where communism was established, it was believed, a new and more dangerous form of imperialism had taken root, its source lying in Moscow. The negative principle of checking communism thus in effect took precedence over the promotion of democracy, leading the United States to offer aid and comfort to certain Third World leaders and movements which could not be termed democratic without straining the meaning of the term beyond recognition.

Anti-imperialism was as important to Soviet as to American revolutionary doctrine. Indeed in Lenin's revision of Marxism, imperialism was held to be a major prop of capitalism. The progress of the world communist revolution would also spell the end of imperialism, though there were disputes among theoreticians in the early years of the Soviet Union about which would take precedence. Lenin himself accorded priority to the revolution in metropolitan centres and was prepared to countenance support of non-communist nationalist movements within independence struggles as way-stations on the road to communism proper. Stalin, smarting under the impact of Chiang Kai-shek's massacre of Chinese communists in 1927, repudiated Lenin's policy of flexibility and denied that full independence could be achieved under non-communist leadership. During the first phase of de-colonization after the Second World War this policy helped to foment violent independence struggles in Southeast Asia without, it should be said, bringing great returns to the Soviet Union.

Khrushchev's policy represented a return to that of Lenin. It allowed for an alternative for new states to strict alignment to either of the cold war blocs. The assumption was that the neutralism of newly independent states contained an inherently anti-Western bias, given the legacy of European colonialism, and that the Soviet Union was in a position to profit internationally from this stance. The promotion of 'zones of peace', announced by Khrushchev at the Twentieth Party Congress in 1956, coupled with his strong endorsement of the Bandung Conference the year before, was intended to 'steer the emerging anti-Western Afro-Asian political identity along lines favourable to the socialist bloc' (Allison 1988: 29). Significantly, Khrushchev embarked in 1955 on extensive travels to Afghanistan, India, and Burma, in stark contrast to Stalin's immobility and isolation from the world beyond the Soviet borders. He also visited Indonesia in 1960, expressing admiration for Sukarno's devotion to neutralism. Personal diplomacy was followed up by return visits by Third World leaders and by offers of trade and aid to Asian and African nations as they joined the ranks of independent states. Khrushchev recounted with pride in his memoirs the efficiency with which Soviet engineers completed a steel plant in India, outstripping the Germans for speed and (so Khrushchev was told by his Indian hosts) quality in their construction of a parallel plant (Khrushchev 1974: 302–3). In some cases there was a clear political pay-off. India declined to condemn Soviet intervention in Hungary or its Cuban missile venture, and also endorsed Soviet opposition to the rearmament of West Germany. In other cases, especially in the Middle East, Soviet aid did not prevent governments such as Egypt's from mounting attacks on communists.

The Soviet stance entailed a delicate balancing act. Excessive pragmatism in supporting non-communist movements invited the charge that the Soviet Union was abandoning the socialist struggle. The growing split with China in the late 1950s made the Soviet leadership particularly sensitive on this score, a major cause of the rift being China's dissatisfaction with the policy of peaceful coexistence with the West. On the other hand, a return to Stalinist revolutionary purism, which in effect China was demanding, risked undermining such influence as the Soviet Union had managed to gain by the policy of flexibility. By the late 1950s Krushchev had produced a new refinement into his Third World policy, one which sought to meet these contradictory demands. The way forward was to promote 'National Democratic Fronts' in which communists would participate and play an increasingly large role. The model was Sukarno's Indonesia where communists were members of the ruling coalition (Lowenthal 1984: 327–8). Few other Third World nations took this route successfully and indeed in 1965 Sukarno himself was discredited and ousted largely because his association with the communists alienated the army.

One's conclusion must be that there were distinct limits to the capacity of the United States and the Soviet Union to determine the course of de-colonization and nation-building in the Third World. It was the negative cast to their policies, particularly those of the Americans who were more active and took greater risks than the Soviets, which betrayed the potential for weakness in the superpowers' positions, since they often found themselves relying on figures whose loyalty to superpower interests was at best open to question. In the record of superpower interventions in the Third World, to which we now turn, these ambiguities will become clearly apparent.

THE MIDDLE EAST: IRAN, SUEZ AND LEBANON

The first major conflict of the cold war had taken place in Iran in 1946. It represented containment in action a year before the policy had been given a name. Since that date Iran had been in a state of upheaval. A struggle for power between the Shah and a succession of prime ministers revolved around the twin priorities of modernization and securing greater control of Iranian oil production which was dominated by the British Anglo-Iranian Oil Company (AIOC).

Events came to a head after 1951 when, following the assassination of Prime Minister Razmara by an Islamic fundamentalist, Muhammad Mossadegh was appointed Prime Minister. New elections brought an increased number of radical nationalists into the Majlis (parliament), sharpening the confrontation between the Shah and the government. A flamboyant and charismatic figure, Mossadegh headed a nationalist coalition formed around opposition to the AIOC. Initially the United States (still under the Truman presidency) was prepared to continue economic aid and technical assistance, though of modest proportions, even after Mossadegh nationalized the AIOC. British intransigence on the oil negotiations found little support in the United States and at this stage Washington regarded its role as one of mediation between the parties. Within two years, however, the United States had reached the view that Mossadegh was a threat both to internal stability in Iran and to American interests. In 1953 the United States employed the CIA in support of a coup against Mossadegh which restored effective power to the Shah and downgraded the power of the elected assembly. The consequence was a long-term American commitment to the Shah which had its denouement in the Islamic revolution of 1979.

What led to the turn in American policy and the first use of the CIA to unseat an elected government? One contributory factor was the change of government in the United States following the election of Eisenhower in 1952. Not only was the Republican administration, and the new Secretary of State John Foster Dulles in particular, inclined to view Third World nationalism with greater suspicion, but the domestic climate of anti-communism, coupled with the Republican majorities in both

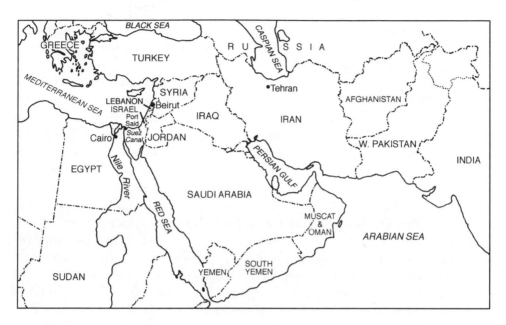

Figure 8.1 The Middle East and the Suez crisis, 1956
Source: Derived from W LaFeber, *America, Russia, and the Cold War, 1945–1992*, New York: McGraw-Hill, 1993, p. 186.

houses of Congress, made compromise on any issue where communism might feature increasingly difficult. The enhanced importance of the CIA, headed by Dulles's brother Allen, further sharpened the anti-communist character of the administration and gave it a distinctly activist slant. Covert operations came into their own in the 1950s, becoming an important and increasingly routine instrument of foreign policy (Rubin 1981: 55–6).

It was the intersection, however, of internal events in Iran and external pressures which provoked the crisis of 1953 and led the United States to intervene directly, if secretly. Following the nationalization of the oil industry in 1951, British and other Western oil companies boycotted Iranian oil, producing a serious economic crisis. Mossadegh's response was to play the communist card, announcing that if the West would not help him he would turn to the Soviet Union. At a critical moment in July 1953 Eisenhower refused a request from Mossadegh for economic aid on the grounds that Mossadegh was a tool of the Tudeh (or Communist) Party. In actuality Mossadegh was a reluctant ally of the communists but as the economic crisis grew he found his support within the Majlis dwindling, forcing him to rely increasingly on the Tudeh. Now in open confrontation with the Shah, Mossadegh sought to gain the Majlis' endorsement of a measure to grant him direct control of the army. When it refused, Mossadegh dissolved the Majlis in early August 1953 by means of a rigged referendum. At the same time, he moved to improve relations with the Soviet Union,

177

hoping that this would force the Americans to come to his aid. In an atmosphere of high tension, violent street clashes between communist demonstrators and the army took place in early August.

As it happened, the United States had already determined on a course of action which would hasten the overthrow of Mossadegh and the restoration of the Shah's power. The coup was originally a British idea, hatched before the 1952 American election and discussed with senior members of the CIA, but delayed since it was known that Truman's Secretary of State, Dean Acheson, would oppose such a step. The precipitating event was the announcement of a decree by the Shah dismissing Mossadegh from office. When he refused, Mossadegh supporters and communists took to the streets, while the Shah fled to Italy, believing that all was lost. It was at that point that the American plan was triggered. It involved feeding money to pro-Shah mobs who on 19 August marched to the centre of Tehran and took over key government buildings. Along the way they gathered thousands of additional supporters, suggesting still 'a reservoir of support for the shah among tens of thousands of Iranians either tired of the chaos of the Mossadegh regime or fearful of the Tudeh' (Rubin 1981: 77, 84, 85). Mossadegh was replaced by General Zahedi whose government quickly received substantial amounts of aid from the United States. The coup also served to cut the Gordian knot of the negotiations on oil, the outcome of which was the establishment of a new international consortium to distribute Iranian oil. The British monopoly broken, the United States now possessed a large economic as well as a political stake in the continued survival of the Shah.

Opinions differ on how decisive the American intervention was in toppling Mossadegh. In most accounts of American foreign policy the American role features large, but a prominent specialist on Iran, Barry Rubin, considers that '"overthrowing" Mossadegh had been like pushing on an open door', the key factor being Mossadegh's own move towards dictatorship which had the effect of alienating many Iranians (Rubin 1981: 89). However, the events of August took place within the framework of the Western boycott of Iranian oil, in which American oil companies participated, and it is reasonable to suppose that this external pressure played a part in pushing Mossadegh towards more extreme positions. If one cannot give a definitive answer to this question, however, one can say that the coup inclined American policy-makers to place great and, as several later instances would prove, misplaced reliance on the CIA as an instrument of foreign policy.

Beyond that, the Iranian crisis illustrated the dynamics of American relations with Third World countries which would be repeated later: American resistance to efforts by Third World nationalists to seize full control of their own resources; the difficulty of finding 'acceptable' nationalist leaders who could chart a third way between communism and right-wing dictatorship; the pursuit by the United States of policies which would tend to polarize internal politics and render a third way more difficult to achieve; and the ultimate decision to back political forces whose chief attraction was the negative one of anti-communism. The outcome was a relationship which on the face of it gave the United States considerable leverage over friendly governments. In actuality, in Iran as elsewhere, much leverage lay with the other party. The Shah too was a nationalist and was able to exploit American desires to build up Iran as a centre of stability in the Middle East by pursuing his own goal of consolidating his internal and external power, above all through military means with arms supplied by the United States.

Finally, the Iranian crisis and its aftermath showed the growing assumption by the United States of the British Great Power role in the Middle East. Mindful, however, of the dangers of alienating Arab nations by following traditional Great Power coercive diplomacy, the United States aimed to keep its distance from British policy even as it sought influence of its own. The short and curious history of the Baghdad Pact shows the ambiguities involved in this stance.

Originally based on a Turkish–Pakistani bilateral security treaty signed in 1954 with the blessing of the United States, the addition under British prompting of Iraq, Britain itself the following year, and also Iran, turned the scheme from an American design for a regional security organization, along the lines of the Southeast Asia Treaty Organization (SEATO), into a means of reinforcing British influence in the area. Not least among American anxieties was that the pact was sure to antagonize other Arab nations, above all Egypt, as indeed it did. Faced with the prospect that American membership would generate as many problems as it might solve, the United States opted not to join but to assume merely observer status. In a sense the United States now had the worst of both worlds. In part because America withheld full backing, the Pact failed to develop an effective military and political capability; because of its association with the Pact (and above all with British ambitions), the United States laid itself open to the full force of anti-Western Arab and especially Egyptian opinion. 'Nasser's persistent vilification of the Baghdad Pact', in the words of a recent account, 'was one factor . . . in increasingly embittering Western and American leaders toward him' (Eilts 1989: 355).

The Suez crisis of 1956 contained some of the same ingredients as the events in Iran, though they were mixed in a wholly different way. Middle Eastern nationalism, the spectre of communism, intervention by a Western power – each played a part. In Suez, as in Iran, the nationalization of a British-controlled resource – in this case the Suez Canal – triggered the Western response. But while the Iranian crisis can be regarded as the first round of the new imperialism of the cold war, the Suez crisis marks the decisive defeat of the old imperialism in the Middle East. Significantly, the United States helped to bury it, even as the Eisenhower administration embarked on new efforts of its own to establish influence in the region. From the point of view of superpower politics – and this is only one of the many angles from which Suez can be viewed – the question to be answered is: what led the United States to move so swiftly and decisively to check radical nationalism in Iran but to dissociate itself with equal determination from Britain and France's attempt to do something similar in Egypt?

The simple answer would be that in the Egyptian case the United States believed communism stood to benefit from a naked display of imperialist military power. As catch-all explanations go this is nearer the mark than any, but on its own it hardly meets the complexities of the case. A brief outline of the events of the crisis will serve to take us further.

Nasser had come to power following a coup against King Farouk in 1952, becoming Prime Minister in 1954 and President the following year. Internally he promoted social and economic reform which included breaking up large landed estates, the extension of cultivation to new areas, and a programme of industrialization – not dissimilar from the path which the Turkish leader Ataturk had set in the 1920s and 1930s for the modernization of Turkey. The key instrument of this programme was to be the building of a dam on the Nile at Aswan which would provide irrigation for new arable land and hydro-electric power for industrial development. Externally Nasser's policies centred on removing the 80,000 British troops from the Suez Canal zone, an arrangement stemming from an agreement of 1888 under which Britain, as the main share-holder in the Canal, assumed both its operation and defence. This was due to expire in 1968.

Nasser pursued both strands of his policy with equal vigour. Removing the British troops was relatively straightforward. The Anglo-Egyptian Treaty of 1954, under which Britain undertook to withdraw its troops from Suez by mid-1956, evidently represented a substantial concession to Egyptian interests, but the treaty also contained some safeguards for Britain in the form of a right to re-enter the Canal zone in the event of an attack on the Arab states or Turkey. Besides, in the age of the H-bomb far-flung military bases seemed obsolete. Nasser for his part appeared anxious to pursue good relations with both Britain and the United States. At the time of the signing of the treaty he seemed, in the word of a British official, 'our best bet' (Louis 1989: 46). The period of the British withdrawal, however, coincided with Nasser's promotion of the other strand of his policy – seeking finance for the building of the Aswan Dam. This proved much more intractable and it was also the issue which brought the United States directly into play.

The United States' attitude towards Nasser and financing the Aswan Dam took a dive in 1955 both because of Nasser's negotiation of an arms deal with Czechoslovakia and because of Nasser's vocal opposition to the Baghdad Pact. Egypt's recognition of Communist China in May 1956 deepened America's disillusionment with Nasser. Nasser, like Mossadegh before him, felt that there was no inconsistency in a sovereign nation concluding such agreements as were believed to be in its interest. From the American and British point of view, however, the arms deal was of particular significance. It threatened to upset the military balance of power in the region, and explicitly violated the British, French, and American Tripartite Declaration of 1950 which was designed to limit arms shipments to the region to these powers and thereby forestall the outbreak of further Arab–Israeli hostilities. In the view of one historian the Czech arms deal was 'the main cause of the [Suez] crisis' (Hewedy 1989: 162).

If this was the chief cause of the crisis, its timing owed much to the coincidence of several key events in the summer of 1956. On 13 June the last British troops left the Suez base. On 19 July the United States announced its final decision to withhold finance for the Aswan Dam after months of temporizing during which Nasser had agreed to conditions which the United States had demanded. Finally on 26 July Nasser announced the nationalization of the Suez Canal itself. With this action the crisis proper began.

The sequel is well-known. There followed three months of fruitless attempts to reach a negotiated settlement, followed by coordinated but in the main poorly executed military action by Israel, Britain and France in late October and early November to re-take the canal; a UN resolution, supported by both the United States and the Soviet Union, calling for a cease-fire and the withdrawal of the invading forces; and subsequent compliance by Britain, France and Israel.

American policy was dictated by a number of considerations. The most immediate was the sheer fury of Dulles and Eisenhower at the absence of consultation with the United States by Britain and France. Secondly, the military campaign coincided exactly with the Soviet Union's crushing of the Hungarian revolt which made it impossible to endorse military action in Egypt, whose aim, like that of the Soviets in Hungary, was evidently to remove a popular leader from power. Significantly, in his memoirs Eisenhower intersperses his account of the Suez crisis with the unfolding of events in Hungary during what he called 'the most crowded and demanding three weeks of my entire Presidency' (Eisenhower 1966: 58).

Thirdly, and in Eisenhower's eyes the most important consideration, to have joined with Britain and France would have been to associate the United States with an untenable position in the Middle East. If the United States had followed the advice of those calling for support of the British and the French, 'where would it have led us? Would we now be, with them, an occupying power in a seething Arab world? If so, I am sure we would regret it.' As for the demands to 'back Israel', 'if the administration had been incapable of withstanding this kind of advice in an election year, could the United Nations thereafter have retained any influence whatever?' (Eisenhower 1966: 99). In this instance, if not in others in the Middle East and elsewhere, the Eisenhower administration rested its case on the status and role of the United Nations. By this means the United States could safely distance itself from British and French action without taking sides with Nasser. This proved to be important in the fence-mending operation on which the United States and Britain quickly embarked. France, by contrast, never recovered trust in the United States and moved quickly towards an independent position within the Western alliance, speeding up the development of its own nuclear weapons and opting eventually for a partial withdrawal from NATO.

The anti-communist factor in American policy was partially screened by the more prominent issues of opposing old-style imperialism and upholding the United Nations. It was nevertheless there. It played a part, as we have seen, in the refusal to back the Aswan Dam, which precipitated Nasser's nationalization of the Canal and the crisis itself. Anxiety at the likelihood of Soviet exploitation of the crisis also figured in America's sponsorship of the UN General Assembly cease-fire and withdrawal resolution. 'At all costs,' wrote Secretary of State Dulles in an NSC memorandum in early November, 'the Soviets must be prevented from seizing a mantle of world leadership through a false but misleading exhibition of concern for smaller nations' (Bowie 1989: 210). The American resolution was designed to head off a more punitive Soviet formula, the tenor of which is suggested by the wording of a letter sent by the Kremlin to the governments of Britain, France, and Israel, and broadcast on Moscow radio. 'In what situation would Britain find herself', it was asked, 'if she were attacked by a stronger power possessing all types of modern weapons of destruction? Indeed, such countries, instead of sending to the shores of Britain their naval or air forces, could use other means, for instance rocket equipment . . . We are fully determined to use force to smash the aggressors and restore peace' (Campbell 1989: 246–7). In such circumstances American support for the UN resolution was an exercise in damage limitation.

The United States similarly quashed a provocative but probably speculative Soviet call for the United States and the Soviet Union to intervene jointly with troops to end the fighting. Eisenhower called the idea 'unthinkable' and warned that 'the entry of new troops into the Middle East would oblige all members of the United Nations, including the United States, to take effective countermeasures' (Eisenhower 1966: 90). In short, American policy all along was formulated with an eye to preventing the Soviet Union from taking advantage of what was regarded as a serious British and French blunder.

The Suez crisis was, as Khrushchev later observed, a 'historic turning point' for the Soviet Union. Having hitherto regarded the Near East as a field of British and French influence, the Soviet Union now embarked on a 'noble mission' to assist the Egyptians and other Arab nations (Khrushchev 1971: 431). Rhetoric apart, Khrushchev's observation contains some justification. The Soviet Union gained enormous credibility in the Middle East and other parts of the Third World by its support for the construction of the Aswan Dam. On the other hand, Khrushchev's account hides much, most notably the extent to which Soviet communism and radical Arab nationalism were partners of convenience when they were partners at all. Nasser was no more inclined to be a slave to Soviet than to American interests, if he could help it. And he generally could, since the Soviet Union always held back from severing its relations with Egypt, however much provoked by Nasser. 'The eventual political reward for ten years of effort and substantial financing for the High Dam', it has been said, 'was humiliating: near-total Egyptian political ingratitude except for a gross commemorative monument in Aswan' (Eilts 1989: 349). In the volatile atmosphere of the Middle East in the late 1950s and early 1960s the fortunes of communists in Egypt, Iraq, and Syria underwent sudden reverses which the Soviet Union was powerless to prevent. In December 1958, following a coup in Iraq whose leaders professed friendship towards the Soviet Union, Nasser took alarm and arrested hundreds of communists in Egypt. For the next few years relations between Egypt and the Soviet Union were distinctly uncordial until in 1964 they were patched up during a visit to Cairo by a Khrushchev determined to check growing efforts by China to extend its influence in the Middle East (Nogee and Donaldson 1988: 170–2).

America's role in the Middle East too was profoundly influenced by Suez. Within two years of condemning European military intervention in Egypt the United States had dispatched marines to Lebanon with the aim of checking a feared coup against its pro-Western president. Once again internal instability and the fear of outside pressure were the ingredients which prompted American policy. The Christian Lebanese President, Camille Chamoun, had provoked the Moslem population by seeking an amendment to the Constitution allowing him to stand for an unprecedented second term. Demonstrators on the streets of Beirut displayed anti-Western and pro-Nasser sympathies. Externally, the formation of the short-lived United Arab Republic, a merger of Egypt and Syria, seemed to presage a strengthening of radical Arab nationalism and the prospect of its extension. Finally, and most importantly, a coup in Iraq in 1958 led to the removal and brutal murder of a pro-Western monarch and brought to power a left-wing government. The dominoes appeared to be falling, and the Eisenhower administration decided on intervention to safeguard President Chamoun's position (Spiegel 1985: 86–91).

It did so under the aegis of the so-called 'Eisenhower Doctrine' which was formulated in the aftermath of Suez with the purpose of filling the 'vacuum' (a notion deeply resented by Arab nationalists) left by the departure of Britain and France. Requesting authorization from Congress for the new policy, Eisenhower said that 'the existing vacuum in the Middle East must be filled by the United States before it is filled by Russia'. The resolution provided for a special economic fund and the use of military force if necessary in the Middle East (Eisenhower 1966: 178). In effect, the outcome of the Suez crisis, as far as American policy is concerned, was to translate its regional Middle East policy into the global terms of the cold war. It was a pattern which would be repeated elsewhere.

SOUTHEAST ASIA

Once the decision had been made to endorse the French effort to pacify Vietnam, the United States embarked on a commitment whose ultimate consequence – the defeat of the United States' goal of containment in Southeast Asia – could hardly have been foreseen. Reading history backwards, as we generally do, we are inclined to view American policy in Southeast Asia in the 1950s and early 1960s in the light of its huge political and military commitment to Vietnam in the period 1965 to 1973. The danger in such a reading is to exaggerate the significance which Vietnam itself held for policy-makers in the earlier period and to underestimate the force of the surrounding context: containment of communism through vigorous defence of Japan, South Korea, and Nationalist China. The stake in Vietnam was a by-product of these primary concerns. That Vietnam itself became the focal point of American policy in the 1960s was less because the United States had a special feeling for Vietnam or the Vietnamese, far less a direct economic interest, than because the persistence and strength of Ho Chi Minh's communist nationalism was perceived as a threat to the larger framework of America's interests in East Asia. The American commitment advanced by stages until the point was reached when the survival of South Vietnam came to be identified with the overall credibility of America's containment policy. If it is going too far to say, as has been said of Britain's acquisition of empire, that the United States assumed its extended role in Vietnam in 'a fit of absence of mind', there is a certain truth in the observation. The 'logic' of America's commitment was established in other places, other times, and other circumstances.

The events of 1949–50 – the communist revolution in China, the Soviet atom bomb test, and the outbreak of the Korean War – transformed a policy of tacit support of the French in Indo-China to one of material aid. American support, however, in line with its declared anti-colonialism, was qualified by its insistence that France be seen to be moving towards granting independence to Vietnam and its neighbouring states of Laos and Cambodia. As half-way houses to this end in 1947 Laos and Cambodia were granted autonomous status within the French Union of Indo-China and the exiled Vietnamese Emperor Bao Dai was returned to power in 1949 to lead a nominally independent Vietnamese republic. This tactic hardly obscured the fact that the Emperor was a creature of French policy. Nor did it solve the political or military problems faced by the French.

Politically Bao Dai was hamstrung by his manifest dependence on France and his slender support among the Vietnamese people. Bao Dai, noted British Foreign Secretary Anthony Eden, 'preferred the casino to the council chamber' (Eden 1960: 80). Even the Americans found it hard to take him seriously, a State Department Asian expert describing him as 'a figure deserving of the ridicule and contempt with which he is generally regarded by the Vietnamese' (Karnow 1984: 177). Most damaging of all, however, was the fact that Ho Chi Minh was the best known and most widely supported Vietnamese nationalist leader. In 1950 he proclaimed the Democratic Republic of Vietnam (DRV), which quickly gained recognition from the Soviet Union and the People's Republic of China. It was this which led the Americans to swallow their doubts about Bao Dai and grant diplomatic recognition to his government. Militarily the French experienced growing difficulties. French casualties of 90,000 between 1946 and 1952, increasing pressure from the DRV army under the leadership of General Giap (using tactics which would later prove equally successful against the Americans), and the constant drain on the French exchequer, strained French resources and internal political stability to the utmost. Governments would fall and rise and fall again on the back of the Vietnam War.

With the ending of Marshall Plan aid in 1952, the French ability to prosecute the war significantly declined, but even before that date the Truman administration had made the decision to grant direct military assistance to France. By 1954 the United

States was paying 75 per cent of the costs of the war. By then, furthermore, France was in deep difficulties in the field and was looking for a negotiated way out.

Other forces too were contributing to the search for a diplomatic solution, which saw fruit in the Geneva conference on Indo-China held between April and July 1954. The post-Stalin leadership in the Soviet Union, in line with its policy of peaceful coexistence, sought means of lessening world tensions, and the People's Republic of China was similarly inclined to establish its credentials as a moderate and statesman-like nation, and moreover as a political force on the world scene independent of the Soviet Union (Karnow 1984: 191–2). Both powers were prepared to place pressure on Ho Chi Minh to negotiate an end to the war. Britain had its own reasons for seeking an end to the war, and Eden was an early advocate of partition of Vietnam. 'My chief concern', he wrote later, 'was Malaya. I wanted to ensure an effective barrier as far to the north of that country as possible' (Eden 1960: 87). Of the Western powers the United States was least happy with the prospect of a settlement which would yield any ground to the communists. Prior to the conference, as the DRV forces tightened the noose around the French garrison at Dien Bien Phu in the north-west corner of Vietnam, Dulles fought hard for British endorsement of an air strike in support of the French, to be accompanied by the immediate formation of a regional security organization, with the aim, as Eden recalled, of 'internationalizing the war' (Eden 1960: 103–4). Neither was forthcoming (though Britain was prepared to join SEATO after the conference had taken place). Eisenhower refused to countenance American intervention without either allied participation or congressional support, which left the United States in the position of going along reluctantly with the negotiations (Ambrose 1984: 178). Not least of Eisenhower's worries, bearing Korea in mind, was the prospect of war with China.

The Geneva conference of 1954 must rank as one of the least satisfactory settlements of the post-war period. It satisfied no one, except perhaps the French who at least managed to extricate themselves from an untenable position. Even so it took a change of government during the conference, consequent upon the defeat of the French forces at Dien Bien Phu, to bring France to the point of accepting a political settlement. The negotiations themselves were carried out in a spirit of deep mistrust on all sides, and in some cases animosity.

The resulting collection of agreements did not have the status of a treaty. It consisted of a series of cease-fire accords, bringing an end to hostilities in Vietnam, Cambodia, and Laos, and a Final Declaration which set out means of implementing the agreements. In Vietnam the French agreed to withdraw their forces south of the 17th parallel and the DRV to withdraw north of the line. No further forces were to enter either zone and within two years elections were to be held throughout Vietnam to unify the country, the process to be supervised by an international control commission. The United States was not a signatory of any of the agreements, and (in company with the Saigon regime) dissociated itself from parts of the Final

Declaration, albeit in a separate statement pledging that it would abide by the agreements.

The Geneva agreements were thus plagued with ambiguities and half-given pledges. Events in Vietnam would follow a pattern well established in other parts of the world where temporary and provisional arrangements hardened into fixed divisions between spheres of influence. Prime Minister and, after 1955, President Diem (following the removal of Bao Dai in a referendum) had no intention of holding nation-wide elections, and the United States did not press him. It was believed that in a popular election Ho Chi Minh would probably receive 80 per cent of the vote. American policy in Vietnam, wrote Eisenhower in a memorandum to his first ambassador to 'Free Vietnam', was 'to maintain and support a friendly and independent non-Communist government in Vietnam and to assist it in diminishing and ultimately eradicating Communist subversion and influence' (Ambrose 1984: 215). At the end of 1954 Eisenhower authorized the establishment of an American military mission in South Vietnam, and the CIA embarked upon its project of bolstering Diem and where possible undermining the DRV. President Diem, in his own very different way as resistant to American dictation as Bao Dai had been, nevertheless became the political instrument of containment in Vietnam. Corrupt and dictatorial as Diem was, so long as he appeared capable of holding the line in South Vietnam the United States was prepared to support him. When his control faltered, as it did by 1963, the United States conspired in his removal and assassination.

For his part Ho Chi Minh moved to consolidate his position in the North through a programme of land reform and the brutal suppression of all those suspected of having worked for the French. He also sought Soviet approval for his plan to liberate the South, which he gained in a visit to Moscow in 1957. Soviet assistance soon rivalled that of China. Most significant of all for the future course of the war, however, were the instructions he gave in 1957 for the formation of communist military units in the South. As yet he held back from ordering them into action against the Diem regime, believing that the time was not yet ripe for revolutionary action. He was unable, however, to resist South Vietnamese Communist (or 'Vietcong') pressure for military action against Diem, and at the end of 1960 he promoted the organization of a National Liberation Front in South Vietnam to embark upon a full-scale political and military struggle to reunify the country (Karnow 1984: 237–9). By the time Kennedy came into the presidency the North was poised to increase substantially the cost to the Americans of sustaining their position in South Vietnam

Ho Chi Minh's capacity to undermine the Saigon regime from within as well as from without rendered the Vietnam conflict critically different from other cold war conflicts such as Korea and Europe where the dividing lines, once established, proved relatively stable and defendable. The line of the 17th parallel in Vietnam with its demilitarized zone was no obstacle to infiltration from the north via Laos and Cambodia. (By comparison the 38th parallel dividing North and South Korea was relatively secure, lying as it did across a peninsula.) Ho Chi Minh was thus always able to exploit the permeability of the north/south line in Vietnam and to exert pressure within Laos and Cambodia to achieve his goals in Vietnam. Ho's support for the communist Pathet Lao in Laos was an important part of his overall strategy (Smith 1983: 169). Indeed when Kennedy came into power his most immediate concern in Southeast Asia was Laos, not Vietnam. The pro-Western government which had taken power after the Geneva agreements had been overthrown in 1960 by a neutralist group. With continued US support of the ousted government, Pathet Lao alignment with the neutralists, and Soviet and Chinese backing for the anti-American grouping, Laos was effectively in a state of civil war during Kennedy's first year of office. American intervention was considered and rejected. The recent memory of the disastrous Bay of Pigs invasion in Cuba and the logistical difficulty of inserting troops into Laos led Kennedy to seek a negotiated settlement. The parties resorted once again to Geneva and in 1962 produced a fragile agreement to neutralize Laos.

If anything the Laos issue served to concentrate Kennedy's mind on Vietnam as the key to Southeast Asia. Given the geopolitical division of the country there seemed no possible neutralist solution which would not involve yielding up power to the communists. Diem himself had been furious at the settlement in Laos and exerted continual pressure on the Americans to sustain their commitment to his regime. Kennedy resolved on sending Vice-President Lyndon Johnson on a fact-finding mission to South Vietnam during the early summer of 1961. Johnson's message was unequivocal. 'The fundamental decision required of the United States', he wrote on his return, 'is whether we are to attempt to meet the challenge of Communist expansion now in Southeast Asia by a major effort in support of the forces of freedom in the area or throw in the towel . . . I recommend we proceed with a clear-cut and strong program of action' (Williams *et al.* 1989: 194). A follow-up visit later the same year by General Maxwell Taylor and Walt Rostow, the President's national security adviser, produced the same message and a specific recommendation to send 8,000 US military advisers to South Vietnam. Anything less risked the loss of South Vietnam.

Kennedy responded to these messages with characteristic caution. While accepting the broad view that Diem must be supported, however distasteful he was as an ally, Kennedy was reluctant to embark on an open-ended and full-scale military campaign. His decision was to pursue a three-pronged strategy: firstly, to place pressure on Diem to introduce reforms and hence, it was hoped, restore political stability to South Vietnam; secondly, to increase the number of American military advisers, and particularly new special forces trained in low intensity counter-insurgency warfare; and thirdly, to strike at the Vietcong's support in the villages of South Vietnam by introducing the 'strategic hamlet' programme developed by the British in Malaya, the object being to isolate the Vietcong by drawing peasants from scattered villages into fortified centres which could be more easily defended. By the end of 1962 the number of American advisers had been increased threefold to 9,000 (Herring 1979: 85–7).

It was the failure of these three strands of policy to produce the desired outcome which ultimately led to President Johnson's decision in 1964 to escalate American involvement into a major politico-military commitment. Diem strongly resisted being a tool of American policy. His attempts to suppress domestic opposition by dis-gruntled generals, Bhuddists, and middle-class professionals led to greater, not less internal instability. Having survived one coup attempt in 1960 and an assassination attempt in 1962, he was overthrown and assassinated in 1963 by a group of generals with the endorsement of a now thoroughly disenchanted United States. Militarily the counter-insurgency effort produced few dividends in the face of increased Vietcong attacks and infiltration from the North. A Vietcong assault on Ap Bac forty miles south-west of Saigon in January 1963, in which a small Vietcong guerrilla unit defeated a much larger South Vietnamese force, produced deep frustration in Washington and despair among the US advisers on the ground (Sheehan 1989: Book III). Nor did the strategic hamlet programme produce the desired results, not least because Vietnamese peasants and Vietcong were indistinguishable from each other (unlike in Malaya where the insurgents were ethnic Chinese). The programme, it has been observed, often alienated the people it was designed to serve and 'converted peasants into Vietcong sympathizers' (Karnow 1984: 257).

The problem facing American policy was now that there seemed no safe third way between abandoning South Vietnam to communism and mounting a major effort to defeat the Vietcong and the DRV. The ending of the illusion that Diem could serve American interests in South Vietnam was critical, in that it resulted not in retrench-ment but in an ever-deeper American involvement in the internal affairs of South Vietnam. 'Incrementalism', it has often been pointed out, defined the process by which a local and regional conflict was transformed into the main front of the cold war in the mid-1960s. The political imperative of finding a South Vietnamese leader adequate to the purpose of serving American interests paralleled the military impera-tive of pacifying the region. Both entailed in effect the Americanization of the war. One significant difference between the Vietnam conflict and Korea was the refusal of either Britain or France to consider joining the Americans, whether under the aegis of SEATO (of which neither Vietnam, Laos or Cambodia was a signatory but were included within the security area defined by the treaty) or independently of that treaty commitment. When SEATO proved to be a dead letter, as Lyndon Johnson acknowledged it was in his report to the President on his visit to South Vietnam in 1961, he affirmed that there was 'no alternative to United States leadership in Southeast Asia' (Williams et al. 1989: 192). Henceforth American policy would be bedevilled by the problem of establishing legitimacy for its actions in South Vietnam.

Whether Kennedy, had he lived, would have expanded the war to the extent Johnson did is difficult to assess. By the time of Kennedy's death in November 1963 the number of American advisers had been increased to 15,000 and they had long been directly involved as helicopter and bomber pilots and in directing ground operations. To the extent that American policy was dictated by the level of enemy military activity – and it is often forgotten that this was a major factor driving American policy – then it seems plausible to suggest that at the very least Kennedy

188

would have been faced in 1964 with the same decision confronted by Johnson: to find some way of cutting American losses by seeking a way out or to expand the American commitment. The momentum and logic of containment would make the first of these options increasingly difficult to contemplate.

LATIN AMERICA: GUATEMALA AND CUBA

The United States had fewer reservations about intervening in Latin America than in other parts of the world since geography and tradition dictated a special American interest in the area. Even without the spectre of communism it is doubtful whether the United States would have stood by in 1959 when Fidel Castro mounted his revolution in Cuba. Indeed the Cuban revolution was not initially made in the name of communism and it was achieved without the aid of the Soviet Union. Such was the heavy imprint of the cold war on American policy-making, however, that well before this revolution efforts by Latin American countries to introduce reforms which affected American interests were interpreted in the light of the cold war. The first and most important of these instances prior to Cuba was Guatemala in 1954.

The broad pattern of events in Guatemala was one with which we are familiar, having considered the case of Iran: a right-wing pro-American dictatorship was overthrown by a leadership pledged to reform, followed by political and economic disarray and the ultimate removal of the reformers in a coup which restored dictatorship with the aid of the blessing of the Eisenhower administration. Only the details are different. Eisenhower relates the essentials of the story thus:

> The troubles had been long-standing, reaching back nine years to the Guatemalan revolution of 1944, which had resulted in the overthrow of the dictator General Jorge Ubico. Thereafter, the Communists busied themselves with agitating and with infiltrating labor unions, peasant organizations, and the press and radio. In 1950 a military officer, Jacobo Arbenz Guzman, came to power and by his actions soon created the strong suspicion that he was merely a puppet manipulated by the Communists.
> (Eisenhower 1963: 421)

Suspicions soon turned to certainties in Eisenhower's eyes as Arbenz moved to expropriate 225,000 acres of unused land owned by the United Fruit Company (UFCO) and instituted an Agrarian Reform Law. The UFCO was the largest producer of bananas, which constituted 40 per cent of Guatemala's exports; the company also owned 42 per cent of the nation's land and controlled the bulk of the transportation system (LaFeber 1993b: 118). Arbenz's denial that his government was communist was 'disproved' in Eisenhower's account by reference to statements by two American officials. The first, Assistant Secretary of State for Inter-American Affairs John Moors Cabot, 'said publicly that Guatemala was "openly playing the communist game"', while the second, the newly appointed Ambassador John E. Peurifoy, declared that 'it

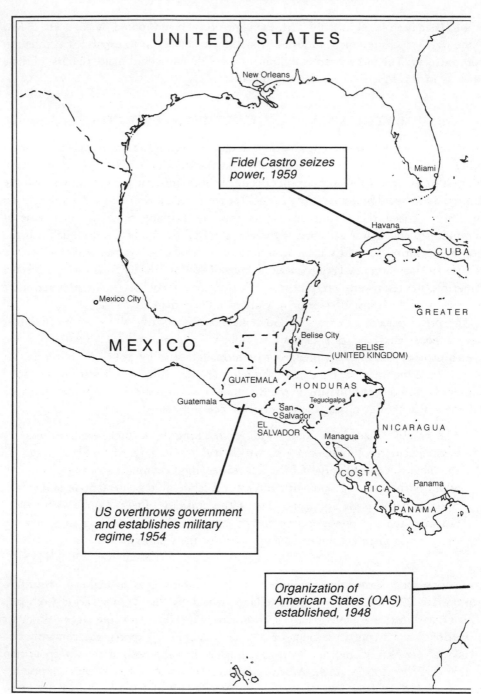

Figure 8.2 The United States in Central America in the 1940s and 1950s
Source: Derived from W. LaFeber, *The Inevitable Revolutions: The US in Central America*, New York: Norton, 1993, pp. 88–9.

ANTILLES

HISPANIOLA

HAITI

DOMINICAN
REPUBLIC

PUERTO
RICO
(UNITED STATES)

Vice-president Nixon
Threatened, 1958

LESSER ANTILLES

Caracas

VENEZUELA

COLOMBIA

Bogota

GUYANA

SURINAME

CENTRAL AMERICA

seemed to me that the man [Arbenz] thought like a Communist and talked like a Communist, and if not actually one, would do until one came along . . . and I expressed . . . the view that unless the Communist influences in Guatemala were counteracted, Guatemala would within six months fall completely under Communist control' (Eisenhower 1963: 422).

If it is difficult to credit such proofs as these, it was nevertheless the case that, like Mossadegh in Iran, Arbenz gained communist support for his reform programme and that communists held leading positions in the Ministry of Education and the labour unions. As things stood in 1954, however, Arbenz's government and his reform programme appear to have been neither dominated by communists nor in receipt of aid from the Soviet Union. Even Dulles admitted that it was 'impossible to produce evidence clearly tying the Guatemalan government to Moscow' (LaFeber 1993b: 124). Furthermore, it is important to weigh such evidence of communist influence against the tight exclusionist policy pursued by the United States government and the UFCO since well before Arbenz's election in 1950. Under United States guidance the World Bank cut off loans to Guatemala, US firms scaled down their operations, including tourism, and American military assistance was stopped. By 1952 banana exports had fallen by 80 per cent over their 1948 level (Barnet 1972: 234). Meanwhile, as Eisenhower took office and Arbenz announced the expropriation of UFCO land, the UFCO mounted a massive publicity campaign in the United States to press for American intervention in the face of a communist take-over in Central America. The company's chances were undoubtedly enhanced by its connections with the Eisenhower administration. The UFCO's legal affairs were managed by the New York firm, Sullivan and Cromwell, of which John Foster Dulles had been a partner, Allen Dulles had served on the UFCO's board of Trustees, and the UFCO's public relations director was the husband of Eisenhower's private secretary (LaFeber 1993b: 120–1).

Intervention itself, however, presented certain problems. It could hardly be mounted successfully without the endorsement of the OAS. As Eisenhower himself admitted, 'United States intervention in Central America and Caribbean affairs earlier in the century had greatly injured our standing in all of Latin America' (Eisenhower 1963: 425–6). It was thus important for Eisenhower to gain the support of the OAS at a meeting in Caracas in March 1954 by means of a resolution declaring that 'the domination or control of the political institutions of any American state by the International Communist movement, extending to the Hemisphere the political system of an extra-continental power, would constitute a threat to the sovereignty and political independence of the American states' (Barnet 1972: 235). Even so the resolution targeted only communist influence from outside and not, as Dulles had wanted, any manifestation of communism within the hemisphere. As it happened, events played into Dulles's hands when in early 1954 Arbenz requested and received a shipment of small arms from the Soviet Union, allowing the United States to tighten the noose around Guatemala. When in June the coup against Arbenz took place, it was with the assistance of American planes, albeit without public acknowledgement of the American role by the Eisenhower administration. The defection of the Guatemalan army from Arbenz in the face of his decision to supply a worker–peasant militia with weapons assured his downfall. His replacement, the American-trained General Castillo Armas, moved quickly to reverse the Arbenz reforms, while American aid flowed back to Guatemala in quantities and the UFCO was restored to its former dominance. 'The situation', Dulles remarked without irony in a television address on 30 June 1954, 'is being cured by the Guatemalans themselves' (Ferrell 1975: 223).

In truth it is impossible to know what a solution favoured by 'the Guatemalans themselves' might have looked like. So many influences – the Monroe Doctrine and its Roosevelt corollary, the virtual eradication in the cold war climate of any distinction between external communist influence and internal reform, and the simple fact of Central America's economic weakness relative to the American giant to the north – combined to render the idea of sovereignty itself questionable for Guatemala and its neighbouring states. Significantly both Honduras and Nicaragua acted as training grounds and staging posts for American-trained Guatemalans in preparation for the coup. American democracy, like international communism, knew no boundaries when vital interests were conceived to be at stake.

It is tempting to see American policy in Cuba as falling into the Guatemalan mould, with the singular difference that in Cuba the policy failed. This, however, is to underestimate the change of emphasis in the Eisenhower administration's stance towards Latin America in the late 1950s. The larger context of this shift was, as Walter LaFeber has suggested, the waning of the old two camps bipolar cold war and the emergence of a more complex form of superpower competition characterized by the new Soviet policy of seeking influence through aid and trade, by increasing Soviet military and scientific sophistication, and by the challenge to US economic supremacy consequent upon Japanese and European Common Market growth. A sequence of recessions in the late 1950s in the United States and a worsening balance of payments suggested that economic self-interest as well as its political stake in a stable Latin America demanded a more enlightened policy of promoting economic growth in the southern American continent (LaFeber 1993b: 140–1). None of this, it should be stressed, implied any let-up in the cold war. If anything competition was intensified as the field of conflict was extended and each side sought new means of waging it. Vice-President Richard Nixon asserted in May 1958 that 'the threat of Communism in Latin America is greater than ever' (Eisenhower 1966: 520).

Indeed an important proximate cause of the change in American policy was Vice-President Richard Nixon's disastrous 'goodwill' tour through Latin America in 1958. Everywhere but in Nicaragua Nixon and his wife were met with anti-American demonstrations of varying intensities, the worst being in Caracas, where their motorcade was stoned and spat upon and the Nixons barely escaped being dragged from their car by the mob. This incident, Nixon later recalled, was one of the 'six crises' which were the decisive events of his political career. 'Caracas', he wrote, 'was a much-needed shock treatment which jolted us out of our dangerous complacency.' On his return to Washington he made a series of recommendations. These included making efforts to reach the opinion-makers of Latin America, developing a new programme for economic progress in Latin America, withholding support as far as possible from dictators and backing genuinely democratic leaders, while recognizing the special conditions which made pure application of the American model inappropriate, and above all showing 'respect for [Latin American] traditions, values and customs'. Perhaps, however, to reassure his fellow policy-makers that he had not lost sight of realities, he emphasized that military assistance to ensure the maintenance of stability was equally necessary. The people of Latin America, he observed, 'want to be on the right side, but they also want to be on the winning side' (Nixon 1962: 229–30).

Not all of these recommendations, Nixon noted, were followed, but in conjunction with other influences Nixon's ideas bore some fruit. After years of refusing to agree to Latin American requests for a regional banking institution to supplement the World Bank and the Export–Import Bank, the United States consented in 1958 to the establishment of the Inter-American Development Bank (IADB). The United States also endorsed the establishment of regional common markets and commodity stabilization agreements with the aim of bringing some stability to the ever-fluctuating prices of the primary products which constituted the chief resources of many Latin American countries. The Eisenhower administration also showed some inclination to withhold unconditional support for dictators. In response to Fulgencia Batista's use of weapons acquired from the United States, including B-26 bombers, to quell demonstrations against his regime, Eisenhower ordered an embargo on further deliveries of weapons to Cuba (Rabe 1988: Ch. 6). Meanwhile, the death of John Foster Dulles in 1959 brought in his place Christian Herter who was more receptive to such measures than Dulles had been. What Kennedy would call the 'Alliance for Progress' was in the making before he entered office.

It was in the context of these shifts in policy that Fidel Castro came to power in Cuba on New Year's Day 1959. The Cuban revolution was thus a particularly stern test for American policy. In one sense it confirmed the assumptions of the revised American stance towards Latin America, in that it showed how vulnerable dictatorships could be to popular discontent and the need therefore for policies to counteract such threats. On the other hand, because the revolution was so successful in achieving its immediate aims and because the Soviet Union reaped such rewards from that success, American policy-makers were inclined to revive the old exclusionist and interventionist policies which had informed American action in Guatemala. The outcome was that any innovations in policy had to run the gauntlet of the old priority of preventing the spread of communism. Castro's revolution meant that the old would generally win out, and in this sense the Alliance for Progress was moribund at birth. This, however, is to run ahead of the story, since during the first year of the Cuban Revolution Castro showed signs of wanting to remain detached from either superpower. What was his political orientation when he came to power?, and was his eventual alignment with the Soviet Union a result of American policy pushing him into it? These are the questions which have preoccupied historians, though neither can be answered with absolute certainty.

As for the first, Castro claimed as he came into power and for some months afterwards that he was not a communist. Nor as late as November 1959 did American officials, including at least some in the CIA, believe that he was a communist. Khrushchev later recalled that Castro was an unknown quantity to them and that he was very cautious in his relations with the Soviet Union for at least a year after the revolution (Smith, W. 1987a: 43–5; Ambrose 1984: 555–6; Khrushchev 1971: 488–90). Castro's initial economic and social policies were moderate rather than revolutionary, involving agrarian reforms and taxation of American companies, neither of which initially met with total American disapproval, despite problems over compensation arrangements for American property. Though Castro legalized the Communist Party soon after assuming power, his government was not dominated by communists. His postponement of promised elections and his rigorous purge of Batista supporters suggested incipient dictatorship, but not necessarily communist dictatorship. Of course, Castro could have been engaging in deception and he later claimed that all along he had been a communist. But this claim itself could have been self-serving, a way of 'insinuating a consistency of purpose' with the aim of retrospectively justifying his chosen course (Smith, W. 1987a: 45–9).

The fact was, however, that by the end of 1959 Castro had shifted towards the Soviet Union, which brought him on a collision course with the United States. Continuing disputes over compensation for American property, Washington's refusal to grant Cuba a loan and the warm reception accorded to Anastas Mikoyan, Soviet Deputy Prime Minister, during his visit to Cuba on 4 February 1960 for trade talks seemed to indicate that Castro had made up his mind to rely on Soviet help. A last attempt by Castro in late February to resolve his differences with the United States was rebuffed, and one month later in a highly charged atmosphere of mutual American–Cuban recriminations a French munitions ship blew up in Havana Harbour, the work, Castro was convinced, of American saboteurs (Miller 1989: 73–5). Soon Castro was receiving oil and arms from the Eastern Bloc and in May Cuba and the Soviet Union established formal diplomatic relations. This was followed by an effective US economic embargo of Cuba, to which Castro responded by nationalizing all US-owned industrial, banking and agrarian enterprises in Cuba (Smith, W. 1987a: 52–8).

Whether a more moderate American response to Castro could have led to a *modus vivendi* between the two nations must remain an open question. The issue of communism itself may have been less important than the fact that, in common with Latin American radical reform programmes before and since, Castro's domestic agenda was bound to arouse American animosity. Communist or not, in January 1959 his programme was undoubtedly radical. The communist factor only intensified the clash of interests. One specialist in Soviet–Cuban relations argues that Castro's shift during 1959 arose from a combination of domestic pressures in Cuba for increasingly radical reform and fear of direct American intervention, with the events of 1954 in Guatemala very much in mind. While 'both sides (at different times) gave out contradictory signals . . . in the highly charged atmosphere between the two countries each chose to concentrate on the hostile signs and ignore any others' (Miller 1989: 66–7).

However, an alternative suggestion, proposed by a former American diplomat who was stationed in Cuba during the revolution, deserves attention. Wayne Smith argues that Castro's foreign rather than his domestic goals served to take him towards the Soviet Union. On coming to power he had hoped that the Cuban example would be repeated in other Latin American countries, enhancing his status as 'leader of a Latin American revolutionary bloc than as leader of a small Caribbean island'. Visions of himself as a charismatic leader along the line of Nkrumah or Nasser drove him on. When the expected revolutions failed to materialize, given the inevitable confrontation with American power and growing suspicion within the OAS of his intentions, Castro was forced to turn to the Soviet Union. As it happened, this turn meshed neatly with Khrushchev's own plan of seeking further influence in the Third World, as announced at a meeting of eighty-one communist parties in Moscow in November 1960. That Castro went further than merely seeking aid and embarked in April 1961 on the wholesale sovietization of Cuban life was because of his pressing need for military protection. 'It was not by accident', Smith observes, 'that Castro declared for socialism on the eve of the Bay of Pigs invasion. He knew that an invasion was on the way, and doubtless expected to face the full impact of US power . . . The motive behind his identification with socialism, then, was transparent. He was in effect saying to the Soviets: "I am a good Marxist-Leninist just like you; if the Americans attack me, you must come to my defence"' (Smith, W. 1987a: 50, 53–4).

Perhaps the two explanations are not mutually exclusive. The push factor from the United States invited, indeed necessitated, pulling the Soviets in. Smith's account does, however, portray Castro as a decidedly active agent in the Cuban–American stand-off. Moreover, it helps to make sense both of the virulence of the American reaction and the willingness of the Soviet Union to take risks in defending Cuba. The bungled attempt by the in-coming Kennedy administration to unseat Castro in the Bay of Pigs invasion of April 1961 and the Soviet emplacement of missiles in Cuba the following year both in their way reflected Castro's success in consolidating his power internally and vindicated his decision to opt firmly for alignment with the Soviet Union. If the outcome of the missile crisis led to the removal of the missiles, it also produced a pledge from the United States that it would not invade Cuba. In short, arguably Castro was as much the manipulator of the superpower relationship as he was manipulated by it.

Doubtless if the United States had been prepared to mount a full-scale invasion of Cuba, Khrushchev would have stood by and reaped the propaganda reward which such a naked display of American aggression would have produced in world opinion. As it was, the constraints on American power opened other opportunities for Khrushchev, which he gladly took. Whether in the long term the benefits to the Soviet Union outweighed the costs involved in sustaining Cuba is less clear. 'Apart from the economic burden', writes Nicola Miller, 'the Soviet Union's connection with Cuba has caused distortion in the development of ties with other Third World nations', alienating conservative regimes and dissillusioning leftists who (along with Castro himself) were dismayed at the Soviet Union's withdrawal of the missiles from Cuba under American pressure and viewed Cuba's all but total economic dependence on the Soviet Union as an unacceptable model for their own economic growth (Miller 1989: 126).

AFRICA: THE CONGO

Belgium's sudden and unexpected decision in June 1960 to grant independence to the Congo precipitated one of the most violent and tangled conflicts of the post-war years. The direct interest of the superpowers was apparently slight in the sense that neither possessed significant economic interests in the Congo. However, the crisis arose at a time when both the United States and the Soviet Union were embarking on new efforts to gain influence in the Third World, and, moreover, at a critical moment in their own relationship. The Paris summit conference had just broken up over the U-2 incident, dashing hopes for a *détente* and a swift move towards the signing of a test ban treaty. British Prime Minister Harold Macmillan confided to his diary in July 1960 that the international mood 'has a terrible similarity to 1914 . . . Now the Congo may play the role of Serbia. Except for the terror of nuclear power on both sides, we might easily slide into the 1914 situation' (Mahoney 1983: 34).

One significant difference from 1914 was the role played in the Congo by the United Nations. Its task was unenviable, given the conflicting forces at work. Within a few days of independence Belgian troops were reintroduced into the Congo following a mutiny of Congolese soldiers against their Belgian officers and the threat to Belgian nationals throughout the country. The secession of the mineral-rich southern province of Katanga, which took place during these early disturbances and with Belgian connivance, created a rival centre of power which was supported by Belgian and other Western mining interests. The UN's initial mandate, at least as it was interpreted by the Secretary-General Dag Hammarskjöld, was to seek restoration of order and the removal of Belgian troops but not to become involved in the Congo's internal affairs to the extent of assisting the central government's efforts to reintegrate Katanga. In the circumstances the Congo's Prime Minister, Patrice Lumumba, sought American support which was refused on the grounds (as Dulles put it) that Lumumba had been 'bought by the Communists', a view which he believed was confirmed by Lumumba's success in gaining the desired military aid from the Soviet Union. An already tangled de-colonization struggle was thus quickly overlaid by superpower conflict (Mahoney 1983: 37–41).

Three subsequent developments are important for an understanding of US and Soviet actions in the Congo. The first was the clash between the Soviet Union and the

UN which followed Hammarskjöld's decision to close the airports to all but UN flights and had the effect of preventing Soviet planes from being deployed to aid Lumumba. Khrushchev then embarked upon a vitriolic campaign against the UN, which he regarded as a tool of Western interests in the Congo. He sought in vain to press for a three-person headship of the UN with one each 'from the capitalists, the socialists, and the nations in between which had liberated themselves from the colonialists but were still nonaligned or neutral' (Khrushchev 1974: 483). The second development was Lumumba's own conflict with the UN which once again focused on Hammarskjöld himself, whom Lumumba accused of conspiring with the Belgians. Lumumba's decision to break with the UN was, it has been said, 'the critical blunder of his brief career . . . By inviting the Soviet Union to intervene, Lumumba became a pawn – and ultimately a victim – of the Cold War' (Mahoney 1983: 45–6). The third important development, which flowed from the first two, was the United States' growing conviction that Lumumba must be removed from power. In September 1960 Lumumba was dismissed from office by President Kasavubu and replaced by Colonel Mobutu, and it was with the CIA's help during the first days of the Kennedy administration that Lumumba was assassinated. Among the many consequences of the assassination was an outburst of racial violence in the United States in reaction to the death of a symbol of black nationalism (Mahoney 1983: 47–8, 69–70, 72).

The end of Lumumba did not immediately produce a solution. On the contrary, as Dean Rusk recalled, if in February 'the situation was a mess', 'things only got worse' when Lumumba was killed (Rusk 1990: 277). By the middle of 1961, besides the secessionist Katanga under Moshe Tshombe, two governments claimed rule over the whole of the Congo: Mobutu's in Leopoldville and another in Stanleyville headed by Antoine Gizenga, a former supporter of Lumumba. On the other hand the death of Lumumba provoked a marked change in Hammarskjöld's policy, inclining him to promote a more prominent and vigorous role for the UN, one which he hoped would win the support of the increasingly vocal African and Asian representation within the organization but also maintain freedom of movement with respect to the superpowers (Holland 1985: 188). If his decision to increase the military and diplomatic pressure on Katanga found favour with Afro-Asian opinion, which viewed the secessionist movement as a creature of Western imperialism, it also disturbed the United States which feared that such a policy played into the hands of the Soviets (Mahoney 1983: 94–8). In the event Hammarsjköld himself was killed in a plane crash in September 1961 as he was en route from the Congo to Northern Rhodesia to meet with Tshombe.

The momentum of his policy, however, was established by the time of his death which, as one account puts it, 'had a cathartic effect on Washington' (Mahoney 1983: 110). In the face of European opposition the United States supported a new UN resolution to put teeth into the UN effort to end the secessionist movement in Katanga and to suppress Gizenga's claims to leadership. By the end of 1961 both aims had been achieved, if only provisionally. Tshombe reopened the civil war during 1962 and it was January 1963 before Katanga was finally reintegrated into the Congo.

Even then, further conflict arose when Simba rebels, Lumumbist in orientation and supported by the Soviet Union, revolted against the central government and took hundreds of Western, mainly Belgian, hostages. This in turn was put down by Belgian paratroopers transported in American planes.

Such a brief account skates over many turns of events and shifts in American policy in the Congo, but in broad outline the overall outcome was clear, if complex in its implications. The initial American and Soviet interventions injected a sharp dose of the cold war into the veins of African politics. Subsequent American policy, however, recognized the force of nationalism in Africa and moreover the utility of the UN in avoiding the extremes of either American disengagement or direct American intervention. 'Kennedy's African record', Mahoney concludes, 'stands out as an exception to the antinationalist tendency of America in the Third World' (Mahoney 1983: 244). The Soviet Union's dissociation from the UN and its support for anti-government groups within the Congo won it some friends among African nations – pre-eminently the so-called Casablanca grouping of Ghana, Morocco, Mali, Guinea, Algeria, Egypt, and Libya – but alienated others. Since neither superpower had close historical links with African nations, their efforts were directed less at promoting particular leaders or clients than in seeking to deny gains to the other superpower in a continent where post-colonial politics were volatile and complex.

CONCLUSION

It will be apparent from the foregoing case studies that the United States was in most situations more prepared than the Soviet Union to intervene directly in Third World conflicts, at least to the extent of sending troops or employing covert means to remove unfriendly regimes. The difference says much about the superior capacity of the United States to project its power around the globe, but also about the two powers' different conceptions of their roles in the post-colonial world. Inasmuch as the United States sought to promote Western-style democracy and capitalism, American power was often found on the side of leaders and regimes who, it was felt, would represent as much continuity as possible with pre-independence institutions and values. To that extent the United States was a *status quo* power, albeit with the proviso that colonialism itself had no place in the new world order. It was a highly ambiguous position, and one which meant straddling awkward gaps between what was desired and what was achievable. What was desired was liberal anti-communist governments; what was achievable more often than not was illiberal anti-communist governments. The risk was that American policy would please neither the European colonial powers, which often resented American pressure to de-colonize, nor the newly independent nations, who wanted aid but not interference, nor the Soviet Union, which sought influence of its own.

In some respects the Soviet task was easier. Its credentials, real or imagined, as the champion of the world's underdogs and symbol of anti-Westernism allowed it some-

199

what greater flexibility in its means of exerting influence. It could go with the flow rather than against it in many instances. In the international communist movement the Soviet Union possessed a political instrument as well as an ideology; in its growing economic power, particularly in heavy industry, it possessed means of backing ideology with material aid. Crucially the Soviet Union in many instances was the beneficiary of American intransigence – in, for example, Mossadegh's Iran, Arbenz's Guatemala, Nasser's Egypt, and Castro's Cuba. In each case the re-exertion of American power, whether successful or unsuccessful, involved costs to the United States in its relations with many Third World countries and in its competition with the Soviet Union. To the evident frustration of the United States, its efforts actively to 'do good' in the Third World frequently met with opposition, while Soviet actions just as often were regarded as being in tune with Third World nationalism.

In truth the Soviet Union's Third World balance sheet by the end of this period was hardly more healthy than that of the United States, probably less so. Its gains in influence, with the singular exception of Cuba, were insecure and its losses were considerable. Both superpowers faced a world of swift change and growing diversity in the mid-1960s. Cold war politics were still a going concern but were progressively less able to determine events in the Third World and elsewhere, as non-alignment became institutionalized, the international communist movement fractured irrevocably, and European nations, East and West, asserted their own interests in defiance of the superpowers. For the United States containment itself came under threat in Vietnam, and a new superpower dispensation seemed called for.

PART IV

DÉTENTE AND ITS LIMITS, 1965–1981

INTRODUCTION

If one were to believe the more extravagant claims made on behalf of *détente*, then it represented a genuine break in the cold war mould of superpower relations. Certainly if one judges *détente* by the aspirations of some leading participants, this was the case. Georgi Arbatov, Director of the USA and Canada Institute in Moscow and a prominent adviser to the Kremlin in the 1970s and 1980s, declared that 'detente is not a continuation of Cold War by other, more cautious and safer, means. It is a policy that, by its nature and objectives, is opposed to Cold War, and is aimed not at gaining victory in conflicts by means short of nuclear war, but at the settlement and prevention of conflicts, at lowering the level of military confrontation, and at the development of international cooperation' (Arbatov 1983: 13). Doubtless this statement served a political purpose of associating the Soviet Union with the most sweeping and publicly appealing conception of *détente*. It was made in 1983, by which time *détente* had run into the ground, and represented an implicit claim that the fault for the downturn in US–Soviet relations lay with the United States. It is noteworthy, though, that *détente* should have been talked about in these terms at all. It fed the popular assumption that US–Soviet relations were an either/or matter – cold war or *détente* (which indeed was the title of Arbatov's book on the subject).

In actuality the line between cold war and *détente* was never so crystal clear, despite the obvious fact that there were periods during which open antagonism predominated and others when negotiation was a central feature of US–Soviet relations. The task of the following three chapters is firstly to examine the conditions which during the late 1960s and early 1970s produced concerted attempts to reduce tension, and secondly to understand the reasons for its limited success.

Something like a consensus has been reached among Western analysts of *détente*. Certain key conditions – among them the Soviet achievement of effective nuclear parity with the United States by 1969, a growing predisposition on the part of bloc members on both sides to assert independent lines of policy, and relative economic superpower decline, greatly increasing the strains of superpower bloc leadership – inclined both powers to seek accommodation within limited areas, pre-eminently nuclear weapons and European security. To the extent that *détente* succeeded it rested on mutual recognition that each side had much to gain from the institutionalization of arms control and confidence-building measures. These saw fruit in the SALT I Treaty and various agreements on means of crisis management, and the lowering of tension in Europe. To the extent that *détente* failed, the argument goes, it did so because each side brought to the process incompatible and mutually misconceived ideas about its scope and goals.

The United States, viewing *détente* as a global process, envisaged across the board changes in superpower relations which would extend beyond the achievement of specific agreements on arms control to, for example, moderation of Soviet ambitions in the Third World. 'Linkage' was the conceptual tool devised to bring coherence to a multi-faceted enterprise which would involve offering inducements to the Soviet Union in some areas (such as improved conditions of trade) in the hope of achieving in return favourable responses in others (such as Soviet pressure on North Vietnam to come to terms with the United States). Essentially, the United States saw *détente* as a means of managing the Soviet Union's emergence as a genuine superpower capable of matching American military power. The Soviet Union, though professing the same hope for a general lowering of tension, saw no incompatibility between reduction of tension in the central arena of nuclear competition and, for example, maintenance of its traditional goal of seeking influence in the Third World. More generally, the Soviet Union regarded *détente* as an opportunity to gain acknowledgement of its superpower status. *Détente* came to grief in the gap between the Soviet preference for compartmentalization of issues and the American assumption of linkage between them. *Détente*, it is said, was thus flawed from the outset by a fundamental philosophical disjunction between the superpowers (Bowker and Williams 1988: Ch. 3 and 260; Garthoff 1985: Chs 2 and 29).

There is much to recommend this view. It establishes links between structural changes in the international system and specific policy changes, and it acknowledges the continued importance of competition during a period of intensive negotiation across a range of issues. The emphasis in this view, however, rests largely on the bilateral superpower relationship, changes in the international system being regarded primarily as enabling conditions of *détente*. If, however, we adopt an international perspective, then the significance of *détente* lies rather in the shift in balance between the US–Soviet relationship considered as a sub-system within the international system of states as a whole and the changing character of the international system itself.

In an essay published shortly before he assumed the post of National Security Adviser to President Nixon, Henry Kissinger wrote that 'in the years ahead, the most profound challenge to American policy will be philosophical: to develop some concept of order in a world which is bipolar militarily but multipolar politically' (Kissinger 1969: 79). (Others would add that economic multipolarity was at least as important as political multipolarity, but Kissinger was curiously incurious about economics.) Arguably neither American nor Soviet policy met Kissinger's challenge, since the superpowers' heavy investment in the arms race and in the maintenance of the bloc system in Europe inclined them towards policies which reinforced bilateralism and the cold war system even as they sought to promote greater flexibility in their encounter with new forces in world politics. *Détente*, as Philip Windsor has written, 'depended on a continuing recognition of spheres of influence, and on a perpetuation of the existing order in Europe. Any threat to this order could rapidly become a threat to *détente* itself' (Windsor 1971: 25). The same was true of arms control. A precondition for *détente* was mutual recognition of each other's pre-eminent stake in the nuclear balance of power. Put another way, there is a sense in which superpower *détente* was an effort to arrest developments which threatened to displace superpower dominance and the cold war system which underpinned it from its position of centrality in world politics.

The result in the period under consideration here was a complex and contradictory process in which the US–Soviet relationship achieved ever-greater formality, interconnectedness, and exclusivity at a time, however, when the international system as a whole was becoming more diverse, more turbulent and unpredictable. The guiding theme of the following three chapters is the encounter between these two sets of forces. Chapter 9 addresses the formative period of *détente* from 1965 to 1973 which saw the signing of major agreements on nuclear arms and European security. Central to this account are profound shifts in the international order: Sino–Soviet conflict, changes in the world balance of economic power, and the challenge posed by Third World turbulence. Chapter 10 examines what appears to be an anomaly in US–Soviet relations: that *détente* coincided with the continuation of America's longest-standing and most costly conflict with communism – the war in Vietnam. Finally, in Chapter 11 we explore the reasons for the erosion of trust between the superpowers during the mid and late 1970s, which produced the so-called new or second cold war of the early 1980s. In truth, the real conflict in world politics by this stage was less between the superpowers than between cold war politics and an emerging world political agenda in which the cold war was increasingly an irrelevance.

9

DÉTENTE IN THE MAKING, 1965–1973

THE INTERNATIONAL ENVIRONMENT

In the absence of cataclysmic events such as wars and revolutions it is rarely easy to explain the crystallization of forces which produce major shifts in relations between nations. In the case of *détente*, though such a crystallization is identifiable in the sequence of agreements on nuclear arms and European security reached between 1971 and 1973, formal agreements do not exhaust what is meant by the term *'détente'*. *Détente* was a process as much as a set of treaties. It emerged out of the competitive nature of superpower relations, and competition remained a feature of those relations even as *détente* took root. Some of the ingredients of *détente* were already present in the legacy of peaceful coexistence and the struggle to reach agreement on the Limited Test Ban Treaty of 1963. Other ingredients were present in the very patterns of conflict between the powers. The superpower relationship was a structured one, in which an element of mutuality underlay the competitive no less than the conciliatory impulses in superpower policy-making. The cold war nexus inclined each to be highly alert to the movements of the other. Our task is to explain why during the late 1960s and early 1970s both powers showed an interest in moving towards accommodation in areas where their differences had been especially critical – above all in nuclear arms and European security.

The key to *détente* lies in the intersection of global, bilateral, and domestic developments. At the global level the consequences of the Sino–Soviet split were clearly evident by the mid-1960s and had developed into open antagonism. The Chinese acquisition of the bomb in 1964 was followed two years later by the opening of Mao's 'cultural revolution', forcing Soviet planners to invest extra military and ideological resources to meet the growing threat from the East. Nor did the winding down of the cultural revolution in 1968 bring any respite to the Soviet Union. Rather the reverse. During 1969 serious clashes took place on the Sino–Soviet border, leading the Soviet Union to increase its troop strength on the Far Eastern front from 25 to 45 divisions between 1969 and 1973 and to deploy new nuclear missiles and aircraft against China (Garthoff 1985: 208). Worse still, at this point the Chinese began to explore contacts with the United States. This new challenge created a complex triangular pattern of relationships between the three powers, in which arguably the United States held the trump card since it possessed the option of *détente* with both the other two and hence of playing one off against the other, a point to which we shall return. In any event, the presence of a substantial new and independent player in the cold war game altered the dynamics between the other two.

A second important development was changing patterns in the world economy which had serious repercussions for the United States. The growing strength of the Japanese and European economies, coupled with the combination of recession and inflation caused in great part by Vietnam War expenditures, severely eroded the United States' trading position and strained the capacities of the international economic institutions which had been established at the end of the Second World War. A growing volume of imports from Japan and Europe narrowed the United States' favourable balance of trade sharply in the late 1960s, until in the early 1970s for the first time since the Second World War the figures showed the United States in the red. With the exception of 1973 and 1975, there they remained through to the end of the 1970s and beyond (Kemp 1990: 148). This and rising inflation placed great strain on the dollar, whose strength and stability had hitherto been the chief prop of the Bretton Woods system. As Europeans converted their dollars into gold, in order to safeguard the value of their dollar holdings, the United States was faced with the prospect of an uncontrolled outflow of gold from Fort Knox. The result in 1971 was Nixon's decision to end the convertibility of the dollar and hence the system of fixed exchange rates with other currencies. Henceforth, despite early efforts to negotiate new fixed exchange rates, the dollar was left to float. Consequent devaluations did not, however, displace the dollar from its pre-eminent position in the world monetary system, in part because 'devaluation . . . gave export industries a reprieve . . . and enabled profits to be maintained'. Furthermore, the raising of interest rates, designed to maintain the value of the dollar, attracted foreign capital and in particular earnings from oil-producing countries (Kemp 1990: 186).

These measures did not, however, entirely compensate for the loss of stability under the old gold-based system. High rates of interest, necessary to support the dollar, cut away at industrial investment and profits, as speculative money sought quick returns. Moreover, these developments came on top of the 'Great Society' reforms of the 1960s which consumed an ever-larger proportion of the Federal budget, part of which was financed by borrowing. The Federal Government thus absorbed a growing proportion of the funds available for borrowing in the economy at large, further squeezing private sector investment. Hence, notes Tom Kemp, 'the phenomenon of "de-industrializa-tion" which began to afflict the so-called "smokestack" industries in the traditional sectors' (Kemp 1990: 187). Viewed from an international perspective, the most important outcome was the increasing vulnerability of the American economy to external forces or, in the terms which became current in the new international relations thinking of the time, the growth of 'interdependence' (Keohane and Nye 1977).

Taken together, these two developments produced a global system in which the lines of conflict were less clear-cut than was the case in the period of high cold war. In effect, the United States and the Soviet Union were each subject to challenges within the spheres which until then they had dominated: the United States within the world capitalist system and the Soviet Union within the world communist system. A degree of loosening in bloc cohesion – the third important element in the international context of *détente* – tested the policies which had hitherto governed alliance management.

In the West, France had long shown signs of resentment of American leadership and influence in Europe. When in 1966 De Gaulle withdrew France from the military structure of NATO, he also made overtures to the Soviet Union. The two policies were intimately related. His determination to assert French leadership in Europe was in part a declaration of French nationalism, a bid to regain Great Power status for France; but it also grew from a wider vision of Europe in which the key political and security decisions would be taken by Europeans, including the Soviet Union. Ultimately, De Gaulle's vision of a Europe which extended from 'the Atlantic to the Urals' was intended to cut away at the tight hold which the bloc system exerted over international politics. In visits to Moscow in 1966 and to other Eastern European nations over the next two years De Gaulle sought to bridge the gap between East and West. If his efforts failed, it was in part because the Soviet invasion of Czechoslovakia in 1968 intervened and in part because France was not in a position to deliver such political goods as might have inclined the Soviet Union to enter into serious negotiations (Garthoff 1985: 107–8). This applies particularly to the German question which lay at the heart of the division of Europe. Only Germany itself, with the endorsement of the United States, could crack that particular nut.

As it happened, conditions in Germany following the formation in 1966 of the 'Grand Coalition' of the Christian Democrats (CDU) and Social Democrats (SPD) made possible a movement, as yet tentative, towards a reduction of tension in this central theatre of the cold war. The coalition, it has been said, 'signalled the end of the Federal Republic's formative period' (Marshall 1990: 55). A new flexibility in relations with the Soviet Union and the nations of Eastern Europe was indicated in a 'Peace Note' in 1966 which promised a modest departure from the orthodoxies of the Adenauer period (1949–1963). While there was as yet no formal abandonment of the 'Hallstein Doctrine' – under which the Federal Republic refused to consider relations with East Germany or with states (barring the Soviet Union) which recognized it – the opening of trade links with Romania and Yugoslavia, and an undertaking to work towards *détente* and demilitarization, began to chip away at the rigidities established in 1949 (Marshall 1990: 58). Only following Willy Brandt's accession to the Chancellorship of West Germany in 1969 would the Hallstein Doctrine itself be officially dropped as one element within Brandt's Ostpolitik, under which a new *modus vivendi* was established with the Eastern Bloc.

The larger significance behind these moves lay in the clear sign that West Germany was now prepared to assert its independent nationhood in a way which had been impossible in the early post-war years when Germany had been under the tutelage of the wartime occupying powers. That tutelage still wielded some force, particularly as regards Berlin, but was increasingly recognized as an anachronism, given Germany's impressive economic growth and evident political stability. Just as important was the American suspicion of the dangers involved in this process. 'It seemed to me', recalled Kissinger in his memoirs:

> that Brandt's new Ostpolitik, which looked to many like a progressive policy of quest for *détente*, could in less scrupulous hands turn into a new form of classic German nationalism. From Bismarck to Rapallo it was the essence of Germany's nationalist foreign policy to manoeuvre freely between East and West. By contrast, American (and German) policy since the 1940s had been to ground the Federal Republic firmly in the West, in the Atlantic Alliance and then the European Community.
>
> (Kissinger 1979: 409)

That Kissinger and Nixon finally 'recognized the inevitable' and opted to work constructively with Brandt (Kissinger 1979: 410) represented an acknowledgement that German–American relations must now be established on a new and more equitable basis. More pointed perhaps is the suggestion that Kissinger and Nixon 'moved to develop an American *détente* with the Soviet Union in part to preclude a West German-led European *détente* with the Soviet Union from excluding the United States and thus splitting the Western Alliance' (Garthoff 1985: 109).

If West Germany's bid for independence within the Alliance posed a challenge to American leadership, it was only one among a number of such anxieties which led observers in the late 1960s to speak of a 'malaise' within NATO (Kissinger 1979: 81–6). It arose from a divergence in European and American perceptions of security needs and defence policy. Since the mid-1960s the United States had been pressing for a shift in the burden of conventional defence on to the 'European pillar' of the Alliance, a result of America's increasing commitment to the Vietnam War, Congressional demands for military retrenchment, and a sense that the likelihood of war in Europe was diminishing. The American pressure for greater defence cooperation among the European NATO allies, however, met with a guarded response, since to European leaders it seemed to imply a downgrading of the American nuclear guarantee for the defence of Europe. An America bent on partial withdrawal from Europe and bilateral nuclear arms control with the Soviet Union looked like a recipe for 'de-coupling' American defence from that of Europe. Would the United States in practice risk nuclear attacks on its own soil in order to defend Western Europe? This question, which had always been present, was now asked with increasing urgency.

Resentful as Europeans were of American efforts, in Kissinger's words, 'to mono-polize the central nuclear decisions', they were nevertheless suspicious of any move which might undermine the credibility of the American nuclear umbrella. 'Our allies', noted Kissinger somewhat acerbically, 'on the whole acted like ostriches. They were as unwilling to confront the changed strategic relationship or make a greater defense effort as they were ready to attribute to complex, sometimes devious, American intentions what was in fact largely the result of an inexorable technological evolution [namely, nuclear *détente* with the Soviet Union]' (Kissinger 1979: 84). In practice, while European political cooperation went ahead at an increased pace during the years of *détente* – with the accession to the European Economic Community (EEC) of Britain, the Irish Republic, and Denmark in 1973 – plans for greater devolution of defence policy, based on an enhanced European pillar, made little progress (Cromwell 1992: Chs 3–4). Both developments in fact represented continual irritants in the American–European relationship, since the United States was as unhappy with EEC protectionist trade policies as with European unwillingness to shoulder increased defence burdens. In short, the Atlantic relationship was pervaded by a deep ambiguity which would have important repercussions in the *détente* process. Managing allies would be an important aspect of managing the Soviets.

Across the Iron Curtain shifts were also taking place, though inevitably they took a different form, given the limits Moscow set on diversity within the bloc. By the mid-1960s, however, those limits showed growing signs of fluidity. Albania in 1961 and Romania in 1963 had already begun to disengage from Moscow, Albania to the extent of taking firm sides with China. Romania's detachment was less absolute. While it succeeded in forestalling integration into Comecon and, inspired by France's partial withdrawal from NATO, established an independent military role within the Eastern bloc, Romania maintained formal, if distant, ties with Moscow (Fejtö 1974: 151–64, 315–18).

Closer to the front line of the cold war, Moscow was less willing to tolerate such bids for independence, but even here there was a noticeable opening up of debate which focused initially on economic reform and then extended to politics and ideology. Khrushchev's successors, Brezhnev and Kosygin, writes Fejtö, adopted a more pragmatic and cautious style in relations with the People's Democracies which encouraged a 'tendency towards emancipation and concentration on national prob-lems' (Fejtö 1974: 192). Increasing industrialization, a desire for greater trade with the West, and the opening of tourism and political contacts with the West (above all with France and Germany) both sensitized Eastern bloc nations to the disparity in living standards between East and West, and prompted demands for reforms which would meet the need for modernization.

Above all, West Germany's diplomatic offensive in 1966, offering trade links and the possibility of diplomatic recognition of Eastern bloc nations, drove a wedge into the bloc, pitting Hungary and Czechoslovakia, who responded favourably, against Poland and East Germany who were firmly opposed (Steele 1985: 96–7). These external pressures reacted most strongly on the internal politics of Czechoslovakia, where the movement for domestic liberalization had gone furthest. This was due, Fejtö observes, 'as much to the country's situation in the heart of Europe as to its high level of industrial, intellectual and technological development and the evidently indestructible nature of its liberal and democratic traditions' (Fejtö 1974: 213). And it was in Czechoslovakia that the limits of diversification within the Eastern bloc were to be most starkly revealed.

The crushing of Alexander Dubcek's 'socialism with a human face' in August 1968 reverberated through all levels of East–West relations. It deepened the rift between the Soviet Union and China, momentarily checked the momentum towards US–Soviet *détente*, and above all sent a clear signal to nations East and West that the Soviet Union would not tolerate any threat to the integrity of the Eastern bloc in its most sensitive central zone. The 'Brezhnev Doctrine' of limited sovereignty was if anything more shocking in its application than the suppression of the Hungarian revolt of 1956 had been, in that the Czechs, unlike the Hungarians, insisted that they had no intention of leaving the Warsaw Pact or of departing from socialism.

The international context of the Czech tragedy, however, was quite different from that of 1956. Rather than reversing the trend towards East–West *détente*, after a 'decent interval' it was resumed, and at a swifter pace. In part this was because the re-establishment of bloc cohesion emboldened the Soviet leadership to move forward on *détente* from a position of strength; in part also because the perception among key Western leaders, particularly Brandt, was that, having asserted the limits of the possible in the *détente* process, the Soviet Union might prove 'more amenable to making concessions' in less contentious fields (Marshall 1990: 65). Furthermore, the American elections in 1968 brought a new administration to power, as did the German elections of 1969, both of which were committed to negotiation with the Soviet Union. Three spare references to Czechoslovakia over 1,500 pages of Henry Kissinger's memoirs for the years 1969–73 suggest that he viewed the events of August 1968 and their repercussions as a sideshow to the larger drama of Great Power politics.

Broadly, then, the shifts within the Eastern and Western blocs meant that East–West relations were subject to currents of West–West and East–East tension, inclining both superpowers to pursue *détente* with one eye firmly on their own friends. To put it another way, the success of superpower *détente* was heavily dependent upon containment of their respective alliance partners.

A fourth factor of great significance for *détente* was the Vietnam War. It is sufficiently important to merit a chapter on its own, but here some preliminary points can be made. As we have seen, Vietnam War expenditures had begun to affect the American economy, but by 1968 the military course of the war and dissent at home had also provoked a fundamental reappraisal, not only of policy in Vietnam but of global containment as it had developed since 1947. As Nixon entered the White House in 1969 calls were heard for retrenchment from the US role of global policeman. Support for Senator Mansfield's demands for withdrawal of substantial numbers of troops from Europe, first put forward in 1966, grew with domestic disenchantment with the Vietnam War, and though they did not succeed, placed continuous pressure on policy-makers to reconsider America's military commitments overseas (Garthoff 1985: 115). 'Linkage', posited by Nixon and Kissinger as a scheme for enmeshing the Soviet Union within a web of interdependence, was in part forced upon them by the manifest connections between different facets of America's own priorities. The need for disengagement from Vietnam – or 'peace with honour' – could hardly be considered in isolation from relations with the Soviet Union, since the tie between Moscow and Hanoi was taken to be integral to the North Vietnamese war effort. Whether *détente* was regarded as a means of securing withdrawal from Vietnam or withdrawal from Vietnam was considered to be a precondition for the success of *détente* – a 'chicken and egg' problem for the historian which is probably insoluble – there could be little doubt that some such connection existed.

The Nixon administration's chosen policy of 'Vietnamization' represented in microcosm the larger policy known as the Nixon Doctrine. This proposed a new international division of labour which would involve America's allies assuming greater shares of local defence, leaving the United States to deal with the larger strategic issues – in effect a return to the Eisenhower–Dulles policy of securing United States interests via a network of security pacts (Bowker and Williams 1988: 56). In Nixon's own words:

> The stated basis of our conventional posture in the 1960s was the so-called 'two and a half war' principle. According to it, United States forces would be maintained for a three-month conventional forward defense of NATO, a defense of Korea or Southeast Asia against a full-scale Chinese attack, and a minor contingency – all simultaneously. These force levels were never reached.
>
> In the effort to harmonize doctrine and capability, we chose what is best described as the 'one and a half war' strategy. Under it we will maintain in peacetime general purpose forces adequate for simultaneously meeting a major Communist attack in either Europe or Asia, assisting allies against non-Chinese threats in Asia, and contending with a contingency elsewhere.
>
> (Chace 1973: 44)

Clearly an important novel feature of this stance was the revised assessment of the Chinese threat. The original rationale for involvement in Vietnam – the perceived need to check Chinese expansionism – was no longer plausible. As Kissinger observed, by contrast with the Johnson administration, 'the Nixon administration, from the beginning, never cited, or even hinted at, an anti-Chinese motive for our Vietnam involvement; we did not agree with the analysis; we needed no additional enemies' (Kissinger 1979: 168). This did not rule out, of course, seeking Chinese help in persuading Hanoi to come to terms, given the ideological connections between these two communist powers, and to that extent the opening to China was related to policy on Vietnam.

Finally, Vietnam had implications too for the United States' relations with its West European allies. Verbal and somewhat grudging endorsement by the British Labour Government of American policy in Vietnam scarcely compensated for Britain's unwillingness to send troops. Other NATO countries were much less helpful, to say nothing of the groundswell of student opposition to the war which merged with wider domestic political protests and peaked in 1968. Neutrals, such as Sweden, became safe havens for Americans seeking to escape the draft. America's isolation in Vietnam (with the exception of Australia, South Korea, and some smaller countries) stood in stark contrast to the Korean War. Not only did the Vietnam War lack the imprimatur of the UN, which the Korean conflict had received, but Europeans would not accept, as they had done in the Korean case, that communist aggression in Asia meant that it was likely to be repeated in Europe (Urwin 1989: 196–7). As far as American relations with Europe were concerned, the Vietnam War was, as in so many other respects, a wasting asset.

Vietnam was only one of a number of conflicts in the Third World which were to exert an important influence on *détente*. While new movements for revolutionary change in Angola, the Horn of Africa, Afghanistan, and Central America erupted only in the second half of the 1970s and are discussed in Chapter 11 in the context of the decline of *détente*, the Middle East was in ferment throughout the early phases of *détente*. From the Six Day War of 1967 to the October War of 1973 and beyond, Arab–Israeli conflict posed a persistent challenge to superpower accommodation. Indeed the intense polarization of the Middle East conflict produced by the Israeli victory over the Arabs in 1967 found the superpowers directly at odds, much as both seemed desirous of avoiding confrontation in the region (Bowker and Williams 1988: 99–100). Within a year of signing the Basic Principles Agreement, designed to establish a code of conduct for crisis prevention, the United States and the Soviet Union came into conflict at a critical stage of the Arab–Israeli War of October 1973. A Soviet threat of unilateral intervention to enforce a cease-fire provoked an American world-wide nuclear alert. While the incident did not escalate further, as Bowker and Williams point out, 'questions remain . . . about the extent to which the behaviour of the superpowers was compatible with *détente*, and especially with the principles of crisis prevention that had been established at the 1972 and 1973 summits' (Bowker and Williams 1988: 110).

Similar tensions arose over the Indo-Pakistan War of 1971, but here there was the added dimension of a Chinese interest. East Pakistan's desire for independence, Indian sympathy for their cause, and West Pakistan's brutal attempt to suppress the movement for autonomy led to war between India and Pakistan. China had long been an ally of Pakistan, while the Soviet Union earlier the same year had signed a security treaty with India. American policy was concerned less with the conflict in the subcontinent itself than with the presumption that the Soviet Union planned to humiliate

Table 9.1 US and USSR nuclear arsenals, 1967–69

	January 1967	September 1968	November 1969
United States			
ICBMs	1,054	1,054	1,054
SLBMs	576	656	656
Bombers	650	565	525
Total	2,280	2,275	2,235
USSR			
ICBMs	500	875	1,140
SLBMs	100	110	185
Bombers	150	150	145
Total	750	1,135	1,470

Source: Labrie 1979, p. 11.

China, to prevent which Nixon and Kissinger ordered a naval task force to the Bay of Bengal. While in actuality the outcome of the war, a defeat for Pakistan and independence for East Pakistan (now Bangladesh), owed little to the machinations of the superpowers during the crisis, the Soviet Union undoubtedly emerged as the gainer in the superpower stakes. The wider point, however, is the vulnerability of *détente* to the eruption of regional conflicts and the tendency of the superpowers to view such conflicts through cold-war-tinted lenses.

The final international factor influencing the development of *détente* was more truly bilateral in character: it was the swift growth of the Soviet nuclear arsenal in the latter part of the 1960s. The figures in Table 9.1 show a clear dynamic in Soviet weapons production as compared with virtual stasis in the American case. The raw figures, however, tell only part of the story. Further refinement would show substantial numbers of Soviet missiles under construction (380 ICBMs and SLBMs in 1969) and also that the total Soviet 'throw-weight' (deliverable megatonnage) was considerably larger than that of the US, arising from the Soviets' preference for heavier missiles. By the time the SALT I Treaty was signed in 1972 the Soviet SS-9 ICBM could deliver approximately four times the megatonnage of the largest US missile, the Minuteman III. On the other hand, the United States had a more even balance between the three prongs of its strategic triad (ICBMs, SLBMs, and bombers) and was ahead in development of multiple independently targetable re-entry vehicles (MIRVs) which multiplied American warheads by a factor of three in the case of the Minuteman and ten in the case of Poseidon SLBMs. America first deployed MIRVed missiles in 1970, the Soviets not until 1975. All these elements of asymmetry in the two arsenals became important points of contention in the SALT talks, to be discussed later.

However, despite differences in their weapons, both sides were aware in 1969, when the first soundings on arms negotiations were made, of the overriding reality: that the

Soviet Union had in broad terms caught up with the United States. In any face-off such as had taken place over Cuba in 1962 there was now less likelihood that the Soviet Union would back down, and indeed the growth in the Soviet arsenal owed much to the perception that its strategic nuclear inferiority in 1962 had put the Soviet Union at a decisive political disadvantage. In short, rough nuclear parity between the superpowers inclined the United States to acknowledge the Soviet Union's status as a military superpower, while it encouraged the Soviet Union to believe that it was now possible to bargain from a position of strength. The fact that each perceived the momentum of the arms race differently – the United States from the position of a front runner being caught up and even overhauled and the Soviet Union from the standpoint of the overhauling competitor – was fundamental to the dynamics of the arms negotiations. Each was faced with the difficulty of adjusting to the pace of the other without losing such advantages as they already possessed. If both sides nominally subscribed to the view that it was no longer plausible or safe to conceive of the nuclear relationship as a race, both nevertheless experienced enormous difficulty in abandoning that assumption.

THE DOMESTIC DIMENSIONS OF *DÉTENTE*

Nations do not respond automatically to changes in their external environments. Indeed there is often a considerable lag between external stimulus and internal response, not least because powerful inertial forces exist in bureaucracies and political institutions. In the case of *détente*, the policy shifts undertaken by the United States and the Soviet Union were complicated by the fact that the rhythms of their domestic politics moved at quite different paces and were subject to different pressures.

In the United States the demands of electoral politics often dictate that a new administration will, at least rhetorically, commit itself to policies which diverge from those of its predecessor. This priority, of course, has particular significance when the election produces a change of party in the Presidency, as took place in 1952, 1960, and 1968. In each of these instances the new administrations announced 'new' dispensations – Eisenhower's 'New Look', Kennedy's 'New Frontier', and Nixon's 'era of negotiation' – despite the fact that they can all be interpreted as variations on the theme of containment. In each case, furthermore, the new dispensation was conceived not merely as a response to a perceived change in the external threat but as a means of addressing domestic political problems. Korea was a huge millstone round the neck of the Truman administration in 1952, and during the election campaign Eisenhower made great political capital out of his declaration that he would 'go to Korea' – an apparently decisive gesture which, however, offered little in the way of substance. In 1960 Kennedy made much of the missile gap, picturing the Eisenhower administration as sclerotic and deficient in ideas, and he promised to close the gap and embark on domestic reconstruction. In 1968, amid the domestic turmoil of anti-war demonstrations and race riots, Nixon appealed to Middle America (what he would later call the 'silent majority') and announced that he had 'a plan' to end the Vietnam War with honour. Like Eisenhower before him he did not reveal what the plan was, but the sense of a new direction weighed heavily in the electoral scales.

For the Soviet leadership, American electoral politics posed a challenge to the Soviet premium on continuity in policy-making, and there was the added problem that politicking did not stop with elections. Who made the running in an American administration – the President, Congress, or even public opinion? What credence could be given to Presidential treaty pledges when they were subject to ratification by a Senate jealous of its rights and privileges? The Nixon administration was particularly aware of these issues, embarking as it was on an ambitious and complex foreign policy agenda, and was hence conscious of the need to maintain tight control over the chain of command.

The result was paradoxical. The chosen course was to centralize policy-making in the White House, by cutting out nominally important Cabinet members, such as the Secretary of State, from key decisions on Vietnam and *détente*, and employing 'back-channel' diplomacy via National Security Advisor Kissinger through to Hanoi and Moscow (Isaacson 1992: Ch. 10). This may have simplified the negotiating process in the short term, but it also produced a dangerous concentration of power which ultimately back-fired on Nixon. Extreme sensitivity to leaks and to any manifestations of opposition promoted a siege mentality in the Nixon White House. Most notoriously that mentality was reflected in the break-in at the Democratic Party headquarters in June 1972, a bungled effort by White House staffers to unearth information which would help to ensure Nixon's re-election and hence the continuity of his policies. 'Watergate' was no isolated incident but a consequence of the growth of what has been called 'the imperial Presidency' (Schlesinger 1974). Apparently at the peak of success in 1973, with the completion of the SALT I Treaty, the opening to China, and the peace accords with North Vietnam, Nixon's achievements were immediately placed in question. From early 1973 until his resignation under threat of impeachment in June 1974 Nixon and his policies were under continual pressure from Congress and the media. The backlash continued after his resignation, as Congress refused funds for military aid to South Vietnam, which fell to the North Vietnamese in 1975, and 'intruded' into the *détente* process by making improved trade terms for the Soviet Union conditional upon the granting of emigration visas for Soviet Jews, of which more later. As James Chace observed in 1973, 'in foreign policy it should never be forgotten that politics dictates policy, the means however pragmatic and the ends however moral' (Chace 1973: 5).

If the Soviet Union found it hard to credit how a world leader with such manifest achievements to his name could be brought down by an apparently minor misdemeanour such as Watergate, it was because Soviet leaders themselves were virtually immune from the pressures of public opinion and governmental opposition. This did not mean that they experienced no challenges to their leadership, but these emerged from within the Party elite and were resolved as far as possible with minimum disruption to the wider Party structure.

True, the death of Stalin had produced upheavals which took several years to settle, and the fall of Khrushchev likewise gave way to a period of collective leadership out of which a single dominant figure emerged only by stages. Following Khrushchev's departure – a consequence of the failure of his domestic policies and of the perception that the Cuban missile crisis had been a defeat for the Soviet Union – a triumvirate was established, with Leonid Brezhnev as General Secretary of the Communist Party, Alexei Kosygin as Prime Minister, and Nikolai Podgorny as Head of State. Primary responsibility for economic reform was intially undertaken by Kosygin who embarked on a re-centralization of the economy following Khrushchev's unsuccessful and contentious efforts to devolve production and distribution. This did not mean a return to Stalinism. Kosygin's reforms included a limited introduction of incentives to managers which gave them some scope for decisions about how their profits should be allocated. Planning was rationalized in an effort to bring greater coordination between demand and supply. A further significant departure from the Khrushchev era was the decision to make up for the Soviet Union's technological backwardness by buying Western equipment and encouraging Western firms to set up manufacturing plants in the Soviet Union. Fiat's automobile factory at Stavropol (home of the young Mikhail Gorbachev) was the most prominent example (Hosking 1985: 364–5).

Party discipline and ideological orthodoxy too were tightened under Brezhnev's leadership. The cultural thaw under Khrushchev, which had seen the publication of Alexander Solzhenitsyn's *One Day in the Life of Ivan Denisovich* (1962), was checked in 1965 when the writers Andre Sinyavsky and Yuly Daniel were placed on trial for spreading 'anti-Soviet propaganda'. Both received sentences in labour camps and were subsequently deported.

Broadly, the watchword in the post-Khrushchev years was 'consensus', an emphasis on consolidation and stable growth after the experimentalism of the Khrushchev period. Following a period of struggle with Kosygin which lasted until the middle of 1968, Brezhnev emerged as the dominant figure in the Soviet hierarchy in both foreign and domestic policy (Breslauer 1982: Chs 8, 9, and 10). Indeed the period of *détente* coincided with Brezhnev's supplanting of Kosygin as the chief Soviet spokesman on foreign policy. In 1967 it had been Kosygin who had met President Johnson in the United States and it was he again whom Johnson was to meet at a proposed summit meeting the following year to discuss arms control. The invasion of Czechoslovakia intervened and the meeting was called off. By the time negotiations with the Nixon administration had advanced to the point where a summit seemed appropriate, Brezhnev had strengthened his position within the leadership. 'In August 1971', writes Garthoff, 'as the United States moved to respond to the new Soviet interest in a meeting, on Kissinger's advice Nixon for the first time wrote to Brezhnev rather than to Kosygin' – the result of information from one of Kissinger's 'back-channel' Soviet contacts that following the 24th Party Congress in spring 1971 Brezhnev had assumed a 'new role' in foreign policy (Garthoff 1985: 95). Nixon's three summit meetings (May 1972, June 1973, and June 1974) were all held with Brezhnev.

By comparison therefore with the instability of the American administration during the crucial period in which *détente* came to fruition (1972–5), the Soviet leadership was achieving ever-greater stability and directedness. The fate of *détente* was closely linked to this disparity in domestic conditions. During the latter half of the 1970s, while the Soviet leadership continued to declare its adherence to *détente*, the Ford and Carter presidencies experienced an uphill struggle to sustain it in the face of the disaffection of influential pressure groups. Part of Nixon's legacy to his successors was a weakened presidency and a divided establishment. By contrast Brezhnev was increasingly secure and indeed the boldness of Soviet policy in the second half of the 1970s was one reason for the disenchantment in the United States with *détente*. Not only, then, were the domestic climates in the two superpowers markedly different, but these gave rise to clashing perceptions which heightened the difficulty of sustaining *détente*. A weakened United States viewed a seemingly confident and aggressive Soviet Union with increased suspicion; an emboldened Soviet leadership felt able to take advantage of what it regarded as a favourable international 'correlation of forces' – by, for example, encouraging the Cubans to intervene in the Angolan civil war – while at the same time protesting its devotion to *détente* with the United States.

DÉTENTE: THE THEORY

It would be a mistake to think that *détente* sprang forth fully formed as Nixon entered the White House. There was no detailed master plan, though there was a broad strategic outlook on global politics. 'After a period of confrontation', Nixon announced in his inaugural address, 'we are entering an era of negotiation.' The words are vague enough, but they denote an important shift of attitude on the part of Nixon and Kissinger. Both, after all, were old cold warriors whose early careers had begun during the years of high ideological tension between the superpowers. Nixon, a freshman Congressman in the Republican-dominated 80th Congress elected in 1946, had been particularly vociferous in his criticism of the Truman administration for the loss of China. As a member of the House Un-American Activities Committee he had pursued the case of Alger Hiss with tigerish zeal. As Eisenhower's Vice-President he had consistently played the role of ideological front man to Eisenhower's pragmatic statesman.

Kissinger, meanwhile, had shown in his early writings considerable militancy with respect to the Soviet Union. Indeed his first book, a study of the 'Concert of Europe' following the Congress of Vienna in 1815, took as its underlying premise a distinction between types of nation-state which had as much relevance to the cold war as to the first half of the nineteenth century. 'Wherever there exists a power', he wrote:

> which considers the international order or the manner of legitimizing it oppressive, relations between it and other powers will be revolutionary. In

such cases, it is not the adjustment of differences within a given system which will be at issue, but the system itself . . . The distinguishing feature of a revolutionary power is not that it feels threatened – such a feeling is inherent in the nature of international relations based on sovereign status – but that nothing can reassure it. Only absolute security – the neutralization of an opponent – is considered a sufficient guarantee, and thus the desire of a power for absolute security means absolute insecurity for all others. Diplomacy, the art of restraining the exercise of power, cannot function in such an environment.

(Kissinger 1957: 2)

Revolutionary France was one such power according to this scheme, but so, one can say without straining Kissinger's point in the least, was the Soviet Union. Furthermore, he could well have been describing the cold war when he wrote that 'because in revolutionary situations the contending systems are less concerned with the adjustment of differences than with the subversion of loyalties, diplomacy is replaced either by war or by an armaments race' (Kissinger 1957: 2).

With a scheme such as this, which is heavily loaded against the possibility of dealing with a revolutionary state, one must ask how Kissinger came to believe that this was both possible and necessary in the case of the Soviet Union and China in the late 1960s. Part of the answer must lie in the changes in the international order, already described, which had the overall effect of exposing limits to American power. 'Our resources', Kissinger noted in his memoirs, 'were no longer infinite in relation to our problems; instead we had to set priorities, both intellectual and material. In the Fifties and Sixties we had attempted ultimate solutions to specific problems; now our challenge was to shape a world and an American role to which we were permanently committed, which could no longer be sustained by the illusion that our exertions had a terminal point' (Kissinger 1979: 57–8). Furthermore, the Sino–Soviet split now rendered the earlier assumption of a monolithic communist ideological threat redundant. Soviet power rather than communist ideology was now the chief danger. As he entered office in the Nixon administration, Kissinger regarded Soviet strategy as one of 'ruthless opportunism' (Kissinger 1979: 119).

Another clue to Kissinger's apparent change of heart lies within his philosophical outlook itself. His yardstick for assessing the character of states and systems of states was a model of legitimacy and stability drawn from the diplomacy of nineteenth-century Europe. Terms like 'order', 'power', 'stability', 'equilibrium', 'legitimacy' are strewn across Kissinger's pages – the coinage of the 'Realist' for whom the ultimate determinant of international politics was the struggle for power and the effort to achieve balance among nation-states. Kissinger's vision, his prescriptive values, were rooted in this outlook and it took only a small shift of gear for him to bring the conceptual apparatus of Realism to bear on the changed international situation.

This did not mean that ideology no longer played a role in Kissinger's thinking about international affairs. It merely meant that it remained implicit rather than explicit. Just as, it has been said, pragmatism is simply a matter of taking your ethics for granted, so Realism as an outlook on international affairs is simply a matter of taking ideology for granted. It was no longer necessary to hammer home one's distaste for Soviet ideology, least of all for card-carrying cold warriors such as Kissinger and Nixon. With plenty of ideology in the bank, invested over a period of years, they could afford to attend to 'realities' of power.

The overriding reality, as Nixon and Kissinger saw it, was that the United States was subject to multiple pressures. 'As I looked at America's foreign policy during the 1960s', recalled Nixon, 'I felt that it had been held hostage, first under Kennedy to the cold war and then under Johnson to the Vietnam War. Our tendency to become preoccupied with only one or two problems at a time had led to a deterioration of policy on all fronts' (Nixon 1978: 343). Policy must therefore be multi-faceted, and its different elements coordinated. Within that broad scheme the Soviet Union nevertheless represented the primary focus of US interest to which, Kissinger urged, the United States should apply three basic principles: concreteness, restraint, and linkage (Kissinger 1979: 128–9). The first of these reflected a distaste for poorly prepared summit meetings and negotiations based on 'general atmospherics' rather than specific causes of tension; the second aspired to a climate in which neither side would seek unilateral advantage.

The third principle, that of linkage, has received much comment, since it is felt to contain the essence of the Nixon–Kissinger approach to diplomacy. As Kissinger describes it, linkage was an unexceptionable notion which simply acknowledged certain givens of diplomacy and international relations:

> In our view, linkage existed in two forms: first when a diplomat deliberately links two separate objectives in a negotiation, using one as leverage on the other; or by virtue of reality, because in an interdependent world the actions of a major power are inevitably related and have consequences beyond the issue or region immediately concerned.
>
> (Kissinger 1979: 129)

The new administration resorted to linkage in the first sense, Kissinger observed, 'when we made progress in settling the Vietnam war something of a condition for advance in areas of interest to the Soviets, such as the Middle East, trade, or arms limitation'. But, he added, 'in the far more important sense, linkage was a reality, not a decision . . . We saw linkage . . . as synonymous with an overall strategic and geopolitical view.' It was ultimately the means whereby the Nixon administration was able to 'free our foreign policy from oscillations between overextension and isolation and to ground it in a firm conception of the national interest' (Kissinger 1979: 129, 130).

Kissinger was evidently keen to play down the first sense of linkage, perhaps since it seemed to imply coercion. It is also clear that Kissinger did not intend linkage to extend to attempting to change a state's internal system or values. Such a tactic risked exacerbating tensions without materially influencing Soviet behaviour. Kissinger consistently resisted justifying policies on moral or ideological grounds. He saw the world, it has been pointed out, in structural and geopolitical terms. Hence his dismay at Congress's insistence on tying a grant of Most Favoured Nation status to the Soviet Union to its willingness to allow Soviet Jews to emigrate (Litwak 1984: 152–3).

Having said that, however, the Soviet perception of linkage was that it was punitive in conception and implementation. There was a good deal more stick than carrot. Linkage seemed designed, as indeed in part it was, to hedge the Soviet Union around with constraints, and to that extent linkage took away with one hand what it offered with the other: namely recognition of the Soviet Union as an equal. Linkage was overtly manipulative, even paternalistic, in its ambition to modify 'Soviet behaviour'. The ambiguity of linkage pointed to an ambiguity in *détente* itself. In principle, according to the American theory, *détente* represented an acknowledgement that the world had changed radically in the direction of multipolarity, a diffusion of the communist threat, and the rise of new economic forces which cut across the rigid lines of the cold war. In practice, however, not only did the Soviet Union remain the consuming interest of American foreign policy, but in instance after instance the American leadership demonstrated that its basic perception of the communist threat had changed little.

In the space of one page of his memoirs Nixon exposed the two sides of *détente* with great clarity. Having just taken Kennedy and Johnson to task for their 'tendency to become preoccupied with only one or two problems at a time', adding that 'I did not feel there should be any single foreign policy priority', Nixon nevertheless concluded that 'as I looked at America's position in the world and examined our relations with other nations, I could see that the same central factor in 1968 on the eve of my presidency was the same as it had been in 1947 when I first went to Europe with the Herter Committee [in connection with the Marshall Plan]: America now, as then, was the main defender of the free world against the encroachment and aggression of the Communist world' (Nixon 1978: 343). American *détente* policy, in short, was not very far removed from the old priority of containment of communism.

The Soviet approach to *détente* similarly showed important elements of continuity with the past. While the name of Khrushchev had disappeared from public life, the policy of 'peaceful coexistence', with a lineage going back to Lenin, was there to be invoked. Peaceful coexistence in its original formulation implied that, in the absence of worldwide socialist victory in the wake of the Bolshevik Revolution, the Soviet Union must perforce coexist with capitalist states if socialism were to survive and prosper. Avoidance of war, particularly with the advent of the nuclear age, was a necessity, even if it was also necessary to be prepared to fight a war should it occur. But peaceful coexistence had never been a passive doctrine. Included within it was the imperative of consolidating and where possible expanding the boundaries of socialism.

222

A statement adopted by an international meeting of communist parties in Moscow in June 1969 glossed peaceful coexistence as follows:

> The policy of peaceful coexistence does not negate the right of any oppressed people to fight for its liberation by any means it considers necessary – armed or peaceful . . . This policy does not imply either the preservation of the socio-political status quo or a weakening of the ideological struggle. It helps to promote the class struggle against imperialism on a national and world-wide scale.
>
> (Daniels 1985: Vol. 2: 355)

Perhaps even more ominously, the same document observed that 'the defense of peace is inseparably linked with the struggle to compel the imperialists to accept peaceful coexistence of states with different social systems (Daniels 1985, Vol. 2: 354–5). A seemingly innocuous doctrine thus proved (like the American doctrine of linkage) to carry deeply threatening implications. It is hardly surprising that Americans rarely adopted the Soviet terminology of peaceful coexistence; to them it seemed so plainly a piece of double-talk designed only to deceive, a view expressed as early as 1960 by George Kennan in an exchange with Khrushchev published in the American journal *Foreign Affairs* (Kennan 1960: 171–90). Nevertheless, Kissinger did endorse the term during a press conference in 1972 in which he discussed the Basic Principles Agreement (BPA) on relations with the Soviet Union (Garthoff 1985: 293). Indeed it appears in the BPA text itself, suggesting the distance travelled in US–Soviet relations in the previous decade.

An important change in the Soviet conception of the international environment and of American power had taken place since Khrushchev's vigorous dialogues with Western leaders. His blustering had barely concealed deep anxiety about the Soviet Union's vulnerability to Western nuclear power. Under his successors, however, that deficiency had been largely repaired, and this, in combination with the view that national liberation struggles throughout the world were placing the West on the defensive, convinced Soviet leaders that the 'correlation of forces' was moving in their direction: 'the contradiction between the imperialist "policy of strength" and the actual possibilities of imperialism is becoming more and more evident. Imperialism can neither regain its lost historical initiative nor reverse world development. The main direction of mankind's development is determined by the world socialist system, the international working class, and all the revolutionary forces.' More particularly, went the same analysis, 'in Vietnam, United States imperialism, the most powerful of the imperialist partners, is suffering defeat, a fact of historic significance' (Daniels 1985, Vol. 2: 352).

As has been well pointed out by two leading students of *détente*, however, 'Soviet ideology taught that the capitalist world was at its most dangerous when it believed that its power was threatened in ways which might prove irreversible.' Hence the achievement of strategic parity enjoined caution rather than adventurism (Bowker and

Williams 1988: 31). Furthermore, the achievement of nuclear parity brought with it a revised assessment of the role of arms control in defence policy. So long as the Soviets were in an inferior position with respect to the United States, a freezing of the *status quo*, which had been proposed by President Johnson in 1964, would place them at a disadvantage. By 1969 relative strength, combined with the conviction that avoidance of nuclear war was the overriding foreign policy priority, put negotiations on arms control high on the agenda (Bowker and Williams 1988: 37–8).

Soviet *détente*, like that of the United States, was Janus-faced. It held out strong possibilities for conciliation without erasing the suspicions which its fundamentally competitive stance towards the United States aroused. Furthermore, the potential for a clash between linkage and peaceful coexistence was evident. The essence of the linkage concept was that events on the periphery could vitally affect relations at the centre and that therefore both powers must take pains to avoid provoking such flashpoints; the essence of peaceful coexistence was that continued promotion of worldwide socialist goals was not incompatible with efforts to rebuild the superpower relationship at the centre. In other words, as Kenneth Dyson has put it, 'the West was disillusioned by the Soviet Union's limited conception of peaceful coexistence, whilst the Soviet Union was frightened and defensive about the expansiveness of Western conceptions of *détente*' (Dyson 1986: 37).

Clearly, theoretical formulations cannot tell the whole story of *détente*, but they do indicate the perceptions which guided the practical policies of each side. In essence both superpowers experienced a conflict between their perceptions that the world was increasingly complex and diverse, and their gut instincts, born of long experience, that the other side was likely to take advantage of such opportunities as the new dispensation offered. The result, perhaps inevitably, was the pursuit of policies which reflected those contradictions: *détente* if possible, cold war if necessary.

DÉTENTE: THE PRACTICE

The superpowers

We can place the agreements reached between the United States and the Soviet Union into three broad categories: firstly, economic, cultural, and scientific cooperation; secondly, crisis prevention and control measures; and thirdly, arms control. The latter has received the lion's share of attention in the West but it is important to understand the role the other two categories played in the overall dynamics of *détente*, if only because the United States and the Soviet Union ascribed very different values to them.

In the first category, as in the other two, the first Nixon–Brezhnev summit of May 1972 laid the main foundations for *détente*. Protocols were signed providing for cooperation in the fields of medicine and public health, space exploration, scientific and technological research, and environmental protection (Nogee and Donaldson

1988: 269–70). None of these on their own could be regarded as make-or-break features of *détente*. They reflect perhaps the popularly held view that nations which established connections at a non-political level – which knew each other as peoples rather than states – were less likely to engage in political or military conflict. Nevertheless, while they meant a good deal to the people directly affected and were important symbolically, they were easily sacrificed or downgraded in the event of a downturn in political relations.

Potentially more far-reaching was the establishment of a Joint American–Soviet Commercial Commission designed to work out a normalization of trade relations. In the October following the first summit these plans bore fruit in the Trade Agreement which offered something to both sides – a settlement of Soviet debts to the United States stemming from wartime lend-lease in return for which the Soviet Union was to receive credits for purchases of US technology and agricultural products. In addition (but also conditional on Soviet repayment of lend-lease debts) the United States would grant Most Favoured Nation (MFN) status to the Soviet Union, allowing entry of Soviet goods into the United States at reduced tariff rates. The Soviet Union undoubtedly had more at stake in the economic field than the United States. The Soviet Union sorely needed American grain and technology, while in the United States economic relations were regarded rather as a means of leverage in the larger scheme of *détente*.

It was the issue of grain sales to the Soviet Union which provided the first demonstration of the fragility of *détente*. Soon after the May 1972 summit the Soviets entered into negotiation with American grain companies for the purchase of large quantities of wheat and other agricultural products. Aided by generous American credit terms and with the backing of the Department of Agriculture, by the end of the year the Soviet Union had purchased effectively the entire American grain surplus at below the world prices. The reaction in Congress, which had played no part in the deal, was to accuse the Nixon administration of having been duped by the Soviets. The so-called 'great grain robbery' provoked Congress into hitting back at the Nixon administration in the one area of the new US–Soviet trade accords which was within Congress's power to influence – the grant of MFN status to the Soviet Union. Over the next two years Congress imposed its own form of linkage on US–Soviet relations by insisting on tying MFN to the easing of restrictions on the emigration of Jews from the Soviet Union, a form of linkage which Kissinger had explicitly ruled out since it meant intervening in Soviet domestic policy. Senator Henry Jackson and Congressman Charles Vanik pushed through an amendment to the Trade Bill of 1972 embodying the emigration condition to MFN status which, in conjunction with another amendment placing a low ceiling on credits to the Soviet Union, had the effect of cutting grain sales to the Soviet Union and leading the Soviets to repudiate the original Trade Agreement. Linkage, as Raymond Garthoff has remarked, had 'run rampant' (Garthoff 1985: 305–11, 453–63). It was only the first of many instances which showed the vulnerability of *détente* to domestic pressures within the United States.

This case also revealed a paradoxical feature of the US–Soviet relationship in this period of rapid change: the Soviet Union was prepared to sacrifice a high priority item in order to maintain its vital interest in autonomy and freedom of movement, while the United States (or at least one branch of its government) was inclined to stand firm on an issue which in material terms was of less than vital significance to the American national interest. Asymmetry of needs was fundamental to the interchanges of *détente*.

Crisis prevention and control measures on the face of it had the potential for a reshaping of the superpower relationship, in that they specified general principles governing exchanges between them. True, general principles do not of themselves enact the shifts they aspire to produce. Like the establishment of the 'hot-line' after the Cuban missile crisis they tend to represent, on the one hand, lessons learned after the fact and, on the other, aspirations to institutionalize those lessons. However, in the sense that such agreements set codes of behaviour, Marquis of Queensberry rules for international relations, they can, in conjunction with agreements on specifics, create a climate of trust and a mutual recognition of possibilities and limits of cooperation.

The most wide-ranging of such agreements was the Basic Principles of Relations Between the United States and the Soviet Union (BPA), signed at the May 1972 summit. The agreement committed the parties to the broad goal of creating 'conditions which promote the reduction of tensions in the world and the strengthening of universal security and international cooperation'. There followed twelve principles, chief among which was their 'common determination that in the nuclear age there is no alternative to conducting their mutual relations on the basis of peaceful coexistence. Differences in ideology and in the social systems of the USA and the USSR are not obstacles to the bilateral development of normal relations based on the principles of sovereignty, equality, non-interference in internal affairs and mutual advantage.' The remaining principles called for mutual restraint, crisis avoidance, a commitment to observe all bilateral and multilateral treaties faithfully, and both sides undertook to work for disarmament and cooperation in economic, scientific and cultural fields. It could hardly have been more comprehensive (text in Grenville and Wasserstein 1987: 456–8).

For all the appearance of mutuality it is clear that the Soviets and Americans accorded different priorities to the BPA. While Brezhnev reportedly considered it 'even more important' than the SALT agreements, neither Nixon nor Kissinger regarded it in this light. Nixon, Garthoff notes, played no part in drafting or discussing the BPA. Kissinger, who had been instrumental in negotiating it prior to the May summit, evidently viewed it less as a code of conduct than as a general yardstick for judging progress in US–Soviet relations, one which should not be interpreted too literally. Furthermore, on the American side the BPA had been planned without reference to officials outside the White House, while the Soviets had fully engaged the major foreign policy planning agencies in preparing the proposals (Garthoff 1985: 291–8).

A similar set of attitudes and circumstances surrounded the Prevention of Nuclear War (PNW) agreement, signed at the second *détente* summit in Washington in June of the following year. In essence it applied the BPA principles to the specific task of lowering nuclear tension, though it was notable also for what it did not contain: namely, a joint pledge of 'no first use' of nuclear weapons, a policy which the Soviet Union had long advocated but which the United States had always resisted on the grounds that it was felt necessary to reserve the option of a nuclear response to a Soviet conventional attack in Europe. At any rate, as with the BPA, there was less common ground than met the eye.

How is the distinction between the United States and the Soviet Union on the BPA and PNW agreements to be explained? Doubtless the American stance owed something to a long-held scepticism about the good faith of the Soviet Union. Memories of the Yalta pledges on free elections in Poland, of Soviet endorsement of the Atlantic Charter and the Declaration on Liberated Europe looked hollow beside the imposition of communism in Eastern Europe. But even if these pieces of history were buried – as they could not entirely be for leaders of Nixon and Kissinger's generation – there was the more general belief, rooted in Kissinger's Realism and distaste for the rhetorical moralism of America's own foreign policy tradition, that such general pledges were easy to make and easy to break. Agreement on specifics was one thing; universalist rhetoric was another. It is perhaps not without significance that the most successful of the crisis prevention measures was also the most limited – the Naval Agreement on the Prevention of Incidents on the High Seas. By contrast, the BPA arguably failed an early test when the superpowers came into conflict during the Arab–Israeli War of October 1973.

This aspect of *détente* presents us with an irony. The United States, so long given to universalist claims and large statements of principle, now regarded them with deep scepticism, while the Soviet Union, formerly inclined to view general statements of principle as screens for capitalist predatory designs, now embraced them as of the essence. Once again the explanation may lie in the different trajectories of the two powers at that particular moment. Inasmuch as the promotion of general principles reflects claims of special responsibility for the ordering of world politics, then the Soviet Union, as the bidder for a new role, had more to gain and the United States more to lose by explicit acknowledgement of Soviet equality and legitimacy as a world power.

The strategic arms limitation talks produced two distinct agreements: an Interim Agreement on limitation of strategic nuclear weapons and the Anti-Ballistic Missile (ABM) Treaty, both signed at the May 1972 summit in Moscow. They took two years of complex and tortuous negotiations which were bedevilled on the American side by frequent lapses of coordination between Kissinger's back-channel deals with Soviet Ambassador Dobrynin and the American SALT negotiating team itself, led by Gerard

Smith. Indeed Smith was left in the dark about key elements of Kissinger's negotiating positions and the resulting agreements were regarded as less than satisfactory by Smith and his colleagues (Hersh 1983: Ch. 25, esp. 343). Raymond Garthoff, one of Smith's team and later a leading scholarly authority on SALT, termed the Interim Agreement 'a crucial failure' (Garthoff 1985: 189).

The Interim Agreement effectively checked the nuclear arms race in only one of its categories – numbers of land-based ICBM launchers – but even these limits (1,054 on the American side and 1,618 on the Soviet) were rendered virtually meaningless by other aspects of the agreement. In the first place, though limits were also placed on SLBMs, the ceilings were set so high that building up to them would represent a marked increase in intercontinental missile capacity. The American position on SLBMs was marked by deep confusion. Kissinger seems not to have understood their significance and at one stage in the negotiations had been ready to exclude them from the agreement – a position favoured by the Soviets who, unlike the Americans, were geared up for a dynamic phase of expansion in submarine and SLBM construction. In subsequent negotiations SLBM limits were restored but in a form, as mentioned, which left planned Soviet growth effectively untouched (Hersh 1983: 342; Garthoff 1985: 158–66).

The second feature of the Interim Agreement which undercut the limits placed on launchers was the absence of a ban on MIRVs. While the United States did at an early stage propose a MIRV ban, it was hedged around with conditions – in the form of on-site inspection to verify compliance – which the Soviets would not accept. It seems to have been offered as a negotiating ploy rather than as a serious position. The fact was that since the United States was ready as early as 1970 to deploy MIRVs, a ban would check US missile growth in a field where it held a clear advantage. The Soviets, knowing they were several years behind in this field, had equally little incentive to negotiate restrictions on MIRVs (Bowker and Williams 1988: 70). The result was an arms limitation regime which contained few effective limitations. Above all, perhaps, it contained no restrictions on modernization. Nevertheless, as an avowedly 'interim' agreement, it was entered into on the presumption that full treaty terms would be negotiated in a second round of SALT talks, with what results we shall see in Chapter 11.

The ABM Treaty was in many respects more successful in that it was more categorical about what was and was not permissible. While permitting each side to deploy two systems – one round their National Command Centres (NCAs) and one other – it also limited the number of interceptor missiles on each site. (In 1974 in follow-up negotiations at Vladivostok the ABM systems were reduced to one.) Furthermore, it prohibited in a seemingly comprehensive fashion the development, testing, and deployment of ABM systems whether sea-based, air-based, space-based, or mobile land-based. Why the willingness to accept such sweeping constraints? There are two possible reasons. In the first place neither side had a marked advantage in this field, and agreement was always easier when the balance was fairly even. Secondly, the state of ABM technology was not yet such as to ensure that such systems could provide comprehensive defence. If this had been the case, and particularly if one side had held a clear advantage, then it is likely that neither side would have been willing to sacrifice ABM development, since it would have rendered their offensive missiles vulnerable. To that extent defensive systems had serious implications for offensive capability. The ABM Treaty was thus closely tied to the agreements on offensive missiles, and indeed without the ABM limits it is possible that neither side would have contemplated limits on their offensive systems. In the early 1980s Reagan's 'Star Wars' proposal, which did initially envisage a comprehensive defensive shield, reopened the ABM issue and temporarily at any rate stalled talks on limiting strategic offensive missiles – another case of technological asymmetry undermining the possibility of agreement.

The details of the SALT I agreements tell only part of the story. Equally important are the political dynamics which underlay them. The main agreements were reached at the Moscow summit of May 1972 which was strategically timed by Nixon to have maximum effect on the presidential election campaign. Some accounts suggest that the ABM Treaty could have been concluded as early as 1970. The evidence indicates that the rhythm of the negotiations on the American side reflected not only electoral considerations but the determination of Nixon and Kissinger to keep tight hold of the substance of the talks in the face of priorities set by the negotiating team itself. The Soviets too were subject to internal pressures, not only within the Soviet Union, where disastrous harvests in 1970 and 1971 produced grain and animal feed shortages, but in Poland, where food riots (triggered by food price increases resulting from bread and meat shortages) broke out in December 1970. The replacement of Gomulka by Gierek following the suppression of the riots solved the immediate crisis but the underlying problem of poor food production in the Eastern bloc could only be resolved by imports. Hence the Soviet eagerness for a grain deal with the United States and hence also, if Seymour Hersh is to be believed, the American interest in linking the supply of grain to the Soviet Union to the conclusion of SALT I (Hersh 1983: 339–40 and Ch. 25 *passim*).

Other influences help to explain both the success in reaching substantial agreements in 1972 and the difficulty in following them up. Among the factors complicating progress from 1972 was the collapse of the trade negotiations already mentioned and Nixon's increasing political vulnerability as Watergate unfolded during that same two-year period. In neither the Washington summit of 1973, which despite the PNW agreement was clouded by the trade issue, nor the 1974 summit, which produced little progress in turning the Interim Agreement into a SALT II treaty, were the two sides able to capitalize fully on the advances of 1972. Nevertheless, another factor operating in the background played a significant enabling role in the 1972 summit and this was the American opening to China, marked publicly by Nixon's visit to Beijing in February 1972. Though Nixon's major priority was probably Vietnam, the significance of the American move was not lost on the Soviets who, in the wake of Nixon's visit, moved quickly to arrange the Brezhnev–Nixon summit for May

(Garthoff 1985: 242). America's China policy will be discussed in Chapter 10 in connection with Vietnam. For the moment it is enough to stress the complex interplay between internal needs and external pressures experienced by both sides.

There should be no surprise in this. In the real world of international politics not only are motives inevitably mixed but the total isolation of one field from another is never possible. In that sense, linkage always operates, as Kissinger observed, irrespective of declared intentions. The distinctive feature of the American approach to *détente* was the presumption that the medley of competing forces and intentions could be managed in a coherent and orderly fashion. There are areas in which linkage can be said to have worked. The Soviets acknowledged that they had exerted some pressure on North Vietnam to come to terms with the United States, and the Soviets did not allow the American mining and bombing of Hanoi and Haiphong in 1972 to disrupt plans for the summit. Furthermore, despite the Soviets' rejection of the Trade Agreement in 1974, after a period of continued restriction of Jewish emigration the limits were eased in the mid and late 1970s (Garthoff 1985: 1003).

It is not clear, however, that there was a simple relationship between the exertion of pressure in one field and a favourable outcome in another. In the case of Vietnam the Soviet decision to ignore the United States' provocative military action in the spring of 1972 might be regarded as an instance of Soviet compartmentalization rather than American linkage (Bowker and Williams 1988: 75). Nor was it necessarily the case that Soviet pressure on North Vietnam was a simple pay-off for American agreement on arms control. In the case of the link between trade and emigration of Soviet Jews, once again the cause–effect relationship is not crystal clear, if only because the easing of restrictions in the late 1970s occurred without the grant of MFN to the Soviet Union. It seems more plausible to suggest that the Soviet predisposition to accede to American demands in certain fields arose less from the direct application of linkage than from a broad assessment that a willingness to compromise in certain areas would ease tensions generally and enhance the possibility of agreement on major problems. Arguably, however, the choice in these instances lay with the Soviet Union, not with the United States. At the very least there was no consistent pattern of the application of leverage producing a desired outcome. There are in any case enough instances where linkage manifestly did not work – above all in the Third World – to cast doubt on American claims.

European *Détente*

European *détente* differed in fundamental respects from superpower *détente* in that it was concerned in large part with territorial and specific political disputes such as the status of Berlin. In effect European *détente* represented the conclusion of unfinished business left over from the Second World War. This gave European *détente* a clarity of focus which was not evident in US–Soviet *détente*, even in the field of nuclear arms. So many grey areas existed in the arms agreements: the issues of verification (which were left to 'national technical means' or spy satellites), of modernization, and the size of missiles, to say nothing of areas which were omitted entirely from the Interim Agreement such as MIRVs and the American Forward Base Systems (FBS – chiefly their bomber forces in Europe). In short, the inherent dynamic of technological innovation remained unchecked. Furthermore, in other aspects of superpower *détente*, such as crisis prevention measures, trade, and the enunciation of general principles governing superpower relations, ambiguity was rife. There were few clear boundaries such as characterized the territorial and political settlements which were the subject of European *détente*.

There was another important difference. While European *détente* certainly looked forward, in the sense that both West Germany and the Eastern bloc aspired to better relations in the future, the substance of European *détente* was retrospective. It involved the ratification of an already existing state of affairs: namely, the division of Europe following the war and the anomalies to which that had given rise – a divided Germany, a divided Berlin deep within the eastern part of Germany, and the radical revision of the German/Polish and Russian/Polish frontiers which the Soviet Union had imposed in 1945. Of course, it is true that the settlements on these issues had long-term consequences which, if the Soviet Union had been able to foresee, would have made them think twice about entering into them. As will be suggested in Chapter 13, it is arguable that the collapse of communism in the Eastern bloc in the late 1980s owed something to the subterranean consequences of the agreements to disagree in the settlements of 1970 to 1972. Meanwhile, however, European *détente*, as it were, brought the formalities of intra-European relations into line with its actual history. This accounts in part for the durability of European as compared with superpower *détente*.

A third difference similarly arose from the facts of political geography in combination with the political personality of Willy Brandt. The proximity of West Germany to the front line of the cold war inclined the German leadership to a political realism which was not always apparent in American leadership circles for all the invocation of *Realpolitik* by Kissinger. Of course, Brandt himself was something of an idealist, and his ambition to combine hard-nosed bargaining with the Soviet Union with a vision of a Germany united in spirit if not in fact was regarded by his political opponents as a vain effort to square a political circle. In the eyes of the West German right Brandt's formula of 'two states within one nation' conceded to the Soviet Union its essential demand that the division of Germany be recognized as legitimate. Such concessions as Brandt gained in return – such as freer movement of people between the two Germanys – hardly compensated, it was held, for the seeming abandonment of the basic principle of West German statehood. But Brandt's concessions – and concessions they surely were – arguably embodied a deeper realism than one based on power and inter-state relations. They sprang from an enlightened acceptance of the limits of the possible in power politics and a corresponding conviction that those limits could be transcended by the promotion of genuine conciliation. Brandt was hardly naive about

Soviet intentions, but he saw what few others saw so clearly, that acknowledgement of the *status quo* had the potential to serve as an agent of change.

West Germany's Ostpolitik took the form of three important bilateral treaties – with the Soviet Union, Poland, and East Germany. In parallel, Four-Power talks were held on Berlin, leading to the Quadripartite Agreement, and European *détente* was capped by negotiations among thirty-five nations (all European but for the United States and Canada) in the Conference on Security and Cooperation in Europe (CSCE).

The first of the bilateral treaties was signed in Moscow between West Germany and the Soviet Union in August 1970. Its two main provisions – mutual renunciation of force and mutual acknowledgement that the frontiers of all European states were to be considered inviolable – met the Soviet Union's long-held goal of gaining recognition for its forcible shift in 1945 of the Polish/East German border to a point on the Oder–Neisse rivers some one hundred miles west of its pre-war position. Six months later West Germany and Poland confirmed this settlement in the second of the bilateral treaties. Though these seemed entirely one-sided agreements, West Germany made them conditional upon conclusion of an acceptable agreement on Berlin. The third bilateral treaty – between East and West Germany – took longer to negotiate and was concluded only after the hard-line East German leader Walter Ulbricht had been replaced in 1971 by the more moderate Erich Honecker. While the treaty stopped short of full *de jure* recognition, the two states agreed to exchange permanent missions (rather than ambassadors) and to approve each other's applications for membership of the United Nations. A further clause granted East German imports to West Germany exemption from EEC tariffs (Nogee and Donaldson 1988: 260–2).

A similar compromise was effected over Berlin in the Quadripartite Agreement signed in September 1971. Again the retirement of Ulbricht acted as a catalyst. Neither the West nor the East gained its maximum demands: the West's that West Berlin be considered an integral part of West Germany nor the East's that Berlin should be established as, in some not clearly specified sense, an independent entity. The Treaty affirmed that the Western sectors 'continue not to be a constituent part of the Federal Republic of Germany and not to be governed by it'. Nevertheless, the Treaty also provided generally for improved contact between East and West Berlin, and specified that permanent residents of West Berlin would be able to visit the East for 'compassionate, family, religious, cultural, or commercial reasons, or as tourists'. Crucially, as far as the West was concerned, the Soviets agreed that transit between West Berlin and West Germany would be 'unimpeded', thus removing the weapon which the Soviet Union had employed in the Berlin crises of 1948, 1958–9, and 1961 (Grenville and Wasserstein 1987: 197).

With these treaties signed the decks were cleared for a more comprehensive settlement of European political and security issues. Indeed Western resistance to the Soviets' long-standing desire for such a conference – going as far back as a proposal of Molotov's in 1954 – had rested on the suspicion that the Soviet Union would use the occasion to destabilize the Western Alliance and ultimately force US withdrawal from Europe. As it happened, the coordination of European and superpower *détente* – at least in the sense that Brandt was careful to pursue Ostpolitik with the broad endorsement of the United States – forestalled this outcome. Nevertheless, the United States never entirely relinquished its doubts about the wisdom of formal acknowledgement of the *status quo* in Europe, and the results of the CSCE were reported with little fanfare in the United States.

The CSCE 'Final Act', concluded in Helsinki in August 1975, consisted of three sets of agreements – or 'baskets' – covering firstly security in Europe, secondly, cooperation in the fields of economics, science, technology and the environment and thirdly, cooperation in humanitarian and other fields. The second of these proved relatively uncontroversial, but the first and the third contained provisions which, if taken literally, would pose difficulties for both the United States and the Soviet Union. The first pledged all parties to a 'Declaration on Principles Guiding Relations Between the Participating States' covering respect for rights of sovereign equality, refraining from the threat or use of force, the inviolability of frontiers, peaceful settlement of disputes, non-intervention in internal affairs, respect for human rights and fundamental freedoms, adherence to self-determination of peoples, cooperation among states, and fulfilment of obligations under international law (text in Grenville and Wasserstein 1987: 463–7).

Basket III expanded on the human rights provision in Basket I, committing all parties to promote contact between peoples in the fields of information and ideas in addition to the physical movement of peoples across frontiers. Provision was made for the facilitation of family visits and transnational marriages (text in Grenville and Wasserstein 1987: 469–71).

To all appearances, which is to say that if one could abstract the agreements from the political realities which underlay them, the Helsinki Final Act was a recipe for full normalization of relations between East and West. In actuality each provision was loaded in one way or another. The reality underlying the Soviet commitment to national self-determination, for example, was the Brezhnev doctrine of limited sovereignty in Eastern Europe. The reality underlying the commitment to human rights and freer movement of peoples was the Soviet system and the Iron Curtain, whose hem was scarcely raised by these grand phrases, at least initially. Nevertheless, subscribing to these agreements was risky for the Soviet Union since they engendered expectations which could only be fulfilled by changes which would put the Soviet system in jeopardy. The risk was worth taking both because certain safeguards were built into other parts of the agreements – in, for example, the principle of nonintervention in the internal affairs of other nations – and because the concessions on human rights were balanced by Soviet gains in other fields: namely, acknowledgement of the political and territorial *status quo*, safeguards against German revanchism, and the promise of further economic cooperation with the West.

What the Soviet Union could not foresee was the extent to which Basket III of the Helsinki accords would become a rallying point for dissidents within the Eastern bloc and a focus for Western pressure. In the event the former, marked by the establishment of Helsinki monitoring groups in the Soviet Union and other Eastern bloc nations, was more significant than the latter. Western pressure on human rights, such as took place under the Carter administration, in the short term at least had the effect of inflaming US–Soviet relations.

Here we confront another irony. The Soviet Union, which regarded the CSCE as the high point of *détente*, could be said to have lost most by it in the long run. The United States, which viewed the CSCE largely as window dressing, was ultimately the long-term gainer by it. Both powers failed to see the degree to which *détente* as a process had the potential to subvert the dynamics of the cold war.

CONCLUSION

This chapter began with the suggestion that the period of *détente* was characterized by a growing disjunction between the cold war system and the wider global context in which it was pursued. *Détente* itself proceeded on two parallel tracks: towards a formalization of bilateral US-Soviet ties and the normalization of relations between West Germany and the Eastern bloc. The CSCE tied these two together. When it is claimed, as it frequently is, that *détente* failed, it must be recalled that by comparison with what went before, relations between the superpowers now operated through networks of regular contacts, from summit meetings to lower level meetings associated with monitoring of the agreements, negotiations on conventional force reductions in Europe begun in 1974, in addition to a growing traffic of scholars, businessmen, and tourists. These created a negotiating culture which to a considerable extent survived even the worsening of superpower relations in the late 1970s and early 1980s. In both the United States and the Soviet Union sections of the bureaucracies now had a vested interest in the continuance of *détente*, interests which could not be entirely dismissed by those who were sceptical of its value.

Less visible at the time, however, was the dialectic between the institutionalization of US–Soviet relations and the existence of forces outside the cold war nexus which were influencing superpower relations and seeping into its foundations. Most important of all, the centrality of strategic nuclear arms talks, understandable in the light of the awesome potential for nuclear accidents or war as a result of unresolvable tension, deflected attention from those areas of US-Soviet relations which were less susceptible to bipolar mediation – pre-eminently in the field of economics and Third World development. To put it another way, the bilateral US–Soviet relationship matured at a time when it was a declining influence in world politics. President Carter's initial agenda attempted to address this problem by reorienting American foreign policy on a North–South rather than an East–West basis. That he failed to capitalize on this project was testimony less to his naivety than to the tenacity of the cold war ethos within both superpowers, a subject which will be treated in Chapter 11. For the moment, we turn to the Asian dimension of superpower relations in the period of *détente*.

10

THE VIETNAM WAR AND THE SUPERPOWER TRIANGLE

INTRODUCTION

Viewed from the West, and more especially from the United States, the Vietnam War has been regarded as a peculiarly American problem. The popular view of the war, as represented in films, documentaries, novels, and first-hand accounts, has issued from questions and anxieties about the war's effect on American society. Historians, with some notable exceptions, have tended to reinforce this perspective, addressing such questions as: How did the United States become involved in Vietnam? Why did America fail? What are the lessons of Vietnam?

It is easy to understand this emphasis. Taken as a whole, the American experience in Vietnam was a decisive event in its post-war history in both domestic and foreign affairs. The year 1968 marked not only a crisis in the conduct of the war itself – witness the North Vietnamese 'Tet' offensive which penetrated the US Embassy compound in Saigon – but also within American society, as race riots and student protests reached a peak, and in the eyes of many American leaders threatened the foundations of American society. Symbolizing the government's crisis of confidence at home and abroad was Lyndon Johnson's withdrawal of his candidacy from the presidential election of 1968.

When Americans uttered the word 'Vietnam' (and the same holds true today) they generally meant, not a country several thousand miles from their shores but a whole complex of social conflicts associated with a great divide in the American experience. The fact that with hindsight we can see that the lines of division were actually more complex than these perceptions suggest – public opinion polls show that the fissures were less clear-cut than portrayed by the media images – did not erase the dominant impression of crisis and division (Erikson *et al.* 1980: 70–1, 94, 162, 172).

Talk of the 'Vietnam syndrome' in the years following the war reinforced the sense that in foreign relations, as in domestic affairs, the war provoked a serious rupture. Initial involvement in Vietnam and the subsequent escalation of the war had rested on a measure of consensus on the need to counter the global threat of communism. The costs of implementing that policy in Vietnam ultimately eroded the consensus, producing a retreat from the assumptions which had underpinned it and ushering in a period of indecision about the means and ends of American power. Once again, there is room for doubt about how deep the divide between Vietnam and post-Vietnam policies actually went. There are good grounds for arguing that the basic pattern of US policy was sustained through the aftermath of the war, despite the shock of defeat. Nevertheless, the dominant perception was of discontinuity and this – above all the fact that it was a defeat – has tended to reinforce the emphasis on the war as an episode in the American experience.

For the historian of international relations the specifically American experience is only one among a range of issues to be addressed. In order fully to understand the war, Gabriel Kolko has written, 'we need constantly to examine and recall the larger trends and interrelations, treating them all as integral dimensions of a vast but unified panorama' (Kolko 1986: 6). The most obvious feature of the panorama relevant to American involvement in Vietnam by the late 1960s was the growing conflict between the Soviet Union and the People's Republic of China (PRC). Its roots, as we have seen, lay in the 1950s, but reached a climax as Richard Nixon entered the White House in 1969. Over the next four years, as the United States sought to achieve 'peace with honour' in Vietnam, it also pursued *détente* with the Soviet Union and the PRC, aiming to exploit the Sino–Soviet split without alienating either. Triangular diplomacy and Vietnamization were linked policies. With this in mind, an understanding of the Vietnam War rests on answers to two questions: (1) how did the United States come to believe that vital American interests were at stake in Vietnam? and (2) what were the connections between those interests and the changing pattern of relations between the United States, the Soviet Union, and the PRC? Underlying both questions is the brute fact of North Vietnamese persistence in pursuing the goal of reunifying Vietnam under communist rule.

VIETNAM AND THE AMERICAN NATIONAL INTEREST

Conceptions of the American national interest in Vietnam did not remain static. Indeed the shifts in the American definition of its objectives tell much about the course of the war. Furthermore, examination of stated policy objectives alongside the policies actually pursued exposes difficulties faced by policy-makers in matching means to ends. Rather than give a chronological account of the war, we shall examine American policy in terms of the goals which were most frequently cited by policy-makers.

The first of these, which goes at least as far back as 1952, was 'to prevent the countries of Southeast Asia from passing into the Communist orbit' (*Pentagon Papers* 1971: 27). Here, in line with the domino theory, the emphasis is regional rather than national and, in line with the main thrust of American cold war foreign policy, targets communism as the generalized enemy. Also important is the ambiguity of the goal itself – between containment of communism within its existing boundaries and

Figure 10.1 Vietnam and mainland Southeast Asia, 1954–1975
Source: Derived from W.A. Williams *et al.* (eds.), *America in Vietnam: A Documentary History*, New York: Norton, 1989, p. 2.

neutralizing its effectiveness as an expansive force, which might imply a more positive or aggressive attack at its roots.

Containing communism, of course, was not of itself a policy, far less a strategy, only a broad goal. A strategy, as John Gaddis has put it, is 'the process by which ends are related to means, intentions to capabilities, objectives to resources' (Gaddis 1982: viii). By this standard the escalation of the war by Lyndon Johnson, which saw an increase from 16,000 US advisers in 1963 to over 500,000 ground troops in 1968, represented a vast expansion of means which were poorly designed to achieve the desired objective. Henry Kissinger put his finger on the problem in an influential essay published in the month Nixon was inaugurated. American military strategy, he noted, 'followed the classic doctrine that victory depended upon a combination of control of territory and attrition of the opponent'. US forces were deployed along the frontiers of South Vietnam to prevent North Vietnamese infiltration and in those areas where the bulk of traditionally organized North Vietnamese forces were located. Destroy the enemy's forces and the guerrillas would 'wither on the vine'. Unfortunately, he continued, the policy failed to recognize the difference between guerrilla war, which depended upon control of populations, and conventional war, which depended upon control of territory. The bulk of the South Vietnamese people lived in the Mekong Delta (in the far south) and the coastal plain, while most US troops were deployed in the frontier regions and the Central Highlands which were virtually unpopulated. Kissinger concludes:

> As North Vietnamese theoretical writings were never tired of pointing out, the United States could not hold territory and protect the population simultaneously. By opting for military victory through attrition, the United States strategy produced what came to be the characteristic feature of the Vietnamese war: military successes that could not be translated into permanent political advantage . . . As a result, the American conception of security came to have little in common with the experience of Vietnamese villagers.
>
> (Kissinger 1969: 102–3)

Furthermore, the pacification programme, designed to promote the South Vietnamese government's control of the countryside, failed in its objectives. The Rural Development Programme, follow-up to the Strategic Hamlet scheme developed under Kennedy, had the effect of destroying the local community structures (and creating millions of refugees who poured into the cities) without achieving the military/political goal of winning the stable allegiance of the local populations (Kolko 1986: 236–51).

What in fact might 'defeating communism' mean if not destroying its roots – that is to say, defeating the North Vietnamese? The problem was that communism had roots in the South too in the form of the 'Vietcong' (or Vietnamese communists) and its political organization the National Liberation Front (NLF). Frustration at slow progress in defeating the Vietcong in the South, and the continued supply of Vietcong forces from the North via Laos and Cambodia, inevitably led to consideration of stepping up pressure directly on the North. From 1965 bombing of the North became an integral part of American military strategy, though initially care was taken to avoid attacks on Hanoi and its port Haiphong. Under Nixon's presidency bombing of the North, including Hanoi and Haiphong, assumed a more central role both because it was seen as necessary compensation for the phased withdrawal of US troops under the Vietnamization policy and because it was regarded as a means of leverage to bring the North Vietnamese to the negotiating table.

The common thread running through American strategy, despite the enormous commitment of troops and the intensive air war on the North, was the concept of limited war inherited from Korea. Johnson's escalation of the war, gradual and partially disguised from American public opinion as it was, was carried out with one eye on the Chinese and the other on domestic opinion. Defeating communism was never a live option if that meant risking all-out war with China and full American mobilization on to a war footing. But the other option of containment of communism in Vietnam was hamstrung by two fundamental difficulties, neither of which had operated in Korea: (1) the North Vietnamese held a strong footing in the South in the form of North Vietnamese cadres who had been infiltrated since the late 1950s and among South Vietnamese peasants who were either apathetic to American efforts to win their allegiance or were alienated by those efforts; (2) the geography of Indo-China which made it virtually impossible to insulate South Vietnam from its neighbouring states, Cambodia and Laos. Richard Nixon was surely right about at least one feature of the war: namely, that it was an Indo-Chinese and not simply a Vietnamese war, and to that extent his decision to invade Cambodia in 1970 and to insert troops into Laos had a logic behind it, damaging and ineffective as these tactics proved to be. As an extension of the existing policy of limited war, however, Nixon's policies could not surmount the familiar constraints of growing dissent at home and the capacity of the North Vietnamese to absorb punishment and continue fighting.

A second American objective commonly cited by policy-makers was 'an independent non-Communist Vietnam' or, in another formulation, 'to permit the people of SVN (South Vietnam) to enjoy a better, freer way of life' (*Pentagon Papers* 1971: 278, 432). This goal might seem synonymous with the one already discussed, but there are important distinctions to be made between them. For one thing, the second objective was the positive one of nation-building rather than the negative one of keeping communism out. For another, it focused on the task of political consolidation of the South Vietnamese government rather than on the military task of clearing communists from South Vietnam. True, there was an important military dimension to this goal, as we shall see, but the ultimate test of success would be the creation of self-sustaining, stable self-government in South Vietnam. Crucial to this aspect of American policy were its relations with the South Vietnamese government and that government's relations with its own people.

In three respects the American presence in Vietnam worked to undermine these objectives. In the first place, the American stake in successive South Vietnamese governments, particularly since the overthrow of Diem in 1963, was such as to render questionable the idea of an independent self-governing Vietnam. Of course, the United States could not always call the tune. Continual pressure on Diem's successors to institute reforms, to eradicate corruption and nepotism, and to broaden the base of the administration's support among the South Vietnamese people came to very little. The United States was caught in the bind of, on the one hand, seeking effective control over the South Vietnamese government in order to achieve its own ends and, on the other hand, recognizing that if South Vietnam was to survive once the United States withdrew it must be capable of standing on its own. The result was a half-way house in which American influence over the South Vietnamese government was substantial enough to undermine its autonomy but insufficient to act as a substitute for a genuinely independent and stable regime. In this, as in the economic and military aspects of US–South Vietnamese relations (the other two limiting factors on the creation of an independent and stable South Vietnam), the 'Vietnam' war became in large part an American war.

Economically South Vietnam became largely a creature of the United States, dependent on it not merely for direct aid but for the infrastructure necessary to support the war effort. That the war destroyed much of the agricultural production in South Vietnam only served to increase its dependency on American imports. Corruption was rife among the officials responsible for administering American aid. The likelihood of a self-supporting South Vietnam emerging from these conditions receded as the war progressed (Kolko 1986: 223–30).

Similar problems plagued the South Vietnamese military effort. From the early stages of the war when American servicemen were present only (at least in a technical sense) as advisers, relations between the South Vietnamese generals and their American advisers had been difficult. Low morale among the South Vietnamese troops and the generals' premium on keeping casualties down meant engaging in low-risk ventures which frequently left their American advisers deeply frustrated (Sheehan 1989: Book III). The Americanization of the war under Johnson 'solved' the problem by transferring effective military command to the United States but created another one by depriving the Vietnamese army of all but the fiction of autonomy. When the South Vietnamese army was called upon to undertake an offensive in Laos in 1971 without American ground support – a Congressional amendment having been passed the previous year forbidding the use of American troops in Cambodia and Laos – the operation failed miserably. Vietnamization was hardly likely to succeed so long as, in Stanley Karnow's words, the South Vietnamese general officers 'represented a regime that rewarded fidelity rather than competence' (Karnow 1984: 630).

The combined effect of these political, economic, and military confusions in the relations between the United States and South Vietnam was progressively to under-mine the goal of creating a self-sustaining South Vietnam. One indication of the difficulty of achieving this aim was a remarkable re-ordering of American priorities in the mid-1960s. In March 1964 Defense Secretary McNamara wrote to President Johnson that the chief US objective was 'an independent non-Communist Vietnam' (*Pentagon Papers* 1971: 278). Only a year later, McNamara's Assistant Secretary for International Security Affairs, John McNaughton, listed American priorities as follows:

> 70% – To avoid a humiliating US defeat (to our reputation as a guarantor).
> 20% – To keep SVN (and the adjacent) territory from Chinese hands.
> 10% – To permit the people of SVN to enjoy a better, freer way of life.
>
> (*Pentagon Papers* 1971: 432)

Even if one accepts that this represents the opinion of only one official within the administration and that others might have assigned the percentages differently, it offers striking evidence of the degree to which reputation and prestige had become a factor in American decision-making. It operated as a powerful negative, inclining policy-makers effectively to rule out the option of unilateral withdrawal which was the rallying cry of the anti-war movement. But just as significant is the extent to which the means of achieving the goal of an independent South Vietnam had become an end in itself, producing a circular justification for American involvement. America was there because she was there. Vietnam itself became incidental to the larger priority of reinforcing American power and prestige in the eyes of friend and foe alike.

Such a stance, adopted on the threshold of Johnson's escalation of the war, could only widen the gap between means and ends and render any realistic assessment of the chances of achieving American goals less and less likely. It locked the administration into a strategy in which the only conceivable alternative to pulling out was to increase the commitment of troops. Lyndon Johnson's final realization that the strategy was not working came only at the moment when, in the aftermath of the Tet offensive in February 1968, the American Commander in Vietnam, General Westmorland, requested a further 206,000 troops to the 543,000 already committed to South Vietnam. That the Tet offensive was a costly military defeat for the North Vietnamese was less significant, as far as American credibility was concerned, than the fact that they had been able to mount it at all and that they had managed to penetrate deep into South Vietnam, indeed into the American Embassy compound. As Richard Nixon put it in a retrospective account of the war, 'the debate over whether we should expand our intervention in the Vietnam war ended with the Tet offensive and the November 1 bombing halt. These foreclosed the option of committing ourselves even deeper. Whatever the merits of our cause and whatever our chances of winning the war, it was no longer a question of whether the next President would withdraw our troops but of how they would leave and what they would leave behind' (Nixon 1986: 96).

At the point, then, when Richard Nixon entered the presidency in January 1969 each of the American aims – containing communism in Southeast Asia, creating a stable, self-sustaining South Vietnam, and maintaining American credibility in the eyes of allies and enemies – had run into the ground. Vietnamization was designed to deal with all three. As a maximal strategy it was intended to achieve these aims in conjunction with an American withdrawal and peace negotiations with the North Vietnamese, with the goal, as Nixon put it, of achieving 'peace with honour'. Minimally, however, it would provide the United States with a way out of Vietnam which, it was hoped, would safeguard at least some vital interests.

Not least of the pressures on the Nixon administration was domestic public opinion. Demonstrations against the war reached new heights in the spring of 1970 in the wake of the incursion into Cambodia. In May four students were killed by National Guardsmen at Kent State University, provoking widespread public outrage. The timing of these events was significant. In February of the same year Kissinger had opened secret talks in Paris with Le Doc Tho, a senior North Vietnamese official, in an effort to reach a negotiated settlement. For the next three years Kissinger would shuttle to and from Paris, keeping the details of his conversations with Le Doc Tho largely secret from his colleagues in the administration, reporting only to Nixon himself.

His efforts, however, were seriously weakened by a number of factors. In the first place, time was on the side of the North Vietnamese. They had been fighting the French and then the Americans for over twenty-five years, and could afford to spin out negotiations and wait for the Americans to tire. By contrast, Nixon's time was strictly limited – by what Congress and the American public was prepared to stand and by the demands of electoral politics. As the Presidential election of 1972 drew closer, American urgency increased, a fact which was not lost on the North Vietnamese who in the Spring of 1972 launched a massive offensive which lasted until June, exerting further pressure on Kissinger to reach a solution. Only American bombing and helicopter support prevented military disaster for the hard-pressed South Vietnamese army. By this stage only a few thousand American combat troops remained in South Vietnam (Karnow 1984: 640–3).

The time factor reinforced the short-term and long-term military problems which had bedevilled the American effort from the beginning. In the long term, one military expert has written, American containment had always taken the form of strategic defence, punctuated by tactical offensives. The North Vietnamese, on the other hand, had pursued strategic offence while on occasion adopting tactical defence in order to consolidate their positions (Summers 1982: Ch. 10). The North Vietnamese willingness to accept huge casualties in pursuit of their goal of victory, an option not open to the Americans, further strengthened the North's long-term advantage. In the short term, in line with the phased withdrawal of American ground troops, the United States was forced to rely on bombing both as a lever in the negotiations and in support of South Vietnamese ground operations.

Bombing, however, had not in the past yielded clear positive results, because of the capacity of the North Vietnamese to shift their command centres and the lack of

substantial economic targets in the North. Furthermore, during Johnson's administration the North Vietnamese had been able to rely on American public opinion's
distaste for the bombing policy to limit both the geographical limits and the scale of
the air war. Johnson resisted the pleas of military advisers to allow them to pound
Hanoi and its port Haiphong. Nixon was less inclined to resist such pleas and at two
critical points in negotiations with the North Vietnamese during 1972 he ordered B-
52s to attack the Hanoi area. The first, which took place in May, helped to produce a
breakthrough in the negotiations and the second, during December, triggered the
final agreement which had been stalled in the latter months of 1972. Significant,
however, as the bombing may have been, it was not the only factor in producing a
conclusion to the negotiations. Chinese and Soviet pressure on North Vietnam was
equally important, as will become clear in the next section. Moreover, not only was the
bombing policy highly controversial in the United States then and since, but it
undercut the fiction of Vietnamization.

The terms of the final agreement reached by the United States and North Vietnam
in January 1973 revealed the fragile political and military foundations on which the
American war effort had been based. From the American point of view, the measure of
a successful agreement would be the extent to which the United States managed to
extricate itself from Vietnam 'with honour', leaving behind a militarily and politically
secure regime in the South. In the event, while the formalities of agreement ensued,
peace did not.

On the face of it the agreement was made possible by a major North Vietnamese
concession – the abandonment of their earlier insistence that political and military
issues be resolved together and more specifically the demand that President Thieu be
removed from the leadership of the South as the price of a cease-fire. So long as the
North Vietnamese set these conditions for a settlement, the Americans would not
agree to a cease-fire, since it would leave the political future of South Vietnam in the
balance. Nor would Thieu be likely to accept such a proposal, and for all the American
doubts about Thieu's leadership, an agreement made at Thieu's expense would put in
question the whole rationale of the war effort. As Nixon wrote to Kissinger, 'Thieu's
acceptance must be wholehearted so that the charge cannot be made that we forced
him into a settlement' (Isaacson 1992: 454). In actuality Thieu's acceptance was less
than wholehearted, and in the months leading up to the January 1973 agreement
Kissinger and Nixon were forced to expend almost as much effort in persuading Thieu
to accede to the proposals as in bargaining with the North Vietnamese. In the face of
the American determination to reach agreement Thieu simply had no choice. In line
with American wishes the agreement separated military and political issues. The first
provided for a cease-fire, American troop withdrawal, and an exchange of prisoners;
the second for bilateral negotiations between North and South Vietnam leading to the
establishment of a 'council of national reconciliation' and subsequently elections to
reunify the country (Karnow 1984: 648). This optimistic scenario, however, could not
hide the substantial concession made by the United States which permitted North

Vietnamese troops to remain in the South following the cease-fire. It left South Vietnam with few defences against a resumption of the war by the North, particularly in the light of a Congressional resolution, passed in March 1973, cutting off funds for any further intervention by the United States in the event of North Vietnamese violations of the cease-fire or non-compliance with other parts of the agreement. Thieu and South Vietnam were in effect left to their own devices – the last and most decisive test of Vietnamization. The denouement came two years later when North Vietnamese troops took Saigon and achieved their aim of reunifying Vietnam by force of arms.

Kissinger wrote in his memoirs that 'I believed then, and I believe now, that the agreement could have worked.' He shared Nixon's conviction that 'in the end, Vietnam was lost on the political front in the United States, not on the battlefront in Southeast Asia'. Kissinger put it down to the collapse of executive authority which resulted from Watergate; Nixon was more inclined to blame 'a spasm of Congressional irresponsibility' (Kissinger 1979: 1470; Nixon 1986: 15, 165). In truth, however, a 'credibility gap' had long existed between publically stated policy, which was relent-lessly optimistic about the chances of achieving American goals, and the military and political realities on the ground in Vietnam. The *Pentagon Papers*, a lengthy in-house study of the war commissioned in 1968 by Defense Secretary McNamara and leaked to the *New York Times* in 1971, reveal a consistent pattern of self-deception as much as public deception among American officials from the Kennedy administration onwards. In an analysis of the Papers Hannah Arendt remarked on the policy-makers' imper-viousness to facts. Time and again intelligence reports and advice which ran counter to government plans for the war would be ignored or suppressed. Policy-makers, she suggested, lived in a defactualized world in which the politics of image took over from the politics of reality. She ascribed this to 'two new genres in the art of lying' – 'the apparently innocuous one of the public relations managers in government who learned their trade from the inventiveness of Madison Avenue', and that of the 'professional problem-solvers' who were drawn into government from the universities and think-tanks. Both groups had a hatred of 'contingency', an unshakeable commitment to an order which could only be brought about by ignoring the facts or manipulating them. The gap between the facts and the desired order was filled by public relations (Arendt 1971: 30–1, 34).

Another perhaps less contentious way of making the same point is to say that the United States had difficulty in conceiving of limits to its own power. Nothing is more striking than the contrast between this posture and that of the North Vietnamese, whose history, it has been observed, had long been characterized by 'subjugation and tributary status', pre-eminently to the Chinese (McGregor 1988: 12). North Vietnam's limited material resources, consciousness of the enormous gap in power and resources between itself and the United States, and consequent dependence on Chinese and Soviet aid enforced a certain realism in North Vietnamese political and military strategy. Above all, while these constraints served to concentrate the North

Vietnamese mind on the overriding goal of ridding Indo-China of Western imperialism, they also encouraged tactical flexibility and a good deal of political ingenuity.

NORTH VIETNAM AND SINO–SOVIET CONFLICT

In the hands of a less skilful leader North Vietnam might well have been crushed between the USSR and the PRC. As it was, Ho Chi Minh pursued policies and military strategies which were designed to promote North Vietnamese interests without alienating either of the communist superpowers. As far as possible Ho Chi Minh maintained neutrality in the Sino–Soviet split and exploited the desire of both powers to be seen to be active sponsors of North Vietnamese interests (Zagoria 1967: 102–4). Among other reasons, geography dictated the maintenance of good relations with both powers: while North Vietnam was dependent primarily upon the Soviet Union for heavy military equipment, the main supply route for these deliveries lay through China. Frequent clashes between the Soviet Union and China over the arrangements for delivery during the Cultural Revolution and the deepening Sino–Soviet split (1965–69) put deliveries seriously at risk without, however, wholly disrupting them. Neither the PRC nor the Soviet Union could afford to let this happen (Funnell 1978: 147–50).

Similar disputes between 1965 and 1968 over military strategy and peace initiatives found North Vietnam in the unenviable position of having to tread a narrow path while, as it were, looking over both shoulders simultaneously. Militarily, Beijing favoured the Maoist strategy of protracted guerrilla war, while the Soviet Union counselled the employment of conventional force strategy, a reflection of the ideological biases as well as material resources of both powers. Worse still, this divide reinforced a rift between the Hanoi leadership and the NLF in the South over military strategy. On the question of peace talks too Soviet and Chinese pressures were opposed: the Soviets pressing for an end to the war and a political settlement and the Chinese urging North Vietnam to 'persevere in a protracted war and oppose capitulation and compromise' (Funnell 1978: 156–60, 161). Coming in the wake of the Soviet invasion of Czechoslovakia, which the Chinese stridently condemned, this statement showed the strain exerted on North Vietnam by the Sino–Soviet split at its most extreme point to date. Hanoi's support for the Soviet invasion of Czechoslovakia worsened relations between Hanoi and Beijing, though not to the point of an open breach. While there were thus clear signs by 1969 of a tilt in North Vietnamese policy towards the Soviet Union – Hanoi's largest benefactor by a considerable margin (Pike 1987: 106 and Ch. 6) – it was not yet such as to sever the connection with China.

It would be misleading to regard the complex Soviet and Chinese machinations with respect to Hanoi as arising only from the war in Vietnam. Each power had larger fish to fry. Vietnam was never more than one factor in their calculations, which centred rather on perceptions of global advantage in their relations with each other and with the West (Zagoria 1967: 27–30). North Vietnam was the gainer from these conditions to the extent that, while they inclined both powers to continue aiding North Vietnam, they also acted as a limitation on Soviet and Chinese desire to dictate a solution. North Vietnam could continue to extract maximum advantage from its measure of independence from both powers, knowing that neither would risk all its foreign policy resources in the Vietnam conflict. On the other hand, North Vietnam's scope for manoeuvre was limited by these same conditions, and one important limiting condition was the relations of the communist superpowers with the United States.

THE AMERICAN OPENING TO CHINA

The vector of forces shifted substantially with Nixon's assumption of the presidency in 1969. We have already seen that *détente* with the Soviet Union was begun in part with a view to enlisting Soviet pressure on North Vietnam to negotiate an end to the war. The opening to China had similar aims, though as with Soviet *détente* it also looked a good deal further than Vietnam. Indeed, well before Nixon came to power the United States and the PRC had signalled their desire to prevent the Vietnam War escalating into a Sino–American war in the form of an understanding, the so-called 'stand-off' agreement, reached in 1966. Reportedly the PRC set three conditions, to which the United States agreed: '(1) that the United States not attack China; (2) that it not invade North Vietnam; and (3) that it not bomb the Red River dike system' (Litwak 1984: 40). It was the first indication of the United States' reconsideration of its policy of non-recognition of Communist China, and during the following three years further tentative moves were made towards an opening of negotiating channels.

That these saw fruition under Richard Nixon's presidency has always provoked surprise and even astonishment. No one had been louder in condemnation of the Chinese communists following the Revolution of 1949, no one more publicly opposed to recognition of the PRC nor stronger in support of Chiang Kai-shek's Nationalist government on Taiwan than Congressman, Senator and later Vice-President Nixon. Perhaps, as Seymour Hersh suggests, 'as with other major foreign policy issues, Nixon's views on China had always been more pragmatic than ideological' (Hersh 1983: 350). As early as 1954 we find Nixon taking a middle position between those who believed that the United States had no alternative but to launch a war against the Communist Chinese and those who advocated recognizing Mao's China and opening up trading links in order to woo China away from the Soviet Union (Chang 1990: 111–12). Furthermore, if one judges by Nixon's own record of his thinking during his long period as a private citizen from 1961 to 1968, he had come to believe that the reality of Communist China could no longer be ignored. It was the PRC's growing strength as a nuclear power, as a political force in Asia and above all in independence from the Soviet Union, which inclined him to realism (Nixon 1978: 272–3, 282–3, 371–4). In a 1967 article entitled 'Asia after Vietnam' he had observed that in the light of the growing strength of China 'for the short run . . . this means a policy of firm restraint, of no reward, of a creative counterpressure designed to persuade Peking that its interests can be served only by accepting the basic rules of international civility. For the long run, it means pulling China back into the world community – but as a great and progressing nation, not as the epicenter of world revolution' (Nixon 1978: 285).

Nixon's timetable was brought forward by three things: (1) evidence that China itself was interested in talking to the United States; (2) a preoccupation with finding a way out of the Vietnam War (coupled with a revision of the earlier conventional wisdom that Chinese aggression lay behind the actions of North Vietnam); and (3) his sense, once he had achieved election to the presidency, that he was in a position to make a personal diplomatic coup.

China's motives

Despite the intense preoccupation with internal affairs during the Cultural Revolution, elements within the Chinese leadership continued to seek ways out of China's diplomatic isolation. Their motives were not entirely due to worsening relations with the Soviet Union. In line with China's growing sense of itself as a major power, it lobbied intensively in the late 1960s for admission to the United Nations, recognizing that there was growing support in the General Assembly for a rectification of the anomaly of Taiwan's position as representative of all China. (The PRC was finally admitted in 1971 after the United States abandoned its fruitless efforts to resist.) China's need for technological aid to develop oil resources also counted for a good deal, and that ultimately meant an opening to the United States as the leader in oil technology. In 1966, just prior to the Cultural Revolution, there had even been an American proposal, prompted by American academic specialists on China but taken up by the Secretary of State, that Chinese scholars and scientists be permitted to visit the United States. This was shelved with the opening of the Cultural Revolution (Spence 1990: 628–9). Mention has already been made of the stand-off agreement between the United States and China in 1966 regarding Vietnam. Finally, within a few days of Nixon's election to the presidency in November 1968 China requested a reconvening of talks between the US Ambassador to Poland and Chinese diplomats which had taken place intermittently since the mid-1950s. Tentative and still-born as some of these moves were, they display a consistent shift in Chinese policy towards the West. The Sino–Soviet border crisis of 1969 and the declining intensity of the Cultural Revolution quickened its momentum.

The larger pattern behind these individual moves, however, rested on Mao's perception of the changing balance of power among the three superpowers. The combination of relative American decline, increasing Soviet strength, and China's own growing power had produced a fundamental shift in the international correlation of forces. The chief threat to China by the late 1960s was the Soviet Union, not the United States. As John Gittings has suggested, Mao applied the same argument in the late 1960s as he had done in the 1930s in the face of Japan's bid for hegemony in Asia: 'one had to identify the "principal contradiction" or major enemy (Japan then and the Soviet Union now) and make common cause against it with those who posed the lesser threat (American imperialism in both cases)' (Gittings 1982: 74). In effect, Mao's vision was a realization of the hope which some American policy-makers had harboured in the 1950s – that Mao might become an Asian Tito. That it had taken so long to materialize was in part due to Mao's own difficulty in establishing Chinese independence from the Soviet Union and in part because the Americans had taken so long to perceive the implications of the Sino–Soviet split.

Finding a way out of Vietnam

The Nixon administration's determination to conclude the war in Vietnam was one important factor in the opening to China. In abandoning the view of previous administrations that North Vietnam was a stalking horse for Chinese expansionism, Nixon was in a position to exploit China's own desire to improve relations with the United States by seeking Chinese help in reaching a Vietnam settlement. While rhetorically the Chinese leadership continued to berate the United States, particularly during the expansion of the war into Cambodia and Laos in 1970 and 1971, behind the scenes the Beijing leadership maintained channels of communication which had been opened soon after Nixon came into office, convinced as they were by Nixon's troop withdrawals that 'the United States was serious about withdrawing from Vietnam'. Furthermore, the Chinese evidently did, as Garthoff records, 'make a concentrated effort to persuade the Vietnamese to compromise' (Garthoff 1985: 255). That the Chinese were willing to run the risk of alienating the North Vietnamese demonstrated where their chief priority now lay.

Nixon: the personal factor

Nixon's personal stake in the opening to China was immense. It was his own rather than Kissinger's initiative, though he employed Kissinger as his emissary in the latter's secret visit to Beijing in July 1971 which laid the groundwork for Nixon's own visit six months later. 'Kissinger', notes his most recent biographer, 'was at first sceptical about any quick opening to China and it was Nixon's dogged vision that propelled the initiative' (Isaacson 1992: 336). Before these path-breaking moves, however, careful preparation had been necessary. Via renewed ambassadorial talks in Warsaw in early 1970 and further contacts with China through intermediaries (Presidents Ceausescu of Romania and Yaya Khan of Pakistan) Nixon conveyed the message that he was prepared to talk about the status of Taiwan, the main sticking point in China's relations with the United States. In April 1970 came a surprise invitation to the American table tennis team to visit Beijing – the advent of so-called 'ping-pong diplomacy' – to which Nixon responded by easing restrictions on Sino–American trade.

Nixon set off for China with a heady sense that he was making history. A few days before he left, he had received the French writer André Malraux at the White House. Malraux had known Mao Zedong and Zhou Enlai during the 1930s and had maintained intermittent contact with them. The writer's final words to Nixon, faithfully recorded in the President's memoirs, doubtless fed his sense of destiny. '"I am not De Gaulle,"' declared Malraux, '"but I know what De Gaulle would say if he were here. He would say: All men who understand what you are embarking upon salute you."' Later, during the flight to China, Nixon noted in his diary that . . . 'there was almost a religious feeling to the messages we received from all over the country' (Nixon 1978: 559). Despite notes of caution and realism in his account of his China trip, these hardly hide his pride of accomplishment. *Détente* with the Soviet Union was business; important business but business nevertheless. The opening to China was pleasure, born of satisfaction with a bold personal achievement which promised much and yielded much, at least symbolically. He warmed to Prime Minister Zhou Enlai in a way he did not to Brezhnev. Brezhnev, he noted had 'a great deal of political ability and a great deal of toughness'. Zhou Enlai, though, 'had the combination of elegance and toughness, a very unusual one in the world today' (Nixon 1978: 619).

Doubtless some of Nixon's satisfaction arose from the pressure his China visit put on the Soviets who, in the wake of Nixon's trip, moved quickly to fix a date for the US–Soviet summit later in the year. Equally important was the achievement of a form of words on the Taiwan issue which allowed each side to edge towards the other without sacrificing basic principles. Of course, the outline of the American position had been prepared well before Nixon's visit, indeed by Kissinger, drawing, as he admitted, on an unused State Department memorandum dating from the 1950s (Kissinger 1979: 783). The result on the face of it was stalemate. In the Shanghai Communiqué which concluded the talks, the American and Chinese positions on Taiwan were simply stated alongside each other, their differences plain to see. The Chinese asserted that 'Taiwan is a province of China', that 'the liberation of Taiwan is China's internal affair in which no other country has the right to interfere', and that 'all US forces must be withdrawn from Taiwan'. For its part, the United States declared that:

> the United States acknowledges that all Chinese on either side of the Taiwan Strait maintain there is but one China and that Taiwan is a part of China. The United States Government does not challenge that position. It reaffirms its interest in a peaceful settlement of the Taiwan question by the Chinese themselves. With this prospect in mind, it affirms the ultimate objective of the withdrawal of all US forces and military installations from Taiwan. In the meantime, it will progressively reduce its forces and military installations on Taiwan as the tension in the area diminishes.
>
> (Grenville and Wasserstein 1987: 305)

The largest concession lay on the American side – its commitment, though at an unspecified date, to withdraw troops from Taiwan – but the US–Taiwan security treaty dating from 1955 remained in force as a reminder of America's continuing role as guarantor of Taiwan's independent status. Furthermore, the final words of the communiqué ('as tension in the area diminishes') reflected the American expectation that the Chinese now had a stake in ending the chief source of tension – the Vietnam War (Garthoff 1985: 238).

Clearly the agreement on Taiwan and on other issues fell far short of full normalization of Sino–American relations. Diplomatic recognition would only come in 1978 under Carter's administration. The resumption of contact, however, after two decades of icy coexistence, was a measure of the enormous external and internal changes which both powers had experienced. Kissinger concluded his account of these events with the remark that 'the bipolarity of the postwar period was over' (Kissinger 1979: 1096).

The impact on Nixon's political fortunes was less clear-cut. While he was able to ride out the storm of protest from the Right over his 'abandonment' of Taiwan, his triumph in China did not over the next two years immunize him against the erosion of his domestic credibility as the Watergate story broke and finally engulfed him. The Chinese, like the Soviets, were mystified that a statesman with such achievements to his credit should be sacrificed on the altar of domestic politics. Mao had made much in his talks with Nixon of his preference for dealing with 'Rightists' among capitalist leaders. 'I voted for you during your last election', Mao told him (Nixon 1978: 562). Mao's 'vote' may have counted in the international arena, but at home what counted was a solid base of support, and the very means which Nixon used to promote his foreign policy initiatives – back-channel diplomacy, secrecy, and surprise – contributed to the fragility of that base even as it smoothed the path to diplomatic solutions.

VIETNAM: THE COSTS OF VICTORY

Accounts of the Vietnam War commonly end with discussion of America's defeat and its implications for policy-making in the 1970s. We shall have much to say about that in the following chapter. For the moment, however, we must consider the implications of the communist victory not only in Vietnam itself but in Indo-China as a whole, since in 1975 Ho Chi Minh's dream of Indo-Chinese liberation was finally achieved with communist victories in Cambodia and Laos following swiftly on the fall of Saigon. Rather than producing unity among the communist regimes in Southeast Asia and between the PRC and the Soviet Union it exposed all the more clearly the differences between them. So long as the American presence in Southeast Asia had lasted, it had served to paper over the many conflicts of purpose among the interested powers in the region.

China had always had ambiguous feelings about Vietnamese nationalism. Aid to North Vietnam in the war against the United States, John Gittings points out, had been offered 'with the purpose of maintaining the north as an effective buffer zone rather than to bring liberation to the South' (Gittings 1982: 85). A strong and united

Vietnam, particularly one backed heavily by the Soviet Union, posed a threat to China's desire for pre-eminence in Southeast Asia. Vietnam's military and political influence in Laos throughout the period of the war further limited Chinese power, and inclined Beijing to seek influence in Cambodia as a counter-weight. Ideological affinity between Chinese communism and the Cambodian Khmer Rouge, who had led the insurgency against the American-backed Lon Nol since 1970 and finally came to power in 1975, created a deep fissure within Southeast Asia. As the Khmer Rouge leader, Pol Pot, embarked in 1977 upon a murderous campaign to 'democratize' Cambodia and mounted raids and massacres in disputed territories on the Cambodian–Vietnamese border, Vietnam responded in December 1978 by invading Cambodia (or Kampuchea, as it was now called). When the Vietnamese took Phnom Penh, the Kampuchean capital, and ousted the Khmer Rouge, for all their misgivings about Pol Pot, China continued to recognize the Khmer Rouge as the legitimate government (as did the United States) and mounted a brief counter-invasion of Vietnam. With Vietnam receiving strong backing from the Soviet Union – a Soviet–Vietnamese Treaty was signed in 1978 – the Sino–Soviet split thus achieved its final destructive denouement in Southeast Asia (McGregor 1988: 35–41).

Vietnam's harvest of victory was thus another war at a time when it was attempting to rebuild the nation after thirty years of conflict. The refusal of the United States to accede to Vietnam's demand for $3 billion dollars in war reparations as a precondition for talks on reconciliation cut Vietnam off from a much-needed source of aid for reconstruction (Karnow 1984: 28). As the Vietnamese economy floundered and political repression deepened, thousands of Vietnamese fled the country in boats, many of them falling prey to piracy and starvation, further increasing Vietnam's isolation and economic disarray. The outcome could hardly have been further from Ho Chi Minh's vision of liberation and peace. Nor, it must be said, did the actuality correspond to the long-held American fears of the consequences of a communist victory in Southeast Asia. If ever there were proof that the chief force at play in Southeast Asia was nationalism rather than communism, then the aftermath of the war provided it.

That in the critical year of 1978 the United States played its 'China card' by opening formal diplomatic relations with the PRC illustrated the global ramifications of this regional conflict. Soviet anger at the American move worsened US–Soviet relations at a moment when progress on SALT II was already stalled. Was it a paradox that *détente* should have flourished at a time when the United States was heavily embroiled in Vietnam and that it should have begun to unravel once the war was over? Or was it rather logical that *détente* was most likely to succeed when the parties were conscious of limits to their bargaining power? Clearly there was more involved in the rise and decline of *détente* than Vietnam. But there was surely more than a coincidental connection between the two. Arguably the Vietnam War was an enabling condition for *détente*. It sustained a measure of common purpose between the PRC and the Soviet Union, if only to the extent that it inclined both to compete for influence in Hanoi and in Washington. The outer limits of competition were set by the need to be seen to be supporting a critical liberation struggle. The United States for its part needed Chinese and Soviet help in extricating itself from Vietnam, and American negotiators were careful to assure the Soviets that the opening to China was not to be regarded as an anti-Soviet move. Once the Vietnam issue was resolved, at least to the extent of removing the United States from the equation, lines of conflict which had always been present were free to flourish. If only for a brief period in the late 1960s and early 1970s, the Vietnam War was the pivot of the triangular superpower balance. With the pivot removed the balance collapsed.

11

DÉTENTE UNDER PRESSURE, 1973–1981

INTRODUCTION

We have been told so often that *détente* failed and that its failure was marked by the coming of the 'second cold war' in the early 1980s that it is often forgotten that to a considerable degree *détente* had become institutionalized – in the form of continuing arms negotiations, both nuclear and conventional, in trade links, and more generally in patterns of expectations and behaviour established in the negotiations and agreements of 1971 to 1975.[1] Clearly these did not override the basically competitive nature of East–West relations, and equally clearly by the end of the decade many of the specific results of *détente* looked hollow.

It is important, however, to establish precisely where the limits of *détente* lay. In the first place, there was a continuing and increasing disjunction between American and European perspectives; the Europeans, admittedly somewhat inconsistently, adhering to the basic principles of *détente*, or at least their interpretation of it, for a good deal longer than the Americans. Secondly, and not unrelated to the first point, the Soviets continued to pay at least lip-service to *détente* as the Americans moved to expunge it from their political vocabulary. Finally, the retreat from *détente* did not mean a simple return to high cold war, except perhaps in rhetoric, and even there not consistently. *Détente* constituted a new baseline for East–West relations and some of its features remained constant, not least because they were rooted in structural shifts in global politics and the world economy which continued to exert effects in the late 1970s and 1980s. *Détente* was more than a set of specific agreements; it was a process set in motion by the agreements themselves. The question therefore is not: why did *détente* fail? but: what precise forms did East–West conflict take in the move from the formulation of *détente* to its implementation?

In thinking about the second half of the 1970s we are presented, as in the 1950s, with contrasting rhythms in American and Soviet domestic development. The point was referred to in Chapter 9 but deserves to be extended here. While in the 1950s the United States experienced continuity in domestic politics (Eisenhower was the only post-war president until Reagan to serve two full terms) and the Soviet Union experienced instability arising from the post-Stalin leadership shifts, in the 1970s the picture was reversed. While the Soviet leadership, despite Brezhnev's increasing frailty, continued on its well-beaten path, the post-Watergate American presidency in the hands of Ford and Carter was a relatively enfeebled institution. (A further reversal came in the 1980s when a two-term American president was confronted with the post-Brezhnev changing of the guard – Andropov, Chernenko, and Gorbachev – heralding an erosion of authority and of the Soviet Union itself.)

It is hardly surprising that this disjunction should have been reflected in the policies pursued by the two powers. Broadly, American policy seems best explained during these years by reference to domestic pressures. In an analysis of public opinion polls over the post-war period, Richard Melanson has noted that, while from the late 1940s through the 1960s foreign policy dominated the public mind, from 1976 economic issues became the most urgent priority (Melanson 1991: 15). Of course, foreign policy is never merely a reflex of public opinion, but public opinion represents a limiting factor on foreign policy, especially so in a climate in which the credibility of the leadership is in question. The so-called 'Vietnam syndrome' – a reluctance to risk intervention and open-ended commitments – did not mean an end to all foreign policy activism but it did mean a heightened awareness of domestic constraints on foreign policy.

The story of the Soviet Union in the late 1970s, certainly from the American perspective, was of an expansion of power and influence abroad. From Angola to the Horn of Africa to Afghanistan, whether directly or through Cuban proxies, the Soviet Union demonstrated a willingness to intervene in local and regional conflicts on a hitherto unprecedented scale. And these were only the more obvious flashpoints. Whatever significance one ascribes to these ventures – and, as we shall see, opinions differ markedly – the contrast between this and the confusions in American policy were plain to see. Before looking, then, at the details of US–Soviet relations in the late 1970s, we shall examine the motive forces behind their policy-making.

THE UNITED STATES: A NATION IN IRONS?

On the domestic front the United States experienced economic, social, and political difficulties which had the combined effect of checking the nation's momentum. Mention has already been made of the economic problems which led Nixon to end the convertibility of gold in 1971. Associated with this was a worrying combination of recession *and* inflation, rendering the New Deal (and broadly Keynesian) methods of employing government spending to get out of recession inappropriate. In any event, the Nixon administration rejected this approach for political as much as economic reasons.

Two additional strains were exerted on the system during the 1970s. The first was the huge rise in government welfare obligations as the Great Society programmes of the 1960s worked through and were drawn upon by growing numbers of poor and unemployed. Secondly, the OPEC oil boycott of 1973–74, which was immediately followed by a quadrupling of the price of oil, contributed further to inflation, but also had the effect of bringing home to Americans the extent of their dependence on forces beyond their control in the outside world. America's relative economic decline was increasingly visible during the 1970s (Chafe 1991: 447).

Socially and culturally, the 1960s had revealed deep splits within the United States, and though street demonstrations and other forms of mass protest declined during the 1970s, the '*Kulturkampf*' continued. If during the 1960s the Left had most visibly set the political agenda, in the following decade it was the turn of the Right. Nixon had begun the process of reclaiming the political and moral high ground for the Right. His removal intensified the search among right-wing pressure groups for means of reversing the legacy of liberalism and promoting national figures to take the conservative message to the people. The victory of the Right, as represented by the election of Ronald Reagan in 1980, was in the making during the 1970s.

Politically, the fall-out from Vietnam and Watergate was a weakened presidency and a general distrust of Washington. Ford's pardon of Nixon proved to be a disastrous miscalculation which hobbled his administration and contributed to his defeat in the election of 1976. Jimmy Carter, presenting himself as the new broom which would sweep Washington clean and restore faith in national institutions and values, was unable to make Washington work for him. His own difficulties in dealing with Congress compounded the already strained relationship between the executive and legislative branches of government which was the product of the Nixon years.

In domestic policy presidents expect to be challenged by Congress. Though they may not like it and may find ways of resisting, presidents expect Congress to make amendments to legislation which may come close to nullifying the original intentions of the bill. Such was the case with Carter's energy policy. Foreign policy, however, has traditionally been regarded as a sphere of executive action, subject only to formal constitutional constraints (Senate ratification of treaties, for example) and to the need for funds to carry out foreign policy. A feature of the 1970s was Congress's determination to limit the power of the executive branch in various foreign policy fields, most notably the war-making power. Congress's chief tool for cutting the executive down to size was its power to withhold appropriations. Among the measures passed was the War Powers Act (1973), a cut-off of funds for the incursion into Cambodia (1970), a refusal to provide funds to prevent the fall of South Vietnam in 1975, and the Clark Amendment denying appropriations for the American-backed faction in the Angolan civil war (1975). As we saw in Chapter 9, the Jackson–Vanik amendment (1972) made favourable trade terms for the Soviet Union conditional upon the right of Soviet Jews to emigrate.

True, the presidency showed some capacity to maintain the traditional prerogatives of the executive branch. One example was the rescue mission mounted by President Ford in reaction to the Cambodian seizure in 1975 of the American freighter *Mayaguez*. Costly in American lives as it proved to be, the *Mayaguez* rescue mission showed the Ford administration ready to assert itself when it felt vital interests were at stake.

However, fields where larger and more complex issues were involved, such as national security and relations with the Soviet Union, were political battlegrounds. Jimmy Carter came to the presidency with a determination to downplay the Soviet problem and East–West conflict in general. While clearly nuclear arms control, and if possible arms reduction, was a high priority, Carter was conscious that 'the heavy emphasis that was placed on Soviet–American competition' in American policy had distorted America's relations with many Third World nations to the extent that dealings with them rested on 'whether they espoused an anti-communist line' (Carter 1982: 142). In line with the conclusions of the 'Trilateral Commission', a Rockefeller-funded study group of businessmen, academics and politicians of which Carter was a member, the United States' greatest challenge was held to lie in managing the transition from a cold war era characterized by American economic predominance and US–Soviet nuclear rivalry to one of relative decline in American economic power and decline also in the utility of military power. The American challenge now lay in economic coordination and cooperation with Western Europe and Japan and in developing the economic resources of the developing world. North–South rather than East–West relations were the key to America's future (Bowker and Williams 1988: 168–9).

Underpinning these assumptions was the conviction that human rights must be placed at the centre of the foreign policy agenda. 'Our country', wrote Carter in his memoirs, 'has been strongest and most effective when morality and a commitment to freedom and democracy have been most clearly emphasized in our foreign policy.' It was not a matter of having to choose between idealism and realism, or between morality and the exertion of power: 'to me, the demonstration of American idealism was a practical and realistic approach to foreign affairs, and moral principles were the best foundation for the exertion of American power and influence' (Carter 1982: 142, 143). Nothing could have been further from the Kissinger–Nixon approach to foreign policy, and indeed Brzezinski noted that the human rights policy appealed to Carter in part because it 'drew a sharp contrast between himself and the policies of Nixon and Kissinger' (Brzezinski 1983: 49).

In promoting this agenda Carter was hampered by developments inside and outside the United States. The developing world was precisely the area which the Soviet Union seemed to have targeted for high profile intervention, which made it difficult to separate North–South from East–West issues.

Nor did the premium Carter placed on human rights reap the hoped-for rewards. To the extent that the policy was politically even-handed, it provoked the ire of liberals and conservatives within the United States and, as Melanson has noted, was bound in any case to be uneven in its application, given the reality that some powers were more able to resist American leverage than others. Because, moreover, Carter made a point of not linking human rights with other issues, it remained 'more an irritating anomaly than an integral part of a coordinated strategy (Melanson 1991: 117). Nowhere was this more true than in relations with the Soviets, who regarded the human rights policy as an intrusion into internal Soviet affairs. In taking the moral high ground Carter thus exacerbated rather than eased US–Soviet tension. Carter himself conceded that the human rights policy 'did create tension between us and prevented a more harmonious resolution of some of our other differences' (Carter 1982: 149).

Inexorably, it seemed, Carter was pulled back to the old cold war agenda. Among the pressures moving in the same direction was a powerful current of elite opinion represented by the recently formed Committee on the Present Danger (CPD), a re-creation of an earlier organization of the same name which had been established in 1950. Among the leading members of the organization in both its old and new guises was Paul Nitze, the main author of NSC 68 (1950) and in the late 1970s an influential critic of *détente* (Talbott 1989: 59, 151–61). Another prominent member was Henry Jackson, a Democratic Senator who had been the moving force behind tying Most Favoured Nation trading status for the Soviet Union to the right of emigration for Soviet Jews. The conservative challenge to Carter's leadership thus came from within the Democratic Party as well as from outside. The CPD upheld containment of Soviet power as the United States' chief foreign policy priority and regarded Carter's revised form of *détente* as misguided and dangerous. It would not be too much to picture the foreign policy debate of the late 1970s as a battle between the Trilateral Commission and the Committee on the Present Danger.

It would be unwise, however, to exaggerate the enfeebled character of American foreign policy in the latter half of the 1970s. If Carter rejected the sort of activism represented by the Vietnam War and the efforts to unseat President Allende of Chile, he nevertheless envisioned a positive, constructive role for the United States. His Assistant for National Security Affairs, Zbigniew Brzezinski, termed the general foreign policy orientation of the Carter administration 'constructive global engagement' (Brzezinski 1983: 53). Carter's chief foreign policy successes – the Panama Canal treaties and the Camp David Accords which brought Egypt and Israel together – were premised on the view that reconciliation of apparently irreconcilable interests was the truest test of American power. That within a few short years he found himself reverting to containment and power politics as usual betokened not a return to activism after a period of quiescence but a retreat from liberal to conservative internationalism.

THE SOVIET UNION: A NATION UNCHAINED?

It was suggested in an earlier chapter that Brezhnev's hold on power became progressively more secure in the late 1960s and early 1970s. This was a consequence not of a complete absence of opposition but of his success in thwarting it. In common with Khrushchev, Brezhnev's control of the Party Secretariat was the key to control of the policy-making process. But unlike Khrushchev, Brezhnev was both more careful to avoid sudden and risky changes in policy and more astute in satisfying the various interests represented in the Politburo. Important among these were senior military figures and their supporters in the Politburo, whose influence had been significant in the coup which toppled Khrushchev in 1964 (Gelman 1984: 76–9, 92–5).

On the face of it Khrushchev's policy of enhancing Soviet missile development had met the needs of the military, but in two respects it had failed to achieve this. Firstly, his brandishing of Soviet missile power, most notably in the Cuban missile crisis, had exposed Soviet weakness rather than strength, and, secondly, he had not only neglected the other armed forces but made it a point of policy to limit their growth, the assumption being that in the missile age the other armed forces were of secondary importance. Though he did not entirely have his way in this regard, his efforts alienated key military leaders. Brezhnev by contrast held that Soviet security demanded balanced growth in Soviet defence forces. His reasons were in part domestic, in that such a policy won the allegiance of all branches of the military, but he evidently also believed in the wake of the missile crisis that the achievement of superpower status and equality with the United States must be founded on a capacity to project Soviet power globally. Hence the build-up of Soviet defence forces from 1965 which continued unbroken into the 1980s. It was begun, moreover, at a point when the Soviet economy was relatively healthy and growing. Only later were its domestic costs to become apparent (Gelman 1984: 79-87).

This, then, was the internal backdrop to the projection of Soviet power in the mid and late 1970s. The fruits of Brezhnev's ambitions appeared in a series of moves which implied a confidence that the 'correlation of forces' was moving in the Soviet Union's favour. Western observers differed in their interpretation of Soviet activity in the Third World and on its implications for *détente*. What might be called the alarmists viewed Soviet support for radical regimes and left-wing insurgent movements as part of a coordinated strategy to undermine and displace Western influence in key strategic areas. Most worrying to Western policy-makers was the ferment of change in the so-called 'arc of crisis', running from Afghanistan through Iran and the Arab Middle East down to the Horn of Africa. The intervention in Ethiopia in 1977 by Cuban troops, air-lifted by Soviet transports (as had been the case in Angola two years earlier), the Soviet acquisition of a naval base in South Yemen, coupled with increased naval activity in the Indian Ocean, and above all Soviet intervention in Afghanistan in 1979 – these suggested, according to worst-case scenarios, a concerted Soviet push southwards with the ultimate goal of reaching the Persian Gulf and seizing control of Middle Eastern oil resources. Coming on top of the Revolution in Iran and the seizure of American hostages, the invasion of Afghanistan seemed to many Americans final confirmation of the most negative interpretations of Soviet goals.

Threatening as these events appeared, they looked all the more menacing when seen against the background of the fall of Indo-China to communism in 1975, the Sandinista revolution in Nicaragua in 1979 and insurgency in El Salvador. These all seemed part of the same pattern of Soviet gains and Western losses, however indirect Soviet influence might have been in these situations. Beyond this, in the United Nations Third World nations were pressing for a 'New Economic Order', and Palestinian terrorism had introduced a disturbing and incalculable element into international conflict. Neither of the latter developments could be regarded as being inspired directly by the Soviet Union, but they appeared to redound to the Soviet Union's benefit and against that of the West.

From the viewpoint of those who were disenchanted with *détente*, which included not only many Republicans and important pressure groups such as the CPD but increasing numbers within the Democratic administration itself, the balance sheet was firmly in the Soviet Union's favour. Moreover, the alarmist interpretation of Soviet foreign policy found its counterpart in studies of Soviet internal politics. Some academic analyses of the Brezhnev Politburo identify a period of crisis in 1974–75 over *détente* policy which threatened Brezhnev's leadership. *Détente*, charged Brezhnev's critics, was yielding no returns, witness the unacceptable conditions the US Congress was imposing on trade and credits for the Soviet Union. In order to fend off such criticisms and hence maintain his leadership position, it is argued, Brezhnev shifted to a more limited conception of *détente*, which meant being less cooperative in all aspects of East–West relations and more aggressive in pursuit of Soviet interests around the world (Gelman 1984: 148–50, 162–4).

There are, however, other ways of interpreting Soviet policy after 1975. In the first place one can question the view that there was a qualitative difference in the Soviet approach to arms control and general East–West issues after 1974. The Soviet Union signed the Helsinki Final Act after the supposed great change of direction in December 1974, and seemed at least as keen as American negotiators to reach a conclusion to the SALT II negotiations (Bowker and Williams 1988: 199). With regard to the Third World, it can be pointed out that each of the crises in which the Soviet Union was either directly involved or from which it supposedly reaped benefits had separate roots. Local and internal conditions rather than the imposition of a Soviet design explain the upheavals. There was no common pattern. The concept of an arc of crisis itself was in part a construction of fevered Western imaginations. Even the invasion of Afghanistan, so often pictured as naked aggression, may have arisen from defensive motives (Halliday 1981: Ch. V).

Nor, according to this standpoint, did the Soviet Union uniformly gain from its Third World ventures. Moscow's main export to the Third World – arms – was 'more a sign of weakness rather than strength', betraying its inability to match the West economically. A further limiting factor on Soviet influence was 'the increasing reluctance of many Third World countries to be drawn into the superpower con-frontation' (Steele 1985: 177, 178). The invasion of Afghanistan, the Soviet Union's most spectacular intervention of the period, alienated many leaders in the Third World no less than in the West.

What changed in the latter half of the 1970s, as one analysis has it, 'was not Soviet policy but the international context' (Bowker and Williams 1988: 199). Always an opportunist power, the Soviet Union could hardly resist exploiting situations as they came up, and the late 1970s was a period of deep instability in areas of the world considered critical by both superpowers. Soviet policy was thus, according to this view, essentially reactive.

Taken to extremes, these two interpretations of Soviet policy are irreconcilable, but the more careful analysts on both sides acknowledge shades of grey. Among the alarmists Harry Gelman does not deny 'the existence of a defensive element in the behaviour of the Soviet leadership' (Gelman 1984: 16). Among the non-alarmists Fred Halliday concedes that 'Soviet policy certainly played its part . . . in worsening the international climate that produced the New Cold War' (Halliday 1981: 113–14). It seems safe to conclude that the Soviet Union did show an increased propensity to project its power because both the means and the opportunity were there. Opportunism rather than the existence of a coordinated plan, however, explains the timing and the character of its interventions. Soviet policy may have been reactive, though none the less threatening to Western observers for that, since the Soviet Union's capacity to react effectively was greatly enhanced.

The growing disjunction between Soviet and American interests and perspectives during the 1970s represented not the shattering of *détente* but the exposure of a gap between the most optimistic expectations and what was actually achievable. In creating new mutual obligations and commitments, *détente* itself had generated new sources of tension. Both parties displayed a heightened sensitivity to alleged breaches of the new codes of conduct. In this sense, as was suggested in Chapter 9, the paradoxical effect of *détente* was to tighten rather than loosen the knot binding the superpowers together. Neither side was able to achieve what both claimed to aspire to, which was to make their mutual relations less consuming. Rather the reverse; *détente* and its sequel confirmed their intense mutual preoccupation even as the world was becoming more complex and less subject to superpower control.

ARMS CONTROL AND THE STRATEGIC NUCLEAR DEBATE, 1974–1981

Efforts to capitalize on SALT I met with two related difficulties. Firstly, quantitative and qualitative enhancement of strategic nuclear weapons took place on both sides in those areas which were not covered by SALT I, creating new levels of threat to be dealt with. This, moreover, is to leave aside comparable innovations in intermediate and theatre nuclear forces which are discussed in the following section on Europe. Secondly, in part because of these developments, the debate about nuclear strategy moved on to the point where the theory of deterrence, as it had been developed in the United States during the 1960s, came into question. Powerful voices suggested that 'assured destruction' was an insufficient basis for deterrence, and urged the need to be able to fight and win a nuclear war, not least because that appeared to be a central part of Soviet doctrine. It was a right-winger, not the anti-nuclear left, notes McGeorge

Bundy, who invented the acronym MAD out of 'mutual assured destruction', with the aim of holding it up to ridicule (Bundy 1988: 552–3).

The fate of SALT II was intimately bound up with these two challenges. While the immediate occasion for Carter's withdrawal of SALT II from ratification by the US Senate was the Soviet invasion of Afghanistan in December 1979, the SALT process had already come under fire from all parts of the political spectrum, but most importantly from conservatives, in the years during which negotiations were taking place.

The American debate over SALT II is well illustrated in an exchange which took place during 1976 in the journal *Foreign Affairs*. The debate was sparked off by Paul Nitze, who over a long career proved to be almost as influential out of office as in. The views expressed in his article 'Assuring Strategic Stability in an Era of *Détente*' were essentially those of the Committee on the Present Danger, which was recreated during this same year and for whom Nitze was writing comparable material at this time (Bundy 1988: 556–9).

Though the details of his exposition were complex, the leading ideas came through with great clarity. SALT I had not produced strategic stability: 'on the contrary, there is every prospect that under the terms of the SALT agreements the Soviet Union will continue to pursue a nuclear superiority that is not merely quantitative but designed to produce a theoretical war-winning capability' (Nitze 1976: 207). The appearance of strategic balance in the 1974 Vladivostok Accords (follow-up talks from SALT I and designed to be a bridge to SALT II) was deceptive. While each side was to have the same numerical limits – an aggregate level of 2,400 launchers and heavy bombers for each side and a sublimit of 1,320 launchers with MIRV capabilities – this disguised the Soviet Union's vastly greater 'throw-weight' which was untouched by the Vladivostok Accords. The Soviet SS-19 and SS-18 had respectively three times and seven times the throw-weight of the largest US missile, the Minuteman III, giving the Soviet Union an advantage of 'at least two-to-one in overall throw-weight' (Nitze 1976: 220). There was the added problem of the new Soviet 'Backfire' bomber, which, it was claimed, represented a new Soviet development in a field in which hitherto the United States had held a marked advantage.

As important as the numbers themselves was the presumed impact of this imbalance on deterrence. One measure of the adequacy of deterrence, wrote Nitze, was 'our ability to hold Soviet population and industry as hostages, in the face of Soviet measures to deter or hedge against US retaliation directed at such targets'. In short, if the Soviet Union could by some means defend population centres against US missile attack, then the deterrent value of American nuclear missiles would be to that extent reduced. In fact, the Soviet Union did appear to have such means in the form of an extensive civil defence programme. Effective civil defence systems, like anti-ballistic missile systems, had a destabilizing effect since they acted to neutralize offensive weapons, and the same arguments which had been used against ABM systems in 1972 applied also to civil defence (Nitze 1976: 223).

A more crucial test, however, wrote Nitze, was the projected advantage which the Soviet Union would possess in a nuclear exchange by virtue of its superiority in throw-weight. Picturing a large-scale nuclear exchange, Nitze concluded on the basis of projections forward from current figures that by 1977 'after a Soviet-initiated counter-force strike [i.e.: an attack aimed at America's nuclear weapons rather than population centres] against the United States to which the United States responded with a counterforce strike, the Soviet Union would have remaining forces sufficient to destroy Chinese and European NATO nuclear capability, attack US population and conventional military targets, and still have a remaining force throw-weight in excess of that of the United States'. After 1977, Nitze added, 'the Soviet advantage after the assumed attack mounts rapidly' (Nitze 1976: 226).

In short, the United States confronted a 'window of vulnerability', just as in 1950 Nitze had foreseen a 'year of maximum danger' only four years away, which could be remedied only by substantial measures to improve the survivability and effectiveness of the US deterrent. Civil defence measures on any large scale were likely to be politically impossible, though Nitze foresaw a time when the Soviet threat might be sufficient to require such a programme. More immediately to the point, the US must firstly improve the accuracy of its missiles (in defence terminology 'hard target kill capability') in order to compensate for the Soviet throw-weight advantage, and secondly, decrease the vulnerability of its strategic nuclear forces. This meant some sort of mobile launching system with an array of shelters well in excess of the number of missiles, which would be moved around among the shelters according to random patterns and time intervals (Nitze 1976: 227–31).

Nitze's article provoked many rejoinders, but we shall focus on that of Jan Lodal, an analyst who had worked for the National Security Council, since he answered Nitze point for point. Lodal firstly claimed that Nitze had greatly overestimated the importance of throw-weight. Not only were US missiles more accurate, but Nitze had discounted America's superior submarine force. The Soviet emphasis on heavy missiles betrayed their weakness in miniaturization technology (necessary to MIRV smaller missiles) and in submarine launched missiles (SLBMs). If number of warheads rather than throw-weight was taken as the standard, then the United States still possessed a marked advantage (Lodal 1976: 463–9).

As for the Vladivostok limits, these were by no means clearly to the Soviet Union's advantage. The Soviets' strategic weapons totals were closer to the Vladivostok limits than were those of the United States, and it appears likely that they 'had planned to expand further with new submarines, bombers and mobile missiles'. Thus the agreement 'probably would have a restraining effect on Soviet strategic planning'. Furthermore, if the United States had given ground to the Soviets on the issue of their heavy missiles, the Soviets had agreed to leave out of consideration the American Forward Base Systems (FBS - land-based and carrier-based bombers in the European theatre and capable of striking Soviet territory). These systems, like the British and French independent deterrents, had long been and would continue to be a source of

Soviet anxiety. In any event, whatever the precise strategic effect of this trade-off, the insistence on 'equal aggregates' for both sides reflected political rather than military judgement. Following SALT I Congress had insisted that all future arms agreements must provide for numerical equality. The Pentagon supported this requirement less on military grounds than on the basis that 'to accept anything less than numerical equality would lead to "political perceptions" of US strategic inferiority' (Lodal 1976: 470–1, 470).

Among the other elements in the strategic balance about which Nitze was concerned, the Backfire bomber, Lodal observed, was 'vastly less capable than our B-52s', and with its short range and low payload did not constitute a major strategic threat. Finally, the Soviet civil defence programme, though more elaborate than that of the United States, was unlikely to reduce Soviet casualties to any measurable degree (Lodal 1976: 473, 477).

Neither a civil defence programme nor Nitze's chief recommendation – a mobile launch system for land-based missiles – would improve American defences or enhance deterrence, Lodal concluded. Both would be enormously costly and posed possibly insuperable technical difficulties. Above all, there should be no abandonment of the SALT process, since this would only 'increase Soviet–American tension and . . . decrease rather than improve our security' (Lodal 1976: 474–5, 477, 481).

This last statement was of paramount significance in the context of the time. Nitze had disclaimed any intention of advocating the abandonment of arms negotiations, but he was convinced that 'the practical fact we now face is that a SALT II treaty based on the Vladivostok Accords would *not* provide a sound foundation for follow-on negotiations under present trends'. If, and only if, he wrote, 'the United States now takes action to redress the impending strategic imbalance, can the Soviet Union be persuaded to abandon its quest for superiority and resume the path of meaningful limitations and reductions through negotiations' (Nitze 1976: 208). In effect, Nitze argued that a precondition for a new treaty was an adequate American force build-up.

There is a striking continuity in this argument with NSC-68, the seminal national security assessment which Nitze had authored in 1950. There he had seen negotiation as decidedly secondary to the task of building American security. Now in 1976 he warned against looking to the SALT process as a means of getting 'relief from our nuclear strategic problems'. We must look at the United States' strategic nuclear posture, he wrote, 'in much the same way we used to look at it before the SALT negotiations began and determine what is needed in the way of a nuclear strategy for the United States and what kind of posture is needed to support it'. *Détente*, particularly as the Soviets interpreted it, was no guide to American security needs. *Détente* in Soviet eyes 'was not that different from what we used to call "cold war"' (Nitze 1976: 222, 210).

Nitze, of course, was not at this stage responsible for policy-making, but to a considerable degree the issues he raised anticipated the terms in which arms control would be discussed over the succeeding three years. President Carter's own views, at

263

least initially, and those of his chief arms negotiator Paul Warnke were closer to Lodal's than to Nitze's, but Nitze's priorities had immense impact in Congress and the media, and exerted a material influence on the final form of SALT II and more especially on the ratification process. These same priorities were an important influence too on the Reagan election campaign and his transition team following the election of 1980. Not least of Carter's problems in the lead-up to SALT II were his decisions not to proceed with two new weapons systems which his critics felt were vital to restoring the strategic balance: the B-1 bomber and the Enhanced Radiation Weapon (or neutron bomb). At the very least, it was argued, these should have been retained as bargaining chips.

The SALT II negotiations were long and tortuous. Post-Vladivostok negotiations under the Ford administration became bogged down in disagreements over the Soviet Back-fire bomber and American Air Launched Cruise Missiles (ALCMs) which the Soviets wanted to count against the 2,400 launcher limit agreed at Vladivostok but which the Americans did not. The incoming Carter administration then began badly with an ill-judged opening gambit offering two possible options to the Soviets for consideration: a proposal for deep cuts in strategic arms and a fall-back position broadly in line with the Vladivostok guidelines but with some additional cuts. The Soviets rejected both, as much, it would appear, because of the way in which they were proposed as because of their content. The Carter administration had publicized its negotiating position before the first formal meeting on SALT II in Moscow, in the hope, Brzezinski observed, that 'it would generate wider understanding of the constructive character of our proposals'. With hindsight he conceded that this was a mistake, since public pronouncement of the deep cuts plan 'might have created the impression in Moscow that an acceptance of them would be a one-sided concession to Carter' (Brzezinski 1983: 163–4, 164). The Soviets evidently found the radical change from the Kissinger method of quiet diplomacy through back-channels unsettling, indeed threatening.

An added irritant in relations with the Soviet Union during the first month of his administration was Carter's adoption of a high profile position on human rights in the Soviet Union, most notably in his sympathetic reply to a letter from the Soviet physicist and dissident, Andrei Sakharov, and in his White House meeting with the recently released Soviet dissident, Vladimir Bukovsky. When in the following month the Soviets arrested leaders of the Helsinki monitoring group in Moscow, the issue of linkage between human rights and arms control was raised sharply. The Soviet position was clear. No linkage could be accepted. 'Moscow approaches the question of human rights as an internal threat', noted William Hyland, 'the impact on foreign policy is secondary.' The Carter administration, however, gave out ambiguous signals. A statement by Brzezinski that human rights and arms control were 'organically related' was quickly repudiated by Carter (Hyland 1988: 207, 205). The incident was indicative of a growing split within the Carter administration between the pragmatists (represented by Secretary of State Cyrus Vance) and the ideologists (represented by

Brzezinski). Carter himself showed both tendencies at various times and sometimes, as in the above case, both at the same time: making firm pronouncements on human rights but rejecting linkage between them and the all-important arms negotiations.

It is difficult to speak of a single breakthrough in negotiations which lasted several years and covered such complex ground. However, according to Brzezinski an important turning point was the Soviet agreement to the American proposal to allow each side to deploy one new type of ICBM, which would permit the United States to go ahead with deployment of the MX missile (Brzezinski 1983: 326). The MX was a new ICBM which, with its proposed mobile basing mode, was seen as one answer to the supposed vulnerability of the American strategic deterrent. At the time the Soviets made this concession (July 1978) Carter had still not taken a firm decision on MX deployment. That Carter made the decision to go ahead with MX shortly before the Vienna Summit in June 1979 at which SALT II was to be signed was an important indication of the pressures both within the negotiating arena and outside it. Carter yielded reluctantly to these pressures. He wrote in his diary of the prospect of MX deployment that 'it was a nauseating prospect to confront, with the gross waste of money going into nuclear weapons of all kinds' (Carter 1982: 241).

By this stage, however, it had become clear that Carter's closest advisers, among them Brzezinski and Defense Secretary Harold Brown, shared the view of the Joint Chiefs of Staff and key Senate leaders that in the absence of MX and other measures to improve American defence a SALT II treaty would put national security at risk. Furthermore, ratification of the treaty by the Senate was virtually conditional upon implementation of these measures (Brzezinski 1983: 336–7). Ironically, despite the fact that Paul Nitze testified to the Senate in opposition to the treaty – above all because it did not resolve the problem of Soviet advantage in throw-weight – it was the case that his analysis of the overall strategic situation had been substantially accepted by the Carter administration by mid-1979. The need for a new ICBM with a multiple launch point system was also accepted. (In the event, this MX basing mode proved unfeasible and too expensive, and was finally abandoned during the Reagan administration. The MX was deployed in the old Minuteman silos, a decision which effectively undermined the original rationale for the new missile.)

There was a further sense in which the Carter administration adopted important elements of the Nitze strategic outlook, and this was in the field of nuclear war planning. The doctrine of deterrence, Brzezinski observed, had been developed in the early 1960s at a time when the United States had possessed clear strategic superiority over the Soviet Union. By 1977 (the year Nitze had seen as critical in the mounting Soviet advantage) Brzezinski records that he had become sufficiently concerned to propose a series of measures which took as their basic assumption that a nuclear war might not necessarily be 'brief, spasmic, and apocalyptic'. The outcome of this programme of 'strategic renewal' was Presidential Directive 59 (PD-59), issued in July 1980, though it had been prepared for in a series of such directives going back to 1977. These 'were concerned with mobilization, defense, command, and control for a long conflict, and with flexible use of our forces, strategic and general purpose, on behalf of war aims that we would select as we engaged in conflict' (Brzezinski 1983: 461).

Though Brzezinski insisted that PD-59 represented an enhancement of deterrence rather than a departure from it, it seemed clearly to be a nuclear war-fighting doctrine, and indeed Brzezinski used such language in a retrospective account of the episode (Garthoff 1985: 790). To that extent, PD-59 could be regarded as a shift away from MAD, and it was widely interpreted as such, becoming a particular target of the growing anti-nuclear movement in the early 1980s.

The shift represented by PD-59 was premised on the assumption that Soviet doctrine envisaged fighting and winning a nuclear war. In reality, while Soviet doctrine did allow for the eventuality of nuclear war and for the need to try to win it, should it occur, in the words of one expert 'there is little evidence that they think victory in a global nuclear war would be anything other than catastrophic' (Holloway, in Bundy 1988: 562). The overriding reality was mutual vulnerability which meant that prevention of war would always predominate in strategic thinking. In fact, it has been pointed out, even the Soviet Union's most strident critics acknowledged that the Soviet Union accepted the fact of deterrence even if they rejected the theory of MAD (Bundy 1988: 562). Furthermore if one goes by the actions rather than the words of those who believed in the 'window of vulnerability', most notably Ronald Reagan during his presidency, they were in practice willing to allow the supposed Soviet strategic advantage to increase. By the end of Reagan's presidency total US ICBM throw-weight was actually less than it had been when he came into office (Bundy 1988: 563). We shall return shortly to the curious gap between stridency of doctrine and pragmatism in action in the arms control process. For the moment it is sufficient to note that there was an element of accommodation between the SALT negotiators and their critics.

The provisions of the SALT II Treaty followed the Vladivostok guidelines but included a number of new elements which reflected each side's concerns about the other's areas of strength. The overall limit of 2,400 launchers was confirmed, with agreement to lower the ceiling to 2,250 by the end of 1981; the Vladivostok sub-limit of 1,320 MIRVed launchers (MIRVed ballistic missiles and heavy bombers with long-range cruise missiles) was similarly confirmed with variations of detail. In addition to these equal numerical limits the Treaty restricted Soviet 'heavy' missiles to its existing number of 308, limited the number of warheads which could be placed on various categories of missiles, and banned testing or deployment of new ICBM systems with the exception of one new type of light ICBM for each side. Various confidence-building measures (such as advance notification of certain ICBM test launches), verification and non-circumvention provisions were also built into the Treaty which was to last until the end of 1985 (USACDA 1982: 242–3).

A separate protocol banned deployment (though not testing) of ground- and sea-launched cruise missiles with ranges of more than 600 kilometres, and a separate letter from Brezhnev to Carter gave assurance that the Backfire bomber would be produced in limited numbers and would not be increased in range or payload. It therefore met the American concern that the Backfire could be converted into a strategic bomber. The third and final element of the Treaty was an undertaking to work towards SALT III and deeper cuts in strategic forces.

To its critics the Treaty was 'fatally flawed', and even its defenders were disinclined to trumpet its virtues. The best that could be said of it was that it slowed the rate of growth of strategic arms. Yet the Reagan administration and the Soviet leadership continued to observe its provisions beyond the 1985 expiry date, despite the fact that it remained unratified by the US Senate. Indeed, as has been pointed out, under the Reagan presidency the total throw-weight of American ICBMs actually declined.

This can be taken two ways. It could mean that, for all its faults, the Treaty reflected a genuine strategic balance between the superpowers. In that sense it could be said to have been important symbolically and, to the extent that symbols are important politically, therefore a force for stability. To have openly reneged on the Treaty would have been wilfully to disturb that balance. For all the sound and fury created by the Treaty's critics, then, and despite the crisis of Afghanistan which provoked Carter to withdraw the Treaty from ratification, both superpowers had an interest in being seen not to be the one to upset the balance.

An alternative explanation is that the Treaty was so innocuous, and the ceilings on weapons so high, as to leave superpower strategic plans essentially untouched. 'Because of the lead-time of Research and Development', noted one commentator in 1983, 'neither government has so far been prevented by SALT II from doing anything in the strategic nuclear field . . . that it had planned to do' (Edmonds 1983: 166). Such a view might be confirmed by the observation that in most categories of weapons in question it was a matter of building up to the SALT II limits rather than down from them (USACDA 1982: 272–4). In fact, as Raymond Garthoff has pointed out, if the Treaty's critics had really been concerned about strict parity, they should have argued for ratification, since 'to reach the agreed equal levels the Soviet Union would have had to dismantle some 250 operational units, the United States none' (Garthoff 1985: 823).

It may be that both the above interpretations of the Treaty are true in that it reflected a rough strategic balance between the powers *and* left them relatively unencumbered in developing new weapons programmes. Either way, the striking gap between the fervent opposition to ratification in the United States and acceptance of its provisions in practice suggests that more was at stake than the strategic balance itself. The furore over SALT II in actuality represented disquiet over the broader political relationship between the United States and the Soviet Union. The rest of this chapter will examine conflict in Europe, the Middle East and the Third World for clues to the worsening of this broader relationship.

EUROPEAN DILEMMAS: WEST AND EAST

Henry Kissinger had grandly declared 1973 'the Year of Europe'. The imminent ending of the Vietnam War, it was believed, would enable the United States to refocus attention on relations with Europe, which were in a state of sad disrepair. Summing up the reasons for the Year of Europe, Kissinger cited 'the growth of European strength, the emerging nuclear parity, the impact of a period of relaxing tensions, the growing interdependence of our economies'. All this, Kissinger concluded, 'was occurring in a changed psychological environment that tended to weaken the moral basis of allied cohesion' (Kissinger 1982: 725). Consultation with European leaders would lead to an Atlantic Declaration designed to act as a framework for improved relations.

In the event, though the Atlantic Declaration was finally signed in July 1974, by then, as Kissinger recalled, 'it had been drained of its moral and psychological significance by a year of bickering'. Kissinger put the failure down in part to the declining authority of Richard Nixon as the Watergate saga unfolded and reached its denouement with his resignation in August 1974. In addition, however, there were substantive policy differences over the Middle East, relations with the Soviet Union, and the movement towards political unity in Europe (Kissinger 1982: 193, 729–35).

The Soviet Union never resorted to such devices as a 'Year of Europe' since there was never a question of allowing Eastern bloc countries the kind of autonomy which would make such symbolic appeals necessary. The invasion of Czechoslovakia in 1968, and the accompanying Brezhnev Doctrine, had set outer limits to the possible in Eastern Europe. Inner allegiances, however, were another matter. After 1968, Charles Gati has pointed out, 'both Czechs and Slovaks . . . joined most Poles, Romanians, Hungarians, and East Germans in adopting an altogether contemptuous attitude toward almost everything Soviet and even Russian' (Gati 1990: 48). Furthermore, *détente* in Europe, in particular the human rights provisions of the Helsinki agreements, gave some leverage to dissident groups within the bloc. Even when they were harassed or ruthlessly suppressed, the Helsinki monitoring groups which sprang up in Eastern Europe and the Soviet Union possessed moral legitimacy by virtue of their connection with an international treaty to which the Soviet Union itself had subscribed. In time this moral legitimacy would come to exert significant political power.

On both sides of the Iron Curtain, then, unresolved problems remained, and these were added to substantially in the late 1970s. There were three major sources of tension: modernization of theatre nuclear weapons, Eurocommunism in the West, and the Polish crisis of 1980–81.

The SALT process, though broadly supported by the United States' NATO allies, served to intensify old fears about the credibility of the US nuclear guarantee. In a speech given in London in October 1977, West German Chancellor Helmut Schmidt remarked that 'SALT codifies the nuclear strategic balance between the Soviet Union and the United States. To put it another way: SALT neutralizes their strategic nuclear capabilities. In Europe this magnifies the significance of the disparities between East and West in nuclear tactical and conventional weapons' (Yost and Glad 1982: 536). In recognition of the growing gap between West and East in nuclear and conventional weapons in Europe, the broad solution adopted by the Carter administration was to recommend a 3 per cent annual increase in military spending among all NATO members, a decision which was formalized in 1978.

More specifically, NATO leaders saw the need to enhance NATO's ability to check any Soviet attack within the European theatre. Well before the decision to increase military budgets, the Ford administration had initiated discussions of the 'neutron bomb' or Enhanced Radiation Weapon (ERW) as a means of strengthening NATO's capacity to stem a Soviet advance. Development was approved by Ford in 1976 but it only became a public issue in June 1977 when the story was leaked to the *Washington Post*.

The story of the ERW reveals much about the dynamics of the relationship between the United States and its European allies. The weapon itself was, as Raymond Garthoff points out, not a bomb but a munition designed to be delivered by artillery or short-range missiles: 'while it did rely on enhanced radiation relative to blast, the radiation effects would not be appreciably greater than the munitions it would replace – while the blast damage would be less' (Garthoff 1985: 851). Its popular reputation, however, was as the arch-capitalist weapon which killed people but not property. Perhaps its greatest significance was that it confirmed fears among many Europeans that the United States was preparing for nuclear war-fighting in Europe. Once news of the weapon leaked out, it became the target of the growing anti-nuclear movement within the West no less than of the Soviet Union.

Most damaging to relations within NATO, however, was the embarrassment which the revelations caused to Chancellor Schmidt whose desire for a strengthening of NATO theatre forces was complicated by deep opposition to the ERW within his own party, the Social Democrats (SPD). Though it appears that Schmidt personally favoured ERW deployment, publically he was reluctant to endorse it. The Carter administration for its part refused to go ahead with production of the weapon without publically expressed European support. West German support was especially vital, since the bulk of the ERWs would be deployed there. By early 1978 a compromise had been reached, according to which West Germany would declare willingness to accept the weapons on their soil on condition that deployment be linked to arms control talks with the Warsaw Pact. If within two years no agreement in this field had been reached, then deployment could go ahead (Yost and Glad 1982: 534).

The outcome proved just about as damaging as it could be for all parties. President Carter, always unhappy with the concept of the ERW, chose to announce deferment of the decision at the very moment West German Foreign Minister Genscher arrived in Washington to finalize the agreement. Carter thus managed, as Brzezinski noted, to destroy his own 'credibility . . . in Europe and at home', while 'personal relations between Carter and Schmidt took a further turn for the worse and never recovered' (Brzezinski 1983: 301).

The tension over ERW was about much more than the specifics of one weapon system. It revealed diverging perspectives and interests between the United States with respect to *détente* and the Soviet threat. The West German position was deeply ambiguous, compounded of equally urgent desires to preserve *détente* – 'we don't want to give the Soviets an alibi that we are increasing East–West tension', said a West German defence official in the midst of the ERW imbroglio – and to ensure United States commitment to West European defence (Yost and Glad 1982: 534). The same ambiguities were present in the more drawn-out and hence even more contentious issue of Intermediate Nuclear Forces (INF) deployment.

The issue arose within the West in response to the Soviet decision to deploy a new intermediate range missile in Europe, the SS-20. The first SS-20s were deployed in Europe in 1976 and it was this which prompted Chancellor Schmidt's speech of the following year expressing anxiety about security in Europe. From the Soviet point of view the deployment was simply a matter of replacing obsolete SS-4s and SS-5s with a new, more accurate missile. It was required, noted Georgi Arbatov, in order to counter the West's 'Forward Base Systems' (FBS), chiefly manned bombers and submarine-based missiles, and was designed to enhance deterrence within the European theatre by increasing the potential cost to the West of launching a 'limited' nuclear strike (Arbatov 1983: 123; Garthoff 1990: 72). The American FBS (and also the French and British 'independent' nuclear deterrents) were of particular concern to the Soviets. Although designated as theatre systems, which were therefore not included in the SALT numbers, they had the capacity to reach Soviet soil and were hence regarded by the Soviets as strategic threats.

As was so often the case in the nuclear arms race, such explanations and justifications mattered less to the other side than the perception that the *status quo* had been unilaterally changed. Western leaders and military planners regarded SS-20 deployment as a dangerous revision of the *status quo*, in political if not in strictly military terms. In Europe, and above all in Germany, it seemed designed to 'decouple' Western Europe from the United States by sowing doubts about the viability of the United States' extended deterrence. According to this scenario, a Western Europe under Soviet pressure, and lacking assurance of America's willingness to go to war to save Europe, might be inclined to come to a separate accommodation with the Soviet Union.

Some analysts doubt, however, whether the Soviets had this in mind. 'Rather than threatening Western Europe, explicitly or even implicitly, with its regional nuclear capability,' writes Garthoff, 'to the contrary the Soviets stressed that *they* regarded any limited use of nuclear weapons as inevitably unleashing general nuclear war' (Garthoff 1990: 73).

Whatever the Soviet perception, however, it was clear that many Europeans regarded the SS-20 deployment as a form of nuclear blackmail, to which they could only respond, not by seeking accommodation with the Soviets, but by seeking new assurances from the United States. (This wholly logical response is perhaps enough to cast doubt on the decoupling theory of Soviet SS-20 deployment.) Hence the NATO decision, arrived at in 1979 after much discussion, to deploy Cruise and Pershing II missiles in Europe. The decision was not exclusively a response to the Soviet SS-20s. Discussions on European theatre nuclear forces modernization had been under way for several years. The Soviet action, however, quickened the pace of decision-making and defined the issues more sharply. Furthermore, the ERW debacle undoubtedly inclined the Carter and subsequently the Reagan administrations to press ahead on deployment with high resolve. Deployment was scheduled for 1983.

At this point we must pause to unravel some of the strands of this complex fabric. In the first place, there is the irony that a decision which was pressed most urgently in the initial stages by the Europeans, and especially by Helmut Schmidt, should come to be perceived later on as a matter of the Americans bullying West European governments into accepting the Cruise and Pershing missiles. In part this can be explained by the growing unpopularity of the proposed deployments within European public opinion. INF deployment became the focus for popular agitation about the nuclear issue on a scale which had not been seen since the late 1950s and early 1960s. Less surprisingly perhaps, the Soviets regarded NATO INF deployment as no less provocative than the West had regarded the SS-20s, and they mounted a vigorous campaign to exploit Western leaders' vulnerability to their domestic public opinion. These developments threw European governments onto the defensive and account for the NATO decision to proceed on a 'twin track': deployment of the new missiles in conjunction with INF talks with the Soviets.

A related point is this: if, as appears to be the case, Schmidt's actions in pushing for new INF deployments were based on political rather than strictly military arguments (Bundy 1988: 567–8), then it is no surprise that Schmidt should have been influenced in his later views by the dramatic deterioration in the political climate of East–West relations which attended the INF deployments. That the INF conflict was swiftly followed by the Iranian Revolution and the Soviet invasion of Afghanistan at the end of 1979 only intensified Schmidt's anxiety about the fate of *détente*. Schmidt was both reluctant to join in sanctions against the Soviet Union over Afghanistan and was inclined to back-pedal on deployment of Cruise and Pershing missiles. He even, Brzezinski recalled with evident irritation, 'floated the idea of a moratorium on theater nuclear weapons deployment'. 'I feared', Brzezinski added, 'that it would further undercut Western European support for the nuclear initiative.' The Schmidt–Carter relationship reached its nadir in November 1980 when the Chancellor announced that West Germany 'would not be meeting the 3% annual increase in defense spending as promised' (Brzezinski 1983: 309, 311).

Finally, it is important to note the intersection between the INF deployments and the issue of limited nuclear war. Soviet spokesmen might insist, pointing to numerous statements by military planners and by Brezhnev himself, that they rejected any notion that a nuclear war could remain limited (Arbatov 1983: 92–8). Western Soviet experts might assert that 'those who argued on the basis of Soviet military doctrine and weapons programs that the Soviet Union was pursuing a war-fighting strategy were simply wrong' (Garthoff 1990: 74). Even figures within the American defence community, such as Carter's arms control director Paul Warnke, might assure Americans that talk of a Soviet nuclear war-fighting doctrine was 'on a level of abstraction which is unrealistic' (Pipes 1981: 135). Such assurances nevertheless cut little ice with the growing body of *détente*-sceptics, most notably Richard Pipes, a Harvard history professor and later an adviser to President Reagan. In an article first published in 1977 he gave chapter and verse for his contention that the Soviet Union thought it could fight and win a nuclear war, adding later that he was gratified to note that in signing PD 59 President Carter had apparently come to agree with him (Pipes 1981: 135).

In truth, the issue of limited nuclear war, like the doctrine of deterrence itself, was such a fertile field for political in-fighting both between and within the superpowers because so many imponderables surrounded it. Technical developments played their part. The increasing sophistication of theatre and battlefield nuclear weapons made it plausible (at least in a narrowly technical sense) to think in terms of less than total nuclear exchanges. But the supposed gain in technical precision, in making possible greater flexibility in nuclear doctrines, only magnified the potential areas of political mistrust. INF modernization, in short, seemed to lower the threshold at which nuclear war would be triggered. It thus compounded the difficulties experienced by both superpowers in other areas of the relationship, most notably with regard to political developments in Europe.

The brief but politically unsettling phenomenon of Eurocommunism in the West arose from two sets of developments, one purely contingent and the other of long-standing. The contingent events were the revolution in Portugal in 1974 and the death in 1975 of Spain's long-lived dictator, General Franco. In the former case, an army-led coup ended a forty-year period of authoritarian rule begun by Antonio Salazar and continued after Salazar's death in 1968 by Dr Marcello Caetano. The coup produced two consequences which were of particular concern to the United States: firstly, the new ruling junta included communists in Cabinet positions and secondly, swift moves were made to grant independence to Portugal's colonies. Among these was Angola where an independence struggle had been waged for more than a decade against Portuguese rule. Indeed, the Portuguese military's frustration with the Angolan quagmire was high on the list of reasons for mounting the coup. The result in any event was the outbreak of civil war in Angola, as the three main components of the anti-colonial movement split, with international consequences which are described in the following section.

As regards internal conditions in Portugal, of particular concern to American policy-makers was the spectre of communists participating in the government of a NATO member. Senate Majority Leader Mike Mansfield, following a visit to Portugal in 1975, reported fears that 'a Communist-infiltrated government in Lisbon could be a conduit for vital defense secrets from NATO to the Soviet Union', and he noted that a meeting of the NATO Nuclear Planning Group had been cancelled in November 1974 'apparently because of this fear' (Facts on File 1976: 5). The feared crisis did not develop, however, since after a period of political instability, opinion turned against the communists. In 1976 a new democratic constitution was established, followed by elections which brought moderate Socialists to power.

In Spain too the ending of a forty-year dictatorship produced inevitable dislocations in the political system, though a measure of public consensus existed on return of the monarchy following a yes vote in a referendum. In the tangled struggle for power in post-Franco Spain the Communist Party emerged as a significant competitor even before it was legalized in 1977. It was a party shorn, however, of some of its revolutionary heritage and inclined to pragmatism at least tactically. Crucially, it embraced constitutional monarchy, chiefly in order to deny to the extreme right any pretext for intervening militarily to crush the left. In elections held in 1977 the Communist Party came third with a popular vote of 9.2 per cent and 20 seats in the lower legislative house (Mujal-Leon 1978: 248–52).

As in Portugal, however, the ultimate gainers on the left in post-Franco Spain were the socialist parties rather than the communists. The communist factor in Spain during the late 1970s was of some importance in East–West relations, however, both because for a time it appeared as if communists might gain a measure of political power in another NATO country and because the Spanish communist leaders had been prominent in the promotion of the ideology of Eurocommunism. It is here that events in the Iberian peninsula intersect with those in France and Italy.

Communism in Western Europe had moved on from the time in 1948 when the General Secretary of the French Communist Party (PCF), Maurice Thorez, had said that if the Soviets marched into Western Europe he would support them. Though the West European communist parties endorsed the crushing of the Hungarian uprising in 1956, they did so with great misgivings. Ironically, earlier that same year the General Secretary of the Italian Communist Party (PCI), Togliatti, had announced the doctrine of 'polycentrism' which asserted the autonomy of all communist parties and the need to acknowledge faults within the communist system, including its 'absurd limitations of democratic rights'. This meant adopting a more positive attitude towards the non-communist left and repudiating the Soviet Union's leading role within the international communist movement (Griffith 1978: 398, 399). Though the PCF rejected Togliatti's revisionist stand at the time, by the mid-1960s it too had embraced the fundamentals of polycentrism. The Soviet invasion of Czechoslovakia in 1968 found the French and Italian parties publically and vigorously opposed.

Eurocommunism was thus a new name for an old idea. Its formal rebirth in the 1970s can be dated from the conference of European communist parties held in East Berlin in 1976. Its most comprehensive statement was the 1977 tract *Eurocommunism and the State* by the Spanish communist leader Santiago Carillo. There he affirmed that 'what is essential is the independence of the Communist parties with respect to the Soviet state and the development in theory and practice of an unequivocally democratic way' (Tökés 1978: 473). The political context of Eurocommunism was the growing electoral power of the communist parties in Italy and France, and their reconciliation with NATO and the European Community. In the 1976 elections the PCI came close to equalling the popular vote of the largest party, the Christian Democrats (34.4 per cent and 38.7 per cent respectively), and the possibility arose of communists taking power in coalition with the Christian Democrats. This so-called 'historic compromise' would, Brzezinski recalled, represent 'a clear shift towards neutralism in Italy's foreign policy'. In the event, the PCI lost votes in subsequent elections, reducing the incentive of the Christian Democrats to go into partnership with them. Efforts to forge ties on the Left between the PCI and the Socialists similarly came to nothing, with the result that by 1980 the PCI was 'isolated in the opposition' (Brzezinski 1983: 312, 313).

The French Communist Party over the years had embraced autonomy with less consistency than the Italian, and when it did so firmly in the mid-1970s it was, writes one analyst, 'under the stimulus, in large measure, of the possibility of national power, which developed suddenly between 1972 and 1974'. The occasion was the opportunity of joining with the Socialists, who had experienced a surge in popularity, to form a coalition of the Left. This plan, like comparable ventures elsewhere in Europe, broke down amid wrangles over strategies and policies, and the divided Left experienced defeat in the elections of 1978 (Tiersky 1978: 161, 162, 140). Even when, following elections in 1980, Socialist President Mitterand appointed four communists to his cabinet, French foreign policy remained firmly oriented towards the West (Steele 1985: 80).

There remains the question of how to evaluate the significance of Western Euro-communism in East–West relations. Neither side's leaderships could be happy with it. Those in the West with memories long enough to recall the Popular Front of the 1930s might be inclined to view the new devotion of Western communist parties to liberal democracy and pluralism as merely tactical. Such observers might also find their scepticism about Eurocommunism confirmed by reference to views expressed at the East Berlin conference in 1976 where 'the PCF, along with the Spanish Communist party, accused the Soviet Union of excessive moderation in its relations with the West, of being too mild in its ideological denunciations of capitalism, too weak in its support of socialist change in Western Europe, and in general more interested in what it can get from great-power *détente* than in its role as a revolutionary vanguard' (Tiersky 1978: 154). And how much credence could be given to the PCI's assurances that it supported Italy's continued membership of NATO? These and other doubts circled around the issue of Eurocommunism. Behind them all lay the encompassing anxiety that Euro-communism threatened the delicate fabric of the East–West division of power.

On the other hand, the West European communist parties' growing accommoda-tion to parliamentary norms was precisely the feature of their development which was most troublesome to the Soviet Union. Eurocommunism seemingly drained Marxist-Leninism of any real meaning and furthermore it was explicitly anti-Soviet. In a bitter attack on Carillo's *Eurocommunism and the State* a Soviet author identified Carillo's cardinal sin as his attempt 'to justify an independent West European model of socialism as the most powerful means of "democratizing" the regimes in Eastern Europe', a more 'hostile and subversive' attack than anything mounted by the imperialists (Levgold 1978: 377).

Perhaps understandably, what neither superpower could easily conceive of at the time was the possibility that Eurocommunism represented the maturation of *détente*, that it was in part a product of their own machinations. A loosening of bloc cohesion was both a cause and a consequence of *détente*. More specifically, even as the European *détente* agreements ratified the division of Europe, the resulting reduction in tension allowed for greater pluralism on both sides of the Iron Curtain and, importantly, increasing links across it.

For the peoples of Eastern Europe greater pluralism and links with the West held out both promise and danger. The promise lay in the chance for increased loans and credits from the West and an increased standard of living, in expectations of liberalization raised by the Helsinki Accords, and more generally in the opportunity to become 'part of Europe' again (Tökés 1978: 490). The danger lay in the reaction which development along these lines might provoke in the Soviet Union. The leaderships of the nations of Eastern Europe were thus bound to maintain a delicate balance between opposing forces. That they possessed long experience in doing just that was a powerful force for stability, but during the 1970s certain new and incalculable elements entered into play which made control less assured.

In addition to the climate of *détente*, the Helsinki Final Act, and the advent of Eurocommunism, Rudolf Tökés cites two further developments in the 1970s which vitally affected Eastern Europe: the global energy crisis caused by the OPEC oil boycott of 1973 followed by the quadrupling of oil prices and the revival of dissidence (Tökés 1978: 438). Nowhere did these developments exert more powerful effects than in Poland. Though perhaps not typical of the nations of Eastern Europe (given their important differences), Poland can be employed as a bell-wether of the kind of forces at work in that region.

Poland's size, economic importance for the Eastern bloc, and its geographical position on the natural invasion route to the Soviet Union from the West ensured that, by contrast, for example, with Yugoslavia or Romania, it would be considered vital to Soviet security (Gati 1990: 48–9; Dawisha 1990: 74–5). The latter point had been made repeatedly by Stalin at Yalta. Historical enmity between Poland and Russia (and later the Soviet Union), based on Russia's responsibility for successive partitions of Poland, if anything tied the knot tighter between the two nations in the post-war period. In particular, the substantial boundary changes at the end of the Second World War, which involved moving Poland westward at German expense, left Poland dependent upon the Soviet Union for security against any possible German attempts to regain that territory. In this context the 1970 treaties between West Germany and Poland and between West Germany and the Soviet Union, ratifying the post-Second

World War Polish borders, if anything increased Soviet insistence on the vital nature of the Polish–Soviet bond because, as Timothy Garton Ash has pointed out, settlement of the territorial issue 'effectively robbed the Polish communist authorities of the bogey of West German revanchism' (Garton Ash 1984: 319). At any rate it seems evident that pragmatic recognition of power realities rather than devotion to socialist ideology underlay the 'special relationship' between Poland and the Soviet Union (Dawisha 1990: 70).

As it happened 1970 was also the year of the first serious political disturbances in Poland since the crisis of 1956. The 1970 demonstrations, which were repeated in 1976, focused on economic issues, primarily the price of food. Neither outbreak produced sustained mass opposition movements, but during the 1976 crisis a Workers' Defence Committee (KOR) was founded by a group of intellectuals, whose activities remained virtually unchecked by the authorities (Garton Ash 1984: 17–21). The decisive change in the internal climate in Poland which gave rise to Solidarity in 1980 was the economic crisis in the second half of the 1970s. The earlier crises had been surmounted in part by huge borrowing from the West. In the late 1970s these debts grew as Poland's ability to repay them declined; a second round of oil price rises in 1979 compounded Poland's economic difficulties. Decline in the supply of food and consumer goods were especially damaging (Dawisha 1990: 169–73, 179–82).

It was these conditions which provoked Polish workers to protest on a scale and with an intensity not seen since 1956. The organizational centre of the movement was the labour union 'Solidarity' which grew within a few weeks of its birth in the Gdansk shipyards during August 1980 into a national force for change, gaining the support of the intelligentsia and the Catholic Church. By the end of the month the government had been pushed into legalizing the organization, and within a few days the Polish leader, Edward Gierek, had resigned.

Initially Solidarity strove to assure the authorities that its platform of 'socialist renewal' did not mean abandonment of the socialist system or the leading role of the Party, but there was an unavoidable ambiguity about the status and goals of Solidarity. 'Party politics didn't interest us,' Lech Walesa wrote later; 'we had no desire to assume power ourselves and to reestablish order through a government of our own.' On the other hand, among the questions debated within the Solidarity leadership was the issue of changing 'the system whereby the Party alone decided on the filling of key posts at all levels of government, not only in the political sphere, but in civic, police, and military activity where its word was law' (Walesa 1987: 145–6, 147). Walesa may have continued to describe Solidarity as a trade union, but the demand for independent status could hardly be regarded by the authorities as anything other than political in nature and potentially subversive of Party rule.

In 1956, in not dissimilar circumstances, the Soviet Union had opted for pressure on the Polish authorities to crush the opposition themselves. The Hungarian and Czech option, direct suppression by the Soviet Union, was available in 1980–1 as a last resort, but was likely to be even more damaging to the Soviets' reputation in world opinion (including the communist world) than in those earlier cases. Besides, an invasion, writes one authority, 'would in all probability have led to a virtual state of war with the workers and the nation'. Preparations were made, however, for that eventuality, and on two occasions – December 1980 and March 1981 – the Soviet leadership was on the point of intervening. In the event, the Soviet Union waited, and applied persistent pressure on the Prime Minister, General Jaruzelski, to restore order. In December 1981 he declared martial law and banned Solidarity. The Brezhnev doctrine was reaffirmed, if less explosively than in 1968 (Bialer 1986: 223; Gati 1990: 53–5).

These events invite two sorts of reflections. Firstly, in contrast to 1956, following the crackdown in 1981 the opposition was down but not out. Solidarity remained a powerful force throughout the 1980s, carrying on an active underground existence, despite internment or imprisonment of many Solidarity members (Garton Ash 1984: 271). Furthermore, the Catholic Church, which had tried to forge a compromise between Solidarity and the government during December 1981, carried on much of Solidarity's work, providing 'a legal channel both to the government and to the people for the promotion of key Solidarity demands, including the release of political prisoners, improvement in living standards, and political reforms that would take non-Party interests more fully into account'. The repeal of the ban on Solidarity, when it came in April 1989, owed much to the efforts of the Church, and in particular of Pope John Paul II (a Pole, the former Cardinal Wojtyla) who received General Jaruzelski at the Vatican during 1987 and visited Poland himself later the same year (Dawisha 1990: 167, 168). It was inevitable that when the communist system cracked in 1989 the people should turn to Solidarity to form the new government. (These events are discussed in Chapter 13.)

A second reflection relates to the connections between the larger framework of *détente* and events in Eastern Europe. In his account of Solidarity and the Polish revolution, Timothy Garton Ash notes the 'embarrassment' of West German political leaders and intellectuals in the face of Solidarity's rise. On the very day when Solidarity's leaders were being 'arrested and herded into internment camps' West German Chancellor Schmidt was meeting with the East German Party leader Erich Honecker. Few West German intellectuals openly protested the banning of Solidarity. Schmidt himself equivocated when he addressed the Bundestag a few days later. The truth was, Garton Ash observes, that the West German investment in *détente* made it very difficult for its leadership to deal with the Polish situation. To embrace the cause of Solidarity would have been to cast in doubt the improved relations between West Germany and the Eastern bloc which had been an important product of Ostpolitik (Garton Ash 1984: 316–19).

Ostpolitik had been entered into in the expectation that a reduction of East–West tension would encourage the East European regimes towards liberalization. The possibility that change might come from below, inviting the regimes to crack down on opposition groups and reassert orthodoxy, and indeed that East European leaders

277

might exploit *détente* (especially Western economic aid) to 'stabilise and strengthen their regimes', was hardly envisaged. Ostpolitik was fraught with ambiguity about whether it was serving the governments or the peoples of Eastern Europe (Garton Ash 1984: 321–4).

By contrast with the West German reaction to the events in Poland, the United States led the Western protests against what looked like imminent Soviet military intervention in Poland during December 1980. Brzezinski credited the United States with a large role in deterring Soviet action by making highly public its intelligence information on Soviet troop movements on the Polish border, and this view has received some confirmation by Soviet specialists (Brzezinski 1983: 465–8; Bialer 1986: 223). From the American standpoint, Poland was thus added to Afghanistan as a nail in the coffin of *détente*.

The gap between the American and West German reactions is instructive. Above all, it confirms the point made earlier that a signal feature of East–West relations in the late 1970s was the bifurcation of superpower and European perspectives and interests. Poland was only one of the points of divergence; another was over the Soviet invasion of Afghanistan, and earlier in the decade West European governments had reacted negatively to the American nuclear alert during the October war of 1973 (treated in the next section). In reflecting on these and other areas of contention between the United States and Western Europe, the Congressional Research Service suggested that:

> Europeans [are] more inclined to regard *détente* as "divisible," to protect the gains of *détente* in Europe. The United States, carrying the majority of Western global military burdens, has a much greater interest in treating *détente* as "indivisible" with Soviet actions outside of Europe seen as providing cause for Western response within a European framework.
>
> (Stuart and Tow 1990: 89)

Europeans, however, and West Germans in particular, could only take the idea of the divisibility of *détente* so far. To fail to take any account of American anxieties would be to put at risk their primary security relationship, which was with the United States. On the other hand, to follow slavishly the American position on such issues as Poland and Afghanistan would be to put at risk their relationship with Moscow, on which the continuation of *détente* in Europe depended. The West Germans therefore, with the help of the French, sought to establish intermediate positions which safeguarded relationships with both superpowers. The West Germans, as one German historian has noted, had most to lose from an abandonment of *détente*; many of the gains of Ostpolitik, such as increased trade and family contacts between East and West Germany, could be easily lost in a worsening of East–West relationships. The continuation of *détente* in Europe was therefore dependent on at least a 'minimum *détente*' between the superpowers (Haftendorn 1986: 140–2).

IRREPRESSIBLE CONFLICT: THE THIRD WORLD

Superpower leaders and opinion-makers characteristically found it hard to accept that instability in the Third World might be due to factors other than the actions of the other superpower. Even when the Soviets did acknowledge, as one leading Soviet analyst did, that 'these processes [of violent change in the Third World] are beyond the control of either the Soviet Union or the United States', this recognition was framed within a larger argument which asserted that the root cause of Third World troubles in the 1970s was American-inspired neocolonialism (Trofimenko 1981: 1026, 1022–7). On the American side, by the end of the 1970s there was little ambiguity about the character of Soviet ambitions in the Third World in the minds of those critics of *détente* who would shortly be advising President Reagan. Richard Pipes placed Soviet Third World policy within the framework of its supposed 'Grand Strategy' of seeking control in countries which lay close to vital supply routes to the West. Among these key points (which corresponded to the geographical boundaries of the 'arc of crisis') were the southern entrance to the Red Sea, giving access to the Suez Canal, and the Strait of Hormuz, giving access to the Persian Gulf (Pipes 1981: 187–8). Both powers found it hard to resist the mentality of globalism which saw the hand of the other in each new crisis, and indeed their actions frequently contributed to the translation of Third World crises into superpower confrontations, however local the origins of the conflicts might be.

There were plenty of opportunities for superpower clashes in the Third World during the 1970s. It is tempting to see a pattern in them. Henry Trofimenko, a leading Soviet specialist on the United States, regarded these upheavals as 'a process of anti-neocolonialist revolution and an aspiration in most of the developing nations to gain economic as well as political independence'. This, he said, was 'the second stage of the process of national and social-economic liberation from external dependence' (Trofimenko 1981: 1022).

There is some merit in this idea, at least in the sense that there was a growing consciousness of common economic problems within the developing world – specifically, inflated prices for manufactured goods from industrialized countries combined with falling prices for commodity exports on which many developing nations depended. Added to these were increasing overseas debt burdens, sharply rising energy costs after the Arab–Israeli war of 1973, and more generally a sense that the global distribution of wealth was unjust. These concerns were voiced by a group of 77 developing nations at a UN General Assembly session in 1974 which formulated proposals for a New International Economic Order (NIEO). Follow-up conferences, some under UN auspices and some outside it, began a process of North–South dialogue on the NIEO, even if actual results by the end of the decade were somewhat meagre. The publication in 1980 of *North–South: A Programme for Survival*, a report by an independent commission headed by Willy Brandt, had some influence in enhancing the visibility of these issues on the international agenda.

Economic crisis was, then, a common thread linking Third World political crisis, but the precise causes and forms of instability varied from region to region. Such a large and complex field can be treated only in a summary fashion. We shall survey it with two issues in mind: internal conditions and the nature of US–Soviet competition, concluding with a rough superpower balance sheet in the Third World. We begin with three crises – Angola, the Horn of Africa, and Afghanistan – in which there was direct Soviet or Soviet–Cuban intervention, and then move to the Iranian revolution, the Arab–Israeli conflict, and the Nicaraguan revolution, where superpower antagonism took more indirect forms.

Angola

Antagonism over Southern Africa was precipitated by Portugal's announcement of independence for Angola, following the Portuguese revolution of 1974. Civil war broke out long before the projected independence date of November 1975, as three forces fought for military and political position – the National Front for the Liberation of Angola (FNLA), the Union for the Total Independence of Angola (UNITA), and the Popular Movement for the Liberation of Angola (MPLA). Tribal rather than political differences separated these movements, and the alignment of foreign support for them proved that international politics can make for strange bedfellows. The United States initially backed the FNLA, nominally the most left-wing of all, in the belief that it represented the strongest faction. China also supported the FNLA but withdrew during the summer of 1975. The MPLA received the support of the Soviet Union, while UNITA was aided by South Africa.

It was during May that the Soviet Union initiated an airlift of Cuban troops to Angola. The effort was stepped up towards the end of the year, eventually reaching a total of 11,000, in response to the arrival of 5,000 South African troops in support of UNITA. The Cuban influx was enough to tip the balance decisively in favour of the MPLA, which at the end of the year took power. In the wake of formal independence the FNLA and UNITA joined forces to continue the struggle with South African support.

What were the motives behind the Soviet–Cuban intervention, and why did the United States not mount an effort on behalf of the FNLA and later UNITA? As for the first question, while the Cubans could not have intervened independently, it is clear now that the Cubans pushed strongly for intervention themselves and were not merely proxies for the Soviet Union (Isaacson 1992: 676). For its part, the Soviet Union claimed that its actions were in response to American and Chinese support for the FNLA, though this was on a relatively small scale and involved no troops. The Soviet concern, besides a desire to increase its influence in the Third World consonant with its growing military power, was the possibility of increased Chinese influence in Africa and the even more dangerous spectre of 'Sino–American collaboration in the competition in the third world' (Garthoff 1985: 528).

280

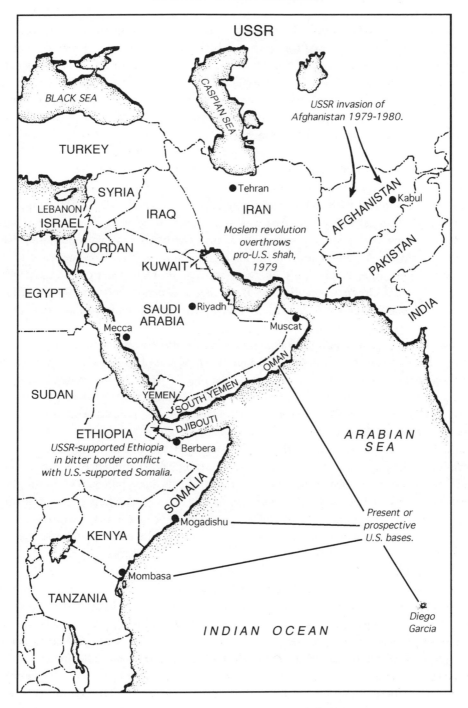

Figure 11.1 The Near East in upheaval, 1980

Source: Derived from W. LaFeber, *America, Russia, and the Cold War, 1945–1992*, New York: McGraw-Hill, 1993, p. 297.

The United States, meanwhile, was constrained in its response by two things. Firstly, it was caught by surprise and had little in the way of a prepared policy beyond the limited effort in support of the FNLA. Even in retrospect Henry Kissinger evidently regarded Angola as of little significance. He referred to it only three times in his memoirs, and then only in passing. Angola became an issue for the United States primarily as a result of Soviet–Cuban involvement, not because of any belief in Angola's intrinsic importance to American interests. Secondly, Congress had no stomach for another intervention so soon after Vietnam, and in December 1975 it denied the administration the authority and the means to undertake it.

In the post-independence period of continued civil war, furthermore, the United States was confronted with the difficulty that support for the UNITA–FNLA opposition would align it with South Africa, and this at a time when black Africa was mounting a powerful propaganda offensive against the vestiges of white minority rule in the continent. A combination of increasing pressure in Rhodesia for the end of minority white rule, stepped up guerrilla activity in Namibia by the Southwest African People's Organization (SWAPO) seeking independence from South Africa, and rising protests against apartheid in South Africa itself made support for South African ambitions in the region a serious political liability.

In this connection a number of commentators have observed the impact of the Angolan situation in provoking a fundamental reappraisal of American policy towards southern Africa. With a speech in Lusaka, Zambia in April 1976, Henry Kissinger announced the new direction in American policy, which was based on 'forthright opposition to white minority regimes and on financial support for emerging black nations'. Though the target of fierce denunciations by Amercian conservatives, the Ford administration's shift in southern Africa policy, later continued by Carter, was a novel and arguably more effective way of countering Soviet influence in Africa than had been previously tried. One practical result of the new policy was Kissinger's application of shuttle diplomacy to the stand-off in Rhodesia, where Prime Minister Ian Smith had maintained white minority rule since his unilateral declaration of independence from Britain in 1965. Kissinger brokered the essentials of an arrangement for transition to majority rule which was implemented under the Carter administration (Isaacson 1992: 686, 687–92; Edmonds 1983: 153–4).

The single most important conclusion which the United States drew from the Angolan situation, however, was the conviction that the Soviet Union had reneged on *détente*, and specifically the undertaking in the BPA to avoid provoking crises. In the American presidential election year which followed the outbreak of the Angolan civil war, the Ford administration retreated from the language of *détente*. The Soviet Union, however, saw no incompatibility between intervention in Angola and commitment to *détente*. The Soviet Union had never, Brezhnev asserted, undertaken to abandon support for liberation struggles. If, as is often argued with some justification, Soviet statements on this issue ring hollow and self-serving, one has to ask whether *détente* at any level would have been possible if the Americans had made, say, arms control explicitly conditional upon Soviet restraint in the Third World. The answer must be no. Nor, it should be said, was the United States entirely innocent of interventionism. Strenuous covert efforts had been made in 1970 to prevent the appointment of the Marxist candidate for the Chilean presidency, Salvatore Allende. Three years later Allende was overthrown and murdered. Though there is no evidence of direct American involvement, and though Allende's fall had important internal causes, the United States' strict economic boycott of Chile and its channelling of funds to opposition groups contributed substantially to the weakening of Allende's government. Furthermore, as we shall see later, during the period of *détente* the United States consistently sought to exclude the Soviet Union from a role in the Middle East.

The Horn of Africa

Some of the Angolan ingredients were present in the Horn of Africa, though the mix was very different. Soviet–Cuban intervention in the conflict between Ethiopia and Somalia was easier to justify in the international arena, since it came at the request of a sovereign government rather than from one party in a civil war. The Soviet Union also showed some concern to prevent escalation of the crisis. Nevertheless, the dominant American perception was of dangerous Soviet adventurism.

War between Ethiopia and Somalia broke out in 1977 as a result of Somalian support for the independence movement in the Ogaden, an Ethiopian province peopled by ethnic Somalis. Somalia clearly wished to annex the Ogaden. Crucial to the dynamics of the conflict and to the character of the international alignments in the war was the coming to power of Colonel Mengistu in Ethiopia in February 1977. Mengistu's accession was the outcome of a fierce struggle within the leftist Provisional Military Administrative Committee (PMAC) which had taken over power following the enforced abdication of Emperor Haile Selassie in 1974. America's long-standing support for Ethiopia was severely strained by the arrival of Mengistu, both because of evidence of serious human rights violations and because Mengistu very soon put out feelers to the Soviet Union for an arms deal. Somalia, meanwhile, until this point firmly aligned with the Soviet Union, sought closer relations with the United States with a view to gaining arms and support for its campaign in the Ogaden region of Ethiopia. In July the United States agreed to send 'defensive arms' to Somalia, an announcement which was widely interpreted as an endorsement of Somali designs on the Ogaden (Steele 1985: 241).

For a time during the summer of 1977, while the future of the Ogaden dispute was still in the balance, the Soviet Union maintained relations with both sides, seeking to mediate between the parties. Indeed, the Soviet Union was supplying arms to both Ethiopia and Somalia until August. Once, however, the Somali leader, Siad Barre, made it clear that he intended to seize the Ogaden by force, the Soviet Union cut off arms to Somalia. At around the same time, in the light of the Somali march into the Ogaden, the United States announced the withdrawal of its promise of arms to

Somalia. It was only in November, when the Somali invasion of the Ogaden was well advanced, that the Soviet–Cuban decision was taken to intervene with troops on the side of Ethiopia.

What had emerged was a reversal of the traditional alignments, a swapping of partners by the United States and the Soviet Union. The process was not entirely symmetrical, however. While the Soviet–Cuban intervention on the side of Ethiopia was decisive by the spring of 1978 in pushing the Somalis out of the Ogaden, the United States continued to refuse arms to Somalia. Once again, the United States had backed the losing side, or rather, as in Angola, had chosen not to match the Soviet–Cuban effort. There were powerful reasons for not doing so, which were acknowledged even by Brzezinski who favoured a much stronger response than Carter was prepared to countenance. As Brzezinski recalled, 'our ability to assist the Somalis was not helped by the fact that they were the nominal aggressors in the Ogaden' (Brzezinski 1983: 178).

Soviet actions in the Horn of Africa contained elements of both restraint and aggressive opportunism. Restraint was manifested in the decision not to endorse a projected Ethiopian incursion into Somalia once the goal of pushing the Somalis out of the Ogaden had been achieved. This policy invited the resentment of the Ethiopian leadership, but these costs were outweighed by the advantage that limiting support of Ethiopia to clearing the Somalis from the Ogaden was in line with the stance taken by the Organization of African Unity (OAU).

Soviet opportunism, on the other hand, was evident in the support given to Ethiopia later in 1978 in suppressing the rebel independence movement in Eritrea, the northern province of Ethiopia. Nominally the Soviet Union's position was that the dispute should be resolved by negotiation. It seems likely, however, that the temptation to help the Ethiopians pacify Eritrea arose from the fact that Eritrea's Red Sea coastline contained Ethiopia's only ports, and hence a means for the Soviets to make good their loss of access to the Somalian port of Berbera (Steele 1985: 242). The result of this operation was the temporary crushing of the Eritrean rebels and the opening of a long guerrilla struggle.

Soviet relations with Ethiopia in the succeeding years, however, were hardly smooth. Many issues divided them, but they can be summed up by reference to the narrow pragmatic base on which their interests met. Each used the other for its own political and strategic purposes. Soviet leverage over Ethiopian politics was largely limited to security issues. In other areas Ethiopian nationalism overrode Mengistu's in any case less than whole-hearted commitment to Marxist-Leninism (Halliday 1981: 97–8).

The United States' involvement in the Horn of Africa was indirect at best and, as in the Angolan case, was stimulated by Soviet actions rather than deep concern for Somalian interests. One significant aspect of American policy was the rift which this crisis exposed between Brzezinski and Vance. It took the form of a very public dispute about the wisdom or otherwise of invoking 'linkage' between Soviet actions in the

Third World and the SALT talks. Brzezinski from the start had favoured a much firmer stance in support of Somalia and always saw the Ethiopia–Somali dispute as 'much more than a border conflict'. 'Coupled with the expansion of Soviet influence and military presence to South Yemen', he wrote, 'it posed a potentially grave threat to our position in the Middle East, notably in the Arabian peninsula' (Brzezinski 1983: 178). He was virtually alone in this view within the Carter administration and was evidently frustrated at his colleagues' unwillingness to recognize what he took to be the reality of the situation. During a press conference, in reponse to a question, he suggested that Soviet intervention would 'complicate' the SALT talks. There followed a 'clarification' by President Carter, in which he denied any deliberate policy of slowing arms talks because of Soviet interventionism but said that Soviet policy 'would lessen the confidence of the American people in the word and peaceful intentions of the Soviet Union and would make it more difficult to ratify a SALT agreement'. Vance left no doubt about his position: 'there is no linkage between the SALT negotiations and the situation in Ethiopia' (Brzezinski 1983: 185).

To all appearances, the President was tilting towards Brzezinski in this dispute. That is at any rate how it was perceived by Vance, for whom SALT far transcended in importance the sideshow in Ethiopia. 'We were shooting ourselves in the foot', Vance wrote in his memoirs. 'By casting the complex Horn situation in East–West terms, and by setting impossible objectives for US policy – elimination of Soviet and Cuban influence in Ethiopia – we were creating a perception that we were defeated when, in fact, we were achieving a successful outcome' (Vance 1983: 88). By successful outcome he meant the ending of the Somali incursion into the Ogaden and pressure on the Soviets to restrain Ethiopia from pushing into Somalia, criteria which in Brzezinski's eyes ignored the single most significant fact about the crisis in the Horn – Soviet–Cuban intervention.

The outcome of this imbroglio was mixed. Actual American policy in the Horn followed Vance's priority of viewing Soviet actions not as 'part of a grand Soviet plan, but rather attempts to exploit targets of opportunity' (Vance 1983: 84). However, Brzezinskian priorities were bubbling up towards the surface in the wake of the crisis in the Horn. An interesting indication of the difference in approach between Vance and Brzezinski lies in the treatments in their memoirs of normalization with China in 1978–79. Brzezinski introduced the topic with reference to the 'troublesome months' during which the crisis in the Horn unfolded. In the light of these events, he wrote, 'we started reviewing more systematically the advisability of developing strategic consultations with the Chinese in order to balance the Soviets' (Brzezinski 1983: 189). Brzezinski received the support of Defense Secretary Harold Brown on this issue. Vance, by contrast, resisted viewing the policy in terms of US–Soviet global competition: 'as I saw it, China was a great country that had an important role to play in the final quarter of the twentieth century, not simply one that might be a useful counterweight to the Soviet Union' (Vance 1983: 79). Predictably, the Soviets themselves perceived Sino–American normalization exclusively in Brzezinskian terms

– as a move in the global superpower contest. Coming in the year of China's brief invasion of Vietnam (see Chapter 10) as well as conflict in the Horn of Africa and slow progress in the SALT talks, the Soviet Union could hardly have perceived it otherwise. What the Americans' use of the 'China card' actually meant, wrote Georgi Arbatov, was an attempt 'to obtain quick gains for the West from the bad state of relations between us and China' (Arbatov 1983: 167).

Afghanistan

If, as Brzezinski declared in his oft-quoted statement, 'SALT was buried in the sands of the Ogaden', then SALT underwent a second burial in Afghanistan. On 25 December 1979 Soviet troops poured into Afghanistan in the first deployment of Soviet combat forces outside the Warsaw Pact area since the Second World War. Claiming that their intervention had been requested by the Afghan leadership, the Soviets quickly installed themselves in Kabul. Within a few hours, the regime of Hafizullah Amin had been toppled, Amin had been killed, and a new leader, Babrak Kamal, had taken power, accompanied with denials by both the Soviets and Kamal that he was a Soviet puppet. For close to ten years, Soviet troops remained there, increasingly beleaguered in Kabul which remained their only solid point of occupation. The war cost the Soviet Union 14,000 combat deaths and, according to some reports, approximately the same number of non-combat deaths (White 1990: 175; Goldman 1992: 198).

The damage to the Soviet Union's international reputation and to East–West relations was severe. Besides the inevitable condemnation from Western leaders, Eurocommunists unanimously excoriated the Soviet Union. The United States boycotted the 1980 Olympic Games and instituted an embargo on export of grain to the Soviet Union. More damagingly, President Carter suspended the SALT II ratification process in the Senate. The events confirmed the worst fears of *détente*'s critics in the West and undercut the position of pro-*détente* moderates such as Cyrus Vance. 'Afghanistan', like Vietnam, came to have associations in both East and West far beyond its geographical meaning.

'Everyone knows', recalled Soviet Foreign Minister Andrei Gromyko with characteristic blandness, 'that these troops were introduced solely as neighbourly assistance between one country and another' (Gromyko 1989: 240). Georgi Arbatov elaborated, if no less evasively, thus:

> We've sent our military contingent there for two closely related purposes: to help the government formed after the revolution in Afghanistan ward off aggression from the outside, and to prevent the turning of Afghanistan into an anti-Soviet base on our southern borders.
>
> (Arbatov 1983: 190)

The revolution referred to by Arbatov took place in 1978, and took the form of a coup against the regime of Muhammad Daoud, a cousin of the former King of Afghanistan.

Daoud himself had come to power in a coup in 1973 with the help of the leftist People's Democratic Party of Afghanistan (PDPA), but he soon repudiated his partners and the reform programme he had promised. It was the PDPA who toppled him in 1978. Once in power, the PDPA, itself a coalition of two major leftist groups, split into its constituent parts, with Hafizullah Amin's faction gaining control. He subsequently embarked on a programme of radicalization which included sweeping and disruptive land reform and a campaign against manifestations of the Moslem religion such as the veil and the Islamic green of the national flag. These changes produced violent popular reaction, intensified by the spill-over effect of the Islamic revolution in Iran during 1979. 'By the spring of 1979', writes one author, 'Moscow was already faced with the dilemma that eventually recurred in a starker form on the eve of their invasion. Should they cut their losses and withdraw support from an unpopular regime that was becoming increasingly unstable, or should they help to prop it up?' Sharp deterioration of the situation during the summer and autumn of 1979 inclined the Soviets towards military intervention (Steele 1985: 124 and 121–5).

It is probably useless, as Harry Gelman points out, to try to distinguish between offensive and defensive motives in Soviet intervention in Afghanistan. Invasion of Afghanistan was a pre-emptive action to forestall the loss of a recent and fragile gain: namely the Afghan revolution of 1978 (Gelman 1984: 169–70). The action was thus defensive in the sense that a failure to act might have weakened Soviet security and have been perceived internationally as a loss to the Soviets; the intervention was offensive in that satisfying these needs meant a sudden and unilateral change in the regional and, arguably, global 'correlation of forces'. A global dimension was involved not merely because the West chose to see it as of a piece with Soviet interventions in Africa but because, in Gelman's words, the Politburo itself regarded it 'as another in a progression of favorable changes that had taken place in different parts of the world in recent years' (Gelman 1984: 170).

Assessing the significance of Soviet intervention in Afghanistan in connection with *détente* is not as easy as it might appear. The Soviet action would have been provocative in any circumstances. In the circumstances of *détente* it was doubly so. The decision was reportedly taken by a small group of no more than four of the Politburo, though that in itself is not greatly out of line with other major Soviet foreign policy decisions. But the intervention was in important respects an aberration from Soviet practice in the Third World. The scale of military involvement was unprecedented and, unlike the Angolan and Horn of Africa instances, the Soviets sought direct control of the Afghan government, despite the fiction of Kamal's independence. This suggests that Afghanistan was conceived to be a vital interest, akin to the United States' interest in, say, Mexico. Of course, outside observers could not be sure that this was not the beginning of a new pattern which might be extended elsewhere. The world reaction must be seen partly in this light.

But outside reactions were not uniform. As mentioned earlier, the Europeans, and especially the Germans, were reluctant to engage in words or actions which would

287

jeopardize *détente*. Indeed many Europeans, one German writer has noted, saw the American reaction as displaced anger and frustration over their inability to resolve the Iranian hostage crisis (Haftendorn 1986: 139). Even Cyrus Vance, who supported all the US counter-measures and worried that the Europeans 'came perilously close to the mistaken idea that *détente* [could] be isolated from events elsewhere', was unwilling to write off *détente*. 'I assured the Europeans', he wrote, 'that the Carter administration was not going to dismantle the structure of *détente* or cut off communication with the East.' Reflecting on the divisions within the American administration, Vance concluded that Afghanistan was 'unquestionably a severe setback to the policy I advocated. The tenuous balance between visceral anti-Sovietism and an attempt to regulate dangerous competition could no longer be maintained. The scales tipped toward those favoring confrontation, although in my opinion, the confrontation was more rhetorical than actual' (Vance 1983: 393, 394).

By this last statement Vance seemed to mean that, unacceptable as Soviet intervention was, it did not pose a serious threat to American interests. Carter evidently disagreed and announced the Carter Doctrine which stated that 'an attempt by any outside force to gain control of the Persian Gulf region will be regarded as an assault on the vital interests of the United States of America, and such an assault will be repelled by any means necessary, including military force' (Carter 1982: 483). In effect the Carter Doctrine was a departure from the Nixon Doctrine of relying on regional allies to secure American interests and a return to the Eisenhower Doctrine of 1957. Among the chief reasons for this shift was the emerging crisis in Iran, the nation which the Nixon administration had envisaged as regional stabilizer in the Middle East. Carter's response to Afghanistan was in part dictated by events in neighbouring Iran.

The Iranian revolution

The full story of the Iranian revolution encompasses a good deal more than the immediate crisis of the 1970s. Behind it lies the experience of encounters between traditional Islamic culture and Westernized secular ideas and institutions. One form which the encounter took was colonialism; the other was indigenous modernization from the top such as took place in the Turkey of Attaturk during the 1920s and 1930s. It was this latter model which the Shah of Iran adopted in the same period and, under the stimulus of growing oil revenues, was continued by his son following his return to power in 1953. In Iran, however, modernization and Westernization was only partial. It barely extended beyond the upper echelons of society and alienated religious leaders and large parts of the masses.

A decisive new factor in Iran's development in the 1970s was the Nixon administration's decision, in line with the Nixon Doctrine, to build up the Shah as a regional stabilizer in the Middle East. The chief instrument of American influence was arms sales, though this by no means guaranteed either the Shah's hold on power or slavish devotion to American interests. In fact the Shah was at one with the oil-producing countries in insisting on steep oil price rises after the Arab–Israeli war of 1973, though Iran did continue to supply the United States with oil during the embargo which followed the war (Rubin 1981: 140). Earlier the same year the Shah had effectively nationalized oil production in his country, thus achieving the goal pursued by Mossadegh during his period in power from 1950–53. Any leverage the United States gained from the Shah's dependence on American arms was matched by the United States' increasing dependence on foreign, including Iranian, oil (Rubin 1981: 139–40). The United States was able to make few dents in the Shah's policy of draconian suppression of dissent.

Internally, opposition to the Shah's dictatorial rule grew sharply during the 1970s but his invariable response to questions from the in-coming Carter administration about violations of human rights and the persistence of civil disturbances in his country was, in Jimmy Carter's words, 'faltering efforts' to meet the demands of the protesters which 'only aroused further dissatisfaction' (Carter 1982: 438). The United States, however, was apparently unable to contemplate any fundamental change in its policy towards Iran. Nor did American intelligence do much to prepare the Carter administration for the upheaval of 1979. In August 1978, in the wake of a sequence of serious riots which had begun in January in the holy city of Qom, a CIA assessment concluded that Iran 'is not in a revolutionary or even a pre-revolutionary situation' (Carter 1982: 438).

In November 1978 a general strike began in Iran which finally pushed the Shah into appointing a Prime Minister and giving him some real power to govern. Among the first acts of Prime Minister Bakhtiar was to call for the Shah to leave the country, which after some hesitation he did. Meanwhile the followers of Ayatollah Khomeini, the religious leader who had long been in exile in Paris, mounted massive demonstrations on his behalf, and Khomeini announced his intention of returning. He arrived in Tehran on 1 February 1979. There followed several months during which the nominal head of the Iranian government continued to be Prime Minister Bazargan (Bakhtiar having been removed as unacceptable to Khomeini), while the real power resided with Khomeini.

By November 1979 the position of the Prime Minister had become untenable in the face of militant demands from Khomeini and his followers for radical Islamic revolution. Increasingly, the United States was identified as the great source of evil and of counter-revolution, a claim made more plausible to the militants by the Carter administration's decision in November 1979 to allow the Shah to enter the United States for medical treatment. It was this which precipitated the 'second' Iranian revolution, marked by the seizing of American hostages in the US Embassy in Tehran by Revolutionary Guards (Rubin 1981: Ch. 10). The year-long hostage crisis, which profoundly affected every aspect of President Carter's domestic and foreign policies, was also the time in which the Islamic revolution was carried through in Iran. This was much more than coincidence. For Khomeini the United States represented the ultimate evil, in opposition to which the Islamic revolution would receive its ultimate validation.

The Soviet Union made no secret of its welcome for the Iranian revolution, and did all it could to promote anti-American sentiment in Iran – not a difficult task, given the direction which the revolution took. Only when the Islamic revolutionaries turned on the Tudeh (Communist) Party did Moscow raise its voice in protest, but there was no inclination to make a major issue of this. On the hostage crisis, the Soviet Union supported a UN resolution condemning the seizure, but this 'legally correct position', noted Cyrus Vance, did not obsure the fact that the Soviet Union 'was clearly seeking to exploit the situation to its advantage' (Vance 1983: 380–1).

The Soviet factor in the Iranian crisis was always an important one for American policy-makers, even if it was overshadowed by the long and drawn out hostage crisis. Following the Soviet invasion of Afghanistan, the possibility of Soviet military intervention in Iran was a regular item on the Carter administration's agenda (Brzezinski 1983: 451–2). It was impossible to separate out the Iranian crisis from the general crisis in the region; even where the Soviet Union was not the direct instigator of upheaval, it could only profit from the embarrassment of American interests. As a response the Carter Doctrine was conceived as an exercise in the setting of limits, a variation of the theme of the Eisenhower Doctrine, which was itself a regional application of the Truman Doctrine.

The Arab–Israeli conflict

In the more complex and tangled Arab–Israeli dispute the United States was ultimately more successful in achieving its goal of excluding Soviet influence, though success was not immediate and there were costs involved. In the wake of Israel's crushing defeat of the Arabs in the Six Day War of 1967, the Soviet Union reassessed its position in the Middle East. The Soviets had given little concrete assistance to the Arabs during the war, and in its aftermath undertook to help Egypt rearm and provide training for Egypt's armed forces. At its height the Soviet presence in Egypt comprised close to 20,000 military advisers. The Soviet motive, it has been observed, was less to salve Arab humiliation in the 1967 war than to stake a claim as an arbiter and peace-maker in the Middle East (Steele 1985: 195). In effect, the Soviets sought a position to rival that of the United States which, under the Nixon administration, established close ties with Israel and promoted a comprehensive peace plan. Nixon in fact was intent as much on wooing Arab sentiment as in assuring Israel's security. Contrary to the conventional wisdom, the 1967 war, he said, had not been a defeat for Soviet interests. As a result of the war, 'they [the Soviets] became the Arabs' friend and the US their enemy' (Spiegel 1985: 179–80).

In the years preceeding the October (or Yom Kippur) War of 1973, through the war, and beyond, the United States held to a delicately balanced set of priorities which, in Kissinger's words, were 'to reduce Soviet influence, weaken the position of

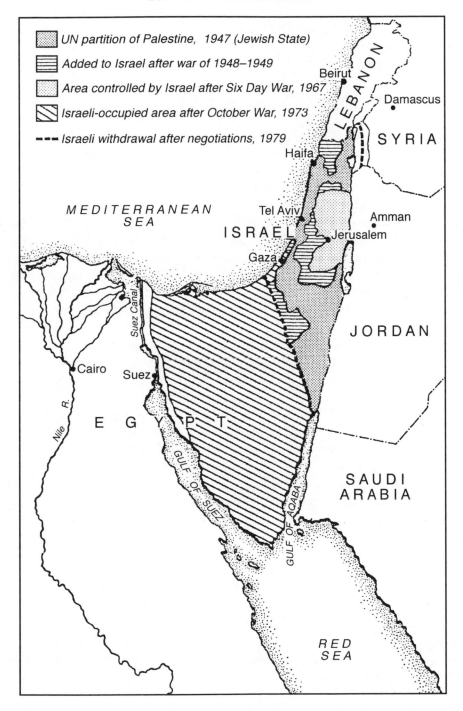

Figure 11.2 The Middle East, 1967, 1979
Source: Derived from W. LaFeber, *America, Russia, and the Cold War, 1945–1992*, New York: McGraw-Hill, 1993, p. 278.

the Arab radicals, encourage Arab moderates, and assure Israel's security' (Spiegel 1985: 172). Soviet influence in Egypt was a blow to this policy, but Soviet–Egyptian relations proved distinctly fragile, in part because the Soviet Union was unwilling to supply the types and numbers of offensive weapons the Egyptians desired to push the Israelis out of the Egyptian territories they had occupied since the 1967 war. The Egyptians were also unhappy with the Soviet Union's apparent lack of energy in pursuing Arab interests at the diplomatic level. The Soviets appeared to be more interested in colluding with the Americans at Arab expense than in promoting Arab interests. A joint American–Soviet communiqué issued at the Moscow summit of 1972 without consultation with Egypt and containing general principles for a solution to the Arab–Israeli conflict was received with anger by Egyptian President Anwar Sadat and precipitated the Egyptian decision to expel the bulk of its Soviet advisers (Garthoff 1985: 315–16).

This dramatic snub to the Soviet Union did not, however, produce a complete break in relations. Both sides had too much at stake: Egypt the need for arms to pursue the goal of retaking the Sinai peninsula, and the Soviet Union the need to maintain influence in the most populous and militarily most powerful of Israel's Arab opponents and to bid for a role as a major player in the region. Soviet arms deliveries, including anti-tank missiles, were resumed later the same year (Steele 1985: 196).

The Yom Kippur War, which began on 6 October 1973, was a crucible for contending Arab–Israeli and superpower forces in the region. Expectations based on the experience of the 1967 war – a swift Israeli victory – proved unfounded. Egyptian and Syrian armies gained the element of surprise and in the early stages of the war seemed poised to overcome the Israelis, though at great cost in men and equipment. Both superpowers experienced strong pressures to resupply their respective allies, with the Soviets responding more swiftly than the Americans. After some hesitation the United States more than matched the Soviets and one week into the war the Israelis had recouped their lost ground and begun to gain the upper hand.

There followed a feverish and complex round of consultations both between Moscow and Washington and between them and their respective allies. Both superpowers appeared intent on preventing a clear victory by either side, conscious that the chances for a settlement acceptable to all parties depended on a degree of balance between them. On 22 October the elements of a cease-fire had been agreed under UN auspices. The next few days, however, saw a deepening of the crisis rather than its resolution.

An ambiguity in Kissinger's discussions with the Israelis about the terms of the cease-fire set off a new round of fighting and a brief but inflammatory confrontation between the United States and the Soviet Union. The problem arose from the Israelis' anger that the cease-fire occurred at a time when they were poised to surround and defeat the Egyptian Third Army in the Western Sinai. Interpreting Kissinger's words that there could be some 'slippage' in the cease-fire deadline as an opportunity to consolidate their military advantage, the Israelis resumed their offensive against the Egyptian Third Army (Isaacson 1992: 527–8).

President Sadat responded with a proposal which provoked direct American–Soviet confrontation. He appealed to both the United States and the Soviet Union to send troops to the Middle East under UN auspices to oversee the cease-fire. The Americans quickly said no, but the Soviets expressed agreement with the proposal and even added the threat that they were prepared to intervene on their own in the event that the United States refused to agree to joint US–Soviet action. The prospect of a Soviet military presence in the Middle East was too much for the United States to stomach, and their response was to mount a worldwide military (including nuclear) alert, combined with placing the 82nd Airborne Division on alert for possible deployment in the region. At the same time, however, Israel was pressed to cease its operations against the Egyptians, and in communications with Moscow, Kissinger included some conciliatory gestures, among which was the suggestion that the Soviet Union be permitted to send representatives to observe the cease-fire. This combination of pressures was sufficient to defuse the crisis. On 25 October the war ended on the basis of a UN Security Council resolution which called for a cease-fire and a return to the positions of the 22nd.

On the face of it, *détente* was the loser in this sequence of events. The United States and the Soviet Union had only recently concluded agreements which enjoined both sides not to provoke crises nor to issue threats of military force. It would seem, however, that while both sides had the capacity to follow through on their threats, they were designed primarily for diplomatic effect. 'A Soviet threat', it has been said, 'had become a ritual at the end of each Arab–Israeli war', and this one, noted a former Assistant Secretary for Near Eastern Affairs, was 'relatively mild' by comparison with earlier ones. Some months after the war, Kissinger spoke of the American alert as 'our deliberate over-reaction' (Spiegel 1985: 264). In his memoirs Kissinger gave this assessment of the fate of *détente* in the war:

> Clearly, *détente* had not prevented a crisis, as some of our critics with varying degrees of disingenuousness were claiming it should have – forgetting that *détente* defined not friendship but a strategy for a relationship between adversaries. After all, a principal purpose of our own Mideast policy was to reduce the role and influence of the Soviet Union, just as the Soviets sought to reduce ours. But I believe *détente* mitigated the succession of crises that differences in ideology had made nearly inevitable; and I believe we enhanced the national interest in the process.
>
> (Kissinger 1982: 600)

There is some irony in the fact that this crisis should have given rise to attacks on *détente*, since one outcome of the war was Kissinger's success in gaining the confidence of Anwar Sadat and in virtually excluding the Soviets from any participation in the post-war negotiations.

The initial approach to a settlement was through a Geneva Conference which was held in December 1973 and attended by all the belligerents in the war (except for

Syria) plus the United States and the Soviet Union. Though the conference was notable for bringing Arab and Israeli representatives face to face for the first time, it achieved little beyond providing a forum for the public airing of differences. It was quickly overtaken by the apparently less tidy but in practice more expeditious method of shuttle diplomacy by Kissinger. Over the next two years Henry Kissinger shuttled from capital to capital in the Middle East in an effort to settle terms of military disengagement and territorial agreements between the parties in the war, including Syria. These efforts were largely successful in resolving immediate issues arising from the war, though they fell far short of a resolution of the Arab–Israeli conflict, and were criticized by some for sacrificing genuine progress for relatively easy short-term gains. This, however, is to underestimate the complexity, even intractability, of political problems in the Middle East; it is to underestimate also the skills necessary to achieve even this amount of progress. Experience would prove, under the Carter, Reagan, Bush, and Clinton presidencies, that progress in the Middle East was achievable only by piecemeal steps, even if at each stage solution of one problem revealed new ones to be dealt with.

At any rate, in this period of shuttle diplomacy, Henry Kissinger was probably at the height of his diplomatic influence and certainly his popularity. During the war itself, and until August 1974, Nixon had been preoccupied by Watergate; American Middle East policy was to a large extent in Kissinger's hands, and it continued to be during Ford's presidency. The result, writes Kissinger's most recent biographer, was to establish the United States 'as the dominant diplomatic force in the region' (Isaacson 1992: 572).

If the personal factor was important in Kissinger's diplomacy, it was no less so in the case of Carter. Carter established an unusually close relationship with Sadat. 'There was an easy and natural friendship between us from the first moment I knew Anwar Sadat', Carter recalled (Carter 1982: 284). This was not the only influence in bringing about the Camp David accords on the Middle East, but it was an important one.

Clearly, a full discussion of the Camp David agreements lies beyond the scope of this book, but the Soviet factor is of some significance in understanding the course and the outcome of the negotiations. In the first place, the Carter administration's initial proposal on the Arab–Israeli conflict called for a reconvening of the Geneva conference, which, of course, implied a role for the Soviet Union. Indeed, in October 1977 a joint US–Soviet communiqué was released which set out general principles for a Middle East settlement. Carter had done little to prepare public opinion, and the proposals immediately ran into protests from Israel and from pro-Israeli groups in the United States who objected both to the Soviet role and to the communiqué's seemingly excessive pressure on Israel to recognize Palestinian rights (Quandt 1986: 122–3).

So long as Carter stuck to the Geneva framework, stalemate seemed to be the only possible result. The log-jam was broken, not by Carter but by Sadat, who seized the initiative in November 1977 by undertaking a historic journey to Israel to meet with Prime Minister Begin. The following month Begin reciprocated with a visit to Egypt.

Ironically, it was the failure of these visits to produce the basis for agreement which 'brought the United States back to center stage in the peace process' (Spiegel 1985: 343). Both Begin and Sadat believed that progress was impossible without participation of the United States, acting not merely as mediator but as a positive factor in negotiations. The result, after eight months of intense diplomacy, which culminated in the meeting of Begin, Sadat, and Carter at Camp David in September 1978, was a two-part agreement. The first established a framework for a 'comprehensive and durable settlement of the Middle East conflict', including a 'basis for peace not only between Egypt and Israel, but also between Israel and each of its neighbours which is prepared to negotiate peace with Israel on this basis'. Provisions for self-government of the West Bank and the Gaza Strip were included, as was recognition of the 'legitimate rights of the Palestinian people and their just requirements'. The second part of the agreement provided the framework for a peace treaty between Egypt and Israel (Quandt 1986: 377, Appendix G).

In practice, only the second part of the Camp David agreement was realized. The Egypt–Israeli peace treaty was signed in March of the following year. Neither Carter nor Sadat had wished for a separate peace between Egypt and Israel, not least because it would alienate the rest of the Arab world, but that is in effect what they got. 'Once Egypt and Israel were at peace', writes William Quandt, who was both a participant in the Camp David process and its leading historian, 'Begin had few remaining incentives to deal constructively with the Palestinian question' (Quandt 1986: 323). In short, the Camp David agreement split the Arab world and left the Palestinian question not only unresolved but further inflamed.

Camp David also finalized the divorce between Egypt and the Soviet Union. In his otherwise even-tempered memoirs, Andrei Gromyko reserves his store of passion and contempt for Anwar Sadat who, having 'betrayed the interests of the Palestinians and all Arabs, went on to put Egyptian territory at the disposal of the USA'. His 'political bankruptcy was total . . . He had an extraordinary ability to distort the facts . . . All his life he had suffered from megalomania, but this acquired pathological proportions when he became President' (Gromyko 1989: 272–3). In the wake of Camp David and into the 1980s, with the Arab world split and Palestinian Liberation Organization (PLO) militancy on the rise, the Soviet Union would seek to exploit the unresolved Palestinian issue to its own advantage.

Crises in Cuba and Nicaragua

As we have seen, 1979 was a year of alarms for the United States. Afghanistan and Iran focused American anxiety sharply on the Middle East, but Central America too concentrated American minds on the Soviet threat. Two crises, one short lived and the other having major repercussions during the Reagan administration, erupted during 1979.

The first was prompted by the 'discovery' of an allegedly combat-ready Soviet brigade (numbering between 2,500 and 3,000 troops) in Cuba. The crisis was precipitated at the beginning of September by a statement by Senator Frank Church, Chairman of the Senate Foreign Relations Committee, who was acting on the basis of a State Department briefing. The State Department had in fact observed some expansion of the military presence in Cuba, including what it took to be a recently installed Soviet brigade, but Church jumped the gun by taking the issue into the public arena before the Department had prepared a response. The result, recalled Brzezinski, was 'disastrous' (Brzezinski 1983: 347). During the next month the scare filled the headlines and air-waves in Washington. It subsided only when President Carter announced that he had received assurances from the Soviet Union that the brigade was a 'training unit' and that there was no intention to enlarge it or increase its capabilities. The United States would take measures to increase its military readiness and would maintain special vigilance with regard to Cuba, but there was no need, the President said, 'for a return to the Cold War' (Brzezinski 1983: 351).

In truth, the Soviet brigade had been in Cuba since 1962, a fact which was confirmed by investigation of the intelligence record during the month of September (Carter 1982: 264; Vance 1983: 362–3). Domestic political considerations drove the crisis forward. Senator Church, a liberal with a dovish record on foreign policy, was evidently concerned to improve his chances for re-election in 1980 by gaining some credibility with the Right in the highly charged and increasingly conservative climate of the late 1970s. Opponents of *détente* and of the ratification of SALT II could be expected to, and did, make a meal of the crisis. It became simply one more item in the debit column of *détente*.

The Nicaraguan revolution, which had been achieved earlier in the same year, received less public attention (and much less space in the memoirs of the Carter administration) than the Cuban crisis but was of greater long-term significance. The revolution in Nicaragua became for Reagan what the Cuban revolution of 1959 became for Kennedy: a cancer in the body politic of the Western Hemisphere. Initially, however, the overthrow of the forty-year dictatorship of the Somoza family found the American administration intent on living with the new government. Nor did the Nicaraguan government, which initially included conservatives as well as a core of avowedly Marxist-Leninist Sandinistas, want to repeat the experience of Cuba and find itself pushed into dependence on the Soviet Union. The Carter administration promptly sent $20 million in aid to the new government, and American businessmen were welcomed in Nicaragua (LaFeber 1993b: 237–8, 239).

However, a seemingly inexorable process of alienation between the United States and Nicaragua had set in by the second half of 1980. The parallels with Cuba from 1959–61 are close. Several sets of forces were at work: consolidation of the revolution in a leftward direction combined with fears of a counter-revolution by Somoza forces, economic collapse, and growing pressure from the United States. Regarding the first of these, announcement of a postponement of the promised elections until 1985 and the defection of moderates from the ruling junta sent warning signals to the

Americans. Equally ominous from the American point of view was the building of a Sandinista army and Sandinista support for the left-wing insurgent movement in El Salvador. Regarding Nicaragua's economic problems, the United States Congress spent eight months debating an aid bill which in any case contained many conditions objectionable to the Nicaraguans. In the meantime, the Nicaraguans established relations with the Soviet Union and gained a highly favourable trade and aid agreement (LaFeber 1993b: 239–40).

By the time of the American presidential election in November 1980, though the lines between the United States and Nicaragua were hardening, there was still some room for movement. This would quickly disappear, as we shall see in the following chapter.

The litany of crises during 1979 described above could hardly have come at a worse time for President Carter. They ensured that the election of 1980 would be to a large degree a referendum on his foreign policy record. The continuing agony of the hostage crisis kept Carter in a political strait-jacket; the failed rescue mission in April 1980, which cost the lives of eight American servicemen, only increased the sense of a paralysed presidency. The Right blamed Carter for the loss of Nicaragua; and even the Panama Canal Treaties, regarded by many as one of Carter's clear foreign policy successes, were seized on by his Republican opponents as a retreat from America's traditional and rightful role in the region. (The treaties provided for the return of the canal zone to Panamanian sovereignty by the year 2000, accompanied by safeguards for the canal's neutrality and for United States security interests.) As we have already seen, Afghanistan dramatically confirmed the views of *détente*-sceptics in the United States and killed SALT II ratification. If, however, we take a more detached view, there are more shades of grey than the above election-driven picture would suggest.

Putting it schematically, the superpower balance sheet in the Third World looked something like this: in the Arab–Israeli dispute the United States was largely successful in denying Soviet influence, though this did not mean a free ride for the United States. There were too many unsolved and seemingly insoluble problems for this to be the case, the Palestinian issue being the most obvious. Iran could be counted as a clear loss for the United States, but Islamic fundamentalism cut across the dividing lines of the cold war, and, except in the short-term, the American embarrassment in Iran produced few benefits for the Soviet Union. In Angola and the Horn of Africa Soviet–Cuban intervention was unencumbered by corresponding American activity, largely because the American will to become involved so soon after Vietnam was absent. The Soviet Union, however, reaped few tangible rewards from its presence in these countries and nor, it should be said, did the Angolans or the Ethiopians. Soviet arms transfers, the Soviet Union's main export to these nations, did little for political or economic stability. They served only to prop up shaky regimes and to postpone treatment of fundamental problems. These surfaced with a vengeance once the cold war ended and the Soviet Union swiftly withdrew, leaving these countries to their own devices. The same happened when the United States abandoned Somalia, as we shall see in Chapter 13.

In Central America, while American policy was once again hobbled by the fall-out from Vietnam, the Soviet Union was cautious about taking provocative action in support of the Sandinistas and the insurgents in El Salvador. In Southeast Asia the United States was effectively out of the picture, but the Soviet Union's ally, Vietnam, soon became embroiled in conflict with Cambodia, as we saw in Chapter 10. Behind Cambodia stood China which, as it drew closer to the United States, became an ever-greater threat to the Soviet Union.

Admittedly, not all the consequences mentioned here were visible at the beginning of the 1980s. However, the Third World was already enough of a patchwork of competing political forces to cast doubt on the idea that US–Soviet competition could be described as a simple zero sum game.

CONCLUSION

This chapter began with the suggestion that to label *détente* a failure was to over-simplify a complex pattern of events. *Détente* evidently had limits, and these were defined broadly by what each superpower considered to be its vital interests. There was no real dispute about the status of their primary mutual interest in arms control, and in essentials that survived in practice despite the rhetorical retreat after 1979. European *détente*, as we have seen, diverged from superpower *détente* as the decade of the 1970s progressed. *Détente* was most at risk in those policy areas – pre-eminently in the Third World – where mutuality of interest had rarely if ever existed, where individual superpower interests were less clearly defined, their likely responses less predictable, and their capacity for control less secure. In the view of one American official who was an assistant to Henry Kissinger in the National Security Council, given the mounting obstacles to *détente*, 'it is surprising how much survived' of the Kissinger–Nixon design (Hyland 1988: 12). In the following chapter we shall examine this judgement.

Part V

COLD WAR VERSUS INTERNATIONAL POLITICS: THE DENOUEMENT, 1981–1991

INTRODUCTION

The final phase of the cold war presents a distinct challenge to the historian. Intensification of cold war antagonism in the early 1980s was succeeded at the end of the decade by the disintegration of the cold war system itself. Moreover, it occurred in the very way which policy-makers such as George Kennan had hoped for when they contemplated the clouded future in the late 1940s – as a result of the collapse of Soviet power. Was this to be regarded as a vindication of containment in general and of President Reagan's hardline cold war policies in particular? Or was the Soviet collapse a result of internal decay, developments in Eastern Europe, the specific policies of Mikhail Gorbachev, or perhaps a combination of all these?

Chapter 13 addresses these issues in detail. For the moment we must draw together some of the threads from previous chapters and indicate the broad patterns they assumed in the 1980s. A recurring theme of the earlier chapters has been the growing gap between the preoccupations of the superpowers, especially their preoccupation with each other, and the changing realities of world politics. To an increasing extent cold war politics, with its emphasis on military rivalry and ideological antagonism, its bipolarism and spheres of influence, and with its tendency to translate all the world's conflicts and problems into the terms of the cold war, was out of keeping with new forces in world politics. The leaderships of the superpowers at various times acknowledged, for example, that the intensity of East–West rivalry hindered the development of serious plans to deal with North–South issues. *Détente* had represented a partial recognition that the cold war had outlived its usefulness; both sides claimed to be concerned with adapting themselves to a more complex international environment as well as with reducing the dangers in their relationship with each other. In the event, despite some advances in the latter priority, they were unable to break the cold war mould.

The 1980s was a remarkable decade for many reasons, but not least among them was that by its end governments could no longer postpone acknowledgement of that more complex international environment. That it took an intensification of cold war to make this plain may have been no accident. President Reagan's revival of the cold war clearly played some part in the demise of Soviet communism, but it also involved costs to the United States. Among these were the enormous budget deficits which Reagan bequeathed to his successors, but more generally an economy which was more vulnerable to external pressures than the one he inherited. By the end of Reagan's second administration the United States had become a net debtor. In short, Reagan's prosecution of the 'new' or 'second' cold war hastened consciousness of, and indeed the reality of 'interdependence'.

Politicians and theorists of international relations had been talking about interdependence for some years. By this they meant a relative decline in the autonomy of the nation-state and a relative increase in the significance of processes which were transnational in nature. Henry Kissinger drew attention to them in a speech given in 1975:

> Progress in dealing with the traditional agenda is no longer enough. A new and unprecedented kind of issue has emerged. The problems of energy, resources, environment, population, the uses of space and the seas now rank with questions of military security, ideology, and territorial rivalry which have traditionally made up the diplomatic agenda.
>
> (Keohane and Nye 1977: 26)

In a world increasingly divided into economic blocs, in which vast amounts of currency and capital were shifted daily across national boundaries, in which the resources of the largest multinational companies exceeded those of most of the world's nation-states, in which environmental damage (acid rain, fall-out from nuclear accidents, dumping of sewage and waste into rivers, seas, and oceans) recognized no national frontiers, and in which growing numbers of refugees from war, famine or oppression sought new lives in new countries – in such a world (and this is to mention only a few of the items on the new agenda) it was increasingly difficult to conceive of the nation-state as being able to supply solutions to a growing array of problems.

Of course a measure of interdependence had always been a fact of international life; nor should we think now that nation-states are of no account. At some point, however, in the middle of the post-war period observers became conscious of a qualitative change in the climate of international politics, which they gave the label interdependence. Perhaps it would be more accurate to say that *American* observers became conscious of interdependence. Indeed, not only was the bulk of the theoretical literature of American origin, it arguably reflected the growing awareness of limits to American power, above all economic power. Other nations understood interdependence, defined as relationships which 'will always involve costs' and which 'restrict autonomy', as a fact of life (Keohane and Nye 1977: 9). For the United States, however, in the wake of the vulnerability of the dollar in the late 1960s and early 1970s, the political and economic costs of the Vietam War, and the oil shock of 1973–74, there was unwelcome novelty in the consciousness that she was, as the title of a book of the period went, merely an 'ordinary country' (Rosencrance, 1976).

As is frequently the case, changes in the world of reality provoked theoretical reflections which went far beyond the circumstances which gave rise to them. Among the central insights of the new theory was the distinction it drew between economic and military power. Indeed, an important contribution of the theorists of transnationalism or 'complex interdependence' lay in their redefinition of power itself.

In traditional or so-called 'Realist' accounts of international relations the world was composed of more or less autonomous nation-states; relations between them took the form of struggles for power in which the decisive, though not the only, instrument of power was military strength. Such a model, however, made it difficult to explain, for example, the international importance of Japan and Germany, whose power was based on economic rather than military might. Japanese penetration of the American automobile and electronic goods markets was in its own way as threatening as Soviet military power. Nuclear weapons could provide no security against such threats. Nor could the realist model easily make sense of the growing importance of 'trans-governmental' organizations, or international 'regimes', such as the Organization of Petroleum Exporting Countries (OPEC), the Organization for Economic Cooperation and Development (OECD), the General Agreement on Trade and Tariffs (GATT), and the European Community (EC), to say nothing of more diffuse processes of economic and financial interpenetration. Finally, the phenomenon of interdependence undercut the Realist assumption of a clear distinction between foreign and domestic policy. In the words of the leading interdependence theorists, in the politics of interdependence 'domestic and foreign policy become closely linked. The notion of national interest – the traditionalists' lodestar – becomes increasingly difficult to use effectively' (Keohane and Nye 1977: 8).

It would be a mistake to think that the theory and the practice of interdependence simply replaced traditional or Realist theories and practices. Military power, for example, continued to be decisive in certain situations. The nation-state remained the key international unit for many purposes and, as has frequently been pointed out, nationalism was and is a 'persisting phenomenon' (Holsti 1988: 228). 'Sometimes', Keohane and Nye stress, 'realist assumptions will be accurate, or largely accurate, but frequently complex interdependence will provide a better portrayal of reality.' It depends on the situation (Keohane and Nye 1977: 24). In an increasing number of situations, however, the model of complex interdependence fitted reality better than the realist model.

If this issue were of merely theoretical importance, there would be no reason to invoke it in a historical examination of international relations in the Reagan years. The reason for doing so is that it helps to make sense in broad terms of the main thrust of Reagan's foreign policy. Briefly stated, Reagan operated with a model of international affairs which was much closer to the traditionalist approach than to the ideas of complex interdependence. His approach was broadly nationalist and unilateralist, it relied heavily on a military definition of power, and it was extremely suspicious of international organizations. Reagan's foreign policy was a conscious attempt to resurrect a pre-*détente* conception of the Soviet Union and of world politics. In practice, however, by the middle of the decade he had been forced into various compromises, in part because his policies came up against the realities of interdependence. There was no Reagan conversion to a concept of interdependence, least of all in the economic sphere, but there was a coming to terms with certain realities. The end of the cold war brought those realities sharply into focus. Clearly this did not mean the end of military power as a decisive instrument of America's or any other nation's foreign policy. The Gulf War of 1991 stood as a clear example of its continuing relevance in certain situations. What it did mean was that the military definition of reality which had been so central to the dynamics of the cold war underwent a transformation. To put it another way, national security could no longer be defined in exclusively military terms.

In the chapters that follow, then, the final phase of the cold war is seen not simply as a seismic shift in US–Soviet relations, but as a transitional period in global politics. The concluding chapter offers some inevitably provisional and tentative ideas about the directions these changes might be taking.

12

REAGANISM AND THE SPECTRE OF COMMUNISM

TRANSITIONS OF POWER

For Ronald Reagan little had changed in thirty years, as far as the Soviet threat was concerned. The Ronald Reagan who had testified as a friendly witness before the House Un-American Activities Committee (HUAC) in the late 1940s and the Ronald Reagan who assumed the presidency in 1981 both saw in the Soviet Union an unrelentingly aggressive and malign presence on the international scene. What was remarkable about his attitude in the 1980s was not his anti-Sovietism but the intensity of his anti-communism. His was a visceral and profoundly ideological opposition to communism. He could not accept the notion that the Soviet Union was a very large and dangerous but in all essentials ordinary nation-state. In this respect he was out of step with the dominant pragmatism of American leadership circles, whether conservatives or liberals, no less than the bulk of academic experts since the mid-1960s. Even Jimmy Carter, who was an idealist in his own way, took a pragmatic line when it came to seeking agreements with the Soviet Union. And when he was in the idealistic vein, his liberal universalism had little in common with Reagan's fighting conservative faith. This emerged clearly in their attitudes towards human rights. Carter announced a single standard which applied in principle to friends and enemies alike. Reagan was frankly disinclined to place pressure on friendly nations whatever the character of the governments or their records on human rights (Dallin and Lapidus 1987: 222). Reagan was, in short, the most unashamedly ideological of post-war presidents.

Armed with this basic philosophy, Reagan came into office with two firm convictions: firstly, that *détente*, particularly under Carter, had been a sorry tale of US surrender to Soviet pressure, and secondly, that the Soviet threat was global. These convictions recalled John Foster Dulles's attacks during the early 1950s on containment for its supposed negativism and also his strident dismissal of the notion that it was possible for any nation to be neutral in the cold war. For both Dulles and Reagan, at least in their most militant public statements, the communist threat was indivisible.

305

There were other connections between Reaganism and the Republican critique of the Democratic record in foreign policy in the early cold war. Most striking of these was the revival of the Yalta issue, occasioned by the fortieth anniversary of the Yalta Conference in February 1985. The 'betrayal' of Eastern Europe at Yalta had been one of the main charges brought by Republicans against the Democrats in the election of 1952. As noted in Chapter 6, in the first month of the Eisenhower administration Republicans in Congress had put forward a 'Captive Peoples Resolution' with the aim of forcing upon the new administration a commitment to undoing Yalta and the subsequent domination of Eastern Europe by the Soviet Union. The resolution had been withdrawn after the death of Stalin in March 1953, but the issue continued to rankle with conservatives, and Reagan's election fostered a climate which was receptive to a reconsideration of Yalta. During 1985 and 1986 a furious debate raged between conservative and liberal scholars in the pages of *Commentary* and the *New York Review of Books* (Kuniholm 1987: 55–7).

There was, of course, no more likelihood in the 1980s than there had been in the 1950s that an American administration would risk war to displace the Soviet Union from Eastern Europe. However, on the fortieth anniversary of Yalta President Reagan did express the view that 'the reason Yalta remains important is that the freedom of Europe is unfinished business'. The issue, he said, was not territory or boundaries but democracy and independence: 'there is one boundary which Yalta symbolizes that can never be made legitimate, and that is the dividing line between freedom and repression. I do not hesitate to say that we wish to undo this boundary' (Reagan 1987, I: 119).

Evidently more than history was at stake in Reagan's mind and in the recondite and often venomous exchanges on Yalta among intellectuals. At stake were the foundations of American foreign policy in the present. The deepest difference between Reaganism in its most ideological form and pragmatism, whether liberal or conservative, was that the Reaganites believed that things could have been otherwise at Yalta and could yet be otherwise in the present. That did not mean risking nuclear war to liberate Eastern Europe but it did mean pursuing active, even aggressive, policies with a view to producing changes in Soviet behaviour.

Within the above basic framework, Reaganism in foreign policy rested heavily on the single theme of restoration of the United States' economic and military strength. The figures for growth in military expenditure are striking. Carter's last defence budget proposed $171.4 billion in military spending, while Reagan's last budget request (presented in January 1989 for fiscal year 1990) was in excess of $300 billion. The figures for 'real growth' in expenditure (i.e.: taking into account inflation) are if anything more revealing. Though clearly a trend towards higher expenditure had begun under Carter – real growth for the years 1979–81 was 4.0 per cent, 3.1 per cent and 4.8 per cent respectively – under Reagan real annual growth for the four budgets of his first term 7.8 per cent, 7.3 per cent, 4.2 per cent, and 9.5 per cent. The trend continued during his second term. A similar story is told by the figures for defence spending as a percentage of gross national product (GNP) (Smith 1990: 63–4).

Associated with these rises and the increase of military 'forces in being' was a predisposition to contemplate their use. In principle at least, interventionism and unilateralism characterized the Reagan approach to foreign affairs. And yet there was no automatic translation of the above principles into practice. The distinction Reagan drew between the territorial and ideological significance of Yalta was of a piece with his general foreign policy stance: a strong ideological position would be staked out but would often be combined with a realistic sense of the limits to which it could be pushed. 'Speak loudly *and* carry a big stick', might have been his motto; that way you might not have to use the stick. The interventions undertaken by the Reagan administration – the sending of troops to Beirut in 1982, to Grenada in 1983, and the bombing of Libya in 1986 – were all highly restricted in scope and duration. Each of them involved costs, in lives in the case of the first two and in political credibility in various quarters in all three cases, but there were few damaging repercussions at home, even in Beirut where more than two hundred marines were killed by a terrorist bomb.

Despite its rhetoric, the Reagan administration proved to be cautious about adopting exposed positions which would involve long-term or open-ended commitments. This was a product in part of restraints imposed by Congress; in part it arose from the administration's own sensitivity to the American public's low tolerance for failure, especially in the case of operations which were drawn out over a long period. This meant a resort to secrecy and deviousness when the administration felt that it could not compromise on a high priority commitment such as support for the Contras in Nicaragua.

On the central issue of relations with the Soviet Union the Reagan administration also proved more flexible than its rhetoric suggested. The new *détente* of the second half of the 1980s, which led to the signing of the INF Treaty and prepared the ground for a Strategic Arms Reduction Treaty (START), is covered in the following chapter, but it is worth observing here that the Reagan administration's move towards arms control predated the advent of Mikhail Gorbachev to the leadership of the Soviet Union. That these moves should have been accompanied by firmness, and even intransigence, in other areas of defence policy – the president's refusal to compromise on SDI being the best example – was part and parcel of the administration's overall approach: negotiate, if at all, from a position of strength.

The tension which existed in the Reagan administration's foreign policy between ideological commitment and a sense of what was practicable was well reflected in the mix of ideologues and pragmatists who comprised the Reagan team. Among the ideologues were Caspar Weinberger, Secretary of Defense, Richard Pipes, adviser on Soviet affairs, and Richard Perle, Assistant Secretary of Defense. All played important roles in setting the tone of the administration's position on arms control and relations with the Soviet Union. Their influence waned, however, as the decade wore on. Pipes left after only two years, and Weinberger resigned in 1987, just prior to the signing of the INF Treaty. The appointment of George Shultz as Secretary of State in 1982 to replace the abrasive Alexander Haig brought a tough-minded moderate conservative into the top foreign policy-making position and also helped to ballast an administration which often gave an impression of unsteadiness.

The final qualification to be made about the picture of Reagan's foreign policy which one gains from his most ideologically charged statements is that for Reagan foreign policy was, at least initially, a secondary concern. During his first year in office, Reagan made no major speeches on foreign policy. His chief priority was domestic policy and above all rebuilding the economy. Of course, economic restoration had important foreign policy implications. America's economic malaise in the 1970s had been, he was convinced, a cause of the loss of America's power and international influence. 'The most important contribution any country can make to world development', Reagan declared in 1981, 'is to pursue sound economic policies at home' (Cohen 1987: 127). The primacy of domestic concerns, however, made for a foreign policy which was nationalist rather than internationalist, unilateral rather than multilateral in character.

It was to be expected that Soviet leaders would show an intense interest in the newly elected president. Carter had been a severe disappointment to them. 'We discovered quickly', recalled Andre Gromyko, 'that he had difficulty in grasping even the most elementary basic features of the US–Soviet relationship' (Gromyko 1989: 288). There was some expectation that Reagan might prove a distinct improvement. The Soviet leadership had generally preferred Republicans over Democrats, both because there was no ambiguity about where they stood ideologically and because they had proved more able than Democrats to deliver arms agreements. 'To put it simply', observed one Soviet specialist, 'the hope of the Soviet leaders was to see another Richard Nixon in the White House' (Bialer 1986: 319). Instead, what they got, as Gromyko put it, was a government 'which did everything it could to undo the work of its predecessors, striking blows at one agreement after another' (Gromyko 1989: 296).

There is no telling how different the future might have been had not Brezhnev died in November 1982 and had not two successors, Yuri Andropov and Konstantin Chernenko, also died after brief periods in office: Andropov in February 1984 and Chernenko in March 1985. It is possible that the reckoning with the Soviet Union's troubled present and past, which Gorbachev's coming to power provoked, would simply have been postponed by a few years. In any event, the most intense period of Reagan's foreign policy offensive (1982–84) coincided with the problems of the post-Brezhnev transition in the Soviet Union. As noted in the previous chapter, this was a reversal of the situation of the 1970s, when the United States experienced uncertainty at the top and the Soviet leadership seemed stable and confident.

It is easier to state that such a situation existed than to know precisely what to make of it. Certainly the leadership transition in the Soviet Union always involved considerable upheaval in the Party and government structures. Being appointed General

Secretary of the Communist Party was only the beginning of a process of consolidating power within the government apparatus. A new leader must establish personal control of key offices, like-minded figures had to be brought into strategic positions, powerful constituencies had to be satisfied, and rivals had to be neutralized or placated. The leadership succession in the Soviet Union, which after all was a relatively rare occurrence, was characterized by uncertainty and unpredictability (Bialer 1986: 82–4).

However, all the initial signs were that Andropov would be successful in stamping his own imprint on the Soviet system. He entered office with a reputation as a tough-minded Party professional who had extensive experience of Soviet politics and of relations with the Eastern European nations acquired during his post as head of the KGB. But he was also considered relatively modern in his thinking and sympathetic to reform. He showed himself ready to address problems of economic stagnation, corruption among political and economic elites, and signs of social decay such as alcoholism, which had been topics of growing discussion among academics during the 1970s. Andropov also responded to the interests of the sizeable and increasingly influential cohort of officials in their middle years whose path to top positions was blocked by figures who were in their seventies. As one Western scholar noted in 1980, this situation existed in the foreign policy establishment no less than in other areas. Given the advanced age of leading policy-makers, it was likely, he noted, that 'by the early 1980s the top Soviet foreign policy elite will have undergone a near-complete transformation' (Hough 1980: 126–7). Hough proved to be substantially right. Andropov was sensitive to the political problems caused by the ageing elite's hold on power, even if he did not have the time to remove it completely. In short, the initial prospect of the Andropov leadership, so far as American observers were concerned, was that it might well serve to strengthen rather than weaken the Soviet Union (Bialer 1986: 84–97).

In the summer of 1983, however, Andropov suffered a heart attack and early the following year he died. His replacement, Chernenko, was a throw-back to the Brezhnev era. He was over seventy and already ill. Why was Chernenko chosen over a younger candidate such as Mikhail Gorbachev? One suggestion is that, given the alternative between the relatively youthful and inexperienced Gorbachev (who had become a member of the Politburo as recently as 1978) and the known quantity of Chernenko, the still-dominant old guard in the Politburo was inclined to play safe. Moreover, as a colourless and formerly loyal lieutenant of Brezhnev, Chernenko would prove compliant to the old guard's wishes. 'The selection of Chernenko', writes Bialer, 'was the "last hurrah" of the old generation' (Bialer 1986: 101–2, 103).

Clearly, Andropov had had insufficient time to break the mould of the politics of the Brezhnev period completely; equally clearly, though, Chernenko's tenure of office was likely to be short, which meant that the question of who would emerge as second in command in the Politburo, and hence his likely successor, would loom large. In his biography of Gorbachev, Zhores Medvedev suggests that the long delay in announcing Chernenko's appointment was due, not to disputes about who should succeed

Andropov but about the direction of policy, and specifically about whether Andropov's policies of reform should be continued. It is likely, Medvedev suggests, that 'people like Ustinov, Gromyko, and Gorbachev agreed to Chernenko's succession only on condition that he did not have a free hand in rehabilitating Brezhnev and possibly turning Andropov into a non-person in revenge' (Medvedev 1988: 138). From this viewpoint, then, Chernenko's success was a highly qualified one; it was no simple victory for the old guard. In the year during which Chernenko held office, Gorbachev acted in effect as Chernenko's deputy, presiding over some Politburo meetings and making important visits overseas, for example, to Britain in December 1984. 'I like Mr Gorbachev,' said Mrs Thatcher; 'we can do business together' (Roxburgh 1991: 22). The British Prime Minister's statement was testimony to the fact that Gorbachev was possibly the first post-war Soviet statesman who appeared to Westerners to be like them. It did wonders for his reputation abroad and initially did him no harm at home. At any rate, with Gorbachev's coming to power, the search for stability in the Soviet leadership seemed to be over.

From the standpoint of American policy-makers, the changing of the guard in the Soviet Union was less significant than the fact that, until Gorbachev arrived, there was substantial continuity in Soviet foreign policy. Even Gorbachev, as we shall see in the next chapter, did not embark immediately on radical changes. What did become apparent during this period of transition in the Soviet leadership, however, was a growing preoccupation within the Soviet Union and among foreign observers with the dismal economic and social legacy of the Brezhnev years. Before looking at Reaganism and US–Soviet relations, we must assess the overall economic position of both powers in the early 1980s. Communism was indeed increasingly a 'spectre', though not in the sense Marx and Engels had in mind when they opened the *Communist Manifesto* with the words: 'a spectre is haunting Europe, the spectre of communism'. Rather than a revolutionary spirit about to be made flesh, communism was increasingly a shadow without substance.

THE ECONOMICS OF SUPERPOWER STATUS REVISITED

Chapter 6 began with an assessment of the economic conditions and relative positions of the superpowers. In that discussion of the 1950s and early 1960s it was suggested that, despite the vast superiority of the United States in absolute terms, Soviet claims to be closing the gap on the United States gained some credence in the West. By the early 1980s there was no mistaking the fact that the Soviet economy was in serious difficulties across all sectors. In his first speech as Brezhnev's successor, Andropov acknowledged that 'there are many problems in our national economy that are overdue for solution. I do not have ready recipes for their solution. But it is for all of us – the Central Committee of the Party – to find answers for them' (Edmonds 1983: 216). Perhaps more revealing are remarks Andropov is reported to have made to a visiting Polish delegation to Moscow in August 1982: 'the Soviet economy is not in much better shape than that of Poland . . . The Soviet Union faces a serious and increasing problem with [our] youth, who are becoming apolitical, pacifistic, and interested only in themselves' (Shultz 1993: 124).

Virtually all economic indicators told a story of sluggishness and inefficiency. Rate of growth in GNP fell sharply in the second half of the 1970s. The 2.7 per cent rise for this period compares with 5.2 per cent for 1966–70. Industrial production, investment, productivity, and consumption all showed declining rates of growth and in some cases negative or near negative growth. Even oil production, a priceless asset which had been a vital factor in sustaining growth in the post-war period, was levelling off in the late 1970s. Only natural gas production showed significant rises, which served to offset the falling off of oil production (Dibb 1988: 72–3, 77, 79).

In agriculture, a perennial problem sector, continued slow growth was accompanied by four years of drought and poor harvests from 1979–82. Hence the importance to the Soviet Union of grain imports from the United States and Canada and also the significance of Carter's grain embargo following the Soviet invasion of Afghanistan. (The embargo was lifted, ironically, by Reagan, a point to which we shall return.) It is also worth noting that these years of agricultural decline coincided with Mikhail Gorbachev's responsibility for agriculture as a recently appointed member of the Politburo. It says something for his political skill and also for the workings of fate that he managed to avoid being blamed for the disaster in agriculture. Fate stepped in in the form of Brezhnev's death in November 1982, which was also the worst year in agriculture in a run of bad years. In the circumstances, writes Medvedev, 'it became more natural to make the deceased responsible for the agricultural and economic failures than to blame those who were alive and well' (Medvedev 1988: 118).

Quantitative data tells only part of the story. As important for the future prospects of the Soviet economy was the slow rate of modernization of equipment in old industries such as steel and the slow introduction of new products and processes such as computers and modern information systems. It is estimated that in the early 1980s the United States held a twenty-five to one lead over the Soviet Union in the use of computers (Bialer 1986: 77). For political as much as technological reasons the distribution of computers and even photo-copiers was strictly limited in the Soviet Union. The result was a failure to keep pace with the West during the key years in which the computer revolution swept the industrialized countries.

Living standards and 'quality of life' issues showed similarly dismal profiles. As already mentioned, the rate of growth in consumption of goods slowed sharply in 1981–82 to near zero, and the quality of those goods remained low. Equally striking was the deterioration in provision of health care, coupled with a rise in infant mortality and a fall in life expectancy from the early 1970s onwards (Nye 1990: 124). An additional burden was military spending, which grew from an estimated 10–12 per cent of GNP in the early 1960s to 13–14 per cent in the mid-1980s or even, according to some estimates, 18 per cent (Dibb 1988: 84).

The overall picture is of an economic and social system which, if not in immediate crisis, suffered from serious systemic flaws. Many of these were of long-standing and had been built into the Soviet system from the beginning. (These systemic issues are dealt with in the following chapter in connection with Gorbachev's reforms.) Indeed that was one reason for the extreme difficulty of addressing them. The Soviet economy had performed some functions very well if one considered the post-war period as a whole. Not only had the nation recovered from the massive destructive effects of the Second World War, but general living standards had been raised to a level unthinkable in the pre-war years. Heavy industrial production in many respects had been a success story, even if the consumer goods sector and agriculture remained underdeveloped. The difference in the early 1980s was that there was a growing recognition of slowing momentum in absolute terms but also, crucially, relative to the Western industrialized nations, above all in those fields which were at the cutting edge of the post-industrial economy – computers and information systems. No one would dare claim in 1980 what Khrushchev had claimed in 1960: that within a decade the Soviet Union would match and even overtake the United States.

Given this state of affairs, it may seem surprising that American leaders persisted in their conviction of Soviet strength. There were three reasons for this. Firstly, the Soviet Union continued to show, as it had done since the war against Hitler, that it was prepared to make sacrifices to ensure national security. When American military planners assessed Soviet military capability they based their judgements on numbers of missiles, tanks, and submarines, not on the quality of shoes, infant mortality rates, or the length of queues for staple foods. During the 1970s and well into the 1980s Soviet arms continued to increase in number and quality, as American Secretary of Defense Caspar Weinberger noted with concern in his introduction to his department's annual review of *Soviet Military Power* in 1987. Not only, he observed, had the USSR 'long followed the Leninist maxim that quantity has a quality of its own', but 'each year . . . we confront a more technologically advanced Soviet Union, which has been aided by theft and legal acquisition of Western technology and growing sophistication of the USSR's own scientific knowledge' (Weinberger 1987: 3).

Secondly, and not unrelated to the first point, for all its systemic flaws, the Soviet system had survived for decades without collapsing. The Brezhnev period in particular had seemed a model of stability; indeed, it has been pointed out, 'this period of eighteen years was one of the most stable in Russian history and certainly the most stable in Soviet history' (Edmonds 1983: 214). This in part, no doubt, accounts for the failure of Western Sovietologists to foresee the collapse of the Soviet system. The rigidity of Soviet political structures did not appear to render them vulnerable to popular discontent. On the contrary, the nation appeared to operate with a high level of social discipline and cohesion. Individual dissidents received a great deal of attention in the West, but their protests seemed marginal to the life of the ordinary Soviet citizen, and indeed it was the Soviet leadership's intention to ensure that this remained so. When individual cases of dissidence threatened to become an international embarrassment, as most notoriously with Solzhenitsyn, the Soviet leaders simply exported the problem by deporting him. A government which was capable of such brazen acts did not look to be in serious trouble.

The third reason for the United States' continued anxiety about Soviet strength arose from worries about America's own economic position. In the 1980s the theme of American decline became front page news. Particular attention was focused on the publication of Paul Kennedy's *The Rise and Fall of the Great Powers*, though the theme had become a matter of public debate from the late 1970s. Kennedy's message gained its force not only from the comprehensiveness with which he treated the subject but from the fortuitous occurrence of a crash on the American stock market in autumn 1987. His book was not in fact primarily an analysis of the United States, but a large-scale historical study of the rise and fall of modern empires since the Renaissance. However, it was the last twenty pages or so of the total five hundred and fifty which aroused most interest and controversy. This last section, entitled 'The United States: the Problem of Number One in Relative Decline', assessed the present conditions and likely prospects of the United States within the framework of the basic thesis of the book: namely, that the history of the rise and fall of empires demonstrated a close relationship between economic strength and military power, that there was a consistent tendency for large powers to overextend themselves militarily in an effort to protect and expand their interests, and that the diversion of resources from wealth creation to military purposes 'was likely to lead to a weakening of national power over the longer term'. The dilemma of 'imperial overstretch' became 'acute if the nation concerned [had] entered a period of relative economic decline' (Kennedy 1988: xvi). Such was the case with the United States. The implication was not that the United States was due for catastrophic decline. Its economic decline, he wrote, was:

> being masked by the country's enormous military capabilities at present, and also by its success in 'internationalizing' American capitalism and culture. Yet even when it declines to occupy its 'natural' share of the world's wealth and power, a long time into the future, the United States will still be a very significant Power in a multipolar world, simply because of its size.
>
> (Kennedy 1988: 533–4)

Kennedy's book evidently touched a raw nerve in a culture which oscillated uneasily between, on the one hand, anxiety about economic decline and social decay and, on the other, confidence in America's ability to overcome it. Kennedy's message in fact touched off two debates: one with academic critics who shared his concern with the long-term issues, and another with those who were preoccupied with the immediate problems of the Reagan years. Of course these debates intersected, but it is noticeable that Kennedy was at one with his sharpest academic critics – the most prominent perhaps being Joseph Nye – in his view that the problems which the United States was experiencing were part of a large-scale transition to a new international order, one in which global shifts of economic power had reduced the capacity of the United States to act independently. Though Nye, for example, objected to the word 'decline' in connection with American power, he noted the 'impossibility of following a strategy of global unilateralism to guide U.S. foreign policy in an era of interdependence'. To the extent that Reagan had adopted unilateralism, it had proved self-defeating, and in practice in some instances Reagan had grudgingly accepted the role of international institutions (Nye 1990: 254).

There were really three positions on the debate about decline: (1) that the United States faced long-term structural problems in adjusting to the new order and that, given historical precedents, there was no guarantee that it could be made with success (Kennedy); (2) that the United States was 'bound to lead' and that it possessed the capacity, if it could muster the will, to meet the challenge of interdependence (Nye); and (3) that in so far as the United States faced problems, these were of local and relatively short-term origin and could be remedied by vigorous action (Reagan).

Reagan's position intersected with the other two in curious ways. Reagan was in a sense himself a 'declinist' in that he accepted that the United States economy was under-performing, but he ascribed this not to systemic economic problems but to the legacy of 'tax and spend' policies which went back ultimately to Franklin Roosevelt's New Deal. Excessive government obligations in the form of social spending, excessive taxation, and excessive government regulation had tied the hands of business, rendering it unable to produce the goods it was capable of producing and to create the jobs it was capable of creating. 'Making America great again' was a matter, not of bending to the winds of international economic conditions but of releasing America's dormant productive power. The result was policies which were intended to assert American independence but which in fact tended to reduce it.

Tax reduction and de-regulation of business were the chosen remedies, and these had the effect of producing the economic boom of the mid-1980s. To these goals was allied the aim of strengthening the dollar, which during the early Reagan years became a symbol of America's international standing. During the Carter administration the dollar had taken a beating. As the dollar declined in 1978 the President's Council of Economic Advisors announced that the 'administration does not believe it is appropriate to maintain any particular value of the dollar'. By this, the Council meant that it would not intervene to stop the dollar falling. Under the Reagan administration, the opposite was true: it would not intervene to stop the dollar rising. Because of the large budget deficits, which meant borrowing in order to finance them, interest rates were high, attracting capital from abroad which in turn pushed the dollar up. According to one account, 'in the first four years of the Reagan administration, the average value of the dollar in terms of the currencies of other major industrial economies, as measured by the International Monetary Fund, rose by some 60 percent before peaking in the spring of 1985'. This made American exports expensive and imports cheap, contributing to a balance of trade deficit which grew from $25 billion in 1980 to $110 billion in 1984. Not only was the United States' domestic debt being financed increasingly by foreign investors, particularly from Japan and Arab oil nations, but so also was the trade deficit (Cohen 1987: 122,

127, 128, 129). By 1986 the United States had become a net debtor nation, ending over sixty years of creditor status.

One further element made a substantial contribution to the growing budget deficits of the 1980s, and this was the huge rise in military expenditures. In theory, from 1985 onwards the growing budget deficits were controlled by the Gramm–Rudman Deficit Reduction Act, which was designed to mandate graduated reductions in annual deficits until the fiscal year 1993 when the permitted budget deficit would be zero. The Gramm–Rudman rules actually specified that 50 per cent of the budget savings for each year until 1993 must come from defence. In the event, the Gramm–Rudman Act was successfully challenged in the courts during the Bush administration, and in any case neither the Reagan nor the Bush administrations had kept to the Gramm–Rudman targets.

A combination of rising government expenditure, doctrinal resistance to raising taxes (one obvious way of covering the fiscal gap, and one which Bush was forced to resort to, despite earlier promises), and indeed reduction in taxation produced the rising deficits. Rather than going into investment, which might have produced new manufacturing jobs, much of the enhanced spending power resulting from reduced taxes went into consumer goods, many of them imported.

Clearly, the economic dilemmas faced by the United States in the 1980s could not be put down entirely to the policies of President Reagan. Whether one talks of decline or the advent of complex interdependence, the basic picture was of a United States in the throes of a transition over which it wielded a decreasing level of control. The Reagan policies nevertheless tended to compound rather than reduce the dilemma.

ARMS AND THE MAN

The Reagan defence budgets were windfalls for defence contractors, and contributed in the short-term to economic recovery once the recession of 1981–82 was over, just as mobilization for war in 1941 had helped the United States out of the Great Depression. Equally important was the effect on the morale of the armed services, which shared Reagan's view that *détente*, particularly under Carter, had undermined the combat effectiveness and prestige of the armed forces. The image of failure associated with American foreign policy in the Carter period, the apparent passivity in the face of Soviet aggression, the paralysis of American will in the Iranian hostage crisis – these could all be reversed by an urgent call to arms. And, indeed, for good or ill they were. However ambiguous the legacy which Reagan left behind him, his presidency was a public relations success, and it enabled him to ride out storms which would have sunk less able communicators.

Defence budget increases were designed not simply to bolster the existing strategy of containment but to regain the initiative in competition with the Soviet Union. This involved upgrading conventional as well as nuclear forces in line with a goal of developing a conventional offensive, as opposed merely to a defensive, capability against the Soviet Union; it also meant an enhanced ability to intervene in the Third World. As regards nuclear forces, again the build-up involved a shift in strategy towards a 'counterforce' doctrine as well as increases in numbers of weapons (Posen and Van Evera 1987: 89–98). Precedents for some of these changes can be found in the Carter administration. In the wake of the Iranian hostage crisis and the Soviet invasion of Afghanistan the Carter administration had taken steps to implement an earlier decision to create a Rapid Deployment Force (RDF); there had also been a move towards counterforce and war-fighting doctrines in the nuclear field, as we saw in Chapter 11. The Reagan administration took the logic of these developments several steps further. Before examining these changes as they affected negotiations on nuclear arms, it will be helpful to outline the general course of US–Soviet relations in the period between Reagan's entry to office and his first summit with Gorbachev in November 1985:

1981: For several months following Reagan's inauguration there was little inclination within the administration to undertake new initiatives with the Soviet Union. NSC director, William Clark, and Defense Secretary, Caspar Weinberger, were firmly opposed; the State Department under Alexander Haig and Reagan himself were also unsympathetic to the idea. The after-effects of Afghanistan and the continuation of martial law in Poland clouded the negotiating atmosphere. Nevertheless, pressure from Europe and to some extent from within the United States, where the nuclear 'freeze' movement was gathering support, inclined the administration to make some limited steps towards negotiation. Towards the end of the year the administration made the decision that it would abide by the terms of SALT II. At the same time, in conjunction with a symbolic change of SALT to START (Strategic Arms Reduction Talks), it was announced that the United States was prepared to re-open strategic nuclear talks with the Soviet Union (Dallin and Lapidus 1987: 226–7). On the INF issue, Reagan offered the 'zero option', under which the United States would undertake not to deploy Cruise and Pershing II missiles if the Soviet Union removed its SS-20s from Europe. The Soviet Union rejected the offer.

1982: Despite halting progress during this year, negotiations were taking place in a number of arenas, and in November, the recently appointed George Shultz, replacing Haig at the State Department, met Soviet Foreign Minister Gromyko in Washington. 'Gromyko clearly wants to keep talking to us', Shultz reported to the president (Shultz 1993: 123).

1983: This year was undoubtedly a low point in US–Soviet relations, by comparison not only with the rest of the Reagan administration but with the previous two decades. Though in February Reagan held his first meeting as president with a Soviet official, Ambassador Dobrynin, during the following month Reagan's 'evil empire' speech and the announcement of plans to develop the Strategic Defense Initiative (SDI or 'Star Wars') ran directly counter to any momentum towards accommodation. A slight thaw during the summer, represented by a letter from Reagan to Andropov, declaring a commitment to 'the course of peace' and an 'elimination of the nuclear threat', was swiftly followed in September by the shooting down by the Soviet Union of a Korean airliner which had strayed into Soviet air space (Shultz 1993: 360, 361–71). Two months later, the first Cruise and Pershing II missiles were deployed in Europe on schedule, as a result of which the Soviet Union walked out of all negotiations with the United States. 'For the first time in fifteen years,' noted Strobe Talbott, 'the Americans and the Soviets were no longer negotiating in any forum' (Talbott 1984: 4).

1984: This election year saw the beginnings of a change of heart in the Reagan administration. The election itself may have been a factor in encouraging this, since public opinion polls in the wake of the Korean airliner incident showed that 51 per cent of Americans disapproved of Reagan's handling of foreign affairs and only 41 per cent approved. On the specific question of relations with the Soviet Union, one observer noted, 'the public was just about evenly split on whether Reagan's handling of the Soviet Union was increasing (43 percent) or decreasing (42 percent) the chances for war' (Oberdorfer 1992: 70). In addition, having taken the steps to ensure that the United States could negotiate from strength, the country now, to adopt words from Kennedy's inaugural address, had 'the strength to negotiate'. Personnel changes, including, as mentioned before, the departure of Richard Pipes, but also NSC director William Clark, helped to clear the way to new initiatives. A speech made by the president in January 1984, which presented in Reagan's characteristically homely fashion an image of the common human qualities of the peoples of the United States and the Soviet Union, pointed the way forward, even if it was dismissed by the Soviet leadership as a 'hackneyed ploy' designed for electoral purposes (Oberdorfer 1992: 72–3). Despite further obstacles during the year, among which was the Soviet Union's withdrawal from the Los Angeles Olympic Games, by the end of the year sufficient ground had been prepared in ministerial meetings for the opening of START talks in Geneva in January 1985.

1985: The year was dominated by the advent of Mikhail Gorbachev to the Soviet leadership in March. Of lesser significance, but still important, was the replacement of the Methuselah-like Gromyko as Foreign Minister by Eduard Shevardnadze who soon developed a close relationship with George Shultz. Within a short time there were proposals on the negotiating table envisaging cuts in strategic arms on a scale which would have been unthinkable only a year before. These are discussed in the following chapter.

Not all developments, however, flowed in the same direction: 1985 was also the year in which the Reagan administration made it clear that it was not prepared to let the fine print of the ABM Treaty (1972) get in the way of the development of SDI. For the Soviet leadership, furthermore, there was the ever-present question of how sincere Reagan was in his desire for cooperative relations. Was it possible to dismiss his rhetoric as being merely for domestic consumption? Could his labelling of the Soviet Union as an 'evil empire' in his March 1983 speech simply be put down to the fact that he was speaking to an audience of evangelical Christians and felt it necessary to speak in their language (Reagan 1985, I: 364)? And what was to be made of the following supposedly light-hearted remark, made in August 1984 during a voice check for a radio broadcast which he thought was not being recorded: 'My fellow Americans, I am pleased to tell you today that I've signed legislation that will outlaw Russia forever. We begin bombing in five minutes' (Oberdorfer 1992: 85)? The Soviets could be forgiven for not seeing the joke.

The fact was that Reagan clearly did believe the worst about Soviet communism, but this did not necessarily mean that such attitudes entirely dictated his approach to negotiation on nuclear weapons. Reagan pursued an agenda which was distinguished both from that of the liberals and in important respects from that of the extreme conservatives. He was closest to the conservatives on the issue of INF negotiations.

As we saw in Chapter 11, the Carter administration had determined on a twin-track approach on INF, going ahead with deployment while also entering into negotiations. The Reagan administration reduced this to a simple formula, known as the 'zero option', which proposed the withdrawal of Soviet SS-20s (including those deployed against China) in return for a NATO undertaking not to deploy its Cruise and Pershing II missiles. There was little chance of the Soviets accepting this, since it required them in effect to make a unilateral concession, while NATO was simply required to refrain from taking an action. Besides, it left in place the American FBS and also the British and French nuclear deterrents. Negotiations nevertheless continued and it seemed in the summer of 1982 that the head of the United States INF negotiating team, Paul Nitze, and his Soviet opposite number had arrived at a compromise which would have balanced a reduction in the number of SS-20s against a limited deployment of NATO missiles. This plan was overrriden by the Reagan administration, and NATO deployment of its INF missiles went ahead as planned in December 1983 (Talbott 1984: Ch. 6). The Gordian knot of INF was cut only in 1987 when, at Gorbachev's prompting, the Soviet Union accepted the essentials of the original zero option.

The issue of SDI was if anything more complex, since it went to the heart of debates about nuclear strategy. One strand of the debate had to do with the meaning of 'parity' in the nuclear arsenals of the two superpowers. *Détente* had been premised on the assumption that rough parity between the two powers had been achieved by the Soviet military build-up since the 1960s. Both sides, that is to say, were believed to possess the capacity to absorb a first strike and deliver a crushing retaliatory blow with their remaining weapons. The signing of the ABM Treaty in 1972 represented the acknowledgement by both sides that, given existing technology, there could be no effective, certainly no complete, defence against offensive nuclear missiles. However, growing missile accuracy, combined with increasing deployment of MIRVs, held out the possibility of effective targeting of the opponent's ICBMs and hence neutralizing the capacity to retaliate following a first strike. In the late 1970s and 1980s the spectre of 'missile vulnerability' loomed large. Furthermore, if it was believed that one side could effectively disarm the other by accurate 'counterforce' strikes, this would place a premium on striking first. Such logic seemed to bring the notion of nuclear war-fighting closer to the centre of nuclear planning.

The details of nuclear strategic theory seemed to have engaged President Reagan very little, but he was profoundly impressed by the apparent fact of missile vulnerability. His concern went as far back as 1967, when he attended a presentation by Edward Teller, a nuclear physicist and the main influence on the development of America's H-bomb. Teller had long been engaged in research on defence against ballistic missiles and he remained a major advocate of such systems. This presentation, writes George Shultz, 'may have become the first gleam in Ronald Reagan's eye of what later became the Strategic Defense Initiative' (Shultz 1993: 261). Equally important, in the run-up to the presidential election of 1980, Reagan made a visit to NORAD (North American Aerospace Defense Command), the command centre for America's response to nuclear attack. He was apparently horrified to learn that a hit by a Soviet ICBM within a few hundred yards of the command centre would destroy it and that there was no defence against such missile attacks. From that point on it appears that Reagan was determined to explore the feasibility of Ballistic Missile Defense (BMD).

The development of SDI itself contained some remarkable features. In the first place, that it saw the light of day was very much the product of Reagan's own vision, combined with the ambitions of a few scientists working at the cutting edge of new, particularly space-based, technologies. The speech which announced the proposals for SDI, made on 23 March 1983, did not go through the channels usually employed in the preparation of innovative policies. Key figures in the Department of Defense, and even the President's science adviser, were informed of the plan only a few days before the speech was made. Unlike most comparable initiatives, this one 'came from the top down' (Smith, S. 1987: 151). Above all, the announcement was made at a time when the project was still in effect an idea in the minds of a few individuals; it came prior to the feasibility studies which would normally precede such new departures.

A second significant feature of the proposal was its sheer ambitiousness. Reagan conceived of it as a means ultimately of ending the nuclear arms race by replacing MAD with MAS (Mutual Assured Survival). Important as offensive strength was under current conditions, defence was more acceptable morally and also pointed the way ultimately to a genuine reduction of nuclear tension:

> Wouldn't it be better to save lives than to avenge them? Are we not capable of demonstrating our peaceful intentions by applying all our abilities and our ingenuity to achieve a truly lasting stability? I think we are. Indeed, we must . . . Let me share with you a vision of the future which offers hope. It is that we embark on a program to counter the awesome Soviet missile threat with measures that are defensive. Let us turn to the very strengths in technology that spawned our great industrial base and that have given us the quality of life we enjoy today.

> What if free people could live secure in the knowledge that their security did
> not rest upon the threat of instant US retaliation to deter a Soviet attack, that
> we could intercept and destroy strategic ballistic missiles before they reached
> our own soil or that of our allies?
>
> (Reagan 1985, I: 442)

Doubts were very quickly raised about this scenario, however. Reagan's vision relied on the assurance that a total defensive shield was conceivable. Few scientists or military experts were willing to confirm this view, and those who were had to confront formidable arguments against the optimistic assumptions on which the plan was based. For the system to work as Reagan conceived it, all its elements must be 100 per cent reliable and accurate. Not a single in-coming missile must remain undetected or undestroyed; the defensive command and control system must remain intact and proof against all interference. Even one ICBM could do untold damage and would nullify the rationale of the system. In short, the system was required to operate to extraordinarily exacting standards.

If the hardware requirements posed unprecedented challenges, so also did the software. The computing capability necessary to control such a system did not yet exist. Even if these difficulties could be met, there remained the probability of Soviet counter-measures. The space-based elements of SDI – sensor devices and X-ray lasers stationed on satellites – would be vulnerable to missile attack. If the Soviet Union were contemplating an attack, these space-based elements would be their obvious first target. Other counter-measures, which were relatively simple and inexpensive, were also available, such as the employment of decoys and 'chaff' (strips of metal foil) to confuse and possibly overwhelm the defensive radars and targeting systems. A more general application of the same principle would be for the Soviet Union simply to saturate SDI with high numbers of offensive missiles. In other words, the logical Soviet response to SDI would involve an escalation of the nuclear arms race rather than, as SDI's advocates claimed for it, a break in the cycle of nuclear competition. Another alternative was for the Soviet Union to develop its own SDI, and indeed it was already engaged on such research. This too would tend to escalate the arms race and would also extend it into space (Smith, S. 1987: 154–9).

It very soon became clear, however, that the original conception of SDI lay in the realms of fantasy. Besides the problems mentioned above, expense was a major obstacle. It was impossible to estimate what the whole system might cost; it would certainly consume enormous resources over a long period of time. Congressional reluctance to contemplate huge outlays, opposition from influential sections of public opinion, and murmurings from NATO allies combined to moderate the original conception. Plans for SDI were scaled back to a much more modest progamme of research than had originally been envisaged. In fact, as former Defense Secretary McNamara pointed out in one of his many contributions to the nuclear debate in the 1980s, there were really two 'Star Wars' programmes – Star Wars I, which was represented in Reagan's 1983 speech and envisaged a 'leak-proof' defensive shield, and Star Wars II, which envisaged only partial defence of specified military and civilian sites. Star Wars II was essentially what strategic analysts believed they could reasonably expect to implement, given economic, political, and technological constraints. The result, however, was a substantial departure from, indeed a reversal of, Reagan's original vision. Reagan had presented SDI as an *alternative* to deterrence, not an addition to it. In his March 1983 speech he had said that if, instead of replacing the offensive systems with defensive systems, the United States added defensive systems to the offensive, the Soviets would consider this aggressive and 'no one wants that'. The consequence of abandoning Star Wars I and embracing Star Wars II was therefore precisely to arouse maximum suspicion in the Soviets and potentially to stimulate a new round of competition in offensive weapons (Charlton 1986: 11). The Soviets could be forgiven, McNamara suggested, for believing that with SDI the United States was seeking a first-strike capability (McNamara 1986: 99–103). A certain amount of public confusion was assured because President Reagan continued to talk as if SDI I was still the system under discussion.

Those with long institutional memories, such as Robert McNamara, found an unwelcome irony in the situation of the mid-1980s. Twenty years earlier a comparable debate had taken place but with the US and Soviet roles reversed. In the mid-1960s it had been the Soviet Union which was putting substantial resources into BMD. The American reaction had been to push ahead with MIRV research, which was initiated, McNamara recalled, '*solely* as a means of countering Soviet anti-ballistic missile development' (Charlton 1986: 26). In other words, the Americans need only have consulted their own history to discover what the Soviet reaction to SDI might be: namely, a build-up of offensive arms. The irony goes deeper yet. During a discussion between McNamara and Soviet Prime Minister Kosygin at Glassboro, New Jersey, in 1967, when accused by McNamara of destabilizing the nuclear balance by developing BMD systems, Kosygin replied hotly in terms that Ronald Reagan later used with respect to SDI: 'defence is moral, offence is immoral' (Charlton 1986: 27).

The true significance of SDI was that in conjunction with the INF issue it reopened fundamental unresolved issues about the American–Soviet nuclear relationship. It placed in doubt the theory of deterrence as it had developed from the mid-1960s. Reagan's devotion to defence posed the most obvious challenge to the concept of MAD. He had never been happy about the ABM Treaty of 1972, and made it clear that he would not allow the ABM treaty to stand in the way of SDI. The text of the ABM treaty seemed quite categorical. Both parties undertook 'not to deploy ABM systems for a defense of the territory of its country and not to provide a base for such a defense, and not to deploy ABM systems for defense of an individual region except as provided for in Article III of this Treaty [which permitted each side to deploy two fixed and limited ABM systems]'. Article V seemed specifically to rule out some of the key elements envisaged for SDI: 'Each party undertakes not to develop, test, or deploy ABM systems or components which are sea-based, air-based, space-based, or mobile land-based' (Garthoff 1987: 109, 110). Not even the most fervent advocates of SDI doubted that deployment of an SDI system, even a relatively modest one, would contravene the ABM Treaty.

There remained some question, however, about how much research and testing of SDI components might be permissible under a reading of the fine print of the treaty. Government lawyers came up with a 'broad interpretation' under which it was claimed that 'testing and development of ABM systems based on "new physical concepts" was approved and authorized by the treaty' (Garthoff 1987: 3). Critics of the Reagan administration's position on arms control, among them individuals who had nego-tiated the ABM Treaty, fervently dismissed such notions. In an article published in the influential journal *Foreign Affairs* at the beginning of 1985, a group of foreign policy heavyweights, McGeorge Bundy, George Kennan, Robert McNamara, and Gerard Smith (head of the American ABM negotiating team), declared that the President's choice was 'Star Wars or Arms Control' (Bundy, *et al.* 1984–85: 264–78). In short, SDI seemed to some prominent foreign policy specialists to undermine not only deterrence but the attendant principle of arms control. Arms control was what had made MAD tolerable.

A second challenge to deterrence, however, came in the 1980s from an unlikely quarter – from Robert McNamara himself. McNamara's writings on nuclear issues after leaving office are puzzling. However effective a critic of the nuclear policies of successive administrations in the 1970s and 1980s, McNamara's criticisms in certain respects sit oddly with the record of his policy-making. In fact, it is arguable that McNamara's writings in the 1980s cast doubt on the rationale behind a quarter century of strategic doctrine which he had helped to formulate.

The nub of the issue was his concept of 'parity' as expressed in a series of lectures given in the mid-1980s. There were, he said, a number of myths that endangered American security. Among these was the idea that the Soviets had nuclear superiority. A survey of the arsenals of both sides showed that, while in some categories one or another of the superpowers had superior numbers, there was no damaging imbalance. Those who claimed that the United States was subject to a 'window of vulnerability' were deceived. 'The fact is that parity exists today'. McNamara then proceeded to provide a further gloss on 'parity'. Parity existed, he wrote, 'when each side is deterred from initiating a strategic strike by the recognition that such an attack would be followed by a retaliatory strike that would inflict unacceptable damage on the attacker'. Drawing on the example of the Cuban missile crisis, at which time the United States possessed a seventeen to one advantage in warheads over the Soviet Union, McNamara declared that 'it would have made no difference to our behaviour whether the ratio had been seventeen to one, five to one, or two to one in our favor – or even two to one against us. In none of these cases would either we or the Soviets have felt we could use, or threaten to use, nuclear power to achieve a political end' (McNamara 1986: 44, 45).

Many critics of the nuclear arms race then and now would applaud this sentiment, but one is tempted to ask why, if a relatively small number of missiles would have served to underpin deterrence, it was felt necessary in practice to build an arsenal of thousands rather than, say, hundreds of weapons. There appears to be a clear contradiction between McNamara the architect of American nuclear policy at a critical stage of the arms race and McNamara the historian and philosopher of the nuclear dilemma in the 1980s. It had been McNamara who had brought the systems analysts and game theorists into the Defense Department, McNamara who had presided over the expansion and modernization of America's nuclear weapons in the 1960s and over the formulation of deterrence theory with its attendant concepts of rationality and balance. If parity really did mean that a few nuclear weapons would have sufficed, this implies that the nuclear arms race had been based on a fiction.

To put the point so starkly is doubtless to simplify a complex issue. Individuals are entitled to change their views as circumstances change, and in any case the point is not that McNamara was a hawk in the 1960s and a dove in the 1980s. In many respects during his tenure as Secretary of Defense he had acted as a moderating influence on the ambitions of the military. During the debates which ultimately issued in 1967 in NATO's 'flexible response' strategy, he had insisted on selective use of nuclear weapons rather than 'massive retaliation' in the event that deterrence failed, and he had fought hard to establish the importance of conventional defence in order to reduce the United States' reliance on a nuclear response to a Soviet bloc conventional attack (Newhouse 1989: 162–5; Charlton 1986: 17). Nevertheless, his fervently expressed views of the 1980s leave open the question of why neither he nor successive administrations felt able to follow the logic which McNamara's revised concept of parity implied: namely, that a few weapons would be enough to deter even a much more heavily armed opponent.

There are three possible answers. Firstly, there is simply the plethora of unknowns. How could one be sure that a few warheads would deter an opponent who had more? How could one know how the Soviet Union would react in a real crisis as opposed to a game-theoretical exercise? Though MAD made assumptions about Soviet doctrine and possible Soviet responses, little was really known about either of these. What was known, or held to be known, inclined American planners to believe the worst – that the Soviets were prepared to fight and win a nuclear war. In such circumstances it seemed to make sense to hedge bets and broadly match the opponent's arsenal. The second and related point has to do with politics. Perhaps, given what was known about the destructive power of one modern nuclear warhead, a convincing case could be made for a minimalist approach to deterrence. Politically, however, an advocate of such a position would be vulnerable to charges of negligence. The numbers game was a vital component of mutual Soviet–American perceptions of military strength and political will, as it always had been in arms races. In that sense the nuclear arms race was no different from previous conventional arms races for all the manifest difference in destructive power between conventional and nuclear arms.

The third answer to the question of why minimalist deterrence was not considered a practical option brings us full circle to McNamara's flexible response. Reliance on a few warheads to do the work of deterrence tied military planners to a limited range of options: in effect to an all or nothing response, or what the Israelis called the 'Samson option' (Hersh 1991: 137n). Willy-nilly, planners seemed bound to deterrence based on a rough balance between the American and Soviet arsenals.

There is one further way of understanding McNamara's stance during the 1980s. Taken together with President Reagan's very different challenge to deterrence we can perhaps view McNamara's position in the light of a general sense in the 1980s that the rationale behind the arms race was hollow and dangerous. The increased tension between the United States and the Soviet Union from the late 1970s had provoked popular concern about the nuclear issue on a scale not seen since the early 1960s. In the United States it took the form of the nuclear 'freeze' movement; in Europe, including Eastern Europe, elements of national anti-nuclear movements coalesced to form END (European Nuclear Disarmament). Sceptics doubted whether either organization had any direct influence on policy; advocates of these groups, particularly END, claimed to have exerted a material influence on the climate of East–West relations and even helped to bring about the end of the cold war (Thompson 1990: 139–46). Whatever the truth of such claims, there is no doubt that governments and experts felt it necessary to respond to public anxiety about the nuclear danger. Indeed, George Shultz argued that SDI, 'an undeniable success with the public at large', provided 'a potent argument against the increasingly forceful nuclear freeze movement – and against those who argued that the Reagan administration was heedlessly taking the nation down the path to nuclear disaster' (Shultz 1993: 259). With SDI Reagan presented himself as a man of peace. That McNamara too was conscious of a shift in public opinion within the United States and outside is clear from his writings in the mid-1980s, by which time Gorbachev had begun to assert himself as a new type of Soviet leader seeking a new relationship with the West. 'The conviction that we must change course', he wrote, 'is shared by groups and individuals as diverse as the freeze movement, the President, the Catholic and Methodist bishops, the majority of the nation's top scientists, Soviet leader Mikhail Gorbachev, and such leaders of the Third World and independent nations as Rajiv Ghandi and the late Olaf Palme' (McNamara 1986: 79). In short, the grounds of the debate about nuclear weapons had fundamentally changed and this was reflected in all parts of the political spectrum.

THE TROUBLED WESTERN ALLIANCE

In the years since the establishment of the Marshall Plan in 1948 and NATO the following year, relations between the United States and Western Europe had undergone a complex evolution. Certain built-in features of the relationship ensured that some tension and ambiguity was bound to exist. The most important of these was Western Europe's dependence on the United States for security. As we have seen in previous chapters, the problem of extended deterrence always left an element of doubt in the minds of Europeans about whether the United States would be prepared to risk its own destruction in the defence of Europe. Beyond that there were disputes over burden sharing and divergences of perspective on major issues affecting relations with the Eastern bloc. These problems tended to worsen as Western Europe's economic strength, and hence its potential for independent action, grew.

A second problematic feature of the relationship was precisely the European Community's emergence as a major manufacturing and trading bloc. The United States, it will be recalled, had vigorously promoted the idea of European economic unity from the time of the Marshall Plan itself. In the event, the United States was forced to settle for far less in the way of unity than they had envisaged in the original economic recovery plan. Nevertheless, the movement towards economic coordination in Europe during the 1950s, which culminated in the establishment of the EEC in 1958, met with strong American approval. In the following decade, the United States, particularly under Kennedy, promoted the idea of an Atlantic community in which Europe was conceived of as an equal partner or 'European pillar' (Cromwell 1992: 16). Such sentiments were often repeated by American officials in the coming decades but the reality was that, as the EC approached and then overtook the United States in trading power, the United States became increasingly concerned that the EC posed a threat to American interests. In the 1970s and 1980s wrangles over economic issues, among them protectionist trade policies and government subsidies to agriculture in the EC, became tediously familiar items on the American–European economic agenda. Nor was it lost on the Americans that an increasingly prosperous and economically unified Europe was still reluctant to shoulder a larger share of the defence burden.

The third important feature of the American–West European relationship bears directly on the first two: it is the lack of coordination between those organizations concerned with security and those concerned with economics. Most obviously, the memberships of the EC and NATO were not identical, the chief difference from the point of view of the Atlantic community being, of course, that the United States had no direct say in EC affairs, while it dominated policy-making within NATO. There existed, William Cromwell has noted, an 'asymmetry between Europeanism in the economic sphere and Atlanticism in the security field' (Cromwell 1992: 14–15).

Europe never fully developed its own security system, though efforts were made in this direction. Among these was the Western European Union (WEU) whose origins went as far back as 1948. There were many reasons for the failure of this and other attempts to create a European security 'pillar'. National differences were in part to blame; the French had been responsible in 1954 for the collapse of perhaps the most promising venture – the European Defence Community (EDC). Britain's well-known Atlanticist leanings made it reluctant to commit itself to Europe if that meant risking its relationship with the United States. But equally important in accounting for the stunted growth of a European security pillar was American anxiety about any organization which was not firmly within the NATO framework. The EDC idea had been acceptable, indeed strongly promoted by the United States, because it satisfied this condition. (Command and deployment of EDC forces was to be the responsibility of the NATO Supreme Allied Commander.) The WEU had no provision for military operations of its own and to that extent it posed no threat to NATO's (and hence American) leadership (Cromwell 1992: 8–14).

However, when the WEU was revived in 1983–84 in circumstances which were very different from those of the 1950s, it provoked American anxieties about a 'European caucus in NATO'. In fact, one motive for the revival of the WEU was the fear that the United States was contemplating troop reductions in Europe. Another motive arose from worry that the increasing pace of superpower arms negotiations following Gorbachev's coming to power would leave Europe vulnerable. SDI too, because it proposed to defend the United States but not Europe, fed the same sorts of anxieties. In the event, despite a good deal of rhetoric about defence cooperation within Europe and even the prospect of a European army, WEU members experienced difficulty in producing coordinated European responses to security issues, and in any case they were always conscious of the overriding need to acknowledge the primacy of NATO, and hence the Atlantic relationship, in considering their security concerns (Cromwell 1992: 171–9).

These developments showed a good deal of continuity with the past. However, tensions arising from the combination of rivalry and dependence rose to new levels in the 1980s. In part this was because Europe was now more able to assert independence from the United States; in part it was because strains which had emerged during the later phases of *détente* were exacerbated by Reagan's tendency to pursue unilateral policies. We saw in Chapter 11 that the Iranian revolution, the Soviet invasion of Afghanistan, and the Polish crisis of 1980–81 had produced serious differences of opinion between the United States and Europe. Comparable differences arose under the Reagan presidency, among the most important being disputes over SDI, European participation in the Soviet gas pipeline, and American policy towards Libya.

European leaders voiced many of the same criticisms of SDI as did critics within the United States. It would undermine the ABM Treaty, which the British Foreign Secretary, Sir Geoffrey Howe, called that 'keystone in the arch of security', it risked extending the arms race into space, and it would provoke a new round of competition in offensive arms. Nevertheless, there was a limit to official European dissent, prompted in part by the fact that Reagan was clearly determined not to compromise on the principle of SDI, but also because the Reagan administration sweetened the pill by parcelling out research contracts not only to various European nations but to Japan and Israel. The technological stakes were high, and participation was felt to be necessary in a field which had such great economic potential. France, which for political reasons refused to follow suit, launched its own high technology initiative, reflecting a consistent French pattern of dissociation from what it regarded as American military dictation to Europe (Boutwell 1988: 88–9).

While it could be said that the American launching of SDI and the European response was in the established mould of Alliance relations, in this instance, given the already tense atmosphere, the unilateral character of American policy deepened European disquiet over the prospects for a balanced reduction of strategic arms. But European reactions were hardly consistent. Ironically, as one observer put it, European leaders 'let out a collective sigh of relief when it was learned that the U.S. refusal to compromise [at the 1986 Reykjavic summit] over SDI had blocked an agreement to cut nuclear forces by 50 percent over five years and to totally eliminate ballistic missiles . . . over ten years'. Nevertheless, this did not salve the fear that SDI might obstruct the possibility 'for a more evolutionary reduction in strategic nuclear weapons and a corresponding increase in East–West stability' (Boutwell 1988: 90, 91). The European reaction to SDI evinced all the old ambiguities in the Atlantic relationship – the combination of European resentment of and reliance on the United States.

The dispute over the gas pipeline, which surfaced in 1982, saw Europe in a stronger position. Despite American efforts to present it as a security issue, it was so only indirectly. Besides, the United States over-played its hand and was forced to back down from an exposed position. The Soviet Siberian pipeline promised to supply the seven contributing West European nations with approximately 20 per cent of their gas needs and also substantial contracts for technological equipment. The jobs created by the project were badly needed by European nations which were experiencing high levels of unemployment – 14 per cent in Britain and (since 1954) an unprecedented 8 per cent in Germany. American companies too hoped to participate until, on Reagan's accession to the presidency, an embargo was declared on participation by American companies. In the summer of 1982, however, the embargo was extended to European subsidiaries of American companies and also European companies producing goods under American licences (Shultz 1993: 135–6).

The American position was that the tie with the Soviet Union would render Europe vulnerable to Soviet pressure, and furthermore that the transfer of technology and credits would ease Soviet economic difficulties, give it access to foreign exchange, and strengthen its capacity to sustain defence spending. When Europeans pointed out the apparent inconsistency between this policy and Reagan's lifting of the American embargo on sales of grain to the USSR, the reply was that, while the gas pipeline enabled the Soviet Union to earn foreign exchange, the grain sales required them to spend it – an explanation which conveniently left out the role of political pressure from the American farm lobby to lift the grain embargo. At any rate, the European reaction was heated rejection of the American attempt to dictate to them. As William Cromwell points out, the issue went beyond the question of East–West relations to 'the far more provocative matter of the US assertion of extraterritorial jurisdiction over the activities of companies located within their own sovereign borders' (Cromwell 1992: 120). Events came to a head when the United States announced sanctions against European firms for defying the embargo. Since they had done so on the orders of their own governments, it was clear that the issue could be resolved only at governmental level. A resolution was reached in November 1982, according to which sanctions would be lifted in return for European agreement that no new gas contracts were to be signed with the Soviet Union and controls on the 'transfer of strategic items' were to be strengthened. Existing European contracts with the USSR, however, were left in place, and the true significance of the agreement may have been that it allowed the United States to make a 'face-saving retreat from its sanctions policy' (Cromwell 1992: 122).

The European reaction to the bombing of Libya in 1986 was part of a larger difference of opinion within the Western Alliance about how to respond to international terrorism. Since the late 1960s international terrorism had been on the rise (see figures in Kegley 1990: 15). Though some of the most serious incidents had their roots in the Middle East conflict, the phenomenon was widespread. Terrorism, it has been said, is the politics of the weak and the politically disinherited. Yet its power to shock allowed such groups, at least in the short term, to achieve visibility and even influence out of proportion to their size. The United States was frequently the target of international terrorists, but relatively few incidents took place on American soil. This complicated the problem, which was intractable enough in any case, of how to respond to terrorist attacks or hostage situations, since generally the resolution of a crisis was beyond direct American control. The failed attempt to rescue the American hostages in Tehran in 1980 stood as a reminder of how difficult and costly such ventures could be.

President Reagan declared at the outset of his first term that terrorism would be a major priority of his administration, but in practice he was cautious about undertaking high-risk policies (Rubin 1987: 450). Selectively, however, the Reagan administration acted decisively when the source of terrorist activity seemed clear. Such, it was held, was the case with Colonel Quaddafi's Libya. Indeed, identifying particular acts of terrorism as state-sponsored – there was some evidence to show Libyan support for bombings at Rome and Vienna airports in 1985 – simplified the problem of mounting a vigorous response. Since 1981 the United States had conducted a campaign against Quaddafi's support for terrorist groups, which led to a severing of political and economic ties with Libya. Clashes between American naval forces and Libyan forces in the Gulf of Sidra took place in 1981 and again in 1986. Later that year, following the bombing of a discothèque in West Berlin believed to have been planned by the Libyan mission in East Berlin, the decision was taken to bomb Libyan military targets and also Quaddafi's living quarters. Though he was unhurt, his adopted child was killed (Rubin 1987: 452–3).

The raid was mounted from American aircraft carriers and from bases in Britain, the only European nation to provide firm support for the American action. France and Spain denied the United States permission for American bombers en route to Libya to overfly their territory, and the raid was widely condemned as a 'Rambo-style' action which threatened to increase rather than reduce the incidence of terrorism. In the aftermath, though the EC implemented somewhat tighter measures against Libya, there was no disguising the fact that American and European views on how to deal with terrorism differed markedly. In Cromwell's apt summary, 'the American emphasis on dealing with Libyan-inspired terrorism "at the source" [is] instrinsically problematic due to the difficulty in marshalling conclusive evidence of responsibility, contrasted with the European emphasis on reducing the risks of terrorism and stronger and more concerted management of anti-terrorist operations within Europe' (Cromwell 1992: 129, 127–30). Doubtless the Europeans' stance owed something to the fact that more terrorist attacks took place on European than American soil. This turned the issue into one of internal security rather than foreign policy.

Opinions differed markedly during the 1980s about how serious the tensions in the Atlantic Alliance were. The opposite ends of the spectrum of opinion are well represented by two books published during the 1980s – A.W. DePorte's *Europe Between the Superpowers* (second edition 1986) and John Palmer's *Europe Without America?* (1988). DePorte's subtitle, 'the enduring balance', announced his thesis that the bipolar European state system established after the Second World War was fundamentally stable, that its structure effectively reflected the power realities, and that it deserved to endure. Such internal and external challenges as the Western Alliance and its counterpart in the East had experienced over the years had done nothing to alter the basic dynamics of the system. The first edition of DePorte's book had appeared in 1978. On its reissue in 1986 he remarked that 'the tumultuous events of the last eight years' had exerted but 'a small impact on the system'. He saw no reason to change his earlier judgement (DePorte 1986: viii, ix–xvi).

DePorte's view was that of an American who had worked in the State Department and who regarded the American role in Europe as both necessary and right. His book was designed in part to promote 'informed support for a continuing American role in Europe' (DePorte 1986: xv). By contrast, John Palmer, European editor of the (London) *Guardian*, believed that 'the economic, military, and political world of the Atlantic Alliance, in which two generations of Americans and Europeans have grown to adulthood since 1945, is visibly crumbling'. Palmer's subtitle was 'the crisis in Atlantic relations'. While noting that 'post-war US economic hegemony was . . . a reflection of the realities of power', he suggested that the growing economic power of the EC now pitted Europe and the United States against each other as rivals in a world which was fast breaking up into trading blocs. Palmer conceded that Europe had not developed its full economic potential – it remained still a 'relatively Balkanized economy' – and it had been even less successful in creating common European foreign and defence policies. Nevertheless, Europe could do without America if Europe's full potential were developed. Indeed Palmer implied that, given the rancorous disputes within the Alliance over defence, relations with the Eastern bloc, and economic policy, Europe must be prepared to go it alone. If the 'unravelling' of Atlanticism was not inevitable, it was highly probable. For Palmer the way forward was through the coalescence of movements of the democratic left and the creation of a genuine 'Europeanism' which transcended national divisions (Palmer 1988: 1, 11, 13, 193). Palmer's book was in its own way as much a political call to arms as DePorte's.

The reality of the American–West European relationship lay somewhere between these extremes. With hindsight DePorte clearly underestimated the potential for structural change. His convinced Atlanticism inclined him to weight the factors making for continuity too heavily over those making for change. Palmer's advocacy led him to do the reverse. Each abstracted from the complex of forces at work in the Atlantic relationship certain contradictory potentialities. With hindsight, Palmer's reading was more accurate in the sense that the revolutions in the East from 1989–91 did force West Europeans and Americans to address the fundamentals of their relationship.

Yet it cannot be said that the new conditions of the post-cold war world created a simple alternative between Atlanticism and Europeanism. The problems of forging a Europeanist mentality were inherent in the European situation, with its heritage of national rivalries, and were not to be explained wholly by residual Atlanticism on the part of some of the European nations. Palmer's book amply documented the difficulties experienced by Europeans in coordinating foreign and defence policies in the 1980s. Following the upheavals in Eastern Europe, there seemed to be scant progress in these areas – witness the attempts to produce a unified response to events in Yugoslavia. Even in the economic arena, the field in which the EC was institutionally best placed to achieve unity, expectations had to be revised downwards in the early 1990s, as efforts to achieve monetary union foundered.

In short, the collapse of communism and the end of the cold war did not resolve the problems within the Atlantic Alliance. Nor can it be said, however, that these events rendered the Atlantic Alliance redundant. There were a number of possible ways in which the Alliance could evolve to meet the new security environment in Europe in the 1990s, though as of mid-1993 no clear direction had emerged.

The fate of Eastern Europe and its relations with the Soviet Union are discussed in the following chapter, but it may be useful here to refer to certain developments in the early 1980s which had a bearing on later events. The most important of these, which affected all East European countries, was a substantial and damaging shift in the Soviet supply of energy (oil and gas) to Eastern Europe. The Soviet Union had always sold energy products to Eastern Europe at prices well below the world market price, its surplus being sold on the world market for hard currency. However, when the world price dropped dramatically in the early 1980s the Soviet Union announced in 1982 an immediate 10 per cent cut in energy deliveries to Eastern Europe, the intention being to recoup its losses of hard currency by increasing the volume of its exports to the world market. As John Kramer observes, 'this action provided a harbinger of the even greater problems that awaited Eastern Europe after Mikhail Gorbachev assumed power in the USSR in March 1985' (Kramer 1990: 4; and see Medvedev 1988: 227–38). The costs of empire had always been a drain on the Soviet Union. The effort to cut them exacerbated the difficulties which the East European economies were already experiencing, most notably, as we have seen, in Poland which in the mid-1980s was in a state of uneasy calm following the crisis of 1980–81.

The above case illustrates clearly an important difference between the alliances on each side of the Iron Curtain. Eastern Europe's enforced dependence on the Soviet Union for crucial economic resources no less than for security and the maintenance of political conformity, rendered the Eastern bloc as a whole both rigid and brittle. There was little room for the kind of pulling and hauling which was the stuff of relations within the Western Alliance and which, despite perennial anxieties about how far it could go without creating serious damage, was a condition of its relative success.

THE SUPERPOWERS, THE MIDDLE EAST AND CENTRAL AMERICA

The Middle East was in continuous turmoil during the 1980s and it is hardly surprising to find that American policy showed some confusions and inconsistencies. The Reagan administration began, however, with a firm commitment to continuing the chief priorities of its predecessor. In a major policy statement of September 1982, Reagan declared that there were two basic issues which his administration had had to address on entering office:

> First, there was the strategic threat to the region posed by the Soviet Union and its surrogates, best demonstrated by the brutal war in Afghanistan; second, the peace process between Israel and its Arab neighbours. With regard to the Soviet threat, we have strengthened our efforts to develop with our friends and allies a joint policy to deter the Soviets and their surrogates from further expansion in the region and, if necessary, to defend against it. With respect to the Arab–Israeli conflict, we have embraced the Camp David framework as the only way to proceed.
>
> (Laqueur and Rubin 1984: 657)

Of course, these two lines of policy were intimately related. The Camp David agreement had not only conspicuously excluded the Soviets but had outlined a path to a resolution of the Arab–Israeli conflict and the Palestinian problem which was totally at odds with the views of the Soviet Union. 'A separate deal between Egypt and Israel', Gromyko said at the time, 'resolves nothing.' Only a 'comprehensive' settlement concluded by an international conference could bring a just and durable peace. The most important substantive, as opposed to procedural, difference between the Soviet and Camp David positions was the Soviet preference for a Palestinian state on the West Bank and Gaza rather than, as the Camp David formula had it, self-government in conjunction with Jordan (Laqueur and Rubin 1984: 618). The Soviet Union reiterated these positions in September 1982 when Brezhnev, evidently in direct response to Reagan's speech, announced his own plan for peace in the Middle East (Golan 1990: 107–9).

It will be well to keep these American and Soviet stances firmly in mind as we proceed, since, when in the wake of the Gulf War of 1990–91 and the collapse of the

Soviet Union, the beginnings of a Middle Eastern peace settlement did begin to appear, it proved to be an amalgam of both approaches. It contained an international element, in the sense that the process took place under the auspices of an international conference, and a step-by-step approach, in that the chosen method within the international framework was to engage Israel in a series of separate bilateral negotiations with its Arab neighbours. In the interim, however, the Arab–Israeli conflict had become polarized to a degree which made it seem unlikely that any settlement was possible.

The year in which the Reagan and Brezhnev plans were announced, 1982, was also the year in which Israel's invasion of Lebanon brought the region close to a state of full-scale war. Indeed the Reagan and Brezhnev plans were designed to meet this crisis. Several sets of forces were at work in the Lebanon crisis. After several years of what amounted to civil war, Lebanon was in a state of virtual ungovernability. The historic arrangements between Lebanon's diverse religious groupings – Maronite Christians, Sunni and Shia Moslems, and Druzes – had until the mid-1970s given Lebanon the reputation of having achieved 'an almost miraculous balance between different communities and interests'. The collapse of these arrangements had important internal causes, but Israeli and Syrian ambitions, in addition to the situation of the Palestine Liberation Organization (PLO), ensured that Lebanon's internal crisis would not remain isolated from surrounding tensions (Hourani 1985: 1, 14–16). The PLO's leadership and many of its 'fighters' were based in Southern Lebanon following their expulsion from Jordan in 1970. PLO shelling and raids over the border, which increased during 1981, posed continual threats to settlements in northern Israel. A further military threat was posed by Syria's installation of Soviet-built SAM (surface to air) missiles in Southern Lebanon. The Israeli invasion of Lebanon, which began in June 1982, was aimed to neutralize both these threats, but the size of the Israeli invasion force and its advance into Beirut itself suggested that the intention was to dictate the political future of Lebanon.

The United States was presented with a sharper version of the problem which had always existed in policy-making towards the Middle East: balancing its support for Israel against the need to maintain credibility with the Arab nations as a Middle East peace-maker. The immediate issue was the fate of the PLO fighters trapped in West Beirut by the advancing Israelis. Deep divisions existed within the American administration, with Secretary of State Alexander Haig refusing to countenance a strong condemnation of Israel. His increasing isolation within the administration led to his resignation and replacement by George Shultz. There followed the United States' first direct military intervention in the Middle East since the earlier Lebanon crisis of 1958. Marines were dispatched as part of a multinational force to secure the safe departure of the PLO from Lebanon. Two months after the Israeli invasion had begun, the PLO was escorted out of Beirut on ships which took them ultimately to Tunisia, where the PLO established its headquarters (Spiegel 1985: 412–18).

The crisis was not yet over, however. The newly elected president of Lebanon was assassinated, as the various factions within Lebanon resumed their murderous power struggle. Shortly afterwards, Israeli forces around the Palestinian refugee camps of Sabra and Shatila allowed Phalangist forces (Lebanese Christian militia sympathetic to Israel) into the camps where they proceeded to kill hundreds of civilians. The outcry forced Israel to establish a commission to investigate the atrocity which served to mollify Israel's friends but did little to bridge the chasm between Israel and its enemies. In the wake of the incident the United States reinserted its marines into Beirut, only to withdraw them again in October of the following year when a suicide truck-bomber drove into the American Marines' HQ, killing 241 and wounding many others. In the interim, Secretary of State Shultz had managed to broker an agreement providing for the withdrawal of Israeli forces from Lebanon, but as the withdrawal proceeded, internal conflict within Lebanon increased. An added complication was that Syria, which had just concluded a substantial arms deal with the Soviet Union, delayed its withdrawal from Lebanon and encouraged the Druze militia to mount attacks on the forces of the Lebanese government, whose stability was in any case seriously in question following the assassination of the recently elected president, Bashir Gemayel (Spiegel 1985: 421–7).

The result of these tense and confused events was paradoxical. What had begun, as far as American policy was concerned, as an exercise in limiting the damage which Israeli policy had caused to the American position in the Middle East, ended by bringing the United States and Israel back into alignment with each other, with consequent expressions of outrage by many Arab nations. The Middle East conflict seemed as far as ever from resolution.

The process by which this unpromising situation was transformed within seven years into the makings of a peace settlement was complex but can be summed up by reference to three developments: the *intifada* (or uprising of Palestinians in the West Bank against Israeli rule), the changes in the Soviet Union, and the consequences of the Gulf War of 1991.

The *intifada*, which began in 1987, had the effect of bolstering the moral and political claims to self-rule of the Palestinian people and, moreover, placed Israel in the court of world opinion as its often brutal attempts to control the uprisings were broadcast nightly on television. In this context the PLO reconsidered its political stance, seeing more to be gained by renouncing its historic commitment to the armed struggle against Israel. In December 1988 PLO leader Yasser Arafat announced a historic shift in PLO policy. In a speech in Geneva he satisfied the three conditions which the United States had set for the opening of dialogue with the PLO: recognition of Israel's right to exist, adherence to UN resolutions 242 and 338 (essentially calling for recognition of the sovereignty and territorial integrity of all states in the area), and the renunciation of terrorism.

As for the Soviet Union, small but significant shifts in Gorbachev's stance took place in 1988–89. In keeping with the basic principle of Gorbachev's 'new thinking' in foreign policy, the Soviet Union became increasingly pragmatic and less inclined to assume automatic opposition to American proposals. Backing away from solid identification with the PLO, Gorbachev became less insistent on the creation of an independent Palestinian state. He also welcomed the opening of US–PLO dialogue. Indeed, Soviet pressure on the PLO had been an important factor in producing the PLO's revised stance (Golan 1990: 274–8). In short, the moderation of cold war tensions consequent upon Gorbachev's new thinking had the effect of loosening fixed positions in the Middle East, as in other parts of the world.

The third factor making for a realignment of political forces in the Middle East was the PLO's support for Iraq in the Gulf War, a politically disastrous decision. In order to re-establish credibility as a major actor in the Middle East Yasser Arafat was forced to make concessions. 'Conciliation', went one newspaper headline in October 1991, was 'the only weapon in Arafat's hands' (*Guardian*, 19 October 1991: 10). With the opening of an international conference in Madrid later that month, to be followed up by meetings in Washington and Moscow, the first outlines of a Middle East settlement began to take shape. At the same time, the remaining Western hostages held by pro-Iranian groups in Lebanon were released.

There was, of course, no guarantee of ultimate success, and in any case much of the real work of negotiation and bargaining went on behind the scenes rather than in the public sessions. The process owed much to the considerable ingenuity of American Secretary of State James Baker and to other less visible intermediaries. When in September 1993 the PLO and Israel finally agreed on mutual recognition and on the principle of Palestinian self-rule on the West Bank and Gaza, it was revealed that a central role had been played by the Norwegian Foreign Minister. Nevertheless, however slow and halting progress towards a Middle Eastern settlement might be, the radical shifts in the alignment of forces described above created more favourable conditions for conciliation than had existed over the previous forty years. As of the end of 1993, much depended on the extent to which the moderates within Israel and the Arab world would be able to sustain momentum in the peace process in the face of fierce opposition from rejectionist elements in both camps.

Reagan's obsession with Sandinista rule in Nicaragua was comparable in its intensity with Kennedy's fixation on Castro's Cuba. Support for the Nicaraguan Contras (opponents of the Sandinista government) was an article of faith with Reagan, a commitment which admitted of no compromise. Famously, or notoriously, Reagan compared the Contra 'freedom fighters' to the American Founding Fathers. Reagan's views were shared by some of his key officials. George Shultz records an encounter with CIA director Bill Casey in 1982 shortly after Shultz had returned from a trip to Europe. Referring to Central America, Casey lamented that 'we're in danger of losing what is by far the most important foreign policy problem confronting the nation. You shouldn't be traveling around Europe. You should be going around the United States sounding the alarm and generating support for tough policies on the most important problem on our agenda' (Shultz 1993: 285). Despite verbal commitment to a negotiated solution, reflecting the influence of Secretary of State Shultz rather than Reagan's own personal conviction, the actions of the Reagan administration betrayed a consistent effort to stymie or circumvent peace proposals which might have left the Sandinistas in power. Attempts by Congress to place restrictions on support for the Contras were also bypassed. As the Iran–Contra hearings of 1987 revealed, elements within the Reagan administration were running what amounted to a private foreign policy, pursuing goals which were at odds with the wishes of Congress and also, judging by opinion polls, of the people of the United States. In sum, in Reagan's policy towards Nicaragua, intense cold war sentiment coalesced with traditional assumptions of American rights of intervention in its 'own back yard'.

The Reagan administration's policy towards Nicaragua was premised on the fear that Nicaragua was likely to become another Cuba. Sandinista rule was therefore dangerous not only in itself but because it provided a further entry point for Soviet influence in Central America. Of particular concern was Nicaraguan support for the insurgency in El Salvador mounted by the FMLN (National Liberation Front).

How much Soviet–Cuban support was there for Nicaragua, and how significant was it in sustaining the Sandinistas in power? It seems clear that the Soviet Union supplied substantial amounts of arms but stopped short of sending heavy weapons such as MIG fighters which the Nicaraguans asked for. Cuba too was an important arms supplier to Nicaragua. Castro's military had played a role in training the Sandinista forces which carried through the revolution in 1979, and Cuba maintained a higher profile than the Soviet Union in support for Nicaragua after the revolution. Economic support from the Soviet Union was considerable, but was more than matched by the levels of aid received by Nicaragua from other nations in Latin America. All the signs were that the Soviet Union, while content to support a Nicaragua which was able to sustain itself, did not consider it a vital interest and was not prepared to go to the lengths in support of Nicaragua to which it had gone in Cuba. Not only would a second Cuba be a huge drain on Soviet economic resources – aid to Cuba cost the Soviet Union between $8–10 billion a year – but the Reagan administration was evidently determined to prevent such a possibility arising (LaFeber 1993b: 292–4; Luers 1986: 839–40; Nogee and Donaldson 1988: 199–200).

The end of the cold war, while not altering the facts of the case, places them within a new perspective. That Soviet aid was limited and that the Soviet Union had good reasons for not wanting to provoke a major confrontation with the United States in the region is not inconsistent with the view that Soviet aid was enough to keep the conflict alive. The withdrawal of Soviet support for Nicaragua as the cold war came to an end produced a collapse of internal support for the Sandinistas. In free and open elections held in 1990, the Sandinistas lost power, to their own surprise and that of many outside observers. In retrospect, the Soviet role in aiding Nicaragua does seem to have been important in the years between 1982 and 1987. Moreover, Soviet aid was associated with a broad reassessment of its policy towards Latin America. Having played a negligible part in bringing about the Nicaraguan revolution of 1979, in the light of the Sandinista victory Soviet policy-makers moved towards the Cuban position on revolutionary change which emphasized armed struggle by rural-based guerrillas rather than (as the Soviet Union had maintained since the 1960s) political struggle under the leadership of urban-based communist parties. A Soviet official wrote in 1982 that 'the victory of the people's democratic revolution in Nicaragua has been a colossal triumph for the popular movement in Latin America in the 1980s . . . which . . . marks the beginning of a new stage in the continent's revolutionary struggle' (Luers 1986: 831–2, 840). It was within this framework that Soviet policy towards Nicaragua took shape in the mid-1980s.

Such a conclusion, however, does not provide retrospective justification for Reagan's contention that Soviet influence was the only important factor in the Nicaraguan situation. Nor does it exempt him from the charge that his administration effectively undermined attempts by Latin American nations to mount peace plans for Central America. The first of these, the so-called 'Contadora Plan', proposed the withdrawal of all outside support, the ending of arms sales to belligerents, the opening of talks between contending parties for national reconciliation, and economic proposals to restore Central American economies. Having initially expressed support for the plan and announced that it was ready to sign, the Reagan administration back-tracked and placed pressure on its friends in Central America – Costa Rica, Honduras, and El Salvador – to follow the American lead and refuse to sign. A second Contadora plan met a similar fate in 1986 (Smith, W. 1987b: 97–8, 100–1). Equally significant was the fate of the Arias plan, put forward in 1987 by the President of Costa Rica and for which he gained the Nobel Peace Prize. It bore great similarity to the Contadora plans with the addition that it required a firmer commitment to internal democratization, including elections. While the Central American nations, including Nicaragua, accepted the plan, the Reagan administration continued its attempts to thwart any proposal which would leave the Sandinistas in a position to retain power. This occurred, moreover, at a time when the Soviet Union under Gorbachev had begun to scale down its aid to Nicaragua dramatically (LaFeber 1993b: 341–5, 340). In the event, under the Bush administration, in the context of continued Congressional refusal to provide military aid to the Contras and the complete withdrawal of Soviet aid to Nicaragua, a Nicaraguan settlement was reached within the framework of the Arias plan. As mentioned, elections held in 1990 produced defeat for the Sandinistas.

If political opponents of Reagan, including some historians and commentators, tended to discount the Soviet factor in the Nicaraguan conflict, it was not merely because this was felt to be a necessary corrective to Reagan's distorted perspective but because of the huge domestic repercussions of the issue. Assessment of American policy in Central America was inseparable from judgements about the impact of Reagan's conduct of policy upon the domestic political process. A balanced view of Reagan's policy in Central America was, and still is, difficult to attain. The administration's persistent efforts to circumvent Congress's attempts to restrict aid to the Contras, it was held by many, flouted the constitutional balance of power between

Congress and the Presidency (Draper 1990). The ploy, mounted by officials within the National Security Council, to trade arms with Iran in return for the freeing of hostages and to use the money to fund the Contras in Nicaragua was a particularly blatant instance of executive irresponsibility run riot. Moreover, Reagan's claim during a press conference in November 1986 (made over the strenuous objections of Shultz) that the sale of arms to Iran had been correct, that Iran had moderated its support for terrorism, and that he was going to 'continue on this path', suggested either that he was breathtakingly naive or badly misinformed – or both (Shultz 1993: 830). Nevertheless, the damning conclusions of the Tower Commission report on Reagan's 'disengaged' style of management and weeks of public hearings on the Iran–Contra connection made only a small dent in Reagan's standing with the American public. His personal popularity, in combination with his seeming dissociation from the details of policy-making, outweighed the damage done by his lieutenants.

CONCLUSION

Discussion of Reagan's role in the ending of the cold war must be left to the following chapter. For the moment it is enough to assess his general stance towards the outside world. Ronald Reagan pursued a small number of large ideas relentlessly and with supreme confidence. By comparison with the architects of *détente* Reagan's conception of the forces at work in international politics was simplicity itself. The restoration of American economic and military strength, coupled with the conviction that Soviet or Soviet-inspired communism lay at the root of most of the world's problems, guided his approach to the foreign policy agenda. More fully than any other post-war president except Truman, whom Reagan profoundly admired, Reagan conceived of the world as essentially bipolar. Indeed, in urging support for the Contras in a speech of April 1983 he cited the Truman Doctrine speech of 1947, including the passage where Truman spoke of the enforced choice between 'two ways of life' – one 'based on the will of the majority' and the other 'based on the will of a minority forcibly imposed upon the majority'. In quoting Truman's statement that 'I believe that it must be the policy of the United States to support free peoples who are resisting attempted subjugation by armed minorities or by outside pressures', Reagan observed that the words were as relevant now as they had been in 1947 (Reagan 1985, I: 604–5).

One way of placing Reagan in historical perspective is to see his presidency as an attempt to address the foreign and domestic legacy of Franklin Roosevelt and if possible to undo it. In domestic policy this meant seeking to reverse the tide which flowed from the New Deal, with its centralization and expansion of government. In this he can hardly be held to have succeeded, not least because the level of public debt required the government to engage in strenuous efforts to service it. As regards foreign policy, the ultimate goal was to undo the effects of Yalta, and indeed within a year of Reagan's leaving office the Iron Curtain was in tatters. The extent to which Reagan's policies contributed to that end is treated in the following chapter.

13

GORBACHEV AND THE NEW WORLD DISORDER, 1985–1991

INTRODUCTION

When Mikhail Gorbachev assumed power in March 1985 the world order in general and US–Soviet relations in particular showed few signs that they were about to undergo revolutionary change. While Gorbachev represented a new generation within the Soviet leadership – he was the first General Secretary of the Soviet Communist Party to have reached maturity after the Second World War – expectations generally were of liberalization within the familiar confines of Soviet orthodoxy rather than of a radical departure, far less of an abandonment of the Soviet system. Gorbachev's widely read tract *Perestroika*, published in 1988, was firmly anti-Stalinist and also deeply critical of the period of 'stagnation' under Brezhnev. But it was not anti-socialist. Through *perestroika* and *glasnost*, he wrote, 'the ideals of socialism will gain fresh impetus', and they would do so through a return to the ideals of Lenin, who 'lives on in the minds and hearts of millions of people' (Gorbachev 1988: 131, 25).

Perhaps it is no surprise that Western observers by and large were no more prescient than Gorbachev himself about where his reforms might lead. The author of an analysis of the Soviet economy published in 1988 affirmed that while the Soviet Union was a declining power and faced enormous difficulties both at home and in Eastern Europe, it 'is not now (nor will it be during the next decade) in the throes of a true systemic crisis, for it boasts unused reserves of political and social stability that are sufficient to endure the most severe foreseeable difficulties' (Dibb 1988: 260). A study of *Russia and Glasnost* by a prominent Western Soviet expert, published in 1989, concluded that 'there is reason to believe that the glasnost era has now reached its climax and that no great advances should be expected for years to come'. More dramatic and far-reaching progress, he wrote, 'would be a near miracle, for cultural revolutions involve not just the replacement of one political elite by another but lasting and radical change in the mentality of a nation. This may happen one day as the result of a major shock, or the culmination of many small steps, or in consequence of the appearance on the scene of a new generation. Such a revolution in the Soviet Union seems not to be at this time part of the historical agenda' (Laqueur 1989: 311).

338

Such statements could be multiplied, but the object of citing such authors is not to crow at their failure to predict the events of 1989 and after. It is rather to point up the enormous gap between the subterranean course of events and our capacity to comprehend them. Frameworks of understanding devised for one set of circumstances served poorly as guides for circumstances which defied all current expectations. While Soviet experts had long debated the capacity or otherwise of the Soviet system to adapt to change, the degree of 'pluralism' within it, the feature of the Soviet system which seemed most to require explanation was 'the political system's remarkable stability' (Cohen 1985: 146). While there were dissenters from this view – one being Zbigniew Bzrezinski in an article which touched off a fierce debate (Brzezinski 1969: 1–34, 151–63) – the conviction of stability appeared to grow during Brezhnev's period of stagnation. At the outset of a major analysis of the Soviet system, published in 1986, Seweryn Bialer wrote that 'it is unlikely that the [Soviet] state is now, or will be in the late 1980s, in danger of social or political disintegration. Thus we must study the factors which made the regime stable in the post-Stalin era and are still at work at the present' (Bialer 1986: 19). Those who did argue that the Soviet system was in crisis were, it has been said, 'written off as anti-Soviet' (Goldman 1992: 51).

On the wider question of the post-war international system stability also seemed to be the thing which called for explanation. A year after Gorbachev came to power the American historian John Lewis Gaddis published an article entitled 'The Long Peace: Elements of Stability in the Postwar International System'. His thesis was that for all its dangers the cold war system had proved remarkably stable and bore comparison, 'in longevity at least, to the great and now wistfully recalled nineteenth-century systems of Bismarck and Metternich'. 'Unlike those earlier systems', Gaddis added, 'after four decades of existence [the cold war system] shows no perceptible signs of disintegration' (Gaddis 1986: 100). A combination of structural factors – chief among them bipolarity and rough equivalence in nuclear arms – and behavioural factors – mutual agreement on such 'rules of the game' as respecting each other's spheres of influence and avoiding direct military confrontation – had served to produce four decades without major war. While declining to predict how long the system might last, Gaddis affirmed that it certainly deserved to endure.

It says something about the limitations of social science that it proved so helpless to predict the collapse of the Soviet Union. No one has been harder on social scientists than Gaddis himself since the events of 1989–91 (Gaddis 1992/3). Revolutionary change, however, by its nature contains a large element of the incalculable. 'People never seem to expect revolution for themselves', it has been said, 'but only for their children' (Brinton [1932] 1965: 66). Even in retrospect it is difficult to keep in view all the relevant explanatory factors, far less be sure that we can comprehend precisely how they relate to each other.

Perhaps the most apt general observation on the causes of revolution is still De Tocqueville's: that revolutions happen not when dictatorial regimes are at their most repressive and tyrannical but when they are seeking to reform themselves. Awareness of weakness, above all economic, is the cue for reform attempts. In seeking to institute and legitimize their reforms, the old regimes make certain political concessions to their opponents and in doing so chip away at the foundations of their own power. This model, generalized as it is, is a useful starting point for an understanding of Gorbachev's revolutionary period in power.

Internal developments within the Soviet Union, however, can tell only part of the story. Equally important are Soviet relations with its 'external empire' in Eastern Europe and with the wider world, in particular with the United States. Taken together, an examination of these three areas can help to explain the connections between Soviet collapse and the end of the cold war. We shall look at each in turn.

THE SOVIET UNION AND THE COLLAPSE OF COMMUNISM

Analysts did not wait for the dust to settle before seeking explanations for the 'Gorbachev phenomenon' deep within Soviet history. Well before there was any question of the end of communism or the break up of the Soviet Union some observers were placing the reforms of Gorbachev's first two years in office (beginning in March 1985) within a long historical perspective. The broad picture is of a social transformation since the 1930s which was not matched by changes in the political system. Urbanization and economic modernization had occurred at an unprecedented speed in the Soviet Union, processses which were promoted by the government but not wholly controlled by it. Social change outpaced the capacity of the state structure to adapt. Most importantly, the needs of a rising 'techno-scientific and intellectual class accompanying the urbanization process' were poorly served by the strait-jacket of the political system. Underneath the carapace of old political dogmas and institutions, therefore, was an emergent 'civil society', described by a prominent advocate of the social interpretation as 'an aggregate of networks and institutions that either exist and act independently of the state or are official organizations capable of developing their own spontaneous views on national or local issues' (Lewin 1991: 49, 80). The potential for conflict was apparent, as the new forces within Soviet society encountered resistance from the old political structures and values.

Gorbachev spoke to and spoke for that 'techno-scientific and intellectual class' for whom 'freedom of movement, choice of profession, multiple choices in many walks of life' came to have more relevance and immediacy than the slogans of Marxist-Leninism. The 'personal dimension' assumed a new importance in the dense and complex texture of urban life, but opportunities for growth and autonomy could hardly exist in a 'coercive environment' (Lewin 1991: 64, 65). Broadly speaking, the goal of Gorbachev's reforms was to release the forces of creativity which were latent in Soviet society but which had been suppressed for decades by the heavy hand of democratic centralism. As Gorbachev himself put it, in terms which earlier generations of communists would doubtless have regarded as purely bourgeois, 'today our main job is to lift the individual spiritually, respecting his inner world and giving him

340

moral strength. We are seeking to make the whole intellectual potential of society and all the potentialities of culture to mold a socially active person, spiritually rich, just, and conscientious' (Gorbachev 1988: 30).

This social interpretation of the Gorbachev phenomenon begs certain questions about its timing but it does help to make sense of the fact that the Soviet system, despite its apparent inertia, was nevertheless able to produce a figure like Gorbachev (Lewin 1991: 129). That there were important long-term factors involved is confirmed when we examine the Soviet economy.

The Soviet economy was not on the point of collapse when Gorbachev came to power. The catastrophic decline of the late 1980s was a direct result of Gorbachev's policies. Patently, however, the collapse would not have taken place had not serious structural weaknesses existed. Some of these were built in to the Soviet conception of the command economy, the most damaging being the inflexibility of the central planning system which rewarded gross output rather than productivity, and conservativsm rather than innovation in production and management techniques. The Soviet central planning system was at its best, writes Marshall Goldman, 'when it was dealing with slow-moving basic technology'. Once the pace of technological change quickened, 'Soviet central planners were simply unable to keep up with the speed with which one innovation superseded another' (Goldman 1992: 36).

A related problem was the absence of any rational relationship between demand and supply within the economy. This was in part a consequence of the central planning system itself, which placed exclusive responsibility for deciding on the overall needs of the economy at the centre. But it was also a consequence of the particular way in which the central planners defined those needs. From the first of Stalin's Five Year Plans (1928) pre-eminence was given to heavy industrial production rather than consumer goods with a view to force marching the Soviet economy into the twentieth century. The main effort of Soviet planners was devoted to large-scale production of producers' goods – coal, steel, machine tools – and military equipment, both areas in which consumer demand played but a little role.

Arguably, the effort succeeded, at least up to a point, albeit at enormous human cost and at the cost of entrenching the primacy of heavy industry in Soviet economic thinking far beyond the point of utility. That point was reached somewhere in the 1970s when the computer and automation revolution overtook the West but virtually bypassed the Soviet Union except in the military sector. And even there the Soviet Union found it hard to keep pace with the West (Dibb 1988: 266). Political reasons as much as strictly economic inflexibility lay behind the inability of the Soviet Union to respond to the high-tech revolution. Even a photocopier represented a threat to centralized control of information; computer networks in the hands of private individuals or even business managers took the potential for autonomy several steps further.

Agriculture had always been a problem sector in the Soviet Union. Forced collectivization in the 1930s had imposed inefficiencies as well as hardship on farmers, who responded by devoting as much of their efforts as they could to cultivating the private garden plots which were legally permitted. The private plots were significantly more efficient than the state-run collective farms where there was little incentive to increase output. The black economy in agriculture, as in other areas of Soviet economic life, was a constant drain on the official economy. Notoriously, much food production was lost in distribution or rotted in the fields (30 per cent and on occasions as much as 50 per cent), further contributing to the spectre of a nation possessed of ample means to feed itself but increasingly forced to import vital foodstuffs such as grain (Goldman 1992: 50).

All these conditions had existed to a greater or lesser degree throughout Soviet history. Two questions suggest themselves: why didn't the Soviet Union fall apart sooner? and why did these conditions become critical in the 1980s? Part of the answer to the first question lies in the legacy of repression and political discipline which enabled successive Soviet governments to exact sacrifices from its population which would have been intolerable in more open societies. But the economic reason, in Goldman's words, is that 'given its abundant resources [above all oil], the Soviet Union was able to mask its basic structural shortcomings'. The hard currency income gained by export of oil was employed to cover shortfalls in production of food and machinery, thus removing incentives to engage in fundamental reform (Goldman 1992: 50–1).

As for the second question, the answer lies in the coalescence in the late 1970s and early 1980s of declining harvests, declining output in certain key industries, and slowing growth in the economy as a whole. And this at a time when military expenditures were increasing. Only in 1988 under the pressure of *glasnost* was it revealed that since 1976 the Soviet Union had been running budget deficits (Goldman 1992: 63, 79, 129–30). Equally damaging, and a point stressed by Gorbachev in his 1987 publication *Perestroika*, was the decline in the quality of public services and public morals which flowed from economic stagnation. The authorities, meanwhile, kept up the fiction of a 'problem-free' reality at a time when 'the world of day-to-day realities and the world of feigned prosperity were diverging more and more' (Gorbachev 1988: 22). The overall picture is of a Soviet Union which was a superpower largely by virtue of its military strength – in Dibb's apt phrase 'an incomplete superpower'.

The social and economic conditions discussed above do not of themselves, however, constitute an explanation for the disintegration of communism. Even the worsening economic conditions in the late 1970s and early 1980s need not necessarily have produced the *political* crisis which attended Gorbachev's period in power. It took a series of specific decisions on the part of Gorbachev to produce that outcome. We can place these decisions under three headings: *glasnost* (or openness), political restructuring, and economic restructuring. In no case were the reform proposals Gorbachev started out with entirely novel; precedents can be found in earlier phases of Soviet history, particularly in the New Economic Policy of the 1920s and in Khrushchev's reforms of the 1950s and early 1960s. Nor was there anything democratic about

Gorbachev's initial steps; this was the classic Soviet (and Russian) model of reform from above. In short, during his first year of office 'Gorbachev's measures resembled those of previous leaderships' (Medvedev 1988: 186). The significant feature of Gorbachev's leadership was the way in which reform advanced to the point of irreversibility, thus breaking the familiar cycle of partial liberalization followed by retrenchment.

Arguably, Gorbachev's primary aim was to restore the Soviet economy, but the earliest, most visible and dramatic effects of his policies flowed from relaxation of censorship of the media. Though criticism of public officials and 'self-criticism' was an established tradition in Soviet life, it took place within very narrow bounds, usually restricted (in, for example, the letters pages of *Pravda* and similar publications) to specific shortcomings and derelictions of duty on the part of individuals and institutions. It did not extend to generalized criticism of the Soviet system. Nor did Gorbachev intend that *glasnost* should be a cue for wholesale denunciations of Soviet life, despite his clear intention to allow much greater liberalization than previous Soviet leaders. *Glasnost* was necessary in order that 'democratization of the atmosphere in society and social and economic changes' could advance (Gorbachev 1988: 75). In a word, *glasnost* was the means by which restructuring would be legitimized, and in that sense it was a step, if only a small one, towards the advocacy of popular consent as the basis of government. Liberalization, however, it has been pointed out, was 'clearly not democratization' (Bova 1991: 119). Gorbachev evidently intended that the people should consent to what *he* wanted. As one observer noted, *glasnost* did not mean unrestricted freedom of speech but rather 'the right to criticise whatever got in the way of Gorbachev's reforms' (Roxburgh 1991: 36). Much would depend on whether Gorbachev would be able to control the expanded means of opinion formation.

All accounts attest to the extraordinary sense of liberation which accompanied the gradual freeing up of controls on the media and other means of cultural expression. From the familiar themes of 'revelations of mismanagement, false accounting, embezzlement, bribery and nepotism' during the first months of Gorbachev's rule, criticism soon extended to the Party itself and the privileges enjoyed by its elite (Roxburgh 1991: 37). Following an important speech by Gorbachev to a Party Plenum in January 1987 *glasnost* was extended firmly into the cultural sphere. Pasternak's *Dr Zhivago*, banned by Khrushchev in the 1950s, was published in 1987 by a Soviet literary journal; the film *Repentance*, an allegorical fantasy about Stalinism, was shown during 1987, having been completed three years before; Soviet history itself was opened up to scrutiny, tentatively at first but eventually to the extent of re-envisioning the entire Soviet past. Pressure was felt too for the release of political prisoners. At the end of 1986 the physicist Andre Sakharov was released from exile in Siberia and allowed to return to Moscow, a personal decision taken by Gorbachev apparently without consultation with the Politburo (Roxburgh 1991: 45–6, 53, 59, 60–61, 63–4). This move was in line with a wholesale revision of Soviet legal concepts which resulted in the 'humanization' and modernization of the law, coupled eventually with the introduction for the first time of the principle of the presumption of innocence of the accused (White 1990: 38).

Some observers, such as Gorbachev's first biographer Zhores Medvedev, saw in these developments little more than a continuation of Khrushchev's anti-Stalinist campaign, though with a new vigour. Writing in a book published in 1988, Medvedev noted that 'Gorbachev's attitude was careful and guarded' (Medvedev 1988: 303, 300–6). In the light of subsequent events Medvedev's judgement looks excessively cautious, but it is a useful reminder that once the process of *glasnost* was set in motion Gorbachev tended to be well behind pro-reform public opinion. Furthermore, once given rein, the direction of the newly released force of public opinion could not necessarily be controlled. There was no guarantee that freely expressed opinion would support *perestroika*, a point well illustrated in the publication of a long and heartfelt defence of socialist principles and Soviet history in the newspaper *Sovetskaya Rossiya* in March 1988. Since the paper was the official mouthpiece of the Russian Republic and was part-owned by the Communist Party's central committee, the article in question was taken as a 'manifesto of anti-perestroika forces' within the government (Roxburgh 1991: 84).

Though Gorbachev was able to quash this effort to undermine *perestroika*, it illustrated an uncomfortable truth: that 'pluralism' released the politically unacceptable as well as the acceptable into the public arena. Gorbachev declared as early as summer 1986 that *glasnost* was necessary because 'we don't have any opposition parties, comrades' (Roxburgh 1991: 89). But the meaning of opposition changed subtly as *glasnost* worked itself out. At first Gorbachev could conceive of himself as constituting the opposition – opposition to the old regime, to the dead hand of Soviet history itself. Once, however, he had established his own agenda, the question was whether he would be willing to allow 'opposition to the opposition' – both from those who wanted to go faster and further than he did and from those who wanted to apply the brakes and even go into reverse. To a degree, as we shall see, *glasnost* worked against the interests of both his political and his economic restructuring proposals.

The logical conclusion of *glasnost* was acceptance of the legitimacy of opposition to the Communist Party and ultimately the abolition of Article 6 of the Soviet Constitution which guaranteed the Communist Party a 'leading role'. The Party was much more than a party in the Western sense; it represented the sinews of the state itself, woven as it was into all the executive and legislative functions of government, indeed into virtually all aspects of social life. It is no surprise that Gorbachev had no thought initially of tampering with Article 6; that would have been to cut at the roots of Soviet life, and his aim was to renew socialism, not destroy it. It was March 1990 before Gorbachev, under considerable pressure, consented to the abolition of Article 6.

Gorbachev's initial approach to political reform – change of personnel in key positions – lay within the established mould. Changes in personnel were an inevitable part of consolidating political power, but because Gorbachev evidently intended to go farther and faster than his predecessors in order to make his reforms irreversible, he eventually arrived at the point where structural change in the political system became unavoidable. He could never hope to make a clean sweep of the Party '*apparat*', and in any case some of the growing conservative opposition to his reforms came from individuals such as Yegor Ligachev whom Gorbachev himself had appointed. Ligachev became the leader of the counter-reform movement within the Party, a movement which reached a peak in early 1988 with the publication of the letter in *Sovetskaya Rossiya* referred to earlier. Gorbachev could only hope to defeat the conservatives by undermining their institutional base; hence the raft of reform measures proposed at the 19th Party Conference in June 1988.

These reforms constituted an important step towards the end of one-party rule, though they did not go all the way. Essentially their effect was to begin the process of separating the Party from the executive and legislative functions of government. The mass of Party committees which oversaw and duplicated the work of the government ministries were to be abolished. A new legislature, known as the Congress of People's Deputies, two-thirds of whose members were to be directly elected, was given the function of electing a new Supreme Soviet which unlike its predecessor of the same name would meet in continuous session (Roxburgh 1991: 96). This was hardly as yet a full parliamentary system. One-third of the Congress of People's Deputies was reserved for delegates from the Party and other public organizations. The Party's role, however, was substantially reduced, it was partially democratized, and, noted one commentator, 'perhaps not coincidentally' Gorbachev's opponents within the full-time apparatus were marginalized (White 1990: 36).

There was always an ambiguity in Gorbachev's stance on democratization, however, which was pregnant with dangers. As he pushed ever harder for democracy within the system, he accrued ever-greater power to himself. Perhaps this was inevitable; it was certainly within the Soviet and Russian traditions of autocracy and reform from above. Perhaps only hectoring speeches, threats of resignation, and the assumption of virtually dictatorial powers (as in the creation of the new 'executive presidency' in 1990) could serve to move the lumbering Soviet bureaucracy and then, once it was roused, control the effects it produced. The danger of opening the process of liberalization to full democratic choice would be loss of control from the centre (Bova 1991: 118–22). Nevertheless, it was hard to ignore the irony of Gorbachev pushing relentlessly for the principle of popular election for Deputies while he refused to submit himself to popular election. The chief cost was his loss of credibility with the Left, which increasingly looked to Boris Yeltsin for leadership, and the ire of the Right, which saw Gorbachev successfully exploiting his position to undermine communism not only at home but in Eastern Europe. From mid-1989 onwards the course of change in the Soviet Union was inseparable from the momentum of communist collapse in Eastern Europe, a subject which is discussed in the following section.

However willing Gorbachev was to contemplate the end of the Soviet Union's external empire in Eastern Europe, the integrity of the Soviet Union itself was another matter. Gorbachev was only intermittently sensitive to the aspirations for autonomy in the republics and among certain ethnic groups within them. At crucial points he proved openly hostile to their wishes and endorsed or failed to prevent the forcible suppression of nationalist aspirations. The frequent charge that Gorbachev's greatest weakness was his failure to grasp the significance of 'the nationalities question' seems borne out by events.

Conflict between Armenians and Azeris over Nagorny Karabakh (an Armenian region contained within and administered by Azerbaijan) first erupted in 1988. The demand of the Armenians of Karabakh for separation from Azerbaijan and incorporation into Soviet Armenia provoked a violent response from Azeris. The plight of the Armenians initially produced expressions of sympathy from Gorbachev, though little else. In fact during a visit to Armenia following the disastrous earthquake of December 1988 Gorbachev comprehensively alienated the Armenians with his remark that the Karabakh situation was being exploited by 'unscrupulous people, demagogues, adventurists, corrupt people, black-shirts . . . and men in beards who [are] hungry for power' (Roxburgh 1991: 123). In siding with the Azeris, Gorbachev was doubtless conscious of the example which Armenian autonomy would offer to other ethnic groups seeking separate status, of which there were an increasing number. The Karabakh situation reached effective stalemate, when Azerbaijani control was confirmed following a brief but unsuccessful attempt to rule Nagorny Karabakh directly from Moscow. By this stage 'most Armenians living in Azerbaijan had fled the republic, and there were few Azeris left in Armenia' (Roxburgh 1991: 152).

The demands for Georgian independence presented perhaps a greater challenge to central control. If that should succeed it would place the integrity of the whole Union in question. In April 1989 twenty demonstrators were killed by Soviet troops in the Georgian capital of Tblisi. Though the order had been given while Gorbachev was on holiday, and though he clearly deplored the violence, he was equally unwilling to concede the demand of full independence for Georgia. In August 1989 the Central Committee of the Soviet Communist Party drew up a new platform on the nationalities question which acknowledged the need for greater devolution of power to the republics but reaffirmed the primacy of the Soviet Communist Party and of the principle of democratic centralism (White 1990: 144–5). Gorbachev was intent on holding the line well short of independence for the republics.

It was not lost on his conservative opponents, however, that nationalism within the Soviet republics could hardly have been given voice had it not been for *glasnost* and the undermining of Party rule from Moscow. Among the many charges brought against Gorbachev in the powerful conservative backlash which took place in the second half of 1990 was his responsibility for the seemingly inexorable break-up of the Soviet Union. Gorbachev's response in the critical latter months of 1990 was to meet the conservatives more than half way by introducing a range of new measures which restored substantial powers to the KGB and the army, further centralized power, and effectively denied a voice and a place to liberal advisers on whom he had relied in some cases for five years. Chief among those who departed during this debacle was Edward Shevardnadze who resigned in December 1990 uttering dark words about coming dictatorship (Beschloss and Talbott 1993: 295–6).

He also announced that he would suppress nationalist movements by force. Since Lithuania had declared independence in March 1990 Gorbachev had maintained an economic blockade. In January 1991, however, the Soviet Defence Ministry announced that it was sending paratroopers to Lithuania and other secessionist republics. Nominally the purpose was to enforce draft calls, but it seemed clear from the actions taken by the troops to suppress nationalist newspapers that their target was nationalism. The storming of the television station in Vilnius, with the death of thirteen people, was not, Gorbachev insisted, at his orders, but his words in the preceding months had done much to encourage such actions and little to prevent them. The events were repeated in Latvia a few days later (Sixsmith 1991: 97–101).

These events formed the backdrop to the coup against Gorbachev in August 1991. If Gorbachev was consistently unable to convince liberals that he was a genuine reformer, he was equally unable to convince conservatives that the Soviet Union was safe in his hands. Having in 1990 effectively broken faith with the reformers, in 1991 he oscillated once more and swung back towards reform. The immediate occasion for the August coup was the imminent signing of a new 'Union Treaty' which would have given substantial autonomy to the fifteen republics which made up the Soviet Union – tantamount in conservative eyes to the breaking up of the Soviet Union itself (Sixsmith 1991: Ch. 3).

The result of Gorbachev's gyrations was that he suffered from a double blow in 1991, first from the conservatives and then from the liberals. The first blow was the coup itself. It failed, but rather than bolstering Gorbachev's position with the liberals, it did the opposite. It was not so much suspicion that he had himself been complicit in the coup. This is unlikely to have been the case, though it was a charge which came easily to those who were already disenchanted with Gorbachev (Sixsmith 1991: Ch. 9). It was rather that Gorbachev's own leniency towards the hardliners seemed patently to have contributed to the mounting of the coup. Indeed among the chief plotters of the coup were conservatives who had been appointed by Gorbachev, including Defence Minister Dmitiri Yazov, Minister of the Interior Boris Pugo, and Deputy President Gennady Yennayev, the latter two as recently as December 1990. Also prominent among the plotters were representatives of the military who were deeply alienated by the decision to withdraw from Afghanistan and the uniliteral reduction in Soviet conventional forces announced in December 1988 (Sixsmith 1991: Ch. 5). Further-more, in the aftermath of the coup Gorbachev seemed incapable of grasping the fact that everthing had changed. In a press conference the day he returned to Moscow he continued to defend the Communist Party and was clearly out of touch with the mood which Boris Yeltsin's courageous defiance of the plotters had created (Sixsmith 1991: 125). The sequel to the failed coup was the final collapse of the Soviet Union itself.

In pursuing political reform Gorbachev ultimately proved able, if only under the pressure of events, to dismantle the old system but unable to push the Soviet Union into the reconstructive phase. His was an exercise in de-structuring rather than re-structuring. Nor should this be a cause for surprise. Gorbachev's own roots lay in the Soviet past, but more importantly the means needed to reconstruct Soviet politics were not yet available. That would require a measure of consensus on the kind of institutions needed, on the speed and direction of the transition to democracy, and on the place of the republics and ethnic groups within the Union. No consensus existed on these vital issues. Indeed the effect of *glasnost* and democratization was to foster diversity and difference rather than consensus. Above all, though, consensus would be most likely to grow out of success or at least out of some assurance that reform would eventually produce it. The immediate fruits of reform, however, were disorder and nowhere more so than in the economy. If economic failure was not itself the cause of the collapse of communism, political collapse exposed the inherent weaknesses of the Soviet economy and hastened its decline. It did so because, as George Schöpflin has pointed out, 'the pivot of the Soviet-type system was that it enforced the construction of a wholly politically determined future, in which all the spheres – economic, social, legal, aesthetic, religious, etc – were subordinated to political criteria, regardless of appropriateness, in the name of an ideologically derived goal' (Schöpflin 1990: 4). Remove the political rationale, and the economy was stripped of the rules and justifications which allowed it to function.

Gorbachev's initial goals, however, were to enhance the efficiency of the Soviet economic system rather than to dismantle it. A streamlining of central planning and a crack-down on private trade were the first fruits of Gorbachev's reforms (Goldman 1992: 89–90). Like the stringent anti-alcoholism drive, a continuation of Andropov's policy, these policies proved ineffective in strict economic terms and failed to satisfy the demands for more radical change which the rhetoric of *perestroika* and *glasnost* had stimulated. Indeed the anti-alcoholism drive alienated most workers and caused drastic shortages of sugar, as people turned to home manufacture of alcohol. The government also lost millions of roubles in tax revenue from the decline in officially sanctioned alcohol sales. The restrictions on the sale of vodka were relaxed in 1988 (White 1990: 204–5).

Genuine economic reform began in 1987 with the enactment of laws legalizing private farming and business cooperatives. Though such ventures were still hedged around with restrictions and though these organizations developed slowly by comparison with similar efforts in China, they did represent a significant departure from communist orthodoxy (Goldman 1992: 111–17).

Potentially more sweeping in its effects, however, was the Enterprise Law, since it dealt with the state-controlled businesses, by far the largest component of the Soviet economy. Coming into effect in January 1988, its aim was to transfer decision-making power from the central ministries to the enterprises themselves. This was not a privatization measure. Government ownership continued. Furthermore, the state remained the principal customer for their goods. What the plant owners did gain was the right to sell a certain percentage of their products, around 15 per cent, to whomever they wished. Managers also gained more control over wage levels (Goldman 1992: 118–20). In short, this measure, like so many others put forward by Gorbachev, attempted to straddle the gap between the command economy and a market system which would provide more incentives on the part of managers to innovate and to produce quality products.

Equally ambivalent were the first tentative steps towards opening up the Soviet economy to foreign investment. The centre-piece of reform in this area was the law on Joint Ventures, published in January 1987. Initially it restricted foreign ownership to 49 per cent but in 1990 the law was modified to allow for 100 per cent ownership. Its potential results were far-reaching, indeed 'explosive' in the words of one observer (Hough 1988: 66). Soviet 'protectionism' had never been simply one policy option among others; it had been fundamental to the project of sustaining communism in the face of a hostile capitalist world. While the Soviet Union had engaged in trade with the West, and at increasing levels since the early 1970s, such trade had been strictly controlled by the Ministry of Foreign Trade and largely limited on the Soviet side to the sale of oil and other natural resources. Joint ventures meant relinquishing monopolistic control by a single ministry in order to allow for more flexible relations between Soviet enterprises and foreign investors. It also meant opening the Soviet economy to Western economic practices, including the repatriation of profits, and to direct economic competition with other nations. Ultimately it would require a convertible rouble. Each of these things was incompatible with the command economy (Hough 1988: 66–72).

Once again, joint ventures were slow to develop, in part because the Soviet bureacracy remained a formidable obstacle to Western investors, and in part also because once a venture looked like being a success the authorities could not resist taxing that success to the hilt and hence reducing profitability and the incentive to expand. The experience of McDonald's in Moscow was one such example (Goldman 1992: 165–9).

In foreign as in domestic economic policy Gorbachev pushed far enough to undermine the old system but was unable to lay firm foundations for a new economic dispensation. This was due in part to the inherent difficulty of the problem. The Soviet Union was engaged in an unprecedented experiment of building down from a command economy. But Gorbachev's own ambivalence about the capitalist market clearly played a role in fostering a confusion of purpose. His well-known visceral distaste for such notions as private property was indicative of the limits to which he was prepared to go in contemplating the abandonment of communism.

The result, at any rate in the short term, was economic chaos and perhaps the worst of both worlds – the capitalist and the communist. The collapse of the Soviet Union itself, following the August 1991 coup, compounded the strains of transition. With the central planning system in abeyance and no well-established market mechanisms to take its place; with prices haywire (some still reflecting heavy government subsidies and some reflecting what the 'market' would stand); with growing shortages of goods, both essential and non-essential, and rampant inflation; and with little consensus on the speed of transition to a more market-oriented system, the Soviet economy between 1987 and 1991 was in deep disarray. As Marshall Goldman points out, 'shock therapy' (a sudden switch to market capitalism) might have worked in a country where there were producers ready and waiting for the optimum market conditions (Goldman 1992: 253). In the Soviet Union this was not the case. Soviet industries had always produced to the order and the timetable of the state. Nor did the requisite mechanisms exist for capital investment, credit, fiscal and monetary controls.

Underlying the difficult economic decisions faced by Gorbachev, and later by Yeltsin, however, was a political problem. The limits on economic reform were set by what was politically possible. Political prudence dictated caution, whatever economic rationality might dictate. In practice, caution meant a dualistic approach which sought to meet the hunger for change without alienating those who resisted change. Consistency in policy was hardly to be looked for in circumstances which threw up such contradictory demands. There was, however, a broad common theme in Gorbachev's domestic policies – a conviction that no system was worth preserving which relied on force or oppression to maintain itself. That ultimately spelled the doom of Soviet communism. His application of the same principle in Eastern Europe had similar results for the Eastern bloc as a whole and indeed, with one or two exceptions, for communism throughout the world.

EASTERN EUROPE IN REVOLUTION

Historians are prone to pile up precedents and anticipations of great events in an effort to explain them. One can, for example, point to numerous signs of dissent from Soviet rule in the history of Eastern Europe since 1945, indicating that the crisis of 1989 had been long in the making. Important as it is to observe the periodic signs of strain within the Eastern bloc since the imposition of Soviet power, however, nothing can or should undo one's sense of the enormity of the communist collapse in 1989. Its speed and comprehensiveness was a challenge to existing theories of political change. Its effects on East–West relations were such that virtually at a stroke cold war notions became redundant.

The collapse of communism as ideology was not the only remarkable feature of these events. Communist ideology had long been largely a matter of form among the people if not the governments of Eastern Europe. As significant was the Soviet Union's unwillingness to wield the instruments of its national power to check the course of events. Rarely can imperial power have been abandoned so precipitately without the pressure of war. Given that Soviet hegemony in Eastern Europe had been at the core of the cold war's origins, and given the extent to which the division of Europe had come to define East-West relations, the ending of that division was an event of global significance.

At the risk of flattening out the curve of history, however, the record of conflict and dissent within the bloc over the previous forty years remains an essential part of an explanation of the revolutions of 1989. The dynamics which produced the communist collapse were present from the mid-1950s onwards and were perhaps even inherent in the way the bloc was formed. The Stalinization of Eastern Europe between 1947 and 1953 represented the imposition of an alien culture and ideology on nations which were not only highly diverse but more often than not had looked west rather than east for political ideas, cultural links, and trade (Brzezinski 1989: 105; Gati 1990: 3–6). Even the most pro-Soviet of East European leaders such as Jakub Berman, Polish Secretary for Ideology in the late 1940s, recalled that as Stalinization took over, the Polish leadership attempted to 'tone down' its worst excesses: 'we knew by then that it was inevitable, but we tried to lend it a more European character. It was an attempt to defend . . . our cultural ties with Western Europe . . . and not allow ourselves at any price to be walled up in only one part of the world' (Dawisha 1990: 18–19).

Khrushchev's liberalization was an effort to accommodate nationalist pressures without compromising the political and military integrity of the bloc. The post-Stalinist leadership, writes Charles Gati, was looking for 'a middle ground made up of old hegemonical habits and slowly evolving pragmatic flexibility' (Gati 1990: 35). Hegemonical habits dictated the crushing of the Hungarian and Czechoslovak revolts of 1956 and 1968; pragmatic flexibility dictated grudging toleration of Yugoslavia's independence, Romania's partial detachment from the bloc, and Albania's shift of allegiance to China. It also meant acknowledging the force of national traditions, including Polish Catholicism and Hungary's relatively liberal economic and social policies (Dawisha 1990: 166–7, 176).

The delicate balance which these policies entailed is perhaps best illustrated in the case of Poland, at once among the most resistant of East European nations to Soviet influence and yet the most sensitive as far as Soviet security was concerned. Poland had avoided direct Soviet intervention in 1956 because a new Polish leader – Wadislaw Gomulka – was selected who proved able to 'police' Poland without Soviet help. Gomulka was far, however, from being a Soviet stooge. In fact his liberal policies – among which were the ending of collectivization of agriculture – were an object of deep suspicion on the part of the Soviets. A measure of 'revisionism' in internal policies could be tolerated, however, if Poland's role within the Warsaw Pact remained uncompromised. The Soviet–Polish relationship existed in a continuous state of tension.

Similar circumstances in 1980–81 produced a similar result, at least initially. From its establishment in 1980 during a shipyard strike, the Solidarity union quickly assumed the status of a quasi-political body, independent of the Party and the state apparatus. Its membership comprised over one third of the Polish population. By late December 1981 it was calling for a referendum on the issues of military relations with the Soviet Union and on the principle of the one-party system. Nothing could have been more calculated to frighten the Soviet leadership into a military response, and doubtless this would have taken place had it not been possible to find a leader – General Jaruselski – who was prepared to undertake a crackdown himself (Gati 1990: 52–5). Having declared martial law and banned Solidarity, Jaruselski was then in a position to pursue a 'Polish' solution, within the limits which were open to him.

There were three important differences between 1956 and 1981, however, which help to explain subsequent events both in Poland and in the rest of Eastern Europe. Firstly, the economic problems which had given rise to Solidarity were part of a general and deepening economic crisis in the Eastern bloc as a whole from the late 1970s onwards. Declining industrial and agricultural production – resulting in part from the kinds of problems described earlier in connection with the Soviet economy and in part from external causes such as increased world oil prices – produced negative or near negative growth in East European economies. The necessity to increase imports, which could be financed only by borrowing, produced an enormous burden of indebtedness to Western banks (Dawisha 1990: 169–73). By contrast, during the 1950s the East European economies had been on an upward curve, albeit from a low base. If not a sufficient condition for the political crisis which ensued in 1989, economic decline was an important contributory condition.

Secondly, dissidence was more firmly institutionalized in the 1980s than it had been in the post-Stalin thaw. Despite the banning of Solidarity, it remained a powerful underground force and a continuing focus of opposition to the Jaruselski regime. Furthermore, the Catholic Church emerged as a champion of Solidarity's reform agenda, carrying on where Solidarity had left off (Dawisha 1990: 167–8). While Jaruselski was prepared to crush public demonstrations against his regime, he tolerated the flood of 'samizdat' materials which circulated within Poland. Nor did his concessions to reality strengthen the legitimacy of his rule. Rather the reverse. His efforts to meet the demands of the increasingly disaffected Polish people only raised more starkly the issue of repeal of the ban on Solidarity.

Looking beyond Poland, organizations such as Charter 77, set up by dissident Czech intellectuals to monitor compliance with the human rights provisions of the Helsinki 'Final Act', presented a continuing challenge to the authorities. Charter 77 was subject to severe repression, as was the comparable organization in the Soviet Union. However, the status these bodies gained in Western eyes from their association with a treaty which the Soviet and other Eastern bloc countries had signed proved an embarrassment to the bloc authorities and made brutal suppression of them a relatively high-risk venture. Once Gorbachev came to power such organizations became rallying points for reform. Perhaps most important of all, both Solidarity and Charter 77 provided key personnel for the new governments which were formed at the end of 1989, most notably Lech Walesa in Poland and Vaclav Havel, who, as a leader of Czechoslovakia's Charter 77, had spent many years in prison and emerged in 1989 as the leader of Civic Forum, the organization which formed the vehicle of

Czechoslovakia's transition to democracy. In short, in the conditions which emerged in the 1980s, dissidence had an afterlife.

Finally, flowing directly from the last point, the example of Soviet *glasnost* and *perestroika* after Gorbachev's entry into office in 1985 undermined the legitimacy of the old regimes in Eastern Europe and gave active and open encouragement to opposition forces. In Poland and Hungary *glasnost* went further and faster than in the Soviet Union and the rest of Eastern Europe. By the middle of 1988 both nations were near the point of ungovernability; communism was an empty shell. The key factor in allowing the logic of change in Poland and Hungary to be played out was the Soviet decision, reportedly taken some time during 1988, not to intervene to bolster unpopular East European regimes (Dawisha 1990: 208). This meant the end of the Brezhnev Doctrine of limited sovereignty. It meant allowing genuinely separate 'paths to socialism' (since one must assume Gorbachev thought socialism in some form would survive in Eastern Europe).

Symbolic of the revised relationship between Moscow and the nations of Eastern Europe was the abolition in September 1988 of the special Central Committee department for relations with the 'fraternal countries'. Its functions were taken over by the International Department, an acknowledgement that relations with Eastern European countries were now a matter of *foreign* relations.

Why Gorbachev made this decision is the subject of much discussion. It may be that he was confident that communism had enough popular support to survive in some form; he may simply have wanted to retrench militarily in order to save money; he may, it has been suggested, have wanted to force the anti-reform leaders of Romania, Bulgaria, East Germany, and Czechoslovakia to sink or swim, hoping that they would sink (Gati 1990: 163). He may simply have doubted whether the Soviet Union had the capacity any more to enforce allegiance to its leadership.

Doubtless each of these reasons played a part, but if one considers the decision within a larger context, then it is plausible to see that maintenance of the Brezhnev Doctrine would have cast doubt on everything that Gorbachev had attempted to do both in domestic and in foreign policy. How could he impose communist orthodoxy abroad when he had built his leadership upon the principle of reform and the task of redefining socialism at home? What credibility could democratization have at home if it were accompanied by the denial of a voice to the people of Eastern Europe? Furthermore, Gorbachev had made much in his book *Perestroika* and in speeches given in Eastern Europe and elsewhere of the idea of a 'common European home'. 'I felt', he wrote, 'with growing acuteness the artificiality and temporariness of the bloc-to-bloc confrontation and the archaic nature of the "iron curtain"' (Gorbachev 1988: 194). Even if at this stage Gorbachev was unwilling to contemplate the complete erosion of difference between the social systems of East and West, his pan-European concept made anything like a repeat of the Czech experience of 1968 extremely unlikely.

Foreign policy too presented clear limits to a reimposition of the Brezhnev Doctrine.

This is discussed in the following section, but it is enough here to observe that as early as November 1986 the Politburo had reached the decision to withdraw from Afghanistan, a recognition both that the war was unwinnable and that its domestic costs were excessive (*Washington Post*, 16 November 1992: 1). The Soviet leadership could hardly embark now on a doubtless even more costly foreign intervention. Besides, at around the same time the Soviet leadership had announced a fundamental revision of military doctrine – 'reasonable sufficiency' – which saw fruit in the Intermediate Nuclear Forces (INF) Treaty of December 1987. This was followed up in 1988 by indications that the Soviet Union was prepared to engage in asymmetrical cuts in conventional forces in Europe. The Soviet Union, wrote a contemporary observer, had made the 'bold decision to plan on the assumption that world war can be prevented by political means, so Europe is no longer central to its security concerns or those of the United States' (McGwire 1989: 15). Perhaps it would be truer to say that, rather than making a deliberate decision not to intervene in Eastern Europe, that conclusion was arrived at by default, given the basic shift in Soviet priorities which had taken place since Gorbachev's arrival in office.

Certainly, once the message was communicated to the Eastern European Party elites that they could not count on Soviet help to sustain them, the East European leaderships engaged in a series of manoeuvres to safeguard their power. They did so with varying degrees of success. In Poland, Jaruselski yielded to popular pressure and repealed the ban on Solidarity as of January 1989. In a further concession he agreed to hold popular elections in June, though retaining the right of communists to dominate the lower legislative house. In the elections themselves, the first free elections to be held in Eastern Europe for over forty years, Solidarity candidates won all but one of the seats in the upper house. All the communists who stood lost (Gati 1990: 167). Even more stunning was Gorbachev's direct intervention in the stalled negotiations between the Polish communists and Solidarity during August 1989, as the former struggled to form a government. At Gorbachev's urging, the communists joined a Solidarity-led government (Dawisha 1990: 155).

The replacement of Janos Kadar in Hungary in May 1988 opened a period of feverish debate within and outside the Communist Party which by February 1989 had issued in the abandonment of the leading role of the Party and the legalization of independent political groupings. The spring and summer of that year saw a steady waning of governmental authority. Each measure it instituted to increase its popularity had the effect of further weakening its grasp on power. This was most notably the case with the removal of the security fence between Hungary and Austria in May 1989. Arguably, this act was the immediate trigger of the general collapse of communism in Eastern Europe in the autumn of 1989. In September the Hungarian authorities allowed thousands of East German tourists to pass across the border and on to West Germany (Gati 1990: 167–75). They voted in their thousands with their feet, proof if ever it were needed that the Iron Curtain had been designed to keep people in and not, as the communist authorities had ritually claimed, to keep the capitalists out.

The sequel represented the puncturing of an illusion – as sudden and decisive as the discovery of how a conjuror works his magic. There was after all no magic, just a skilful pair of hands and a plausible manner. The East German leadership attempted to sustain the illusion by replacing Erich Honecker with Egon Krenz, evidently with the endorsement, perhaps even the pressure, of Gorbachev who visited East Berlin in the first week of October. In this, East Germany was following an old tradition of Soviet-type systems which was 'their propensity to try and avoid paying the high political price that goes with the redistribution of power and to change leaders rather than policies'. It had been tried in Hungary the year before with the dropping of Janos Kadar and in Czechoslovakia the same year when Husak was replaced by Jakes; it was repeated in Bulgaria in November 1989 with the retirement of Todor Zhivkov (Schöpflin 1990: 7).

These proved to be only stop-gap measures. The pressure in East Germany and elsewhere was for the repeal of communism itself. The process was carried through perhaps most decisively in Czechoslovakia where the government attempted during the month of November to resist the inevitable in the face of mass demonstrations. Once again, under pressure from the Soviets to refrain from using force to suppress the demonstrations, the government fell in December and within a week the former dissident writer, Vaclav Havel, had been elected as interim president of the Czechoslovak Republic. Only in Romania did the transition take violent form, a consequence perhaps of the peculiarly personal and rigid form which Ceausescu's dictatorship had taken and of his immunity to pressure from Moscow. After what amounted to a brief and bloody civil war in December, Ceausescu and his wife were hunted down and executed.

Transition to what? East Germany was a special case, a state whose legitimacy had always been open to question, since it was entirely the product of Soviet fiat. Once the Berlin Wall fell in November of 1989 the issue of reunification was on the agenda, resistant to the idea as Gorbachev and many observers in the West initially were. As it happened, once the process began to happen of itself, driven forward by the popular demand in East Germany and by the West German government, Gorbachev gave it his blessing and entered talks in the early months of 1990. 'If there was a single point at which the Cold War ended', it has been said, 'it was probably . . . the moment [in July 1990] when Gorbachev acceded to German unification within NATO' (Beschloss and Talbott 1993: 238).

Despite the social and economic strains of East Germany's absorption into the West, the long-term outlook held promise. For the other former People's Democracies no such solution was available. What they desired was much clearer than the means of achieving it. Writing in February 1990, as a plethora of new political organizations and movements emerged in Eastern Europe, a British observer noted that:

> If you look at what these diverse parties are really saying about the basic questions of politics, economics, law, and international relations, there is a

remarkable underlying consensus. In politics they are all saying: there is no 'socialist democracy', there is only democracy. And by democracy they mean multiparty, parliamentary democracy as practised in contemporary Western, Northern, and Southern Europe. They are all saying there is no 'socialist legality,' only legality. And by that they mean the rule of law, guaranteed by the constitutionally anchored independence of the judiciary.

(Garton Ash 1990: 21)

Translating these aspirations into stable government would prove a daunting task, rendered all the more difficult since the removal of the communist carapace released destructive social and ethnic conflicts along with the urge for freedom. Yugoslavia, where communism had been dying a slow death since the death of Tito in 1980, descended into a sequence of civil wars as the nation broke up into its constituent parts after 1989. By the end of 1992 Czechoslovakia was split into two, albeit peaceably. Poland, Hungary, Bulgaria, Romania, and Albania (whose communist leadership held on some months longer than the others) were confronted with awesome economic problems, comparable with those of the Soviet Union.

There can be no single explanation for the communist collapse, but the manner of its fall suggests that a rigidity inherent in its ideology and institutions rendered it incapable of adaptability to change. Force, or more accurately the threat of force, held it together. Once that threat was removed, the stimulus to change which had always been present within East European societies achieved full expression. Not least of the forces making for the collapse of communism was the manifest alienation of East European peoples from communism and their desire for freedom.

Thus far we have concentrated on internal pressures in producing the communist collapse, but these interacted crucially with forces in the international environment. To these we now turn.

THE UNITED STATES, THE SOVIET UNION, AND THE END OF THE COLD WAR

In seeking explanations for the end of the cold war there are those who would place the impact of American policies at the head of the list. President Reagan's repudiation of *détente* and his determination 'to make America great again', the argument goes, set the scene for the dramas which were played out during George Bush's presidency. More specifically, Reagan's arms build-up in the first half of the 1980s, and in particular his devotion to the Strategic Defence Initiative (SDI), forced the Soviet Union either to match the United States and thereby bankrupt itself or to seek accommodation. Gorbachev chose the latter in order to concentrate attention and resources on domestic restructuring, though it proved insufficient to repair the damage. In short, American strength of will and material resources at a critical moment in Soviet history tipped the scales in the United States' favour.

Discussion of this issue in the United States inevitably contained heavy party political overtones. In fact it was its emergence as a presidential election campaign issue in 1992 which prompted a *New York Times* article by George Kennan entitled 'The G.O.P. Won the Cold War? Ridiculous'. Kennan questioned both the historical claim and the spirit in which it was made:

> The suggestion that any Administration had the power to influence decisively the course of a tremendous domestic political upheaval in another great country on the other side of the globe is simply childish. No great country has that sort of influence in the internal development of any other one . . . Nobody − no country, no party, no person − "won" the cold war. It was a long and costly political rivalry, fueled on both sides by unreal and exaggerated estimates of the intentions and strength of the other party . . . That the conflict should now be formally ended is a fit occasion for satisfaction but also for sober re-examination of the part we took in its origin and long continuation. It is not a fit occasion for pretending that the end of it was a great triumph for anyone, and particularly not one for which any American political party could properly claim principal credit.
>
> (Kennan 1992: A21)

In response to Kennan, Richard Pipes, a former Reagan adviser on Soviet affairs and a Harvard history professor, asked: why deny Bush 'recognition for a happy event that occurred on his watch?' He also questioned Kennan's premise that one nation was unable to influence another's internal development decisively, and suggested that Kennan's own concept of containment had been based on the assumption that containment would 'encourage an internal implosion in the Soviet Union' (Pipes 1992: A28).

It will be apparent from the foregoing sections of this chapter that broad credence is given here to Kennan's emphasis on the internal causes of the communist collapse. But Kennan and Pipes stated the issue too narrowly. The either/or character of their dispute obscures important interactions between change in the Soviet Union and the international environment during the 1980s. Specific policies of the Reagan and Bush administrations were not the only external forces operating on the Soviet Union, though as we shall see these played a role. Equally important were more diffuse influences arising from shifts in the relative power of the Soviet bloc with respect to the non-communist world. These had as much to do with non-material factors, such as the attractive power of Western culture within the Soviet bloc, as with relative economic decline.

As regards economic factors, in the late 1980s much attention was focused upon American relative economic decline, most notably by the publication of Paul Kennedy's *Rise and Fall of the Great Powers* in the wake of the Wall Street crash of autumn 1987. However, from the point of view of East−West relations Soviet relative economic decline was arguably more important, since it took place in the context of substantial overall growth, above all in trade, within the world economic system. The Soviet share of world manufactures and of world trade fell in the 1970s (Kennedy 1988: 430–2; Brzezinski 1989: 35–6). Moreover, this occurred at a time when the volume of East–West trade was increasing as a result of *détente* policies. One reason for the disparity in the figures is that the fastest growing trading nations were among the newly industrialized countries of Asia, not the Eastern bloc. Another reason is that most East-West trade was one-way. In all categories of East–West trade, except Soviet oil, Eastern bloc exports fell while imports rose. The gap was covered by borrowing from the West which gave rise in the course of the 1970s to the build-up of heavy debt to the West (Van der Wee 1987: 398–9). Not only did autarky have its limits, but efforts to overcome it tended to increase rather than reduce the Eastern bloc's vulnerability to external and internal pressure. In effect the relationship of the Soviet Union to the capitalist world was not unlike that of a developing country: a supplier of raw materials and a victim of increasing indebtedness. Indeed it was the Soviet Foreign Minister, Edward Shevardnadze, who posed the question in the spring of 1990: 'in what do we, who have virtually the highest infant mortality rate on our planet, take pride?' (Oberdorfer 1992: 438). (In fact, the Soviet Union in the mid-1980s held fiftieth position among the world's nations in this category, still a miserable figure. See Oberdorfer 1992: 214.)

Ironically, the gradual revision of Soviet views about the economic viability of socialism – in particular, its capacity to generate growth – was most clearly apparent in its assessments of economies in the developing world. By the early 1980s many Soviet economists were abandoning the orthodox view that developing nations which accepted Western investment inevitably became semi-colonial dependencies. Many even argued, Jerry Hough observes, that 'integration of such countries into the world economy led to stronger growth than autarky and "socialist orientation"' (Hough 1988: 58). In terms of Leninist principles this was sheer heresy. In terms, however, of the actual economic record of many developing nations since the mid-1970s, it made a good deal of sense. Nations in Asia, Africa, and Latin America which had communist or 'socialist oriented' governments experienced serious socio-economic deterioration (Brzezinski 1989: 213–24). The fastest-growing developing countries, by contrast, were those which embraced capitalism and modernization, most notably the newly industrializing countries (or NICs) of the Pacific rim – Taiwan, Hong Kong, Singapore, South Korea, Malaysia, and Indonesia.

In purely economic terms it was not a huge step to argue that the same tests should be applied to the developed socialist economies. For political reasons this argument was difficult to make, though it seems that by 1983 or 1984 some economists were implying as much in the tenor of their comments on developing countries. The fact that they were now able to argue against autarky and, even if only indirectly, for a gradual reintegration of the Soviet bloc into the world economic system, suggests, in the view of one specialist, that their opinions were shared by some high officials (Hough 1988: 59).

The ability to make such comparisons was deeply subversive of the communist faith, as was the increasing exposure of Soviet bloc countries to Western culture through television (West German TV, for example, was widely watched in East Germany and in Czechoslovakia), radio, travel, and pop music. Opinion polls from the late 1970s onwards taken by Radio Free Europe among Eastern European travellers to the West suggest that support for some form of Western democracy far outweighed commitment to communism (Halliday 1990a: 19; Brzezinski 1989: 138). Difficult as it is to measure the significance of such evidence, there is little reason to doubt its essential validity, if only because the actions of the newly liberated peoples of Eastern Europe in 1989 bore it out. Cumulatively, recognition of comparative disadvantage undercut the fundamental Marxist-Leninist assumption that Soviet communism was the wave of the future. In a sense it represented confirmation of Trotsky's conviction that an island of communism could not ultimately survive in a capitalist sea.

These developments formed the backdrop to the opening of negotiations on nuclear weapons between Reagan and Gorbachev which in December 1987 produced the first arms reduction agreement between the two powers – the Intermediate Nuclear Forces (INF) Treaty – and later issued in more comprehensive agreements on strategic nuclear and conventional weapons. As we have seen in Chapter 12, some of the necessary groundwork for the ultimately momentous shift in superpower relations had been laid before Gorbachev came to power in March 1985.

It is important, however, not to exaggerate the speed of the change in US–Soviet relations. In particular, American suspicion of Gorbachev's motives remained a feature of the negotiating process until the autumn of 1989. Paul Nitze, Reagan's arms control adviser, wrote in December 1988 (a full year after the signing of the INF Treaty) that stability was the goal of arms control and that 'reductions per se are not necessarily good'. 'We must always remember', he continued, 'to base our security policies on Soviet capabilities rather than hoped or expressed intentions. There is no evidence to date that their military capabilities have changed.' Furthermore, he added, 'we should resist the entreaties of some "to help Gorbachev out"' (Nitze 1988: 4, 6). The incoming President Bush appeared to agree. His Secretary of State-designate, James Baker, used his first foreign policy statement just prior to Bush's inauguration 'to signal a go-slow on rapprochement with the Soviet Union' (*Guardian*, 18 January 1989: 8). Secretary of Defence Cheney was even more sceptical of Gorbachev, remarking in May 1989 that the Soviet leader was likely to fail with *perestroika* and to be replaced by a hardliner (*Guardian*, 3 May 1989: 26). Even though Bush and Baker were quick to distance themselves from Cheney's remarks, his views did represent a significant body of opinion in the United States. The overall implication of the above facts is that, despite the INF success, relations between the superpowers between 1985 and autumn 1989 were still characterized by certain basic cold war attitudes, at least on the American side.

Following Bush's election, it was September 1989 before arms negotiations were resumed. By this time Eastern Europe was in turmoil and within a few months the entire structure of East–West relations had changed, with the swift collapse of the Warsaw Pact, the prospect of German reunification, and demands by the nations of Eastern Europe for the withdrawal of Soviet troops from their soil. By March 1990 one Western arms expert observed that 'with his domestic position weakening, Mr Gorbachev has all but given up attempting to bargain. These days if a Western position is stated with any degree of firmness it soon becomes the Soviet position' (Freedman 1990: 22).

Viewed in this light, there are some grounds for the contention that, in the words of one commentator, 'hanging tough paid off' for the Americans (Gaddis 1989: 11–14). It is important, however, to be clear about precisely what is being claimed for the American policy of negotiating from strength. The larger claim – the one which Kennan addressed in his letter – is that it effectively ended the cold war. The narrower claim is that it forced the Soviet Union to make unprecedented concessions in arms negotiations, of which the INF Treaty is the clearest example. Both rest on the same basic assumption: that American policy was the decisive factor in producing key changes in Soviet policy. There is a second assumption, however: namely, that Soviet policy during these years is to be interpreted solely as a series of concessions. Both assumptions deserve to be questioned. This can best be done through an examination of the record of negotiations between the two powers.

Soviet diplomacy between 1985 and 1989 may well have been that of a nation in decline, but the full story is more complex and more interesting than the word 'decline' might suggest. In the first place, if American hardball diplomacy had been the only or chief factor in bringing about the INF and subsequent agreements, then it is reasonable to ask why it had not produced that effect prior to Gorbachev's assumption of office (Risse-Kappen 1991: 163). Clearly, these results were as much the product of a new philosophy of international relations on the part of the Soviet Union as of American pressure. We must therefore address Gorbachev's 'new thinking' in foreign policy.

New thinking was announced at the 27th Party Congress held in January 1986. Its main thrust lay in the contention that with modern weapons of mass destruction, against which there was no sure defence, security was more and more a 'political task' which could be solved only by 'political means'. Relations between the United States and the Soviet Union must therefore be based on mutuality and cooperation. Shared dangers meant a necessary recourse to 'common security'. Underlying these precepts was a fundamental shift in Soviet philosophy of international relations: from a conception of class struggle and irreconcilable conflict between capitalism and communism to a conception of an interdependent world in which nations faced common global challenges. Gorbachev added a specifically military dimension to these ideas in his notion of 'reasonable sufficiency' as a basis for thinking about arms control and arms reduction. Not only did this mean an explicit renunciation of offensive motives and means but it implied a willingness to accept asymmetrical reductions of weapons and conventional forces, a hitherto unthinkable standpoint in arms negotiations for both sides (Oberdorfer 1992: 159–61, 231).

Translating these precepts into policy was less straightforward than announcing them. There were years of mistrust on the American side to overcome and resistance at home, particularly among the military. As new thinking worked itself through into policy changes, Gorbachev's star rose in the outside world and declined at home, not least because the most dramatic effects of the new philosophy coincided with the disintegration of communism in Eastern Europe and deepening economic crisis in the Soviet Union.

Among the specific policy changes which managed to convince American negotiators that Gorbachev meant what he said were a number of concessions which helped to produce the INF Treaty. The Treaty (signed in Washington in December 1987) provided for the removal of all intermediate range nuclear weapons in Europe – SS-20s on the Soviet side and Cruise and Pershing II missiles on the American – and established a stringent set of verification procedures. The first substantial shift on the Soviet side was the decision to 'de-couple' INF from agreement on strategic weapons; the second was abandonment of the insistence that an INF Treaty be conditional upon the United States agreeing to curtail development of SDI; the third was acceptance by the Soviet Union of highly intrusive means of verification; the fourth was the Soviet abandonment of its desire to reserve one hundred SS-20 missiles for deployment against China; and finally, the Soviet Union consented to the exclusion of the British and French nuclear deterrents from the INF deal. In effect, the Soviet Union accepted in all essentials the 'zero option' which Reagan had proposed in 1981.

However, while most of the movement was on the Soviet side, this did not represent an undiluted victory for an American hard line. On SDI, Gorbachev's judgement was that continued Soviet opposition to SDI was in danger of bolstering support for it in the US Congress. In fact, once he softened his position, Congress moved to limit funds for SDI and to restrict development and testing in space. In doing so, Gorbachev became a participant in the heated debate which erupted in the United States in 1985 over whether SDI violated the ABM Treaty of 1972. US government lawyers reached the conclusion that on a broad interpretation of the Treaty, development and testing of SDI (though not deployment) was permissible, a conclusion much disputed by experts in the arms control field (Garthoff 1987: 96–107), but supported by key Reagan administration figures such as Defense Secretary Weinberger and arms control negotiator Nitze. In the event, the Reagan administration chose to straddle the issue, reserving the right to a broad interpretation of the ABM Treaty but announcing that it would abide for the moment by the 'narrow' interpretation (Oberdorfer 1992: 123–7). SDI remained on the agenda as an irritant in US–Soviet relations but its sting was drawn by a combination of Gorbachev's 'tactical retreat' and misgivings about the SDI programme within the United States.

Verification too proved to be a double-edged sword, since under the regime proposed, the US military and the arms industry would have to submit to detailed inspection in areas which had always been of the highest secrecy. Overcoming the military's traditional anxieties about inspection was a factor on the American no less than the Soviet side (Oberdorfer 1992: 233–4). More generally, although the INF Treaty was widely acclaimed as a breakthrough in arms negotiations, it also had severe critics both in the United States and in Europe on the grounds that 'denuclearization' left Europe vulnerable to the Soviet Union and de-coupled from the United States. The Western INF weapons in question – Cruise and Pershing II missiles – had, after all, been originally proposed in part in order to calm European fears on precisely these points. In short, negotiation on the INF Treaty was not entirely a one-way street. On Gorbachev's side it was envisaged not as a giveaway to the United States but as part of a controlled process in line with the principle of 'common security'. In that sense it paralleled his efforts for domestic reform. The loss of control came only later – in both fields.

An equally, perhaps even more momentous, practical consequence of new thinking in foreign policy was the decision to withdraw from Afghanistan, an involvement often described as the Soviet Union's Vietnam. 'The decision to leave Afghanistan', Edward Shevardnadze said later, 'was the first and most difficult step [in reorienting Soviet foreign policy]. Everything else flowed from that.' Documents declassified in 1992 indicate that Gorbachev proposed the decision to the Politburo in November 1986, some nine months before it was communicated to the United States. They also show that the American supply of 'Stinger' missiles to the *mujaheddin* guerrillas in 1986 was decisive in making up Gorbachev's mind. (The Stinger was a shoulder-held weapon used with considerable effect by the *mujaheddin* against Soviet helicopter gunships.) In fact, as early as October 1985 the Politburo had worked out a new line on Afghanistan, one which bore a striking resemblance to Nixon's Vietnamization plan of 1969. Within the overriding goal of withdrawal, Soviet policy would be 'a more vigorous prosecution of the war in the short-term, combined with an attempt to broaden the political base of the Afghan government' (*Washington Post*, 16 November 1992: A16).

It was the failure of this policy, in combination with the American supply of high-tech weaponry to the *mujaheddin*, which provoked Gorbachev's decision. His action also reflects perhaps his view of the way the original decision for intervention was made. It had been arrived at in 1979 by a small committee of the Politburo which did not include Gorbachev, a recent appointment to that body. Not least of his concerns was the domestic cost of the war – in money and in the mounting list of casualties which by the time all the troops left in the middle of 1989 had reached 15,000 dead.

Implementing the decision brought its own difficulties. It was announced only after Gorbachev had achieved a house-cleaning of key military leaders, rendered easier after the bizarre flight of the West German student, Matthias Rust, to Red Square in 1987. Leaving from Finland in a one-engine Cessna he had managed to penetrate the Soviet Union's sophisticated air defences, a feat which cost the Defence and the Air Defence ministers their jobs. Newly armed with authority, Gorbachev moved ahead with the

Afghanistan decision. On 15 February 1989 the last Soviet troops left Afghanistan, well within the deadline he had set in his public announcement of the policy in early 1988. Military aid, however, was continued until the end of 1991 (as was American support of the *mujaheddin*), at which point the collapse of the Soviet Union rendered further underwriting of the Kabul regime financially and politically impossible. By April 1992 the Kabul regime had been driven from power (*Washington Post*, 16 November 1992: A16).

Finally among the substantive changes brought about by new thinking in foreign policy were the 'Theses' of the Central Committee of the Soviet Communist Party, adopted by the 19th Party Conference in 1988 and driven home by Gorbachev in a speech to the United Nations in the same year. In part the Theses simply restated the new internationalism and revised military doctrines announced in 1986 at the 27th Party Congress. But they were now given fuller expression and were accompanied by specific proposals for total nuclear disarmament by the year 2000 and, in Gorbachev's UN speech, by the dramatic announcement of a unilateral reduction in numerical strength of the Soviet armed forces by 500,000, coupled with the withdrawal of 10,000 tanks, 8,500 artillery systems, and 800 combat aircraft from Eastern Europe (White 1990: 159–61; Oberdorfer 1992: 316–19).

It was these developments which helped to open the way, albeit with some delay, to the conclusion of the START I (Strategic Arms Reduction Treaty) in July 1991 and START II in January 1993. Begun in 1982, the START talks had limped along under the Reagan administration through a series of summit conferences and detailed negotiations. Bush's initial caution in relations with the Soviet Union, the revolutions in Eastern Europe, and the disintegration of the Soviet Union brought new delays. The latter posed particular problems, since shortly after START I was signed three 'new' nuclear powers had appeared on the scene – Ukraine, Kazakhstan, and Belarus. All refused to ratify the Treaty, fearing for their security as newly independent states faced by a powerful and, it was perceived, hostile Russia. When the United States and Russia concluded START II – which proposed a reduction of strategic weapons to a third of current levels by 2003 – the Ukraine and Belarus had still not ratified START I. Since START II could only come into effect when START I had been ratified, the future of negotiations on strategic arms remained uncertain at the beginning of 1993.

A further and related complication was noted by the *New York Times* in an assessment of the future of nuclear arms control. Bilateral US–Russian negotiations could deal with only a part of the nuclear danger in the new instability of the post-cold war world. Nor were the Ukraine and Belarus the only problems. Whereas until 1991 the issue of nuclear proliferation had been overshadowed by the compelling fact of US–Soviet antagonism, 'it is the small powers who are now the big threats, countries like Iran, Iraq, China, North Korea, Israel, South Africa, Libya, Pakistan, Algeria, and India' (*New York Times*, 10 January 1993: E3).

For all its unintended consequences, Gorbachev's new thinking and the actions which flowed from it served to unlock the door to a fundamental reorientation of US–Soviet relations. This would not have happened in the way it did, however, without certain shifts on the American side too. Gorbachev's concessions may, as *Newsweek* suggested, have been 'a brilliant way to play a losing hand' (Oberdorfer 1992: 319), but the outcome was due in part also to new American perceptions of itself and of the Soviet Union.

It may appear paradoxical that President Reagan, the arch cold warrior, should also in a moment of euphoria at the Reykjavik summit in October 1986 have agreed to the elimination of all nuclear weapons – an apparently astonishing transformation of the Reagan who three years before had spoken of the Soviet Union as an evil empire. The moment passed when the question of SDI was raised once again by Gorbachev. To Gorbachev's insistence that SDI research must be strictly confined to the laboratory Reagan responded that 'I have promised the American people that I will not give up SDI' (Oberdorfer 1992: 203).

The contradiction between Reagan the cold warrior and Reagan the advocate of the ultimate abolition of nuclear weapons is more apparent than real. As we saw in Chapter 12, Reagan had never really believed in the doctrine of mutually assured destruction (MAD) as the basis for American defence and had been shocked to discover on a visit to the North American Aerospace Defense Command (NORAD) that there was no defence against Soviet missiles. He had clutched at the idea of SDI as a means both of defending the United States and of breaking the deadlock of deterrence. His background and experience put him at several removes from the bureaucratic consensus of the defence intellectuals, and in particular from the somewhat arcane science of nuclear deterrence theory. Notoriously unconcerned with detail and disinclined to put himself in Soviet shoes, Reagan was baffled that anyone could be opposed to a new defensive system, overlooking the fact that a secure American defensive system, should it ever be feasible, would nullify Soviet offensive power. In any event, Reagan's evidently sincere distaste for the nuclear balance of terror, coupled with his high confidence in the power of American know-how to finesse a solution to that terror, allowed him to toy with more radical proposals for resolving US–Soviet conflict than his more careful advisers were prepared to countenance. At Reykjavik, as one account has it, while Reagan and Gorbachev 'engaged in a bout of feverish one-upmanship, with each trying to outdo the other in demonstrating his devotion to the dream of a nuclear-free world', Reagan's advisers looked on in astonishment (Mandelbaum and Talbott 1987: 175). Once the news of what had gone on at Reykjavik was made public, many commentators were quick to express relief that no agreement on a nuclear-free world had been reached. Not only, it was said, would the West be at a disadvantage with respect to Eastern bloc conventional forces, but 'abolishing nuclear weapons forever was simply not possible because the understanding of how to make them would always remain' (Mandelbaum and Talbott 1987: 175). Reagan's radicalism consisted in a degree of emancipation from the conventionalities of diplomacy, even if his more grandiose notions remained still-born.

A further clue to Reagan's willingness to reconsider American relations with the Soviet Union lies in the often remarked fact that those on the right of the political spectrum – Nixon is a comparable example – were freer than liberals to make such choices, since they did not have to fear attacks on their credibility as true defenders of America. In building up American military power substantially during his first term of office, Reagan had, so to speak, earned the right to negotiate in his second. Once Reagan the ideologist had had his say, Reagan the pragmatist was free to emerge. In foreign as in domestic affairs, those who had hoped most fervently that the Reagan presidency would at last enthrone genuine conservatism in the White House and in the country at large were to be disappointed. Furthermore, as John Gaddis has pointed out, Reagan's view of the Soviet Union had always been characterized by ambivalence; his deep pessimism about the dangers of Soviet power had always been matched by a 'strong sense of self-confidence' and a conviction that capitalism would prevail over communism (Gaddis 1992: 123).

Reagan's curious mixture of stubbornness and willingness to entertain substantial changes would probably have yielded little without the steadying hand of his Secretary of State, George Shultz, and other policy advisers who were charged with the task of translating Reagan's general ideas into detailed negotiating positions. The relationship which Shultz established with Edward Shevardnadze, the Soviet Foreign Minister, rivalled in significance that of Gorbachev and Reagan themselves, since the two foreign secretaries met on numerous occasions to prepare the four Reagan–Gorbachev summits. Moreover, personnel changes were important on the American as on the Soviet side during Reagan's second term of office. In the run-up to the Washington summit of December 1987 Defense Secretary Caspar Weinberger and Assistant Defense Secretary Richard Perle – both hawkish on SDI and on arms control generally – left office and were replaced by less doctrinaire figures (Oberdorfer 1992: 265–6). Similarly, under the Bush administration, considerable credit must go to Secretary of State Baker in converting the improved climate of relations between the two powers into workable agreements. Baker's role in the American decision-making process was matched by Shevardnadze's in the Soviet Union. Baker's relationship with Shevardnadze was as close as Shultz's had been. Their key joint contribution to the improvement of US–Soviet relations, it has been suggested, was to privately urge 'their bosses to pay less heed to domestic hard-liners' (Beschloss and Talbott 1993: 61).

On balance, one's conclusion must be that, while American policy exerted great influence on Soviet policy changes, it was never a simple matter of an American hard line yielding up Soviet concessions. There was some movement too on the American side, an element of accommodation to the new realities brought about by the upheavals in the Soviet Union.

On the wider question of the relative importance of internal Soviet and external causes of the end of the cold war, once again it seems wise to resist a strict either/or explanation. The internal decay of Soviet communism must count as the primary cause, but this cannot be considered in isolation from the relative economic decline of the Soviet bloc and the political consequences this had for the global status of the 'incomplete superpower'. These consequences were evident not only in the collapse of the Soviet Union itself but also in the worldwide collapse of Soviet-inspired communism.

THE END OF THE COLD WAR AND THE WIDER WORLD

The developments which led to the end of the cold war had repercussions throughout the international system. Most notably, the declining capacity of the Soviet Union to continue aid to socialist regimes and insurgent movements set in motion the partial resolution of a number of so-called 'regional conflicts'. It is necessary to use the adjective 'partial' since these conflicts were resolved only in the sense that they were now removed from the arena of superpower antagonism. Internal problems remained which in many cases required continued involvement by outside bodies such as the United Nations. If there was such a thing as a 'new world order' following the end of the cold war, then its ordering principles were as yet only partially delineated.

Among the first nations to feel the effects of the Soviet cutback of aid to the Third World was Angola. Since the deployment of Cuban troops in 1975 a state of virtual civil war had existed between the Cuban-backed MPLA (Popular Movement for the Liberation of Angola) government and the opposition UNITA movement which received support from South Africa. The beginning of the end of the war came in December 1988 when Angola, Cuba and South Africa signed an agreement providing for the phased withdrawal of Cuban troops from Angola in conjunction with independence for Namibia. (South Africa's claim on Namibia had its roots in a League of Nations mandate dating from 1919, under which it gained control over this former German colony. The mandate was superseded by later United Nations action, but South Africa continued to resist compliance with it.) South Africa's agreement to Namibian independence, which represented its final compliance with a UN resolution dating from 1978, was granted only on condition that Cuban troops leave Angola. As the last troops left in May 1991, the MPLA and UNITA signed a peace accord to end the war. In elections held under UN supervision in September 1992 the MPLA gained a convincing victory. While there was no assurance of domestic peace and stability, the UNITA leadership agreed to abide by the results, and for the first time in seventeen years Angola was free of military conflict (*Manchester Guardian Weekly* 29 November 1992: 16). The peace was to be short-lived, however. In 1993 there was a resumption of what amounted to civil war.

In Southeast Asia too military conflict came to an end, though once again without promise of domestic peace, perhaps even less so in this instance. Under pressure from the Soviet Union, Vietnam agreed in January 1989 to withdraw its troops from Cambodia which had been inserted in 1978 to oust the regime of the Khmer Rouge leader, Pol Pot. Though the troops had left by September 1989, Cambodia remained in chaos, as the Khmer Rouge (still at that point officially recognized by the UN as the legitimate government of Cambodia) stepped up pressure to regain power. Furthermore, the Vietnamese withdrawal did not represent a formal end to the war between Vietnam and Cambodia. This was reached only in October 1991, after which a UN peace-keeping force attempted to sustain a new Cambodian government composed of elements from the four leading factions. Indeed, under accords reached in Paris in 1991 Cambodia became virtually a ward of the UN in a complicated and unusual arrangement under which the Cambodian Supreme National Council 'delegated to the United Nations all the authority needed to ensure that the accords would be successfully implemented' (Helman and Ratner 1992–93: 15).

An important aspect of the resolution of the Cambodian problem was the associated *rapprochement* between the Soviet Union and China. As we saw in Chapter 10, the Vietnamese invasion of Cambodia in 1978 had ranged the Soviet Union and China on opposite sides, serving to intensify the already existing antagonism between the two powers. The withdrawal of Soviet support for Vietnam was the trigger for direct negotiations between China and the Soviet Union over Cambodia and for broader moves to improve relations. Though Gorbachev's visit to Beijing in May 1989 took place amid mounting student demonstrations on behalf of democracy, leading to the violent suppression of the democracy movement in Tiananmen Square in June, Sino–Soviet relations, declared Gorbachev, were entering a 'qualitatively new stage'. This was marked by agreements to reduce troop levels along the Sino–Soviet border and to resolve territorial disputes through international law (White 1990: 172–3).

In Central America also the reshaping of US–Soviet relations had significant effects. Most important was the withdrawal of Soviet support for Cuba and hence Cuba's declining capacity to aid Nicaragua and the rebels in El Salvador. The Sandinista government in Nicaragua, long subject to the continuous pressure of American support for the Contra rebels and to an American economic embargo, finally agreed to hold elections in February 1990. To the surprise of the Bush administration, as well as to the Sandinistas themselves, the Sandinistas lost to a coalition of opposition groups. In June 1990, Bush announced an 'Enterprise for the Americas' initiative, which was followed up in December by a six-day Presidential visit to Latin America. 'Latin America', it was reported, 'stands poised to enter a new economic relationship with the United States, as free market policies sweep through the region and Washington adapts to a rapid shift of economic blocs' (*Guardian*, 12 December 1990: 5). In the autumn of the following year the United Nations brokered an agreement between the government of El Salvador and the rebels, bringing to an end eleven years of virtual civil war in that nation. Fidel Castro's Cuba remained the sole socialist outpost in Latin America, though with the continuance of the American economic embargo and the ending of Soviet aid, Cuba's economic and political future was uncertain.

Perhaps the most obvious victims of the end of the cold war were Ethiopia and Somalia. Since the US–Soviet-fuelled war in the Horn of Africa in the late 1970s

Ethiopia had received aid from the Soviet Union and Somalia from the United States. So long as the Soviet Union continued support for Colonel Mengistu's regime in Ethiopia, it was in the United States' interest to maintain Siad Barre in power in Somalia, not least because the Somalian port of Berbera offered the United States a strategic naval base. Once the Soviet Union abandoned Ethiopia, the United States followed suit in Somalia. When Siad Barre's government fell in January 1991, Somalia, riven by tribal conflict, descended into chaos. While Mengistu stayed in power, Ethiopia too was wracked by civil war. The plight of both countries was compounded by drought and famine which was only partially alleviated by international relief efforts. At the end of 1992 the United States sent 25,000 troops to Somalia with the aim of trying to ensure that international food aid reached the starving. There was, however, no assurance that this could do any more than provide temporary relief, far less that it could solve the problem of political anarchy. Somalia and Ethiopia, according to one view, were instances of 'a disturbing new phenomenon': 'the failed nation-state, utterly incapable of sustaining itself as a member of the international community' (Helman and Ratner 1992–93: 3).

If there was a pattern in the worldwide consequences of the end of the cold war, in the Third World no less than in the Soviet Union and Eastern Europe it lay not so much in the re-emergence of nationalism as the dominant force in world politics as in the exposure of the fragility of the nation-state itself. More precisely, it exposed deep contradictions between the claims of the nation-state and of ethnic components within them. In those states where communism had served to suppress the aspirations of competing ethnic and religious groups, nationalism – in the sense of a stable fit between a sense of national community and statehood – in effect was still-born. Clearly the crisis of the nation-state extended beyond the former communist countries and those which were aligned with the Soviet bloc. It was in these countries, however, that the crisis manifested itself most sharply, with consequences which the international community would be forced to deal with for years to come.

14

CONCLUSION

THE ISSUE OF STABILITY

The events of 1989–91 provided a rare sense of history in the making. Such turning points reshape our sense of the past as well as future possibilities. By way of conclusion, then, we shall reflect on the ways in which the upheavals of 1989–91 have influenced perspectives on the cold war and on the shape of things to come.

The end of the cold war confounded the expectations of virtually all observers and none more so than those who had come to view the cold war as a stable system. Theorists had long debated the issue of whether bipolar or multipolar systems were more conducive to stability (Deutsch and Singer 1964; Waltz 1964). The longer the cold war lasted the more plausible it seemed to regard bipolarity as more stable than multipolarity. In fact, one of the strongest arguments for bipolar stability, John Gaddis's 'The Long Peace: Elements of Stability in the Postwar International System' (1986), was published only a few years before the cold war collapsed. Very soon, of course, the question of the moment became the sources of instability in the cold war system, as journalists and scholars scrambled for explanations of why such an apparently solid structure had melted into air.

In retrospect there were two sorts of problems associated with stability theories. Firstly, there was a tendency to regard the relationship between the United States and the Soviet Union, or more precisely between East and West, as being symmetrical in character. The competing ideologies, each defining itself explicitly in contradistinction to the other, the parallel alliance systems, the neat slicing of Europe into two, the closely matched nuclear arsenals, and the almost ritual polarization of Third World conflicts according to the dictates of the cold war – these all lent the East–West conflict the appearance of balance and symmetry. Above all, perhaps, nuclear weapons seemed to freeze the relationship into virtual immobility. A second and related problem with stability theories was the assumption, explicit in some and implicit in others, that the major antagonists in the cold war 'needed' each other; in effect, that the cold war was functional for each side. The United States, one account has it, 'came to depend upon Stalinism to legitimize its general cold war strategy' (Cox 1986: 26).

Neither of these arguments was wholly wrong. There *were* striking elements of symmetry in the superpower relationship. Clearly too the leaderships of both sides used the threat of the other to justify their own policies and strategies. The issue is not whether these features were present – they clearly were –but the degree to which they can be held to explain the superpower relationship. Both arguments tended towards determinism and made it difficult to account for change, not least the changes which brought the fall of communism. Such theories also underestimated the extent to which the cold war was dysfunctional, not only for the superpowers but also for those many smaller nations which became theatres of cold war conflict (Brecher and Wilkenfeld 1991: 85–104).

In the light of the collapse of the cold war system it seems clear that an adequate interpretation of the post-war years must satisfy two requirements: firstly, it must be able to account for the forces of change as well as the forces making for stability and, secondly, it must take account of the differences in the status and roles performed by the United States and the Soviet Union in the international system.

As has been suggested in the course of the foregoing chapters, at the root of cold war conflict lay important asymmetries in American and Soviet power. This was not simply a matter of Soviet economic weakness and American economic strength but of differences in the kinds of power they possessed and their means of employing it. In the initial phase of the cold war American economic power was pre-eminent, and despite its relative decline this continued to be the case. American nuclear superiority was also a feature of the first two decades of cold war. However, the Soviet Union's relative economic weakness was counterbalanced by its conventional military strength and later its growing nuclear power, its geographical proximity to the major theatre of potential conflict, and its autarkic economic development which rendered it effectively immune, at least until the early 1970s, from Western economic pressure. Autarky and the communist system itself were ultimately unsustainable not merely because of long-term structural problems within Soviet bloc economies but because of differential rates of growth between the Soviet bloc and the West. Furthermore, the ideological attraction of the Soviet system, which had gained some prestige as a result of the Second World War and some adherents among newly independent Third World nations, waned over the period. By contrast, Western culture and economic methods proved eminently exportable and adaptable to local conditions in many parts of the world, even when politically the United States and the West in general were pushed on to the defensive.

In the light of these considerations it seems plausible to argue that what was at issue in US–Soviet relations was not one system but two overlapping but distinct systems: (1) a cold war system defined by the geopolitical division of Europe and its extension to parts of the Third World, the existence of nuclear weapons, and ideological conflict, and (2) a world capitalist system which was defined by the expansion of production and trade, growing economic interdependence, and the establishment of international 'regimes' for the management of various transnational processes (Keohane and Nye

1977: Chs 3 and 4). The development of international relations theory, as was mentioned in Chapter 1, mirrors this bifurcation. Realism, with its source in the early cold war but continued and developed by such neo-realists as Kenneth Waltz, stressed inter*state* relations, the political and military dominance of the United States and the Soviet Union within a bipolar international system, and the notion of the balance of power as the operational force making for system stability. Pluralist theories, with roots in the economically multipolar world of the 1970s, stressed the growing importance of transnational processes, especially economic, the declining saliency of the US–Soviet bilateral relationship and of military/security concerns associated with it, and interdependence as the chief systemic force. 'Interdependence', it has been well said, 'is to many pluralists what balance of power is to the realists' (Viotti and Kauppi 1993: 243).

Arguably both approaches were justified within the terms of the realities they set out to explain, but neither on its own seemed capable of accommodating the full reality, which was that while the Soviet Union's capacity to sustain itself was limited to and by the cold war system, the United States was never so constrained, since it had access to the resources of the world system. The United States could, so to speak, afford to fight the cold war with one hand while making money with the other. Put differently, we could say that the Soviet system, born in war, developed by Stalin as a military command system with power centred in the state, tempered further by the Second World (or 'Great Patriotic') War, and steeled by the cold war, was above all a society permanently mobilized as if for war and effectively only for war. This was the source both of its appearance of strength and its long-term weakness. Arguably this was the real meaning of totalitarianism, of Hitler's Reich no less than of Soviet communism. Significant as the military-industrial complex was and is within American society, it never became the all-encompassing reality which it did in the Soviet Union.

Viewed in this light, the cold war system was subject to a dynamic – the growth of the capitalist system – which was tangential to the cold war itself. The cold war did not so much collapse as it was bypassed. Ironically, because the costs of the cold war weighed less heavily on the United States than the Soviet Union, the United States had less reason than the successor states of the former Soviet Union to abandon the assumptions which underpinned its policies during the cold war. Adapting policies which were designed for cold war conditions to the new agenda of world politics would prove difficult.

THE SHAPE OF THINGS TO COME

The mass of commentary on the post-cold war world proves that it is wellnigh impossible for observers to separate their interpretations of the cold war from conceptions of the kind of order (or disorder) that is emerging from it. Those who had been inclined, for example, to interpret the cold war system as stable, and for that reason to view it as fundamentally benign for all its dangers, tended to emphasize the dangers of the new and as yet unstructured condition of Eastern and Central Europe. Calling the cold war 'the long peace', as John Gaddis did, suggested an ominous prospect for the period following the cold war (Gaddis 1986, and 1990b: 19).

The functionalist argument – the view that the antagonists in the cold war could scarcely do without each other – was also embarrassed by the end of the cold war. It is by no means obvious, as has been claimed, that 'without the Soviet Union the rehabilitation of bourgeois rule on a global scale would have been impossible in the postwar period' or that Stalinism had been 'a necessary condition for bourgeois hegemony' (Cox 1986: 36). For one thing, the necessary condition for American absolute and relative economic strength in the post-war world was supplied by the Second World War itself: the combination of the boost which the war gave to the American economy and the temporary destruction of its competitors. This is not to say that the emerging cold war did not sharpen the edge of American expansionism or influence the shape it took, but it is to say that the United States was not entirely dependent upon the goad of the Soviet Union to achieve it. Secondly, and closely related to the last point, the functionalist argument assumes, as do many interpretations of the cold war, that the superpowers were the only significant actors on the international scene. But surely the revival of capitalism after the war owed much to the internal dynamism of Western European and Japanese capitalism and the presence of a developed industrial infrastructure. The Marshall Plan would scarcely have succeeded if this had not been the case.

Finally, despite the evident challenge which the demise of the Soviet Union posed to American policy-making in the 1990s, the United States was not suddenly bereft of resources in formulating new policies. As we shall see later, in the post-cold war world the United States returned for good or ill to lines of policy which long pre-dated the cold war. Indeed they had never disappeared. The American foreign policy tradition, as described in Chapter 2, was continuous with the cold war and largely survived it.

Many commentators, however, viewed the post-cold war world entirely through the lens of the cold war. Having been persuaded that the cold war was a stable system, they could envision only instability resulting from its end. The most striking version of this sort of argument was put forward by John Mearsheimer in a deeply pessimistic prognosis for Europe in the post-cold war world. The euphoria greeting the collapse of communism, he wrote, was misplaced. The absence of war since 1945 had been the consequence of three factors: 'the bipolar distribution of military power on the Continent; the rough military equality between the two states comprising the two poles in Europe, the United States and the Soviet Union; and the fact that each power was armed with a large nuclear arsenal'. Should the superpowers depart from Central Europe, the result would be power inequities among the European states and a multipolar system 'prone to instability'. The danger of 'hyper-nationalism', which the cold war had effectively suppressed, increased the likelihood of war. The best guarantee against such an outcome would be 'the managed proliferation of nuclear weapons', since nuclear weapons had proved to be 'a superb deterrent' to war in Europe since 1945 (Mearsheimer 1990: 6–7, 20–1, 31). Mearsheimer later developed similar arguments with respect to potential conflict between Russia and the Ukraine following the break-up of the Soviet Union. The conventional wisdom – that Europe was likely to be more stable with fewer nuclear powers – was quite wrong: 'in fact, as soon as it declared independence Ukraine should have been quietly encouraged to fashion its own nuclear deterrent' (Mearsheimer 1993: 50).

The reactions to Mearsheimer's highly contentious arguments went to the heart of the theoretical debates about international politics which had developed during the cold war. Mearsheimer's analysis, responded Stanley Hoffmann, was 'almost a carica-ture of neo-realism' in its theoretical abstraction and its dogmatic assertion that bipolarity necessarily bred stability. Structural factors did not of themselves explain outcomes. Any structure, Hoffmann pointed out, 'can lead either to peace or war; it depends on the domestic characteristics of the main actors, on their preferences and goals, as well as on the relations and links among them' (Hoffmann 1990: 191–2). Robert Keohane responded in line with the theory of interdependence which he had been instrumental in developing since the 1970s. Mearsheimer's effectively Hobbesian vision of virtually unrestrained international conflict, Keohane suggested, underesti-mated 'the impact of international institutions on world politics, particularly in contemporary Europe'. The fact that there were no (and never had been) global institutions which possessed enforcement powers comparable to those exerted by national governments within their own territories did not mean that incentives for cooperation did not exist. Nor did it mean that the disciplining effect of the bipolar cold war structure and of nuclear weapons had been the only restraint on nations' ambitions since 1945: 'the nature and strength of international institutions are also important determinants of expectations and therefore of state behaviour.' 'Insofar', Keohane concluded, 'as states regularly follow the rules and standards of international institutions, they signal their willingness to continue patterns of cooperation, and therefore reinforce expectations of stability' (Keohane 1990: 193).

Relating these somewhat abstract points to the situation in Europe since 1989, it is probably wise to resist making dogmatic assertions about the kind of political and security structures emerging from the wreckage of the cold war. The fact that the American role in Europe was rooted in the cold war did not mean that there was now no role for the United States in Europe. On the contrary, many Europeans, not least those in the former Soviet bloc, were insistent that an American presence must continue. Nor did the collapse of the Warsaw Pact mean that NATO was now redundant. There were indications that it might evolve into a pan-European security organization. Indeed, in January 1994 at the NATO summit in Brussels consideration was given to the eventual admission of some Eastern European nations – in the first instance Poland, Hungary, the Czech Republic, and Slovakia. Meanwhile, NATO offered them a 'partnership for peace' holding out the prospect of an evolution towards membership.

On the other hand, given the surge of nationalism in Russia following the elections of December 1993 and continued economic and political chaos, a NATO which included some nations of Eastern Europe but excluded Russia might be a recipe for instability in Europe. One could even envisage a new cold war resulting from a face-off between an expanded NATO and an isolated Russia, with a new Iron Curtain some hundreds of miles east of the old one. It was doubtless with some such prospect in mind that President Clinton went to great lengths to assure Russia that any moves to expand NATO would be part of a gradual, evolutionary process. Along with such assurances went the promise of greater coordination between the G7 (or major industrialized) nations and Russia. Finally, during President Clinton's visit to Moscow following the NATO summit in January 1994 it was announced that both nations had agreed to stop targeting their strategic nuclear missiles on each other. In short, in a highly fluid situation it was apparent that all parties were striving to move cautiously from the known to the unknown. Needless to say, the potential for instability and conflict remained large, given the continuous state of crisis in Russia and the former Yugoslavia.

The above considerations by no means exhausted the possibilities opened up by the ending of the cold war. The forces at work in the post-cold war world were sufficiently diverse as to provide fuel for virtually any speculation about the future. To some, global economic change indicated the splitting of the world into large and increasingly exclusive trading blocs – a North American free trade bloc, comprising the United States, Mexico, and Canada (formalized in 1993 as the North American Free Trade Association); an Asian bloc centred on Japan; and the European Community. In the most extreme version of the view that economic competition would dominate world politics the United States and Japan were depicted as mortal rivals. The prospect for America, it was said, was of a 'coming war with Japan' (Friedman and Lebard 1991).

A very different conception of the future and of the United States' place in it was the view that the end of the cold war had left the United States presiding over a 'unipolar moment' in which American political and military power was the only effective global stabilizing force. 'In the Persian Gulf', for example, wrote Charles Krauthammer, 'it was the United States acting unilaterally and with extraordinary speed, that in August 1990 prevented Iraq from taking effective control of the entire Arabian peninsula' (Krauthammer 1990–91: 24). Perhaps the most widely discussed vision of the future was that of Francis Fukuyama who regarded the end of the cold war as 'the end of history'. Not, he emphasized, that international conflict would cease, merely that fundamental ideological conflict such as had characterized the cold war was over. Western liberal democracy had prevailed and seemed likely to constitute 'the end point of man's ideological evolution' and 'the final form of human government' (Fukuyama 1992: xi). Nor was the appetite for large-scale speculation confined to optimists about the West's future. In an argument which recalled the writings of Arnold Toynbee, Samuel Huntington proposed that the fault lines in the world which was emerging from the cold war lay between civilizations or cultures rather than between nation-states or economic blocs (Huntington 1993).

There can be no way of fully reconciling these various views. They seize on different levels of power (economic, political, military, or cultural), employ different units of analysis (nation-state, economic bloc, civilization), and are underpinned by different philosophical assumptions (realist, pluralist, idealist). However, two considerations are present in all these speculations: firstly, an awareness that, however diminished the role of the nation-state might be, it still had a role to play; secondly, a preoccupation with the position of the United States in the new world order.

The issue of nationalism presented a paradox. On the one hand, it seemed clear that the notion of sovereignty had been undermined from two directions. Transnational processes took crucial areas of decision-making out of the hands of national governments, while ethnic and religious conflicts ate away at many nations from within. Yet, on the other hand, the urge to assert national identity – to bring nation-state boundaries into line with ethnic identities – had never been stronger. As a result of the end of the cold war the number of new nations was increased through the achievement of independence by the successor states of the Soviet Union. Indeed, the whole post-Second World War period had seen a burgeoning of nation-states from around 50 in 1945 to 184 in 1994. In this sense, the second half of the twentieth century more appropriately deserved the title of the 'era of nationalism' than did the nineteenth century.

The issue, however, was not one of nation-states versus other forms of political organization, or the simple development of one at the expense of the other, but of the specific ways in which nation-states interacted with new forces in world politics. One important feature of international politics in the post-cold war years was the growing recognition that sovereignty was a negotiable quantity, not an absolute value. One indication of how this operated in practice can be seen in the activities of the United Nations. Between 1990 and 1993 the United Nations engaged in four major interventions: the Gulf War, Somalia, Cambodia, and Bosnia. Some observers came to regard the Gulf War as a paradigm case of the new internationalism of the post-cold war world. With the Soviet veto effectively gone from the Security Council, the United Nations could now act in the way intended by its founders – as a collective security organization. Genuine internationalism was poised to achieve its long-delayed entrance on to the stage of world politics. By contrast, others saw the Gulf War as no more nor less than a case of the United States hijacking the United Nations for its own national purposes.

In actuality, the Gulf War was no paradigm case for either view. While the maintenance of the Gulf War coalition was undoubtedly dependent on enormous pressure from the United States, it was also dependent upon the consent of nations in the Gulf region. The Gulf War was a case neither of pure internationalism at work nor simply of American national ambition but of an *ad hoc* trade-off between the two. For the particular purpose of checking Iraqi aggression, a goal which received widespread international support (at least until the immediate task of removing Iraqi troops from Kuwait had been achieved), regional needs and American national purposes coincided. Because this measure of consensus existed, the United Nations proved to be an appropriate instrument.

The other cases of United Nations intervention show very clearly that the Gulf War was a unique event rather than a new paradigm for internationalist action. Though it is too early to say whether United Nations intervention can be ultimately successful in Somalia in producing political and economic stability, towards the end of 1993 it was already evident that a large United States role could not guarantee these outcomes. Resistance within Somalia to the American role on the part of key groups and a lack of regional consensus on the means and goals of the intervention threatened to undermine the rationale for the attempt to rescue Somalia from chaos. Equally important was the growing dissent within the United States to an extension of the American role. In October 1993 the Clinton administration announced that it would withdraw its troops from Somalia by March 1994. It was more difficult in the Somalian case than in the Gulf War to convince the American people that American interests were vitally at stake. In short, neither internationalism (as embodied in the United Nations) nor the exertion of American power could ensure a desired outcome where other vital ingredients – such as regional and local consensus – were absent.

The case of Cambodia was different again, but demonstrated the same fundamental point: that internationalist ventures were most likely to succeed when they took account of local and regional needs and interests. The composition of the UN mission in Cambodia reflected these interests, in that the mission was headed by a Japanese diplomat and the peace-keeping forces included contingents from Thailand, Malaysia, Indonesia, India, Holland (a former colonial power in the region), and Australia, which supplied the military commander. There was, in short, a potentially fruitful intersection between internationalism, regionalism, and local needs.

In Bosnia few of the conditions which might help to resolve the conflict seemed to be present. At the local level, for a period of two years after the fighting broke out in 1992, a murderous three-way conflict between Serbs, Croats, and Moslems allowed little scope for consensus on outside intervention beyond bare toleration of a humanitarian initiative by the UN. Until early 1994 successive attempts by various bodies to mediate produced only short-lived cease-fires. In February 1994, following the highly publicized lethal shelling of Moslems in Sarajevo by Bosnian Serb artillery, the UN was moved to enforce its fragile mandate with the aid of NATO troops and planes, and temporarily Bosnian Serb ambitions appeared to be checked. It remained to be seen whether this could last and whether the new-found international resolve could be extended from Sarajevo to other parts of Bosnia.

It was significant that these cases saw international efforts mounted on behalf of nation-states (or in the case of the former Yugoslavia, would-be nation-states) with the goal of restoring their integrity and sovereignty. It was significant also that the process could not be divorced from power political considerations. In that sense, the traditional opposition between internationalism and nationalism no longer held water. An idealist internationalism which ignored the reality of conflicts of power between nations was no more capable of comprehending the forces at work in international politics than a notion of realism based on the supposed imperviousness of national ambitions to any supranational influences. If there was a new paradigm for internationalist actions in the post-cold war world, it lay in the requirement that each new operation be the product of a specific negotiation of the relationship between national, regional, and international interests in the conflict in question.

One implication of the above discussion is that while the United States may be 'bound to lead', it is not necessarily bound to lead in every instance even if she wanted to. Economic power, military strength, and political influence mean that the United States will be a major player in many international and regional conflicts. As compared, however, with the cold war years, the United States may often have the luxury of choice, or at least the appearance of choice, with respect to intervention. In the absence of the Soviet threat, what will the rationale for such choices be?

In a major speech of September 1993, President Clinton's National Security Advisor, Anthony Lake, outlined such a rationale, one which he felt was consistent with the traditions of American foreign policy but which also met the needs of new global conditions. His prime concern was to discourage any tendency towards isolationism – one choice which now appeared to be open to the United States. It was an illusory choice, he insisted. The line between foreign and domestic policy, he noted, 'has evaporated'. 'Our choices about America's foreign policy will help determine', he continued:

- Whether Americans' real incomes double every 26 years, as they did in the 1960s, or every 36 years, as they did during the late '70s and '80s.
- Whether the 25 nations with weapons of mass destruction grow in number or decline.
- Whether the next quarter century will see terrorism, which injured or killed more than 2,000 Americans during the last quarter century, expand or recede as a threat.
- Whether the nations of the world will be more able or less able to address regional disputes, humanitarian needs and the threat of environmental degradation.

(Lake 1993: 2)

Having appealed to Americans' self-interest as well as to their idealism, he outlined four salient features of the new era which enjoined American engagement in the world: the broad acceptance in the world of America's core concepts (democracy and market economics), America's dominant global position, the explosion of ethnic conflicts, and the acceleration of information flows and of the pace of human life itself. The first two of these developments invited American engagement; the other two necessitated it. Engagement, however, must be made on a new basis. During the cold war 'we contained a global threat to market democracies; now we should seek to enlarge their reach, particularly in places of special significance to us'. 'Enlargement' was the successor to containment – enlargement of the 'world's free community of market democracies' (Lake 1993: 3-4, 5).

It may be doubted whether enlargement would carry anything like the same rhetorical and political force as containment since the term lacked specific focus. On the other hand, precisely because it lacked focus it could be suspected of blurring any distinction between pragmatically conceived American interests and the interests of other powers. Was enlargement not simply 'manifest destiny' and Woodrow Wilson's 'making the world safe for democracy' writ large for the late twentieth century? Enlargement seemed dangerously close to ethnocentrism, which invited undiscriminating definitions of American interests. At the very least, this new doctrine displayed the fundamental continuity in American foreign policy over the previous century and a half.

If, as was argued above, a central dilemma in the post-cold war world lay in the tension between global, regional, and national interests, then coordination between these levels was a prerequisite for global stability. No structure can endure which does not reflect the existing distribution of power. For that reason, given the pre-eminent power of the United States, much depends upon whether that power is exerted in a generous or a narrow spirit.

NOTES

1 INTRODUCTION: THE FIFTY YEARS' WAR

1 Clearly, the status of international law as compared with law within nations is a complex subject. Much debate surrounds the issue of whether international law deserves to be called law at all, given the absence in the international arena of any 'sovereign' power above that of nations themselves. For present purposes it is not necessary to resolve this question; we need simply note the fundamental distinction between international law and national law, arising from the fact that international law is not backed up by an international government. A full discussion of this and related issues can be found in Bull 1977: Ch. 6.

2 The issue of stability in the post-war international system has been most fully treated by John Gaddis in an important and much discussed article published in 1986. For a critique of his tendency to underplay the asymmetries in the US–Soviet relationship, and hence the potential for instability, see Crockatt (1993).

3 THE SECOND WORLD WAR AND THE STRUGGLE FOR PEACE, 1941–1946

1 However dissolution of the Comintern was accepted in Britain and the United States at the time, it seems clear that Stalin was as concerned to send a message to communists abroad as to the Allied leaders. Stalin believed that he could control communist parties abroad more easily through direct relations with each organization individually than through the cumbersome machinery of the Comintern (Mastny 1979: 95–7).

2 This problem was moderated but not entirely removed during the Korean War by the passage of the 'Uniting for Peace Resolution', designed to enable the Security Council veto to be circumvented via a General Assembly resolution (Howard 1989b: 34).

4 'TWO WAYS OF LIFE': THE COLD WAR IN EUROPE, 1947–1953

1 A good example of how the debate between revisionist and orthodox historians has continued to appear in new guises is an article by Melvin Leffler (1984: 346–81) with accompanying responses by John Gaddis and Bruce Kuniholm (382–400). Leffler's approach, which he has reinforced in his massive study of the Truman administration (1992), might be termed neo-revisionist just as Gaddis and Kuniholm retain elements of orthodoxy.

2 Raymond Garthoff makes the same point in (1992: 128).

11 *DÉTENTE* UNDER PRESSURE, 1973–1981

1 Many examples could be cited, but a particularly cogent version of this view is Breslauer (1983).

BIBLIOGRAPHICAL NOTE

References to writings on special aspects of United States and Soviet foreign policies are given in the text. Here are included only general surveys and books which offer broad perspectives on cold war history and international politics.

GLOBAL PERSPECTIVES

Peter Calvocoressi's *World Politics Since 1945* (6th edition, 1991) has gone through several editions since its first publication in 1968. Though containing a wealth of information, its organization by region blunts one's sense of change over the period. T.E. Vadney, *The World Since 1945* (1987) is an eminently readable narrative which pays particular attention to Third World issues. A more analytical study of global politics since 1945 is Seyom Brown's *New Forces, Old Forces, and the Future of World Politics* (1988). No one should miss Paul Kennedy's *The Rise and Fall of the Great Powers* (1988) which, among other things, is a reminder that in many important respects there is nothing new under the sun. The best overview of the world economy is Herman Van der Wee, *Prosperity and Upheaval: The World Economy 1945–1980* (1987).

A good introduction to international relations theory is Paul R. Viotti and Mark V. Kauppi, *International Relations Theory: Realism, Pluralism and Globalism* (2nd edition, 1993). It contains a wide selection of readings from various schools of theory plus commentary by the editors. An exceptionally clear account of the philosophical issues underlying international relations theory is Martin Hollis and Steve Smith, *Explaining and Understanding International Relations* (1991).

STUDIES OF THE COLD WAR

First mention must go to a book which appeared just as this one was being completed – Martin Walker's *The Cold War and the Making of the Modern World* (1993). It is the first comprehensive history of the Cold War written from a post-cold war point of view. Walker's experience as a journalist covering the Soviet Union during the Gorbachev period and the United States at various times shows to good effect. John Gaddis, *Russia, the Soviet Union and the United States* (1990a) begins with the founding of the United States and effectively conveys the entire sweep of two centuries of Russian–American relations. Louis Halle's *The Cold War as History* (1967), though covering only the first two decades of the cold war, contains much that is not to be found elsewhere – especially on geopolitics – and stands up well.

George Liska considers the patterns of superpower relations in *Re-thinking US–Soviet Relations* (1987). *The Global Rivals* (1988) by Seweryn Bialer and Michael Mandelbaum is a fairly brief interpretive account which approaches the material thematically rather than in

381

narrative form. The combination of Bialer's expertise in Soviet studies and Mandelbaum's in security issues makes for a powerful analysis. Paul Dukes's *The Last Great Game: USA Versus USSR* (1989) contains a wealth of material on the structure of US–Soviet relations and on each nation's perceptions of the other. Though his many flashes of insight do not add up to a sustained analysis, he has certainly made the case for placing the cold war in a long historical perspective. Adam Ulam's *The Rivals* (1973) takes the story of US–Soviet relations up to *détente* and can be supplemented by his *Dangerous Relations: The Soviet Union in World Politics, 1970–1982* (1983). Walter LaFeber, *America, Russia, and the Cold War* (7th edition, 1993a) is an updated version of a by now standard moderately revisionist account. Richard Crockatt and Steve Smith bring together essays from a number of hands, organized around the themes of the first cold war, *détente*, and the second cold war, in *The Cold War Past and Present* (1987). John Gaddis's *The Long Peace* (1987) is a collection of essays rather than a survey and covers mainly American policy. However, the title essay (originally published in *International Security* in 1986) proposes a framework for understanding the cold war as a whole and is sufficiently arresting to have inspired numerous responses. Among the best of these are collected by Charles Kegley in *The Long Postwar Peace: Contending Explanations and Projections* (1991). History and political science feed off each other here to good advantage.

There are some excellent surveys of the cold war which focus on the nuclear arms race: C.G. Jacobsen, *The Nuclear Era* (1982); John Newhouse, *The Nuclear Age: From Hiroshima to Star Wars* (1989); and McGeorge Bundy, *Danger and Survival: Choices About the Bomb in the First Fifty Years* (1988). Each includes material on the lesser nuclear powers as well as on the Soviet Union and the United States.

AMERICAN FOREIGN POLICY

Any of the following general surveys of US foreign policy will serve as a useful entry point into the subject: James E. Dougherty and Robert L. Pfaltzgraff, *American Foreign Policy: FDR to Reagan* (1986); Robert D. Schulzinger, *American Diplomacy in the Twentieth Century* (1984); Stephen E. Ambrose, *Rise To Globalism: American Foreign Policy Since 1938* (1988); though John Spanier, *American Foreign Policy Since World War II* (1977) is still valuable. Specifically on American policy towards the Soviet Union Peter Boyle's *American–Soviet Relations from the Russian Revolution to the Fall of Communism* (1993) is an excellent survey which contains a thoughtful concluding chapter on the larger implications of American cold war foreign policy. William Appleman Williams's *The Tragedy of American Diplomacy* (revised edition, 1972), the classic text of cold war revisionism, remains important for the force and scope of its argument even if, as I believe, its main contentions have been discredited. John Gaddis, *Strategies of Containment* (1982) manages to combine a clear analytical framework with an impressive use of primary sources, his thesis being that the policies of the various post-war administrations are to be understood as variations on the theme of containment. Michael Hunt's *Ideology and US Foreign Policy* (1987) tackles what the author admits is a 'big and slippery subject' and does so illuminatingly. There are many stimulating insights in Ernest May, *The Lessons of the Past: The Use and Misuse of History in American Foreign Policy* (1973). Finally, the following two books examine the institutions and processes of American foreign policy-making: Charles W. Kegley and Eugene Wittkopf, *American Foreign Policy: Pattern and Process* (1987), and John Dumbrell, *The Making of US Foreign Policy* (1990).

SOVIET FOREIGN POLICY

The standard history of Soviet foreign policy in the post-war period is Joseph Nogee and Robert Donaldson, *Soviet Foreign Policy Since World War II* (3rd edition, 1988), though Adam

Ulam, *Expansion and Coexistence: Soviet Foreign Policy 1917–1973* (1968) remains important, not least because of its coverage of the formative period of the Soviet state. As mentioned above, Ulam's *Dangerous Relations* (1983) carries the story forward into the early 1980s. Robbin Laird and Erik Hoffmann (eds), *Soviet Foreign Policy in a Changing World* (1986) is a compendious collection of articles. Most are from the 1970s and 1980s but many throw light on the whole period. Robert V. Daniels (ed.), *A Documentary History of Communism,* Volume 2: *Communism and the World* (1985) contains many key sources.

Some of the best writing on Soviet foreign policy and its domestic roots is contained in relatively old books: Philip E. Mosely, *The Kremlin and World Politics: Studies in Soviet Policy and Action* (1960), and Robert C. Tucker, *The Soviet Political Mind: Stalinism and Post-Stalin Change* (1972). Richard Lowenthal, *World Communism: The Disintegration of a Secular Faith* (1964) is also an old book, but Lowenthal's insights into the complex dynamics within world communism at a critical period in its history – 1955–64 – remain unsurpassed.

BIBLIOGRAPHY

Acheson, D. (1969) *Present at the Creation: My Years in the State Department*, New York: Norton.

Acton, E. (1986) *Russia*, Harlow: Longman.

Adler, S. (1961) *The Isolationist Impulse: The Twentieth Century*, New York: Collier.

Allison, G. (1971) *Essence of Decision: Explaining the Cuban Missile Crisis*, Boston: Little, Brown.

Allison, R. (1988) *The Soviet Union and the Strategy of Non-Alignment in the Third World*, Cambridge: Cambridge University Press.

Alperovitz, G. (1985) *Atomic Diplomacy: Hiroshima and Potsdam, The Use of the Atomic Bomb and the American Confrontation with Soviet Power*, 2nd edition, New York: Elizabeth Sifton Books.

Ambrose, S. (1984) *Eisenhower the President, 1952–1969*, London: Allen and Unwin.

Ambrose, S. (1988) *Rise to Globalism: American Foreign Policy Since 1938*, Harmondsworth: Penguin.

Arbatov, G. (1983) *Cold War or Détente? The Soviet Viewpoint*, London: Zed Books.

Arendt, H. (1971) 'The Art of Lying: The Pentagon Papers', *New York Review of Books*, 18 November, 30–9.

Barnet, R.J. (1972) *Intervention and Revolution: The United States in the Third World*, London: Paladin.

Barraclough, G. (1967) *An Introduction to Contemporary History*, Harmondsworth: Penguin.

Beschloss, M. (1986) *Mayday: Eisenhower, Kennedy and the U-2 Affair*, New York: Harper and Row.

Beschloss, M. (1991) *Kennedy v Khrushchev: The Crisis Years 1960–1963*, London: Faber and Faber.

Beschloss, M. and Talbott, S. (1993) *At the Highest Levels: The Inside Story of the End of the Cold War*, London: Little, Brown.

Bialer, S. (1986) *The Soviet Paradox: External Expansion, Internal Decline*, New York: Knopf.

Bialer, S. and Mandelbaum, M. (1988) *The Global Rivals*, London: I.B. Tauris.

Blair, B. (1993) *The Logic of Accidental Nuclear War*, Washington, DC: The Brookings Institution.

Blight, J. and Welch, D. (1990) *On the Brink: Americans and Soviets Reexamine the Cuban Missile Crisis*, New York: Noonday Press.

Blight, J., Allyn, B. and Welch, D. (1993) 'Kramer vs. Kramer: Or How Can You Have Revisionism in the Absence of Orthodoxy', *Bulletin* of the Cold War International History Project, Issue 3, Fall: 41 (continues on 47–50).

Blum, J.M. (ed.) (1985) *Public Philosopher: Selected Letters of Walter Lippmann*, New York: Ticknor and Fields.

Boutwell, J. (1988) 'SDI and the Allies', 87–109 in J. Nye and J. Schear (eds), *On the Defensive? The Future of SDI*, Lanham, Md.: University Press of America.

Bova, R. (1991) 'Political Dynamics of Post-Communist Transition: A Comparative Perspective', *World Politics* 44, No. 1, October: 113–38.

Bowie, R. (1989) 'Eisenhower, Dulles, and the Suez Crisis', 189–214 in W. Louis and R. Owen (eds), *Suez 1956: The Crisis and its Consequences*, Oxford: Clarendon Press.

Bowker, M. and Williams, P. (1988) *Superpower Détente: A Reappraisal*, London: Royal Institute of International Affairs/Sage.

Boyle, P. (1993) *American–Soviet Relations from the Russian Revolution to the Fall of Communism*, London: Routledge.

Brands, H. (1989) 'The Age of Vulnerability: Eisenhower and the National Insecurity State', *American Historical Review* 94, No. 4, October: 963–89.

Brecher, M. and Wilkenfeld, J. (1991) 'International Crises and Global Stability: The Myth of the "Long Peace"', 85–104 in C. Kegley (ed.), *The Long Postwar Peace: Contending Explanations and Projections*, New York: HarperCollins.

Breslauer, G. (1982) *Khrushchev and Brezhnev as Leaders: Building Authority in Soviet Politics*, London: George Allen and Unwin.

Breslauer, G. (1983) 'Why *Détente* Failed: An Interpretation', 319–40 in A.L. George (ed.), *Managing US–Soviet Rivalry: Problems of Crisis Prevention*, Boulder: Westview.

Brinton, C. ([1932] 1965) *The Anatomy of Revolution*, New York: Vintage.

Brodie, B. ([1945] 1989) 'The Atomic Bomb and American Security', 64–94 in P. Bobbit, L. Freedman, and G. Treverton (eds), *US Nuclear Strategy: A Reader*, London: Macmillan.

Brown, S. (1988) *New Forces, Old Forces, and the Future of World Politics*, Washington, DC: Brookings Institution.

Brzezinski, Z. (ed.) (1969) *Dilemmas of Change in Soviet Politics*, New York: Columbia University Press.

Brzezinski, Z. (1983) *Power and Principle: Memoirs of the National Security Advisor 1977–1981*, New York: Farrar, Straus and Giroux.

Brzezinski, Z. (1989) *The Grand Failure: The Birth and Death of Communism in the Twentieth Century*, New York: Scribners.

Buchan, A. (1972) *Power and Equilibrium in the 1970s*, London: Chatto and Windus.

Bull, H. (1977) *The Anarchical Society: A Study of Order in World Politics*, London: Macmillan.

Bull, H. (1984) 'The Revolt Against the West', 217–28 in H. Bull and A. Watson (eds), *The Expansion of International Society*, Oxford: Clarendon Press.

Bundy, McG. (1988) *Danger and Survival: Choices About the Bomb in the First Fifty years*, New York: Vintage.

Bundy, McG., Kennan, G., McNamara, R. and Smith, G. (1984–85) 'The President's Choice: Star Wars or Arms Control', *Foreign Affairs* 63, No. 2, Winter: 264–78.

Calvocoressi, P. (1991) *World Politics Since 1945*, 6th edition, London: Longman.

Campbell, J. (1989) 'The Soviet Union, the United States, and the Twin Crises of Hungary and Suez', 233–53 in W. Louis and R. Owen (eds), *Suez 1956: The Crisis and its Consequences*, Oxford: Clarendon Press.

Carr, E.H. (1942) *The Twenty Years' Crisis, 1919–39: An Introduction to the Study of International Relations*, London: Macmillan.

Carter, J. (1982) *Keeping Faith: Memoirs of a President*, New York: Bantam Books.

Chace, J. (1973) *A World Elsewhere: The New American Foreign Policy*, New York: Scribners.

Chafe, W. (1991) *The Unfinished Journey: America Since World War II*, 2nd edition, New York: Oxford University Press.

Chang, G. (1990) *Friends and Enemies: The United States, China, and the Soviet Union, 1948–1972*, Stanford: Stanford University Press.

Charlton, M. (1984) *The Eagle and the Small Birds: Crisis in the Soviet Empire from Yalta to Solidarity*, London: BBC Publications.

Charlton, M. (1986) *The Star Wars History: From Deterrence to Defence, The American Strategic Debate*, London: BBC Publications.

Chen, J. (1992) 'The Sino–Soviet Alliance and China's Entry into the Korean War', Working Paper No. 1, Cold War International History Project, Woodrow Wilson Center, Washington, DC, June: 31 pages.

Chomsky, N., Steele, J. and Gittings, J. (1982) *Superpowers in Collision: The New Cold War*, Harmondsworth: Penguin.

Churchill, W.S. (1953) *The Second World War: Triumph and Tragedy*, Boston: Houghton Mifflin.

Cohen, B. (1987) 'An Explosion in the Kitchen? Economic Relations with Other Advanced Industrial States', 115–43 in K. Oye, R. Lieber, and D. Rothchild (eds), *Eagle Resurgent?: The Reagan Era in American Foreign Policy*, Boston: Little, Brown.

Cohen, S. (1985) *Rethinking the Soviet Experience: Politics and History Since 1917*, New York: Oxford University Press.

Cox, M. (1986), 'The Cold War and Stalinism in the Age of Capitalist Decline', *Critique* 17: 17–82.

Cox, M. (1990) 'From the Truman Doctrine to the Second Superpower *Détente*: The Rise and Fall of the Cold War', *Journal of Peace Research* 27, No. 1: 25–41.

Crankshaw, E. (1963) *The New Cold War: Moscow v Peking*, Harmondsworth: Penguin.

Crankshaw, E. (1966) *Khrushchev*, London: Collins.

Crockatt, R. (1993) 'Theories of Stability and the End of the Cold War', 59–81 in M. Bowker and R. Brown (eds), *From Cold War to Collapse: Theory and World Politics in the 1980s*, Cambridge: Cambridge University Press.

Crockatt, R. and Smith, S. (1987) *The Cold War Past and Present*, London: Allen and Unwin.

Cromwell, W. (1992) *The United States and the European Pillar: The Strained Alliance*, London: Macmillan.

Dallin, A. and Lapidus, G. (1987) 'Reagan and the Russians: American Policy Toward the Soviet Union', 193–254 in K. Oye, R. Lieber, and D. Rothchild (eds), *Eagle Resurgent?: The Reagan Era in American Foreign Policy*, Boston: Little, Brown.

Daniels, R. (ed.) (1985) *A Documentary History of Communism*, Vol. 1 *Communism in Russia*, Vol. 2 *Communism and the World*, London: I.B. Tauris.

Darby, P. (1987) *Three Faces of Imperialism: British and American Approaches to Asia and Africa, 1870–1970*, New Haven: Yale University Press.

Dawisha, K. (1990) *Eastern Europe, Gorbachev and Reform: The Great Challenge*, Cambridge: Cambridge University Press.

Department of State ([1949] 1967) *United States Relations With China With Special Reference to the Period 1944–1949*, Vol. I, Stanford: Stanford University Press.

DePorte, A. (1986) *Europe Between the Superpowers: The Enduring Balance*, New Haven: Yale University Press.

Deutsch, K. and Singer, J. (1964) 'Multipolar Systems and International Stability', *World Politics* 16, No. 3: 390–406.

Deutscher, I. (1960) *Stalin: A Political Biography*, New York: Vintage Books.

Deutscher, I. (1961) *The Great Contest: Russia and the West*, New York: Ballantine Books.

Deutscher, I. (1970) *Russia, China, and the West, 1953–1966*, Harmondsworth: Penguin.

386

Dibb, P. (1988) *The Soviet Union: The Incomplete Superpower*, London: International Institute for Strategic Studies/Macmillan.

Divine, R. (1965) *The Reluctant Belligerent: American Entry Into World War II*, New York: John Wiley.

Divine, R. (1978) *Blowing on the Wind: The Nuclear Test Ban Debate 1954–1960*, New York: Oxford University Press.

Djilas, M. (1962) *Conversations with Stalin*, New York: Harcourt Brace.

Dobson, A. (1988) 'The Kennedy Administration and Economic Warfare Against Communism', *International Affairs* 64, No. 4, Autumn: 599–616.

Dougherty, J.E. and Pfaltzgraff, R.L. (1986) *American Foreign Policy: FDR to Reagan*, New York: Harper and Row.

Draper, T. (1990) 'The Constitution in Danger', *New York Review of Books* March 1: 41–7, and responses May 17: 50–3.

Drucker, P. ([1956] 1971) 'America Becomes a "Have-Not" Nation', 556–68 in R. Goldwin (ed.), *Readings in American Foreign Policy*, 2nd edition, New York: Oxford University Press.

Dukes, P. (1989) *The Last Great Game: USA Versus USSR*, London: Pinter.

Dulles, F.R. (1972) *American Policy Towards Communist China*, New York: Thomas Y. Crowell.

Dulles, J. (1954) 'Policy for Security and Peace', *Foreign Affairs* 32: 353–64.

Dumbrell, J. (1990) *The Making of US Foreign Policy*, Manchester: Manchester University Press.

Dyson, K. (1986) 'European *Détente* in Historical Perspective: Ambiguities and Paradoxes', 14–55 in K. Dyson (ed.), *European Détente: Case Studies of East–West Relations*, London: Frances Pinter.

Eden, A. (1960) *Full Circle: The Memoirs of Anthony Eden*, London: Cassell.

Edmonds, R. (1983) *Soviet Foreign Policy: The Brezhnev Years*, Oxford: Oxford University Press.

Edmonds, R. (1991) *The Big Three: Churchill, Roosevelt and Stalin in Peace and War*, New York: Norton.

Eilts, H. (1989) 'Reflections on the Suez Crisis: Security in the Middle East', 347–61 in W. Louis and R. Owen (eds), *Suez 1956: The Crisis and its Consequences*, Oxford: Clarendon Press.

Eisenhower, D. (1963) *The White House Years: Mandate for Change, 1953–1956*, London: Heinemann.

Eisenhower, D. (1966) *The White House Years: Waging Peace, 1956–1961*, London: Heinemann.

Erikson, S., Luttberg, R. and Redin, K. (1980) *American Public Opinion: Its Origins, Content, and Impact*, 2nd edition, New York: Wiley.

Etzold, T. and Gaddis, J. (eds) (1978) *Containment: Documents On American Policy and Strategy, 1945–1950*, New York: Columbia University Press.

Facts on File (1976) *Portuguese Revolution 1974–1976*, New York: Facts on File.

Fejtö, F. (1974) *A History of the People's Democracies: Eastern Europe Since Stalin*, Harmondsworth: Penguin.

Ferrell, R. (ed.) (1975) *America in a Divided World, 1945–1972*, New York: Harper and Row.

Fitzpatrick, J.C. (ed.) (1940) *The Writings of George Washington*, Washington, DC: US Government Printing Office, Vol. 35: 214–38.

Foot, R. (1985) *The Wrong War: American Policy and the Dimensions of the Korean Conflict, 1950–53*, Ithaca: Cornell University Press.

Freedman, L. (1981) *The Evolution of Nuclear Strategy*, London: Macmillan/International Institute for Strategic Studies.

Freedman, L. (1990) 'Parade's End', *New York Review of Books* 37, March 29: 22.

Friedman, G. and Lebard, M. (1991) *The Coming War with Japan*, New York: St Martin's Press.

FRUS (= *Foreign Relations of the United States*) (1945) Diplomatic Papers: 194–6.

FRUS (1947) Vol. III, British Commonwealth/Europe.

FRUS (1950) Vol. I, National Security Policy, 234–92.

FRUS (1952–54) Vol. II, National Security Affairs, Part I: 577–97.

FRUS (1955–57) Vol. XIX, National Security Policy: 638–61.

Fukuyama, F. (1992) *The End of History and the Last Man*, London: Hamish Hamilton.

Funnell, V. (1978) 'Vietnam and the Sino–Soviet Conflict, 1965–1976', *Studies in Comparative Communism* XI, Nos. 1 and 2, Spring/Summer: 142–69.

Gaddis, J. (1972) *The United States and the Origins of the Cold War, 1941–1947*, New York: Columbia University Press.

Gaddis, J. (1982) *Strategies of Containment: A Critical Appraisal of Postwar American Security Policy*, New York: Oxford University Press.

Gaddis, J. (1986) 'The Long Peace: Elements of Stability in the Postwar International System', *International Security* 10, No. 4, Spring: 99–142.

Gaddis, J. (1987) *The Long Peace: Inquiries into the History of the Cold War*, New York: Oxford University Press.

Gaddis, J. (1989) 'Hanging Tough Paid Off', *Bulletin of the Atomic Scientists* 45, No. 1, January: 11–14.

Gaddis, J. (1990a) *Russia, the Soviet Union and the United States: An Interpretive History*, 2nd edition, New York: McGraw-Hill.

Gaddis, J. (1990b) 'Beyond the Triumph of Liberty', *The Guardian* (London), 1 June: 19.

Gaddis, J. (1992) *The United States and the End of the Cold War: Implications, Reconsiderations, Provocations*, New York: Oxford University Press.

Gaddis, J. (1992/3) 'International Relations Theory and the End of the Cold War', *International Security* 17, No. 3: 5–38.

Gardner, L. (1993) *Spheres of Influence: The Great Powers Partition Europe, from Munich to Yalta*, Chicago: Ivan Dee.

Garthoff, R. (1985) *Détente and Confrontation: American–Soviet Relations Nixon to Reagan*, Washington, DC: Brookings Institution.

Garthoff, R. (1987) *Policy Versus the Law: The Reinterpretation of the ABM Treaty*, Washington, DC: Brookings Institution.

Garthoff, R. (1988) 'Cuban Missile Crisis: The Soviet Story', *Foreign Policy* 72, Fall: 61–80.

Garthoff, R. (1989) *Reflections on the Cuban Missile Crisis*, revised edition, Washington, DC: Brookings Institution.

Garthoff, R. (1990) *Deterrence and the Revolution In Soviet Military Doctrine*, Washington, DC: Brookings Institution.

Garthoff, R. (1992) 'Why Did the Cold War Arise, and Why Did it End?', 127–36 in M. Hogan (ed.), *The End of the Cold War: Its Meaning and Implications*, Cambridge: Cambridge University Press.

Garton Ash, T. (1984) *The Polish Revolution: Solidarity*, New York: Charles Scribner's Sons.

Garton Ash, T. (1990) 'Eastern Europe: The Year of Truth', *New York Review of Books* 37, February 15: 17–22.

Gati, C. (1990) *The Bloc That Failed: Soviet–East European Relations in Transition*, Bloomington: Indiana University Press.

Gelman, H. (1984) *The Brezhnev Politburo and the Decline of Détente*, Ithaca: Cornell University Press.

Gittings, J. (1982) 'China: Half a Superpower', in N. Chomsky *et al.*, *Superpowers in Collision: The New Cold War*, Harmondsworth: Penguin.

Golan, G. (1990) *Soviet Policies in the Middle East: From World War II to Gorbachev*, Cambridge: Cambridge University Press.

Goldman, M. (1992) *What Went Wrong with Perestroika*, New York: Norton.

Gorbachev, M. (1988) *Perestroika: New Thinking for Our Country and the World*, London: Fontana.

Green, D. (1974) 'The Cold War Comes to Latin America', 149–95 in B. Bernstein (ed.), *Politics and Policies of the Truman Administration*, New York: New Viewpoints.

Greenstein, F. (1982) *The Hidden-Hand Presidency: Eisenhower as Leader*, New York: Basic Books.

Greiner, B. (1990) 'The Cuban Missile Crisis Reconsidered, The Soviet View: An Interview with Sergo Mikoyan', *Diplomatic History*, No. 2, Fall: 205–21.

Grenville, J. and Wasserstein, B. (eds) (1987) *The Major International Treaties Since 1945: A History and Guide With Texts*, London: Methuen.

Griffith, W. (1978) 'The Diplomacy of Eurocommunism', 385–436 in R. Tökés (ed.), *Eurocommunism and Détente*, New York: New York University Press.

Gromyko, A. (1989) *Memories*, London: Hutchinson.

Guardian (London) January 18, 1989: 8.

Guardian (London) May 3, 1989: 26.

Guardian (London) December 12, 1990: 5.

Guardian (London) October 19, 1991: 10.

Haftendorn, H. (1986) *Sicherheit und Stabilität: Aussenbeziehung der Bundesrepublik zwischen Ölkrise und NATO–Doppelbeschluss*, Munchen: DTV.

Halle, L. (1967) *The Cold War as History*, New York: Harper and Row.

Halliday, F. (1981) *Soviet Policy in the Arc of Crisis*, Washington, DC: Institute for Policy Studies.

Halliday, F. (1983) *The Making of the Second Cold War*, London: Verso.

Halliday, F. (1990a) 'The Ends of the Cold War', *New Left Review* 180, March/April: 5–23.

Halliday, F. (1990b) '"The Sixth Great Power": On the Study of Revolution and International Relations', *Review of International Studies* 16, No. 3 July: 207–22.

Halliday, J. and Cumings, B. (1988) *Korea: The Unknown War*, London: Viking.

Harsch, J. (1950) *The Curtain Isn't Iron*, London: Putnam.

Hartz, L. (1955) *The Liberal Tradition in America*, New York: Harcourt Brace.

Hastings, M. (1988) *The Korean War*, London: Michael Joseph.

Hathaway, R.M. (1981) *Ambiguous Partnership: Britain and America, 1944–1947*, New York: Columbia University Press.

Heath, J. (1976) *Decade of Disillusionment: The Kennedy–Johnson Years*, Bloomington: Indiana University Press.

Helman, G. and Ratner, S. (1992–93) 'Saving Failed States', *Foreign Policy* 89, Winter: 3–20.

Herken, G. (1980) *The Winning Weapon: The Atomic Bomb in the Cold War 1945–1950*, New York: Alfred Knopf.

Herring, G. (1979) *America's Longest War: The United States and Vietnam, 1950–1975*, New York: Wiley.

Hersh, S. (1983) *The Price of Power: Kissinger in the Nixon White House*, New York: Simon and Schuster.

Hersh, S. (1991) *The Samson Option: Israel, America, and the Bomb*, London: Faber.

Hershberg, J. (1992) 'Before "The Missiles of October": Did Kennedy Plan a Military Strike Against Cuba?', 237–80, in J. Nathan (ed.), *The Cuban Missile Crisis Revisited*, New York: St Martin's Press.

Hersey, J. ([1946] 1986) *Hiroshima*, Harmondsworth: Penguin.

Hewedy, A. (1989) 'Nasser and the Crisis of 1956', 161–72 in W. Louis and R. Owen (eds), *Suez 1956: The Crisis and its Consequences*, Oxford: Clarendon Press.

Hoffmann, S. (1990) Correspondence, *International Security* 15, No. 2: 191–2.

Holland, R. (1985) *European Decolonization 1918–1981: An Introductory Survey*, London: Macmillan.

Hollis, M. and Smith, S. (1991) *Explaining and Understanding International Relations*, Oxford: Clarendon Press.

Holloway, D. (1984) *The Soviet Union and the Arms Race*, 2nd edition, New Haven: Yale University Press.

Holsti, K. (1988) 'Interdependence, Integration or Fragmentation: Scenarios for the Future', 216–30 in C. Kegley and E. Wittkopf (eds), *The Global Agenda: Issues and Perspectives*, 2nd edition, New York: Random House.

Hoopes, T. (1974) *The Devil and John Foster Dulles*, London: André Deutsch.

Horowitz, D. (1967) *From Yalta to Vietnam*, Harmondsworth: Penguin.

Hosking, G. (1985) *A History of the Soviet Union*, London: Fontana.

Hough, J. (1980) *The Soviet Leadership in Transition*, Washington, DC: Brookings Institution.

Hough, J. (1988) *Opening up the Soviet Economy*, Washington, DC: Brookings Institution.

Hourani, A. (1985) *Political Society in Lebanon: A Historial Introduction*, Cambridge, Mass.: Center for International Studies, Massachussetts Institute of Technology.

Howard, M. (1985) 'Introduction' to O. Riste (ed.), *Western Security: The Formative Years, European and Atlantic Defence, 1947–1953*, Oslo: Norwegian University Press.

Howard, M. (1989a) 'Ideology and International Relations', *Review of International Studies* 15, January: 1–10.

Howard, M. (1989b) 'The United Nations and International Security', 31–45 in A. Roberts and B. Kingsbury (eds), *The United Nations, Divided World*, Oxford: Clarendon Press.

Hunt, M. (1987) *Ideology and US Foreign Policy*, New Haven: Yale University Press.

Huntington, S. (1993) 'The Clash of Civilizations?', *Foreign Affairs* 72, No. 3, Summer: 22–49.

Hyland, W. (1988) *Mortal Rivals: Understanding the Hidden Pattern of Soviet–American Relations*, New York: Simon and Schuster.

Isaacson, W. (1992) *Kissinger: A Biography*, New York: Simon and Schuster.

Jacobsen, C.G. (1982) *The Nuclear Era*, Nottingham: Spokesman.

Janis, I. (1972) *Victims of Groupthink*, Boston: Houghton Mifflin.

Jensen, K. (ed.) (1991) *Origins of the Cold War: The Novikov, Kennan, and Roberts 'Long Telegrams' of 1946*, Washington, DC: United States Institute of Peace.

Jervis, R. (1976) *Perception and Misperception in International Politics*, Princeton: Princeton University Press.

Jones, J.M. (1955) *The Fifteen Weeks*, New York: Harcourt Brace.

Kahn, E.J. (1975) *The China Hands: America's Foreign Service Officers and What Befell Them*, New York: Viking Press.

Kaplan, L. (1985) 'An Unequal Triad: The United States, Western Union, and NATO', 107–27 in O. Riste (ed.), *Western Security: The Formative Years, European and Atlantic Defence, 1947–53*, Oslo: Norwegian University Press.

Karnow, S. (1984) *Vietnam: A History*, Harmondsworth: Penguin.

Kaufmann, W. ([1956] 1989) 'The Requirements of Deterrence', 168–87 in P. Bobbit, L. Freedman, and G. Treverton (eds), *US Nuclear Strategy: A Reader*, London: Macmillan.

Kegley, C. (1990) 'The Characteristics of Contemporary International Terrorism', 11–26 in C. Kegley (ed.), *International Terrorism: Characteristics, Causes, Controls*, New York: St Martin's Press.

Kegley, C. (ed.) (1991) *The Long Postwar Peace: Contending Explanations and Projections*, New York: HarperCollins.

Kegley, C. and Wittkopf, E. (1987) *American Foreign Policy: Pattern and Process*, New York: Macmillan.

Kemp, T. (1990) *The Climax of Capitalism: The US Economy in the Twentieth Century*, London: Longman.

Kennan, G.F. (1947) 'The Sources of Soviet Conduct', *Foreign Affairs* 25, July: 566–82.

Kennan, G.F. (1960) 'Peaceful Coexistence: A Western View', *Foreign Affairs* 38, January: 171–90.

Kennan, G.F. (1967) *Memoirs 1925–1950*, Boston: Little, Brown.

Kennan, G.F. (1992) 'The G.O.P. Won the Cold War? Ridiculous', *New York Times*, October 28: A21.

Kennedy, D. (1980) *Over Here: The First World War and American Society*, New York: Oxford University Press.

Kennedy, J.F. (1962), *Public Papers of the Presidents of the United States: John F. Kennedy 1961*, Washington, DC: US Government Printing Office.

Kennedy, J.F. (1964) *The Public Papers of The Presidents of the United States: John F. Kennedy 1963*, Washington, DC: US Government Printing Office.

Kennedy, P. (1988) *The Rise and Fall of the Great Powers: Economic Change and Military Conflict, 1500–2000*, London: Unwin Hyman.

Keohane, R. (1990) Correspondence, *International Security* 15, No. 2: 192–4.

Keohane, R. and Nye, J. (1977) *Power and Interdependence: World Politics in Transition*, Boston: Little, Brown.

Khariton, Y. and Smirnov, Y. (1993) 'The Khariton Version', *Bulletin of the Atomic Scientists*, 49, No. 4: 20–31.

Khrushchev, N. (1971) *Khrushchev Remembers*, Boston: Little, Brown.

Khrushchev, N. (1974) *Khrushchev Remembers: The Last Testament*, Boston: Little, Brown.

Khrushchev, N. (1990) *Khrushchev Remembers: The Glasnost Tapes*, Boston: Little, Brown.

Kimball, W. (ed.) (1984) *Churchill and Roosevelt: The Complete Correspondence*, Vol. 3, London: Collins.

Kissinger, H. (1957) *A World Restored: The Politics of Conservatism in a Revolutionary Age*, New York: Grosset and Dunlop.

Kissinger, H. (1969) *American Foreign Policy: Three Essays*, London: Weidenfeld and Nicolson.

Kissinger, H. (1979) *The White House Years*, London: Weidenfeld and Nicolson.

Kissinger, H. (1982) *Years of Upheaval*, Boston: Little, Brown.

Kolko, G. (1986) *Vietnam: Anatomy of a War*, London: Allen and Unwin.

Kramer, J. (1990) 'Eastern Europe and the "Energy Shock" of 1990', Paper delivered to the Conference of the British International Studies Association, Newcastle-upon-Tyne, December.

Kramer, M. (1993) 'Tactical Nuclear Weapons, Soviet Command Authority, and the Cuban Missile Crisis', *Bulletin* of the Cold War International History Project, Issue 3, Fall: 40–6.

Krauthammer, C. (1990–91) 'The Unipolar Moment', *Foreign Affairs* 70: 23–33.

Kuniholm, B. (1980) *The Origins of Cold War in the Near East: Great Power Conflict and Diplomacy in Iran, Turkey, and Greece*, Princeton: Princeton University Press.

Kuniholm, B. (1987) 'The Origins of the First Cold War', 37–57 in R. Crockatt and S. Smith (eds), *The Cold War Past and Present*, London: Allen and Unwin.

Labrie, R. (ed.) (1979) *SALT Handbook: Key Documents and Issues, 1972–79*, Washington, DC: American Enterprise Institute.

LaFeber, W. (1993a) *America, Russia, and the Cold War, 1945–92*, New York: Knopf.

LaFeber, W. (1993b) *Inevitable Revolutions: The United States in Central America*, New York: Norton.

Laird, R. and Hoffmann, E. (eds) (1986) *Soviet Foreign Policy in a Changing World*, New York: Aldine.

Lake, A. (1993) 'Remarks to Johns Hopkins' School of Advanced International Studies', United States Information Service, US Embassy, London, September 22: 13 pages.

Laqueur, W. (1989) *The Long Road to Freedom: Russia and Glasnost*, London: Unwin Hyman.

Laqueur, W. and Rubin, B. (eds) (1984) *The Israel–Arab Reader: A Documentary History of the Middle East Conflict*, 4th edition, New York: Facts on File.

Larson, D. (1985) *The Origins of Containment*, Princeton: Princeton University Press.

Lattimore, O. (1945) *Solution in Asia*, Boston: Little, Brown.

Lebow, N. (1988) 'Provocative Deterrence: A New Look at the Cuban Missile Crisis', *Arms Control Today*, July/August: 15–16.

Leffler, M. (1984) 'The American Conception of National Security and the Beginnings of the Cold War, 1945–48', *American Historical Review* 89, April: 346–400.

Leffler, M. (1992) *A Preponderance of Power: National Security, The Truman Administration and the Cold War*, Stanford: Stanford University Press.

Lenin, V.I. (1925) *Collected Works of Lenin*, Moscow, Vol. XVII.

Levgold, R. (1978) 'The Soviet Union and West European Communism', 314–84 in R. Tökés, (ed.), *Eurocommunism and Détente*, New York: New York University Press.

Lewin, M. (1991) *The Gorbachev Phenomenon: A Historical Interpretation*, Berkeley: University of California Press.

Liska, G. (1987) *Re-thinking US–Soviet Relations*, Oxford: Blackwell.

Litwak, R. (1984) *Détente and the Nixon Doctrine: American Foreign Policy and the Pursuit of Stability, 1969–1976*, Cambridge: Cambridge University Press.

Lobanov-Rostovsky, A. (1965) 'Russian Expansion in the Far East in the Light of the Turner Hypothesis', 79–94 in W.D. Wyman and C.B. Kroeber (eds), *The Frontier in Perspective*, Madison: University of Wisconsin Press.

Lodal, J. (1976) 'Assuring Strategic Stability: An Alternative View', *Foreign Affairs* 54, No. 2, April: 462–81.

Louis, W. (1989) 'The Tragedy of the Anglo-Egyptian Settlement of 1954', 43–71 in W. Louis and R. Owen (eds), *Suez 1956: The Crisis and its Consequences*, Oxford: Clarendon Press.

Low, A.D. (1976) *The Sino–Soviet Dispute: An Analysis of the Polemics*, Rutherford, N.J.: Farleigh Dickinson University Press.

Lowe, P. (1986) *The Origins of the Korean War*, London: Longman.

Lowenthal, R. (1964) *World Communism: The Disintegration of a Secular Faith*, New York: Oxford University Press.

Lowenthal, R. (1984) 'The Soviet Union and the Third World: From Anti-imperialism to Counter-imperialism', 323–33 in H. Bull and A. Watson (eds), *The Expansion of International Society*, Oxford: Clarendon Press.

Luers, W. (1986) 'The Soviets and Latin America: A Three Decade U.S. Policy Tangle', 824–52 in R. Laird and E. Hoffmann (eds), *Soviet Foreign Policy in a Changing World*, New York: Aldine Publishing Company.

Lundestad, G. (1978) *The American Non-Policy Towards Eastern Europe, 1943–1947*, Oslo: Norwegian University Press.

Lyon, P. (1984) 'The Emergence of the Third World', 229–37 in H. Bull and A. Watson (eds), *The Expansion of International Society*, Oxford: Clarendon Press.

McCagg, W. (1978) *Stalin Embattled, 1943–1948*, Detroit: Wayne State University Press.

McCarthy, J. (1951) *America's Retreat from Victory: The Story of George Catlett Marshall*, New York: The Devin–Adair Company.

McGregor, C. (1988) *The Sino–Vietnamese Relationship and the Soviet Union*, London: International Institute for Strategic Studies, Adelphi Paper 232.

McGwire, M. (1989) 'About Face in Europe', *Guardian* (London) November 15.

McMahon, R. (1981) *Colonialism and Cold War: The United States and the Struggle for Indonesian Independence, 1945–1949*, Ithaca: Cornell University Press.

McNamara, R. ([1962] 1989) 'Speech to NATO Council, Athens, 5 May', 205–22 in P. Bobbit, L. Freedman, and G. Treverton (eds), *US Nuclear Strategy: A Reader*, London: Macmillan.

McNamara, R. (1986) *Blundering into Disaster: Surviving the First Century of the Nuclear Age*, New York: Pantheon.

Mahoney, R. (1983) *JFK: Ordeal in Africa*, New York: Oxford University Press.

Manchester Guardian Weekly, November 29, 1992: 16.

Mandelbaum, M. and Talbott, S. (1987) *Reagan and Gorbachev*, New York: Vintage.

Mark, E. (1981–82) 'American Policy Toward Eastern Europe and the Origins of the Cold War, 1941–46', *Journal of American History* 68: 313–36.

Marshall, B. (1990) *Willy Brandt*, London: Sphere Books.

Mastny, V. (1979) *Russia's Road to the Cold War: Diplomacy Warfare and the Politics of Communism, 1941–45*, New York: Columbia University Press.

Matusow, A.J. (ed.) (1970) *Joseph R. McCarthy*, Englewood Cliffs, N.J.: Prentice-Hall.

May, E. (1973) *The Lessons of the Past: The Use and Misuse of History in American Foreign Policy*, New York: Oxford University Press.

May, E. (ed.) (1993) *American Cold War Strategy: Interpreting NSC 68*, Boston: St Martin's Press.

Mearsheimer, J. (1990) 'Back to the Future: Instability After The Cold War', *International Security* 15, No. 1: 5–56.

Mearsheimer, J. (1993) 'The Case for a Ukrainian Nuclear Deterrent', *Foreign Affairs* 72, No. 3, Summer: 50–66.

Medvedev, R. (1982) *Khrushchev*, Oxford: Blackwell.

Medvedev, Z. (1988) *Gorbachev*, Oxford: Blackwell.

Mehnert, K. (1964) *Peking and Moscow*, New York: New American Library.

Melanson, R. (1991) *Reconstructing Consensus: American Foreign Policy Since the Vietnam War*, New York: St Martin's Press.

Merk, F. (1966) *Manifest Destiny and Mission in American History: A Reinterpretation*, New York: Vintage.

Miller, N. (1989) *Soviet Relations with Latin America 1959–1987*, Cambridge: Cambridge University Press.

Mosely, P. (1960) *The Kremlin and World Politics: Studies in Soviet Policy and Action*, New York: Vintage.

Mujal-Leon, E. (1978) 'Communism and Revolution in Portugal', 271–313 in R. Tökés (ed.), *Eurocommunism and Détente*, New York: New York University Press.

Munting, R. (1982) *The Economic Development of the USSR*, London: Macmillan.

New Republic (1945) 'World Government', September 24: 366–7.

New York Times (1993) 'Beyond START: A New Level of Instability', January 10: E1, E3.

New York Times (1993) '1st Soviet A-Bomb Built From US Data, Russian Says', January 14: A12.

Newhouse, J. (1989) *The Nuclear Age: From Hiroshima to Star Wars*, London: Michael Joseph.

Nitze, P. (1976) 'Assuring Strategic Stability in an Era of Détente', *Foreign Affairs* 54, No. 2, January: 207–32.

Nitze, P. (1988) 'Security and Arms Control: A Number of Good Beginnings', *NATO Review* 36, No. 6, December: 1–6.

Nitze, P. (1989) *From Hiroshima to Glasnost: At the Centre of Decision*, London: Weidenfeld and Nicolson.

Nixon, R. (1962) *Six Crises*, New York: Doubleday.

Nixon, R. (1978) *The Memoirs of Richard Nixon*, London: Sidgwick and Jackson.

Nixon, R. (1986) *No More Vietnams*, London: W.H. Allen.

Nogee, J.L. and Donaldson, R.H. (1988) *Soviet Foreign Policy Since World War II*, New York: Pergamon.

Nove, A. (1970) *An Economic History of the USSR*, Harmondsworth: Penguin.

Nye, J. (1990) *Bound to Lead: The Changing Nature of American Power*, New York: Basic Books.

Oberdorfer, D. (1992) *The Turn: From the Cold War to a New Era*, New York: Touchstone Books.

Oppenheimer, J. (1953) 'Atomic Weapons and American Policy', *Foreign Affairs* 31, No. 4, July: 525–35.

Owens, J. (1990) 'The Legacy of Reaganomics', 36–59 in M. Pugh and P. Williams (eds), *Superpower Politics: Change in the United States and the Soviet Union*, Manchester: Manchester University Press.

Padover, S.K. (ed.) (1943) *The Complete Jefferson*, pp. 384–86, New York: Duell, Sloane and Pearce.

Palmer, J. (1988) *Europe Without America? The Crisis in Atlantic Relations*, Oxford: Oxford University Press.

Paterson, T. (1988) *Meeting the Communist Threat: Truman to Reagan*, New York: Oxford University Press.

Paterson, T. (1990) 'The Defense-of-Cuba Theme and the Missile Crisis', *Diplomatic History* 14: 249–56.

Pelling, H. (1988) *Britain and the Marshall Plan*, London: Macmillan.

Pentagon Papers (1971), New York Times Edition, New York: Bantam Books.

Pike, D. (1987) *Vietnam and the Soviet Union: Anatomy of an Alliance*, Boulder: Westview Press.

Pipes, R. (1981) *US–Soviet Relations in the Era of Détente*, Boulder: Westview Press.

Pipes, R. (1992) Letter to the Editor, *New York Times*, November 6: A28.

Pollard, R.A. (1985) *Economic Security and the Origins of the Cold War, 1945–1949*, New York: Columbia University Press.

Posen, B. and Van Evera, S. (1987) 'Reagan Administration Defense Policy: Departure from Containment', 75–114 in K. Oye, R. Lieber, and D. Rothchild, (eds), *Eagle Resurgent?: The Reagan Era in American Foreign Policy*, Boston: Little, Brown.

Quandt, W. (1986) *Camp David: Peacemaking and Politics*, Washington, DC: The Brookings Institution.

Rabe, S. (1988) *Eisenhower and Latin America: The Foreign Policy of Anti-Communism*, Chapel Hill: University of North Carolina Press.

Reagan, R. (1985) *Public Papers of the Presidents of the United States: Ronald Reagan: 1983*, Book I, Washington, DC: United States Government Printing Office.

Reagan, R. (1987) *Public Papers of the Presidents of the United States: Ronald Reagan, 1985*, Book I, Washington, DC: United States Government Printing Office.

Remnick, D. (1993) *Lenin's Tomb: The Last Days of the Soviet Empire*, New York: Random House.

Risse-Kappen, T. (1991) 'Did "Peace Through Strength" End the Cold War? Lessons from INF', *International Security* 16, No. 1, Summer: 162–88.

Rockefeller Brothers Fund (1958) *International Security: The Military Aspect*, Garden City, N.J.: Doubleday.

Rosenberg, D. (1983) 'The Origins of Overkill: Nuclear Weapons and American Strategy, 1945–1960', *International Security* 7, Spring: 3–71.

Rosencrance, R. (1976) *America as an Ordinary Country*, Ithaca: Cornell University Press.

Roskamp, E. (1977) *The American Economy, 1929–1970*, Detroit: Wayne State University Press.

Roxburgh, A. (1991) *The Second Russian Revolution*, London: BBC Publications.

Rubin, B. (1981) *Paved With Good Intentions: The American Experience and Iran*, Harmondsworth: Penguin.

Rubin, B. (1987) 'The Reagan Administration and the Middle East', 431–57 in K. Oye, R. Lieber and D. Rothchild (eds), *Eagle Resurgent? The Reagan Era in American Foreign Policy*, Boston: Little, Brown.

Ruggie, J. (1986) 'Continuity and Transformation in the World Polity: Toward a Neorealist Synthesis', 131–57 in R. Keohane (ed.), *Neorealism and its Critics*, New York: Columbia University Press.

Rupnik, J. (1989) *The Other Europe*, London: Weidenfeld and Nicolson.

Rusk, D. (1990) *As I Saw It*, New York: Norton.

Sagan, S. (1989) *Moving Targets: Nuclear Strategy and National Security*, Princeton: Princeton University Press.

Sagan, S. (1993) *The Limits of Safety: Organizations, Accidents, and Nuclear Weapons*, Princeton: Princeton University Press.

Sainsbury, K. (1985) *The Turning Point: Roosevelt, Stalin, Churchill and Chiang Kai-shek, 1943: The Moscow, Cairo, and Teheran Conferences*, Oxford: Oxford University Press.

Saivetz, C. and Woodby, S. (1985) *Soviet–Third World Relations*, London: Westview Press.

Sanders, D. (1990) *Losing an Empire, Finding a Role: British Foreign Policy Since 1945*, London: Macmillan.

Schaller, M. (1986) *The American Occupation of Japan: The Origins of the Cold War in Asia*, New York: Oxford University Press.

Schlesinger, A.M. (1963) 'The One Against the Many', 531–8 in A.M. Schlesinger and M. White (eds), *Paths of American Thought*, Boston: Houghton Mifflin.

Schlesinger, A. (1974) *The Imperial Presidency*, New York: Popular Library.

Schöpflin, G. (1990) 'The End of Communism in Europe', *International Affairs* 66, No. 1, January 1990: 3–16.

Schöpflin, G. (1993) *Politics in Eastern Europe*, Oxford: Blackwell.

Schulzinger, R.D. (1984) *American Diplomacy in the Twentieth Century*, New York: Oxford University Press.

Seward, W. (1849) *Life of John Quincy Adams*, Philadelphia: Porter and Coates.

Sheehan, N. (1989) *A Bright Shining Lie: John Paul Vann and America in Vietnam*, London: Jonathan Cape.

Sherwin, M. (1977) *A World Destroyed: The Atom Bomb and the Grand Alliance*, New York: Vintage Books.

Sherwood, R. (1948) *Roosevelt and Hopkins: An Intimate History*, New York: Harper and Row.

Shulman, M. (1963) *Stalin's Foreign Policy Reappraised*, Cambridge, Mass.: Harvard University Press.

Shultz, G. (1993) *Turmoil and Triumph: My Years as Secretary of State*, New York: Charles Scribner's Sons.

Singer, J. (1969) 'The Level-of-Analysis Problem in International Relations', 20–9 in J. Rosenau, (ed.), *International Relations and Foreign Policy*, New York: Free Press.

Siracusa, J. (ed.) (1978) *The American Diplomatic Revolution: A Documentary History of the Cold War, 1941–47,* Milton Keynes: Open University Press.

Sixsmith, M. (1991) *Moscow Coup: The Death of the Soviet System*, New York: Simon and Schuster.

Smith, D. (ed.) (1964) *American Diplomatic History: Documents and Readings*, Vol. II, Lexington, Mass.: D.C. Heath.

Smith, R. (1983) *An International History of the Vietnam War*, Vol. 1 *Revolution Versus Containment, 1955–1961*, London: Macmillan.

Smith, S. (1987) 'SDI and the New Cold War', 149–70 in R. Crockatt and S. Smith (eds), *The Cold War Past and Present*, London: Allen and Unwin.

Smith, S. (1990) 'The Reagan Legacy and the Bush Predicament', 60–81 in M. Pugh and P. Williams (eds), *Superpower Politics: Change in the United States and the Soviet Union*, Manchester: Manchester University Press.

Smith, W. (1987a) *The Closest of Enemies: A Personal and Diplomatic Account of US–Cuban Relations Since 1957*, New York: Norton.

Smith, W. (1987b) 'Lies About Nicaragua', *Foreign Policy* 67, Summer: 87–103.

Smith, W.B. (1950) *Moscow Mission*, London: Heinemann.

Spanier, J. (1977) *American Foreign Policy Since World War II*, New York: Praeger.

Spence, J. (1990) *The Search for Modern China*, London: Hutchinson.

Spiegel, S. (1985) *The Other Arab–Israeli Conflict: Making America's Middle East Policy, From Truman to Reagan*, Chicago: University of Chicago Press.

Steele, J. (1985) *Soviet Foreign Policy: The Limits of Power*, Harmondsworth: Penguin.

Stuart, D. and Tow, W. (1990) *The Limits of Alliance: NATO Out-of-Area Problems Since 1949*, Baltimore: Johns Hopkins University Press.

Stueck, W. (1981) *The Road to Confrontation: American Policy Toward China and Korea, 1947–1950*, Chapel Hill: University of North Carolina Press.

Summers, H. (1982) *On Strategy: A Critical Analysis of the Vietnam War*, Novato, Calif.: Presidio Press.

Talbott, S. (1984) *Deadly Gambits: The Reagan Administration and the Stalemate in Arms Control*, New York: Knopf.

Talbott, S. (1989) *The Master of the Game: Paul Nitze and the Nuclear Peace*, New York: Vintage.

Taubman, W. (1982) *Stalin's American Policy*, New York: Norton.

Thomas, B. (1969) 'What's Left of the Cold War?' *Political Quarterly* 40: 173–86.

Thompson, E.P. (1990) 'The Ends of Cold War', *New Left Review* 182, July/August: 139–46.

Tiersky, R. (1978) 'French Communism, Eurocommunism, and Soviet Power', 138–203 in R. Tökés (ed.), *Eurocommunism and Détente*, New York: New York University Press.

Tökés, R. (1978) 'Eastern Europe in the 1970s: *Détente*, Dissent and Eurocommunism', 437–511 in R. Tökés (ed.), *Eurocommunism and Détente*, New York: New York University Press.

Trachtenberg, M. (1990) 'Commentary: New Light on the Cuban Missile Crisis?', *Diplomatic History* 14: 241–7.

Treverton, G. (1989) 'From No Cities to Stable Vulnerability', 190–204 in P. Bobbit, L. Freedman, and G. Treverton (eds), *US Nuclear Strategy: A Reader*, London: Macmillan.

Trofimenko, H. (1981) 'The Third World and the US–Soviet Competition: A Soviet View', *Foreign Affairs* 59, No. 5, Summer: 1021–40.

Truman, H.S. (1955) *Year of Decisions*, Garden City, N.Y.: Doubleday.

Truman, H.S. (1963) *Public Papers of the Presidents of the United States: Harry S. Truman, 1947*, pp. 176–80, Washington, DC: US Government Printing Office.

Tucker, R. (1972) *The Soviet Political Mind: Stalinism and Post-Stalin Change*, London: Allen and Unwin.

Ulam, A. (1968) *Expansion and Coexistence: The History of Soviet Foreign Relations*, New York: Praeger.

Ulam, A. (1973) *The Rivals*, London: Allen Lane.

Ulam, A. (1983) *Dangerous Relations: The Soviet Union in World Politics, 1970–1982*, New York: Oxford University Press.

Urwin, D. (1989) *Western Europe Since 1945: A Political History*, 4th edition, London: Longman.

USACDA (1982) *Arms Control and Disarmaments Agreements*, Washington, DC: United States Arms Control and Disarmament Agency.

Vadney, T.E. (1987) *The World Since 1945*, Harmondsworth: Penguin.

Van der Wee, H. (1987) *Prosperity and Upheaval: The World Economy 1945–1980*, Harmondsworth: Penguin.

Vance, C. (1983) *Hard Choices: Critical Years in America's Foreign Policy*, New York: Simon and Schuster.

Viotti, P. and Kauppi, M. (1993) *International Relations Theory: Realism, Pluralism and Globalism*, New York: Macmillan.

Volkogonov, D. (1991) *Stalin: Triumph and Tragedy*, New York: Grove Weidenfeld.

Walesa, L. (1987) *A Way of Hope*, New York: Henry Holt.

Walker, M. (1993) *The Cold War and the Making of the Modern World*, London: Fourth Estate.

Walker, S. (1990) 'The Decision to Use the Bomb: A Historiographical Update', *Diplomatic History* 14: 97–114.

Wall, I. (1991) *The United States and the Making of Postwar France*, Cambridge: Cambridge University Press.

Wallace, H. (1943) *The Price of Victory* in *Prefaces to Peace*, New York: Simon and Schuster *et al.*

Waltz, K. (1964) 'The Stability of the Bipolar World', *Daedalus* 13, Summer: 881–909.

Waltz, K. (1979) *Theory of International Politics*, New York: Random House.

Waltz, K. (1986) 'Reflections on *Theory of International Politics*: A Response to my Critics', 322–45 in R. Keohane (ed.), *Neorealism and its Critics*, New York: Columbia University Press.

Ward, B. ([1955] 1962) *The Interplay of East and West*, New York: Norton.

Washington Post (1992) 'Dramatic Politburo Meeting Led to End of War', November 16: A1, A16.

Weathersby, K. (1993) 'Soviet Aims in Korea and the Origins of the Korean War, 1945–1950: New Evidence From Russian Archives', Working Paper No. 8, Cold War International History Project, Woodrow Wilson Center, Washington, DC, November: 33 pages.

Weinberger, C. (1987) 'Preface' to *Soviet Military Power*, (pp. 3–5) Washington, DC: US Government Printing Office.

Wells, S.F. (1985) 'The First Cold War Buildup: Europe in United States Strategy and Policy, 1950–1953', 181–97 in O. Riste (ed.), *Western Security: The Formative Years, European and Atlantic Defence 1947–1953*, Oslo: Norwegian University Press.

Werth, A. (1965) *De Gaulle*, Harmondsworth: Penguin.

Whelan, R. (1990) *Drawing the Line: The Korean War, 1950–1953*, Boston: Little, Brown.

White, B. (1987) 'Britain and the Rise of *Détente*', 91–109 in R. Crockatt and S. Smith (eds), *The Cold War Past and Present*, London: George Allen and Unwin.

White, S. (1990) *Gorbachev in Power*, Cambridge: Cambridge University Press.

Wight, M. (1979) *Power Politics*, Harmondsworth: Penguin.

Williams, W., LaFeber, W., Gardner, L. and McCormick, T. (eds) (1989) *America in Vietnam: A Documentary History*, New York: Norton.

Williams, W.A. (1972) *The Tragedy of American Diplomacy*, New York: Dell.

Williamson, E. (1992) *The Penguin History of Latin America*, Harmondsworth: Allen Lane, the Penguin Press.

Wilson, W. (1983) *The Papers of Woodrow Wilson*, Vol. 41, edited by A. Link, Princeton: Princeton University Press.

Windsor, P. (1971) *Germany and the Management of Détente*, London: Chatto and Windus for the Institute for Strategic Studies.

Wolfe, B.D. (1964) *Three Who Made a Revolution*, 4th edition, New York: Dell.

Yergin, D. (1980) *Shattered Peace: The Origins of the Cold War and the National Security State*, Harmondsworth: Penguin.

Yost, D. and Glad, T. (1982) 'West German Party Politics and Theater Nuclear Modernization Since 1977', *Armed Forces and Society* 8, No. 4, Summer: 525–60.

Zagoria, D. (1967) *Vietnam Triangle: Moscow, Peking, Hanoi*, New York: Pegasus.

Zuckerman, Lord (1987) 'Technology for a Cold War', 24–34 in R. Crockatt and S. Smith (eds), *The Cold War Past and Present*, London: Allen and Unwin.

INDEX